Alfred A. Ring, S.R.A., M.A.I., Ph.D.

Chairman
Department of Real Estate and Urban Land Studies
University of Florida

The Valuation of

Real Estate

SECOND EDITION

PRENTICE-HALL, INC.
Englewood Cliffs, New Jersey

To:
E
and
K
A
G
E

Prentice-Hall International, Inc., London
Prentice-Hall of Australia, Pty. Ltd., Sydney
Prentice-Hall of Canada, Ltd., Toronto
Prentice-Hall of India Private Ltd., New Delhi
Prentice-Hall of Japan, Inc., Tokyo

Preface

During the years since the first edition of *The Valuation of Real Estate* was published in 1963, great strides have been made in perfecting the art of property valuation, and in elevating the status of appraising as a field of specialization. The role of the appraiser, too, as a professional practitioner in the broad area of real estate economics is increasing in importance. The bulk of national wealth, both public and private is invested in realty consisting of land and its fixed improvements, and no significant transfer of ownership of real property is likely to take place without professional assistance from experts in the field of valuation.

The ever increasing importance of ownership of real property as an estate building asset, as a hedge against inflation, as a tax shelter device, and as a permanent and secure investment has caused ownership of realty to become popular and widespread. This is evident from the increasing number of realty transactions that are presented annually for public recording. To assure "arms-length" bargaining in these transactions at prices reflecting market supply and demand, an expert opinion concerning value is deemed essential.

This book is written essentially as a training and teaching guide for candidates who seek membership in one or more of the principal appraising societies: The American Institute of Real Estate Appraisers, The Society of Real Estate Appraisers and The American Appraisal Society. This book has been revised specifically to serve as a text for class room use and study in schools of business and commerce, in vocational schools, and in case study and extension course work sponsored by professional appraisal societies. Every effort was made to keep this writing and the applied theory and practice of property valuation "down to earth." There is, however, no easy road to learning. A book, no matter how masterly written, can by self-study alone contribute little to an expansion of human wisdom or to the perfection of human judgment. These human attributes can best be obtained through the broad school of field experience and professional involvement. A well written book, nevertheless, can simulate experience, challenge the reader to reach for perfection, and encourage him through interesting arrangements of facts and explanatory statements to seek mastery of the art of a chosen profession.

It is important to remember that *value* is the heart of economics. More important still is the indisputable fact that only *people* can make value. A sound theory of value, thus, must keep the human factor in focus and be attuned to practices that are the outgrowth of socio-political forces that operate within a capitalistic economy where dollar democracy expresses itself in free and open market operations.

This book is an outgrowth of nearly three decades of college teaching in appraising principles and practices at New York University and the University of Florida. Although the topical presentation of subject matter is traditional and follows procedure recommended for use by leading appraisal societies, new concepts of valuation theory and practice are introduced to stimulate classroom study and discussions and to aid in the modification of field practices where tested results warrant their application.

The author wants to acknowledge the special contributions made to this writing by his many students at the professional, graduate and undergraduate level, who enthusiastically welcomed the opportunity to test and evaluate alternate teaching methods as an improved vehicle for learning. Grateful acknowledgement is made for valuable assistance and continued encouragement and support over more than a quarter of a century to my long time friend and colleague Dr. Herbert B. Dorau, Professor of Economics Emeritus and formerly Chairman of the Department of Real Estate at New York University. To this outstanding teacher and scholar goes credit for many of the thought-provoking ideas that are given expression in this writing. Special thanks goes to Ronald O. Boatright, a doctoral candidate and instructor in real estate and urban land studies at the University of Florida, for constructive suggestions that contributed to greater clarity of subject matter presentation.

For valuable suggestions offered during the manuscript stages of this publication and for constructive editorial comments our thanks are expressed to Dr. William N. Kinnard, Jr., M.A.I., S.R.A., Director and Professor of Finance and Real Estate at the University of Connecticut and to Mr. H. Grady Stebbins, Jr., S.R.E.A., M.A.I., Vice Chairman of the Subcommittee for Course Development, of the Society of Real Estate Appraisers. Also recognized is valuable assistance from my colleagues on the faculty of the College of Business Administration at the University of Florida.

For diligent and loyal aid in the compilation and typing of the manuscript we express gratitude and wish to commend our departmental secretary Miss Geraldine Bourne. To our secretarial assistant, Miss Jane McDavid, we express thanks for the drafting and typing of charts and tables and for editing the manuscript. Last but not least, the author wishes to express his deep appreciation to Donald E. Snyder, Staff Vice President of the Society of Real Estate Appraisers for soliciting valuable and constructive comments from the Society's teaching faculty who had tested the author's approach to learning in classroom work throughout the country. To the tasks of these teachers and to the thousands of students who seek to master the art of appraising this book is dedicated.

ALFRED A. RING

Contents

4

Importance of Cost, Price, Income and Market . . . 43

Replacement Costs Versus Reproduction Costs 44; Price as a Measure of Value 45; Income as a Measure of Value 50; The Real Estate Market 52.

5

Impact of Political, Social and Economic Forces . . . 55

Political Forces Influencing Value 56; Social Forces Influencing Value 58; General Economic Forces Influencing Value 60; State or Regional Forces Influencing Value 64.

6

Impact of Urban Forces Upon Property Value . . . 68

The Nature and Character of Cities 69; The City's Plan and Land Use Pattern 70; Population Trends and Characteristics 72; Economic Measures of Community Growth 73; The Economic Value of Good City Government 75; The Problem of Urban Renewal 76.

7

Value Analysis of Neighborhood Characteristics . . . 78

The Neighborhood Age Cycle 78; Neighborhood Characteristics 81; Location Characteristics 81; Social Forces Influencing Neighborhood Values 85; Neighborhood Economic Characteristics 86; Neighborhood Attributes of Commercial Districts 90.

8

Factors and Considerations in Site Analysis . . . 93

The Need for a Location Sketch 94; Nature of Terrain and Soil Characteristics 99; Street Improvements and Availability of Essential Public Utilities 99; Location Analysis 101; Size, Depth, Shape, and Corner Lot Location Influences 102; The 4-3-2-1 Depth Rule 103; Odd-Shaped Lot Valuation 104; Corner Lot Valuation 106; Zoning and Contractual Limitations on Ownership 109; Title Considerations and Encroachments 110; Site Improvements 111.

9

Fundamentals of Land Valuation . . . 114

The Market or Comparison Approach to Value 115; Market Data Summary and Correlation 118; The Ideal Neighborhood and Site Comparison Method 123; The Income, or Residual Earnings, Approach to Value 125; The Land Development or Cost of Land Production Approach to Value 127; The Ratio of Improvement Value to Value of the Site 129.

10

The Market Sales Comparison Approach to Value . . . 131

Verifications of Sales 132; Price Adjustments to Compensate for Time and Transfer Terms 133; Market Comparison Adjustment Techniques 134; Construction Detail Analysis and Price Rating Technique 135; Overall Construction and Building Condition Rating Technique 138; Percentage Adjustments —Their Use and Limitation 140; Assessment Ratios as a Guide to Market Value 141; The Market Data Approach for Commercial and Industrial Properties 142; Rent or Gross Income Multipliers as a Guide to Market Value 145.

11

Building Construction and Plan Reading . . . 149

Plan Reading for Proposed Construction 155; The Importance of Written Specifications 157; Computing Building Value Measurements 159; Basic Attributes of Good Floor Planning 161; Importance of Construction Knowledge 163.

12

Building Cost Estimating and Valuation . . . 165

Builders' Detail Inventory Method 166; Subcontractors' or Quantity Survey Method 166; Unit-in-Place Construction Method 171; The Comparative Market Method of Cost Estimating 173; Estimating the Standard or Base House 173; Estimating the Subject House 175; Commercial Cost Services 178.

13

Depreciation Theory and Practice . . . 184

Depreciation Versus Amortization 185; Depreciation Theory 186; Economic Life and Effective Age Versus Physical Life and Chronological Age of Property 187; The Engineering or Observed Method for Measuring Accrued Depreciation 189; Theoretical Methods for Measuring Accrued Depreciation 195; Depreciation Estimates—Their Limits of Use 203.

14

Income Forecasting and Analysis . . . 205

Actual Versus Average Income 206; Economic Versus Contract Rents 207; Importance of Typical Management 208; Estimating the Quantity of Income Flow 209; Quality and Duration of Income 213; Rental Schedule Construction and Analysis 214; Owner's Income Statements and Adjustments 215; Income Adjustment for Changes in the Purchasing Power of the Dollar 217.

15

Operating Expense Forecasting and Analysis . . . 219

Income Deductions Versus Operating Expenses 220; Income Tax and Property Tax Considerations 222; Operating Expense Outlays and Classifications 223; Operating Expense Schedule Reconstruction 226; The Significance of Operating Expense Ratios 228; Capital Expenditures 230.

16

Determining the Rate of Capitalization . . . 232

Kinds of Interest Rates and Capitalization 236; Available Methods for Selection of the Rate of Capitalization 241; The Market Investment Quality Comparison Method 241; The Band of Investment Method 243; The Banker's Rate Selection Method 244; The Built-Up Method 245.

17

Mathematics of Property Valuation . . . 247

Compound Amount of 1 (Interest) Table 248; Present Worth of 1 (Discount) Table 249; Future Worth of an Annuity of 1 Table 251; Present Worth

18

The Income Approach to Value . . . 266

19

Residual Techniques of Capitalization . . . 283

20

Leasehold Estates and Leased Fee Appraising . . . 299

21

Equity Appraising and Financing . . . 315

22

Condemnation Appraising Practices and Procedures . . . 330

Data 469;   Floor Plan 471;   Market Approach to Value 472;   The Cost Approach to Value 474;   Depreciation Schedule 476;   Income Approach to Value 478;   Correlation of Value Estimates 479;   Statement of Limiting Conditions 481;   Certification 482.

Appendix II . . . 483

Cases and Problems in Property Appraising 485;   Suggested Solutions to Cases and Problems 521.

Appendix III . . . 563

Index . . . 650

Property valuation may rightfully be designated as the heart of all real estate activity. In fact, valuation is the heart of all *economic* activity. Everything we do as individuals or as groups of individuals in business or as members of society evolves about and is influenced by the concept of value. Whether we are buying, selling, investing, developing, lending, exchanging, renting, assessing, or acquiring property for public use, a

1 *Nature, Importance, and Characteristics of Value*

working knowledge of sound valuation is essential in all sorts of decisions relating to real estate buying, selling, financing, developing, managing, owning, leasing, trading, and in the ever more important matters involving tax considerations. Sound valuation too is basic to zoning, ad valorem taxation, city planning and to sound management of urban affairs in order to put land and its improvements to the highest, best, and hence, most profitable use.

Although the importance of value as an economic measure is generally recognized, there exists a wide variance of understanding as to the character, nature, and meaning of value, especially among laymen who comprise the broad market for real property. This wide variance, and the lack of understanding as to available uniform means of measuring the magnitude of value, may be explained by the failure of most laymen to differentiate thoughtfully between *individual worth*—or *subjective value*—on the one hand, and *market worth*—or *objective value*—on the other.

SUBJECTIVE VERSUS OBJECTIVE VALUE

In the final analysis all value, no matter how defined, has its origin in individual measures of worth. Everyone has a scale of preference for given goods or services. This preference, or *desire-pull relationship* between an individual and the object or service wanted, is influenced continuously and in varying degrees by personal traits and by cultural, religious, and governmental forces which influence each person as a member of society. This subjective value can readily be demonstrated by a scatter diagram, wherein each circle represents the worth (or sacrifice a person would willingly make for it) of a given quantity of a good or service as measured in units of dollars. Each circle may stand for one or more individuals, or it may represent a second or third measure of worth by one or more individuals for additional units of the same good or service.

Thus someone may be willing to pay, or sacrifice the equivalent amount, $12,000 for a modest home, offer no more than $10,000 (as an investment in a like residence), and express no desire (demand) for ownership of a third property. Another person may offer no more than $11,000 for the same property and express no interest in another even as a recommended investment on a reduced or discount basis. Each individual thus expresses his preference (or estimate of subjective worth) for one or more units of a commodity or service by bidding along a scale as shown in Figure 1.1. The fitted curve may then appropriately be labeled as a composite diagram that projects the relationship of offering prices for given goods or services to quantities of such goods, or services offered for sale at a given time and place in an open, free, and generally normal market.

Demand for goods or units of service arises from necessity or from possessory human desires which are backed by purchasing power, cash, or credit. As individual or group desires are modified or molded by environmental influences, human behavior reacts accordingly and expresses itself in a changed pattern for the kinds of goods or services sought after in the marketplace. To gain a better understanding of the ever changing socio-economic forces which underlie the concept of objective value, a study of the basic law of market supply and demand is therefore deemed essential.

An offer to exchange a quantity of dollars for a quantity of goods or services does not, by itself, create a market or an opportunity to barter. There must be owners who supply these goods and services and who are ready, willing, and able to meet the demand at the prices offered. Each

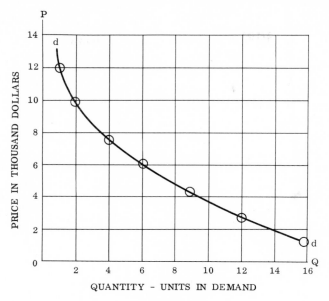

FIGURE 1.1

unit of an economic good or service must be *produced* or supplied at a certain sacrifice of the various factors of production involving land, labor, capital, and entrepreneurial effort. Some suppliers are more efficient than others; and as a result of volume of production, increased mechanization, or other factors which lower construction or manufacturing costs, they are able to market their wares at lower prices.

In market areas where producers' earnings are relatively high, and where market demand is considered expandable, other suppliers of goods and services are competitively attracted. Ignoring for the moment customers' ability or willingness to pay even the warranted cost of an efficient producer, a scale of increasing individual producer costs can be plotted as a scatter diagram, as illustrated in Figure 1.2. The most efficient producers are able to supply the wanted product at lowest possible cost; they are followed along the scale by producers of lower quantities and generally lower efficiency and higher per unit costs.

By superimposing the demand curve in Figure 1.1 on the cost of production curve in Figure 1.2, it is possible to measure the interaction of market supply and demand for given quantities of goods or services. As shown in Figure 1.3, where the supply and demand lines intersect at this point, the individual or subjective value forces of users and producers merge into an objective market measure of value. The demand below the

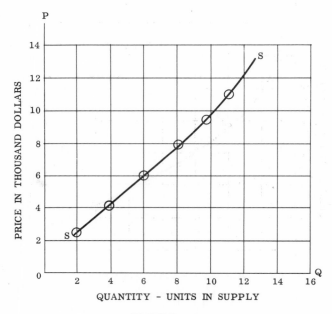

FIGURE 1.2

point of merger is classified as submarginal, or inadequate to meet the marginal costs of production. The supplier's costs above the point of merger are likewise submarginal—that is, above the highest bids offered at the time and place for the good or service in demand.

MARKET CONDITIONS AND TERMS OF SALE INFLUENCING VALUE

Where analysis of market data permits accurate presentation of the interacting economic forces which influence the shape of the supply and demand curves shown in Figure 1.3, the resulting findings offer conclusive evidence in support of the equilibrium price or objective value as verified by actions in the open market. The market price thus obtained is in effect a synthesis or equilibrium of the interacting subjective values or forces which comprise a *market*. No informed person who buys with due care is warranted to pay more than the market price, and no equally informed seller will accept less. Attention is called to the fact that in all value discussions here it is assumed that the forces of supply and demand are in equilibrium and that no artificial or temporary barriers impede either supply or demand, causing the market to be designated as "gray" or "black" in character. Scarcity in supply as well as over- or undercon-

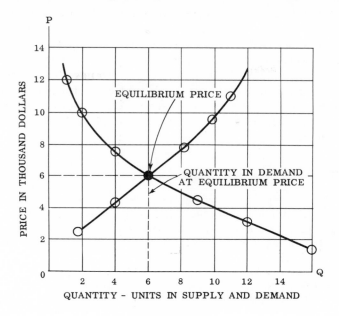

FIGURE 1.3

sumption will temporarily influence the price of the product and cause payments of either premiums or discounts, depending on the nature of market conditions. Therefore, in solving a value problem it is essential to stipulate either whether or not market conditions are normal; or, if they are not, the dollar extent to which value adjustments must be made to reflect peculiarities of the market.

To illustrate: After World War II the scarcity of residential properties due to a moratorium on construction was so great that market prices of homes available for sale reflected a premium for occupancy ranging from 15 to 20 percent above depreciated replacement cost. To reflect this abnormal market condition, a home that sold for $23,500 in 1947 un-doubtedly represented a composite of market value as follows:

Depreciated value of property	$20,000
Premium for occupancy due to excessive demand in relation to available supply	3,500
Market value—as of date of sale	$23,500

Another condition requisite in a determination of objective (or market) value is that the exchange of dollars for quantities of goods or services is in *present* dollars on a cash or cash equivalent basis. Promises of future dollars create interest costs and hazards of collection which must be compensated for over and above the value ascribable to a good or service on a *cash* or cash equivalent basis.[1] Just as favorable terms of sale increase the price at which realty is exchanged in the open market, conversely restrictive terms, such as high mortgage interest rates, can decrease the price below the amount a property would command if available for transfer on typical—that is, conventional—terms of sale. Further consideration will be given in Chapters 3 and 4 to the impact of *terms* of sale on *prices* of goods and services.

TYPES OF VALUE

Although logic would dictate that only *one* type of value could possibly measure the economic significance that individuals attach to a good or service in a given market, common usage has put in vogue many types of value, a few of which are listed below:

1. Economic value	16. Sales value
2. Stable value	17. Salvage value
3. Appraised value	18. Intrinsic value
4. Potential value	19. Extrinsic value
5. Book value	20. Tax value
6. Sound value	21. Use value
7. Fair value	22. Rental value
8. Real value	23. Speculative value
9. True value	24. Reproduction value
10. Depreciated value	25. Nuisance value
11. Warranted value	26. Liquidation value
12. Face value	27. Mortgage loan value
13. Cash value	28. Improved value
14. Capital value	29. Insurance value
15. Exchange value	30. Leasehold value

This listing by no means exhausts the many uses to which the term *value* is being put today. A complete enumeration would take many pages, especially if the variations of value related to political, social, and religious matters were added to those used to define the importance of business and economic operations. Is it any wonder that a learned U.S. Supreme Court Justice once said that "value is a word of many meanings"? Undoubtedly, the late Justice Brandeis had in mind the many uses of the term that prove puzzling to businessmen even to this day.

The question may now be asked, Can there really be that many types of value? Is there one value for the buyer, another for the seller, a third

---

[1] 'Cash equivalent' as used here and in subsequent chapters refers to typical financial terms, i.e. equity down payment plus mortgage loan amounts which are currently available to a typical purchaser.

for the lender, and so forth? The answer is Yes where value sought is subjective in character, and where the estimate of value is to serve a special or limited purpose. To illustrate, value for fire insurance purposes would differ in amount from value for mortgage loan purposes. In the former case, emphasis is placed on the replacement cost of improvements which are subject to fire hazards regardless of the marketability or income-producing capacity of the subject property. Where the value estimate is to serve as a basis for mortgage loan determination, principal reliance must be placed on the earnings capacity of the property and on its marketability in case of default in mortgage payment. This illustration points up the fact that a property can have different values for different persons where subjective, commercial, or special-use purposes must be considered and given due weight in the value estimate.

To prevent misinterpretation and error in acting on the basis of a value estimate it is most important that the purpose of the value problem be clearly stated in the letter of transmittal as well as in the body of the appraisal report, and that a definition of value be fully expressed as a guide to action by the reader or client to whom the report is submitted.

Where the estimate of value is to establish the most probable amount that a property can command if exposed for sale in a relatively free, open, and competitive market, and at a given time, place, and under specified market conditions then there can be only *one* value. This kind of value, which most frequently is the object of economic search and analysis, is created by the multitude of buyers and sellers who cause a synthesis or interaction of the forces of supply and demand for specific goods or things which are traded in an open market.

THE MEANING OF MARKET VALUE

Although by the exclusion of subjective and special purpose property uses we have narrowed the economic realm in which the forces that forge market value operate, we still find divergence in professional judgment as how best to define the concept of market value. Therefore, to pinpoint the problem, it is necessary that a single clear-cut definition be formulated. The meaning of value can best be expressed in two closely related ways:

1. "The power of a good or thing (service) to command other goods or things in exchange," and
2. "The present worth of *future* rights to income."

The first concept of value generally known as the "barter" or purchasing power definition of value is useful in measuring the worth or power of exchange of one commodity directly for another; in short, how much fish for how much game, or how much wheat for how much corn. Under this definition of value no money as a medium of exchange is necessary to measure the value-power of one good compared with another. If a standard dwelling of a given size and quality is worth the equivalent of five automobiles of a given kind and make in a given year, and ten years later the relationship of these commodities remains the same, then no change in value has taken place so far as autos and houses are concerned—no matter what happened to the value of money or to the level of prices.

During World War II, Adolf Hitler dramatically demonstrated the concept of value based on the power of a good to command other goods in exchange. When the Allied Powers cut the flow of gold and world dollars to impede if not cripple Hitler's war efforts by withdrawing the international medium of exchange, Hitler was little affected. He merely bartered for needed war supplies by exchanging German products elsewhere for oil and other critical supplies on the basis of the prevailing exchange power of one product for another. Even today, we measure to a large extent the welfare of a group or a nation by the hours of labor (value) necessary to achieve a given standard of living or quantity of goods and services.

The second definition of value is more helpful and more readily applicable as a measure of value where *money* serves as a medium of exchange. Most goods and services are sold for specific purposes—generally to render buyer satisfaction (utility) for one or more years into the future. Thus a home is purchased for a sum of "X" thousand dollars to provide, throughout the economic life of the dwelling, rental savings as well as psychic income (amenities) derived from the pleasure and prestige of home ownership. Where the direct and/or indirect income from goods and services over future years through study of market behavior of buyers and sellers can be translated into money or money's worth, the present worth or value of such goods and services can be determined by *discounting* these future rights to income into a present sum or *present value*. This process of discounting, better known as *capitalization,* will be explained more fully and demonstrated in Chapters 18 and 19.

With the introduction of money as a medium of exchange the barter relationship of one commodity to another became more complex. In a dollar economy, prices essentially serve as a measure of the exchange power of goods for dollars and dollars for goods. This price relationship in a free market has caused acceptance of the meaning of value as being synonymous with the term *exchange* (or *market*) value. As used by real estate appraisers, and as sanctioned by court decisions, market value is currently defined under the "willing buyer, willing seller" concept as follows:

Market value is the highest price estimated in terms of money which a property will bring if exposed for sale in the open market allowing a reasonable time to find a purchaser who buys with knowledge of all the uses to which the property is adapted and for which it is capable of being used.[2]

Market value is the price which a property will bring in a competitive market under all conditions requisite to a fair sale, which would result from negotiations between a buyer and a seller, each acting prudently, with knowledge, and without undue stimulus.[3]

These definitions like most others that concern value, were judicially enunciated and currently are widely used by practicing appraisers everywhere. Nevertheless, the concept that market value is the *highest* price that a property will bring suggests to the lay reader a valuation report that there also must be a *lowest* or at least a lower price which a purchaser should initially offer. Under the equilibrium market value theory, the price that a property commands in the open market is in fact neither the highest nor the lowest—as measured by individual worth—but rather one balanced or equated by all the prevailing forces of market supply and consumer demand. To reinforce the understanding that an estimate of value is a studied and considered approximation of the most probable amount for which a property can be exchanged under cash or cash-equivalent terms of sale, a more precise definition of market value for use in appraisal reporting is offered as follows:

Market value is the warranted price expressed in terms of money which a property is estimated to bring, at a given time and place where buyers and sellers act without compulsion and with full knowledge of all the uses to which the property is adapted and for which it is capable of being used. The warranted price is further contingent on the sellers' ability to convey title with all rights inherent in the property and allowing sufficient time for the transaction to mature normally under cash or cash-equivalent terms of sale.

As this definition suggests, the time of sale, the terms of sale, the relationship of the parties, knowledge concerning rights to be conveyed, present and possible potential uses to which the property may be put, time for the transaction to mature and close normally, and the immediate transferability of good and marketable title all influence the estimate of a warranted price. More detailed consideration to the impact of conditions and terms of sale will be given in succeeding chapters.

---

[2] V. Viliborghi, Prescott School, District 55, Arizona 230, 100 Pac. (2nd ed., 1940), p. 178.

[3] See *Real Estate Appraisal Principles and Terminology* (Chicago: The Society of Real Estate Appraisers, 1960), p. 85.

WHAT MAKES VALUE?

The question most frequently posed is: "What makes value?" Is a property or a commodity valuable because it possesses *intrinsic* qualities such as are attributed, for instance, to gold or silver, or is value entirely *extrinsic* to the object and being created wholly in the minds of people who seek to possess that object? Theoretically, support can be given to a contention that, to be valuable, a product must possess certain qualities which attract the buyer and user and thus create a desire for ownership. Such qualities, if indeed assignable to an inanimate object, are then classified as intrinsic and, thus inherent in the product per se. Those subscribing to a humanistic philosophy of value hold that value is a product of the mind, and that in the final analysis *people* create value—not wood, steel, brick or mortar. Adherents to this school of thought hold that value is extrinsic in character, and that logically an object or service cannot possess intrinsic value. This contention they illustrate as follows. If gold or silver, for instance, should suddenly rain like manna from the heavens, its so-called intrinsic value would disappear; in fact its superabundance might create a nuisance that would give it a negative rather than a positive value under the circumstances. Changes in modes and fashions, too, it is pointed out, cause an object (through no fault or diminution of its intrinsic qualities) to be classed as obsolete or relatively useless.

Progress in the arts and sciences, development of new and rapid modes of transportation, and changes due to computerized technology all give weight to the concept that to a large degree it is people who make value and that value, therefore, must be considered as basically being extrinsic in character. Nevertheless, at a given place and moment of time, the object under value study must possess certain economic and legal characteristics in order to be wanted and thereby claim attributes of value.

VALUE CHARACTERISTICS

For a good or service to have value it must possess certain economic and legal characteristics, specifically the following: (1) utility, (2) scarcity, (3) demand, and (4) transferability.

Utility may be defined as the power of a good to render a service or fill a need. Utility must be present for a good or service to be of value. Utility, however, is only one of the characteristics that make up value. Thus where utility is present but demand or scarcity is absent, market value will not exist. For instance, water and air possess utility—yes, total utility, for both are essential to life itself. The value of neither air nor water, however, is measurable in terms of dollars for each is abundant and free to all. To have market value, therefore, a useful good or service must be scarce. The influence of utility on value, too, must be considered in relation to the size, shape, or form of the property, its geographic or spatial location, and its mobility and availability at given times. Variations in utility characteristics influence value; value differences, therefore, are caused by form, space, or time utility, as the case may be.

Scarcity is a relative term, and must be considered in relation to demand and supply and the alternate uses—present or prospective—to which the good or service may be put. Thus Christmas trees may be scarce the day before Christmas, and most abundant the week after. Value, too, will fluctuate accordingly. Gold and silver are relatively scarce, but their degree of scarcity, and hence value, can be affected by discovery of new sources of supply or the introduction of a new metal offering equal or even greater utility. Everything else remaining equal, value differences will result with changes in the relative scarcity among market goods and services. Generally, the greater the scarcity, the more spirited becomes the competitive bidding for goods or services and the higher, as a rule, the transaction price or market value.

Demand is an economic concept that implies not only the presence of a "need" but also the existence of monetary power to fill that need. Wishful-buyer thinking or necessity alone, no matter how strong, does not constitute demand; to bring about the latter, purchasing power must be available to satisfy the need or to back up the coveted demand. Builders, developers, and investors in particular should keep the purchasing-power aspects of demand in mind. For example, large-scale housing developments are often planned and carried out to fill a long-felt "need," only to end in financial grief because of failure to consider accurately the effective buying power of the prospective tenants. Hotels, amusement enterprises, and large commercial projects have also experienced a high rate of economic mortality chiefly because of failure to distinguish between need and demand, and because of inability to measure accurately the effective purchasing power of their customers.

Transferability is a legal concept that must be considered in the determination of property value. Even though the characteristics of utility, scarcity, and demand are present, if the good or thing cannot be transferred in whole or in part, market value cannot exist. The moon, for instance, has utility; it is scarce (there is only one); and there might possibly be a demand for it if ownership and use of it could be controlled. The lack of transferability, however, keeps the moon a free good marketwise. Transferability does not necessarily mean physical mobility—it means rather the possession and control of all the rights which constitute ownership of property.

Assuming that other things remain relatively equal, a change in any one of the characteristics of a property—be it utility, scarcity, demand, or transferability—will inevitably be reflected in its value. Consequently, an increase in utility as evidenced by greater soil fertility will increase the net income productivity of farmland and thus enhance its value. An increase in relative scarcity resulting from an increase in population, all other things being equal, will also be reflected in higher values for the remaining, or marketable, properties. An increase in demand caused by a rising standard of living will increase competitive bidding for more and better home sites, increasing the values of the properties so affected. Transferability, too, has an important influence on value. Generally, the greater the liquidity of a commodity, the greater its value because of the greater opportunity and flexibility present to exchange one property for another or its price equivalent. The appraiser must therefore consider with great care possible changes in value characteristics, especially where forecasts need be made for the economic life of properties extending over thirty, forty, or more years into the future. The nature, kind, and impact of forces which influence value characteristics of real properties will be more fully discussed in Chapters 4 through 8 inclusive.

READING AND STUDY REFERENCES

1. *Acquisition for Right-of-Way* (Washington, D.C.: American Association of State Highway Officials, 1962), chap. 22.
2. *The Appraisal of Real Estate* (Chicago: American Institute of Real Estate Appraisers, 1967), chaps. 2–4.
3. Babcock, Frederick M., *The Valuation of Real Estate* (New York: McGraw-Hill Book Company, Inc., 1932), chaps. 1–2.
4. *Condemnation Appraisal Practice* (Chicago: American Institute of Real Estate Appraisers, 1961), pp. 38–45.
5. Davis, W. D., "What is Market Value," *The Appraisal Journal* (Chicago: American Institute of Real Estate Appraisers, January, 1960), pp. 42–46.
6. Kinnard, William N., Jr., *An Introduction to Appraising Real Property* (Chicago: Society of Real Estate Appraisers, 1968), chap. 6.
7. Ratcliff, Richard U., *Real Estate Analysis* (New York: McGraw-Hill Book Company, Inc., 1961), chaps. 3–4.
8. Ring, Alfred A., "The Labyrinth of Value," *The Appraisal Journal* (Chicago: American Institute of Real Estate Appraisers, January, 1965), pp. 9–14.
9. Schmutz, George L., revised by Edwin M. Rams, *Condemnation Appraisal Handbook* (Englewood Cliffs, N.J.: Prentice-Hall, Inc., 1963), chap. 2.
10. Wendt, Paul F., *Real Estate Appraisal* (New York: Henry Holt and Company, 1956), chap. 1.

Development and progress in any art or science depends heavily on the knowledge which accumulates throughout history. In a way, we must stand on the shoulders of those leaders in a given field who have gone before us in order that we may raise our sights beyond the horizon of present-day knowledge and perfect the application of established principles and practices.

The art of valuation has a rich his-

2 *History and Importance of Value Thought*

tory. Much of the value thought that has developed over the past centuries is of significance today, and an understanding of the history of this thought is essential for those who seek professional status as real estate appraisers. It is the purpose of this chapter to trace the landmarks of value thought and to demonstrate their impact on prevailing methods and theories in the field of property valuation.

The concept of value as a ratio measuring the significance of goods or services demanded in exchange for other goods or services dates back to the Middle Ages. Religious beliefs, moral customs and philosophical reasoning influenced the measures and standards by which men judged the fairness of servitude, trade or barter as practiced among people. St. Thomas Aquinas, in his greatest work *Summa Theologica* (1266–1273) as translated from Latin, speaks of true value and just price. To sell a thing for more than its worth he regarded as immoral. Economic motives were thus subjected to ethical appraisal. To this day we find social, political and other non-market measures influencing the thoughts of men, judges and jurors who are called on to rule what constitutes fair, true, real, sound, or just value, especially where the taking of property is compulsory as in "eminent domain" proceedings or in instances where there is absence of unimpeded trade and barter.

MERCANTILISM

The first organized theory of value is ascribed to a group of thinkers and writers known as *mercantilists*. Under the theory of *mercantilism*—which held sway for nearly three centuries before the American Revolution in 1775—the power and well-being of a nation depended on ever increasing stocks of gold and silver or bullion and the maintenance of a favorable balance of export-import trade. Manufacturing and employment of productive labor (for exportable goods) were encouraged in order to increase national wealth through truck and international barter. The goal of mercantilists in guiding and shaping economic policy was to strengthen and increase the status of national and military power. Economic planning, generally, was directed to further national productive capacity. By edict or decree, export was encouraged and imports discouraged in order that a greater share of the world's stock of precious metals might be secured by the individual nation as a measure of national power and security.

During the sixteenth, seventeenth, and part of the eighteenth centuries (the mercantilistic period in the history of trade), a transition took place from religious, moral, and philosophical concepts of value to pseudo-economic concepts based on intrinsic and extrinsic values. The latter constituted objective value as molded by the forces of market supply and demand, whereas intrinsic value was a measure of the objects' inherent utility to render service or satisfaction in use. Development, too, of the natural sciences gave rise to a "natural" value based on competitive forces in place of "just" value that primarily rested on philosophical and moral supports. The mercantilists also emphasized production rather than distribution of wealth, and counted merchants among the best and most profitable members of the commonwealth.

Although mercantilism as an economic policy is long outdated, the theory underlying this nationalistic value and power concept is still very much relevant. The relative international power status of a nation continues to be basic not only to the welfare of its individuals but also to the value of the goods and services it trades in the open market. Appraisers as well as economists should pay careful heed to data which evidence or measure national well-being and prestige as measured for instance by balance of international trade and value of domestic currency in terms of gold. These and other economic measures such as employment, fiscal policy, inflation, etc. should be carefully observed in order to be alert to changes that influence property value.

THE PHYSIOCRATS

A revolt against mercantilism, with its emphasis on balance of trade, wealth, power, and frequent national wars took place in France. François Quesnay, a brilliant court physician to Louis XV, undertook at the monarch's request a study of the production and distribution of the national wealth. As a by-product of this study—and to support his findings—Quesnay conceived his famous *Tableau economique,* in which the production, distribution, and circulation comprising the economic activity in France was diagrammatically demonstrated. Quesnay is recognized as the founder of the physiocratic school, which is credited with laying the groundwork for the study of economics as a science as well as for the related field of political economy.

The physiocrats effectively demonstrated that production rather than trade constituted the life of a nation and that trade in fact was a "sterile," derived, and secondary economic activity depending wholly on that nation's vigor, strength, and volume of production. In the eighteenth century this production was principally agricultural in character and later writers, beginning with Adam Smith, labeled the physiocratic theory as the "Agricultural System."

It is interesting to note that the Physiocrats did not regard value as intrinsic or inherent in things. Further the concepts of price and value were accepted as interchangeable terms, both reflecting a market ratio of exchange that could far exceed the cost of production. Generally, the physiocratic theory may be viewed as a revolt against trade and the role attributed to nonproductive (money) wealth.

Study of physiocratic economic doctrine is rewarding to a student of appraising, since it reveals historical support for the productivity theory of value and the application of the net income or earnings approach as a measure of value.

CLASSICAL ECONOMICS

No attempt will be made here to discuss the writings of all those individuals in many nations who contributed to the science of economics as it developed after the publication of Adam Smith's *Wealth of Nations* in 1776. Emphasis will be placed rather on the individuals and the important theories which brought about the evolution of the concept of value specifically.

Classical economics and the development of early value theory were chiefly founded on the lectures and writings of Adam Smith, Thomas Malthus, and David Ricardo. In fact, Adam Smith is often called the founder of economics as a science. Although this is not strictly true, he was nevertheless the first to bring together in one comprehensive volume a logical and well-written treatise on the operation of those economic forces which create value and control the well-being of a nation. Smith effectively reasoned that labor constituted the foundation of national wealth, and that the *value* of any good or service is equal to the quantity of labor which it allows its owner to purchase or command. Even though the importance of land and capital as factors of production were minimized by Smith, his *barter* definition of value ("the power of a good to command other goods or labor services in exchange") remains valid to this day.

Two other significant contributions to modern value theory were made by Adam Smith. First, he stressed the important distinction between "value in use" and "value in exchange." He logically demonstrated that it was only when the utility of a service or good was accompanied by conditions of scarcity and demand that exchange or market value could arise. His second important contribution to value thought was the noteworthy distinction between the concepts of "market value" and "market price." Market (or "natural") value undoubtedly referred to "normal" prices that covered long-term costs of wages, rent, and profit. Market prices—to the extent that such differed from natural prices—reflected short-run influences exerted by temporary forces of scarcity or monopoly. To Smith, value was basically a cost-of-production theory. Since technological changes were slow in developing during the eighteenth century, it was left to later thinkers to stress the importance of *replacement cost* rather than *reproduction cost* as a better and more reliable measure of value.

Smith's greatest contribution to economics as a science was his analytical study of the impact of the division of labor and his logical development of the price system in which exchange value was the center of economic life. In retrospect, Smith's economic philosophy—in which he viewed national progress as best secured by freedom of private initiative within the bounds of justice—is judged overindividualistic and unrealistically motivated by "unreal" economic men.

The optimistic outlook of Adam Smith—that the uncontrolled economic interests of the individual (the laissez-faire economy) will best tend to increase the wealth of nations—was given a pessimistic twist by his classical-theory successors. Malthus, for example, was to gain prominence with a startling theory—that the world's natural population growth would eventually outstrip the possible and effective growth of its food supply. The tendency for man to increase in number geometrically, as compared with the arithmetic increase in agricultural production capacity, forecast a dire economic state at low subsistence levels for society at large unless artificial measures could be taken to check the birthrate. Although technological developments in the century following Malthus' writing appear to have disproved his population theory, modern economists—in pointing to present-day population growth problems in China, India, and even in much of the western world find Malthus' scholarly analysis of population-growth tendencies essential to a better understanding of current economic theory and practice.

In the development of value thought, Malthus was the first to work out a theory of underconsumption. He warned that production does not create its own demand (as was held by Adam Smith and Ricardo) and that overproduction or underconsumption may in fact create market gluts. The economic experience during the deep business depressions of later years proved not only the validity of Malthus' early theory but also his deep understanding of economic phenomena. Malthus, too, made a noteworthy contribution to a better understanding of the role of *rent* as a price-determined (surplus) return to the landowner and not, as held by Adam Smith, a price-determining cost of production. This rent theory was enlarged upon and refined by his contemporary and friend David Ricardo.

The residual theory of land value as taught today has its documentary beginning in David Ricardo's work, *Principles of Political Economy and Taxation*. Although Malthus in prior writings stressed the importance of soil quality as a rent-producing source of income, it was Ricardo who developed the theory that long-term prices (value) equalled the cost of production at the marginal point where the last and poorest land was brought into cultivation. On this marginal soil (no-rent land) the price of the product exactly equalled the cost of labor and cost of capital. Thus the greater productivity possible where more fertile land was employed yielded a surplus, or land residual return—*rent*—which accrued to the landlord and not to the employing capitalist. With an ever expanding population and the need to bring poorer and less desirable land into production increased costs of production would cause prices to rise, thus yielding an ever higher return to the better and relatively more fertile lands.

Rent as defined by Ricardo was the excess payment over the amount necessary to bring land into production and consisted of that portion of total income paid to the landlord for the original and indestructible powers of the soil. In analyzing this residual earning capacity of land, Ricardo developed the theory of the interacting margins of intensive and extensive development of land that is valid and important in land utilization studies to this day. Where (after "apparently" full capacity of land use) it was possible to make the land more productive by an expenditure of additional units of labor or capital, and by doing so produce an excess of income above that derived where like amounts of labor or capital were expended on adjacent land of like or inferior quality, then the more intensive or vertical use of land would produce a higher residual rent than could be realized by extensive or horizontal land utilization.

This theory of the interactions of margins in the intensive and extensive utilization of land is of vital importance presently whenever appraisers are charged with the responsibility to ascertain the highest and best use of land, as will be more fully developed in the following chapter. For a continuity of value thought, Ricardo's concept, that land has no claim on income and the residual economic rent has no influence on price, which is established on "no rent land," should be kept firmly in mind.

The rather cold and dismal picture of an "economic man" struggling for bare subsistence was disputed by later writers and critics of the classical school of economics. Two writers who took exception to the pessimism of Malthus and Ricardo were the French economist Frédéric Bastiat (1801–1850), and the American writer Henry Carey. Both were optimists who saw a great future, with mankind enjoying the wonders of bountiful nature. To Bastiat, value was measured not by the labor expended but rather by the labor *saved* through effective use of investment capital. The harmony he saw in the economic system was later attacked by socialistic writers such as Karl Marx, as a theory of exploitation of the labor class and a means to perpetuate the class struggle.

Carey's optimism sprang from the seemingly limitless economic opportunities which were open to all in the new and virgin territory of America. He is best known for taking exception to Ricardo's theory of rent, which was based on the extensive utilization of successively poorer (marginal) land. Carey, on the contrary, held that the poorest land was generally cultivated first and that better and more fertile land was reached as population growth made clearing of forest lands and draining of river-bottom land a necessity. Carey's theory, overinfluenced by the special and short-run conditions peculiar to virgin territory, had no lasting impact or influence on the development of value thought.

An attempt to restate the classical school of economic thought and to humanize the theory of political economy was made by a brilliant and clear-thinking writer, John Stuart Mill. Mill's greatest service was to clarify the classical economic doctrine and to inject his social philosophy in order to help formulate a concept of welfare economics. So far as the theory of value is concerned, Mill agreed with Adam Smith to the "truck and barter" concept of the power of a good to command other goods in exchange.

In his book *Principles of Political Economy,* published in 1848, Mills differentiates between *normal* value and market price. The former concept of value, he reasoned, is set and determined at the lowest point of profitable production cost; whereas, market price may be higher because of temporary or disturbed market situations. Since a rise in price above normal value will increase the supply of goods, an equilibrium of price and value is bound to be established over the long run of economic activity.

Mills was also the first economist to use the term "unearned increment" as applied to rising land values. Ascribing this increment in value to social (increased population) causes rather than landlord's capital improvements, he favored the taxing of such excess and unearned windfalls of value. This at the time, appealing mechanism to establish a more equitable distribution of wealth was readily supported by other welfare economists, and sparked a political campaign for a single (land) tax and the ultimate public ownership of land. The implementation of such a tax was espoused dramatically as the true remedy for economic injustice by Henry George in his well-known book *Progress and Poverty—The Remedy,* published in 1879. The fallacy of a single tax as well as the error of the classical school to take a minimum market demand for granted was belabored by a later school of economists, as will be noted below.

A further significant contribution to the development of value thought was made by the German estate owner and economist Johann Heinrich von Thünen. In his book, published in 1826, entitled *Der Isolierte Staat* (The Isolated State), von Thünen improved on Ricardo's rent theory by introducing the effect of economic location. Although largely hypothetical, von Thünen's writings offered a valuable study of how the economy of a region is affected by distance from the imaginary city and with changes in prices and taxes. Von Thünen was the first economist to treat clearly and systematically the influence of distance from the marketplace on cost and production of agricultural economics. Stress was laid in his writings on the interacting forces of intensive and extensive land utilization. Von Thünen pointed out that as intensive utilization of land near villages caused the cost of production to rise, extensive utilization of land at more distant places became profitable. Cost of transportation served as a balancing factor between the extensive and intensive margins of land use. Thus even at equal fertility, rent as a measure of land value was ascribable to location in reference to marketability for the products in demand. Von Thünen laid some of the groundwork on which the marginal utility economists in later years built their theory of value. He is also recognized as the founder of the economic theory of agriculture, which is based on land location and the market theory of supply and demand.

THE AUSTRIAN SCHOOL OF ECONOMICS

The classical economists conceived value to be influenced and determined by cost of production. The nature of the economy prevailing at the close of the eighteenth century caused classical writers to take the demand for a product largely for granted. Evolution in production and increasing importance of product utility gave rise to a new theory, and school, of economic psychology, founded in Austria by a trio of writers: Karl Menger (1840–1921), Friedrich von Wieser (1851–1926), and Eugene von Böhm-Bawerk (1851–1914). These writers developed the Austrian or *marginal utility* theory of economics which greatly influenced economic thought for nearly half a century.

The shortcomings of the classical school in overemphasizing one extreme of economic analysis—production—were overcompensated for by the Austrian-school adherents to the other extreme of economic analysis —demand. Menger, in fact, held that the value of any good or product was determined by the marginal utility of the last unit essential to meet demand irrespective of the cost necessary in its production. The principal weakness of the utility theory, when judged with hindsight, rested on its failure to distinguish the effects on value of both short-run and long-run economic tendencies and market forces as influenced by supply and demand. Considering short-run market conditions alone, however, the dominant role of utility as a concept of value unquestionably must be acknowledged.

Another important contribution to economic analysis made by the Austrian school was the theory of *imputation*. As logically presented by von Wieser, the value of the whole (product) in essence is derived or inferred from the value of the respective component parts. The theory of imputation served to explain the distribution of the value product— income—over the factors of production as measured by rent, wages, and profits. Von Böhm-Bawerk further refined the utility theory by developing a *market-merger* measurement (a market synthesis) of the individual scales of consumer preferences for market goods. Market price was held to be a compromise of marginal preferences supported by the subjective valuation of buyers and sellers. Von Böhm-Bawerk was also the first to develop a logical and practical theory of interest. He conceived interest to be a measure of time preference for the immediate use or consumption of capital, and present value as a discounted sum of future rights to capital income. This Austrian-school theory thus became the cornerstone of the present utility or income concept as a measure of economic value.

Since value from the individual point of view is largely subjective in character, it follows that utility in a sense "sanctions" sacrifice and thus the cost of production of a good or service. The weakness of this applied theory as espoused by the Austrian school rests chiefly in the concept that costs have no price-determining importance. The pendulum of economic theory marking the actions of the classical school had by the beginning of the twentieth century reached the extreme reaction where causation of value was explained by a search for the greatest utility at the least possible sacrifice.

THE HISTORICAL AND INSTITUTIONAL SCHOOL

This school made no direct contribution to the theory of value, but aided greatly in the growth and development of economics as a mature social science. It had its origin in Germany, where the philosophy of Hegel stressed the importance of the *state* as an institution. Under this philosophy, importance was placed on the value of historical study as an aid to better understanding of human relations. In essence this school rejected the rugged individualism of the classical school, epitomized by the "economic man" and the "iron law of wages" in a laissez-faire society, and emphasized instead the evolutionary and historical importance of economic doctrine in an ever-changing society. Representatives of this school included the German writers Werner Sombart, Max Weber, and Richard Ehrenberg. In this country, Thorstein Veblen is best known as an outstanding economic institutionalist. His famous writings included *The Theory of the Leisure Class* and *The Theory of Business Enterprise.* Other American members of the institutional and historical school included Wesley C. Mitchell, best known for his study, *Business Cycles,* and John R. Commons, best known for his *History of Labor in the United States.*

Historical economics as a *school of thought* did importantly contribute to a better understanding of the interaction of "noneconomic" motives on economic activity. Adherents to this school of thought appropriately emphasized the fallacies of extreme individualism and the doctrine of unbridled laissez-faire. The foundation was thus laid for historical and institutional adherents to broaden the scope of economics as a social science.

THE NEOCLASSICAL AND EQUILIBRIUM SCHOOL OF ECONOMICS

The important and lasting impact on value theory made by the Austrian or utility school of economics was principally because of the importance placed on the *human* or *demand* concept of value. People, it was argued, in the final analysis determine value—not objects or things. Since the wishes and economic needs of people are given expression on the demand side of the economic equation, the pendulum of value reasoning swung to the opposite extreme of that held by the adherents of the classical school of value thought.

The need for a reappraisal of economic principles grew steadily greater in a world becoming increasingly mechanistic and industrial in character. Alfred Marshall (1842–1924) a brilliant, scholarly individual trained for the ministry in his youth. Drawn into economic studies by the widespread existence of poverty and exploitation nurtured by monopolistic competition, he dedicated his life to economic teaching and writing and brought his influential concepts to the world's attention in his world-famous book *Principles of Economics,* first published in 1890. Alfred Marshall is best described as the father of modern economic thought and modern economic analysis.

Recognizing the importance and validity of the utilitarian concepts of value, Marshall reintroduced with diagramatic skill the importance that production costs exert in affecting an equilibrium of market value in the interplay of the forces of supply and demand. Marshall expertly likened the underlying causes and value influences of cost versus marginal utility (or demand) to the functions served by the blades of a pair of scissors. Each blade, he reasoned, is important, but both are needed to effect smooth and efficient cutting. This balance or interplay of economic forces in the determination of value as seen by Marshall caused his teachings to be called the *equilibrium school.*

Another noteworthy contribution to economic analysis made by Marshall was the development of a *dynamic* as opposed to a *static* theory of value. He effectively demonstrated that the separation and study of any given economic force or cause under the doctrine "everything else remaining equal" was fraught with pitfalls and errors of logic. This he made clear by referring to the position and gravity force interplay of billiard balls in a glass bowl. The removal of any one of the balls in a bowl would bring about a realignment and repositioning of the remaining balls. Modern textbooks on appraising stress the Marshallian theory of value by emphasizing the importance of correlating the social, political, and commercial activities of individuals and society in the final determination of value. The impact of changes in the purchasing power of money, in economic potential and social prosperity, in population growth and composition, and finally, in fashions, taste, and habits of society all influence forces of supply and demand and the relative prices or values at which goods and services can be exchanged.

After its publication in 1890, Marshall's *Principles of Economics* served as the bible of economic theory in all the leading universities for nearly a generation. It was left to later economists—identified with the neoclassical school—not to supplant but rather to build on the equilibrium theory in areas which during the fading years of the nineteenth century did not pose current problems in applied economics as it then served business, industry, and commerce. Development of economic thought as deduced from the study and operation of the business cycle theory and the imperfect, or monopolistic competition theory was a task left to later writers such as Joan Robinson, A. C. Pigou, Edward Chamberlain, Dennis H. Robertson, and John Maynard Keynes.

CURRENT VALUE THEORY

The periodic impact on employment, consumption, capital flow, interest, prices, and value caused by variations in the business cycle as measured by economic booms, recessions, and depressions logically led to a restudy of "traditional" economic theory in the light of social welfare and public policy. Paving the way for current value theory and practice was the scholarly contribution made by Wesley Clair Mitchell in the field of business cycles. Based on extensive and analytical research into the causes and effects of cyclical business behavior, Mitchell drew the substantiated conclusion that cyclical business behavior was not due to accident or acts of God but rather to the inevitable results of unrestricted workings of the economic system within the framework of capitalistic society. Mitchell's studies exploded the theory of an economic norm, or equilibrium, and strengthened the acceptance of an ever-changing norm in accordance with the economic principle of change and the resultant integration and disintegration of economic components—in time. To Mitchell, an equilibrium as conceived by the classical and Austrian schools of economics was nonexistent. He saw instead a continual cumulative change from one phase of a business cycle to another. Thus a boom contains seeds of recession that lead to a depression, and the latter contains seeds of prosperity that bring recovery and a recurring boom.

Another shock to traditional classical and neoclassical economics was administered by the influential writings and teachings of John Maynard Keynes. His unorthodox theories, born in depression years, were at first rejected. Today, however, Keynesian economics is taken seriously not only as a theory but also as a basis for influencing, if not guiding, public economic and fiscal policies.

It is generally recognized that Keynes has made far-reaching contributions to the theories of consumption, employment, savings, interest, and investment. Specifically, Keynes rejected the equilibrium concept as conceived by the classical and neoclassical schools even where applied to dynamic economic society. Keynes demonstrated that in a rising economy, the propensity to consume diminishes as individual incomes climb to higher brackets. Conversely, the propensity to save increases proportionately. Thus Keynes held that underconsumption rather than overproduction was the basic cause of lasting depressions. To prevent money hoarding by saving, he advocated a fiscal policy that would encourage investment and plant expansion to increase employment and consumption in times of economic stress. Conversely, at "full employment" the reverse fiscal policy is called for, savings are encouraged by rising interest rates (tight money policy) to avoid or at least mitigate inflation. The Keynesian theory of full employment and deficit financing where necessary to maintain maximum productive capacity had significant influence on economic and political policies throughout the world.

After three decades of experimentation with fiscal and economic policies on a national level, Keynesian or modern economic theory designed to achieve a dynamic equilibrium of the forces of supply and demand is now a firm and nationally accepted policy. Modern writers and teachers of economics, in an attempt to bridge the classical concepts of a premechanized and largely agrarian society to the complex workings of a series of megalopolis-populated regions, have divided the study of economics as a science into *microeconomics*—a study of the individual firm or firms, and *macroeconomics*—the study of sociopolitical economics of society as a national whole.

The operations of the national economy, at least so far as total investment, employment, and money-spending power is concerned, can no longer be left to an uncontrolled laissez-faire system. In fact the latter system lacked a stabilizer or an economic thermostat designed to adjust excess savings as well as under- or overinvestment at a level to maintain "full employment." To achieve a viable equilibrium level of income and production and to safeguard the purchasing power of the dollar, government fiscal and political policy attempts to stabilize the national economy by:

1. Changing tax rates with a rise or fall in national income.
2. Increasing or decreasing public expenditures to "heat" or "cool" the economy.
3. Priming the economic pump in times of recession through payments of unemployment compensation and increased welfare (Social Security) transfer.
4. Providing subsidies through farm-aid programs.
5. Establishing financial aids or interest rate controls to encourage or discourage corporate and family savings.

These government policies and socio-economic measures are a first line of defense to prevent recurring hardships caused by economic booms and busts. Since a stabilized economy also effects a stabilized value for real and personal property, the appraiser must know and study government socio-economic activity which now serves as the fifth and "steering" wheel that controls and directs the wheels of production—land, labor, capital, and entrepreneurial management—on which the capitalistic value system is dependent.

INFLUENCE OF VALUE THEORY UPON APPRAISAL PRACTICE

As stated in the introductory paragraph of this chapter, today's appraiser depends heavily on the body of ideas and knowledge created by past thinkers in the fields of value and economics. The value theories briefly outlined here have each contributed a link to the chain of value thought. Value theory and practice as taught by leading appraisal societies today are largely a synthesis of the important ideas and economic concepts developed by leaders of the classical, Austrian, historical, neoclassical and modern schools of value theory. The three approaches to value applied in current appraisal practice evidence especially the impact of value theory as it has developed over the past two centuries. The cost approach to value largely follows the teachings of the classical school, with greater emphasis placed perhaps on replacement cost than on reproduction cost—as was the case at the time of Adam Smith. The income approach in effect is a utilitarian measure of value which yields the present worth of future rights to income without reference to relevant cost of the agents of production. The market sales comparison approach places emphasis on short-run market forces of supply and demand, and yields an index of prevailing prices at a given time and place which may or may not equal a measure of long-term, stabilized, or warranted value. These three approaches to value are really three different ways of measuring the *same* value and are useful as a check one upon the other in judging the accuracy of the end (value) results. The correlation of the three approaches and the estimation of *market value* as defined in Chapter 3 is in effect an equilibrium of all the value forces which come to bear, at a given time and place, on typical prudent buyers and sellers.

To understand these value forces better, a first-hand study of the principal writings of the masters in economic literature, as referenced here, is a "must" for those appraisers seeking attainment of a truly professional status. The evolution of value theory, no doubt, will continue in the future as it has in the past. Alertness and awareness of ever-changing value tendencies must therefore be the watchwords of the appraisal profession.

READING AND STUDY REFERENCES

1. *Acquisition for Right-of-Way* (Washington, D.C.: American Association of State Highway Officials, 1962), chap. 22.

2. Kahn, Sanders A., Frederick E. Case, and Alfred Schimmel, *Real Estate Appraisal and Investment* (New York: The Ronald Press Company, 1963), chap. 3.

3. Kinnard, William N., Jr., *An Introduction to Appraising Real Property* (Chicago: Society of Real Estate Appraisers, 1968), chap. 6.

4. McSweeney, Thomas F., "Proposed Code of Technical Standards: Economic Background of Value," *Technical Valuation* (June 1959), pp. 27–33.

5. Rams, Edwin M., *Principles of City Land Values* (Worthington, Ohio: Academy Publishing Co., 1964), chap. 1.

6. Ratcliff, Richard U., *Real Estate Analysis* (New York: McGraw-Hill Book Company, Inc., 1961), chap. 10.

7. Schmutz, George L., revised by Edwin M. Rams, *Condemnation Appraisal Handbook* (Englewood Cliffs, N.J.: Prentice-Hall, Inc., 1963), chap. 2.

8. Unger, Maurice A., *Real Estate* (Cincinnati: South-Western Publishing Company, 1964), chaps. 2 & 25.

9. Weimer, Arthur M., "History of Value Theory for the Appraiser," *The Appraisal Journal* (October 1960), pp. 469–89.

10. Wendt, Paul F., *Real Estate Appraisal* (New York: Henry Holt and Company, 1956), chap. 2.

Although the history of value thought supports the contention that value is the heart of economics, and that all things of value created or wanted by man are objects with which economics as a science is concerned, there are nevertheless valid arguments that "property" valuation as a practiced art is greatly influenced by legal and institutional constraints. The basis for such arguments is the contention that real property and real estate—

3

Nature and Principles

of Property Valuation

which are the subjects of valuation—are principally legal and not physical or economic in character. The terms *property* and *estate* denote measures of rights and ownership which are legally identified and constitutionally guaranteed to the true owner under the *allodial* [1] system of land ownership which prevails in the United States. It stands to reason that the larger the rights, the larger the measure of value—all other things remaining equal.

The legal concept of property value and ownership, as will be demonstrated, is very important. Without a thorough understanding of the nature and character of rights in realty as recognized and supported by law, appraising as a profes-

---

[1] Private land ownership is subject to broad governmental limitations as opposed to ownership under a state-controlled (communistic) or feudal system under which absolute ownership of land rests with the king or the sovereign government.

sional practice would not be feasible. In the final analysis, no doubt, the appraiser is concerned not so much with the physical aspects of the property under value study but rather with the possible and legal uses to which the property may be put—under competent ownership and effective control.

WEALTH VERSUS PROPERTY

All tangible and useful things owned by man which have attributes of economic value are classified as "wealth." Thus an inventory of wealth would include all material and physical things controlled and owned by man to which an economic or monetary scale of value could be applied. Property, on the other hand, is an intangible concept, being the right to own or possess wealth and to put it to legal uses if one wishes. Property thus is a legal right that expresses the relationship between owners and their possessions. To illustrate: A forty-acre farm in North Carolina may possess certain given physical characteristics and measurable natural qualities of fertility. These physical facts are known, and the land can rightly be classified as wealth. The value of this farm, however, depends on the legal and permissible uses (property rights) to which this farm may be put. If only cotton can be grown commercially, one value will result; but under corn or truck farming, another and higher value will accrue to land. If a government allotment makes possible the growing of leaf tobacco, a still higher—and perhaps maximum—farm use value will result. This illustration should make it clear that the appraiser is concerned only secondarily with physical attributes of wealth. His chief and prime interest must be the valuation of rights or property in land and its improvement.

The distinction between wealth and private property can further and more dramatically be illustrated by considering the impact that national decree effects under which the ownership of all land is transferred (confiscated) from the estates of individuals to the nation as a whole. Such a shift of ownership actually did occur in Cuba in 1960, and presently is a matter of national policy in all communistic countries. Confiscation of wealth and the shifting of property rights which control this wealth from one person or persons to another or to the state as a whole does not alter the inventory or magnitude of total national wealth, but it does destroy the value of such property (rights) as were vested in the individual. To safeguard Americans from such governmental decrees the Fifth and Fourteenth Amendments to the constitution provide that no life, liberty or property may be taken from anyone without due process of law and without just compensation where such taking is for public use and in the public interest.

THE ECONOMIC CONCEPT OF PROPERTY

Land is the original and basic factor of production. Without land man could not exist. No commodity can be produced and no improvement erected without using land. Land as nature provided it consists of the earth's crust, including the underlying soil which provides life-sustaining fertility and supporting power for structures and other man-made improvements. Legally, possession of a given part of this crust of land includes rights to the control of minerals, gas, and oil below the earth's surface as well as the air space above the ground. Thus the boundaries of any parcel of land extend in the shape of an inverted pyramid from the center of the earth upward to the limits of the atmosphere.

Land as originally provided by nature no longer exists anywhere on earth. All land has been directly or indirectly modified by man—directly by the construction of improvements on the site and indirectly by improvements related to the site, such as access roads, bridges, canals, and parks. Land, together with its improvements, is designated as *realty*.

The ownership of realty is classified as *property*. Where this ownership is for a term of years, the property (right) becomes *personal* property. Where the ownership of realty extends for a lifetime, or longer to heirs, or forever to assigns, the property (right) becomes *real* property. Thus a lessee possesses personal property in realty, whereas a lessor—to whom the realty reverts at the termination of the lease—owns real property subject to conditions and terms of the lease. Where the term *estate* is used to designate an interest owned, the meaning of real estate and real property are one and the same. *Real estate,* however, as a term is also used to identify the business engaged in by those who conduct commercial transactions in real property. The term realty as used in this book includes not only the land and building improvements, but also anything permanently affixed to land or building where the reasonable intent—as supported by the method of annexation and the relationship of the parties involved at the time of annexation—causes the article to be classified as a *fixture:* to wit, furnaces, wall-to-wall carpets, built-in cabinets and similar (fixture) improvements.

THE "BUNDLE OF RIGHTS"

The largest possible estate in real property is known as *fee simple.* Where such ownership exists to the exclusion of all others, the possessor is said to have the complete *bundle of rights.* That is, the "bundle" contains all the individual "sticks" or interests essential to fee simple ownership, including the right to use or not to use the property, the right to lease all or parts of the property (air rights, surface rights, mineral rights, easements, and rights of way), the right to sell or not to sell, and the right to donate or grant the property as a gift. Care must be taken by the appraiser to ascertain whether the entire bundle of property rights is to be conveyed by sale or included in the valuation. Since property rights are both separable and divisible it is likely that the bundle of rights is incomplete—whether by partial sale, lease, or by private or governmental limitation—in which case the value of the property is bound to be affected.

All land in the United States—whether owned in *fee simple, fee upon conditions, fee determinable,* or as a *life estate*—is subject to certain Government limitations on ownership, imposed for the mutual welfare of all citizens. These limitations fall under: [2]

1. The police power of government.
2. The right of eminent domain.
3. The right of taxation.
4. Escheat to the state.

POLICE POWER

The police power is a sovereign power inherent in state government and exercised or delegated by it to the village, city, county, or other governing agency to restrict the use of realty in order to protect the well-being of its citizens. Under police power the rights in property, its use, and occupation may be restricted—without any compensation whatever—when government deems such restrictions necessary in the interest of the welfare, morals, or safety of its citizens. It is to this power that citizens take recourse for city planning and zoning as well as for building, urban, and subdivision control. Regulations of rent control authorities and building, fire, and health departments are exercises of the police power and are in fact limitations on the "use" of land.

EMINENT DOMAIN

The right of *eminent domain* is the power inherent in the governmental body to "take" an owner's land, or any part of it (air rights, road easements, etc.) by due process of law, when the necessity arises. Only two requirements must be met: the use must be public, and just compensation must be made to the owner. Whether or not the owner wants to surrender his land makes no difference—nor can he set his own price. His desires are

---

[2] For a full discussion of real estate interests and ownership, see Chapter 4 of Alfred A. Ring and Nelson L. North, *Real Estate Principles and Practices,* 6th ed. (Englewood Cliffs, New Jersey: Prentice-Hall, Inc., 1967).

not consulted; but a fair valuation, fixed, as a rule, by expert appraisers, is paid him. Land is obtained for streets, parks, public buildings, and other public or social purposes through the exercise of this power.

RIGHT OF TAXATION

Under the right of taxation, the state levies taxes for its support and for the maintenance of all its varied branches which protect and benefit its citizens. It is fair that citizens should pay for the protection and benefit they receive. Land, because of its permanence and accessibility, is a convenient article to tax and is usually the basis for local taxation. If such taxes, when levied, are not paid in due course the owners may lose their land as the result of tax law enforcement. Taxes, too, are a cost of land use and operations. Where such taxes are excessive, the value of land and its improvements is adversely affected.

ESCHEAT

Under the allodial system *escheat* does not limit land ownership but rather provides for the reversion or escheat of land to the state when an owner of land dies, leaving no heirs and not disposing of the land by will. This, however, seldom happens for generally—difficult as it may sometimes be—heirs can be found. Since it is not possible to conceive of land becoming "unowned," the law of escheat to the state provides a logical solution.

In addition to the governmental limitations, real property is often subject to private or contractual limitations on ownership. Such limitations are usually contained in deeds, easements, and leases for mortgage instruments. Where the bundle of rights is limited, the appraiser must note such restrictions and estimate the effect on value as reflected by typical market operations.

THE CONCEPT OF HIGHEST AND BEST USE

In order for land to be productive and income-yielding it must be combined (improved) with capital and labor. This is accomplished by the coordinator or entrepreneur. Since capital and labor are relatively mobile and free to be employed where compensation in the form of interest and wages is highest, these factors of production cannot be attracted unless a competitive return is assured them. Labor, under provisions of law as well as of necessity, must be compensated first or it will cease to operate. Capital, too, unless profitably employed will seek investment opportunities elsewhere. It is true that once capital is committed to land it becomes semifixed in character—but capital can be withdrawn in one form or another through neglect of maintenance or through accelerated depreciation charges.

Because labor, capital, and entrepreneurial compensations have priority claims on the income or products of land only the balance remaining after the due shares to the mobile factors of production (labor, capital, and entrepreneurial compensations) are paid serves as a measure of the earning power of land. Because land receives what is *left* as a *residue* of the total income stream, land is said to be *residual* in character.

The passive nature of land, which causes its income to be residual, makes it of prime importance that land be employed under its *highest and best possible use*. Only under such use can land attain its maximum return of income and hence its maximum value.

Highest and best use is logically defined as "that possible and legal use or employment which will preserve the utility [usefulness] of the land and yield a net income flow that forms, when capitalized at the proper market rate of interest, the highest present value of the land." It must be kept in mind that a given parcel of land may be available for alternative and competitive uses. Nevertheless, a site can have only *one* highest and best use at a given time. Thus, for instance, the highest and best use of an urban site may be to leave it vacant in order that it may "ripen" into an anticipated use that forms a higher present value than it would under the immediate and alternate uses to which the land might be put. This may be the case, for instance, where a tract of land can be developed for apartment-house purposes, but an urban study has disclosed that the site location will prove ideal as a neighborhood shopping center in three to five years. The proper choice in this instance should be supported by an appraisal study in which the value findings will serve as a guide to appropriate economic action. No doubt the present worth of future rights to income will be higher under a commercial use in this instance although the property is to be idle during the years of ripening.

The determination of the highest and best use of a given parcel of land at a given time requires careful study and expert analysis of the social, political, and economic forces which influence land utilization and land income over the economic life of the improvements. Basically, the amount of net income that can accrue to a parcel of land is essentially limited by the *law of diminishing returns*. Under this law employment of additional units of production will yield an increasing residual (net) income to land until a maximum of income per unit of investment is reached, after which diminishing returns set in until a point is reached at which the last unit of input yields only an income great enough to cover its cost with no return to land. It is at this point that the aggregate income to land is highest. By analysis of the hypothetical uses to which a site can legally be employed—now and in years to come—the appraiser is able to select that use which will yield to land its highest present value.

The ability of land to absorb additional units of labor and capital profitably is economically classified as land *capacity*.[3] Capacity refers to the volume of input. Some sites have the capacity to absorb millions of

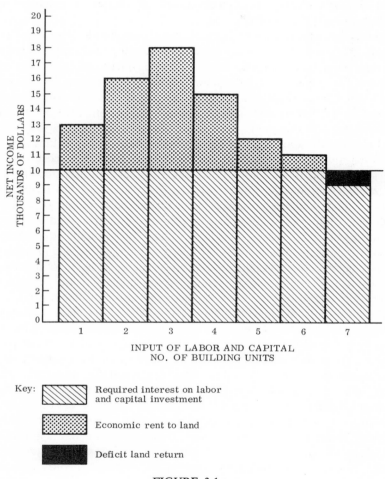

FIGURE 3.1

---

[3] The concepts of capacity and efficiency of land utilization were originally and ably introduced by H. B. Dorau and A. G. Hinman in *Urban Land Economics* (New York: The Macmillan Company, 1928).

dollars before the point of no return (to land) is reached. Other sites reach maximum capacity on the expenditure of a few thousand dollars. In the illustration shown in Figure 3.1, the capacity of the site is reached on expenditure of labor and material sufficient to erect a six-story building. Construction of less than six stories in this instance would constitute an underimprovement, and construction of a higher structure an overimprovement. Either under- or overimprovement will cause a diminution in the overall property value of this site.

The construction of a one-story building as shown in Figure 3.1 results in a net income sufficient to cover not only building operating expenditures, but also required earnings to meet interest payments on labor and capital investment plus an excess or residual return (rent) to land in the amount of $3,000. The addition of a second-story unit further increases excess rent income by $6,000. A third-story addition yields another $8,000 as excess land income. At this point, and under this selected use, the efficiency of land per unit of labor and capital input is at its highest. So long, however, as added units of labor and capital cover their investment costs and yield excess rent returns, the property warrants further and more *intensive* land utilization. As shown in Figure 3.1, the parcel's capacity to absorb added units of labor and capital is reached with the construction of a six-story building. Adding a seventh floor would result in a deficit land income, thus diminish both land income and land value. The economic loss caused by an overimprovement of a subject property is chargeable, as will be demonstrated below, as economic obsolescence (depreciation) to the building improvements and not to the value of the land. For the latter's value logically is established under the highest and most profitable use.

A study of land capacity by itself, however, is insufficient in a determination of highest and best use. The appraiser need further consider the efficiency of land return in relation to land capacity under alternative types of uses. Two sites with equal capacity may differ in efficiency of land return and hence differ in value. Sites developed for apartment housing have often greater capacity (to absorb construction dollars profitably) than commercial sites in downtown areas. The greater efficiency of business property, too, may more than offset the lack of land capacity. Whereas capacity refers to the ability of land to absorb capital outlays profitably, efficiency refers to a measure of quality as represented by the ratio of dollar land input to dollar land output in terms of income and capital expense. Figure 3.2 is intended to demonstrate a case where alternate land uses provide the same capacity but differ in efficiency, and hence value, as determined by the amount of residual land income.

The more efficient land use, as shown in Figure 3.2, is to improve the property with a six-story office building. Zoning permitting, the residual rent under an office building substantially exceeds that realized under an

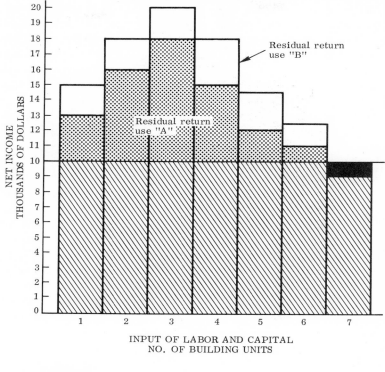

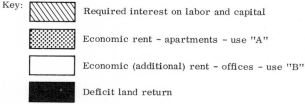

FIGURE 3.2

apartment-house development. As demonstrated in Figure 3.3, the cumulative economic rent under use "A" is $25,000 as compared with $38,000 under the more efficient use "B." The ratio of efficiency per unit of labor and capital input is 38 ÷ 6 or 6⅓ under the highest and best use and 25 ÷ 6 or 4⅙ for the next best or alternate use. The higher the ratio of output in relation to input, the greater the efficiency of land use. As demonstrated, the highest and best use of a site is not necessarily that use which permits development to the greatest capacity nor that use with the greatest efficiency. It is rather that use in which the composite results of

CUMULATIVE ECONOMIC RENT
UNDER ALTERNATE DEVELOPMENT

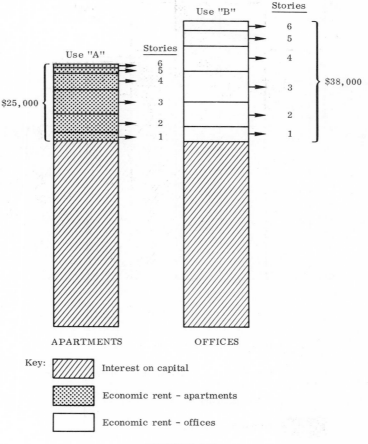

FIGURE 3.3

CUMULATIVE ECONOMIC RENT UNDER ALTERNATE DEVELOPMENT

capacity and efficiency of land use brings the greatest net return that forms a basis for the land's highest present value. Capacity and efficiency bear the same relation to the quality of a parcel of land that length and breadth do to the area of a rectangle. An examination of Figure 3.3 shows that the more efficient land use represents an income area of thirty eight unit squares (6⅓ efficiency ratio times 6.0 capacity). The larger the area, other things remaining equal, whether due to greater capacity or greater efficiency of land use, the higher the net income and hence value. Only by careful study and analysis of permissible and economically feasible alternative land uses can the appraiser determine professionally the highest present value of a site.

Once the highest and best use of a site has been determined, and the value under such use fixed, it stands to reason that the misuse of a site either through over- or underimprovement cannot subtract from this value. Man-made errors arising from improper land utilization must be charged against the value of the improvements as a form of functional or economic obsolescence (depreciation). To illustrate: Assume that there is a two-story apartment building costing $30,000. Assume further that the land value under this use is $10,000. If because of miscalculation an improvement costing $60,000 is placed on this land, and the total value of land and building upon completion proves to be only $65,000, then the value of the component parts is derived as follows:

Total value	$65,000
Value of land under highest and best use	10,000
Value of improvement	$55,000

The difference between building cost of $60,000 and building value of $55,000 is a functional loss (depreciation) in the amount of $5,000 due to an overimprovement.

To restate the land utilization principle: Land value is based on residual land income under the highest and best use of the land. Under any other use both income and value diminish and the value loss incurred constitutes "built-in" depreciation. *Only under the highest and best land use are costs of improvement equal to market value of such improvements.*

The income which is ascribable to land under its highest and best use is known as *economic rent*. It is that rent which the land is capable of producing when employed to its optimum capacity and efficiency. Any other income or rent agreed on between owner and tenant is known as *contract rent*. Where the contract rent is less than the economic rent, the owner in fact transfers a portion of the land value to the user. Where contract rent exceeds economic rent, the owner realizes a bonus value which is computed by capitalization of these excess earnings at an appropriate risk rate (capitalization rate) as will be demonstrated in Chapter 20.

In addition to the concept of highest and best land use and the principle of increasing and decreasing return resulting from intensive land utilization it is essential for the student of appraising to understand the operations of other principles, quasiprinciples, and market rules of operations as follows:

1. Substitution or opportunity cost.
2. Contribution or marginal productivity.
3. Market supply and demand.

4. Balance in land use and development.
5. Anticipation of future rights to income.
6. Change in socio-economic patterns.

SUBSTITUTION

All properties, no matter how diverse their physical attributes or how varied in geographic location, are substitutable economically in terms of service utility or in income productivity. The economic concept of substitution thus sets an upper limit of value that is set by the cost of acquisition of an equally desirable substitute property, provided such can be fashioned without undue (costly) delay.

The theory of substitution is applicable not only to the replacement of a new property of reasonably equal service utility or earnings capacity but also to an existing old or equally depreciated replica. It is this theory of substitution that warrants application of the direct market, income, and cost comparison approaches to value which will be demonstrated more fully in the following chapters.

THE PRINCIPLE OF CONTRIBUTION

Whereas in the development of land the principle of highest and best use is guiding as to the type of improvement that should be erected to support the highest present value of the land, in expenditures for modernization or property betterment the principle of *contribution* must be observed. Briefly, the principle provides that an investment (sacrifice of factors of production) is warranted when the added income flow is sufficiently large to cover all costs of operation and maintenance ascribable to the investment, and leaves a surplus sufficiently great to cover interest and amortization provisions over the economic life of the improvement.

The late George L. Schmutz, M. A. I., stated the principle of contribution as follows: [4]

> The value of any individual agent in production [of gross income] depends upon how much it adds to the net income because of its presence, or detracts from it by reason of its absence.

Practical application of this principle can be demonstrated in this manner: Suppose the owner of a large apartment building considers air-conditioning the entire structure. This project should not be undertaken unless the capitalized value of the anticipated added net income equals

---

[4] George L. Schmutz, *The Appraisal Process* (Studio City, California: published by the author, rev. ed., 1953), p. 64.

or exceeds the costs of the air-conditioning improvements, including installation and cost of maintenance. Should the capitalized added net income—derived from increased rentals—support a maximum value of $10,000 and the capital costs for air-conditioning exceed this amount, then the betterment would not be economically justified. To proceed with it would be in violation of the principle of contribution.

An understanding of the principle of contribution is also important in a determination of highest and best land use. A feasibility study undertaken to test economic advantages of alternate land uses requires a study of marginal productivity at the point where intensive or vertical land use balances output (income) realized at the margin of horizontal or extensive land utilization. When productivity under intensive and extensive land uses are in balance, the two margins merge into one (of equal productivity) in conformity with the principle of contribution.

SUPPLY AND DEMAND

In applying the principle of contribution the practical appraiser essentially undertakes an effective comparison between capital input and output under proposed or alternate improvement plans. Since the output of income from rentals or operation is governed by the economic law of supply and demand the value of a given improvement may or may not equal costs, depending on the status of the market and the present and potential quantity and quality of competition. Care must be taken to analyze thoroughly the market operation under *typical* conditions in order to avoid the pitfall of capitalizing excess income, which is temporary in nature and due to consumer time preference as to the moment of purchase, caused by scarcity or transitional monopoly. Like water seeking its natural level, so excess income (profit) will seek its natural level through the increased competition it will attract.

Where market forces are competitively free to operate, and where population is unrestricted in movement and migration from farm to urban and from urban to suburban areas, the shift in balance or changes in the interaction of supply and demand for housing causes prices to fluctuate from a high point at extreme scarcity to bargain prices below cost of replacement in a buyers market and generally in areas where supply is superadequate. Economists characterize this trade imbalance by reference to long-range values and short-run prices. Since appraisals are made as of a given date or moment in the overall sequence of time, it is important that market forces which abnormally influence supply and demand for real property in a given community be carefully analyzed and their impact on present value noted and explained.

THE ROLE OF BALANCE IN LAND USE
AND DEVELOPMENT

An understandable error to which many field appraisers are prone is evaluating property without due consideration of the principle of *balance*. If the value of a site under the Empire State Building or some other well-known skyscraper has been reasonably established, it does not necessarily mean that the site adjacent to it warrants a like value. A market study may disclose that one skyscraper will amply serve the space needs of a community for many years, while the construction of another may spell economic loss if not disaster to the owners of both. The resulting loss in property value would be a direct measure of the degree to which the principle of balance had been violated. The presence of too many hotels, motels, restaurants, drugstores, or other building facilities brings about a "buyer's market" in which lowered values will reflect the degree of imbalance in relation to demand.

To guard against value losses caused by lack of property balance, an appraiser must know his community and be thoroughly conversant with effective land utilization as well as with community planning policies. This will be more fully discussed in Chapter 6.

The principle of balance and its influence on value can also be effectively considered in judging interior design and the efficiency of a floor plan. Too many or inadequate bathrooms, bedrooms, or storage areas; wasted space in kitchen, hall, or living rooms; ceilings which are too high or too low; and over- or undersized heating, piping, or cabinet facilities— all are symptoms of interior imbalance that may be reflected in value losses. The technique used to measure the amount of such losses will be more fully treated in Chapter 12.

ANTICIPATION OF FUTURE RIGHTS TO
INCOME

Market value, although limited in amount by the operation of the forces of supply and demand, does to the owner and user of real property reflect a measure of anticipated property utility and hence is defined as "the present worth of future rights to income." It is the future and not the past with which the appraiser must be concerned. The history of operation of the subject, or, like properties in a market area, is important only in ascertaining a trend in anticipated earnings over the remaining economic life of the property under evaluation. Past operations and other than "typical" management practices may hinder or in the case of accumulated good will accelerate (at least for a time) income production. Such assets or liabilities as attach to a property must be considered in the measure of present value.

Changes in anticipated demand caused by improvements "to" the land in forms of highways, freeways, bridges, schools, and parkways have an important impact on market value even though such improvements are in the planning stage and not visible at the time of the appraisal. The principle of anticipation thus points up the importance of being fully informed in community affairs and with economic changes anticipated in the market area of which the subject property forms an integral part.

CHANGES IN SOCIO-ECONOMIC PATTERNS

To the student of appraising it must now be apparent that the principles of property valuation as outlined above are interrelated and that all of them must be considered separately and as a whole if a reliable and accurate estimate of value is to be derived. Perhaps the single greatest error in value judgments is traceable to a form of phlegmatism that causes inexperienced appraisers to take the present status quo for granted. Next to death and taxes, nothing is as certain as the impact of change. Change, of course, is a product of technological progress and the resulting shift in socio-economic patterns of living. One need only reflect on causes which led to a decline in the value of horses and buggies, bicycles, passenger ships, and railroads. Even the airplane may soon join other declining modes of transportation should rocket power be harnessed economically and with safety for use by individuals. An appraiser must not only be conscious of the forces of change, but learn to also evaluate their impact. This is essential in measuring the degree of anticipated changes causing functional and possible economic obsolescence as well as the ever-present value losses caused by age, wear, tear, and actions of the elements.

READING AND STUDY REFERENCES

1. *Acquisition for Right-of-Way* (Washington, D.C.: American Association of State Highway Officials, 1962), chaps. 21 & 23.
2. *The Appraisal of Real Estate* (Chicago: American Institute of Real Estate Appraisers, 1967), chap. 3.
3. Babcock, Frederick M., *The Valuation of Real Estate* (New York: McGraw-Hill Book Company, Inc., 1932), chap. 13.
4. Cherney, Richard A., "The Principal of Highest and Best Use," *The Real Estate Appraiser* (February 1964), pp. 12–15.
5. *Condemnation Appraisal Practice* (Chicago: Amer. Instit. of Real Estate Appraisers, 1961), pp. 25–37.

6. Kahn, Sanders A., Frederick E. Case, and Alfred Schimmel, *Real Estate Appraisal and Investment* (New York: The Ronald Press Company, 1963), chaps 3 & 7.

7. Ring, Alfred A., *Real Estate Principles and Practices,* 6th ed. (Englewood Cliffs, N.J.: Prentice-Hall, Inc., 1967), chap. 22.

8. Robbins, Richard M., *et al.* "Highest and Best Use," *The Appraisal Journal,* (April 1968), pp. 255–262.

9. Schmutz, George L., revised by Edwin M. Rams, *Condemnation Appraisal Handbook* (Englewood Cliffs, N.J.: Prentice-Hall, Inc., 1963), chaps. 1–2.

10. Unger, Maurice A., *Real Estate* (Cincinnati, O.: South-Western Publishing Company, 1964), chaps. 22–23.

11. Weimer, Arthur M., and Homer Hoyt, *Real Estate,* 5th ed. (New York: The Ronald Press Company, 1966), chap. 15.

Perhaps no single concept in the theory of value gives rise to greater miscalculations by both laymen and appraising practitioners than the concept of *cost*. Cost and value are confused because sacrifices in terms of dollars or in labor and materials are necessary in order to supply goods or services in demand, and in the long run such sacrifices or costs must equal value if construction (production) is to continue and prove eco-

4 Importance of Cost,
Price, Income, and Market

nomically rewarding. Then too, as was explained in Chapter 3, under highest and best use, cost influences the *supply* side of value—and since value without expenditure or cost of production is unthinkable, it would appear that the reliance on cost as a measure of value is justified.

There are a number of reasons, nevertheless, why due care must be exercised before accepting costs as a measure of value. First, cost and value are only equal if, among other considerations, the property is new or proposed. Since improvements age physically from the day of construction, and since forces of obsolescence—both functional and economic —are operating constantly because of changes in style, use, and demand, depreciation must be accounted for accurately and subtracted from cost when new in order that *depreciated cost* may reflect a truer measure of value. Second, cost and value are one and the same only where the improvements represent the highest and best use. Since many properties are under- or overimproved—or misimproved—cost and value may differ significantly. Finally, costs must be economically warranted if the sacrifice of the agents of production is to equal value. To illustrate: Digging a hole in the ground for no purpose whatever except to satisfy a whim does not create value. In fact, the hole in the ground may constitute "negative" value because it may have to be filled again in order to make the site economically usable. Costs which are not justified cannot equal value because no "informed" buyer will pay more for a good or service than is warranted at a given time or place and under prevailing economic conditions. The proverbial "hotel built in a desert" is an illustration of this. Cost is always a measure of a past sacrifice either of labor or materials or both, and always represents a measure of *past* expenditures. Value, on the other hand, always lies in the future because value, by definition, constitutes the *present worth* of future rights to income.

REPLACEMENT COSTS VERSUS REPRODUCTION COSTS

Even when costs are accounted for and deemed acceptable as a measure of value it is *replacement* cost and not *reproduction* cost that must be considered in a determination of value. The valid question facing an informed buyer or a professional appraiser is what it would cost to duplicate the subject improvements. By *duplication* is meant a replacement of the utility or amenities which the property is expected to offer a typical buyer. Where modern methods of construction and design offer savings in both labor and material costs as compared with methods in vogue many years ago, it stands to reason that reproduction costs could not truly measure value. Ceilings may be too high or too low, walls excessively thick or not properly reinforced, the floor plan outmoded or simply wasteful in space utilization, and convenient built-ins lacking. To reproduce such a structure—even on paper for hypothetical calculation of value—would be a wasteful practice. Only where required by law—as in condemnation trials, where the owner's property is to be left intact—may a reproduction cost estimate be in order. But even here the law in most states requires the owner's property to be left intact in terms of *value,* and only a replacement of like improvements, or what typical buyers value as such in open market transactions, can effectively serve as the final guide to just compensation.

Replacement cost is defined as "the necessary expenditure or sacrifice of the agents of production required to replace the improvements with one having the same utility." Reproduction costs, on the other hand, measure the sacrifice necessary to reproduce a replica of the building improvements. There are currently two schools of appraisal thought. One holds that to apply replacement costs as a measure of value constitutes "lazy" appraising, inasmuch as many forms of functional and economic depreciations are circumvented and not accounted for unless a reproduction cost estimate is first obtained. From this estimate of reproduction cost subtraction should then be made for all evidences and forms of accrued depreciation resulting from wear and tear, action of the elements, and all forms of functional and economic obsolescence. Thus if the present building walls are of brick twenty-four inches thick, the reproduction cost adherents would estimate the cost to reproduce these walls even though modern methods of construction call for steel reinforced walls with a maximum thickness of twelve inches. The other school of appraisal thought (to which this writer subscribes) maintains that it is wasteful to estimate reproduction cost when factual evidence supports the conclusion reached by typically informed buyers that replacement costs set the ceiling of value, and that reference to costs of reproducing an outmoded replica is not a realistic approach to accurate value measurement.

In choosing replacement cost rather than reproduction cost as a measure of value, the appraiser must take care not to double up depreciation losses. Such doubling of value losses takes place when faulty methods of construction or design are eliminated in the calculation of replacement cost and then included again in the estimate of accrued depreciation. To state it differently, where replacement costs are lower than reproduction costs of a subject property the estimate cannot be reduced again for faults which theoretically have been cured by the cost estimator. Such practice distorts the facts and places a property as well as its owner in double jeopardy. The application of the cost approach and the technique of measuring accrued depreciation will be dealt with fully in later chapters.

PRICE AS A MEASURE OF VALUE

Price paid simply represents an expression of value—i.e., market value—in terms of dollars. Before accepting a price as bonafide evidence of value, however, it is essential that the appraiser verify the transaction in order to learn the extent to which the purchase price in relation to value should be adjusted upward or downward because of the following:

1. The relationship of the parties.
2. The terms of sale and the market conditions.
3. The date of sale.
4. The effect of changes in the purchasing power of the dollar.

The importance of the relationship of parties is self-evident. Unless the buyer and the seller deal on a reasonably objective and impersonal basis, little reliance can be placed on their transaction as representing *typical* attitudes of market buyers and sellers. Thus a sale from father to son, or brother to sister would hardly represent typical market exchanges. Neither would sales from one corporation to a subsidiary company, nor from an employer to an employee be considered evidence of *market* value. Such sales, even though validly recorded on public records, must be disregarded in favor of impersonally objective transactions by sellers and buyers who have bartered freely and independently in an *open* market in which the sale was offered with full and open knowledge of the property's potential uses and where its availability to all concerned is readily and widely known.

The greatest single factor responsible for differences in the price-value relationship is the underlying conditions, or terms of sale. Where the sale is made on time, where down-payments are extremely low, and where the mortgage payments are spread over many years at favorable (below market) rates of interest, the price paid for a property will reflect these favorable terms. In such cases, the buyer has in effect purchased two things: (1) the property, and (2) time preference (terms) for paying conveniently out of future earnings in the years to come. Suppose two residences, equal in every respect as to location, quantity and quality of construction and valued at $20,000, each sell on terms as follows:

House A   All cash
House B   10 percent cash as down-payment and the balance payable in equal installments over 20 years at 6 percent interest.

House A, if sold objectively at $20,000, represents a price equal to property value. House B will realize a price of $20,000 (property value) plus the value of favorable terms that accrue because of the low cash payment, the high mortgage-to-equity ratio, and the below-market interest rates. Assuming House B sold for $21,000, the price paid represents the following:

Value of the property	$20,000
Value of terms	1,000
Total transaction price	$21,000

The appraiser, in accepting sale B for market comparison purposes, would have to consider the low down-payment and other favorable terms when relying on this sale for evidence of value.

In judging prices as evidence of value, care must also be taken to determine whether the market is *normal,* whether the buyer and seller acted with *typical* care, and whether the buyer was fully informed as to the present and potential utility (income) which the property can render under the existing and potential uses to which it can legally be put. By normal market is meant conditions when market supply and demand are in balance, or equilibrium, and when prices paid neither reflect a premium, because of scarcity of supply (seller's market), nor a discount, because of oversupply (buyer's market). Furthermore, it stands to reason that, unless the parties to the transactions are mature and fully informed as to the present and potential uses of the subject property, the price paid cannot be guiding as evidence of value. At all times it is essential to judge market transactions with typical informed buyers and sellers, acting in a typical market without duress, in mind.

In analyzing market transactions, the date of sale is also of great importance. Appraisers as a rule rely on the date of the transaction as shown on the deed of record as evidence of time of sale. It is essential to recognize that the date of sale, guiding in courts of law, is not the date of deed-recording or date of transfer of title but rather the day on which a meeting of minds of the parties to the contract for deed took place. Since it is possible that months, or even years, may elapse between the date of contract and the date of transfer of title by deed, adjustments must be made to account for possible economic effects on market prices occurring during the interval between the date of contractual agreement and the date of appraisal of a given property.

Perhaps the most confusing aspect in price adjustment due to lapse of time over either past or future years is attributable to *inflation,* i.e., changes in the purchasing power of the dollar. Assume that a property constructed twenty years ago for $10,000 sold today for $20,000. What has been the change in value? Certainly the price has risen to double the number of dollars; but if the purchasing power of the dollar has shrunk to 35 percent in the time interval, the value of the property today, assuming no depreciation, in terms of constant (uninflated) dollars is $7,000, showing a loss of 30 percent rather than in increase of 100 percent as indicated by inflated dollar prices. This illustration is intended to give emphasis to the economic truth that *market prices* merely provide a measure of the purchasing power of the money (dollars) paid. The economic impact of changes in the purchasing power of money can perhaps be better realized if a parallel situation could be visualized in a nonmonetary field of practice. Suppose that by governmental decree the number of inches in the standard measure of a foot were altered and thus varied from month to month or year to year. The resulting confusion in the construction industry would almost be incalculable. If 24 inches are finally accepted as the inflated parts of a "foot," does that make all mankind twice as tall? Conversely, doubling all wages at times when all goods and services have doubled in price does not make a wage earner twice as rich. In effect such price inflation may harm the typical worker where his savings melt in power to exchange for other economic goods, and where lagging adjustment to income-tax rates exact a higher levy through payroll deductions.

Fortunately for the appraiser, where the task is to estimate value in *present* dollars, anticipated inflation is of little or no concern provided the sale of property is to be on a cash basis and the bundle of rights to be conveyed is typically unencumbered or unimpaired. Like ships which maintain their size and position no matter how high the waves rise, so unencumbered properties in a free economy should retain their purchasing-power position, unaffected by the rising or falling level of prices. The power of a good to command other goods in exchange, other things remaining equal, cannot logically be affected by inflation. Changes in the level of prices are only significant where such affect the equilibrium of supply and demand for given goods and services. This would occur where savings are wiped out or changes in the pattern of living become mandatory.

There are, however, circumstances and conditions when inflation, or the threat of it, is of serious concern to the appraiser. This would be the case where the property or its income cannot adjust itself as readily as a ship in a rising sea to changes in the level of prices. Under price or rent control, for instance, the income is "anchored," and rising price levels in effect economically diminish if not "drown" the power of that good to be exchanged for other goods which are free from such controls.

The relationship of changing (inflated) prices to value can effectively be demonstrated by comparing the price-value ratio of a property with the price-value ratio of another commodity—let's say coffee—in times of inflation. Assuming, all else remaining equal, that the purchasing power of the dollar declined 33⅓ percent, and that as a consequence prices increased threefold, a valid comparison of the property—coffee value-price relationship would be as follows:

Year	Price of Property	Purchasing Power of Dollar in Terms of Coffee
19—	$10,000	$10,000 @ $.25 per lb. obtains 40,000 lbs.
20 years later	$30,000	$30,000 @ $.75 per lb. obtains 40,000 lbs.

As the above table indicates, the price of the property increased in terms of dollars over a twenty-year period from $10,000 to $30,000. A relative price change has also taken place with coffee, which went from 25¢ per pound to 75¢ per pound. Though prices for both goods increased 200 percent, the value relationship of one good to another remained the same. The property exchanged for 40,000 pounds of coffee now as it did twenty years ago. This is as it should be where prices of properties are economically free to adjust themselves. Under such circumstances the appraiser need not be concerned with inflation if charged to find present value in present dollars.

The impact of inflation on fixed income can effectively be demonstrated again by use of the property-coffee relationship assuming, for purposes of this illustration, a 60 percent first mortgage on a residential property as follows:

Year	Price of Property	Purchasing Power of Dollar in Terms of Coffee
19—	$10,000 Total	$10,000 @ $.25 per lb. obtains 40,000 lbs.
	6,000 Mortgage	6,000 @ $.25 per lb. obtains 24,000 lbs.
	4,000 Equity	4,000 @ $.25 per lb. obtains 16,000 lbs.
20 years later	$30,000 Total	$30,000 @ $.75 per lb. obtains 40,000 lbs.
	6,000 Mortgage	6,000 @ $.75 per lb. obtains 8,000 lbs.
	24,000 Equity	24,000 @ $.75 per lb. obtains 32,000 lbs.

Here again the exchange value of the property as a whole in relation to coffee has not changed. The property commanded 40,000 pounds of coffee today as it did 20 years ago. The relative value positions of the equity and mortgage interests, however, have been materially altered. Whereas the mortgagee could purchase 24,000 pounds of coffee with his holding twenty years ago his interest today has shrunk to one-third, or 8,000 pounds. On the other hand, the equity interest has increased from an equivalent purchasing power of 16,000 pounds of coffee twenty years ago to double, or 32,000 pounds, today.

Whereas in an inflationary market, when prices move upward, purchasing power is shifted from the creditor or mortgagee to the debtor or the equity interests, the reverse takes place in a deflationary market when prices move downward. To illustrate, again using the property—coffee price and value relationship—let's assume a decline in purchasing power from a base of 100 percent to a level of 60 percent. The relative mortgage —equity positions shift as follows:

Year	Price of Property	Purchasing Power of Dollar In Terms of Coffee
19—	$10,000 Total	$10,000 @ $1.00 = 10,000 lbs.
	6,000 Mortgage	6,000 @ 1.00 = 6,000 lbs.
	4,000 Equity	4,000 @ 1.00 = 4,000 lbs.
20 years later	$ 6,000 Total	$6,000 @ $ .60 = 10,000 lbs.
	6,000 Mortgage	6,000 @ .60 = 10,000 lbs.
	Zero Equity	Zero @ .60 = Zero lbs.

In the above illustration a 40 percent decline in purchasing power caused a fixed debt in dollars to wipe out completely the equity interest, thus transferring value from the debtor to the creditor. During the severe depression in the years 1932–1935, nearly one fifth of all residential homes in the United States were on the verge of foreclosure, necessitating federal banking and refinancing relief measures to bridge the deflationary gap. With fiscal and monetary controls now firmly manipulated by federal agencies, deflation and economic busts may only rarely be experienced, but the threat of inflation and the consequent redistribution of accumulated wealth appears politically expedient. The appraiser must, therefore, consider the impact of changes in the level of prices and in the purchasing power of the dollar, and measure the impact on value where rentals or incomes are fixed or where a market comparison study involves sales which were transacted in diverse markets and at different levels of prices.

To summarize, inflation need not concern the appraiser so long as his task is to find value on a "cash" basis of unencumbered property in terms of *present* dollars. However, where the income is fixed or controlled —as may be the case under long-term leases or rent control, or where the property is encumbered by a mortgage and a split interest is to be appraised—the impact of inflation on risk of ownership must be given careful value consideration.

INCOME AS A MEASURE OF VALUE

Although replacement cost under the theory of substitution establishes the ceiling of value, the lower limit of the value range is set by the present or discounted worth of the anticipated net income stream. It is assumed that this net income is reasonably obtainable from the improved property during its economic lifespan and under typical ownership. Income, therefore, especially for industrial and commercial properties, is an important index of value. Care must be taken to consider only income which is ascribable to the property under typical management. Income that is attributable to superior management or good will attaches to people or to the business and not to the property for which an estimate of value is sought. The technique of estimating income and the method of capitalizing it into a sum of present value will be discussed fully in Chapters 15 and 18. Stress in this chapter is placed only on the basic principles underlying income forecasting.

Property income in previous references has been characterized as a "stream." The words "income stream" were deliberately chosen to create in the minds of both reader and appraiser a pictorial concept of the ups and downs of dynamic income productivity. Nothing is static, as the principle of change has taught us. Past income experiences may indicate a certain trend, and present income flow may substantiate this trend; nevertheless the anticipated future income expectancy may radically differ on the basis of important changes in national, regional, and local business activity—of which the real estate market is a part. Income forecasting must not, however, be thought of as crystal gazing. The subject property in nearly all instances can be classified as belonging to a certain group of properties for which income experience data is known from prior appraisal analysis or from study data published by management, accounting, or appraisal institutes. If experience data is unobtainable from file or published sources, a rental or income flow study of similar, or *bench mark*, properties (comparable properties from which value indexes are derived) must be undertaken as a guide to income forecasting.

By income for appraisal purposes is always meant *net property income,* after all operating expenses and contingencies have been accounted for, but, as a rule, before deductions are made for interest "on" the investment and provisions made for amortization or depreciation "of" the investment in capital improvements. Logically, there is no reason why depreciation charges should be excluded as operating expenses. In practice, this is done under the assumption that depreciation is a loss in value and that this loss cannot be ascertained until value through the process of appraising is found. As one author expressed it: "Since value is the end and object of valuation, the process cannot include an expense item (depreciation) based upon the answer." [1] This holds true in a determination of total accrued depreciation, but not in estimating the amount of *annual* provisions for future depreciation. If the *rate* of depreciation is known, then this rate as a percentage of the combined rate of capitalization can be applied to the stabilized net income to determine the amount of depreciation that should be subtracted as operating costs, in the same manner as other related costs, to yield a net income constituting a return on invested capital only for the property as a whole. Under this recommended procedure, it would be necessary to separate income to land from income to building as must be done whenever future depreciation or amortization is treated as a rate rather than as an operating expense under the income approach to value. To illustrate: When an appraiser estimates capital recapture to occur at the rate of 2 percent per year and required interest earnings to be 8 percent per annum, a stabilized income (before depreciation) of $1,000 would yield a capitalized value of $10,000 ($1,000 ÷ .10). In selecting 10 percent as the rate of capitalization the appraiser in effect estimates that 2 percent out of 10 percent (2 ÷ 10) or 20 percent of income before depreciation represents recapture of capital and 80 percent of the remaining income a return on the invested capital. The income problem can now be restated as follows:

---

[1] Frederick M. Babcock, *Valuation of Real Estate* (New York: McGraw-Hill Book Co., Inc., 1932), p. 420.

Net income before depreciation	$1,000
Allowance for recapture of capital 2/10 or 20 percent =	200
Net income after depreciation	$ 800
Value of property: $800 ÷ .08 (8 percent) =	$10,000

Thus whether the appraiser capitalizes $1,000 at 10 percent (8 percent interest plus 2 percent recapture) or $800 at 8 percent (interest only) the estimate of value remains the same. The advantage of the expense method for the provision of recapture of depreciable property is that it conforms to investment practices followed by accountants, lawyers, income tax agents, and the investor for whom presumably the appraiser reports most of his estimated findings. Further and more detailed treatment of the subject of provision for capital recapture (depreciation) will be given in Chapter 16.

THE REAL ESTATE MARKET

To understand more fully the nature and predictability of property income, the appraiser must be aware of the peculiar characteristics of land and how these affect income and the market for real estate. Immobility, indestructibility, and nonhomogeneity of land cause the market for real estate to be *local* in character. As a commodity, real estate cannot be moved from place to place. An oversupply of land in one community cannot be used to balance an undersupply in another. Real estate must be employed where it is, and, because of its fixity in geographic location, it is extremely vulnerable to economic effects caused by shifts in local demand.

Land dissimilarity—nonhomogeneity—further imposes special market conditions. Because of location, no two parcels of real estate are physically alike. Each parcel is geographically fixed and has distinct legal descriptions which as a rule are accurately set forth in public plat book records. Since no one parcel of land may be legally substituted for another without the purchaser's consent, value considerations must reflect this market immobility.

The durability of real estate, too, causes maladjustments in both supply and demand on a local market level. Thus where demand for any reason suddenly falls, the inability to adjust supply will cause real estate to become a drug on the market. An oversupply of real estate creates a buyer's market, which in turn results in lower price offerings and hence lower market values. A sudden increase in demand also is difficult to meet. The resultant scarcity causes market prices of realty to rise, creating an upward swing in the real estate cycle.

The appraiser must take great care to study objectively the underlying forces creating supply and demand for real property. Since value, by definition, is a measure of the present worth of future rights to income, temporary booms or depressions must be analyzed to determine their cause and to forecast their duration and effect on typical buyer-seller bargaining power. The real estate cycle, sometimes induced by land speculations, more often reflects the state of general business and housing or construction cycles. The business cycle operates on the demand side, positively or negatively, through increased or decreased overall employment, wage levels, supply of mortgage funds, interest rates, and personal savings. The construction or building cycle, on the other hand, operates on the supply side, reacting to population changes, family formation, vacancy ratios, and cost of land and housing supply in relation to prevailing and anticipated income or rental levels.

Though physically abundant, land which is economically usable is often in short supply. Improvements, in the form of access roads, drainage facilities, water, and other community utilities, must be added to raw land before it ordinarily can be subdivided and offered for sale through marketing channels. Because such improvements are costly and can be successfully carried out only with community sanction and on a relatively large scale, a scarcity of economic land often occurs. This lack of building sites in turn causes upward pricing of real estate holdings to a point where community development and real estate market activities may be adversely affected. On the other hand, speculative optimism, unchecked by community foresight and planning, may cause economic land to be produced in quantities too great to be absorbed by prevailing demand and creating an oversupply which may depress the market for real estate for many months or even years.

There is a definite relationship between business booms and depressions on the one hand, and real estate market activity on the other. As a rule the downward swing of the real estate cycle precedes the downward swing of business activity caused by business recession, and lags long beyond the period of general business recovery. As economic adjustments or recessions cast their shadows, typical home and land buyers prefer to wait and to maintain a cash position during periods of adversity. In a like manner, when business recovery takes place, expenditures for fixed investments are undertaken only after all immediate needs for clothing, food, and other necessities are met. Thus the economic inflexibility of real estate as a commodity is directly accountable for the greater intensity of real estate booms and depressions and the longer life of the real estate cycle as compared with the normal upward and downward swing of general business activity. It is important, therefore, that the appraiser keep his finger on the pulse of business as well as on real estate market activities in order to forecast with reasonable accuracy shifts in market conditions and changes in the anticipated income flow that forms, for a given property and at a given time, the basis of real estate value. The impact of social, political, and economic forces on the market for real estate from a national, state, and community level will be discussed at length in the succeeding chapters.

READING AND STUDY REFERENCES

1. *Acquisition for Right-of-Way* (Washington, D.C.: American Association of State Highway Officials, 1962), chap. 23.

2. *The Appraisal of Real Estate* (Chicago: American Institute of Real Estate Appraisers, 1967), chap. 3.

3. Babcock, Frederick M., *The Valuation of Real Estate* (New York: McGraw-Hill Book Company, Inc., 1932), chap. 3.

4. Kahn, Sanders A., Frederick E. Case, and Alfred Schimmel, *Real Estate Appraisal and Investment* (New York: The Ronald Press Company, 1963), chap. 7.

5. Kinnard, William N., Jr., *Industrial Real Estate* (Washington, D.C.: Society of Industrial Realtors, 1967), chap. 12, part III.

6. McMichael, Stanley L., *McMichael's Appraising Manual* 4th ed., (Englewood Cliffs, N.J.: Prentice-Hall, Inc., 1951), chap. 3.

7. Ring, Alfred A., *Real Estate Principles and Practices,* 6th ed. (Englewood Cliffs, N.J.: Prentice-Hall, Inc., 1967), chap. 22.

8. Schmutz, George L., revised by Edwin M. Rams, *Condemnation Appraisal Handbook* (Englewood Cliffs, N.J.: Prentice-Hall, Inc., (1963), chap. 3.

9. Weimer, Arthur M., and Homer Hoyt, *Real Estate,* 5th ed. (New York: The Ronald Press Company, 1966), chap. 16.

10. Wendt, Paul F., *Real Estate Appraisal* (New York: Henry Holt and Company, 1956), chap. 3.

Every parcel of land located anywhere within the United States, no matter how small its dimensions, is subject to national, social, political, and economic forces which influence its value. In fact the general forces that influence property values on a local level often reach beyond the borders of our country into the international community of nations. If World War III should be started by any nation and our country becomes again

5

Impact of Political, Social,

and Economic Forces

embroiled, the impact of the struggle would influence the value of real estate everywhere to a greater or lesser degree, depending on the geographic position and importance of the sites in the war economy.

There is no doubt, for example, that the outbreak of a shooting war would adversely affect the value of property developed and employed for recreational use. Travel restrictions, gas rationing, and possible food shortages would compel ocean, lake, and mountain vacation resorts to restrict or close their operations, with resultant losses in property income and property value. Hotels, motels, restaurants, and places of amusement serving resort cities would immediately feel the negative value impact of a war economy. Educational cities would also generally be adversely affected. Students and faculty personnel would be drafted for war purposes, and community service facilities surrounding a campus area would suffer as a consequence in property income and value. A big segment of our economy, however, might experience an acceleration of activity essential to and associated with the war effort. Manufacturing centers, iron and coal mines, oil, and public utilities would intensify production; and property so employed would immediately benefit from increased incentive efforts necessary to win the war.

The appraiser, therefore, must evaluate the world situation and consider the impact, if any, that a cold or a shooting war may have on a given property in a subject location. Of course, it isn't the appraiser's opinion that counts, but rather the actions of buyers and sellers as reflected by the opinion of political and economic experts who study market operations and who make it their business to publish the effects of world trends and shifts in international relations. A number of national services, such as the Prentice-Hall Real Estate Guide, Roy Wenzlick Research Corporation Trends, Dodge Corporation Appraisal Service, Downs Market Letter and others in related economic fields keep an ear to the international ground, warning their reader of probable coming events and their consequent effects on the value of real property. In every valuation it is the appraiser's duty to stipulate whether the value reported does or does not reflect possible and impending changes in international relations and, if, so, to what degree and amount. The client or reader of the appraisal report is then in a position to make his own value adjustments based on personal observation of market operations and his investment risk position.

POLITICAL FORCES INFLUENCING VALUE

Under our allodial system of property ownership (as opposed to state or feudal control of land and land improvements) property values are derived from property rights—the bundle of rights. Although these private rights are constitutionally guaranteed to the fee owner they are nevertheless subject to important modification by legislative, executive, and judicial action. Even the form of government and the underlying philosophy guiding political leadership can influence market operations and investment choices made by individuals or corporations. In Russia, and the other Communist-controlled nations of Europe and Asia for example, ownership of land was seized in the name of the "people," and private rights and value in realty for these nations have been liquidated as a result of Communist political policy.

In America, England, and other "free" European nations attempts, too, have been made to transfer to the state or nation the value increments in land which—as claimed—unjustly accrue to private owners. The so-called unearned land value increment theory reached its popular peak with the effective writing of the American economist Henry George who, in his book *Progress and Poverty,* published in 1879, suggested the "single-tax" remedy whereby value increments in land created by community life and action could be returned to the "people," from whence it came. In America, adherents of the single-tax doctrine made a concerted and powerful effort to have this socialistic theory implemented by legislative action. Since the power to tax, in the hands of unwise or biased government, is tantamount to the power to destroy property values, special safeguards are provided in the U.S. Constitution (the Fifth and Fourteenth Amendments) and by statutory law in the various states to protect property owners.

The political attitude and national policy toward home ownership, slum clearance, and public housing is also of interest to the appraiser, since changes in national policy as expressed in housing legislation have a direct and often significant effect on property values. To illustrate, passage of the Home Owners Loan Corporation Act as an emergency measure by Congress to prevent disastrous and large-scale mortgage foreclosures during the depression years of 1932–1935 stabilized the real estate market and prevented foreclosure action for about four out of five home borrowers who sought the Corporation's aid. Enactment of rent control during World Wars I and II prevented runaway prices threatened by war-induced home scarcities and limitations of home construction. Retention of rent control, however, beyond the period of an emergency—for political rather than economic purposes—depresses values of property so affected and discourages investment in rental real estate wherever such controls are still operative, as in New York City or overseas in France, Italy, and England to this day. Whereas housing and home-ownership legislation as a rule tend to stabilize and protect home investment, public housing, no matter how justified from a welfare or socialistic point of view adversely affects the market for rental real estate and, hence, real estate values. On the other hand, slum clearance and urban renewal legislation provide a direct subsidy by the federal government to a given county or city government and indirectly contribute to the enhancement of values of property located adjacent to or in the immediate vicinity of rehabilitated slum areas.

The significant increase in home ownership and home construction everywhere in the United States is directly traceable, in a large measure, to federal financing aids and fiscal policy controls. The Federal Housing Administration and the Veterans' Administration loan programs are largely responsible for the increase in home ownership and home construction during the last two decades. These loan programs, too, have encouraged suburban land development and have thus brought about a shift of urban land values from the central city to outlying residential areas. Government fiscal policies and their effect on money interest rates also must be watched closely by the real estate appraiser in order to measure the effect of rate changes on value of income-producing real property.

As a rule, changes in the rate of interest or interest rate structure have an inverse relationship to real property values. Everything else remaining equal, a rise in the rate of interest lowers property value, and a fall is reflected in higher value. This is due to the direct relationship which income bears to value, with the interest rate serving as leverage for conversion of income into value. To wit, a $1,000 income in perpetuity at 10 percent interest is worth $10,000 ($10,000 @ 10 percent equals $1,000); whereas a rate of 5 percent interest produces double the value ($20,000 @ 5 percent equals $1,000).

SOCIAL FORCES INFLUENCING VALUE

Since people create value it is important to keep abreast of changes in number, age distribution, and ethnological composition of the total popula-

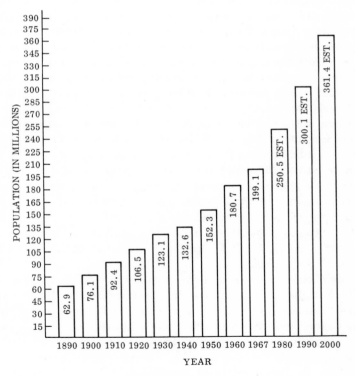

FIGURE 5.1

Source: U. S. Department of Commerce, Bureau of the Census; *Current Population Reports,* Series P-25, Nos. 368, 381, and 393.

tion. A vigorous growth and a positive trend in the national population may not necessarily be reflected in an equally beneficial population pattern on a state or local level. Nevertheless, the impact of local population forces cannot be effectively understood or interpreted unless the national pattern is used as a background for growth comparison. As shown by the chart in Figure 5.1, the total U.S. population steadily increased from approximately 62.9 million in 1890 to 199.1 million in 1967. The forecast for total population by 2,000 is 361.4 million. This increase of over 136 million people during the past seventy-seven years is also reflected in the increase in population per square mile of land from 21.2 persons in 1890, to 56.2 persons in 1967.

Although the concentration of people took place largely in metropolitan areas, the overall increase in population is nevertheless remarkably related to an increase in the value of all U.S. lands. From 1929 to 1967, based on estimates in current dollars, values of all private and public land increased from 113.3 to 452.5 billion dollars. Adjusting this increase to account for inflation and the consequent decline in the purchasing power of the dollar since 1929, the net increase in U.S. land values is directly proportional to the rise in the overall population shown in Figure 5.1. The significance of the population-value relationship is thus of prime importance, and must be considered carefully in appraising the impact on the value of a given property of general economic forces anticipated for future years.

Another significant trend which is important to the appraiser is the steadily increasing demand for dwelling units per 1,000 population as shown in Table 5.1. Dwelling units increased from 12.69 million in 1890, to 58,845 million in 1967—or by 463 percent—as compared with an increase in population of 316 percent for the same period. This housing

TABLE 5.1

TOTAL DWELLING UNITS IN THE UNITED STATES, 1890–1967

Year	Dwelling Units (Thousands)	Population Per Dwelling Unit
1890	12,690	4.93
1900	15,964	4.76
1910	20,256	4.54
1920	24,352	4.34
1930	29,905	4.11
1940	34,949	3.77
1950	42,857	3.52
1960	53,021	3.38
1967	58,845	3.28

Source: U. S. Department of Commerce, Bureau of the Census, *Population Series Reports,* 1960; and *Current Population Reports,* Series P-20, No. 116.

demand, brought about by early marriages and "undoubling" (where two or more families were living together) has reduced the average population —as shown in Table 5.1—from 4.93 persons per dwelling unit in 1890, to 3.28 persons per dwelling unit in 1967. In effect this means that whereas 493 persons exerted a demand for 100 dwelling units in 1890, the same number of persons demanded and occupied 150 dwelling units in 1967. Even if no growth in population had taken place during the past seventy-seven years, housing on the basis of changes in family formation alone would have increased by 50 percent. Since the trend toward smaller families is expected to continue, this factor also must be considered in the appraisal of real property, especially in areas where high standards of living prevail.

Another factor of increasing importance in the evaluation of general forces which affect changes in property values is the longevity of life as reflected in the changing age composition of the U.S. population. People not only live longer but, through pension and Social Security plans, are economically and medically better cared for. These aging citizens demand independent dwelling units in increasing numbers, most often seeking retirement opportunities in geographic areas where mild climate keeps housing and related costs at a minimum. As a result, states such as California, Arizona, New Mexico, and Florida have experienced during recent years greater than average population gains, which have been directly reflected in rapidly advancing market activity and prices of real property. Whereas 6.8 percent of the total U.S. population was 65 years old and over in 1940 (9.0 million persons), this percentage of senior citizens is expected to increase to 9.0 percent by the year 1990 (27.0 million).

GENERAL ECONOMIC FORCES
INFLUENCING VALUE

Since real estate activity, property price levels, and real estate values are directly influenced by the general economic activity and economic well-being of the country as a whole, the appraiser must be seriously concerned with the general economic forces which influence value. Important indexes that should be observed as a barometer of general economic progress include the following:

> Gross National Product.
> Per capita income and real wage levels.
> Unemployment as a measure of full employment.
> Personal savings and investments.
> General business and real estate activity.

Although all the above are related as measures of economic well-being the year-to-year variations, or lag of one index as compared with another, may provide an important clue to anticipated changes in general economic activities which are bound to influence the value of real property. The measure most widely used as a yardstick for economic progress in the United States is the Gross National Product, which aggregates in dollars the annual value of all goods and services produced, consumed, saved, and invested by individuals, business corporations, and government operations. Using 1940 as a base, the G.N.P. has grown from 99.7 billion dollars in that year to 785.1 billion in 1967. The percentage growth in economic activity from year to year over the twenty-seven years may be observed by study of the chart in Figure 5.2. Attention is called to the fact that general economic activity prior to and during war conflicts is accelerated, and that readjustments following a war cause overall business operations and consumptions to decline. The steep rise in the G.N.P. from 1940 through 1967 also reflects rising prices caused by dollar in-

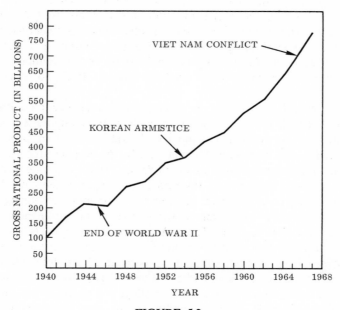

FIGURE 5.2

Source: U. S. Department of Commerce, Office of Business Economics; *The National Income and Products Accounts of the United States, 1929–1965,* and *Survey of Current Business.*

flation and a consequent loss in the purchasing power of the dollar of 62.5 percent during this time period. Generally, the economic health of the United states as judged by past performance is excellent; and the future outlook based on the *Economic Report of the President* is for steady and continuous growth in all phases of economic activity. The experienced rate of economic progress in constant dollars has averaged 4 percent per year over the past two decades. Continued growth at this rate is aimed at by economic planners during the decade ahead.

Per capita income and changing level of real wages provide another and more refined measure of economic well-being as seen from the consumer's point of view. Although overall dollar productivity for the country as a whole is of prime importance, the appraiser must temper his value conclusions for given types of real property in accordance with the distribution of this total income flow to the factors of production, including tax payments to government. The steadily rising standard of living is a direct result of increasing wage payments to the labor force. Disposable personal income (income after state and federal taxes) has risen from 75.7 billion dollars in 1940, to 544.6 billion dollars in 1967. This constitutes an increase of 719.4 percent. In constant dollars, based on the purchasing power of the dollar in 1958, the increase is 286.2 percent. Disposable income has in effect almost tripled over this twenty-seven-year period. It is this continuing rise in the financial well-being of individuals that largely accounts for the significant increase in the number of home owners from 43.6 percent of all dwelling units in 1940, to 63.6 percent in 1967.

This significant increase in the number of owner-occupied dwellings, when coupled with the extraordinary growth in total population, presages a continued and increasing demand for desirable suburban sites suitable for residential and commercial development. As a consequence, overall land values are expected to increase in future years at a rate faster than the value of goods and services invested in the improvements on the land.

Another and more sensitive measure of economic well-being that is important to property appraisers is the degree of unemployment in relation to the total available labor force. Accepting labor analysts' conclusions that labor turnover and willfully unemployed persons comprise a "normal" unemployment rate of approximately 2 percent of the total labor force, an increase in the percentage of idle workers above this rate—discounting seasonal unemployment—will adversely affect the value of real property. This is understandable, since expenditures for ownership of shelter are less important for subsistence than outlays for food and clothing. There is a direct correlation between unemployment, property foreclosures, and property tax delinquencies. When unemployment reached the peak of 24.9

percent of the civilian labor force in 1933, property values also hit the century's lowest ebb; and, as pointed out, government emergency laws were passed to create a debt moratorium to halt the avalanche of foreclosures. In recent years, unemployment has fluctuated from a low of 2.9 percent in 1953 to a high of 6.8 percent in 1958. The rate in 1967 is at 3.8 percent. These changes in the level of unemployment are of national concern because they are accompanied by changes in economic progress and rates of increase in land values throughout the nation. Thus the appraiser should reflect in his value estimates the prospect for property demands as based on a forecast of the health of the labor-consumer market as a whole.

Investor confidence and national economic stability can also be judged by the amount of personal savings as related to total disposable personal income after all taxes. Patterns of expenditures change, as does consumer saving philosophy; hence the importance of time preference in consumption. The cause for a decreasing rate of personal savings should be carefully analyzed, for a continued downward trend in savings will decrease investment capital and hence the demand for and value of real property. The percentage relationship of personal savings to disposable personal income for selected years since 1940 is shown in Table 5.2.

TABLE 5.2

PERSONAL SAVINGS AS PERCENT OF TOTAL DISPOSABLE INCOME,
1940–1967[1]
(IN BILLIONS OF DOLLARS)

Year	Disposable Personal Income	Personal Outlays	Personal Savings	Savings as Percent of Income
1940	75.7	71.8	3.9	5.1
1945	150.2	120.7	29.5	19.7
1950	206.9	193.9	13.0	6.3
1955	275.3	259.5	15.8	5.7
1960	350.0	333.0	17.0	4.9
1965	472.2	445.0	27.2	5.8
1967	544.6	505.8	38.8	7.1

[1] *Economic Report of the President,* transmitted to the Congress, February, 1968.

Although no fixed percentage of savings to disposable income is recommended as an optimum guide to capital reinvestment, it is apparent that venture capital is dependent on this source for capital funds. A decrease in the rate of savings below 5 percent may foreshadow economic readjustment if not depression. An increase, however, in the annual rate of savings above 7 percent may prove equally disconcerting if the increased thrift reflects *underconsumption* or lack of investor confidence in the economic progress and stability of the United States. In any case, changes in this index as a barometer of economic climate call for analysis and value interpretation by professional real estate appraisers.

A composite of all the forces that motivate economic activity within a nation is reflected in the position of the business cycle that measures the intensity of general business operations. A historical study of business cycles in the United States discloses a rhythmic recurrence of business booms and depressions to such a degree that economic forecasts on the basis of past experience with a high degree of accuracy were deemed possible. The Cleveland Trust Company has made studies of general business activity since the year 1850, and has computed business indexes in relation to a "norm" of business activity. A review of their published cyclical business behavior supports the contention that, under normal unimpeded economic behavior in a capitalistic nation, business reflects consumer and investor cycles of optimism, overoptimism, caution, or pessimism. Cyclical business behavior, it seems, is attributable to violations of the economic laws of supply and demand and the lack of central business control. In studying past cyclical behavior of business activity to forecast future business operations, the appraiser must keep in mind that in recent years federal government controls have successfully counteracted adverse economic behavior and, with varying degrees of success, have revitalized business operations by means of pump-priming government expenditures in a vast variety of public construction projects and general improvements. The necessity for increased government action is a sign of maladjustment in the private sector of the national economy, and requires careful attention by the real estate appraiser translating the impact of the general national economy, especially in times of extreme booms or depressions affecting real estate activity on a regional, state, and local level.

STATE OR REGIONAL FORCES
INFLUENCING VALUE

The same pattern of statistical analysis which guides the real estate appraiser in interpreting the value influence of general forces on a national level should be used in the analysis of state or regional forces which influence property values. Here again the nature, character, and comparative general quality of social, political, and economic forces must be carefully studied and interpreted as a basis for reaching a professionally sound and reliable value conclusion.

Unless the population within a state or region increases as favorably as that of the nation as a whole, local property values will reflect—on a broad level—the area's retarded growth. The center of population within the continental United States has steadily shifted west by southwest since the formation of this country. A continued rapid population increase in states such as California, Arizona, New Mexico, and Florida seems assured so long as people and industry, aided by advances in rapid transportation and electric power, seek milder climates and areas where natural resources can more advantageously be exploited. Accelerated growth in these states by necessity is accomplished at the expense of a decelerated growth—if not a decline—of population in other states and regions. Thus, though the nation as a whole may experience a favorable growth in total population, care must be taken to relate this growth to economic area prospects and developments.

Although for the country as a whole total population was used as a measure of growth significance, the population analysis of a state or region must give greater emphasis to population quality and characteristics. The influx of people aged sixty and over in search of retirement homes, for example, may create economic problems that far outweigh the economic benefits which normally accrue from favorable immigration. Likewise, the ethnological pattern of people and their effect on property values must be considered. Significant changes in age composition, nationality, race, creed, and even in color of skin within the population are bound to influence the economic well-being and value of real property as recent events in many states and regions have demonstrated. With the aid of federal and state census data, appraisers should keep abreast of population changes and interpret for their clients the long-term effects of regional population trends on the value of real property.

Equally important as a population factor affecting the value of real properties is the political climate in which people and industry find opportunity to prosper. Many states have passed legislation—often by constitutional referendum—to favor business, industry, or resident homeowners in order to spur state economic growth. The relatively simple and economically favorable laws of incorporation in Delaware, the homestead exemption tax law of Florida, and freedom from state income taxes in Maine and other states are instances where the law has been designed to foster state growth and development. In some states, however, what once was considered beneficial to a growing economy may prove in later years an investment handicap—even a financial burden—to a more mature economy. The rent control laws still in effect under state law in New York City and Chicago discouraged apartment developments for years until such laws—at least for new constructions—were made inapplicable. The homestead tax exemption law in Florida, too, has long since outlived its economic usefulness, and the revenue burden which this law places on populous counties often necessitates oppressive indirect and business taxation to offset this outdated legislation—which politically oriented state representatives lack the courage or power to correct.

Since property values reflect the present worth of *future* rights to income, the appraiser must not only analyze the nature and character of present state laws and the quality of government but he must interpret the trend of government and legislation for better or worse in the years to come. The stability and quality of government, as will be demonstrated in subsequent chapters, is directly reflected in the rate of interest at which capital for investment purposes becomes available. The higher this rate of interest, as a rule, the greater the risk of investment ownership and hence the lower the investment value for a given anticipated flow of income dollars.

The current economic status and prospects for anticipated economic development must also be given careful attention. To judge effectively the economic status of a given state or region the appraiser must gather for ready reference and use in his office or appraisal plant statistical data from which comparative value judgment conclusions can be drawn. The importance of the state or region to the economy of the nation as a whole should be ascertained. To what extent is dollar or resource competition threatened? Is the state economy sufficiently diversified to withstand rapid technological changes in production and marketing demands? The economic hardships of the "cotton" South, the "shipping" Northeast, the "corn-belt" Midwest, the "cattle" Southwest, and the coal mining and steel smelting regions of the country are still fresh enough in memory to serve as vivid reminders that the principle of change is ever active. No appraiser can hazard a judgment based on an extension of the status quo. Unless a state or region is strong enough to resist strains of powerful economic readjustments caused by changes in technology— as, for example, having the resources to adjust itself to new developments in atomic energy and space—the remaining economic life of property because of anticipated obsolescence is shortened. The possible loss of future productive income years is translated, of course, into lower property values by informed investment buyers.

It is the appraiser's responsibility to gather pertinent social, political, and economic data on a national, state, or regional level, and to interpret the meaning of such data in the light of action taken by *typical* buyers and sellers in the market place. Generally, the appraiser should decide whether the outlook for real estate investment over the years to come is good, bad, or uncertain. Data should then be supplied to support the appraiser's conclusions and to aid the reader of the valuation report in reaching his own value judgment where circumstances warrant subjective rather than objective considerations.

READING AND STUDY REFERENCES

1. *Acquisition for Right-of-Way* (Washington, D.C.: American Association of State Highway Officials, 1962), chap. 24.

2. *The Appraisal of Real Estate* (Chicago: American Institute of Real Estate Appraisals, 1967), chap. 5.

3. Babcock, Frederick M., *The Valuation of Real Estate* (New York: McGraw-Hill Book Company, Inc., 1932), chaps. 7–9.

4. Coffman, Paul F., "Effect of Business Conditions Upon Value," *Technical Valuation* (February 1956), pp. 3–6.

5. McEntire, Davis, "Population and Land Value," *The Appraisal Journal* (July 1949), pp. 311–317.

6. Seyfried, Warren R., "Predicting the Economic Growth Potential of the Community," *The Appraisal Journal* (January 1958), pp. 54–60.

7. Smith, Walstein, Jr., "The Appraiser and the Real Estate Cycle," *The Real Estate Appraiser* (March 1963), pp. 2–19.

8. Weimer, Arthur M., and Homer Hoyt, *Real Estate,* 5th ed. (New York: The Ronald Press Company, 1966), chap. 23.

9. Wendt, Paul F., *Real Estate Appraisal* (New York: Henry Holt and Company, 1956), chap. 4.

All but a fraction of the total number of private appraisal assignments currently originate in urban areas, and the value of property appraised is principally urban in character. Studies of U.S. wealth also disclose that less than 5 percent of the total value of all U.S. structures is located on farms. Land values, too, which at the beginning of the twentieth century were approximately two-thirds farm and one-third urban, are presently re-

6 *Impact of Urban Forces Upon Property Value*

versed in order of value significance. It is this tremendous investment in, and growth of urban areas, that make the study of the city and its suburban developments of essential interest to the real estate appraiser.

A city may be conceived as a corporate entity offering cultural, social, and economic advantages to present and prospective community residents. In this effort the city must compete with other cities near and far which vie for national recognition and a share of the total urban market. The ability of a city to retain its present citizens and to continue attracting new residents at a rate favorable when compared with growth of the state and the nation is thus of great significance. All cities must have reasons for their existence. Unless the social, economic, and political forces which caused the formation of the city continue to exert their influence favorably within a given area as compared with urban services and facilities offered elsewhere, community growth may be arrested—or even wither—as property investment is withdrawn through accelerated depreciation or neglect of essential maintenance of private and public improvements. This possibility was brought home with disastrous effect to real estate investors and home owners in so-called ghost towns that once represented thriving communities in now neglected mining, fishing, shipbuilding, and specialized (such as cotton) farm areas.

THE NATURE AND CHARACTER OF CITIES

Cities, broadly speaking, may be classified as *primary* and *secondary* urban centers. A primary community is one which has its own economic base, and whose existence is not dependent on the operations or welfare of other communities within the state or the metropolitan region. A secondary community, on the other hand, is in effect a satellite whose length and strength of orbit depends on the principal cities to which it owes its existence. These satellite communities are better known as "bedroom" cities where commuters (people who work where they would rather not live) reside. The economic strength of a satellite community is entirely dependent on the strength of the primary community, of which it is often an unwilling part. To appraise property in such a community necessitates careful evaluation of the forces which keep the primary community operative.

Primary communities may be subclassified into cities which reflect their cause of urbanization, as follows:

Industrial cities such as Detroit, Michigan, and Pittsburgh, Pennsylvania.

Commercial cities such as Chicago, Illinois, and San Francisco, California.

Mining cities such as Scranton, Pennsylvania, and Wheeling, West Virginia.

Resort cities such as Miami Beach, Florida, and Atlantic City, New Jersey.

Political cities such as Tallahassee, Florida, and Washington, D. C.

Educational cities such as Chapel Hill, North Carolina, and Ann Arbor, Michigan.

Many communities have assumed a diverse economic base and may fall with equal importance into two or more subclassifications. Thus New York City is both industrial and commercial in character. Miami, Florida, which started as a resort city, is presently one of the most important commercial cities in the South having the largest international airport facilities in the country. New Orleans, which served as the fishing and commercial center of Louisiana, is important today as an international shipping center second only to the harbor facilities and shipping tonnage of New York City.

In evaluating property within a city it is important that a clear understanding is had not only of the city's origin but also of the economic base that presently and prospectively will support continued city growth and development. A city with a single dominant industry or service activity, no matter how prosperous currently, must be evaluated with caution. Having all its eggs in one basket is hazardous for a city, and technological changes or competition within the area may cause economic slumps that severely depress its property values. Even though the appraiser is unable to forecast with accuracy future changes in economic patterns, he must call potential value hazards to the attention of his client and reflect the concern of informed investors for the higher rate of interest which the market will deem necessary to attract investment and venture capital.

THE CITY'S PLAN AND LAND USE PATTERN

City planning is an art more often talked about than practiced. Most cities with a simple village origin grow like Topsy until economically costly growing pains call for hindsight actions which foresight actions could well have avoided. (The growth of Boston along its early cowpaths is a vivid example of this kind of chaotic growth.) Generally, the development of a city should be planned ten or even twenty years in advance under a comprehensive master plan. Communities, like people, are dynamic in character, and their expanding or changing needs must be served through orderly expansion beyond the city's limits where necessary. Like a business enterprise, a city as a whole must prosper if it is to continue effectively as a going concern.

As a requisite to better understanding of a city's potential growth and development, the appraiser should inventory the physical and economic resources of the subject community and maintain an active file to keep such data up to date. The first step in the collection of pertinent data is to obtain an official city map on which the legal boundaries are delineated and the street pattern sketched. Wherever possible, land use data about contiguous county areas, too, should be obtained to observe facilities for street and utility service expansion. A well-planned city, as a rule, reduces per capita urban operating costs and facilitates the ready flow of people and commerce during normal as well as rush hours.

Next in importance is checking the adequacy of land use patterns and city zoning in relation to public needs for sites suitable for improvements as follows:

Residential homes.
Commercial buildings.
Industrial parks.
Public administrative and school buildings.
Recreational parks and playgrounds.

Residential areas should be free from natural or man-made hazards, and should provide the opportunity for privacy and enjoyment of the amenities of home ownership. Through streets should be routed around residential areas to reduce traffic flow and noise, especially during evening hours. Streets should be paved, curbs, gutters, and sidewalks provided, and all essential utilities—including water, electricity, telephone, sanitation, and storm sewerage—made available for service connection. Effective zoning should call for uniform building setback, minimum plot width, and building construction and population-density regulations. Nonconforming uses of an industrial and commercial nature should especially be screened out by natural or man-made buffer zones, such as landscaped plantings. The degree to which good planning is lacking, and the extent to which private or public hazards are permitted to encroach on residential areas, will significantly affect the lifespan of the neighborhood and the duration of economic life throughout which property values are assured freedom from economic obsolescence.

Commercial facilities—including retail stores, bank and office buildings, and wholesale establishments—should be grouped together in an orderly pattern, with ample off-street parking to permit uncrowded commerce and safe shopping. Spot and faulty business zoning impede orderly city growth and adversely affect the value of surrounding property. Generally areas chosen for commercial development are level, of even contour, and readily accessible by surface transportation. Commercial areas should also be strictly zoned and protected by building ordinances to promote public interests and to safeguard private ownership of a city's most valuable investment—the 100 percent shopping district.

Industrial sites, which prior to World War II were given little protection from encroachment by other though higher uses, have often been hampered in potential development and in relation to the principle of highest and best land use. Manufacturing, whether heavy or light, provides for many communities the "bread and butter" resources on which much of the secondary commercial and service industries depends. Planned industrial parks should play an important part in every master plan. Such industrial locations should be situated near major highways, railroad rights of way, waterways, and airports. Ready road and rail access, adequate utility service, and freedom to expand give assurance to established industries that they are wanted and respected for the part they play in the corporate structure of the city. In communities where residential, commercial, and industrial growth complement rather than encroach upon each other, the values of real estate properties will reflect the increased income stability and the stronger holding power of property owners.

Public administration buildings, school buildings, and recreational parks and playgrounds should all be carefully planned and located to serve public needs adequately and efficiently. Even quasi-public buildings such as churches, libraries, museums, and exhibition halls should be placed as near as possible to the community areas they serve. In political, educational, and resort cities great care must be taken in planning the location of public structures that may influence the character and extent of private building investment and thus, indirectly, influence the very structure of city growth. Familiarity with the principles of good city planning will better enable the real estate appraiser to judge economic forecasts in the light of regional and state developments in which the subject community plays a part.

POPULATION TRENDS AND CHARACTERISTICS

Because of the direct correlation between growth of population and rising values of real property, the real estate appraiser must be fully informed as to the history of population changes in his community, especially over the preceding two or three decades. In addition, population shifts, deaths, and birth and migratory patterns must be analyzed to forecast the population status over periods extending forty or fifty years into the future—or, in any case, a period not shorter than the remaining economic life of the property under appraisal. The city's growth pattern, whether favorable or unfavorable, can best be ascertained by comparison with the rate of growth for the state and the nation. Where community population increases faster than that of the nation and the state, real estate values, all other things being equal, will also keep pace with the accelerated growth. A study of the number of people alone, however, is inadequate. A meaningful population study must also consider among other things the following:

1. *Age-group analysis.* It is important to know the number of persons aged under 20, 20 to 40, 40 to 60, and 60 and over. A favorable ratio of persons in the 20-to-60 age group provides the work force on which the community depends for economic support. Excessive ratios of young or dependent old people may pose community problems the effects of which, if any, must be known and evaluated.
2. *Ethnological pattern of population.* As a rule, the more homogeneous the population as to race, creed, and origin of birth the more tranquil

the community life and the more stable the property value. Based on the latest census count, a breakdown of total population should be obtained showing the percentage of native-born blacks and whites and foreign-born blacks and whites—by country or origin. The trend of population composition should be noted and evaluated. Generally, minority groups comprising the disadvantaged in the social stream are found at the bottom of the economic ladder. A large percentage of basically poor families create built-in tensions and are the principal cause of community social unrest. Poor schools, poor housing, and racial discrimination (often de-facto segregation) pose socio-economic problems which hinder community growth and depress overall property values especially where breakdown of law and order denigrates a city's national reputation. Where racial minorities as a rule exceed 20 percent of the total community population, political statesmanship and enlightened civic leadership must play an important role to achieve coordination of diverse community interests for the overall benefit of the city.

ECONOMIC MEASURES OF COMMUNITY GROWTH

Although measures of economic growth may be equally well applicable in small as in large communities, it must be kept in mind that the hazards of economic forecasting increase with a decrease in community size. An estimate of probable changes in economic standing for a city of 100,000-and-over population can be made with greater certainty than a similar estimate for a community of 25,000-and-under population. The loss of a dominant industry, for instance, due to plant relocation may prove economically disastrous in a small community. A similar loss in a metropolitan city, however, may go wholly unnoticed because of the constant readjustments that take place in the everyday economic life of a large city. For instance, thousands of businesses come and go each year in and around New York City and Chicago without creating a noticeable effect on the balance of their overall economic growth and activity. Indicators of economic growth which warrant observation and provide a basis for judging the quality of investment prospects in a community include, among others, the following:

1. Number of banks, bank deposits, and savings.
2. Postal operations and receipts.
3. Construction and building permits (volume and dollar amounts).
4. Automobile and truck registration.
5. Railroad, airline, and bus passenger traffic.
6. Assessed value of real property.
7. Number of light meters and telephone service connections.
8. Retail sales and buying income per household.
9. Number of gainfully employed by type of employment.

As a rule, the economic growth of a community can best be judged by comparison with other communities of like size and character within the region or by a per capita or per family basis comparison with similar cities anywhere in the country. The census of housing and population income and characteristics, and the special census of manufacturing, provide excellent source data for such comparative growth studies. Ready access to economic growth data listed above should enable the real estate appraiser to formulate accurate forecasts of what the future holds in store for a given community. The number of banks and their total deposits and savings reflect on a per capita basis the degree of well-being as well as the extent of optimism or pessimism that motivates the general economy. Construction volume in dollars and the number of building permits issued during a given period are excellent measures of speed of growth or retardation. Registration statistics of automobiles and trucks, compared with state or national averages, provides further proof of conclusions supported by commercial indexes. Saturation measures of electric and telephone service on a per household basis are useful in ranking a community on the economic "totem pole." Most informative of all as a statistical measure of community standing, however, are retail expenditures, buying income per household, and number of gainfully employed by type of employment.

Employment data should be analyzed as to number and percent engaged in primary occupations as compared with those employed in secondary or service establishments. A primary source of employment involves a product or service that is exported from the community, and which channels into it purchasing power from outside areas that supports service and community economic life generally. As a rule, each primary worker supports two secondary workers engaged as butchers, tailors, barbers, shopkeepers, and general servicers. Thus a new industry providing jobs for 100 family breadwinners in effect accounts for 200 more families which are needed to provide essential social, educational, economic, and recreational community services.

Generally, it is not too difficult to ascertain the status and past performance record of a city and to keep one's finger, so to speak, on the economic pulse of the community under study. Economic source data as a rule can be obtained from utility companies which are called on to forecast community needs for many years into the future. State development agencies as well as local and state chambers of commerce take periodic inventories to ascertain the relative impact of economic growth on the city, the region, and the state. The appraiser should keep himself well informed as to the economic health of his community and be in a position, when compiling a report for an appraisal client, to support his judgment concerning the prospects for growth, decline, or stability of property values within the confines of the city over the economic life of the realty for which he forms a value judgment.

Care must be taken not to rely too strongly on past performance. Every effort should be made to forecast accurately, on the basis of experienced trends, the prospects for continued economic growth as well as the anticipated rate of progress compared with past performance. Value of property, as previously emphasized, lies in the future; and the ups and downs of property income, and hence property worth, are closely tied to the economic strings of the city to which real property is irrevocably attached.

THE ECONOMIC VALUE OF GOOD CITY GOVERNMENT

Just as a business acquires a reputation for honesty, efficiency, reliability, quality of merchandise, and dependable service, so a community acquires a reputation for being subject to good, poor, or corrupt government. There is little doubt that efficient, honest, competent, and forthright government is directly reflected in greater amenities of property ownership and lower costs per unit of municipal service. The overall economic value of good city government—whether its form be manager, mayor, council, or some hybrid combination—must be measured not only by the capitalized savings in the cost of government, but also by the capitalized increased income that accrues to owners of real property as a consequence of effective and economical municipal administration. It may prove misleading if not fallacious to judge the quality of good government by the size of the tax burden per dollar of taxable property. To do so would be to imply that high taxes necessarily lower net income and, as a consequence, account for lower property values. The error of such logic becomes apparent when one considers the fact that cities with the highest property tax burdens, such as New York, Chicago, and Los Angeles, are cities where values per front or square foot of property are also the highest.

Property taxes, of course, are important. To measure the economic burden of such taxes, however, consideration must be given to the value of the municipal services rendered to property owners. Municipal expenditures, for instance, for maintenance of a top-rated fire department may result in the lowering of insurance rates the benefits of which far outweigh the cost of such fire protection service. Similarly, excellent police protection reduces crime and is directly and indirectly reflected in savings to life and property. Expenditures for city planning, zoning, building code enforcement, and traffic control, if wisely undertaken, definitely contribute to orderly city growth and to the enhancement of property values. The attitude of city government toward quality schools, safe housing, and adequate park and recreational facilities is also important. Where expenditures promote equity in law enforcement and increase the level of community well-being, such outlays may prove to be investments which are directly measurable in advancing market prices as reflected in overall property sale transactions.

THE PROBLEM OF URBAN RENEWAL

Practically every city in the United States, large or small, contains slums and other blighted areas. These are the result of city growth, transition to lower economic or faulty use, or simply the result of structural age, decay, and functional obsolescence. Slums constitute a cancer in the body politic, and unless treated and confined in their early stages will contaminate surrounding areas into which urban blight ultimately is expected to advance. Appraisers must become aware of the unsound social and economic effects of slums and blight, especially in communities where local government is financially unable or politically unwilling to cope with this major civic liability.

One of the main obstacles to clearance of slums and blighted areas is the high cost in relation to value recreated. The cost of acquiring affected land, razing it, clearing it, and resubdividing and improving it generally far exceeds the value of the land when redeveloped for a higher and better use. Since slums sap the strength of city government and weaken the moral fiber of its inhabitants, the federal government under the Housing Act of 1954 authorized a new agency—the Urban Renewal Administration—to provide grants and subsidies for eliminating, where possible with local aid, existing slums and controlling the causes of urban blight. Urban renewal programs, both privately and government financed, have been vigorously applied in major metropolitan communities throughout the country, and the anticipated effects have proved economically rewarding to a degree where the broadening of slum clearance legislation is urged as a matter of national policy. The entrance of the federal government as an investor in community welfare provides food for new appraisal thought concerning the socio-economic destiny of American cities. It now appears that the prophets of doom who predicted for more than two decades that American cities could not survive are being proved wrong, and that the centrifugal forces of urban service and culture have reversed the trend of decentralization which got its impetus through the widespread use of rapid transportation and the economical transmission of electric power. Nevertheless, the future of an individual city must rest on the stability of its economic base. It is the appraiser's function to measure the width, depth, and strength of this base—on which a given community supports its property values.

In collecting and analyzing city data, the appraiser must avoid the common pitfall of getting lost in history. Data by itself—uninterpreted—is of little significance to the lay reader. In fact such data may prove to be highly misleading in the case of a "has-been" community. It matters little how a city secured its name, or what heights were reached in designated socio-economic fields of accomplishment. What is important in the formulation of a sound value judgment is what lies ahead for the community—what may reasonably be anticipated from a sound analysis of past performance. It must be kept in mind that the appraisal client is entitled to professional guidance based on a thorough study of community growth trends and their impact on property values, for better or for worse. For illustrative coverage of socio-economic forces that influence property value the reader is referred to the demonstration appraisal report included in Appendix I.

READING AND STUDY REFERENCES

1. Babcock, Frederick M., *The Valuation of Real Estate* (New York: McGraw-Hill Book Company, Inc., 1932), chaps. 5–6, 11.
2. Kahn, Sanders A., Frederick E. Case, and Alfred Schimmel, *Real Estate Appraisal and Investment* (New York: The Ronald Press Company, 1963), chaps. 4–5.
3. Kinnard, William N., Jr., *An Introduction to Appraising Real Property* (Chicago: Society of Real Estate Appraisers, 1968), chap. 8.
4. McEntire, Davis, "Population and Land Values," *The Appraisal Journal* (July 1949), pp. 311–17.
5. Rams, Edwin M., *Principles of City Land Values* (Worthington, Ohio: Academy Publishing Co., 1964), chaps. 2 & 3.
6. Ratcliff, Richard U., *Real Estate Analysis* (New York: McGraw-Hill Book Company, Inc., 1961), chaps. 2 & 4.
7. Ring, Alfred A., *Real Estate Principles and Practices,* 6th ed. (Englewood Cliffs, N.J.: Prentice-Hall, Inc., 1967), chap. 25.
8. Weimer, Arthur M., and Homer Hoyt, *Real Estate* 5th ed. (New York: The Ronald Press Company, 1966), chaps. 18–19.
9. Wendt, Paul F., *Real Estate Appraisal* (New York: Henry Holt and Company, 1956), chap. 5.

The smallest geographic unit—*a neighborhood*—represents a single area in which housing and population characteristics are qualitatively homogenous. As defined by the Society of Real Estate Appraisers, a neighborhood is "that part of an area or community whose physical characteristics are influenced by a similarity of its residents from the standpoint of their economic and social tendencies." [1] Usually it is not difficult to delineate a

7 Value Analysis of Neighborhood Characteristics

neighborhood, because of natural or man-made barriers which enclose it or because of physical attributes or development practices that characterize the area. In most planned communities, neighborhoods come into existence as a result of deliberate platting by subdividers or developers who, with the aid of deed restrictions, control neighborhood growth and expansion. In Figure 7.1, a desirable neighborhood has formed about a spring-fed creek that winds its way alongside a dual-lane, oak-tree-shaded boulevard. Mere size, of course, does not determine a neighborhood. However, the larger the size, the better the protection from infiltration by inharmonious influences or detrimental property uses.

THE NEIGHBORHOOD AGE CYCLE

An important step in the valuation process is the determination of a neighborhood's *age-cycle position*. All neigh-

[1] *Real Estate Appraisal Principles and Terminology* (Chicago, Ill.: Society of Real Estate Appraisers, 1967), p. 71.

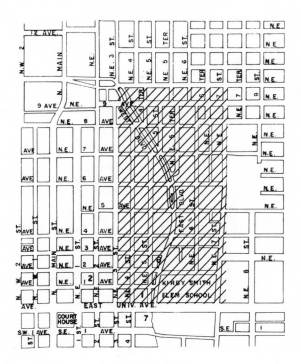

FIGURE 7.1

HIGHLAND SUBDIVISION, GAINESVILLE, FLORIDA

borhoods have a beginning, and most follow an age pattern that reflects growth, maturity, decline, and transition or rehabilitation as influenced by socioeconomic forces that shape community land use patterns. A typical neighborhood age cycle may be diagrammed as in Figure 7.2.

As indicated in Figure 7.2, the *development* period of any neighborhood is the period of growth. The length of time to reach neighborhood maturity will vary with the size of the area under development, but fifteen to twenty years is generally considered typical. Peak neighborhood values are reached during the period of maturity, when improvements generally are at their prime appearance. The length of the maturity period will vary with the kind and size of the community and the economic well-being of those who reside in the neighborhood. Generally, a period of twenty to twenty-five years may be regarded as a typical stretch of time during which a neighborhood remains static in quality.

As buildings pass the prime of their economic life, and as a new gen-

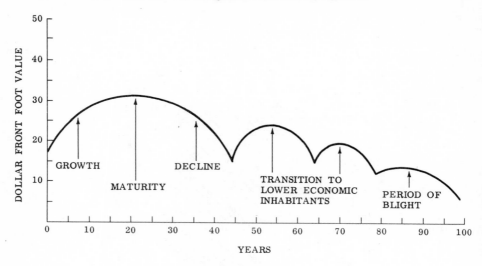

FIGURE 7.2

TYPICAL NEIGHBORHOOD AGE PATTERN

eration replaces the old, properties that no longer fulfill the needs of the original buyers are placed on the market and a new and generally lower class of economic buyers infiltrates the area. This is the stage of neighborhood decline. At first, the trend of property values gently turns lower, as shown by the diagram in Figure 7.2. As demand for properties increases with the transition to the new class of residents (who tell their friends and relatives of the better residential district now available at costs they can all afford) property values again rise, but rarely to the heights reached in prior years. This cyclical economic behavior repeats with successions of transitory ownership-clan changes until the neighborhood reaches a status of blight and prospective slum condition. At this stage, or in prior periods, public or private (renewal) efforts may change the character of a neighborhood to a higher and better use.

It is the appraiser's responsibility to determine the position of the neighborhood's age cycle, and to estimate the effect of neighborhood age and obsolescence on amenities of ownership or income from its use over the remaining economic life of the subject property. As will be demonstrated in Chapter 15, the income productive capacity of a property, as a rule, lessens with age; and, under the impact of forces of obsolescence, consideration must be given to the value effect of such contingencies by stabilizing in the appraisal the anticipated declining income flow or by increasing the risk rate at which such prospective diminishing income must be capitalized.

NEIGHBORHOOD CHARACTERISTICS

In judging the quality of a residential neighborhood the following physical, social, and economic factors warrant analysis:

A. *Physical features*
    1. Location within the city.
    2. Nature of terrain.
    3. Quality of soil.
    4. Features of natural beauty.
    5. Drainage facilities, both natural and man-made.
    6. Street pattern and street improvements, including essential public utilities.
    7. Type of architecture and quality of housing.
    8. Nature, frequency, and cost of public transportation facilities.
    9. Proximity to schools, stores and recreational facilities.
    10. Freedom from hazards and adverse influences.

B. *Population characteristics*
    1. Kind of residents—as to race, creed, and nationality.
    2. Living habits and care of homes.
    3. Attitude toward law and government.
    4. Homogeneity of cultural and civic interests.
    5. Age grouping and size of families.

C. *Economic data*
    1. Extent (percentage) of development.
    2. Percentage of homes owner-occupied.
    3. Frequency of property turnover and vacancies.
    4. Professional or occupational means of earning a livelihood and income stability.
    5. Taxation and assessment levels, and tax burdens.
    6. Zoning and deed restrictions.
    7. Investment quality of area for V.A., F.H.A., and institutional mortgage-loan financing.
    8. Price range and rental value of neighborhood homes.

LOCATION CHARACTERISTICS

The first step in the analysis of a neighborhood is to delineate the boundaries which encompass the area under value study. This can readily be done by identifying the names of streets which enclose the neighborhood north, south, east, and west. Generally, the boundaries of a neighborhood are not difficult to establish because of physical features—natural or man-made—that distinguish the area characteristically as a unit of development. Normally, the neighborhood is referred to by name as originally recorded on public plat book records or by reference to a distinguishing natural feature that marks the area. Often a neighborhood, because of qualitative location within the city, acquires a favorable reputation which to status-seeking buyers enhances the location or status value of the area thus described.

The nature of terrain, too, may influence development practices and should be described and noted as to its effect on value. For residential purposes, gently rolling land is preferable to a flat plateau. People, it seems, prefer to live on hillsides which make possible the enjoyment of a more extensive view of the community's skyline. Elevations, and sometimes valleys, provide a sense of security which attracts residents to that location in preference to others. A flat terrain, on the other hand, is preferable for commercial and industrial development. It is costly and difficult to make building store-fronts conform to sloping sidewalks, and an uneven area is hazardous in a wintery climate where ice and snow make travel on sloping streets dangerous. The nature of the terrain may thus, as noted, exact an important influence on the marketability of a given site for a particular type of intended and permissible use.

In most appraisal reports that have come to the attention of this writer, and which are concerned with urban properties, reference to the *quality of soil* has been omitted. The reason for this oversight, no doubt, is ascribable to the fact that a "normal" load-bearing quality of the soil is taken for granted and that quality of soil for other purposes is considered of negligible importance. An appraiser, however, has no right to take anything for granted. It is his obligation to gather factual data and to report it without prejudice instilled by custom or personal preference. In commercial uses of land the presence of rock, quicksand, hard pan,[2] and high or low water levels may significantly influence costs of construction and hence—since the income to land under a highest and best use is residual in character—the value of the land. Even for residential use, the quality of soil for lawn development and general landscaping may prove of value significance and of deciding importance to a purchaser.

Features of natural beauty that distinguish a neighborhood also deserve careful attention. Majestic trees which line an avenue or provide welcome shade in summer months add value to the abutting land far beyond the price of cords of wood that can be realized if the same trees (as is often, sadly, the case) are cut down and sold for lumber. The presence or nearness of creeks, streams, rivers, lakes, or even man-made reservoirs, enhances the value of sites to varying degrees, depending on land use, beauty of terrain, and utility of the waterways. In any case, the appraiser in formulating a final value decision should carefully inventory the influencing value features for the use and information of the report reader.

---

[2] Layers of dense sand or limestone that prevent the percolating (penetration) of surface waters to subsurface levels.

Of increasing importance in suburban developments, where the extension of public sewerage facilities proves too costly, is the adequacy of soil drainage both natural and man-made. Existence of hard pan or inadequate (safe) soil drainage as based on *percolating* soil tests [3] may cause a site or area to be declared unsafe for installation of sanitary septic tanks, and may result in the denial of building permits in order to safeguard public health. Drainage of surface or flood waters during periods of seasonal rains or storms also must be considered. Failure to do so is a serious omission of factual data, and may subject the appraiser to lawsuit and court charges for professional negligence.

The impact of neighborhood street patterns and street improvements, including essential public utilities, must next be carefully evaluated. Subdivision cost studies confirm that development expenditures for road grading, paving, curbing, gutter, water mains, storm drains, and sanitary sewage facilities aggregate from a minimum of 60 to as high as 90 percent of the value of a developed site. Conversely, the value of raw land may be as little as 10 and seldom more than 40 percent of the value of a fully developed neighborhood site. The presence or absence of street improvements must therefore be emphasized and evaluated by market comparison studies, as demonstrated in the following chapter on site analysis. The street pattern, too, should be noted and its influence on value stressed. The grid street pattern which characterizes older neighborhoods, and which is still favored to this day by economy-minded builders and developers, is frowned on by modern planners and discouraged in proposed subdivisions submitted for loan approval to the V.A. or the F.H.A. Curvilinear streets and cul-de-sac avenues cause automobile traffic to slow down and usually limit their use to residents in the immediate area, creating greater enjoyment and safety for neighborhood occupants both young and old. Market prices confirm buyer preference for *safe* lot locations, and the appraiser must recognize this in the adjustment of comparable sales where neighborhood street patterns are unsatisfactory.

In judging the quality of a neighborhood it is essential to observe the type of architecture and the quality of housing. In design, a distinction should be made between "homogeneity" and "monotony." Houses may appear to be alike but yet be different. Qualitative homogeneity, dignity of design, and pleasing variety of setting and construction elevation give a neighborhood a character rating that can be measured on the preference scale of market value. A good neighborhood will not be marred by irregular setbacks, extremely unorthodox designs, and clashing periods of architecture. The appraiser should be conversant with the features and

---

[3] Soil penetration or drainage tests taken by county, F.H.A., and other agencies to determine soil fitness for installation of private sanitary sewage tank systems.

characteristics of basic architectural styles and be able to classify the ancestry of a residence at least in terms of its relationship to colonial, English, Latin, contemporary or native-conventional periods of construction.

Although the automobile has diminished the importance of intracity transportation, nevertheless the quality of a neighborhood is enhanced by the ready availability of public transportation. Pedestrians are still the rule rather than the exception in community life, and the use of public surface transportation to reach schools, shopping, and recreational centers provides an essential convenience—if not being an absolute necessity. In considering the value added by convenient public transportation, the type, frequency, and cost of service should be ascertained and reported. All other things being equal, a neighborhood with ready accessibility to quality public transportation is preferable and deemed more valuable than one isolated from arteries of public surface travel.

Spreading decentralization, aided by the increasing use of electricity for the performance of essential household chores, has encouraged the development of residential subdivisions far from the public conveniences offered to residents of central urban areas. Although efforts are made to provide essential public conveniences for these outlying developments through the construction of neighborhood shopping centers, church missions, schools, parks, and recreation areas, there is nevertheless a considerable time lag from the period of original neighborhood development to the period when neighborhood shopping facilities and schools become a reality. Years often elapse without such public conveniences, and the values of suburban sites will reflect their absence. An appraiser, therefore, must accurately report the distances in blocks or miles from the subject neighborhood to nearby schools, stores, and churches as well as to the central business area. He must also estimate the effect that distance from these public service facilities may have on the value of the subject property.

The last, but by no means the least of the physical features that make or break a neighborhood from a value point of view is the relative freedom which residents of the area enjoy from *health hazards and other adverse influences*. The danger of through automobile traffic was mentioned before. Other hazards to be checked are smoke, dust, noise, and the gradual infiltration of nonconforming land uses. A check of area residents, public officials, and the opinions of informed persons, along with a thorough neighborhood investigation, should disclose the absence or presence of neighborhood nuisances. Where evidence points to man-made or natural conditions which presently or potentially will impair the health or peace of area residents, the effects on the present value of neighborhood sites must be ascertained and disclosed in the value correlation and report of area influences.

SOCIAL FORCES INFLUENCING
NEIGHBORHOOD VALUES

People create value—hence the compatibility and congeniality of people in an area are important to sustain and enhance neighborhood desirability and property values. A quality neighborhood will disclose homogeneity as to *kind of residents* in regard to race, creed, and national origin. Despite educational and legal efforts to bring about the acceptance of true democratic doctrines, enforced—even when inadvertent—mixing of residents with diverse historical backgrounds within a neighborhood has immediate and depressing influences on value. Often just the threat of infiltration—like rumors within a stock market—causes market values of real properties in the area to be adversely affected. Therefore the necessity and importance of inventorying and reporting the background characteristics of neighborhood residents appears obvious. It must be kept in mind, however, that it is not the opinion or personal preferences of the appraiser that are to be reflected, but rather an objective prediction of the anticipated action or reaction of typical buyers who may purchase properties for use and occupancy in the subject area.

Inspections of the neighborhood by sight and by interrogation will give additional value clues as to the *living habits* of residents and their *care of property*. These external evidences give the neighborhood a character of its own. Well-kept lawns, attractive landscaping, neat and well-maintained buildings, and clean, quiet thoroughfares, provide self-supporting evidence of pride of ownership—an important ingredient in the forecasting of value stability.

Attitude toward government is another essential social trait that enters into a neighborhood quality rating. Ownership and possession of property are legally backed and sanctioned. Respect for law and judiciary opinions minimizes vandalism and the violation of constitutional rights to the quiet enjoyment of life, liberty, and property. Law-abiding citizens, too, will refrain from the illegal and illicit use of premises—use that undermines the moral character of the area. A breakdown in moral fiber, respect for law, and law enforcement itself destroys neighborhood value more swiftly than do the physical forces of wear, tear, decay, and the actions of the elements. A statement of the apparent attitude of local residents toward law, order, and government is an essential part of a report on property value.

Another social characteristic lending support to neighborhood stability and value is the relative *homogeneity of cultural interests*. Generally this homogeneity is evidenced by friendly relations among neighbors, membership in the area's civic and protective organizations, organized neighborhood social and cultural events, the extent of resident participation in social clubs, and the sharing of recreational facilities. This social aspect of neighborhood population is, of course, closely linked to homogeneity of occupational and professional economic interests that will be discussed below.

With the increasing longevity of life, another point of appraisal interest concerns the neighborhood's *age groupings and size of families.* Extreme age differentials among heads of households is not conducive to neighborhood value stability. Older citizens acquire different habits and modes of living and may find the active and seemingly frivolous conduct of younger neighbors distracting and disquieting. An area devoid of age-group conflicts, of course, will be rated better qualitatively than one where consciousness of social and age differences is noticeable. Size of family, too, must be observed and rated, especially in relation to the space availability of the typical home. Young couples wanting families cannot long remain residents of a neighborhood where two- or even three-bedroom houses with single bathroom facilities are typical for the area. Where variation in family size is observed, possible transfers of occupants to quarters where their needs can be better served must be anticipated.

NEIGHBORHOOD ECONOMIC CHARACTERISTICS

A matter of important interest to mortgage lenders, and of prime concern to real estate investors, is the extent or percentage of neighborhood development. The image of investment failures and mass property foreclosures during the early 1930s—although more than a generation removed —is still much talked and read about in informed real estate circles. The danger then and the fear now are based on overexpansion caused by thinly supported hypothetical demands envisioned as a projection of a temporary "boom" psychology rather than a projection based on the analysis of long-term trends and socioeconomic resource studies. An area thinly developed or improved below 50 percent of its land capacity holds investment hazards which must be reflected in value estimates and stressed in appraisal report writing. Undeveloped sites, too, tempt owners and speculators into premature, hasty, and often faulty land utilization that may adversely affect the value of abutting and neighboring properties. The appraiser is duty-bound to remove the "blinds" which cause the uninformed to evaluate an apparent "jewel" of a property without an objective study of its situation.

If the neighborhood is of residential character, it is important to determine the number of percentage of total homes that are *owner occupied.*

Tenants, no matter how desirable, are transient in character,[4] and frequent changes in the kind and composition of tenant families create a sense of insecurity and area instability which impairs the investment quality of a neighborhood. Tenants, too, lack a feeling of belonging, and generally their lack of pride of ownership is reflected in lax lawn and home care. Owner-occupancy status can readily be secured from public tax-record data or from tax officials, especially in states where homestead tax exemptions are accorded owner occupants.

Frequency of *property turnover* and percentage of home, apartment, or store vacancies provide another measure of economic rating. All else being equal, a neighborhood with well-established owner occupants of long standing poses fewer investment risks than one characterized by frequent property transfers. Excessive property sales, no matter how valid the reason, create a feeling of investment insecurity or a climate of speculation, resulting in distorted market prices that reflect a transitory time-position along the ever-moving real estate business cycle. Since property values—unless otherwise stated—reflect the present worth of future rights to income, at least over the remaining economic life of property improvements, the appraiser must take into account the influence of temporary price determinants and objectively predict future expectancy under anticipated typical market operations. Vacancies, too, if in excess of normal ratios varying from 0 to 5 percent of total space supply—depending on geographic location and kind of real property—must be analyzed with care. Excessive vacancies may indicate a glutting of the market or a violation of the principle of balance in area development.

The economic status of neighborhood occupants, their means of livelihood, and their income stability is of further economic importance. The predominating professional or occupational interests of area residents should be established. The order generally descends from executives to professionals (doctors, lawyers, etc.), junior executives, white-collar office workers, skilled mechanics, clerks, and skilled laborers. Although a neighborhood can normally be classified as housing one or more of the occupational or professional interest groups, it is the relative income and status of the area occupants (assuming compatible social status) that matter most. Generally, there is a direct relationship between range of annual earnings and range of property values. Executives earning $20,000 to $30,000 annually generally seek homes in the price-range of $40,000 to $60,000. White-collar workers, on the other hand, earning from $8,000 to $10,000 annually create a demand for housing in the $20,000 to $30,000 price range. Of equal significance is income stability. Certain occupations,

---

[4] Studies of tenancy in metropolitan areas support the fact that the average tenant moves at least once each year.

though lower on the scale of earning power (such as teachers and salaried technicians) enjoy greater job security and stability of income. Neighborhoods occupied by this group, or any similar group—such as retired persons—whose stability of income is relatively certain, will experience greater stability in their level of property values.

The economic impact of property taxation and assessment levels and burdens must be carefully analyzed in the valuation process. Although property taxation is generally a matter for study and analysis as a political policy of county and city governments, it is a commonly recognized fact that in most communities tax differentials exist among newer and older neighborhoods. This is caused by the political expedient of shifting the burden of taxation onto incoming residents in newly developed subdivisions while slowing down the upward adjustments of assessed values for older, established neighborhoods where the area's real voting power generally rests—with their long-time, influential residents. Where such tax differentials exist, they must be noted and evaluated over the immediate years as being, at best, a form of community "good will." Conversely, neighborhoods may have been overburdened with heavy assessments for road and area improvements that have brought little if any benefits to the properties affected. To illustrate: In a court case, property owners in Miami Beach, Florida, challenged the right of the municipality to levy assessments for the widening of Indian Creek Drive. The property owners contended that the improvements were made to relieve congested traffic on another street, and that as a result of the widening the affected street had turned into a noisy thoroughfare that had caused neighboring values to lessen. The State Supreme Court, in a 4–3 decision, ruled against the city and in favor of the property owners by recognizing that benefits which may accrue from road widening in a residential area are questionable. The majority opinion at one point asked, "Whoever heard of making a traffic count to locate a home?" Where uneconomic assessments, however, are enforced the appraiser must estimate their effect (considering both amount and duration) on the market value of neighborhood properties.

Since the typical buyer, contrary to accepted opinion, is not especially informed on matters concerning public zoning and deed restrictions it is the appraiser's responsibility to evaluate the benefits or detriments constituted by the presence or absence of protective zoning and private deed restrictions. Care must be taken to recognize that zoning by itself does not create value. For example, to zone an area for business counter to good planning or in excess of such land use demands may not only lower the value of the property so zoned but may also lessen the value of surrounding properties in the neighborhood. Zoning, moreover, is designed to restrict *land* uses, and does not and cannot legally separate people by race, color, creed, or mode of living. Good zoning, however, does assure uniformity of land use and thus provides protection against inharmonious land uses which exploit the public good for purposes of excessive private gain. The presence, need, and adequacy of deed restrictions must also be evaluated. Zoning ordinances can often be rescinded or adversely amended. Deed restrictions, however, have stronger legal sanctions which attach to and run with the land and cannot be violated without consent of the property owners affected, as well as without compliance to stipulated contractual provisions under which land use exceptions may be made. The period of time during which deed restrictions are effective must be noted along with permissible extension of existing deed restrictions where they are deemed essential to protect the character of neighborhood over the economic life of the neighborhood improvements.

Of interest to investors and home owners, as well as being of value significance, is whether a neighborhood warrants approval for F.H.A., V.A. *or institutional mortgage-loan financing.* In the current market, where an increasing number of marginal home buyers depend on high-ratio mortgage-to-value loans, the unavailability of government-underwritten or institutional loans—especially if caused by a lack of required neighborhood improvements such as sewerage, water, paving, etc.—may curb sales of residential properties to an extent where a buyers' market will reflect in its lower values the absence of liberal financial aid. The loss in property value in a restricted mortgage market is often far in excess of the costs of street and utility improvements the absence of which disqualify the neighborhood for government-approved or conventional mortgage loans.

An important guide to the price quality of a neighborhood is the value range of residential homes. In fact the first step in classifying a neighborhood is to establish the value range within which typical homes can be exchanged in the open market. It is this price range that guides the appraiser in his selection of comparable properties to serve as a market guide for estimating the worth of a particular property in the subject neighborhood. Care must be taken not to attempt a narrowing of the range to the point where "guesstimating" becomes a strong temptation. As a rule, the spread of values may range from a minimum of 25 to a maximum of 50 percent of typical sale values. The appraiser thus may conclude a range, for instance, of from $10,000 to $12,500, or $20,000 to $25,000; or a maximum spread of from $10,000 to $15,000, or $20,000 to $30,000 respectively. Although circumstances may warrant exceptions, it should be kept in mind that a typical and not an extreme range is sought in categorizing a neighborhood. The actual, or imputed, rental value per month or per annum of typical neighborhood structures, too, is of interest. This information serves importantly in helping to check market sales estimates against the capitalized value found under the income or earnings approach to value.

No appraisal is complete without a thorough analysis of environmental forces and improvements that affect the value rating of a neighborhood. Every appraisal form in use currently provides for entry of data which aids the field appraiser in reaching a value conclusion concerning the quality of the area under study. An appraisal form used by the Veterans Administration for G.I. loans provides for evaluation of neighborhood data as follows:

1. Character of neighborhood.
2. Neighborhood development activity.
3. Type of major structures.
4. Nature and quality of construction.
5. Typical condition.
6. Percentage built up.
7. Age of typical building.
8. Percent owner-occupied.
9. Percent vacancy.
10. Zoning classification.
11. Transition of neighborhood.
12. Available utilities (water, sewerage, gas, electricity, septic tank).
13. Street improvements (walks, curb, gutter, paving, alleys, fire protection).
14. Civic conveniences and distances to grade schools, high schools, stores, churches, and transportation.
15. Typical influences as to occupants (occupation, income, rentals, and range of property values).

NEIGHBORHOOD ATTRIBUTES OF COMMERCIAL DISTRICTS

Greater dependence by shoppers on private means of transportation has accelerated the developments of suburban shopping centers where ready access and ample parking invites unhurried and carefree shopping. Contrary to hasty predictions made by prominent urban economists the central city as a commercial entity is, however, far from oblivion. In fact the downtown shopping areas, which in major cities have struck a low point in unit land value in the 1960–1965 period, are now readjusting, modernizing, and effectively competing for their share of the community trade dollar. The revitalizing of the downtown Philadelphia area, initiated and pioneered by the John Wannamaker Department Store firm, is an illustration that marks the comeback of the downtown areas of major cities.

It is the appraiser's responsibility to analyze the qualitative importance of the commercial shopping area, and to designate the grouping of stores which marketwise constitute the 100% trade location. Other locations that radiate from this 100 percent area can then be qualitatively and percentage-wise rated in the process of estimating comparative unit land values.

The shopping center itself must be analyzed in accordance with the principle of balance to ascertain the adequacy in number as well as the variety of essential retail establishments. Based on a recent analysis by *Sales Management,* the magazine of marketing, twenty-three retail stores are needed to serve the needs per 1,000 family units as follows:

Number of Stores	Kind of Retail or Service Establishment
3	Food stores
1	Bakery
2	Apparel stores
1	Drug store
2	Eating places
1	Furniture and Household
2	Automotive supplies
2	Gas service stations
1	Lumber, building materials, and hardware
1	Package liquor store
2	Barbershops
2	Beauty parlors
1	Shoe repair
1	Variety
1	Dry cleaning and pressing

The kind and number of retail establishments in a subject commercial area depends, of course, on community custom, climate, and the general characteristics of the inhabitants.

The valuation of industrial and farm properties is deemed too specialized a field to be covered even superficially in a general text on property valuation. The interested reader and practitioner is referred for study materials in these fields to publications made available by the Society of Industrial Realtors and the Farm Brokers Institute through their Chicago offices.

READING AND STUDY REFERENCES

1. *Acquisition for Right-of-Way* (Washington, D.C.: American Association of State Highway Officials, 1962), chap. 25.

2. Albert, Sterling H., "Neighborhood Factors Affecting Residential Values," *The Appraisal Journal* (January 1960), pp. 81–89.

3. *The Appraisal of Real Estate* (Chicago: American Institute of Real Estate Appraisers, 1967), chap. 6.

4. Kahn, Sanders A., Frederick E. Case, and Alfred Schimmel, *Real Estate Appraisal and Investment* (New York: The Ronald Press Company, 1963), chap. 6.

5. Kinnard, William N., *An Introduction to Appraising Real Property* (Chicago: Society of Real Estate Appraisers, 1968), chap. 9.

6. McMichael, Stanley L., *McMichael's Appraising Manual*, 4th ed. (Englewood Cliffs, N.J.: Prentice-Hall, Inc., 1951), chap. 13.

7. Rams, Edwin M., *Principles of City Land Values* (Worthington, Ohio: Academy Publishing Co., 1964), chaps. 5 and 6.

8. Ratcliff, Richard U., *Real Estate Analysis* (New York: McGraw-Hill Book Company, Inc., 1961), chap. 4.

9. Weimer, Arthur M., and Homer Hoyt, *Real Estate,* 5th ed. (New York: The Ronald Press Company, 1966), chap. 17.

10. Woltz, Seth P., "Analyzing Residential Neighborhoods," *The Residential Appraiser* (August 1960), pp. 2–5.

Since the characteristics of a neighborhood do not uniformly extend to all locations within the area, and since some sites are superior to others because of geographic situation, land improvement, size, shape, and other physical or economic attributes, it is important that land per se be analyzed separately and evaluated as if free for development, in conformity with the principle of highest and best use. There are, of course, other

8

Factors and Considerations

in Site Analysis

reasons why the value of the land, as distinct from the improvements which it supports, must be known:

1. Local tax assessment regulations, in most jurisdictions, require the allocation of total property value to land, buildings, and other land improvements. This division aids the assessor in the allocation of units of value with greater consistency and uniformity. Improvements, too, are made subject to adjustment for loss in value due to depreciation, whereas land historically has shown tendencies to appreciate.
2. Federal internal revenue regulations also require the separation of land from improvement value for purposes of depreciation allowance on the latter.
3. Where land is not improved with structures that constitute the highest and best use, it is necessary to determine the value of land as if free and clear and to charge the improvements with value losses resulting from over-, under,- or faulty improvements.

4. For insurance purposes, a separation of land from value of building improvements (which are subject to fire and other hazards) is essential in order to measure accurately the nature and extent of insurable risks.
5. For investment purposes, a study of shifting land to building value ratio may prove important and useful in measuring changes in the duration of economic building life.
6. Some appraisal techniques too, as is the case under the cost and building residual income approaches to value, require separate handling of site and improvements in the valuation process.
7. Unimproved or vacant land too must be evaluated as available under a potential and legally permissible highest and best use.

THE NEED FOR A LOCATION SKETCH

Every appraisal should include a legal description which definitely and unmistakably fixes the geographic location of the subject property. Where the land is improved, the legal description should be reinforced by street name and building number for added reference. Within the city limits and in suburban subdivisions, a description by lot and block number as shown on a given page in a plat book on official record best serves this purpose. For property locations in suburban or rural areas, or where subdivision designations by lot and block numbers are unavailable, the appraiser should obtain accurate legal descriptions prepared under either the "metes and bounds" or government survey system.

Because of the technical competency required to derive directional bear-

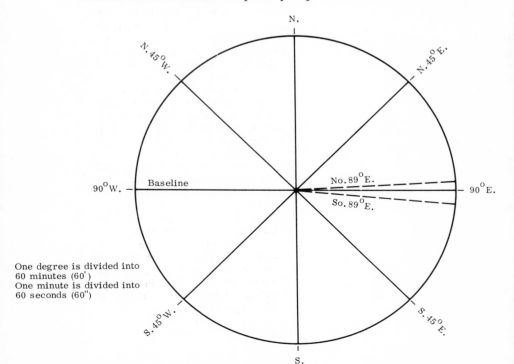

ings north, south, east, and west with accuracy to minutes and seconds of degrees, metes and bounds descriptions should be prepared only by registered land surveyors. In metes and bounds descriptions as shown in the circular diagram on page 94, the bearings or course of a line of direction is the angle which that line makes from the central point of departure parallel with a meridian. As shown on the facing page, the bearing of any line cannot exceed 90 degrees. A line running almost due east might have a bearing of "north" 89 degrees east. If this same line were rotated three degrees in a clockwise direction, its bearing would become "south" 88 degrees east.

Bearings may be measured and described either from the magnetic north and south (in which case they are called *magnetic bearings*) or from a true astronomic meridian north and south (in which case they are called *true* bearings). The bearings of a given line as expressed under the two systems will differ by the amount of the magnetic declination for that date and locality.

To make available accurate legal descriptions, particularly in rural areas, the federal government adopted in 1785 the rectangular survey of land locations.

This system is based on surveying lines running north and south, called meridians and east and west, called base lines. These are established through the area to be surveyed and each is given a name and number by the land office in Washington, D.C. A map showing the location of the several prime meridians and their base lines in the United States is shown on page 96.

Beginning at the intersection of the meridian and base lines, the surveyors divided the area between intersections into squares, called "checks," twenty-four miles on each side. These squares were further subdivided into sixteen areas each measuring six miles by six miles, called "townships." The townships containing an area of thirty-six square miles were again subdivided into "sections," each a square mile containing 640 acres, and the sections were then divided into halves, quarters, or smaller subdivisions as the need called for to describe individual land holdings.[1]

To identify the various townships, the rows east and west and parallel to the base line were numbered as "tiers" 1, 2, etc., north or south, of a given base line. The rows north and south and parallel to the meridians were called ranges and were numbered 1, 2, etc., east or west of a principal or guide meridian. The numbering system is illustrated by the diagram at the top of page 97.

---

[1] For a full explanation of Land Surveying and Property Descriptions, see Chapter 6 of Ring and North, *Real Estate Principles and Practices* (Englewood Cliffs, New Jersey: Prentice-Hall, Inc., 6th ed., 1967), pp. 86–97.

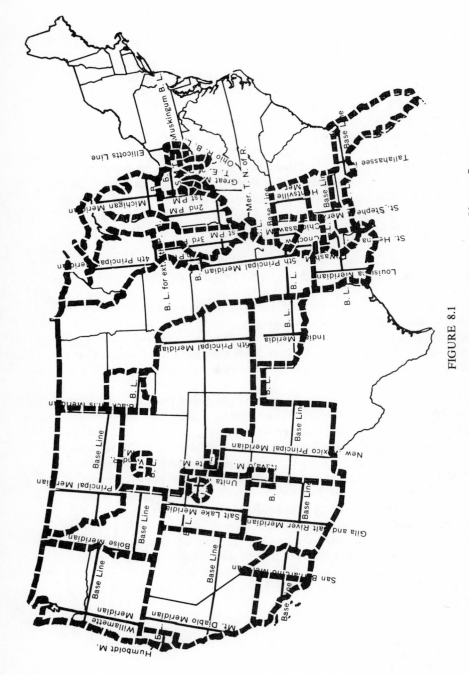

FIGURE 8.1

MAP OF PRIME MERIDIANS AND THEIR BASE LINES WITHIN THE UNITED STATES

N

3rd STANDARD PARALLEL NORTH

				TIER	12	NORTH		

TIER 12 NORTH
" 11 "
WEST = = 2nd PRINCIPAL MERIDIAN EAST = = = " 10 " = =
" 9 "

2nd STANDARD PARALLEL NORTH

RANGE 4 3 2 1 1 2 3 4 TIER 5 6 7 8
RANGE = = = = " 8
" 7 "
" 6 "

1st STANDARD PARALLEL NORTH

1st GUIDE MERIDIAN WEST

T4N R4W	T4N R3W	T4N R2W	T4N R1W	TIER	"	4	"		2nd GUIDE MERIDIAN EAST
T3N R4W	T3N R3W	T3N R2W	T3N R1W	"	1st GUIDE	3	"		
T2N R4W	T2N R3W	T2N R2W	T2N R1W	"		2	"		
T1N R4W	T1N R3W	T1N R2W	T1N R1W	BASE LINE		1	"		

|← 24 MILES →|← 24 MILES →|← 24 MILES →|

INITIAL POINT

24 MILES 24 MILES 24 MILES

Sections are identified by number as indicated on the following diagram:

6	5	4	3	2	1
7	8	9	10	11	12
18	17	16	15	14	13
19	20	21	22	23	24
30	29	28	27	26	25
31	32	33	34	35	36

6 MILES

6 MILES

Owing to the spherical shape of the earth, the meridians converge as one goes north—the north side of a township is approximately fifty feet shorter than the south side. To correct this error, the government established certain principle meridians and others, called guide meridians, which are changed at each parallel to make allowances for the earth's curvature. This problem really concerns only the surveyor and is mentioned only so that the reader may not be confused in studying the diagram.

In describing a section, it is customary to state first the number of the section, then the township and range: "Section 12, Township 3 North, Range 2 East of the principal (named) meridian." It may be abbreviated: "Sect. 12 T. 3 N. Rge 2 E, ... County, State of ...."

The description of a part of a section is simple. For example, the plot A on the diagram below is, "West ½ of Southwest ¼, Sec. 12." The same diagram indicates the description of other parts of the section.

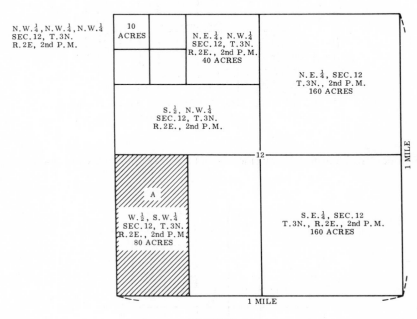

FIGURE 8.2

To avoid any possible misunderstanding as to the exact location of the site under value study, it is recommended that a location sketch, such as shown in Figure 8.3, be made a part of every appraisal report. This sketch should designate a prominent point of reference, such as a court house, police station, museum, or other well-known public building, and should indicate by reference to public roads or streets the direction and location of the subject property. With the aid of this sketch, even a stranger to the community should be able to reach the location without fail. As shown,

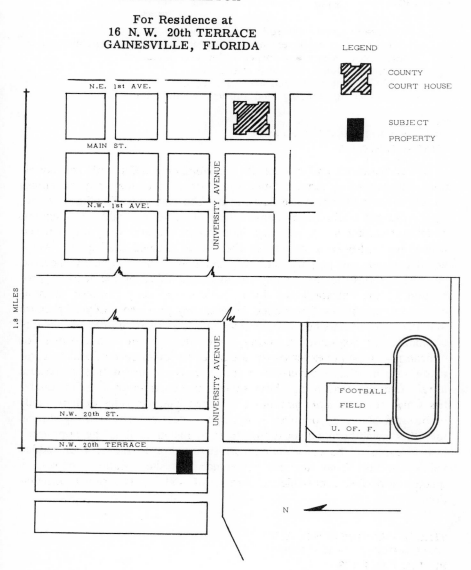

LOCATION SKETCH

For Residence at
16 N. W. 20th TERRACE
GAINESVILLE, FLORIDA

LEGEND

COUNTY
COURT HOUSE

SUBJECT
PROPERTY

N.E. 1st AVE.

MAIN ST.

N.W. 1st AVE.

UNIVERSITY AVENUE

1.8 MILES

UNIVERSITY AVENUE

N.W. 20th ST.

N.W. 20th TERRACE

FOOTBALL
FIELD

U. OF. F.

N

FIGURE 8.3
LOCATION SKETCH

distances in blocks or miles should be noted to avoid further unnecessary delays in pinpointing the subject location.

The location, once accurately established, should then be analyzed in regard to:

1. Nature of terrain and soil characteristics.
2. Kind of street improvements and availability of essential public utilities.
3. Size, depth, shape, and corner-lot location influences.
4. Zoning, building, and deed restrictions.
5. Title encumbrances and encroachments.
6. Landscaping, building, and subsurface land improvements.

NATURE OF TERRAIN AND SOIL CHARACTERISTICS

Site preparations and cost of site developments differ with soil conditions and nature of terrain. Sites below street level may require filling; others, because of subsurface flaws, costly shoring; and still others, terracing to prevent washouts or construction of retaining walls to safeguard building foundations. Rock may have to be blasted or pilings driven where the load-bearing quality of the soil is deemed inadequate. Additional costs of site preparation, over and above those typically incurred in building construction, usually diminish the value of the land in proportion to the extraordinary dollar outlays necessary because of nontypical site conditions. Some sites, in fact, may prove so costly to prepare that the land is classified *submarginal* and defaulted in title to the city or county for tax saving purposes, or deeded to public authorities for utilization—at public expense—as a park or for other recreational or community-use benefits. Conversely, a site, because of orientation or natural terrain features, may bring about savings in construction or offer amenities which result in *situs qualities* (economic characteristics of land made or brought about by popular acceptance) over and above those typical for other neightborhood locations. In such instances it is the appraiser's task to estimate the construction cost savings, or to measure the added value resulting from demand preference for site locations possessing quality attributes ascribable to nature of soil or geographic orientation.

STREET IMPROVEMENTS AND AVAILABILITY OF ESSENTIAL PUBLIC UTILITIES

Street accessibility and extent of street frontage are of substantial value importance for all urban uses. This is supported by the fact that the *unit* value for such sites is quoted on a front foot rather than on a square foot or acre basis, as is the case with industrial or agricultural land. This front-foot value is considerably enhanced where streets are properly improved and provide for service connections to essential public utilities. Street improvements recognized as adding value include paving, sidewalks, curb, gutter, storm drains, sanitary sewage, and connections for water, gas, telephones, and electricity. Care must be taken to make certain that all improvements are fully paid for. The value of a site is generally based on "as is" condition on a given date. If assessments for street and capital improvements are outstanding, the present worth of the future dollar obligations must be subtracted from the site value derived under a "free and clear" assumption of land ownership. To avoid misunderstanding the appraiser should stipulate that the value findings assume the discharge of all outstanding debt obligations and assessments due and payable, including accrued taxes to date of the appraisal. Where essential street improvements or public utilities are lacking, the appraiser must measure with care the "negative value" market reactions that penalize a site, often in excess of cost of such utilities or of road improvements.

LOCATION ANALYSIS

An interesting table for rating a location for mortgage loan purposes was developed by the Federal Housing Administration to be used by their appraisers. This form, which is reproduced on the facing page, requires field inspectors to exercise sound judgment in rating site features as follows:

1. Protection against inharmonious land uses.
2. Physical and social attractiveness.
3. Adequacy of civic, social, and commercial centers.
4. Adequacy of transportation.
5. Sufficiency of utilities and services.
6. Level of taxes and special assessments.

Each feature is rated from "reject" to excellent (in column 5). Columns signify (1) Poor, (2) Fair, (3) Satisfactory, (4) Good, and (5) Excellent. Under F.H.A. regulation, a loan is denied if any feature is sufficently poor to warrant a *reject* classification. The overall rating must equal 60 or better for the location to be acceptable under the F.H.A. mortgage insurance risk program. This, or a similar rating grid for evaluating location features, may prove of great assistance in the development of an accurate neighborhood reference file as part of the appraisal plant (office). Especially when comparing comparable sales for one location with location features of the subject property does the rating grid serve a most useful purpose.

Site Desirability Features	Reject	1	2	3	4	5	Rating
Protection against inharmonious land uses		4	8	12	16	⑳	20
Physical and social attractiveness		4	8	12	⑯	20	16
Adequacy of civic, social, and commercial centers		4	8	12	16	⑳	20
Adequacy of transportation		4	8	12	⑯	20	16
Sufficiency of utilities and services		2	4	6	⑧	10	8
Level of taxes and special assessments		2	4	6	⑧	10	8
Rating of Site Desirability							88

RATING OF LOCATION GRID [2]

In appraisal practice, the above form would be used only as a work sheet. The location features would be discussed in a narrative report, and the final rating reflected in value conclusions reached under the market and income approaches to value.

SIZE, DEPTH, SHAPE, AND CORNER LOT LOCATION INFLUENCES

It is recognized that a site must be of a minimum size and shape to permit effective utilization in conformity with the principle of highest and best use under existing zoning, building, and deed restrictions. A site 10 feet wide and 100 feet deep in a residential area where building restrictions call for a minimum size lot containing 10,000 square feet of area has no value except as it may attract offers from neighboring property owners who may, at a price, be interested in adding this strip of land to their holdings. It is important, therefore, to make certain that a site under valuation meets minimum lot-size requirements. The value of a rectangular site (if residential or commercial in character) depends on the number of units, or front feet, along the abutting street, and on the depth of the lot if the same is deeper or shallower than that considered standard for the neighborhood.

To illustrate: Assuming a standard lot depth of 100 feet in a given neighborhood and a front foot lot value of $50 (as supported by market

---

[2] See Federal Housing Administration, *Underwriting Manual*, F.H.A. 2049 (Washington, D. C.: Government Printing Office, rev. April 1, 1965).

comparison lot sale analysis), then a 100-foot wide by 100-foot deep lot is estimated to bring 100 x $50, or $5,000, if exposed for sale. For every street foot added or subtracted from this lot, provided the lot depth remains 100 feet, the value will increase or decrease by $50 in amount. In many instances, however, lots are either substandard or in excess of a depth considered standard for the area. To measure the value influence of depth—in conformity with the principle that the front of a lot (because of street access and utility) is more valuable than the rear—depth rules have been devised to measure changes in value resulting from variations in depth size—all other things remaining equal.

In applying depth rules, it should be kept in mind that rules by themselves do not make value but rather reflect the market actions of typical buyers in a community. Then too, rules applied should merit acceptance by professional appraisers in the area and prove acceptable in court practice.[3] Most of the depth rules have been devised as an aid to tax assessors to permit uniformity of value treatment. However, these rules appear to check out with market sale transactions and are applied when other and more accurate means of measuring the value of nonstandard size lots are unavailable.

THE 4-3-2-1 DEPTH RULE

This depth rule has gained prominence because it is general in character and not tied by name to any person or location. The rule is based on the theory that a standard lot, if divided into four equal parts, will differ in value as follows: First quarter, 40 percent; second quarter, 30 percent; third quarter, 20 percent; and fourth quarter, 10 percent. This value allocation accounts for the rule's classification as *4-3-2-1*. For every additional quarter of lot depth added beyond standard depth the value increment decreases by 1 percent from that of the last quarter. Thus the next 25 feet beyond a 100-foot standard lot adds 9 percent of value. The next 25 feet beyond that, 8 percent, the next, 7 percent, and so forth. A depth value comparison table and diagram for three of the more widely used depth rules is presented on the next page.

Where a "standard" lot in a given neighborhood exceeds 100 feet in depth, and typical lot depth in either 120 or 140 feet, then under the 4-3-2-1 rule the total market value is allocated to each quarter—be it 30 feet or 35 feet or more—and applied to nonstandard lots in accordance with depth rule practice as illustrated above.

---

[3] During testimony in an Alabama District Court a witness referred to the use of a "New York depth rule in measuring damages for land taken under eminent domain proceedings." Opposing counsel asked, "Why do ya'll use a Yankee rule in the Southland?" The jury got the message, at least so the verdict indicated.

Feet of Depth	4-3-2-1	Davies Rule	Milwaukee Rule
175	7	11.7	4
150	8	12.8	6
125	9	13.7	9
100	10	15.9	13
75	20	18.7	17
50	30	23.7	21
25	40	41.7	49
0			

Street Frontage

DEPTH COMPARISON BASED ON PERCENTAGE OF VALUE

(STANDARD LOT = 100 FEET)

ODD-SHAPED LOT VALUATION

Irregular plots often present a problem in appraising. Assuming no disutility because of odd shape and no impairment of utilization under a highest and best land employment program, an irregular site should be evaluated in accordance with the customary unit measure applied in practice for similar and regular-shaped lots, plus value allowance for odd plot portions as demonstrated in Figure 8.4. Residential and commercial sites

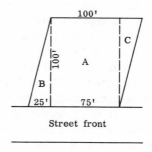

Street front

FIGURE 8.4

are generally evaluated in relation to the number of feet fronting on a city street. Where the shape is a parrallelogram as shown in Figure 8.4, no value adjustment is necessary for lot irregularity since the two triangles marked B and C in effect form a rectangle the combined value of which is equal to a rectangle of like street frontage.

Odd-shaped lots such as shown in Figure 8.5 are valued as rectangular lots, plus the additional value of the triangular lots. Based on market study, a triangular lot, provided the base fronts the street such as Lot 2

PERCENTAGE COMPARISON DEPTH VALUE TABLE FOR LOTS FROM
5 FEET TO 175 FEET IN DEPTH [4]

Depth in Feet	4–3–2–1	Davies Rule	Milwaukee Rule
5	9.4	12.6	17.
10	17.8	21.7	28.
15	25.6	29.2	37.
20	33.0	35.8	44.
25	40.0	41.7	49.
30	46.7	47.1	54.
35	53.1	52.1	59.
40	59.1	56.8	63.
45	64.7	61.3	67.
50	70.0	65.4	70.
55	74.9	69.5	74.
60	79.4	73.4	77.
65	83.4	77.1	80.
70	86.9	80.6	84.
75	90.0	84.1	87.
80	92.2	87.4	90.
85	94.2	90.6	93.
90	96.2	94.0	95.
95	98.1	97.0	98.
100	100.0	100.0	100.
110	103.8	106.0	103.
120	107.4	111.2	107.
130	110.6	116.2	110.
140	113.8	121.6	113.
150	117.0	126.5	115.
160	119.8	131.2	117.
170	122.6	136.2	118.
175	124.0	138.2	119.

[4] Standard lot depth equals 100 feet.

in Figure 8.5, is worth 65 percent of a rectangular lot of the same frontage. A triangular lot with its apex on the street such as Lot 1 in Figure 8.5 is worth 25 percent of a rectangular lot with a street frontage equal to the base of the triangle. To illustrate, assuming a value of $50 per front foot, the lots illustrated in Figure 8.5 would be appraised as shown below the figure.

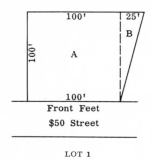

LOT 1

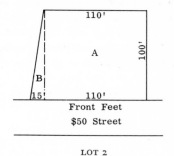

LOT 2

FIGURE 8.5

Lot No. 1

A	100 fee @ $50.00	=	$5,000.00
B	25 feet @ $50.00 × .35	=	437.50
	Total value Lot No. 1		$5,437.50

Lot No. 2

A	110 feet @ $50.00	=	$5,500.00
B	15 fee @ $50.00 × .65	=	487.50
	Total value Lot No. 2		$5,987.50

CORNER LOT VALUATION

With the increasing width of standard residential lots—from 20 and 25 feet to 100 feet or more in suburban subdivisions—the advantages which corner locations once offered in providing better light, more convenient access and, perhaps, greater privacy have diminished to a point where the additional hazards encountered at corner locations from automobile traffic have completely neutralized corner location advantages. In residential areas, therefore, the recommended appraisal practice is not to ascribe a value increment because of corner location, unless market sales in a community or area clearly demonstrate preference for such locations.

Commercial corner locations, however, do have value advantages over inside lots because of greater accessibility, increased pedestrian traffic, better merchandise display, and store visibility from two street locations. Corner lots typically command better rentals, and the net income to land is higher at corner store locations whether they are under owner or tenant occupancy. Under the income approach—as will be demonstrated in Chapter 18—the added corner value is directly accounted for by capitalization of the increased income ascribable to a site location. Under the market approach, however, comparison sales data generally relate to inside lots, and adjustments are required to account for corner value influences. As stated previously, rules do not create value; nevertheless, they do offer, where tested by field practice, an opportunity to check value findings derived from other approaches to value.

A corner value rule which has gained prominence and wide acceptance in appraisal practice is that developed by John A. Zangerle of Cleveland, Ohio. Under the Zangerle-Cleveland Rule, corner value influence extends for a maximum of 100 feet along the main street from the point of intersection with the side street, and is based on a percentage of side street lot value up to a distance of 100 feet as follows:

Lot Width on Main Street	*Corner Value as Percent of Side Street Value*
5	15
10	25
15	33
20	40
25	46
30	51
35	55
40	58
45	61
50	63
55	64
60	66
65	67
70	68
75	69
80	70
85	71
90	71
95	72
100	72

Based on this table, a lot as illustrated in Figure 8.6 is valued as shown below the figure.

As indicated in Zangerle's table, the land closest to the corner benefits most from the corner location influences and the corner value diminishes to a negligible or fractional amount for the last portion of the corner lot. Assuming separate ownership of a corner lot as marked in Figure 8.7, the corner value benefits would be derived as shown below the figure.

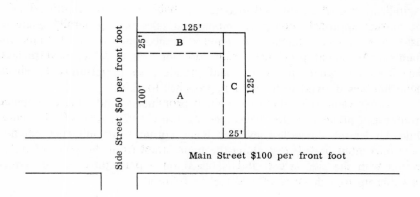

FIGURE 8.6

Lot A	100 feet @ $100	=	$10,000
	Corner value: 100 feet @		
	$50 × .72	=	3,600
	Total Lot A		**$13,600**
Lot B	25 feet @ $50	=	1,250
Lot C	25 feet @ $100 × 1.09 (depth factor)		2,725
	Total value A, B, and C		**$17,575**

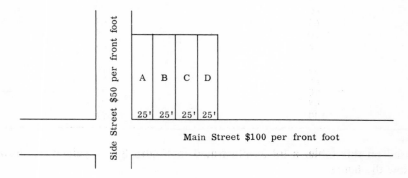

FIGURE 8.7

Lot A	25 feet @ $100	=	$2,500
	Corner value: 100 feet @		
	$50 × .46	=	2,300

	Total value A			$ 4,800
Lot B	25 feet @ $100	=	$2,500	
	Corner value: 100 feet @			
	$50 × .17 (.63 — .46)	=	850	
	Total value B			$ 3,350
Lot C	25 feet @ $100	=	$2,500	
	Corner value: 100 feet @			
	$50 × .06 (.69 — .63)	=	300	
	Total value C			$ 2,800
Lot D	25 feet @ $100	=	$2,500	
	Corner value: 100 feet @			
	$50 × .03 (.72 — .69)	=	150	
	Total value D			$ 2,650
	Total value A, B, C, and D			$13,600

Assuming lots A, B, C, and D to be in single ownership, the value of the parts will equal the value of the whole as follows:

100 feet along Main Street		
@ $100 front foot	=	$10,000
Corner value: 100 feet @		
$50 × .72	=	3,600
Total value		$13,600

Where the assembled lots, because of single ownership and unified control, permit more intensive utilization of the land, the added value increment is known as *plottage*. This plottage value is best measured by capitalizing the actual or anticipated increased income attributable to an assembled property rather than by any arbitrary percentage such as 10, 20, or more percent as was customary in years past.

ZONING AND CONTRACTUAL LIMITATIONS ON OWNERSHIP

The highest and best use of land is often limited by the legal and permissible use for which a site may be developed. Again attention is called to the fact that zoning by itself does not create value. There must be a demand for land so zoned. If this demand is lacking, the period of years required for land to ripen into the highest and best use must be estimated, and the value as of a future date discounted into a sum of present value at an appropriate (capitalization) rate of interest.

Often changes in the character of a neighborhood support a strong possibility that changes in zoning regulations will follow in order that utilization of land be adapted to changing and dynamic community needs.

Where this is the case, the appraiser should recognize such added value influences, provided current prices of similar land indicate investor expectation of higher and better land uses under anticipated changes in zoning or deed restrictions. Arbitrary denial of land use changes may be overruled by judiciary decree in courts of equity, if not in courts of law.

Contractual limitations on ownership are generally noted in deeds of record, and hence are referred to as "deed restrictions." Such restrictions as a rule are initiated by subdividers for the protection of property owners, and are intended to govern future land utilization in conformity with preconceived building plans and in the interest of owners and users as a whole. Deed restrictions which go with or attach to the land may control items as follows: minimum lot sizes, maximum building area, building height and minimum building value, building set back requirements from front, side and rear property lines, occupancy by single family and other customary and reasonable limitations on ownership to safeguard property values.

Other contractual limitations which must be noted and evaluated by the appraiser include easements, leases, and mortgages. Easements are rights extended to others for ingress and egress over the property, or to air or subsurface rights for utility installation, soil removal, flood control or mining operations. The effects of such easements on property value must be measured and accounted for in appraisal reporting. Leases give tenants or lessees the right to use land and its improvements for certain periods of time. In effect leases create "split" interests that divide property values among the parties involved. The technique of appraising lease interests will be fully illustrated in the chapter entitled "Leasehold Estates and Leased Fee Appraising." Mortgages in effect encumber a property. Where terms of the mortgage debt are at typical market rates of interest and for typical periods of years no impact on property value will result. However, where mortgage contract terms are favorable or unfavorable as measured by market loan standards, the resulting plus or minus income adjustments when discounted to present worth will affect the price at which the property will exchange when exposed for sale.

TITLE CONSIDERATIONS AND ENCROACHMENTS

The appraiser, in seeking values, operates within the field of economics. He is cautioned not to usurp the functions or assume the responsibilities that are rightfully those of abstractors, title companies, lawyers, architects, or construction engineers. For appraisal purposes it must be assumed that the title to the subject property is free and clear, unless otherwise and expressly stated, and that no encumbrances restrict the full use of the property except those covered by zoning and deed restrictions as shown on public records. If the appraisal client, in addition to value, seeks assurance that the title is good and marketable or that lot measurements are accurate and the property is free from encroachments, then qualified professionals in the respective fields should be consulted and the cost of their services added to the fees deemed compensatory to cover the appraisal service.

Furthermore, the validity of title and the accuracy of survey lines and measurements for appraisal purposes must be assumed to be correct, except for encroachments and property use violations that are apparent at the time of field inspection. Where violations or *easements* (rights for public ingress or egress to or over the site) are apparent it is the appraiser's responsibility to report them and to estimate their effects upon the value and marketability of the property.

SITE IMPROVEMENTS

All improvements classified as *fixtures,* the ownership of which legally "runs" with the land, must be inspected and appraised. To guard against errors and omissions, it is recommended that a plot plan be prepared as a guide for better appraisal reporting. As indicated on the plan shown in Figure 8.8, the lot dimensions and lot improvements are drawn to scale and in proportion to boundary line measurements which enclose the property. The plot plan should further sketch walks, driveways, and roof plans of the various structures that improve the property. This plan, together with pictures of the site and neighboring street and lot improvements, is deemed essential to effective site analysis in the appraisal process.

Other land improvements which should be inventoried and analyzed include landscaping and subsurface land improvements. Not all shrubs are classified as fixtures, and care must be taken to specify in the appraisal report the extent and amount to which landscaping contributed to total value. An allocation of 1, or at most 2 percent of final value for lawn sodding and foundation plantings may prove typical for most residential properties. Amounts expended in excess of 2 percent constitute *costs,* which may or may not be a measure of market value, depending on the circumstances at the time the property is exposed for sale to typical buyers.

Subsurface improvements, too, must be given value influence considerations. Underground utilities such as gas, telephone, sewerage, drainage, water, electricity, and steam piping are assets adding to site value. *Site data* of other on-site improvements to be included in site valuation include paving, curb, gutter, and sidewalk installation. (See demonstration report in Appendix I.) Especially when comparing comparable land sales for

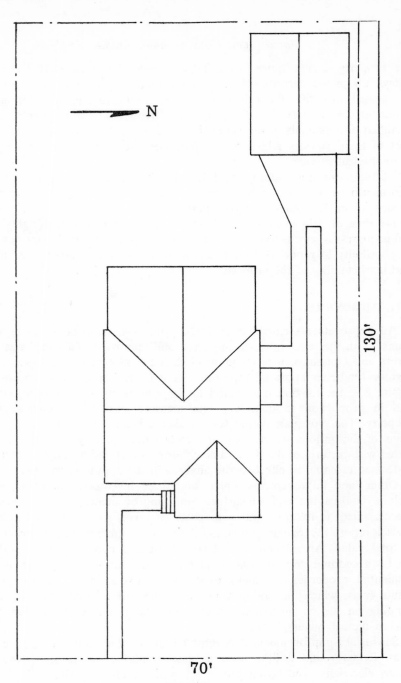

N

130'

70'

FIGURE 8.8

PLOT PLAN

16 N.W. 20TH TERRACE

112

differences in site location, care must be taken to adjust transaction prices to reflect the presence or absence of the various site improvements.

READING AND STUDY REFERENCES

1. *Acquisition for Right-of-Way* (Washington, D.C.: American Association of State Highway Officials, 1962), chap. 26.
2. *The Appraisal of Real Estate* (Chicago: American Institute of Real Estate Appraisers, 1967), chap. 7.
3. Kahn, Sanders A., Frederick E. Case, and Alfred Schimmel, *Real Estate Appraisal and Investment* (New York: The Ronald Press Company, 1963), chap. 6.
4. Kinnard, William N., Jr., *An Introduction to Appraising Real Property* (Chicago: Society of Real Estate Appraisers, 1968), chap. 10.
5. Lersk, Herbert N., "Formula's for Irregular Plots," *Technical Valuation* (October 1954), pp. 43–47.
6. McMichael, Stanley L., *McMichael's Appraising Manual,* 4th ed. (Englewood Cliffs, N.J.: Prentice-Hall, Inc., 1951), chaps. 31, 35, 36, 37 & 38.
7. Ring, Alfred A., *Real Estate Principles and Practices,* 6th ed., (Englewood Cliffs, N.J.: Prentice-Hall, Inc., 1967), chap. 24.

In appraisal procedure it is customary to derive an independent estimate of the value of the land, whether or not it is free and clear of all building improvements and available for development under a program of highest and best land use. The durability and relative indestructibility of land obviates the necessity to provide for land depreciation and causes income from land to be capitalized into perpetuity. This is in contrast

9 Fundamentals of

Land Valuation

with site and building improvements which are subject to inevitable losses in value because of physical, functional, and economic causes of depreciation.

Often, the purpose of the appraisal necessitates the separation of land value from the value of the improved property as an integral whole. To illustrate: Fire insurance is generally placed on the destructible portions of a property and not on the bare land used to support the site improvements. Also, in most jurisdictions, land value and the value of the improvements are recorded separately for ad valorem purposes. For income tax or ownership accounting reasons, too, the separation of land and improvement values serves useful purposes.

In estimating the value of land, reliance is placed on one or more of the following methods, or approaches:

1. The market, or comparison, approach.
2. The income, or residual earnings, approach.
3. The land development, or cost of land production, approach.
4. The ratio of improvement value to site value.

Generally only one of these approaches to land value is accepted as guiding, although a second approach if applicable and appropriate data are available may prove useful as a check for accuracy. For purpose of clarity, the various approaches to land value will be discussed as independent appraisal techniques. In theory and practice, nevertheless, all valuation irrespective of method or approach is related and imputed to market operations. The interrelationship of the various approaches to value will become apparent from the discussion of recommended appraisal procedure as presented below.

THE MARKET OR COMPARISON APPROACH TO VALUE

The most reliable method of estimating land value is based on a comparison of the subject property with similar properties in like locations which have sold in recent times. Where the market is active and the sales recent and similar in kind, the comparison approach yields satisfactory value estimates. The mechanics of the market approach are relatively simple, and no great skill is required to master the method.

The first and most important requirement in the market or comparison approach to value is ready access to up-to-date sources of real property sale transactions. The sources of sales data in order of availability, accuracy, and convenience are as follows:

1. Abstract or title insurance company records.
2. Tax assessor's record files.
3. County clerk's official public records.
4. Appraiser's personal office files.
5. Real estate brokers' multiple listing or general sales record files.
6. Financial news or newspaper reporting services.

The appraiser may use one or more of these sources for sales data depending on appraisal volume and procedure adopted for maintenance of an appraisal plant file. In many communities copies of official deed records are made available by the county clerk's office at reasonable costs. This information, when promptly posted in geographic order or by alphabetical name of subdivisions, furnishes a ready and convenient source for market sales information. This recommended practice, where available, keeps the appraiser abreast of market operations and thus provides him with ready information concerning volume of transfers, price trends, and community growth patterns.

Irrespective of the source from which sales record data are obtained, it is the appraiser's responsibility to verify the price and terms of sale by a personal or telephone interview with the buyer, the seller, or both. Real estate transactions historically are considered private in nature and public records may or may not reveal factual circumstances which "cushioned" or "sweetened" a sale. Interviewing the parties to the transaction, or informed persons such as lawyers or brokers who guided the sale, enables the appraiser to formulate judgments in adjusting market prices paid to the prices obtainable for the subject property were it exposed for sale in the open market. If a sale cannot be confirmed, or where the prices or terms are deliberately held secretive, it is best to disregard the transaction in favor of another and more reliable sale property. When applying the market approach to value, caution must be exercised in accepting state revenue stamps affixed to deeds as reliable evidence of the transaction price. Legally, a deed is considered an instrument of "conveyance" in which the actual consideration agreed on in a prior and unrecorded contract need not be stipulated. Although most state laws require that revenue stamps based on the exact transaction price be attached to the deed, there are, nevertheless, circumstances under which these stamps do not indicate the price for which the property was exchanged.[1] For instance:

1. A buyer may wish to give the impression that he paid an amount greater than the actual purchase price and for that reason affixes more revenue stamps than the law requires. There is no limit to the number or amount of stamps that may be purchased, and the tax agent will gladly sell all the buyer wants. The attaching of excess stamps may be a device to have future buyers believe that the property is worth a great deal more than the "bargain" price at which it is offered to them.

2. Sellers who must deliver the deed at time of closing—with revenue stamps attached—may attempt, unlawfully, to save on this expenditure by purchasing fewer stamps than the sale price calls for. The county clerk from whom the revenue stamps are obtained does not question the transaction price quoted by the seller, nor the intent of the seller in obtaining more or fewer stamps than the law requires.

3. Many states do not have deed revenue stamp laws, and even where such laws are in force the requirements regarding the effects of existing mortgages differ. In some states, only the cash portions of transactions need be considered; whereas in others, state revenue stamps representing the full consideration must be attached to the deed.

4. In the case of property exchanges, the interested parties may understate or overstate the transaction price for tax or other purposes which prove mutually advantageous.

---

[1] See Alfred A. Ring and Nelson L. North, *Real Estate Principles and Practices* (Englewood Cliffs, N. J.: Prentice-Hall, Inc., 6th ed., 1967), pp. 354–55.

Seller_____ Type of Instrument_____

Dated_____

Recorded_____

Book_____ Page_____

To

Revenue Stamps_____

Cons. Indicated $_____

Cons. Shown $_____

Buyer_____ Area_____

Legal Description_____

_____

_____

_____ County_____

Location_____

_____

Cons. Paid was $_____ or $_____per_____

_____as confirmed by_____to

_____ on _____ at___ AM/PM

The property was inspected by_____ on _____

Land_____

_____

_____

Improvements_____

_____

_____

Assessment: County $_____Year___City $_____Year___

Remarks and Analysis of Sale (continued on back)_____

_____

MARKET DATA REPORT FORM

INDEX SALE NO._____

Although in many jurisdictions revenue stamps do reflect fairly well the actual transaction price of the property, the possible exceptions noted above should be kept in mind when accepting deed revenue stamp data as evidence of market price or value. In most condemnation trials, too, revenue stamp data as evidence of market sale price is inadmissible or subject to challenge when introduced by an expert witness.

To aid the appraiser in the analysis of market sales, a data report form such as shown on preceding page is recommended for use.

In securing information from court house or file records for entry on the work form, it should not be taken for granted that the date of title closing represents the date of sale. Often land is sold under a *contract for deed*,[2] in which case months and years may separate the date of contract from the date of title closing. The date of contract, in fact and in law, determines the time at which a meeting of minds took place, and it is that date which must serve as a basis for time adjustments reflecting changes in economic or market conditions up to the date of appraisal. Furthermore, the appraiser must make certain that the sale was concluded under objective, impersonal bargaining and that the terms of sale were fully disclosed. Sales from father to son, or from one relative to another, or where circumstances indicate undisclosed terms and conditions, or where prices paid appear unreasonable or questionable should be discarded in favor of other clear-cut, bona-fide sale transactions.

Where market data for comparable properties is unavailable, recourse may be had to property listings. A study of the relationship of listing to market sales prices conducted by Dr. Clayton C. Curtis, Associate Professor of Real Estate at the University of Florida, disclosed a reliable tendency for listing prices, where used in groups of three or more, to range at a variance of 0 to 5 percent in relation to market value at time of sale for improved residential properties valued at $15,000 or less.[3] For higher-priced properties listings proved unreliable as an accurate guide to market value, and they must therefore be used with caution.

MARKET DATA SUMMARY AND
CORRELATION

After a minimum of four comparable sales has been selected, confirmed, field-inspected and analyzed, the appraiser is in a position to transfer the

---

[2] An agreement under which transfer of title to the land is deferred until partial (periodic) payments aggregate the entire or agreed-upon amount of the purchase price.

[3] Research study sponsored by the Research Committee of the Florida chapter, American Institute of Real Estate Appraisers. Findings published in July, 1961 issue of *Appraisal Journal,* American Institute of Real Estate Appraisers, Chicago, Illinois, p. 311.

individual sales data to a recapitulation, or summary, sheet for adjustment and correlation purposes to derive an estimate of market value for the subject property. A sample summary sheet on which the derivation of a market value estimate for a residential site is illustrated, is shown on page 120. The property under appraisal measures 110 feet along the street front, and is 150 feet in depth. In this instance, it is compared with four reasonably similar market sale transactions that are adjusted to reflect and equalize for economically better or poorer conditions of the subject property as demonstrated. The standard depth for a typical residential site in the neighborhood is 120 feet.

In following the step-by-step correlation of comparable market sales data as indicated in the market value summary sheet, it will become apparent that the accuracy of the final value conclusion reached depends largely on the exercise of sound appraisal judgment. This judgment cannot be gained by textbook reading or classroom study alone, but follows as a result of diligent application of the valuation principles in field practice. Individual maturity and thought discipline based on an inquiring and energetic mind are essential ingredients of good appraising.

The first entry on the summary sheet is the *date of sale* for each comparable property. This entry is important as a measure of elapsed time to date of appraisal, allowing consideration to be given where necessary to changes caused by economic forces which influenced market value during the interval.

The second entry shows the *indicated price* paid for the sale property. This price as a rule is based on revenue stamp tax data. Where tax stamp information appears to be out of line, and where sale confirmation fails to yield supporting facts and explanations, the sale should be rejected in favor of another and more reliable source of market value evidence.

The third entry notes *size of lot*. With the aid of these measurements the appraiser is in a position to compute the price paid per unit (front foot) of land, and to adjust unit value where necessary to compensate for variation in lot depth.

The fourth entry is the *price paid per front foot of land*. This amount is derived by dividing the total price paid (Entry 2) by the number of front feet (Entry 3) of the comparable lot.

The fifth entry indicates a *time adjustment factor*. If, because of economic conditions, the comparable sale property would bring more or less were the sale to take place today (i.e., on the date of appraisal) then an adjustment factor should indicate the percentage of increase or decrease as market conditions warrant. Where no adjustment is necessary, the entry is 1.00. A 5-percent-plus adjustment would be noted as 1.05.

The adjustment factor in Entry 5 is then multiplied by the unit foot value given in Entry 4, and the resulting *unit price adjusted for time* is then shown in Entry 6. This time adjustment must not be made arbitrarily but rather must be based on considered study of market conditions —or at least on the opinions of *informed* persons such as experienced appraisers, builders, and realtors in the community.

Entry 7 provides for *depth factor* consideration. Where all sales are

---

MARKET VALUE SUMMARY SHEET

Sales Reference No.:	1 one	2 two	3 twelve	4 eight
1. Date of sale:	mth. ago	mths. ago	mths. ago	mths. ago
2. Indicated price:	$3,500	$3,150	$2,900	$3,100
3. Size of lot:	100' × 150'	80' × 200'	90' × 120'	100' × 90'
4. Price per front foot:	$35.00	$39.37	$32.22	$31.00
5. Time adjustment factor:	1.00	1.00	1.15	1.10
6. Unit price adjusted for time:	$35.00	$39.37	$37.05	$34.10
7. Depth factor (4-3-2-1 rule):	.9174	.8197	1.00	1.111
8. Unit price adjusted for depth:	$32.10	$32.27	$37.05	$37.88

Subject property is rated as follows in regard to:

9. Neighborhood:	Same	Better	Same	Poorer
10. Location:	Better	Same	Same	Same
11. Site facilities:	Better	Same	Same	Poorer
12. Subject comparative per cent rating:	1.10	1.05	1.00	.90
13. Adjusted value:	$35.31	$33.88	$37.05	$34.09

Market Value Correlation

14. Estimated (correlated) unit value of land: $ 35.00
15. Value of subject site: 110' × 150' = 110 × $35.00 = $3,850.00
16. Value adjusted for depth: $3,850.00 × 1.09 = $4,196.50
17. Value adjusted for corner or plottage influences: None
18. Final estimated land value: $4,200.00

of the same depth as the subject property, this and the following entry can be omitted from the summary sheet. However, whenever lot-depth variations influence the price paid, the appraiser must adjust his figures accordingly and in conformity with an appropriate depth value rule.

To adjust unit prices paid for nonstandard lots to prices which reflect standard depth in the subject neighborhood, a reciprocal of the depth factor is applied in order to obtain the adjusted unit prices by simple multiplication. To illustrate: Sale No. 1 involved a lot with a depth of 150 feet. The depth factor, as explained in Chapter 8, under the 4-3-2-1 rule is 1.09 percent as compared with 1.00 percent for a standard lot depth of 120 feet. To reduce the unit price of $35 paid for a depth of 150 feet to a unit price reflecting a depth of only 120 feet, the amount of $35 must be either divided by 1.09 or multiplied by the reciprocal of 1.09 which equals 1 $\div$ 1.09 or .9174. Thus, whether we divide $35 by 1.09, or multiply $35 x .9174, the answer obtained is identical, i.e., $32.10. Because experience has proved that mathematical results obtained by multiplication are less subject to error than are those obtained by division, the reciprocals of applicable depth factors were used, as shown in Entry 7, for adjustment of prices paid for "nonstandard" lots. By multiplying the unit prices in Entry 6 by the reciprocal depth factors shown in Entry 7, the unit prices adjusted for depth are obtained as indicated in Entry 8.

Entries 9, 10, and 11 constitute judgment conclusions concerning the relative quality of the subject property as compared with each comparable property in regard to (a) neighborhood, (b) location advantages, and (c) site facilities. Considering the status of the *subject* property as compared with the *sale* property, the appraiser establishes a quality rating for each of the features as being better, poorer, or the same. An overall percentage rating is then reached for the subject property (Entry 12).

In the narrative section of the valuation report as shown in Appendix 1—the Demonstration Appraisal Report—the appraiser explains *why* the neighborhood, location, and site facilities of the subject property are deemed better, poorer, or the same, thus justifying the overall comparative percentage rating assigned in the market value summary sheet. Some appraisers prefer to rate each feature on a percentage basis, and to multiply the separate percentage ratings for a weighted or combined average. There is danger, however, in such a practice. Suppose each of the features (i.e., neighborhood, location, and site) is judged to be 50 percent when compared with the sale property; by multiplying .50 time .50 times .50, an overall average of 12.5 percent is obtained. This method has a tendency to overadjust for comparative deficiencies and to underadjust for superior features. To illustrate: Where one adjustment calls for a 50 percent minus rating and another adjustment calls for a 50 percent plus rating, it would appear logical that the two ratings should cancel out. By multiplying .50 by 1.50, the net result is nevertheless 75 percent, which constitutes an overadjustment on the minus side of the rating scale.

Even when percentage adjustments are added—plus and minus—to overcome the errors derived by percentage multiplications, the separate adjustment for each category of variation is fraught with hazards which lead to "guesstimating" rather than "estimating." For this reason it is recommended that ratings be judged descriptively, and that only *one* final percentage quality rating be arrived at and entered as shown under Entry 12 of the market summary sheet.

The overall quality percentage rating is then multiplied by the adjusted unit price (Entry 8) of the comparable property to derive an estimated value per unit measure of land for the *subject* property. This value is listed in Entry 13. The next step calls for correlating the adjusted values derived from four or more sales into a single estimate of unit value. This final unit value is found in Entry 14. In this instance, correlation does not mean averaging but rather assigning judgment weights to each sale on the basis of comparability, terms of sale, and reliability of sales data. The correlation procedure should be explained in the narrative section of the appraisal report as follows:

Sale No. 1 is located in the same block as the subject property, is identical in size, and required no time adjustment. A judgment weight of 50 percent was given to this sale.

Sale No. 2 is also located in the same block, but the property depth of this sale is nonstandard. For this reason a judgment weight of only 30 percent was given to this sale.

Sales No. 3 and 4 are in an adjacent neighborhood, and both sales required time adjustments of 1.15 percent and 1.10 percent respectively. For these reasons the correlation weight assigned to these sales was 10 percent each.

The value of the subject property—for a standard depth of 120 feet is then derived as shown below:

Index Sales	Adjusted Value	Weight of Sale	Value Component
1	$35.31	50	$17.66
2	33.88	30	10.16
3	37.05	10	3.71
4	34.09	10	3.41
			$34.94

Rounded to $35.00

The value of the subject land is then derived by multiplying the number of unit feet of land by the unit value as was done under Entry 15 and by adjusting this site value for depth of lot, if need be, as demonstrated under Entry 16. Similarly, adjustments for corner locations or plottage if called for should be made and noted under Entry 17. The final estimate of land value, rounded to the nearest $50 or $100 value bracket, should then be listed in Entry 18. The market value procedure as outlined,[4] when applied with professional care, should yield accurate estimates that will reasonably reflect the market price that may be anticipated were the subject property exposed for sale in the open market on the date of appraisal.

THE IDEAL NEIGHBORHOOD AND SITE COMPARISON METHOD

In the conventional market comparison method as demonstrated above, each comparable sale represents a market rating of 100 percent and the subject property is adjusted plus or minus to reflect quantitative and qualitative differences. This approach to value necessitates a re-evaluation or re-comparison of the sale property each time the index sale is used as a value base in subsequent appraisals involving other subject properties. In order to streamline appraisal practice and to permit instant reuse of rated sale properties a novel market evaluation procedure known as the "Ideal Neighborhood and Site Comparison Method" has been developed and successfully tested in practice and in court valuation cases.[5] Instead of using a variable base—as in the market approach to value explained above, under which each of many comparable sales is used as a standard of comparison—an *ideal* neighborhood is used as a base for comparison of all comparable sales as well as for the subject property. The percentage components of the ideal neighborhood are as follows:

Features	*Percent Rating*
1. Location: access, transportation to center of city, nearness and quality of schools and shopping	15
2. Surroundings: percent developed, age, price range of homes, upkeep, quality of neighbors	15
3. Zoning: protection, land use trends	10
4. Traffic: safety, parking, accessibility	10
5. Street improvements and services: paving, sidewalks, curb, gutter, sewer, water, garbage, fire protection	15
6. Lot features: size, topography, shape appeal, landscaping, trees	15
7. Amenities and trends: prestige, popularity, competitive position	20
Total rating	100%

[4] An alternative market comparison method provides for direct adjustment of the comparables using the subject property as a 'norm' or 'standard' in terms of which variations or deviations in the comparables are measured. Either method, of course, if diligently applied should yield identical end results.

[5] The ideal market comparison method is exclusively used by Talmadge D. Campbell, M.A.I., president of Campbell Realty Company, Ocala, Florida.

The subject property, as well as each comparable sale property, is now rated against the ideal neighborhood as follows:

NEIGHBORHOOD AND SITE COMPARISON DATA TABLE

Rating Features	Ideal *	Subject	Sale No. 1	Sale No. 2	Sale No. 3	Sale No. 4
1. Location	15	10	12	8	15	12
2. Surroundings	15	15	9	10	10	12
3. Zoning and protection	10	5	4	6	5	8
4. Traffic	10	5	5	4	5	10
5. Street improvements and services	15	10	8	12	10	5
6. Lot features	15	10	12	10	10	10
7. Amenities	20	10	9	12	10	15
Total rating	100	65	59	62	65	72

* These ideal percentage weights are judgment ratings derived from market analysis of comparable sales to measure the relative significance of the rating features.

The next step is to establish an adjustment percentage ratio by comparing the subject property with each index sale as follows:

LAND VALUE ADJUSTMENT TABLE

Sale No.	Subject Property Rating		Comparable Sale Rating		Adjustment Ratio		Unit Price of Sale Property		Adjusted Unit Price
1	65	÷	59	=	1.10	×	$32	=	$35
2	65	÷	62	=	1.05	×	32	=	34
3	65	÷	65	=	1.00	×	37	=	37
4	65	÷	72	=	.90	×	38	=	34

The steps necessary to obtain the unit sale price for each comparable property, and the thought process essential to a market correlation of the adjusted prices for a final estimate of unit land value are the same as outlined previously under "Market Data Summary and Correlation."

Both the conventional and the ideal neighborhood and site comparison methods are intended only as guides in helping the appraiser consider fully the differences in market sales data in order to reach a sound value conclusion. No valuation table, method, or procedure can ever serve as a substitute for sound judgment sharpened by experience. Conversely, it is inconceivable that sound judgment can be exercised without a data-study program such as outlined above.

THE INCOME, OR RESIDUAL EARNINGS, APPROACH TO VALUE

In the final analysis, the value of all land is based on its productivity, or income producing capacity under a program of highest and best land use. Whenever the market approach is inapplicable, either because of absence of market transactions or nonexistence of unimproved land in the subject or comparable areas, the appraiser must take recourse to the earnings or income approach to value. Land income, as discussed in Chapter 3, is residual in character. Costs of labor, management, maintenance, operation, and a fair market return *on* and *of* the invested capital in improvements must be met first. What is left, if anything, under a program of highest and best use belongs to land. This residual income, when capitalized at an appropriate rate of interest—assuming continued and unending (perpetual) use—forms a capital sum of money that measures the *present* worth of the subject property.

To apply the income approach to land value, the appraiser cannot and must not assume that the existing building improvements necessarily constitute the highest and best use of the land. The appraiser, in fact, must undertake a land utilization study of the area and site, and determine what type and size of improvement should be placed on the land in order to reap for it the highest possible return and present value. Since few improvements—even when considered to represent the highest and best use— are in new condition, it is necessary under the income approach to land value to assume first a reasonable highest and best land use, and second that improvements *are* in new condition.

The procedure for selecting the highest and best use and the process of capitalizing the residual income into a sum of present value can best be illustrated as follows: [6] Suppose a building site in a given community can be developed for residential purposes only under existing and reasonably anticipated zoning restrictions. Suppose, further, that preliminary analysis of neighborhood characteristics and of housing demand narrows the choice of possible and profitable site improvements to one of the following types of structures:

1. A single-story duplex building, each rental unit containing two bedrooms, dining-living room, kitchen, and tiled bath. Total improvement cost, $20,000.
2. A three-family apartment building, each apartment containing two bedrooms, dining-living room, kitchen, and tiled bath. Total improvement cost, $30,000.

---

[6] For a more detailed discussion of the Nature, Importance and Character of Land, see Alfred A. Ring and Nelson L. North, *Real Estate Principles and Practices* (Englewood Cliffs, New Jersey: Prentice-Hall, Inc., 6th ed., 1967), pp. 1–15.

Since the *highest* use of the building site was prescribed by zoning law for residential purposes, the determination still to be made is which of the alternate types of improvements described above constitutes the *best* use. Under the definition of highest and best use, it is necessary to ascertain the income-producing capacity of the land under the alternate types of improvements and to find by the process of capitalization which income yields to the land its highest present value. Based on prevailing rentals of similar residences in comparable neighborhoods at $150 per month per four-room and bath duplex unit, and $135 per month per four-room and bath apartment unit, the procedure to derive land income and land value at a market rate of interest of 7 percent is as follows:

ANALYSIS OF LAND INCOME AND LAND VALUE
UNDER ALTERNATE TYPES OF IMPROVEMENTS

	Single-Story Duplex	3-Family Apartment
Gross annual income:		
Duplex units $150 x 2 x 12 (month) =	$3,600	
3-Family apartment $135 x 3 x 12 (mo.) =		$4,860
Less vacancy and collection losses @ 5%	180	243
Effective gross income	$3,420	$4,617
Less operating expenses:		
10% Management (Entrepreneur)	$ 342	$ 462
Real estate taxes	400	500
Maintenance and repairs	200	275
Hazard insurance	70	100
Fuel and utilities	240	315
Janitor service		120
Total operating expenses:	$1,252	$1,772
Operating income	$2,168	$2,845
Less income attributable to building improvements. Interest "on" the investment:		
Duplex $20,000 @ 7% =	$1,400	
Apartments $30,000 @ 7% =		$2,100
Amortization "of" the investment		
Duplex $20,000 @ 2%	400	
Apartments $30,000 @ 2%		600
Total capital costs	$1,800	$2,700
Net income remaining to land	368	145
Value of land at 7% rate of capitalization:		
Duplex $368 ÷ .07 =	$5,257	
Apartment $146 ÷ .07 =		$2,071

The valuation procedure as outlined above is one generally practiced by informed investors to determine the present worth of land under the income or earnings residual approach to land value. Based on the analysis, as illustrated, the conclusion can be drawn that the highest and best use of the building site under value study is a single-story duplex to be constructed at a cost of $20,000 and renting at $150 per month per dwelling unit. Under this highest and best use, the land warrants a present value of $5,257. Under the next best type of improvement or utilization, both land income and land value diminish.

The residual techniques of capitalization under the income approach to value are more fully described and demonstrated in Chapter 19.

THE LAND DEVELOPMENT OR COST OF
LAND PRODUCTION APPROACH TO VALUE

Throughout the historical development of appraisal thought, and in the writing of most appraisal literature, the existence of land has been taken for granted. In effect it is implied that land cannot be produced and hence should not be evaluated via the cost approach to value. This classical theory of land as being permanent, indestructible, immovable, and unique (heterogeneous) is valid only if applied to raw land as God created it for man's eventual use. The appraiser, however, is concerned with "economic" land, modified and improved by man; and in this economic sense, such land *can* be produced, duplicated, and its situs qualities shifted to other locations.

Man's ability to modify land and thereby produce land value is illustrated by the following story: A farmer, after years of grueling work cutting trees, pulling stumps, and plowing, had converted an overgrown forest region into a fertile and productive farm. One day while harvesting he was talking with a city cousin who was mightily impressed by the lush appearance of the farm and said: "Aren't you lucky to own this land, which God created and presented as a gift to man." The farmer looked bemused at his calloused hands and replied: "It's true. But you should have seen this land when God had it all to himself."

Today, raw land as nature provided it no longer exists. All land has been directly or indirectly modified by man. Direct modification has included the construction of buildings, fences, dykes, drainage canals, land filling and grading, and the conversion of forests into grazing, farming, or building sites. Land has been modified indirectly by the construction of access roads, bridges, canals, modes of rapid transportation, and other means of public improvements which increase land utility.

Where land is anticipated to ripen into higher economic uses, or where the conversion of farm or rur-urban (land in transition, being neither farm nor suburban in use or character) acreage into suburban building sites is justified by community growth and demand, the appraiser can logically and accurately apply the land development or cost of land production approach to value as follows: Suppose an appraisal problem calls for finding the value of 50 acres or rur-urban land which a subdivider seeks to purchase and develop into residential building sites. As a result of a highest and best land use study, it appears best to subdivide the 50-acre tract into 150 lots each measuring 100 feet by 120 feet, or 3 lots per acre. Under this development plan the 150 building lots comprise 82.5 percent of the total land area, while the balance, or 17.5 percent of land, is deemed necessary for construction of access streets, avenues, traffic isles, and other public uses. Based on study and analysis of comparable property sales, it is concluded that the lots can be marketed as follows:

> 1st year—50 lots at $2,000 each
> 2nd year—50 lots at $2,250 each
> 3rd year—50 lots at $2,350 each

Based on these market findings the appraisal cost approach yields the following results, assuming a developer's discount and profit rate of 10 percent:

Present worth of lot sales:		
1st year, 50 lots @ $2,000 = $100,000 discounted to present worth at 10% for one year or $100,000 × .9091 =		$90,910
2nd year, 50 lots @ $2,250 = $112,500 discounted to present worth for two years or $112,500 × .8264 =		92,970
3rd year, 50 lots @ $2,350 = $117,500 discounted to present worth for three years or $117,500 × .7513 =		88,489
Total present worth of anticipated lot sales		$272,369
Less development cost:		
Street grading and paving @ $300 per lot =	$45,000	
Sanitary and storm sewers @ $400 per lot =	60,000	
Curb and gutters @ $150 per lot =	22,500	
Water mains @ $200 per lot =	30,000	
Other costs: (Legal, filing, sales brokerage, property taxes, and overhead)	$50,000	
Developer's profit (10% of gross sales)	27,237	
Total development costs and profit		$234,737
Residual value of "raw" land		$ 37,632

Value per acre = $37,632 ÷ 50 = $752.66
Rounded to $750.00 per acre

The above illustration does not include costs of sidewalks, extension of gas, electric, or telephone utilities, nor expenditures for other public or recreational facilities. Should such expenditures be incurred by the developer they must, of course, be added into the land production cost approach to value.

THE RATIO OF IMPROVEMENT VALUE TO VALUE OF THE SITE

Under conditions where the market, income, or cost of land development approach to value is not applicable, an estimate of land value may be derived from a study of typical ratios of improvement value to value of comparable sales. Under highest and best utilization of land, studies disclose certain optimum improvements to land ratios on which the appraiser may rely for value guidance. At the outset, stress is laid on the fact that ratios, like depth or corner land value rules, do not *make* value but rather reflect typical land-improvement relationships which serve a useful purpose in the allocation of total value to the component parts of land and building improvements.

Where land value equals improvement value, the ratio is said to be one to one; if the investment in building improvements is double that of the land value, the ratio is two to one and so on. Commercial land in the downtown area is generally characterized by a low (but efficient) land-to-improvement ratio, and the ratio increases as the land is put to lower (less efficient) uses. Guiding ratios for a typical community may range as follows:

Land Use	Land-to-Improvement Ratio
Commercial	1 to 1
Office	1 to 4
Residential	1 to 6
Apartment house	1 to 10
Industrial	1 to 20

Once a study of typical land uses within a community discloses a guiding relationship of improvement to site values, the appraiser may use the results as a basis for or check on the accuracy of value findings by other and more direct appraisal methods. For instance, if typical residential properties are improved with buildings costing six times the value of the building site, improvement ratios as low as four to one or as high as eight or more to one may warn of under- or overdevelopment of the site. In either case, faulty improvement will cause a loss in building value reflected by the difference between actual and estimated potential dollar return realizable under a program of highest and best site utilization.

A 6 to 1 residential-building-to-land-value ratio, in essence, implies that typical investors or developers purchase building sites at 14.3 percent of the price at which new properties sell. Thus where residential properties sell at a price of $25,000, the 6 to 1 improvement ratio indicates a site value of $25,000 times .143, or $3,575. The prevailing ratio of improvement value to site value for a given class of real property also aids the appraiser in deriving, by abstraction, appropriate market rates of capitalization, as will be explained and demonstrated in Chapter 17.

READING AND STUDY REFERENCES

1. *Acquisition for Right-of-Way* (Washington, D.C.: American Association of State Highway Officials, 1962), chap. 26.
2. *The Appraisal of Real Estate* (Chicago: American Institute of Real Estate Appraisers, 1967), chap. 8.
3. Babcock, Frederick M., *The Valuation of Real Estate* (New York: McGraw-Hill Book Company, Inc., 1932), chap. 30.
4. Kahn, Sanders A., Frederick E. Case, and Alfred Schimmel, *Real Estate Appraisal and Investment* (New York: The Ronald Press Company, 1963), chap. 8.
5. Kinnard, William N., Jr., *An Introduction to Appraising Real Property* (Chicago: Society of Real Estate Appraisers, 1968), chap. 11.
6. Miller, C. Marc, "Estimating Basic Land Value," *Right-of-Way* (April 1959), pp. 34–35, 40.
7. Ratcliff, Richard U., *Real Estate Analysis* (New York: McGraw-Hill Book Company, Inc., 1961), chap. 4.
8. Schmutz, George L., "Two Approaches to Land Value," *The Review* (December 1951), pp. 3–4.
9. Wendt, Paul F., "Economic Growth and Urban Land Values," *The Appraisal Journal* (July 1958), pp. 427–443.

For standardized goods and services, prices paid at "arm's length" bargaining in an open and normal market provide a reliable *index* of value. As a rule, little difficulty is encountered in obtaining reasonably accurate estimates of market price quotations for commodities such as wheat, coffee, sugar, corn, eggs, poultry, or for bonds and stocks which are freely traded. The greater the dissimilarity of the product and the less frequent

10 *The Market Sales Comparison Approach to Value*

the trading, however, the greater the required skill necessary to adjust for product differences in order to attain price comparability, and the greater the chances for error in the final estimate of value via the market approach.

With real estate, which is heterogeneous in character, exact comparability can never be obtained, if only because of differences in the fixed geographical location of the property. It is possible, nevertheless, through study and analysis of market operations, to adjust for price effects caused by differences in "physical" characteristics in order to obtain "economic" equality essential to an accurate estimate of market value.

The greater the number and the more recent the sales of comparable properties, the greater the accuracy and the more convincing are the results obtained via the market approach to value. Ready access to market transaction source data is, therefore, of first importance. Most active appraisers maintain a market sales-data file as part of their appraisal plant, at least for the geographic community area in which the majority of their appraisal assignments originate. The appraisal report file itself provides an important source of market transaction information. It is a gratifying experience to receive an appraisal request and to find that a comparable property in the same neighborhood, or better still in the same block, was recently appraised. Where office files are insufficient or incomplete, ready access to sales data must be had through abstract companies, county tax or record offices, or through commercial services which computerize sales data for multiuse research purposes. Abstract companies, for title search and title insurance application, maintain accurate records of property ownership and title transfer data which generally are filed in geographic or alphabetical order by legal descriptions for a county area. With aid of these data, abstract companies render specialized services in all matters concerning the acquisition date and type of real property ownership. For appraisal purposes abstract record data are deemed most reliable and, in the long run, most economical when the appraiser's time is an important consideration.

VERIFICATIONS OF SALES

Market sale transactions should never be used as value source data unless the appraiser personally, or through a responsible assistant, has taken steps to confirm the sale, and to inquire into the circumstances causing the sale or affecting the transaction price. The verification, as a rule, can readily be obtained from the seller or purchaser of the property. It is rare that a seller or purchaser refuses information, especially if informed that the sales information was obtained from public records and is to be used as one of many sale transactions in deriving a measure of objective value. Circumstances surrounding and affecting the sale must be known—especially if extraordinary terms or conditions of sale appear likely or if lack of objective, impersonal bargaining or forced-sale motivations are suspected. Where the sale was not clear-cut, and when adjustments for conditions or terms of sale cannot readily and accurately be made, it is best to refrain from using the particular transactions and to select another and more reliable guide to market value.

Sales prices, too, should never be deduced from the amount of documentary stamps affixed to a deed of record. Real estate transactions are still largely deemed private and confidential in character, and stamps may be over- or understated deliberately for devious tax or investment gain purposes. Stamp data, too, is deemed unreliable and unacceptable as evidence for an index of market value in most court jurisdictions, unless the sales price was directly confirmed with a party to the transaction.

PRICE ADJUSTMENTS TO COMPENSATE
FOR TIME AND TRANSFER TERMS

Comparable sales selected for price analysis under the market approach to value must be adjusted, if necessary, to compensate for the effect of economic forces that influenced the real estate market during the time interval elapsed between the date of the index sale and the date of subject property appraisal. Market prices of real estate are dynamic in character and move upward or downward with changes in building supply and demand, variations in business and real estate cycles, and changes in the value of money as a result of dollar inflation or deflation. The more recent the index sale, the better and the more reliable are the market comparison results. Sales which are six months old or older must be analyzed in the light of current market conditions (to measure the price effect, if any) that are attributable to the passage of time. The appraiser should ask himself the question: Suppose the comparable sale were exposed for sale today (on the date of the appraisal)—would it bring the same price at which it sold some time ago? If the answer is in the negative, price adjustments are called for, and the reason for them must be explained in the narrative section of the appraisal report. Adjustments are generally shown in relation to 100 percent and applied as ratios of 1.00—such as .95, 1.02, 1.05, etc.—of prevailing market prices.

Where it is known or evident that the terms of sale influenced the price at which the index property exchanged, price adjustments, too, are called for. Value, by market definition, is based on property transfer on a cash or cash equivalent basis. Where the impact of terms is difficult to measure, or where the sale was not on an open and competitive basis, it is best to disregard the transaction and to select another for market comparison purposes.

Adjustment for terms of sale, when known, can readily be made by computing the present worth of savings which accrue to the purchaser. Suppose a residential property sold for $22,000, subject to a $20,000 existing mortgage which remains to be amortized over the next twenty years at 6 percent interest. Assuming a current mortgage market rate of 7 percent, the value of the terms of sale are estimated as follows:

1. Savings in mortgage placement and closing costs. These average a minimum of 3 percent of the value of the mortgage,[1] or in this instance 3 percent of $20,000, or $600.

---

[1] Brokerage fee of 1 percent, title insurance costs of 1 percent, and 1 percent covering legal expenses, appraisal fee, credit report expense, stamp taxes on note and mortgage, and notarizing and recording fees.

2. Savings resulting from existing favorable rate of interest which is 1 percent below prevailing mortgage market rates. A $20,000 mortgage to be amortized over 20 years at 7 percent interest requires monthly payments of interest and pricipal in the amount of $155.06. A like mortgage at 6 percent interest calls for monthly payments of $143.29. The difference of $11.77 per month, capitalized over a period of 100 months,[2] results in savings to the purchaser of $11.77 x 75.60 (present worth of an annuity of one dollar *per month* at 7% per annum for one hundred months or $889.81.

The combined savings resulting from existing and favorable financing in the amount of $600 + $889.81 or a total of $1,490 (rounded) must be subtracted from the selling price to derive the price that would have been realized had the property been sold on cash or cash equivalent terms.[3]

MARKET COMPARISON ADJUSTMENT
TECHNIQUES

The market approach to value, as applied to the appraisal of unimproved land, and the adjustments necessary to equalize for differences in sale prices caused by neighborhood, location, and site advantages was illustrated and explained in Chapter 9. The data sale form shown on page 117 can with slight modification also be used for entry of improved property sales information from public records. The only suggested change in the form, as shown, is to provide for field entry of a description of the kind and condition of on-site improvements. To adjust for value differences attributable to variations in age, quantity, and quality of building construction, one of the following techniques may be employed:

1. Construction detail analysis and price rating technique.
2. Overall construction and building condition rating technique.

The application of these market comparison techniques as applied to the subject property and to the comparable sales are for purposes of illustration based on building construction data obtained as follows:

> *Subject property.* Frame construction, 1,450-square-foot area. Exterior walls of redwood siding. 3 bedrooms, 2 tiled bathrooms, living room, kitchen, and dinette. 1-car garage, screened porch, and concrete patio. Central forced-air ducted gas heating, suspended oak flooring over pine subflooring, asbestos shingle roofing over four-inch rock-wool insulation. Building condition good, deferred maintenance—none. Effective age 8 years. Lot value by market comparison, $4,500.

---

[2] Although most residential mortgages are issued for twenty or more years, the average mortgage life because of frequent refinancing is estimated at 8.5 years.

[3] Typical financial terms currently available to the typical (accredited) purchaser.

Index Sale No. 1. Concrete block structure, 1,650-square-foot area, 4 bedrooms, 3 tiled baths, living-dining room combination, kitchen, and utility room. Carport storage area and open entrance porch. Central forced-air—oil heating system. Terrazzo flooring over concrete slab subflooring. Asphalt shingle gable roof. No attic insulation. Building condition good, deferred maintenance (decorating) $600. Effective age 10 years. Lot value by market comparison, $5,000. Total sale price: $21,000. Date or sale: 1 month ago.

Index Sale No. 2. Brick veneer over concrete block structure, 1,503-square-foot area. 3 bedrooms, 1 tiled bath, living room, sun porch, and kitchen. 1-car garage, open porch. Central oil heating and 3-ton air-conditioning system. Oak parquet flooring over concrete slab subflooring. Asphalt shingle roof over 4-inch rock-wool insulation. Floored attic storage area. Condition good, no deferred maintenance. Effective age 12 years. Lot value by market comparison, $4,000. Total sale price: $22,500. Date of sale: current.

Index Sale No. 3. Cedar-shingled frame structure, 1,400-square-foot area. 3 bedrooms, den living-dining room, kitchen and 2 partially tiled bathrooms. 2-car garage. Open entrance porch. Suspended floor, wall-to-wall carpeting over plywood base and pine subflooring. Built-up roofing covered with marble chits, four-inch insulation, circulating gas heater, thirty-six-inch attic fan. Built-in reverse-cycle air-conditioning wall unit. Effective age 5 years. Deferred maintenance $200.00 (repaint kitchen, bath, and hallway areas). Lot value by market comparison, $4,500. Total sale price: $22,600. Date of sale: 6 months ago.

Index Sale No. 4. Concrete block structure, stuccoed exterior, 1,550-square-foot area. 3 bedrooms, 1 tiled bathroom, living room, kitchen, utility room, and screened porch. 2-car carport. Suspended oak flooring over pine subflooring. Asphalt shingle roof over four-inch insulation, hip-roof construction, boxed eaves, thirty-six-inch roof overhang. Central duct oil-fired—forced-air heating system. Built-in kitchen fan, electric wall heater in bathroom, and garbage disposal unit. Condition good, no deferred maintenance. Effective age 12 years. Lot value by market comparison $5,250. Total sale price: $20,500. Date of sale: 20 months ago.

CONSTRUCTION DETAIL ANALYSIS AND PRICE RATING TECHNIQUE

After confirmation of the sales prices and terms of sale with respective buyers, sellers, or real estate brokers, the index properties are inspected and inventoried for size and details of construction in order that price adjustment can be made to make each sale as nearly as possible comparable to the subject property. The appraiser, in effect, must ask himself as he considers differences in age, quantity and quality of building construction: How much more or less will a typical purchaser pay—as compared with the subject property—because of the presence or absence of major construction features? The successful application of this technique requires:

1. Building construction know-how.
2. Detailed property inspection and keen observation.
3. Knowledge of construction costs and building unit prices.
4. Knowledge of typical buyer preferences and price reactions.
5. Application of sound judgment to obtain reasonable results.

The adjustments required to bring about price comparability of the index sales with the subject property are shown in Table 10.1. The first adjustment equates differences in time of sale. As noted, Index properties 3 and 4 would bring $500 and $1,000 more if exposed for sale on the date of the appraisal as compared with sale prices realized six months and one year before respectively. Differences in lot value, based on market sales, are adjusted next. Other adjustments reflect differences in quantity and quality of building construction. Building volume was equalized at a current building rate of $7.50 per square foot, exclusive of fixtures, heating, electrical, and plumbing costs in kitchen and bathrooms. Further adjustments were calculated at estimated construction expenditures at time of construction new, less accrued depreciation due to wear and use over the period of economic age of the index property. Differences in economic ages were equated at uniform rates of 2.5 percent per year on the basis of straight line accounting over an economic age period of forty years. Differences in building conditions were adjusted on the basis of estimated expenditures to cure deferred maintenance. Based on these adjustments and assignment of correlation (judgment) weights, in accordance with the importance of each sale as an index of market value, a final estimate of $22,500 indicates the value for the subject property under the market approach using the construction detail analysis and price rating technique.

The four comparable sales used in the market data approach to value were correlated in accordance with assigned judgment weights as shown in Table 10.1. The reasons that justify the selection of the correlation weights are as follows:

> *Sale No. 1* was given a weight of 30 percent because no time adjustment was necessary to update this sale for market changes in the price level of residential properties. This sale also is located in a similar setting as the subject property, both being in the same neighborhood. Further, an opportunity to inspect this sale property with care made possible accurate adjustments for variations in building features and construction.
> *Sale No. 2* was given a weight of 40 percent because this property is located in the same block as the subject property, and because this sale represents the most recent transaction of all the sales considered in the market approach to value. Sale No. 2 also comes reasonably close to the space volume of the subject house (1,450 square feet), as compared with 1,503 square feet for the sale property. Similarity of building condition, too, made this sale superior to Sales 1 and 3.
> *Sale No. 3* is located in a comparable neighborhood, one-half mile

TABLE 10.1

MARKET SALE PRICE RECAPITULATION SCHEDULE BASED ON CONSTRUCTION
DETAIL ANALYSIS AND PRICE RATING TECHNIQUES

Sale Index No.:	1	2	3	4
Indicated price	$21,000	$22,500	$22,600	$20,500
Time adjustment	0	0	500	1,000
Lot value difference	−500	500	0	−750
Construction variations: (1)				
Building volume	−1,500	−400	375	−750
Exterior walls	775	−750	−350	500
Interior finishes	800	0	250	0
No. of baths	−350	350	0	350
Tile in baths	−275	275	300	275
Roof construction	300	300	0	200
Insulation	175	0	0	0
Heating—cooling	0	−900	600	0
Equipment	0	0	−425	−225
Finished flooring	0	0	−500	0
Attic area	0	−400	0	0
Garage construction	500	0	−800	0
Porches and utility rooms	250	300	375	0
Building age	500	1,000	−500	1,000
Building conditions	600	0	200	0
Total adjustment + or −	$ 1,325	$ 275	$ 25	$ 1,600
Adjusted market price	$22,325	$22,775	$22,625	$22,100
Correlation (judgment) weight	.30	.40	.20	.10
Correlated value	$22,542			
Rounded to	$22,500			

(1) Price variations are based on *market* evidence (*not* cost to install) of how much
more or less buyers are willing to pay for the presence or absence of construction
features.

from the subject property. The sale took place one year ago and a time
adjustment of $500 was made to reflect the estimated increase in market
prices caused by rising property values in the community. Because of
substantial variations in time of sale and location, this comparable sale
was given a weight of only 20 percent.

Sale No. 4, although most comparable as far as physical features are
concerned, took place nearly twenty months ago, thus necessitating a
time adjustment of $1,000. This sale, too, is located in a similar but
distant neighborhood, causing a significant adjustment in the property
lot value. Because of the substantial adjustments necessary to make this
sale comparable, the weight assigned was judged at 10 percent. (A summary of the sale prices and adjustments is provided in Table 10.2.)

The market approach to value under the construction detail analysis
and price rating technique as illustrated is ideal, provided good reasons

TABLE 10.2

MARKET SALES PRICES AND ADJUSTMENT SUMMARY

Index Sale	Market Price	Price Adjustment	Indicated Value	Percent Weight
1	$21,000	$1,325	$22,325	30
2	22,500	275	22,775	40
3	22,600	25	22,625	20
4	20,500	1,600	22,100	10

are given for the use of the different correlation percentage weights. When applied with care, the market comparison method produces accurate appraisal estimates. This method, however, can be used successfully only where the appraiser through available plant or other source data has construction features for each sale property readily at hand. In practice, few appraisers can afford the time required to complete a thorough field inspection of each comparable sale (assuming owner's permission) used as an index to market value. Nor do appraisal fees customarily paid in the amount from $50 to $100 for appraisals of residential properties economically warrant the expenditure of effort necessary to secure and analyze essential market and construction data as outlined above. For this reason a less detailed but still sufficiently accurate market comparison technique is recommended for appraisal purposes.

OVERALL CONSTRUCTION AND BUILDING CONDITION RATING TECHNIQUE

Under this approach to value, market comparison is based on an overall judgment as to percentage-price adjustment called for in order to make each index sale comparable with the subject property. The overall percentage applied to each property in turn is justified by a statement that the subject property is deemed better, poorer, or the same (comparable) in relation to its construction as to type, size, features, age, and building condition. Since the subject property in every value problem represents "X" (unknown price) each index sale for comparison purposes is accepted as a measure of market forces of supply and demand equal to 100 percent at a given time and place. By adjusting the index rating upward or downward in accordance with characteristics of the subject property, a market value estimate is derived. The greater the number of truly comparable index sales used for market analysis purposes the greater, as a rule, the accuracy of the final value estimate. Individual errors in fact or judgment generally cancel out or are at least mitigated in their effect on the end results.

The application of the overall construction and building condition technique is demonstrated in Table 10.3. The judgment ratings shown

TABLE 10.3

MARKET SALES PRICE RECAPITULATION SCHEDULE BASED ON OVERALL CONSTRUCTION
AND BUILDING CONDITIONS RATING TECHNIQUE

Sale Index No.:	1	2	3	4
Indicated price	$21,000	$22,500	$22,600	$20,500
Time adjustment	0	0	500	1,000
Price adjustment for time	21,000	22,500	23,100	21,500
Lot value difference	−500	500	0	−750
Adjusted price	20,500	23,000	23,100	20,750

Subject property rating in regard to:

Construction:

Type	Poorer	Poorer	Poorer	Same
Size	Poorer	Poorer	Better	Poorer
Features	Better	Poorer	Same	Better
Age	Better	Better	Poorer	Better
Condition	Better	Same	Better	Same
Subject property percent rating	1.10	1.00	.95	1.10
Adjusted value	$22,550	$23,000	$21,945	$22,825

Index Sales Weights and Market Correlation

Index Sale	Adjusted Market Value	Weight of Sale	Value Components
1	$22,550	.30	$6,765
2	23,000	.40	9,200
3	21,945	.20	4,389
4	22,825	.10	2,283

Correlated market value—total $22,637

Rounded to $22,600

are supported by property descriptions as detailed on pages 134 and 135, and are based on a general rather than detailed field inspection of the physical property improvements. For the reader's benefit, further explanatory statements can be made in the appraisal report as follows: "The subject property, as compared with Index Sale No. 1, is poorer in type of construction because the index property has 4 bedrooms and 3 fully tiled bathrooms as compared with 3 bedrooms and 2 bathrooms contained in the subject building. The subject also is smaller in size, containing 1,450 square feet of area as compared with 1,650-square-foot area of the index sale. The subject property is deemed better in construction features, age, and condition because it has an asbestos-shingled roof and rock-wool insulation compared with the asphalt-shingled roof without insulation of the index property. The subject property has an effective age of 8 years; the index property age is 10 years. The subject property is in good condition with no deferred maintenance. Index Sale No. 1 requires an expenditure of $600 to redecorate the interior. The overall adjustment rating for the subject property is estimated at 110 percent, and the adjusted market price ascribable to the subject property is $22,550." A like comparative analysis of each of the other index sales with the subject property aids the client for whom the report is prepared in following step by step the procedure and logic used by the appraiser in arriving at the final estimate and value conclusion.

Although the percentage adjustment method does not appear as refined as the dollar equalization method, the former method is more realistic and in conformity with thought processes which motivate buyers and sellers when bargaining. It must be kept in mind that appraising is an art and not a science, and that final estimates of value are deemed reasonably accurate if within 5 percent, plus or minus, of actual market value realized by a subsequent and open sale. Then, too, the market approach to value is rarely used alone. Generally the cost approach and, where applicable, the income approach to value, or both, are used as checks and counterchecks on each other to insure the accuracy of the final value estimate as certified in the appraisal report.

PERCENTAGE ADJUSTMENTS—THEIR USE AND LIMITATION

To achieve comparability and to adjust for price differences caused by variations in type, size, features, age, and condition of the improvements, most appraising practitioners rather than using the "better, poorer, same" judgment analysis as illustrated in Table 13.3 apply percentage ratings to reflect superior or inferior market factor relationships. The use of a sequence of percentage ratings poses serious pitfalls and limitations. First, to ascribe to a number of structural deviations precise percentage ratings such as 5 percent superior, 10 percent inferior, and so on, presumes appraising to be a science—which it is not. Then, too, an appraiser would be hard put to justify whether a given quality of construction should be rated exactly 10 percent or perhaps 9 or 11 percent superior respectively. A jury or even an investor might get the impression that the appraiser is playing a number game that borders on "guesstimating" rather than professional estimating. Second, and more serious, is the mathematical distortion that results from given equal weight to percentage minuses and percentage pluses. A given market value can decline only 100 percent but can possibly increase a million or more percent—perhaps large and long enough to reach the moon. To illustrate, a minus of 50 percent is not offset by a plus of 50 percent, for a multiplication of .50 ×

1.50 equals .75; and if percentages are divided, the results obtained are 1.00/.50 $\times$ 1.00/1.50 or .667. If percentages are to be used at all, they should be added and then divided by the number of ratings employed to obtain an average adjustment factor. The nature of things, however, that permit an unlimited upward percentage adjustment, but limit a decline to a maximum of 100 percent will still cause value distortion no matter which percentage adjustment method is employed. For this reason the appraiser is advised to judge structural differences qualitatively and to report and describe these differences narratively in justifying an *overall* percentage relationship that justifies professionally the adjustments made to achieve comparability among the subject and the selected index sale properties.

ASSESSMENT RATIOS AS A GUIDE TO MARKET VALUE

A useful check on the accuracy of the market approach is provided by application of the property assessment ratios of the sale properties to the assessed value of the subject property. In every county or parish the tax assessor generally attempts to assess real property for tax "ad-valorem" purposes at uniform ratios in relation to market value. It is true that individual properties may be grossly out of line in being over- or underassessed, but where many properties are combined in an assessment-to-market-value ratio analysis, the results are often quite accurate. This, it is realized, may be due to compensating errors whereby inequities in individual property assessment are cancelled out through the use of a larger sample as a base for study. In many counties, too—especially in the larger and the more progressive smaller ones—responsible appraisal firms are periodically called in to establish equitable assessments based on fair-market value.

The application of the assessment ratio method as a guide to market value is a relatively simple procedure. This method, by the way, is facetiously referred to as the "fourth approach to value." In gathering market sales data from public records, the appraiser can readily obtain from tax records in the county clerk's office the assessed value for each of the index sales. The work form shown and recommended for market study use in Chapter 9, page 117, provides for entry of assessment data and computation of sale-to-assessment ratios. By combining the sale-assessment ratios for all index sales used in the market approach to value, a typical or average ratio can be derived and applied to the assessed value of the subject property as a guide to market value. To illustrate: Suppose the index sales described above yield sale-to-assessment ratios as follows:

Index Sale	Sale Price		Assessed Value	Sales-Assessment Ratio
1	$21,000	÷	$13,550	1.55
2	22,500	÷	14,060	1.60
3	22,600	÷	14,850	1.52
4	20,500	÷	13,650	1.50
Total	$86,600	÷	$56,110	1.54

Assuming that the subject property is assessed for $14,500, the indicated market value based on the typical sale to assessment ratio of 1.54, as computed above, would be $14,500 × 1.54, or $22,330. This appears to compare favorably with the values of $22,500 and $22,600 derived above under the conventional market approaches to value. Should the results obtained under the assessment ratio guide to value be considerably out of line, the appraiser would have good cause to recheck his data for possible errors in the market value analysis. Where no errors are found and the conclusions point to an over- or underassessment of the subject property, this information may also prove of useful interest to the client or owner of the property. This writer has experienced numerous occasions where his value findings brought about a lowering of property assessments and welcome tax savings to the grateful property owners. The sales-assessment ratio method as described above is graphically presented in Figure 10.1.

THE MARKET DATA APPROACH FOR
COMMERCIAL AND INDUSTRIAL PROPERTIES

The larger and more complex the physical improvements, the more detailed and difficult the market comparison approach. Whereas with residential property the structure as a whole served as a basis for comparison, a more detailed and manageable microstructural unit basis must be devised to permit realistic comparison and logical adjustments for building differences caused by size, age, quality, and quantity of construction.

Market price equalization is generally achieved by the unit comparison approach selecting for comparability one or more of the following:

1. Price per square or cubic foot of building volume.
2. Price per square foot of non-rentable area.
3. Price per apartment exclusive of land investment.
4. Price per room inclusive of bath, closet, and storage areas.
5. Gross annual or monthly multiplier.

For industrial, warehouse, or office buildings the cubic foot method of comparison (giving weight to the third dimension, i.e., height of ceilings and depth of basement area) yields more accurate results than the square

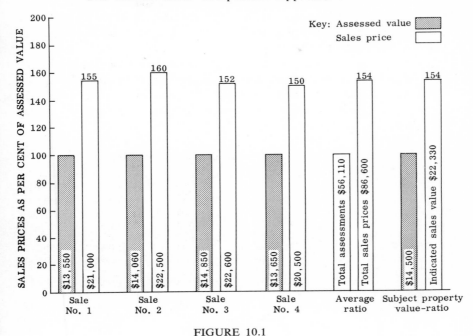

FIGURE 10.1

THE MARKET COMPARISON APPROACH BASED ON RATIOS OF SALES PRICES
TO ASSESSED VALUATIONS

foot comparison approach to value. Care, however, must be taken to exclude land value from the total market price paid for the property and to
adjust the cubic foot cost of each sale or index property for differences
caused by age, quality, condition, economy of building size, and equipment
features when compared with the subject property. Where sale properties
are selected with care, this market approach to value yields reliable results.
The gross annual multiplier, as explained below, can also be applied as a
check on the direct and usually more accurate unit comparison approach
to value.

Apartment properties offer greater flexibilities in the application of
the market or unit comparison approach to value. Because of greater
uniformity in construction design and building technique, and competitive
demand and supply for apartment housing, it is readily possible to apply
the unit comparison method more effectively on the basis of construction
cost (exclusive of land) [4] per apartment, per room as well as per square

---

[4] Where building to site ratios are essentially the same, the appraiser may be
justified in using the square foot cost measure with the land included.

or cubic foot. All these various unit cost indexes can then be rechecked by the gross annual multiplier for derivation of a market-correlated index of value for the property as a whole.

Given a subject property that is effectively in new condition and which contains 30 apartments and 70 rooms, and for which the underlying land value was estimated at $26,000, and the effective gross income at $33,200 a sales recapitulation summary schedule for the estimation of market value may be constructed as follows:

MARKET APPROACH TO VALUE OF APARTMENT PROPERTY

Sale No.	1	2	3	4
Sale price	$235,000	$120,000	$245,000	$288,000
Time adjustment	0	0	0	1.10
Adjusted price	$235,000	120,000	245,000	316,800
Less land value	$22,500	11,000	24,000	30,000
Building value	$212,500	109,000	221,000	286,800
Percent condition	.90	.80	1.00	.96
Adjusted improvement costs—new condition	$236,100	136,250	221,000	298,750
No. Apartments	35	20	33	43
No. Rooms	79	47	76	103
Cost new per Apt.	$6,745	6,813	6,697	6,948
Cost new per Room	$2,989	2,899	2,908	2,900
Gross Income	$34,100	17,200	35,250	42,000
Gross Multiplier	6.89	6.98	6.95	6.86

MARKET VALUE OF SUBJECT PROPERTY

1.	30 apartments @ $6,700[1]	=	$201,000	
	Add land value of		26,000	
	Indicated value—based on Apartments			$227,000
2.	70 rooms @ $2,900[1]	=	203,000	
	Add land value of		26,000	
	Indicated value—based on Rooms			229,000
3.	Gross Income		$33,200	
	Gross Income Multiplier		6.95[1]	
	Indicated value—based on Multiplier			230,700
	Correlated Market Value			$230,000

[1] Market indexes based principally on sale No. 3, because no adjustment for age of building was necessary and room and apartment count were closest to subject property.

The procedure employed in the comparative analysis presented above is relatively simple. The price paid for each comparable sale property is adjusted for changes attributed to passage of time from date of sale transaction to date of the appraisal. From this adjusted total the land value, derived by a market comparison approach, is subtracted to obtain the residual value attributable to the building improvements. Next comes an important percentage adjustment that reflects, in the appraiser's judgment, the age and condition of each sale property as compared with the subject property. Thus if a property sold for $80,000 and is deemed to be in 80 percent condition as compared with the subject property, then it follows that the comparable sale would have realized $100,000 ($80,000 ÷ .80) if equal in all respects to the subject property. The adjusted sale prices, are then allocated on a per-apartment and a per-room basis as shown. By correlating the derived units of measurement, giving greater judgment weights to sales which require little or no percentage adjustment, the appraised value of the subject property is obtained as demonstrated.

RENT OR GROSS INCOME MULTIPLIERS AS A GUIDE TO MARKET VALUE

The gross income multiplier as a device to convert monthly or annual gross income into a sum of market value has gained popularity as a rule of thumb and as an index of value. Like all rules which are based on the law of averages, the gross income multiplier can serve a useful purpose when applied intelligently and with care.

At the outset, it should be realized that the use of the gross income multiplier cannot and should not be considered as part of the income or capitalization approach to value. To capitalize, means to convert the estimated *net* income anticipated over the remaining economic life of the subject property into a sum of present value. The gross income multiplier does not give weight to amounts of operating expense ratios, or to variations in the remaining economic life of properties. In fact the user of the multiplier assumes that all properties within a given classification, such as residential, commercial, or industrial, are identical in operating characteristics and in their economic age-span of remaining productive life.

It may be fair to state that, by custom, many appraisers have been compelled to give recognition to the gross income multiplier as an index of value. In many areas, lay investors use the multiplier as a cardinal guide in judging the quality of property purchase offers. In New York City, for instance, apartment properties appear to sell consistently at prices approximately seven times the annual gross income of this class of property. In fact, an article published in the *Appraisal Journal*.[5] gave credence to the "mystic seven." The article labeled the multiplier as unscientific but nevertheless rated it as a market phenomenon that cannot be ignored.

The writer agrees that as an index of value the gross income is useful,

---

[5] Leonard H. Scane, "The Mystic Seven," *The Appraisal Journal* (April, 1958).

but only as a secondary device—a check on the result obtained by other and professionally recommended methods under the market, cost, and income approaches to value. Should the multiplier indicate results inconsistent with those obtained under more refined and analytical procedures, it would be the appraiser's duty to explain the variation and to give reasons for the cause of the exception to the rule-of-thumb findings.

By custom, the gross income multiplier is used for conversion of monthly rentals in establishing the value of residential properties and applied to the annual gross income valuation of industrial and commercial properties. Studies disclose that multipliers vary from region to region, often among communities within a region—and conceivably among neighborhoods within a city. The multiplier is simply derived for any given area by relating market prices of a given class of properties which have recently sold to the gross income actually or hypothetically derived from these properties if offered for rent in the open, competitive market at the time of sale. For residential properties—using the four index sales described on page 135—the procedure for obtaining and using the multiplier is as follows:

The market analysis detailed in Table 10.4 indicates a monthly multi-

TABLE 10.4

DERIVATION OF MONTHLY RENT MULTIPLIER FOR RESIDENTIAL PPOPERTIES

Index Sale	Established Market Value	Actual or Estimated Monthly Rental	Gross Monthly Multiplier
1	$21,000	$160	131
2	22,500	170	132
3	22,600	165	137
4	20,500	150	137
—	——	——	——
Totals and average	$86,600	$645	134

plier of 134. This multiplier can now be applied to the actual or estimated rental of the subject property to yield a measure of market value. Based on an estimated rent of $165 per month, the resultant market value equals $165 × 134 of $22,110. Conversely, the multiplier may also prove useful in estimating fair rentals for residential properties offered for lease. Given a market value of $22,100, and a prevailing monthly rent multiplier of 134, the fair-market rent is $22,100 ÷ 134 or $165 per month.

As indicated, in the hands of an informed person the multiplier may prove a useful aid in approximating prevailing market value. The professional appraiser, however, is well advised to use this valuation tool with caution for the following reasons: First, the multiplier converts into value *gross* rather than *net* income. It is entirely possible that a property which produces a comparable gross income may yield inadequate or even no net income because of excessive operating or maintenance cost due to faulty construction or inequitable contractual commitments written into long-term lease agreements. In either case the existence of gross income gives an illusion of value that could not be justified by an expert appraiser. It is for this reason that users of the gross income multiplier should pay heed to the saying, "The accountant can estimate our gross, but only God can give us our net."

Second, the use of the multiplier assumes uniformity among properties in their operating ratios. Even among residential properties, where operating experience supports claims for relative constancy of expense outlays, individual properties may vary significantly from the norm as a result of differences in construction, quality of insulation, kind of heating, amount of built-in equipment, equity of property taxation, and other causes.

Third, consideration of remaining economic life appears entirely ignored. It is a rare coincidence that properties selected as index sales are identical in relation to effective age, and a rarer coincidence still that the subject property should be of the same age as those of the index sales. Uninformed use of the gross multiplier would ascribe equal value to properties of equal income even though one may be in the last stages of its economic life and the other in new condition. It may be argued that such properties are not comparable; but be that as it may, the gross income multiplier *never* provides for adjustment of differences in properties which are by nature heterogeneous in character.

Fourth, care must be taken not to adjust the gross income, nor the "raw" market prices, paid for comparable properties for age, condition, or location of the sale property. To do so will overadjust for physical, functional, or economic factors which both the renters and the investors have already considered in the price paid for rental and in the purchase amount offered for the property in its "as is" condition.

With these limitations in mind, the gross income multiplier may be used as a straw in the bundle of straws to which the appraiser clings in formulating and justifying his final judgment of market value.

READING AND STUDY REFERENCES

1. *Acquisition for Right-of-Way* (Washington, D.C.: American Association of State Highway Officials, 1962), chap. 29.

2. Anderson, Robert E., "The Comparison Approach on Appraising

Residential Properties," *The Appraisal Journal* (April 1960), pp. 177–81.

3. *The Appraisal of Real Estate* (Chicago: American Institute of Real Estate Appraisers, 1967), chaps. 20–21.

4. Babcock, Frederick M., *The Valuation of Real Estate* (New York: McGraw-Hill Book Company, Inc., 1932), chap. 30.

5. Denton, John H., "Market Theory in Real Estate Appraising," *The Real Estate Appraiser* (September 1963), pp. 2–13.

6. Kahn, Sanders A., Frederick E. Case, and Alfred Schimmel, *Real Estate Appraisal and Investment* (New York: The Ronald Press Company, 1963), chap. 8.

7. Kinnard, William N., Jr., *An Introduction to Appraising Real Property* (Chicago: Society of Real Estate Appraisers, 1968), chaps. 13 & 14.

8. Opelka, F. Gregory, "Market Data Approach on Apartments," *The Real Estate Appraiser* (September 1963), pp. 19–22.

9. Ring, Alfred A., "New Techniques of the Market Comparison Approach," *The Residential Appraiser* (July 1962), pp. 2–8.

10. Wendt, Paul F., *Real Estate Appraisal* (New York: Henry Holt and Company, 1956), chaps. 7 & 9.

A competent appraiser, to be professionally qualified, must possess a working knowledge of the arts of building design and building construction. As will be demonstrated, this knowledge is essential in the accurate application of each of the approaches to value as well as in deriving a reliable measure of accrued depreciation. Under the cost approach to value, knowledge of construction quantity and quality is essential in order that

11 *Building Construction*
and Plan Reading

the applicable unit cost per square foot or per cubic foot can be computed to reproduce or replace the structure in new condition. Under the market approach to value, structural differences between the subject and the comparable properties must be recognized in order to make reasonable qualitative and quantitative value adjustments. Under the income approach, too, an estimate of remaining building life expectancy is necessary for correct capitalization of building income. Even an estimate of theoretical depreciation cannot be made without an estimate of the effective structural age as reflected by a building's condition, its functional and economic obsolescence, and the structural resistance it offers to forces of wear, tear, and action of the elements.

The anatomy of a building [1] may be

---

[1] Since the bulk of building construction is residential rather than commercial or industrial in character, emphasis in this chapter for illustration purposes will be placed on the anatomy of a single family building structure.

studied in the order of its structural components as follows:

1. Footings, piers, and foundation walls.
2. Exterior walls.
3. Sub- and finish floor framing.
4. Partition framing and interior walls.
5. Roof framing and roof cover finish.
6. Windows and doors—kind, quality.
7. Cabinet work.
8. Plumbing and electric wiring.
9. Heating and air-conditioning systems.
10. Insulation and other improvements.

Footings, piers, and foundation walls as a rule are constructed in accordance with local or national (F.H.A. or V.A.) building codes. Footings generally consist of reinforced concrete that is poured on undisturbed soil below the frostline, as specified for the geographic area. The width of the footing must be at least twice that of the foundation wall to be supported, and equal to the thickness of the foundation wall in depth, and in no instance less than six inches. Foundation walls typically are of concrete blocks eight by eight by sixteen inches in size. Where needed for extra strength, reinforcing rods are placed at corner and wall supporting locations. Waterproofing is a requirement where subfloor or basement areas are subject to surface water penetration. The appraiser, unless informed of structural weaknesses, or unless he sees evidence of excessive settlement at the time of building inspection, assumes proper compliance with applicable construction codes in all foundation work. Where doubt exists, or conditions warrant it, a construction engineer should be called on to inspect the premises for building flaws and to render a certified report on which the appraiser may rely for value adjustments or repair expenditures.

Exterior walls are constructed in a variety of frame, metal, or masonry materials and generally in conformity with community customs and owners preferences. Again, unless evidence points otherwise, structural soundness must be assumed. The appraiser should chiefly be interested in costs differentials of the materials used, and in the comparative utility (or disutility) of exterior wall construction in relation to expenditures for building maintenance and repair. More expensive exterior wall material may be warranted from a value point of view (brick versus frame) where the additional construction cost—other things remaining equal—does not exceed the present worth of anticipated dollar savings in building management and upkeep. Amenities offered by attractiveness of exterior design or appearance must, of course, be considered as plus items in the value estimate.

Where exterior walls are of frame or of brick or stone veneer, the supporting wood framing consists of studs either two by four inches or two by six inches in size that rest on sills which are bolted to the foundation wall. In geographic areas where termite infestation is prevalent, soils enclosed by the foundation walls are poisoned by licensed entomologists and metal termite sheets are placed on top of foundation walls and piers to safeguard against these wood-destroying subterranean pests.

In checking the kind and quality of sub- and finish floor construction the appraiser should make certain that the underlying and surrounding soil shows no evidence of poor surface drainage and that no telltale signs point to the existence of, or possible damage from, subterranean pests or surface varmints. The subsurface building area should be checked for size, quality, and utility of basement area. Many residential buildings today are constructed without basements, and most throughout the South and Far West are built on concrete slab poured directly on the ground without crawl space or excavation of any kind. This type of construction, in milder climates where ground frost presents no danger, offers savings of $500 to $1,000 per residential structure depending on size of building area. Where the subfloor is suspended and of frame, a check should be made of the size of girders, size and spacing of floor joists, proper cross bridging of joists (at least every eight feet apart) to assure floor stability, and creakproof construction. Subfloor planking should be diagonal to further strengthen building rigidity. The kind and quality of finished flooring should be noted, and inspected for uniformity of placement and appearance. Wall-to-wall carpet should be mounted over felt underlay for even and longer wear. Where rugs are intended as partial floor covering, the finished wood surface should be of hard clear wood strips or parquet wood tiles nailed over diagonal, rough-finished pine or equal subflooring. Kitchen floors generally are covered with grease-resistant linoleum or vinyl tile. Bathroom floors, for long lasting use as well as appearance, are recommended to be finished with ceramic tile firmly cemented in place over concrete slab subflooring. Concrete flooring in basement, commercial or industrial areas, should be four inches in thickness and for reinforcement be poured over continuous wire mesh.

Construction details of partition framing and of interior walls should be considered. Particular checks should be made where exterior walls are of metal or masonry to discern whether the inside of these walls are fitted with furred strips of kiln-dried or moisture-treated wood to create airspace between the wall surface and the plaster or other interior wall finishes. This airspace is important wherever climatic conditions cause walls to sweat because of extreme differences in indoor-outdoor temperatures. Where plaster is placed directly on the wall rather than on rock lath over furring strips, the appraiser should reflect this "economy" construction in his value estimate and possibly consider penalizing the property under functional obsolescence, especially in areas where lending companies reject such substandard construction for mortgage loan purposes. Interior finishes, too, should be noted for quality attributes. Where wood paneling is used, check for quality workmanship in the mitering of joints, and for type and grade of wood and excellence of finish. Height of walls from floor to ceiling are important, and where less than standard (eight feet) or in excess of a nine-foot clearance, a plus or minus adjustment should be made to reflect the lack of, or increase in, resulting amenities to owner-occupants.

Type of roof construction, method of framing, and roof shingle or surface finishing should next be given due attention. Depending on the period of architecture, the principal roof types are as follows: flat (built-up), gable, hip, gambrel, mansard, or pyramid, as shown in Figure 11.1.

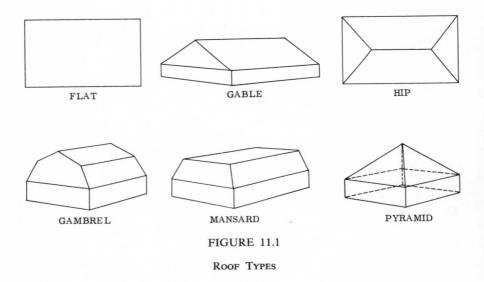

FLAT   GABLE   HIP

GAMBREL   MANSARD   PYRAMID

FIGURE 11.1

Roof Types

Where roofs are sloped and roof shingles are conventionally nailed (and not cemented), it is important that the rise in slope is not less than four inches for every twelve inches of roof slope distance, as shown in Figure 11.2.

The higher the rise in slope, the costlier the roof construction—but the larger the attic area and the safer and more lasting the roof shingle coverage because of lessened wear and tear from rain, hail, snow, or tornadic winds. A rise in slope below four inches in twelve inches permits rain and wind to drive under the shingles, weakening the shingle fastenings and the undercover roof seal. Ceiling joists and roof rafters should be at least

FIGURE 11.2

two inches by six inches in size for residential buildings, and placed not less than sixteen inches on center (from the center of one joist or rafter to the center of the adjacent joist or rafter). The roof extension, or eaves, should be at least twelve inches beyond the exterior wall surface, and larger where protection is sought from sun and rain for windows and exterior finishes. A typical roof section shows details as in Figure 11.3.

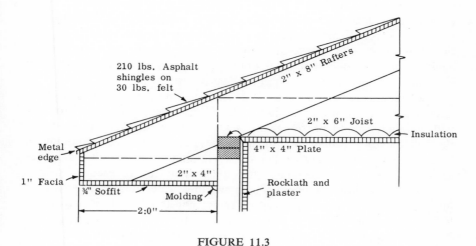

FIGURE 11.3

Roof Section View

Windows and doors should be inspected to ascertain the manufacturer, the kind of wood or metal sash, the quality of fitting, and the extent of trouble-free operation. Weakness of construction or poor lintel support over wall openings manifests itself in plaster and wall cracks at corners of windows and doors. Where cracks are due to structural settlement, inspection of floor beams and piers should be made to determine the necessity for and cost of corrective repairs. Windows should be tested and checked for airtightness, and exterior doors should be fitted with full-length screens and weatherstripped saddles and frames. Windowsills and stools, where of special construction and finish, should be noted as quality attributes which must be reflected specifically in the cost approach to value.

Windows are either double-hung or casement type and of wood sash in northern and midwestern states, and of jalousie or awning type and of aluminum-sash in subtropical climate states. Jalousie windows are largely used in closed-in porches and in industrial and commercial buildings. Better home construction practices confine window types to double-hung, casement or awning manufacture. Quality windows are recognized by fineness and strength of glass—sheet, crystal, plate, or thermopane. Ease of operation and weatherstripping are further marks of quality noticeable by careful inspection.

Sufficiency in number, size, and quality of closets, built-ins, and cabinet work in general should be evaluated and described for the benefit of the report reader. Quality construction is apparent when closets are cedar-lined, fitted with switch-controlled lights, and contain carpentry details such as shoeracks and special shelf-and-rod arrangements. Sliding, louvered, or mirrored closet doors, too, may warrant special value consideration. Built-in vanities, bookcases, mantles, china closets, and extra kitchen cabinets that increase functional utility and amenities of living must be itemized and considered for appraisal purposes.

Adequacy, convenience, and safety of plumbing and electrical installations are a *must* in a modern home. Each bathroom, unless back-to-back with another, should be separately vented with a metal stack extending through the roof. Similar venting for the kitchen sink is a requirement. Water faucets should have individual valve shutoffs to permit emergency repairs or washer replacements. The piping should be checked as to kind of metal (galvanized or copper) and whether water flow is adequate or impeded by inadequate pipe size or faulty construction. It is important, too, to ascertain whether sewage disposal is by a public, community, or individual septic tank system. In the latter case, the number and size of septic tanks should be considered and reported. Increasing reliance on electrically operated household conveniences such as ranges, refrigerators, dishwashers, garbage disposals, and washing machines make proper and adequate wiring for regular lighting and power use of utmost importance. Modern construction calls for a three-wire (220-volt) panel wiring, of 100-ampere or greater capacity, and fitted with circuit breakers rather than old-fashioned fuses. Wall receptacles, at least three to each room, should be conveniently located. Switches, whether conventional or mercury (silent) type, should be noted. All plumbing and wiring should be concealed, including wiring for telephone outlets to various rooms and television aerial connections.

Most often underestimated is the kind and quality of an adequate heating and air-conditioning system. In many southern and far-western homes heat is supplied simply by a single gas, electric, or oil-fired stove (the space heater). Such a method of heating—no matter how warm the climate during most of the year—is inadequate and often unhealthy because of faulty venting or inadequate air circulation. The cost of central heating, with adequate duct and register controls, may vary from $500 to $2,000, depending on quality of furnace and intricacy of pipe or duct work installation. This wide cost range is reason enough for an appraiser to confirm the kind and quality of heating, and to reflect the appropriate value attributes in his appraisal estimate. Air conditioning in most parts of our country is still in a luxury classification, and care must be taken to study the demand for homes so equipped in order to reflect market value rather than necessary cost of construction expenditures.

Last but not least, accessory building details should be inventoried. Included in this category are ceiling and wall insulation, finished attic space, outdoor flood-lighting, patios, landscaping, driveways, walks, porches, garages, stoves, refrigerators, laundry equipment, disposals, fireplaces, incinerators, elevators, storm sash, fences, wells, water tanks, water softeners, water pumps, sprinkler systems, and other related improvements.

PLAN READING FOR PROPOSED
CONSTRUCTION

It is said that the best time to appraise a property is before it is built. Ideally this would give the best protection to builders, investors, and home buyers. In practice, however, this precaution is not generally taken. It is assumed by the public at large that cost and value are synonymous. Not until a resale takes place do errors come to light as to under-, over-, or faulty improvements and resultant value losses. Fortunately, as a protection to mortgage lenders, the practice of appraising proposed buildings prior to construction became mandatory—at least where governmental agencies or private institutional lenders are involved.

Every appraiser must be capable of analyzing building plans and specifications, and must know how to estimate from architectural specifications the cost of constructing proposed improvements. Whether costs are warranted will depend on the kind and character of the described improvements in the light of prevailing demand and market conditions, as was discussed in preceding chapters and as will be further outlined in chapters concerned with the cost, market, and income approaches to value.

Typical construction drawing, as a rule, contain the following:

1. Foundation plan.
2. Floor plan.
3. Elevations.
4. Sectional views.
5. Mechanical, heating, and electrical plan layouts.

The *foundation plan* is generally drawn to a scale of one-quarter inch to one foot and provides the essential details concerning size of footings, size and dimensions of piers, and construction measurements and details of the subfloor area. Where the building foundation is of concrete slab, the plan will show thickness of slab, kind and size of steel wire reinforcement, as well as areas where foundations are to be thickened for placement of load-bearing interior walls. Location of concrete expansion joints and foundation areas to be termite-shielded are also marked for ease of reference and worker's guide. Where basement area or subfloor crawlspace is called for, the foundation plan will note the exact location and size of girders and beams as well as the kind and quality of floor joists—generally two by eight or two by ten inches in size and placed, as a rule, twelve or sixteen inches on center, depending on the type of superstructure and the permissible building codes.

The *floor plan* (See Figure 11.4) is an important guide to accurate

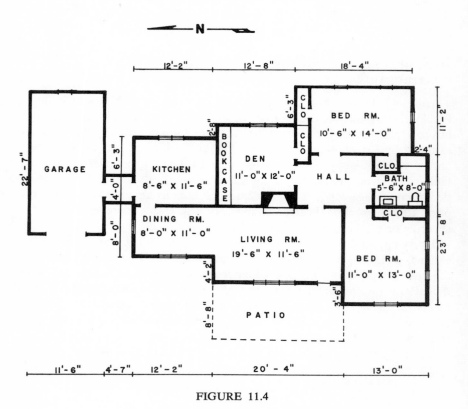

FIGURE 11.4

FLOOR PLAN FOR RESIDENTIAL STRUCTURE

building layout. From this plan, measurements are. taken for the calculation of square foot or cubic foot space volume that serve as a basis for construction-cost estimating. The floor plan, as shown, indicates wall-to-wall dimensions, room sizes and exposures, and placement of windows, doors, partitions, fireplace, chimney, fixtures, cabinets, patio, breezeway, and attached garage. The floor plan is normally drawn to an exact scale of one-quarter inch to one foot and includes, where separate mechanical drawings are not called for, construction details concerning placement of lighting outlets, telephone jacks, plumbing, and heating fixtures.

Elevations show the exterior sides of a building as it appears after all structural work has been completed. As a rule, each building side is viewed by an elevation and, for identification, marked as north, south, east, and west or by structural designation as front, rear, left, and right side elevation. Symbols on elevation drawings indicate the kind of exterior materials, their placement, and the height of their construction. The type and slope of roof is noted, as well as the kind and placement of roof shingles. Type and placement of windows are detailed, as are other openings such as doors, dormers, vents, and skylights. Typical elevations, from which an overall view of the finished building can be obtained at a glance, are shown in Figure 11.5.

To provide a detailed guide to specific construction practices, sectional views of exterior and interior walls are made a part of every set of building plans. Sectional views permit detailed considerations of specific construction methods, from footings and subflooring to ceiling, attic, and roof construction. Special elevation drawings, too, are provided for built-in items such as bookcases, china closets, and kitchen cabinets.

THE IMPORTANCE OF WRITTEN
SPECIFICATIONS

No matter how completely plans, elevations, and related drawings and sketches are prepared, they still would fail to convey an accurate picture of the structural elements to be incorporated in a building without the important and supplementary aid of written specifications. In fact written instructions are deemed of greater importance than graphic illustrations, and where these two are in conflict it is the written word that is guiding and legally binding.

The reason for the importance of written specifications can be readily illustrated. Plans may indicate construction and placement of materials. In the specifications, however, structural quality and quantity is specifically spelled out. Thus the specifications may call for a concrete mix of one part cement, two parts sand, three parts stone, and a minimum supporting strength of 2,400 pounds per square inch at a time interval of forty-

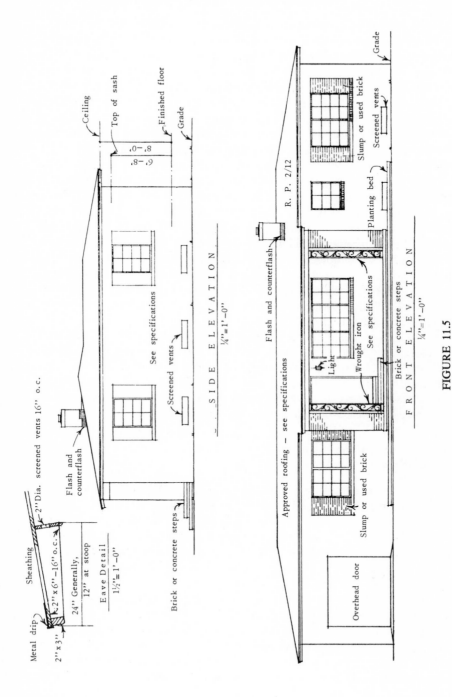

Metal drip

Sheathing

2'' Dia. screened vents 16'' o.c.

2'' x 3''

2'' x 6'' –16'' o.c.

24'' Generally,
12'' at stoop

Flash and
counterflash

Eave Detail
1½"= 1'–0"

Ceiling

Top of sash

Finished floor

Grade

8'–0''

6'–8''

See specifications

Screened vents

Brick or concrete steps

S I D E   E L E V A T I O N
¼"= 1'–0"

R. P. 2/12

Flash and counterflash

Approved roofing – see specifications

Slump or used brick

Planting bed

Screened vents

Grade

Light

Wrought iron

See specifications

Brick or concrete steps

Slump or used brick

Overhead door

F R O N T   E L E V A T I O N
¼"= 1'–0"

FIGURE 11.5

158

eight hours after pouring. Or the plans may show two-by-six-inch floor joists placed twenty-four inches on center. The specifications will indicate the kind of timber—whether pine, oak, or other—and the grade of timber as rated in accordance with quality and manufacturer's tensile strength. Specifications, too, may stipulate whether timber is to be treated, processed for protection against termites (Wolmanized) or kiln dried to minimize shrinkage.

Specifications historically have served as a contract document between builder and owner, and are intended to avoid disputes or misunderstandings concerning details of construction. Other and equally important purposes are to permit accurate estimating of required labor, quality of materials, and costing of contractors' and subcontractors' services in accordance with plan requirements. Specifications also safeguard against expensive omissions when construction costs are estimated and minimize construction delays due to misunderstanding of building plans. Written specifications generally are prepared in one of two forms:

1. The narrative or report form.
2. The standard specification form.

For multiple-story residential and for commercial and industrial buildings the narrative or report form is generally used. For a skyscraper, for instance, the specifications contain sufficient pages to comprise a book.[2]

COMPUTING BUILDING VALUE
MEASUREMENTS

Depending on local custom and building practices, construction areas are quoted in terms of square feet or cubic feet measurements. The latter method of sizing a building is more accurate, since weight is given to height of structure from six inches below the finished surface of the lowest floor to and including the roof and attic area. Where given structures, such as residences, are of uniform height, however, the use and application of the square foot method of costing a building is justified and does yield accurate results, as will be demonstrated in the following chapter. All building measurements are based on exterior rather than interior wall dimensions. This practice gives consideration to thicknesses of walls which importantly contribute to the cost of building construction.

In illustrating the procedure of "squaring" a building, reference is made to the floor plan shown in Figure 11.6. For computation purposes the floor area is divided into rectangular units as shown below the figure.

---

[2] Alfred A. Ring and Nelson L. North, *Real Estate Principles and Practices* (Englewood Cliffs, N. J.: Prentice-Hall, Inc., 6th ed., 1967), pp. 470–474.

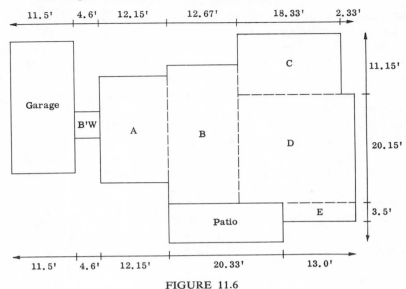

FIGURE 11.6

Building Square Feet Computation:

Area A	12.15′ × 18.25′	=	221.74 square feet
Area B	12.67′ × 25.07′	=	317.64 square feet
Area C	18.33′ × 11.15′	=	204.38 square feet
Area D	20.66′ × 20.15′	=	416.30 square feet
Area E	13.0′ × 3.5′	=	45.50 square feet
	Total building area		1,205.56 square feet

Other building units:

Garage	11.5′ × 22.6′	=	259.9 square feet
Breezeway	4.0′ × 4.6′	=	18.4 square feet
Patio	8.7′ × 20.3′	=	176.6 square feet

Where cubic feet measurements are required, an additional multiplication for each rectangular unit must be made in accordance with the building height taken from six inches below the finished basement floor to the outside measurement of a flat roof. Other roof plans must be computed to reflect accurate cubic foot volume of gable or other type roof areas. For a detailed discussion and illustration of methods to figure square or cubical contents of buildings, see Chapter 15 of *McMichael's Appraising Manual*.[3] For detailed illustrations and instructions on building measure-

3 Stanley L. McMichael, *McMichael's Appraising Manual* (Englewood Cliffs, New Jersey: Prentice-Hall, Inc., 4th ed., 1951).

ments, reference may also be made to the various cost services (Boek, Marshall-Stevens, Dodge Corp., Dow Cost Calculator, etc.) and to the F.H.A. Underwriting Manual.

BASIC ATTRIBUTES OF GOOD FLOOR PLANNING

It is the appraiser's responsibility to develop sound judgment in classifying attributes of good or poor floor planning, and to evaluate the effects on the marketability of the property of excellence in layout and design or lack of functional utility. Where the principle of balance in interior space allocation is violated the market will reflect the degree of functional obsolescence in sales resistance that is measurable in dollars, either directly by market comparison or by the extent to which such obsolescence is curable or incurable in estimating this cause of loss in value.

Attributes of good floor planning which increase the amenities of living in residential structures and which make for more efficient use of space include, among others, the following:

1. Orientation of rooms to capture prevailing breezes, sunshine, and beauty of area views surrounding the property.
2. Proper placing of picture window and large window areas to assure adequate light and fenestration for all rooms.
3. Provision for entrance hall or foyer (with guest-closet space) to shield living room from direct view and drafts.
4. Grouping of bed and bathroom areas to assure maximum of privacy. A separate entrance to the bedroom wing or access without a view from or crossing of living room area is considered a must.
5. Proper functional layout of kitchen area to conserve steps in housekeeping.
6. Location of kitchen near entrance and side doors to minimize traffic flow.
7. Adequate bedroom, linen, and storage closets and necessary utility space.
8. Proper wiring and location of household utility equipment and economical but adequate provision for central heating.
9. Accessibility to attic space area via conveniently located hatch or concealed stairway.
10. Minimum room sizes at least equal in square feet area and dimensions as provided by minimum property standards for residential units adopted by the Federal Housing Administration as follows: [4]

Under F.H.A. regulations, halls must be at least three feet wide, and closets at least three feet wide, two feet deep, and five feet high. Closet

---

[4] See *Minimum Property Standards for One and Two Living Units,* Federal Housing Administration, F.H.A. No. 300 (Washington, D. C.: Government Printing Office, January, 1965), page 32.

Dwelling	Living Room	Dining Room	Kitchen	Total Bedrooms	Minimum Bedroom
One-bedroom	160	80	60	120	—
Two-bedroom	160	80	60	200	80
Three-bedroom	170	95	70	280	80
Four-bedroom	180	110	80	380	80
Least dimensions	11'	8'	3'4"	—	8'

space must be a minimum of 200 cubic feet, with an additional seventy-five cubic feet of storage per bedroom. Thus a three-bedroom house must contain a minimum of 425 cubic feet of storage space of which 50 percent must be provided out of doors in carports, garages, or exterior (enclosed) storage closets.

The functional utility of commercial, industrial, or farm buildings can in like manner be tested by the principle of balance. In appraising large and multistory structures—especially if old or intricate in design—professional aid from contractors, builders, architects, or construction engineers may have to be obtained to report in detail on matters such as structural condition, deferred maintenance and repair, adequacy, safety and speed of elevators, and functional conditions which affect the cost of servicing the building. In some court jurisdictions (The New York Supreme Court, for example) appraisers are not qualified to testify as experts on matters concerning construction or costs thereof, unless they are also licensed as building. In some court jurisdictions (the New York Supreme Court, for structural design affecting revenue, maintenance, management and, possibly, the remaining economic building life include the following:

1. Adequacy of foyer, halls, and public areas to accommodate traffic flow of tenants, employees, and business clientele.
2. Proper washroom facilities assigned where possible for private use to minimize general janitorial services.
3. Modular construction that permits space repartitioning to suit tenant needs.
4. Good lighting and adequate, concealed telephone and electric wiring to serve anticipated maximum service loads.
5. Sufficiency of central heating under individual unit or zone control.
6. Capacity and readiness to supply air conditioning where competitively necesary.
7. High ratio of net rentable area as percentage of total building square foot area.
8. Necessary off-street parking.

In the appraisal of old structures, special care must be taken to recognize functional disutility. For example, structures built of thick masonry walls, which were designed under the old post-and-lintel system to support by sheer dead weight the stresses and strains of tall, multistory buildings, may offer as much as 10 percent less net rentable space than modern structures where exterior walls are built of steel or of steel-reinforced masonry.[5] In such instances, the capitalized income loss due to outmoded type of construction will reflect the amount of depreciation caused by this type of functional disutility.

IMPORTANCE OF CONSTRUCTION KNOWLEDGE

Since improvements on and to land comprise the major portion of total property value, it is important that the appraiser become thoroughly familiar with the essential details of building construction and building-plan reading. In this chapter, an attempt was made to stress the importance of construction principles and practices knowledge in order that the appraiser may effectively differentiate and evaluate the vast variety of building improvements. Many books have been written on construction subjects, and many colleges and universities throughout the country offer courses in this important field of study. A qualified appraiser who seeks to serve his profession well should familiarize himself with the types of architecture and construction practices which typically prevail in the state or region in which he serves his clients. Reading and course work is important to lay a foundation for appraisal knowledge; but nothing can take the place of field experience gained from the inspection of buildings at various stages of construction. Every appraisal presents a challenge to inventory correctly the details of construction, and to evaluate accurately the utility of building improvements. Effective application of the construction guides discussed above should contribute importantly to accurate consideration of building improvements under the cost, market, and income approaches to value, as will be demonstrated in succeeding chapters.

READING AND STUDY REFERENCES

1. Anderson, L. O., and O. C. Heyer (*Wood-Frame House Construction.* Washington: U.S. Department of Agriculture, 1955).
2. *The Appraisal of Real Estate* (Chicago: American Institute of Real Estate Appraisers, 1967), chap. 11.
3. *Building Trades Blueprint Reading and Sketching* (Albany: Delmar Publishers Inc., 1956).

---

[5] Construction under the modern *birdcage* building method, where outer walls are mere protection sheaths, may offer further space advantages or construction-cost economies.

4. Kahn, Sanders A., Frederick E. Case, and Alfred Schimmel, *Real Estate Appraisal and Investment* (New York: The Ronald Press Company, 1963), chap. 21.

5. Polley, Joseph H., "Anatomy of a House," *The Real Estate Appraiser* (November-December 1968), pp. 40–44.

6. Prussiano, Joseph B., "Blueprint Reading," *The Real Estate Appraiser* (March 1968), pp. 18–24.

7. While, Edward L., "Appraising from Plans and Specifications," *The Real Estate Appraiser* (June 1966), pp. 13–26.

In a normal market, when building supply and demand are in equilibrium replacement cost in current dollars will set the ceiling of value—provided the structure is new and conforms in design, size, and mode of construction with the principle of highest and best land use. As a first step in the field-data program it is essential that the appraiser make a detailed inventory of the existing or proposed land and building improvements

12 Building Cost
Estimating and Valuation

in order that an accurate estimate can be made of the cost to *replace* the form utility of the structure under up-to-date but generally typical methods of building construction. Where *reproduction* costs of a replica building—using current labor and similar materials—rather than replacement costs are considered more accurate as an approach to value, the appraiser should give reasons for his preference and choice of methods in costing the improvements. No doubt the purpose of the appraisal and the nature of the value problem will guide the appraiser in selecting the costing method which, at the proper time and place, will yield the most reliable results.

The art of cost estimating is taught in vocational schools and in colleges of architecture and building construction. The cost estimator as a technician is generally not concerned with value. It is the appraiser's task to convert cost into value by giving effect to market conditions and causes of depreciation, as explained in Chapter 13. Cost estimating methods presently in use by architects, builders, and appraisers are classified as follows:

1. Builders' detail inventory method.
2. Subcontractors' or quantity survey method.
3. Unit-in-place construction method.
4. The comparative market method.

BUILDERS' DETAIL INVENTORY METHOD

This method is generally used by experienced cost specialists when estimating project expenditures on large-scale construction proposals which are to be completed in accordance with detailed building plans and specifications. Under this method, a detailed cost estimate is made for each major labor and material construction item in the order of specification requirements. Every unit of labor essential in the building process from ground-breaking to final decorating and cleaning-up is itemized and costed. To this is added the detailed cost of the various quantities of building materials and equipment items. To the summation of the labor and material costs is then added a percentage rate to cover prevailing architect fees and builders' field and general overhead costs and profit. To demonstrate the application of the builders' detail inventory method, a cost breakdown for a 1,000-square-foot concrete block residence is demonstrated on pages 167–172.

The builders' detail inventory method of cost estimating as illustrated yields, when applied with care, accurate results. The application of this method, however, is time-consuming and costly. The typical appraiser, in fact, is not technically trained or qualified to undertake such minute and detailed cost studies. For this reason recourse is made to other, quicker, and more suitable methods of applying the cost approach to value.

SUBCONTRACTORS' OR QUANTITY SURVEY METHOD

This method of cost estimating is simpler in application, less time-consuming and preferred by architects in the costing of residential structures. Under this method, bids for major construction work are obtained by the general contractor from subcontractors and summarized to derive the composite cost estimate. Since each subcontractor is a specialist in his limited field of operation, the resulting economy generally offsets the overlapping of field and overhead expenditures. An illustration of this costing method is shown on page 172.

The subcontractors' or quantity survey method, if expertly applied,

"Construction Cost Estimate
Based on
Builder's Detail Inventory Method
for a Single Family Residence"

Building Description: Two bedroom, living room, kitchen and
bath, concrete block (painted) residential structure. Interior
walls of frame and plaster. Asphalt shingled roof with 4" in
12" pitch over 2" rock wool ceiling insulation. Concrete subflooring and terrazzo finished flooring. Aluminum doulbe hung
windows. Equipped with 40 gallon automatic electric water
heater, built-in electric stove and oven and 85,000 B.T.U. oil
fired, forced air central heating system. Construction methods
and specirications to meet F.H.A. minimum property standards
for one and two living units.

Cost Breakdown

Specifi-cation No.	Type of Construction	Material	Labor	Total
	Water tap			$40.00
	Building permit			30.00
	Electric service			35.00
	Site clearing			60.00
	Architect fee			100.00
1	Excavation:			
	Layout and batter boards	$ 16.50	$ 11.00	$ 27.50
	Excavation--130 x 1 1/3 = 173 1/3 ÷ 27 = 6.41 cu. yds.			
	Labor--6.41 c.y. x $3.75		24.04	24.04
	Backfill--approx. 1 c.y.		1.75	1.75
	Dirt fill--1000 s.f. x 2/3' = 667 c.f. ÷ 27 = 24.7 c.y.			
	24.7 c.y. x $1.75	43.23		43.23
	Puddling and tamping --1000 x $.08		80.00	80.00
2	Foundation:			
	5/8" Rods--364 1.f. x $.12	43.68		
	Labor--364 x $.03		10.92	54.60
	Footings--130 1.f. x 2/3' x 1 1/3 = 115.5 c.f. ÷ 27 = 4.3 c.y. x $20.00	86.00		
	Labor--4.3 x $2.50		10.75	96.75
	1 Course dapped-out block M. 98 x $.45	44.10		
	L. 98 x $.20		19.60	63.70
3	Chimney-Masonry:			
	Brick	60.00	40.00	100.00
	Flashing	5.00	10.00	15.00
4	Exterior Walls: Concrete blocks 8 x 8 x 16)-- 130 x .75 = 98 x 12 (tiers)			

167

	1176 x $.28	329.28		
	Labor--1176 x $.20		235.20	564.48
	Gable ends (8 x 8 x 16) --200 (blocks) x $.28 x 2	112.00		
	Labor--200 x $.19 x 2		76.00	188.00
	Steel rods--364 l.f. x $.12	43.68		
	Labor--364' x $.03		10.92	54.60
	8 x 8 Concrete lintel --2/3 x 130 = 57.77 c.f. ÷ 27 = 2.13 c.y. x $21.00	44.73		
	Labor		5.26	49.99
	Mortar mix and sand ($.05 per block)-- 1274 x $.05	63.70		
	Labor on setting forms and removing--6 hrs. @ $4.95		29.70	93.40
5	Floor Construction: Membrane (2 15# felt hot mopped)--1000 x $.06	60.00		
	Labor--1000 x $.25		25.00	85.00
	Wire mesh--1100 s.f. x $.045	49.50		
	Labor--1100 x $.0062		6.82	56.32
	Expansion joint (1" x 4")--156 l.f. x $.096	14.99		
	Labor--156 x $.02		3.12	18.11
	Concrete slab 4"--1000 s.f. x 1/3' = 334 c.f. ÷ 27 = 12.4 c.y. x $20.00	248.00		
	Labor--12.4 x $2.00		24.80	272.80
	Bolts (1/2" x 6")--31 x $.15	4.65		
	Labor--31 x $.08		2.48	7.13
	Finishing--$.05 per ft.	3.00	50.00	53.00
6	Partitions: Sole plate (2 x 4 trea- ted)--94 x 2/3 x 2 = 126 l.f. x $.18	22.68		
	Labor--126 x $.10		12.60	35.28
	Studs (2 x 4)--94 x $.75 = 70.5 or 71 + 8 (waste) 79 x 8' = 632 l.f. x 2/3 423 b.f. x $1.3	54.99		
	Labor--423 x $.075		31.72	86.71
7	Ceiling Framing: Top plate (2 x 6)-- 130 s.f. x $.18	23.40		
	Labor		10.00	33.40
	Joists, ceiling (2 x 6)--33 x .75 = 24.75 + 4 = 29 x (28 + 2) 30 = 870 s.f. x $.13	113.10		
	Labor--870 x $.10		87.00	200.10
	Bridging (1 x 3)--33 x $1.34 = 44.22 l.f. x 2 = 88.44 x 2 = 177 l.f. x $.04	7.08		
	Labor--177 x $.06		10.62	17.70
	Rough & finish not otherwise included	110.00		110.00

168

8	Roof Framing:			
	Bolts (1/2" x 6")--130			
	÷ 4 32 x $.15	4.80		
	Labor--32 x $.06		1.92	6.72
	Top plate (2 x4)--94			
	x 2 x 2/3 126 b.f.			
	x $.13	16.38		
	Labor--126 x $.10		12.60	28.98
	Facia (1 x 6)--80 1.f.			
	x 1/2 40 x 2 80 x			
	$.19	15.20		
	Labor--80 x $.13		10.40	25.60
	Boxed cornice--84 x			
	1.5 = 126 b.f. x $.14	17.64		
	Labor--126 x $.10		12.60	30.24
9	Roofing:			
	Rafter (2 x 6)--1040			
	b.f. x $.13	135.20		
	Labor--1040 x $.10		104.00	239.20
	Purlins (2 x 4)--35'			
	x 2 = 70 x 2/3' = 47			
	b.f. x $.14	6.58		
	Labor--47 x $.12		5.64	12.22
	Bracing (2 x 4's)--			
	4' o.c. 35 ÷ 4 = 8.6			
	x 2 = 17.2 x 6 = 103			
	b.f. x $.13	13.39		
	Labor--103 x $.12		12.36	25.75
	Roof decking (1 x 6			
	or 1 x 8)--35' x 37			
	1295 b.f. 1295 +			
	(waste) 333 = 1628			
	x $.13	211.64		
	Labor--1628 x .10		162.80	374.44
	Roofing (15# felt 2			
	layers T.T.)--1628			
	x $.02	32.56		
	Labor--1628 x $.015		24.42	56.98
	210# Roofing--13.33			
	squares x $9.25	123.30		
	Labor--13.33 squares			
	x $5.75		76.65	199.15
	Eave drip (36.4 x 2)			
	--73 x 10% = 7 + 73			
	80 1.f. x $.075	6.00		
	Labor--80 x $.025		2.00	8.00
10	Gutters and Downspouts (None)			
11	Windows:			
	Windows--11 x			
	$33.00	330.00		
	Labor--11 x $6.00		66.00	396.00
12	Entr. & Ext. Detail:			
	Doors, outside (1			
	jalousie 1 comb.)--			
	2 x $43.50	87.00		
	Labor--2 x $10.00		20.00	107.00
	Doors, screen--2 x			
	$12.00	24.00		
	Labor--2 x $5.00		10.00	34.00
	Louvres--2 x $9.50	19.00		
	Labor--2 x $2.00		4.00	23.00
13	Insulation 2" rock			
	wool	50.00	30.00	80.00
14	Stairs (None)			

#		Material	Labor	Total
15	Lath and Plaster: Furring strips (1 x 2 treated 130 x 8)-- 1040 l.f. x $.07	72.80		
	Labor--1040 x $.03		31.20	104.00
	Plastering (lath and plaster)--Material --386 sq. yds. x 1.20	463.20		
	Labor--386 sq, yds. x $.75		289.50	952.70
16	Finish Flooring Terrazzo	350.00	450.00	800.00
17	Tile and Resilient Floor (None)			
18	Interior Door and Trim: Exterior walls Baseboard--130 l.f. x $.13	16.90		
	Labor--130 x $.08		10.40	27.30
	Moulding--130 l.f. x $.05	6.50		
	Labor--130 l.f. x $.03		3.90	10.40
	Interior partitions Baseboard--92 l.f. x 2 = 184 + 18 (waste) 202 x $.13	26.26		
	Labor--303 x $.05		15.15	41.41
	Shoe mould--202 x $.05	10.10		
	Labor--202 x $.03		6.06	16.16
	Interior doors--10 x $45.00	450.00		
	Labor--10 x $12.50		125.00	575.00
	Weatherstripping (2 outside doors)-- 2 x $2.00	4.00		
	Labor--2 @ $3.50		7.00	11.00
19	Cabinet Work: 8' Base--finished with formica top & splash @ $18.00	144.00		
	Labor--8 x $5.40		43.20	187.20
	Wall cabinets--12 lin. ft. -- Labor & material @ $9.00			108.00
	Medicine cabinet	25.00	5.00	30.00
	Shelves and rods	15.00	15.00	30.00
20	Painting and Decorating: 2 Coats undercoat and 1 coat enamel-- material 3556 sq. ft. @ $.05	177.80		
	Labor--3556 sq, ft. @ $.06		213.36	391.16
	11 Windows @ $9.00			99.00
	Exterior walls and gable			92.00
21	Plumbing: Plumbing w/40 gallon HWH, 5 yr. guaranty	400.00		
	Labor		418.00	818.00
22	Heating:			750.00

170

```
23        Electric:
          Electrical--37 outlets
          x $6.00 (L & M)                             222.00
          Service--100 amp.      50.00
          Labor                            60.00      110.00
          Range and heater
          wiring                 20.00     35.00       55.00
          Fixtures                                     85.00

             Total Labor and Material Cost      $9,860.20
             Add:    Field overhead @ 3%           295.81

                                               $10,156.01

                                               $10,156.01
          Contractor overhead & profit @ 12%      1,218.72

             Total Construction Cost - New      $11,374.73

          Rounded to:   $11,400.00


          Cost per square foot of building       $    11.40
```

produces fairly accurate results. The application, however, is still too time-consuming and costly to be recommended for use by the average appraiser. In fact it would take thoroughly trained cost estimators, who are conversant with the operational details and technology of the building industry, to apply this method with assurance and relative accuracy. The typical appraiser is by necessity, therefore, referred to still simpler and more objective methods of cost calculation.

UNIT-IN-PLACE CONSTRUCTION METHOD

Under this method only costs of structural units installed in place as charged by the various subcontractors or incurred by the general contractor are itemized and summarized. Under this method, for instance, the number of cubic yards of concrete poured is multiplied by the unit cost per yard in place. The same is done for the number of squares of roofing of a given type and grade. Typical unit-in-place costs are as follows:

Asphalt shingle roofing	per square (100 sq. ft.)	$23.50
Plaster in place	per yard (27 cu. ft.)	1.35
Brick veneer wall	per lineal foot	21.50
Parquet finished flooring	per square foot	.85
Ceramic tile wall or floor	per square foot	1.15
Vinyl tile flooring—⅛″	per square foot	.70
Gutter and spouts	per lineal foot	1.35

This method of cost estimating is useful for estimating costs of substitute materials, and for estimating construction additions or deletions from

Construction Cost Estimate
Under
The Subcontractor's or Quantity Survey Method
For A Single Family Residence
Containing 1,000 Square Feet of
Building Area

Building Description: Two bedroom, living room, kitchen and bath,
concrete block (painted) residential structure.   Interior walls of frame
and plaster.   Asphalt shingled roof with 4" in 12" pitch over 2" rock wool
ceiling insulation.   Concrete subflooring and terrazzo finished flooring.
Aluminum double hung windows.   Equipped with 40 gallon automatic
electric water heater, built-in electric stove and oven and 85,000 B.T.U.
oil fired, forced air central heating system.   Construction methods and
specifications to meet F.H.A. minimum property standards for one and
two living units.

Cost Breakdown

Spec'n. No.	Type of Construction	Material	Labor	Total
	Architect's fee			
	Permits and utility connections			$ 100
	Site clearing			105
	Excavation			60
	Foundation			177
	Chimney-masonry			215
	Exterior walls			115
	Sub-flooring			950
	Framing, carpentry			492
	Roofing			1,780
	Windows and doors			262
	Lath and plaster			560
	Finished flooring			1,057
	Cabinet work			800
	Insulation			355
	Painting			80
	Plumbing			582
	Heating			818
	Electrical			750
	Fixtures			387
	Insurance			85
	Miscellaneous			30
	Field overhead -- 3%			100
	Contractor's overhead & profit			296
	Total			$11,375

Rounded to $11,400

Cost per square foot of building $11.40

given plans and specifications. Because of the difficulty to reduce accurately carpentry and finishing work to a unit basis, this method of cost estimating is only infrequently employed by builders and developers and is not recommended as a valuation tool for real estate appraisers.

THE COMPARATIVE MARKET METHOD OF COST ESTIMATING

The comparative square- or cubic-foot method is used almost exclusively by appraisers and by builders and architects when cost estimates must be had speedily. Under this method, the applicable unit cost per square or cubic foot of a building is derived by dividing the total building costs of similar structures recently completed by the volume of square or cubic feet contained within the exterior wall dimension of the building's structural surfaces—including attics, dormers, basements, and subfloor areas. Where the building to be costed is similar in size, design, quality, and quantity of construction of buildings completed within a three- to six-month period, the results obtained should prove quite accurate. The unit cost thus obtained is then multiplied by the total number of square- or cubic-foot space area, and to this total is added a percentage for architect's fees and builder's overhead and profit.

The principal difficulty and inaccuracy of the comparative costing method is that—except for large developments—no two buildings are exactly alike in kind and quality of construction; and unless adjustments are made to reflect these differences, the margin of possible error may prove too great to make the estimate reliable as a guide to building costs. In order to minimize errors and to perfect this costing method, square-foot or cubic-foot costs are calculated for a *standard* or *base* house of a given size, exclusive of land costs, and adjustments are then made for differences in size, perimeter, or shape of building as well as for quality and quantity of features such as extra bathrooms, special flooring, fixtures, equipment, and other exceptional improvements. The application of the modified comparative method of cost estimating is demonstrated below.

ESTIMATING THE STANDARD OR BASE HOUSE

Since a comparison with anything in any field is best attained if a reliable standard of measure is available, a base house typical for a given geographic area is selected and priced under the quantity survey or unit-in-place method by competent, reliable, and active builders. Generally specifications complying with F.H.A. minimum property standards are set up and given to at least two, preferably three, community builders for detailed cost estimating. The several estimates are then analyzed, checked, and correlated into one composite estimate representative of local building costs for the selected base house. The 1,000-square-foot house as described and estimated on pages 167 to 171 is used for purposes of illustration. Attention is called to the fact that items subject to frequent variations, such as the size of a house, its perimeter shape, special type or kind of flooring, paneled walls, extra equipment, built-in cabinets, air conditioning, to name a few, must be separately priced and added to the basic unit cost at the time when adjustments are made to account for differences between the base or standard house and the subject house under cost study. This is similar to the practice of pricing automobiles where the costs of extras are added to the factory price of a "standard" model as quoted f.o.b. at the factory location.

As shown on page 171 the total cost of the described standard or base house in a given geographic area is $11,400 inclusive of contractor's overhead and profit caluculated at the rate of 12 percent. This amount, divided by the size of the base house of 1,000 square feet, equals a market unit cost of $11.40 per square foot. The next step is to adjust the unit cost of the base house to a unit cost applicable to a specific or subject house under cost study.

Variations in unit cost most frequently encountered are caused by the following:

1. Differences in community construction costs and standards.
2. Differences in building size.
3. Quality of design and construction.
4. Added construction cost of built-in features.
5. Built-in fixtures and appliances.

Unit costs per square foot or cubic foot of building construction are generally available for metropolitan areas as well as for principal cities with populations of 100,000 persons and over from individual sources or commercial cost valuation services. For communities of lesser size, or where unit-building cost quotations are unavailable, it is necessary to adjust the best available and most reliable cost index for a given community in accordance with cost differentials known to exist between it and the community in which the subject property is located. Cost variations, as a rule, are ascribable to differences in wage rates, costs of locally delivered materials, local construction standards, and labor practices enforced in given areas. Assuming a cost average of 1.00 for the United States as a whole, location cost differentials for selected cities have been calculated by the Dow Valuation Service as follows: [1]

---

[1] *Dow Building Cost Calculator and Valuation Guide,* Edition No. 153A (New York, N. Y.: Copyright 1968, by F. W. Dodge Corporation).

Metropolitan Area	Local Cost Modifier
Atlantic City, N. J.	1.505
Augusta, Me.	1.285
Baltimore, Md.	1.323
Baton Rouge, La.	1.303
Bismarck, N. D.	1.390
Boston, Mass.	1.422
Chicago, Ill.	1.501
Cleveland, Ohio	1.649
Dayton, Ohio	1.492
Denver, Colo.	1.374
Detroit, Mich.	1.542
Flint, Mich.	1.559
Fort Worth, Tex.	1.429
Greenville, S. C.	1.049
Hartford, Conn.	1.479
Indianapolis, Ind.	1.487
Jacksonville, Fla.	1.259
Lansing, Mich.	1.526
Las Vegas, Nev.	1.538
Milwaukee, Wisc.	1.510
Minneapolis, Minn.	1.477
Montreal, Quebec	1.295
New Orleans, La.	1.309
New York, N. Y.	1.674
Oklahoma City Okla.	1.255
Omaha, Nebr.	1.419
Philadelphia, Pa.	1.447
Pittsburgh, Pa.	1.541
Portland, Me.	1.262
Portland, Ore.	1.315
Quebec, Quebec	1.183
Raleigh, N. C.	1.060
Richmond, Va.	1.139

ESTIMATING THE SUBJECT HOUSE

As a prerequisite to the application of the cost approach it is essential that an accurate and detailed word picture of the building and related improvements under value study be obtained. Without full and firsthand knowledge of building construction features it is not possible to compare effectively the subject house with the standard house, and to adjust applicable construction unit costs to reflect the differences. To illustrate the application of the comparative market method of cost estimating where the square foot of building volume is accepted as a unit of construction cost, it is assumed that the property under appraisal consists of a building site 100 feet by 125 feet valued by comparison at $4,000, and that the building improvements (new) are described as follows:

Single-story masonry residence containing 3 bedrooms, 2 tiled baths, living room, kitchen-dining room combination and hall area. Exterior walls are of concrete block 4" x 8" x 16" painted. Interior walls are of frame and plaster. Built-up 5-ply roof with 1-in-12 pitch. Terrazzo flooring with concrete slab subflooring. Ceiling is insulated with 2" rock wool fibers. Both bathrooms have ceramic floor tiling and full tiling around the walls. Windows are of aluminum frame and awning type over tile window stools. There is an attached patio, a carport and utility-storage area. Equipment includes a 64,000 B.T.U. oil-fired G.E. central heating system, a 1000-watt wall heater in master bedroom, a 52-gallon automatic electric water heater, a 10" kitchen exhaust fan, a garbage disposal unit and Venetian blinds throughout. The one-line floor plan diagram discloses room layouts and perimeter measures of the subject house as follows:

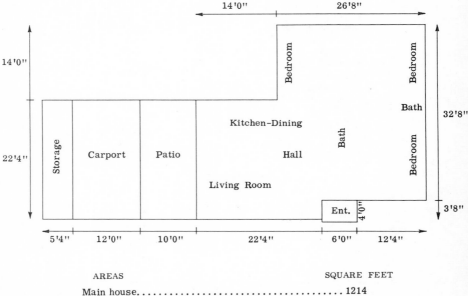

AREAS	SQUARE FEET
Main house	1214
Carport	268
Patio	224
Entrance	24
Utility	119

FIGURE 12.1

FLOOR PLAN

Based on the above building data, property value under the market comparison cost approach is derived in the following manner:

COST APPROACH TO VALUE

Base cost per sq. ft. of standard (1,000 sq. ft.) house =	$11.40
Base cost of subject house (1,214 sq. ft.) = $11.40 x .95 [2] =	10.83
Adjustment for cost variation due to location =	None

[2] See page 180 for variations in base costs due to building size.

Cost Adjustments for Variation from Standard Construction

Item	Amount
Built-up roof	$ 125.00
Extra bathroom with full tiling	675.00
Perimeter wall adjustment 7 ft. @ $13.80	96.60
Sliding glass doors (2)	180.00
Extra windows 2 @ $55.00	110.00
Extra interior door 2 @ $57.50	115.00
Garbage disposal	90.00
Kitchen fan 10″	80.00
Bathroom fan 8″	60.00
1,000-watt bath wall heater	115.00
Built-in bookcase	200.00
Built-in vanity	110.00
Double kitchen sink	45.00
Washing machine connections	125.00
Wind wall 4 ft. @ $5.50	22.00
Extra kitchen cabinets and counter	120.00
Extra closet	80.00
Gutters & spouts	40.00
Exterior construction details & finishes	225.00
Total Extras	$2,613.60
Cost of extras per sq. ft. = $2,613.60 ÷ 1214 =	$ 2.15
Adjusted square foot cost—subject house	12.98

Cost Calculations

Cost of:	Main house	1,214 sq. ft. @ $12.98 =	15,758
	Carport	268 sq. ft. @ $ 4.00 =	1,072
	Patio	224 sq. ft. @ $ 2.75 =	616
	Entrance	24 sq. ft. @ $ 6.00 =	144
	Utility	119 sq. ft. @ $ 5.50 =	655
	Total costs of improvements		$18,245
Add:	Cost of Venetian blinds		200
	Value of land—by comparison		4,000
	Landscaping		250
	Walks and driveway		225
	Total value via cost approach		$22,920
	Rounded to: $23,000		

At the end of this chapter, the reader will find a list of typical unit costs for construction items which are often added as extras to increase the utility of a structure.[3] For items not listed, the appraiser should contact a building contractor or a building supply agency to obtain needed cost data.

---

[3] All cost data are provided to illustrate application of the cost approach to value. In practice the appraiser must consult applicable local builder's services or employ current national building cost references and adjust same to reflect local cost variations.

Attention is called also to the necessity of adjusting the base cost per square foot of a building to account for variations in building size. Since certain basic construction costs are relatively inelastic (plumbing, electrical equipment, and bathroom and kitchen facilities) the principle of decreasing unit cost is operative with an increase in building size. The percentage relationship of building size to building unit costs is shown on page 180. On the same page information is also given as to the number of perimeter feet of exterior walls contained in typical houses of varying building size. The base or standard house, as a rule, is slightly rectangular in shape. Where architectural design calls for an elongated L-type or a ranch-type residence, the extra number of feet of perimeter wall must be reflected in the cost estimate. To illustrate: A structure 20 feet by 20 feet and a structure 40 feet by 10 feet both contain 400 square feet of building area. However, the latter requires 100 feet of perimeter wall as compared with 80 feet of perimeter wall of the former. The cost of the perimeter wall per lineal foot (inclusive of exterior and interior wall finishes) varies as shown on page 181 from $13.80 to $22.80, depending on the type of construction as noted.

The comparative building cost method, as demonstrated, provides a speedy and fairly accurate means for obtaining value estimates for appraisal purposes. Where variations in ceiling heights or building practices necessitate cost quotations on a cubic-foot rather than a square-foot basis, this costing method can be converted by adding the third, or height, dimension and dividing total building costs by the number of cubic-foot units contained in the base house.

With experience and years of appraisal practice, an ever-expanding file of building cost material and construction data can be accumulated. This, as part of the overall appraisal plant, should prove a valuable aid in perfecting appraisal cost estimates. It is important, of course, to keep building construction costs up to date. It is suggested that a check of overall labor and material costs and practices be made at least every six months, or preferably every three months.

From the replacement or reproduction cost estimate, as is the case with existing structures, a deduction must be made for accrued depreciation caused by age, wear, tear and action of the elements. For a detailed study of the causes of depreciation, and the various methods in use for estimating and accounting purposes, the reader is referred to Chapter 13.

The format of the cost approach for existing buildings is recommended as outlined on page 179.

COMMERCIAL COST SERVICES

The cost approach, as a measure of value, becomes increasingly tenuous as the size and age of a structure increases. In fact the cost approach is

Replacement Cost New – all building improvements
  inclusive of all direct and indirect costs $_____

Less: Accrued Depreciation (see Schedule)

  1. Deferred maintenance $_____
  2. Reserve for replacement
      of major units – roof,
      heating, etc.   _____
  3. Incurable loss due to
      age of structure   _____
  4. Functional obsolescence,
      curable   _____
  5. Functional obsolescence,
      incurable   _____
  6. Economic obsolescence   _____

      Total Accrued Depreciation $_____
  Depreciated replacement cost   _____

  Add Land Value – by comparison   _____
      Landscaping   _____
      Walks and drive   _____
      Other land improvements
        (fences, etc.)   _____

Total Value via Cost Approach $_____

the least reliable measure of market value, and is recommended for use only as an overall check of the reliability of other market measures of value or where the cost approach—as is the case with fire insurance or with special purpose properties—represents the principal if not the only measure of value.

No appraiser, unless he also is a trained cost specialist, a contract builder, or a construction engineer, is capable to estimate with any degree of accuracy the costs of proposed construction or the replacement costs of existing structures where the same are of complex commercial, industrial, or special purpose use and architectural design. In such cases, it is best for an appraiser to rely on comparative cost studies made available on a periodic updated subscription basis by commercial cost services such as the F. W. Dodge *Dow Building Cost Calculator and Valuation Guide,* published by the McGraw-Hill Information Systems Company at 330 West 42 Street, New York City, or the *Boeckh Building Valuation Manual,* published by the American Appraisal Company at 525 East Michigan Street, Milwaukee, Wisconsin. In these and other more regionally or localized cost services information is published for typical commercial, industrial and commercial buildings as follows:

  Apartments.
  Hotels, motels, and clubs.

Offices, banks, and lofts.
Stores and shopping centers.
Warehouses.
Garages and service stations.
Theaters.
Educational and public buildings.
Industrial structures.
Hospitals and churches.
Restaurants, bowling alleys, and stadiums.
Other special purpose buildings.

The commercial cost units generally are quoted on a base cost, i.e., cubic-foot basis exclusive of foundation and excavation costs and exclusive of architects' fees and builders' overhead and profit allowances. The latter costs generally average 20 percent of quoted base costs which further must be adjusted to reflect local conditions that vary due to differences in labor, material, sales tax, insurance and finance costs, and building construction regulations.

It is deemed a "must" that every appraiser subscribe to at least one major cost service, and further subscribe to a competent market newsletter or economic business publication that keeps him informed of national and state laws and general market conditions which are bound to have an impact on building construction costs.

Building cost services, at best, serve as a guide to the establishment of replacement costs when the building is in "new" condition. The difficult task of estimating accrued depreciation remains a valuation weakness. For a more detailed study of the causes and measures of accrued depreciation, the reader is referred to Chapter 13.

VARIATION IN BASE UNIT COST AND PERIMETER WALL DIMENSIONS
RESULTING FROM CHANGES IN BUILDING SIZE

Building Size Square Feet	Percentage of Base Cost	Exterior Walls Perimeter Feet
700	115	105
750	110	109
800	108	113
850	106	117
900	104	121
950	102	125
1,000	100	130
1,050	99	134
1,100	97	138
1,150	96	142
1,200	95	147
1,250	94	151
1,300	93	155

1,350	92	159
1,400	91	163
1,450	90	167
1,500	89.5	171
1,550	89	175
1,600	88.5	180
1,650	88	184
1,700	87.5	188
1,800	86.5	197
1,900	85.5	205
2,000	85	213

Note 1: For buildings in excess of 2,000 square feet, use maximum adjustment of 85 percent of cost of standard house.

Note 2: For quality workmanship, add 5 to 10 percent to final cost estimate. For poor workmanship, subtract 5 percent or more as justified.

ILLUSTRATIVE COST VARIATIONS CAUSED BY DIFFERENCES IN CONSTRUCTION FEATURES

Exterior Construction	*Labor and Material Per Sq. Ft.*
Frame (wood) siding	$ .15
Brick veneer	1.10
Brick-solid	1.30
Concrete Block 4″ x 8″ x 16″	.20

Wall Perimeter—Complete exterior and interior finish	*Per Lin. Ft.*
Concrete block—slab floor	$13.80
Concrete block—suspended floor	15.60
Frame—slab floor	16.20
Frame—suspended floor	17.40
Brick veneer—slab floor	19.80
Brick veneer—suspended floor	21.60
Brick solid—slab floor	21.00
Brick solid—suspended floor	22.80

Roof Construction	*Per Sq. Ft.*
Built-up roof (5 ply)	$ .12
Hip roof	.13
Boxed eaves—each ft. over 1st ft.	.10
Overhang—each ft. over 1st ft.	.12
Roof pitch—more or less than 4″ in 12″ (per inch of pitch)	.08
Insulation—2″	.10
—3″	.12
—4″	.15

Floor Construction	*Per Sq. Ft.*
Asphalt tile B net floor area	$ .22
C net floor area	.24
D net floor area	.29
Grease-proof	.35

Cork tile 5/16″	.75
Terrazzo—monolithic	.65
Terrazzo—strip	1.00
Parquet floor	.80
Quarry tile	.95
Rubber tile 3/16″	1.30
Rubber tile ⅛″	1.05
Ceramic tile	2.00
Select oak—suspended floor construction	1.10
Vinyl tile 1/16″	.45
Vinyl tile ⅛″	.70

TYPICAL COST VARIATIONS FOR SELECTED CONSTRUCTION FEATURES

Other Improvements

Full tiling in bathroom	$300.00
Tile over tub only	85.00
Tile on floor only	70.00
Tile per sq. ft.	2.25
Fireplace—extra chimney (no mantle facing)	500.00
Extra bath	400.00
Extra ½ bath—including stack	250.00
[4] Extra windows—each	45.00
[4] Extra doors—each	47.50
Tile window stools—each	6.00
Electric outlets—each	6.00
Kitchen exhaust fan 10″	75.00
Sky vent—each	65.00
Mercury switches—each	1.25
Septic tank	175.00
Gutter & downspout	1.25 per lin. ft.
Carport (sealed ceiling)	3.75 per sq. ft.
Garage—concrete block	5.25 per sq. ft.
Screened porch—concrete floor	4.25 per sq. ft.
Screened porch—suspended floor	4.75 per sq. ft.
Open porch	4.00 per sq. ft.
Stoop (4′ x 6′) and storage closet	175.00
Paneled walls—add cost of lumber over and above cost of plaster in place	
Cypress #1	.40 board ft.
Spruce #2	.22 board ft.
Plaster in place	1.35 yd.

[4] Basic 1,000-square-foot house has ten interior doors and eleven windows. Percentage adjustments for size of structure include one additional door and window for each 100-square-foot increase in building size.

READING AND STUDY REFERENCES

1. *Acquisition for Right-of-Way* (Washington, D.C.: American Association of State Highway Officials, 1962), chap. 27.

2. *The Appraisal of Real Estate* (Chicago: American Institute of Real Estate Appraisers, 1967), chaps. 12 and 14.

3. Armstrong, William Y., "Is the Cost Approach Necessary?" *The Appraisal Journal* (January 1963), pp. 71–80.

4. Babcock, Frederick M., *The Valuation of Real Estate* (New York: McGraw-Hill Book Company, Inc., 1932), chap. 31.

5. Boeckh, E. H., "Use of Cost Indexes," *The Review* (July 1953), pp. 19–20.

6. *Dow Building Cost Caluculator and Valuation Guide*, Myron L. Matthews, Manager-Editor (New York: F. W. Dodge Corp., 1961).

7. Kahn, Sanders A., Frederick E. Case, and Alfred Schimmel, *Real Estate Appraisal and Investment* (New York: The Ronald Press Company, 1963), chap. 13.

8. Kinnard, William N., Jr., *An Introduction to Appraising Real Property* (Chicago: Society of Real Estate Appraisers, 1968), chap. 15.

9. Ring, Alfred A., "Cost Pitfalls," *The Review* (May 1956), pp. 3–6.

10. Ring, Alfred A., "What's Behind the Cost Estimate?" *The Residential Appraiser* (December 1956), pp. 6–9.

A loss in value—from any cause—as measured by the difference between replacement cost new of a property in current dollars and the market value of the same property, actual or estimated, is classified as *depreciation*. In fact it is possible that a property may appreciate rather than depreciate, as is the case when abnormal scarcity exacts a market premium for possession or where uniqueness (classification as antique) makes

13 *Depreciation Theory*

and Practice

the property a collector's item. Appreciation may also be apparent rather than real where inflation has diminished the purchasing power of the dollar. Appreciation in fact, however, is the exception rather than the rule and its causes and measures will not be dealt with in this chapter.

In appraisal practice, it is an established maxim that an estimate of value via the cost approach is no more accurate than the underlying estimate of depreciation through which measures of cost are converted into measures of value. The difficulties encountered in obtaining accurate dollar expressions of accrued depreciation are ascribable, generally, to lack of the sound appraisal judgment essential to an evaluation of the causes which contribute to a loss in value of a given property at a specific time and place. Judgment is a subjective mental attitude difficult to teach and which generally must be developed through experience and maturation of thinking. In this chapter, an attempt will be made to outline and discuss the theory underlying the causes of depreciation and to explain and demonstrate the methods most suitable in measuring the resultant losses in value.

DEPRECIATION VERSUS AMORTIZATION

It is the appraiser's task to estimate the amount of accrued depreciation without concern as to whether depreciation reserves have been established to compensate the owner for losses in the quantity and quality of the original investment. It is on this point that recognition should be given to the differences in functions of, and responsibilities assumed by, the accountant versus the appraiser. The accountant, with the aid of effective bookkeeping, traces and records the *history* of dollar expenditures for capital outlays and those spent for maintenance and operation of an enterprise or property. The accountant is principally concerned with *original cost,* and his interest in value (in current dollars) is as a rule incidental and secondary. The appraiser, on the other hand, is principally interested in the *present worth* of future rights to income which flow from the productive use of the subject property. The original or historical cost of the property is data which may be gathered by the appraiser in order to be fully informed, but the importance of such data is secondary, if not negligible, in the valuation process. What someone pays for a property may or may not be equivalent to value. In fact, the property may have been given to the present owner, or purchased at a token price from a friend or a relative.

Once an estimate of value is ascertained and certified to by an appraiser his task, generally, is completed. The accountant may take over from here to check the book value against the economic value reported by the appraiser, and to make or recommend changes in accounting procedure to accelerate or decelerate depreciation reserve provisions.

It would prove less confusing, and contribute to greater clarity of thinking if in practice and in literature all reference to reserve provisions for the recapture of investment capital be classified as *amortization* rather than *depreciation.* The term "future depreciation" is a misnomer. The best that one can do is provide for the recapture of anticipated value losses in accordance with a preselected schedule of capital amortization which at the investment rate of interest will equal in amount the replacement cost of the subject property at the end of its economic life. A schedule of amortization of an investment of $10,000 over an economic investment life of fifty years is illustrated in Appendix 3 pp. 629-630. The cumulative amount of capital recapture, computed at an investment interest rate of 8 percent, represents at the end of a given period of years depreciation as an *amount* or *book depreciation* derived under the annuity or debt amortization method, as will be more fully explained below. Depreciation as an economic *fact* at any given time first necessitates an estimation of value. Thus if we know that the replacement cost new of a residential property is $20,000, and that market sales of like properties in condition "as is" are exchanging for $15,000, then depreciation as a market fact is $5,000 or 25 percent.

It is important to recognize that accrued depreciation is a loss in market value from *all* causes and that this loss, measured in a lump sum, is automatically reflected in the prices which comparative properties sell for in the open market. The same holds true when value is derived under the income approach. Old properties, as a rule, produce less net income than like properties when in new condition. The income from old properties, too, must be capitalized over a shortened remaining economic life. As in the market approach, the difference between the dollar amount as represented by replacement costs new and the value derived by capitalization of income for the property in condition "as is" measures the loss in value (depreciation) from all causes. Thus under the market and income approaches to value the appraiser is freed from the responsibility to measure depreciation independently as a loss in value. The market, through lower prices and reduced rentals or income, automatically reflects the property's diminished utility from all causes be they age, wear, tear, actions of the elements or man-made, functional or economic obsolescence. Only under the cost approach to value is the appraiser compelled to estimate independently and directly the amounts ascribable to the various causes which have lessened value as a result of age, and so on. For this reason the cost approach is deemed the least accurate measure of value. The accuracy of the cost approach in fact, as explained in Chapter 4, is no more reliable than the appraiser's judgment estimates which are basic to an accurate measure of accrued depreciation.

DEPRECIATION THEORY

Depreciation is defined as a *loss in value from any cause*. The principal causes are recognized as follows:

1. Physical deterioration.
2. Functional obsolescence.
3. Economic obsolescence.

The forces within these causes may be further subclassified for purposes of identification as shown below:

Physical Deterioration.
1. Wear and tear through use.
2. Action of the elements (including ravages of storms and extreme temperatures), age, and destruction by termites and other varmints.

3. Structural impairment through neglect, fire, water, explosion, acts of war, and vandalism.

Functional Obsolescence.

1. Faulty design: ceilings too high or too low; improper location of kitchen, bathroom, bedrooms, etc.; waste space; and general disutility arising from poor floor planning.
2. Inadequacy of structural facilities: exterior walls not furred out; ceilings and walls not insulated; inadequate wiring, plumbing, heating, fenestration and other functional deficiencies which limit effective utilization of the property as a whole.
3. Superadequacy of structural facilities: oversized heating or cooling systems; oversized plumbing and electric wiring; and excessive number of closets, bathrooms, and built-in facilities.
4. Outmoded equipment: old-fashioned cast-iron tub and kitchen sink; exposed wiring and plumbing; coal-burning kitchen stove; manual control water heating; etc.

Economic Obsolescence.

1. Neighborhood hazards and nuisances: heavy traffic flow; smoke; dust; noise; offensive odors; or the intrusion of incompatible, inharmonious uses.
2. Change in zoning and highest and best land use classification: lower land uses and less stringent zoning and building regulations impair utility of use and ownership.
3. Infiltration of less desirable neighbors: people create value and lower economic classes generally cause impairment of property values.
4. Over or underimprovement of land: a $20,000 home in a $10,000 neighborhood or a $10,000 home in a $20,000 neighborhood lessen overall property value as a result of violation of prevailing site (land)-to-improvement ratios.
5. Decreasing demand: population shifts; depression; or other economic factors that lessen demand cause economic obsolescence as reflected in lower property values.

ECONOMIC LIFE AND EFFECTIVE AGE VERSUS PHYSICAL LIFE AND CHRONOLOGICAL AGE OF PROPERTY

Since a property, in order to be productive, must produce an income commensurate with dollar investments in land and building improvements over and above the expenditures necessary to operate and maintain the property, it stands to reason that when a property ceases to be productive it may have reached the end of its economic life. A structure thus may conceivably be physically sound but economically dead and constitute a financial burden on the land on which it rests. Experience has demonstrated that more properties are torn down to make room for more economically productive replacements than fall down.

Studies by the National Association of Real Estate Boards have disclosed that the typical economic age of a well-constructed improvement is fifty years. It is true that many buildings reach chronological ages well beyond that age figure; but experience discloses that most buildings at the ripe old age of fifty years must be overhauled, modernized, and generally rejuvenated to warrant their continued existence. Capital improvements generally extend the remaining economic life of a building or, conversely, lower its effective age. Properties, too, with identical chronological age, may differ significantly in their effective age depending on quality of construction, maintenance practice, operational care, and expenditures made for capital improvements or modernization.

To determine the effective age on which calculations of accrued depreciation are based, the appraiser subtracts from the total (typical) economic life for the type of building under value study his estimate of the remaining economic life over which the structure is deemed to be productive. This estimate, as a rule, is derived after careful field inspection and a conclusion of the extent of condition new ascribed to the building improvements. To illustrate: Assuming a total economic life of fifty years, and an estimated remaining economic life of thirty-five years [1] (based on a degree of newness, judged to be 70 percent) the effective age employed in depreciation calculations is fifteen years. This data is shown as follows:

Total (average) economic building life	50 years
Remaining (estimated) economic building life	35 years
Effective age of improvements	15 years

The actual or chronological age of the structure is, of course, of interest to the appraiser. If, for instance, judgment based on field study supports an effective age of fifteen years, but building history discloses a chronological age of thirty years, then evidence should be gathered to support the reason and justification for this difference. In this case, no doubt, structural improvements were added or substantial rehabilitation must have taken place. Chronological age, too, is important in giving effect in depreciation calculations to structural decrepitude resulting from wear and aging of the building's supporting structures, and for estimating the effective age of component building parts such as roof shingles, plumbing, electrical wiring, and heating equipment—which have a limited service life, shorter than the remaining economic life of the property as a whole, and for which

---

[1] Remaining economic life can also be measured by the period over which a competitive net return is anticipated by typical buyers.

a replacement reserve must be established under the category "Physical Deterioration—Deferred Curable" as is demonstrated below.

THE ENGINEERING OR OBSERVED METHOD
FOR MEASURING ACCRUED DEPRECIATION

There are two principal methods of measuring accrued depreciation:

1. The engineering, or observed condition breakdown method.
2. The theoretical, or age-life, method.

The *engineering,* or *observed condition breakdown* method bears a descriptive title. It is so named because (1) the method is frequently used by engineers in structural analysis, and (2) because field inspection and observation are essential in the gathering of depreciation data. The engineering method is an *applied* method that yields informative and accurate results if professionally compiled. Under this method the causes of depreciation are analyzed as follows:

Physical deterioration—curable. Under this heading, based on careful and detailed inspection, a listing is made of all deferred maintenance and repairs necessary to bring the structure into first-class operating order. The test of curability is based on 1. necesity to cure defects to provide for efficient (economical) operation, and 2. the cost to cure relative to value added or the increase in operating net income for the property as a whole. Provision is also made for depreciation reserves necessary to cover anticipated expenditures for capital items and major units of maintenance which must be replaced or refurbished periodically. The latter items include heating, roofing, plumbing, electrical wiring, and periodic painting and refinishing of exterior and interior surfaces. Prices for maintenance and repair work need to be obtained from service men and subcontractors who typically engage in this type of work. For illustration of this and other sections of the observed depreciation schedules, see page 193.

Physical deterioration—incurable. Under this part of the depreciation schedule, an attempt is made to measure the accrued loss in dollars due to wear and tear of long-lived structural load-bearing parts of the building improvements. Since the supporting parts of a structure such as footings, foundations, and supporting walls and partitions are economically as well as mechanically incurable (without tearing the building down) the appraiser must establish a pro rata estimate of the expired portions of the various substructures in relation to their total unit replacement cost—in place. This can be accomplished by one of two alternate suggested methods:

1. The direct component value method, or
2. The liability to replace method.

Under the direct component value method, the appraiser applies the estimated accrued percentage loss of the substructural component parts to the replacement cost estimate of such parts as follows:

Component—Structural Parts	Replacement Cost
Excavation	$ 400
Footings	800
Walls	3,300
Partitions	1,200
Roof construction	700
Beams and joints	950
Piers	220
Total	$7,570
Add: 8% Architectural costs	606
12% Overhead and profit	908
Total Components Replacement Costs	$9,084
Estimated observed incurable physical depreciation 15% [1]	$1,363

[1] Based on ratio of chronological age to total effective life-span of building improvements.

The "liability to replace" method measures directly the economic impact caused by increasing effective age or, conversely, diminishing remaining economic life. Suppose a structure has a total economic life of fifty years when in new condition, and at the time of appraisal has an estimated remaining economic life of thirty-five years. The liability to replace the property which was fifty years removed when improvements were new is now only thirty-five years removed as a result of the increased effective age. The effective liability to replace varies, of course, with prevailing interest rates at which similar properties are purchased. Based on an investment rate of 7 percent, the present worth of an income stream which was 100 percent at the time the property had an economic life of fifty years stands at 93.82 percent when remaining economic life is reduced to thirty-five years. Conversely, the liability to replace has advanced from zero percent on date when the property was new to 6.18 percent (100%— 93.82%) as a result of an effective age of fifteen years. This percentage loss was derived as follows:

Present worth factor of $1.00 at 7% [1] for 50 years	=	13.801
Present worth factor of $1.00 at 7% for 35 years	=	12.948
Liability to replace factor—difference		.853

Liability percentage loss equals .853 divided by original 50
year value factor of 13.801 $=$ .0618 or 6.18%

(1) The choice of the correct or applicable rate of interest to measure the liability to replace is critical and care must be taken to reflect market conditions and investors market actions.

If the replacement cost new of the building improvements is $18,500, then the liability to replace is 6.18 percent of $18,500 or $1,143. (See "Demonstration Schedule for Measuring Accrued Depreciation" on page 193.) A table indicating percentage losses due to incurable physical deterioration as measured by effective building age for interest rates of 7 to 12 percent, inclusive, under the liability to replace method and for economic lives of five to fifty years at five-year intervals is given in Appendix 3 pages 620-628.

As demonstrated, the direct component value method of measuring accrued physical deterioration—incurable and the liability to replace methods can be effectively applied as measures of physical-incurable depreciation.[2] The liability to replace method, however, will be applied whenever the cost approach to value is demonstrated in this and following chapters. A diagram showing progressive increases in the liability to replace physical improvements as a result of increasing effective age over an economic life of fifty years at 7 percent interest is shown below.

The liability-to-replace method as demonstrated above is applied to replacement cost new and presumes that the improvements, except for their effective age, are inefficient operating conditions. Hence, any value loss caused by deferred maintenance or by functional or economic obsolescence must be cured or reflected as a value loss in the schedule of accrued depreciation.

Functional obsolescence—curable. Under this heading, the appraiser lists recommended modernization and improvements which are essential and economically justified (or feasible) and which would be found in a new and comparable building. Into this category generally fall expenditures for modernization of bathrooms, kitchen, insulation, central heating, additional closets, and other built-in fixtures. Whether such improvements are warranted and thus curable depends on market demand and on compliance with the principle of contribution. Cost estimates to cure items subject to modernization are obtained from building contractors or subcontractors who specialize in the areas of construction involved. Care must be taken

---

[2] Whichever mechanical process is employed for measuring incurable physical deterioration, great care must be taken in the selection (estimation) of the total as well as of the remaining economic life of the improvements that are under value study.

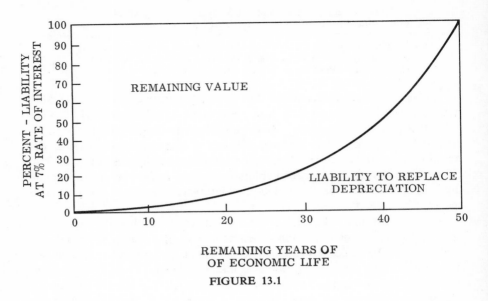

REMAINING YEARS OF
OF ECONOMIC LIFE

FIGURE 13.1

not to duplicate estimated outlays. If, for instance, it is considered that the bathroom and kitchen are subject to modernization, and the cost of painting and decorating of these rooms is included in the modernization estimate, then this expenditure must be excluded from items covered under physical deterioration—curable under which category repainting of the entire structure may have been called for.

Functional obsolescence—incurable. This item of the depreciation schedule rests heavily on the application of sound appraisal judgment. An attempt is made here to reflect the sales resistance encountered from typical buyers as a result of flaws deemed economically incurable such as poor floor planning, lack of privacy, or low ceilings. This sales resistance is generally measured in rounded dollars—$100, $500, $1,000, etc.—or as a percentage of total replacement costs new—1 percent, 5 percent, 10 percent, and so on.

Economic obsolescence—incurable. Losses resulting from economic obsolescence are always caused by forces outside of the structure and within the immediate or market environment of the property. Since the typical property owner cannot control these exterior economic forces, the resultant losses are classified as "incurable." The economic loss ascribable to the subject location, as compared with an ideal, like a neighborhood free from such environmental hazards or nuisances, is determined by capitalizing the actual or estimated rental or income loss through the use of a rent multiplier for residential buildings (see Chapter 10) or through the use of the capitalization process for income-producing properties as explained in Chapter 18. Since the schedule of depreciation should aggregate losses ascribable only to the building improvements, care must be taken to exclude losses attributable to the land. This is accomplished by multiplying the capitalized income loss (depreciation) resulting from economic forces by the typical ratio that building improvements bear to the value of the property as a whole, including the land. To do otherwise would penalize the land twice—once here and again under the market comparison approach to land value, under which the environmental hazard or nuisance would also be reflected. For application of the depreciation procedure to reflect economic obsolescence, see the demonstration schedule below:

DEMONSTRATION SCHEDULE OF THE OBSERVED METHOD
FOR MEASURING ACCRUED DEPRECIATION

Building statistics based on field observation indicate the following:

Effective age	15 years	
Remaining economic life	35 years	
Replacement cost—new	$18,500	

Physical Deterioration:

Curable:

Deferred Maintenance:

Exterior painting	$ 300	
Repair porch screening	40	
Paint kitchen, bath and hall	120	
Scrape and refinish floors	135	
Replace linoleum in kitchen	80	
Total deferred maintenance		$ 675

Reserve for Replacement:

Roof shingles 20% of $350	70	
Interior painting 40% of $250	100	
Heating unit 40% of $375	150	
Plumbing & wiring 20% of $600	120	
Total reserves for replacement		440

Incurable:

Liability to Replace, based on diminished utility and caused by effective age of 15 years, at 7% rate of interest

Present worth factor 50 years	=	13.801
Present worth factor 35 years	=	12.948

Liability Factor   =   .853

Incurable Loss:
  .853 ÷ 13.801 = .0618 or
  6.18% of $18,500   =   1,143

Total physical deterioration $2,258

Functional Obsolescence:

Curable:

  Modernize bathroom (exclusive of painting) $ 220
  Insulate ceiling   115

     Total functional—curable $ 335

Incurable:

  Sales resistance due to low 7.5 foot ceilings
  and poor floor plan (lack of privacy in
  bedroom areas) 10% of cost to replace.
    Total functional—incurable   1,850
      Total functional obsolescence $2,185

Economic Obsolescence:

Incurable:

  Rental loss due to heavy traffic and road
  hazards and noise $15 per month. $15
  times monthly rent multiplied for area =
  $15 × 135 = $2,025.

  Ratio of land value to property value is
  1:6. Loss of rental value attributable to
  building is 5/6 of $2,025 or   1,687

    Total estimate of accrued depreciation $6,130

    Percent accrued depreciation
    $6,130 ÷ 18,500 =   33.13

Value via Cost Approach:

  Estimated replacement cost new (buildings) $18,500
  Less accrued depreciation   6,130

  Depreciated replacement cost $12,370

  Add: Land value by market comparison   3,000
      Walks and driveway   100
      Landscaping   150

    Total value via cost approach $15,620

      Rounded to $15,600

THEORETICAL METHODS FOR MEASURING
ACCRUED DEPRECIATION

The *theoretical* methods, although recommended for use by appraisers as a check on the accuracy and reasonableness of the estimate derived through use of the observed method, were in fact developed for accounting and bookkeeping use as a guide to consistent periodic write-offs of property investments for business and income tax purposes. The theoretical methods are based on the *age-life* property concept under which depreciation is measured by the ratio which effective age bears to the total estimated economic life of the property. There are many theoretical depreciation methods in vogue at the present time, each yielding different results, and some more than double the amount derived by others. If the theoretical measure of depreciation is given principal weight by an appraiser, it is his professional responsibility to select that method which best reflects the age-life experience of comparable properties and is compatible with market actions of typical buyers and investors who bid for like properties in the open market. The theoretical depreciation methods to be explained below are known as follows:

1. The straight line method.
2. The years digit method.
3. The equal percentage method.
4. The sinking fund method.
5. The annuity method.

The straight line method. This, currently, is the most widely used method to account for accrued depreciation. The popularity of this method stems from the simplicity of application and the ready acceptance of it by the Internal Revenue Bureau for income tax determination. To derive depreciation under the straight line method, all that is necessary is to estimate the annual rate of depreciation by dividing the total economic age of the property into 100 percent (of value). The resultant annual rate is then multiplied by the effective age to give the accrued rate, or percent, of depreciation. By multiplying the percent of depreciation thus obtained by the replacement cost new of the building improvements, the total dollar amount of accrued depreciation is derived. To illustrate: Assuming an effective age of twenty years, a total economic life of fifty years, and a replacement cost new of $20,000, the amount of accrued depreciation under the straight line method is:

1. 100% divided by 50 (total economic life) = 2% per year.
2. 2% (per yr.) times 20 (effective age) = 40% accrued depreciation.

3. 40% (depreciation) times $20,000 (replacement cost new) = $8,000 accrued depreciation.

The straight line method, although excellent for accounting and income tax purposes, should be used with caution by the professional appraiser. This method is recommended for use in measuring loss in value due to age of short-lived items such as refrigerators, stoves, heating equipment, or for establishing reserves to replace such items when due. For the property as a whole, however, the straight line method is *not* recommended for it ignores the important function of interest (cost of money) which funds—whether set aside or not—should earn, actual or by imputation, as a result of the passage of time. To ignore interest is to ignore the principle of present worth (discounting) on which the concept of value by definition and in economic analysis does rest. The loss in value under the straight line method may be shown diagrammatically, as in Figure 13.2.

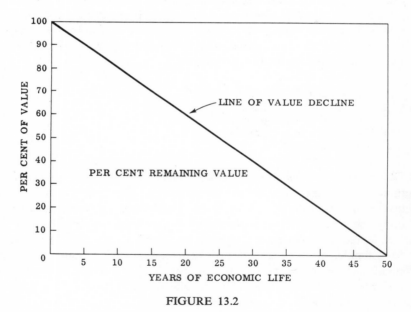

FIGURE 13.2

Value Decline Under the Straight Line Method of Depreciation Over an Economic Life of Fifty Years

The years digit method. This method is a variation of the straight line method. The difference being that instead of giving equal weight to each passing year, a property is considered to be depreciating in accordance with the number of digits contained within the elapsed years of age as compared with the total aggregate number of digit years ascribed to the property when in new condition. To illustrate: The digit years contained in a property with an economic life of fifty years equal $1+2+3+4+5+6+\ldots.50 = 1,275$. If the remaining economic life is thirty years, then the year digits remaining equal $1+2+3+4+\ldots30 = 465$. The digit years applied as depreciation equal 1,275 minus 465, or 810 and the percent accrued depreciation equals 810 divided by $1,275 = 63.5$ percent. This method ascribes heavy depreciation during the initial years of property age (or, conversely, very little depreciation if used inversely as a years digit loss for the first twenty years) and steadily declining depreciation amounts throughout the property's remaining service life. The years digit method is not realistic as a factual measure of accrued depreciation, and is not recommended for use by professional appraisers. For those wishing to use it, a shortcut formula $\left(\dfrac{a+1}{2} \times n\right)$ is offered to enable rapid computation of digit years. In this formula a equals the first (year) number, 1 the last (year)

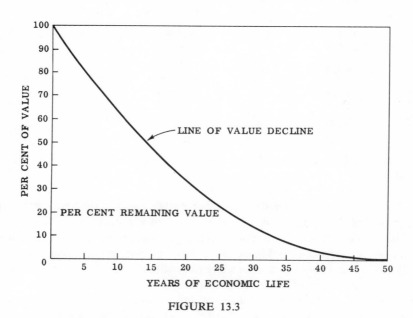

FIGURE 13.3

VALUE DECLINE UNDER THE YEARS DIGIT METHOD OF DEPRECIATION
OVER AN ECONOMIC LIFE OF FIFTY YEARS

number, and n the total number of years over which digit years are to be accumulated. Thus total digits for fifty years equal $\dfrac{1+50}{2} \times 50 = 1,275$.

Digits for thirty years equal $\dfrac{1 + 30}{2} \times 30 = 465.$

The equal percentage method. Whereas under the straight line method depreciation is assumed to occur in equal amounts throughout the economic life of a property (thus constituting increasing annual percentage losses in relation to remaining value), under the *equal percentage* method each year's remaining value forms the base to which a selected constant percentage is applied to obtain the declining amounts of accrued depreciation. To illustrate: Assuming a constant rate of depreciation of 3 percent per year, and a building value of $20,000, depreciation losses during the first ten years of building life would be derived as follows:

SCHEDULE OF DEPRECIATION OF AN INVESTMENT OF $20,000 UNDER THE EQUAL PERCENTAGE METHOD AT 3 PERCENT PER ANNUM OVER THE FIRST TEN YEARS OF AN INVESTMENT LIFE OF FIFTY YEARS

Year	Value Beg. of Year	3 Percent Depreciation(1)	Value End of Year	Accrued Depreciation Amount	Accrued Depreciation Percent
1	$20,000	$600	$19,400	$ 600	3.0
2	19,400	582	18,818	1,182	5.9
3	18,818	565	18,253	1,747	8.7
4	18,253	548	17,705	2,295	11.5
5	17,705	531	17,174	2,826	14.1
6	17,174	515	16,659	3,341	16.7
7	16,659	500	16,159	3,841	19.2
8	16,159	485	15,674	4,326	21.6
9	15,674	470	15,204	4,796	24.0
10	15,204	456	14,748	5,252	26.2

(1) Amounts obtained by multiplying value at beginning of each year by .03 (3 percent).

The loss in value under the equal percentage method over an economic life period of fifty years is sketched as shown in Figure 13.4.

The equal percentage method, although more equitable in the distribution of depreciation losses in relation to remaining value, appears designed to fit investment characteristics suitable to a particular owner rather than the loss of value characteristics of the property as influenced by operation of the market forces of supply and demand. This method also requires a more or less arbitrary selection of the rate of constant depreciation, a rate which, based on regulations of the Internal Revenue Bureau, cannot exceed 3¾ percent of permissible replacement or acquisition cost to the reporting owner. This method, too, never fully depreciates a property even if extended over thousands of years and into perpetuity. It can be assumed, of course, that the remainder at any given life moment equals the salvage value of the property at that moment.

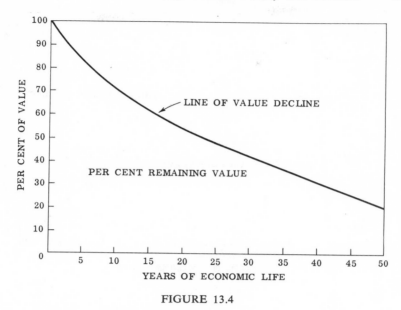

FIGURE 13.4

Value Decline Under the 3 Percent Equal Percentage Method of
Depreciation Over an Economic Life of Fifty Years

The sinking fund method. This method of providing for or measuring accrued depreciation has characteristics of the straight line method in that the amounts actually or theoretically to be set aside annually remain constant—the difference being that the periodic deposits are deemed to be made into a savings, or *safe,* fund on which interest is earned and compounded over the investment or economic life of the property. To illustrate: To accumulate $1.00 over a period of fifty years under the straight line (no interest) method necessitates an annual provision of $.02. Under the sinking fund method, assuming compounded interest payments at the rate of 3 percent, only $.00887, or approximately 45 percent as much as required under the straight line method need be set aside for depreciation purposes. Since valuation is an economic concept, and since economic considerations must be based on time preference, cost, and interest functions of money, the sinking fund method is deemed more logical as a measure of depreciation than any of the theoretical methods thus far explained and illustrated.

The loss in value under the 3 percent sinking fund method over an economic property life period of fifty years is diagramed in Figure 13.5.

The percentage of accrued depreciation under the sinking fund method at the end of any year during a given economic life of a property can

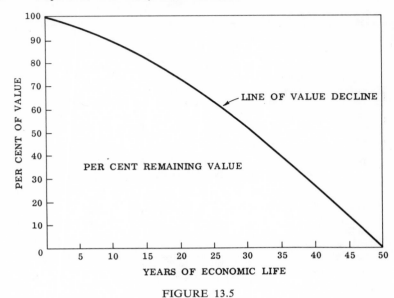

FIGURE 13.5

VALUE DECLINE UNDER THE 3 PERCENT SINKING FUND METHOD OF DEPRECIATION
OVER AN ECONOMIC LIFE OF FIFTY YEARS

readily be computed by using two established mathematical tables: The Sinking Fund, or Amortization Rate, Table, and The Compound Amount, or Future Worth of One Dollar Per Annum, Table. For illustrations of these tables at selected rates of interest see Appendix 3, pages 566 to 589. To derive the percent accrued depreciation, reference is first made to the Sinking Fund Table at the applicable (safe) rate of interest. Assuming an economic life of fifty years, this table at 3 percent interest indicates an annual provision per dollar of investment value of .00887 (see page 569). The Future Worth of One Dollar Per Annum Table (see page 568) indicates the accumulation of $1.00 per annum at the end of each year. Assuming twenty years as the effective age this table at 3 percent indicates an accumulation in the amount of 26.870. By multiplying the fifty-year sinking fund rate of .00887 by the twenty-year accumulation rate of 26.870, a sum of .2383, or 23.83 percent is obtained as a measure of accrued depreciation. At the end of thirty years, .00887 is multiplied by the accumulation factor of 47.575 to yield a rate of .4220, or 42.2 percent. This method of measuring accrued depreciation, because of its conformity to conservative investment practice, appears to be gaining in popularity as an accounting device for accrued depreciation measurement.

The annuity method. In procedure and application the *annuity* method is similar to the sinking fund method, the difference being the selection of a higher rate of compound interest which generally is referred to as a *risk* rate as opposed to a safe rate of interest. In theory the annuity method does not call for the establishment of a sinking fund to accrue depreciation losses but rather is based on the concept of reinvestment of the annual provisions for depreciation at an interest rate equivalent to that earned by the property as a whole. Mortgage investment companies, for instance, operate under this procedure. As amortization payments of outstanding loans become available, such are promptly reinvested in similar mortgage loans at equal or prevailing market rates of interest. The annuity method, where it can be effectively applied, keeps the entire investment operating at maximum market rates of interest, like a revolving fund.

Small or single-property investors, however, have little opportunity to reinvest fractional sums that are annually returned as compensation for depreciation losses at rates of interest which the entire property as an operating entity can command. Thus it may be feasible to earn 8 percent interest on an investment fund of $10,000, but the likelihood of earning this rate on the sums of $80, $100, or even $200 that become periodically available is rather remote. The annuity method, in theory, is undoubtedly more realistic than the sinking fund method because typical investors—home buyers, for instance—do not as a rule set aside funds to offset depreciation losses.

For certain types of properties, or for certain institutional investors, the annuity method nevertheless is applicable and, where applied—assuming 6 percent as the going market (risk) rate of interest—the loss in value follows a curvilinear pattern as shown in Figure 13.6.

To compute the percent of accrued depreciation for any given year of effective age, the necessary annual provision per dollar of investment based on total economic life as shown in the Amortization or Sinking Fund Rate Table (see page 200) is multiplied by the accumulation factor or Future Worth of One Dollar Per Annum Table (see page 574) for the years of effective age. The annual provision for depreciation per dollar of investment over an economic life of fifty years at 6 percent rate of interest is .00344. The accumulation factor—assuming an effective age of twenty years at the same rate of 6 percent—is 36.787 (see page 574). Multiplying the two rates (.00344 $\times$ 36.787), a sum of .1265, or 12.65 percent is obtained as a measure of accrued depreciation under the annuity method. The same percentage results can be obtained by a shortcut method under which the annuity (or Inwood) factor for the remaining economic life of thirty years is subtracted from the annuity (or Inwood) factor for

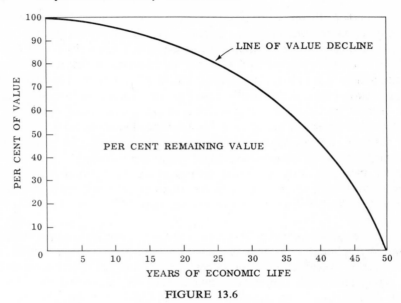

FIGURE 13.6

VALUE DECLINE UNDER THE 6 PERCENT ANNUITY METHOD OF DEPRECIATION
OVER AN ECONOMIC LIFE OF FIFTY YEARS

the total economic life—in this case fifty years. By dividing the loss in factor value by the factor for total (fifty-year) life, a percentage loss is indicated as follows:

Inwood factor at 6% for 50 years	=	15.762
Inwood factor at 6% for 30 years	=	13.765
Factor loss due to age	=	1.997
1.997 divided by 15,762	=	12.65%

The annuity method, if applied as illustrated, assumes that net income remains constant. This assumption, of course, is false because "net" income as a rule is derived from "remaining" value and not the original or replacement value.

Recapitulation. The five theoretical methods of measuring accrued depreciation yield, as demonstrated above, significant differences in their end results. The variations among the theoretical measures are indeed of such magnitude that great care must be exercised in selecting the method deemed best applicable and most representative under given circumstances as an accurate measure of loss in value from all causes of depreciation. As a guide and check, a recapitulation of the five theoretical depreciation methods is presented in summary form at five-year intervals over an economic property life of fifty years.

COMPARATIVE TABLE OF THEORETICAL MEASURES OF PERCENT ACCRUED
DEPRECIATION AT FIVE-YEAR INTERVALS OVER AN ECONOMIC LIFE PERIOD
OF FIFTY YEARS

Effective Age	Years Digit	Straight Line	3 Percent Equal Percentage	3 Percent Sinking Fund	6 Percent Annuity
5	18.8	10.0	14.1	4.7	1.9
10	35.7	20.0	26.2	10.2	4.5
15	50.6	30.0	36.7	16.4	8.0
20	63.5	40.0	45.6	23.8	12.7
25	74.5	50.0	53.3	32.3	18.9
30	83.5	60.0	59.9	42.2	27.2
35	90.6	70.0	65.6	53.6	38.4
40	95.7	80.0	70.4	66.8	53.3
45	98.8	90.0	74.6	82.2	73.3
50	100.0	100.0	78.2	100.0	100.0

DEPRECIATION ESTIMATES—THEIR LIMITS OF USE

Fortunately for the professional appraiser, estimating accrued depreciation directly is usually of secondary importance. In fact, depreciation cannot accurately be determined until value is known. Then, by comparing present worth with estimated cost new, the amount of accrued depreciation is fixed with certainty. Under the market and income approaches to value, as will be explained in succeeding chapters, depreciation as a separate measure is of little importance. The appraiser's problem is to find the value of the subject property by comparison with comparable properties which have sold in recent times, or by capitalizing the rights to net income derived from the subject property over the remaining economic life of the property. Once this value is found, the appraiser's task is, as a rule, completed. Only where the cost approach is deemed of importance must accrued depreciation—as a separate calculation—be taken into account. The cost approach is a most useful tool in the appraisal process, but in the hands of uninformed or unskilled appraisers it can result in grossly misleading calculations. A closing caution: Use depreciation estimates with care. Apply the observed method for measuring accrued depreciation whenever possible. Use the appropriate theoretical measure only as a check against amounts of value losses estimated by the observed method, and where results are at great variance (5 percent or more) seek to find and explain the reason for the difference.

READING AND STUDY REFERENCES

1. Alexander, Robert H., "Measuring Accrued Depreciation in the Market," *The Residential Appraiser,* (April 1960), pp. 22–24.
2. *The Appraisal of Real Estate* (Chicago: American Institute of Real Estate Appraisers, 1967 chap. 13.
3. Babcock, Frederick M., *The Valuation of Real Estate* (New York: McGraw-Hill Book Company, Inc., 1932), chaps. 9 & 29.
4. Kahn, Sanders A., Frederick E. Case, and Alfred Schimmel, *Real Estate Appraisal and Investment* (New York: The Ronald Press Company, 1963), chap. 14.
5. Kinnard, William N., Jr., *An Introduction to Appraising Real Property* (Chicago: Society of Real Estate Appraisers, 1968), chaps. 12 & 16.
6. Knowles, Jerome, Jr., "Estimating Accrued Depreciation," *The Appraisal Journal* (January 1967), pp. 34–43.
7. Louie, Charles F., "Depreciation and the Cost Approach," *The Appraisal Journal* (October 1961), pp. 507–16.
8. McMichael, Stanley L., *McMichael's Appraising Manual,* 4th ed. (Englewood Cliffs, N.J.: Prentice-Hall, Inc., 1951), chap. 5.
9. Pope, Lonnie H., "Depreciation in the Cost Approach," *The Real Estate Appraiser* (June 1964), pp. 2–10.
10. Ring, Alfred A., "Depreciation Expense vs. Depreciation Rate Methods of Capitalization," *The Appraisal Journal* (July 1962), pp. 325–332.
11. Wendt, Paul F., "Depreciation and the Capitalization of Income Method," *The Appraisal Journal* (April 1963), pp. 185–93.

One of the basic characteristics that a commodity must have to possess value is *utility*.[1] Everything else remaining equal, the greater the utility, the greater the value. One of the best measures of utility is the amount of income or rental which a property can earn or command in an open and competitive market for the space facilities it offers at a given time and place.

As previously emphasized, valuation,

14 *Income Forecasting*

and Analysis

especially under the income approach, necessitates a determination of an estimate of the present worth of future rights to income. The term *future* in this definition of value imposes on the appraiser an obligation to forecast with reasonable accuracy the pattern of income expectancy that may be anticipated over the remaining economic life of the subject property. Forecasting in any enterprise is fraught with hazards, as is testified by the thousands of business failures and bankruptcies reported every year. But forecast the appraiser must, or change his profession to another in which he can search the annals of history, looking backward with reasonable certainty rather than forward into a realm of economic uncertainty. Every business venture requires prediction of future

---

[1] Utility as used here refers to the power of a good to satisfy human wants or to render service or to produce income to its owner. See Chapter 1, page 10 for discussion of value characteristics.

operations, and every property is improved in anticipation of estimated revenue from rental or owner use.

The quality of prediction of an anticipated income flow varies directly with the proximity of future estimates to the date of the appraisal. As a rule, income for the year ahead can be established with a high degree of certainty. Income for the second, third, and fourth years ahead can be forecast with reasonable dependability; but thereafter, and to the end of the economic life of a property (extending up to fifty or more years) the accuracy of the forecast becomes tenuous. Fortunately under the capitalization process the early and relatively accurate years of income forecasting are accorded substantial weight in the valuation process, with the importance of latter years diminishing as indicators of value. To illustrate this point, let's assume that two properties, A and B, are estimated to yield equal annual net incomes of $1,000 each, but that property A has an economic life of fifty years and property B, one of one hundred years. At 8 percent interest, applying the present worth of an annuity of 1 table, property A is worth $1,000 × 12.233, or $12,233, while property B is valued at $1,000 × 12.494, or $12,494. The difference is $261, or approximately 2 percent of the value of property A. In this instance, a 100 percent difference in the span of the economic life causes no practical impact on the value estimate of the two properties as a direct result of the discounting process.

ACTUAL VERSUS AVERAGE INCOME

Reliance on *average* rather than on *factual* anticipated income may, under the income approach to value, result in substantial errors in the appraisal estimate. This is clearly demonstrated in the analysis of two income producing properties as shown below:

In this illustration two income-producing properties with identical total and average incomes were discounted over a period of ten years to a sum of present worth at a rate of 6 percent interest. Property A, with a total income of $5,500, and an average income of $550 ($5,500 ÷ 10), yields a capitalized value of $3,696.31. Property B, though experiencing the same total and average income—but derived from a reversed income experience, as compared with property A—yields a present worth of $4,399.91, or a sum approximately 20 percent greater than that derived from property A. The difference in valuation is a direct result of the nature of the income flow and the degree of time preference expressed in the rate of capitalization. A dollar due one year from today has a greater value than one due ten years from today because the early dollar may be put to work for a period of nine years, and the wages which this capital amount earns are reflected in the higher present value. The difference in value estimate of

ANALYSIS OF PRESENT WORTH OF TWO INCOME-PRODUCING PROPERTIES—HAVING
IDENTICAL TOTAL AND AVERAGE INCOMES—UNDER DIVERGENT INCOME ASSUMPTIONS

| | *Net Income* | | *Present Worth* | *Present Value* | |
| | *Property* | *Property* | *Factor* | *Property* | *Property* |
Years	*A*	*B*	*6 Percent*	*A*	*B*
1	$ 100	$1000	.9434	$ 94.34	$ 943.40
2	200	900	.8900	178.00	801.00
3	300	800	.8396	251.88	671.68
4	400	700	.7921	316.84	554.47
5	500	600	.7473	373.65	448.38
6	600	500	.7050	423.00	352.50
7	700	400	.6651	465.57	266.04
8	800	300	.6274	501.92	188.22
9	900	200	.5919	532.71	118.38
10	1000	100	.5584	558.40	55.84
Total	$5500	$5500		$3,696.31	$4,399.91
Average	550	550		100%	119%

the two diverse income-producing properties will vary directly, of course, with the rate of capitalization employed in the income approach—increasing with higher rates, and decreasing with lower rates until equality in present worth is reached at a rate of zero percent.

It may be argued that the illustration offered is extreme in nature and that it does not conform to general practice or experience. Perhaps so. But insistence on the use of unweighted income averages in the process of capitalization is dangerous and may, as demonstrated, result in a substantial error in the value estimate. It is well to keep in mind that as a rule realty, because of its heterogeneous nature and fixity of location, varies in revenue productivity and hence in quantity and quality of income flow. Some income from realty is ascending because land and, indirectly, its improvements is ripening into higher use. Other properties may exhibit declining yields due to transition into lower uses, particularly during the last stages of their economic life cycle.

ECONOMIC VERSUS CONTRACT RENTS

Too much importance is often placed, especially by amateur appraisers and "guesstimators," on past or present income or lease commitments. The present, it must be remembered, is merely a fleeting moment dividing the past from the future. Properties may be underimproved, overimproved, or faultily managed, or income may be attributable to personal skill or business operations rather than to the property itself.

It is the appraiser's duty to evaluate a property as if owned under fee simple title, free from all encumbrances except for use limitations imposed by public authorities and deed restrictions shown on public records. The property, too, must be considered in the light of its earning capacity in conformity with the principle of highest and best use. After value under these normal conditions has been established, appropriate adjustments should be made to reflect economic advantages or disadvantages ascribable to limited contractual agreements or temporary managerial operating policies.

Economic rent, which should form the basis of value, is defined as *that maximum net market rental which a property (land and improvements) can produce over a given period of time.* The phrase "period of time," generally refers to the estimated remaining economic life of the property. *Contract rent,* on the other hand, is that rental income ascribable to the property as a result of contractual commitments which bind owners and tenants for a stipulated future time. As stated, this contract rent may be greater or lesser than the economic rent under the highest and best—and legally permissible—use of the property.

IMPORTANCE OF TYPICAL MANAGEMENT

All property must be considered to be under some form of management, either by the owner himself or by a professional manager. In either case, operating expenses must reflect a charge—whether or not incurred—for the expenditure of time and effort customarily employed in operation and property supervision. Such managerial costs, as will be shown in the following chapter, are generally considered a percentage of revenue and vary from 5 to 10 percent of realized revenues or rent collections.

In forecasting income, it is important to consider property productivity under the operation of *typical* management. To do otherwise would ascribe to the property a value that is influenced by personal characteristics of the management. By *typical* management is meant that which most frequently prevails in the ownership and use of given types of properties. Income considerations, too, are based on typical future managerial practices. This does not mean that effects of past managerial control and operation which linger on are not to be considered under the income approach to value. Exceptional management during past years may, like business good will, be the cause of surplus income extending over two or more years depending on the degree of exceptional property maintenance and the amount of excess rentals under existing lease terms. Poor management during past years, on the other hand, may burden future operation as a result of deferred maintenance, or may reduce income because of unfavorable tenant commitments such as rental concessions.

ESTIMATING THE QUANTITY
OF INCOME FLOW

The amount of income, all else being equal, will vary with the quantity or volume of land and its improvements. Industrial property offered under land use contracts will produce revenue in proportion to the number of square feet of area offered for lease. The presence or absence of railroad siding, highway access, and proximity to market and to community facilities will affect directly the quantity of payments offered per unit of space. The unit of income and value for commercial property is based on the number of either square feet or front feet of land in the property—depending on business use and land location—and the number of square feet of building area contained within the improvements. Apartment buildings produce revenue on a per room or per apartment basis depending on local market customs. Single residences are rented on a "property" basis of stated dollars per month. The amount of revenue generally varies with the size of the building, quality of construction, neighborhood, location and site characteristics, and amount and quality of furnishings and fixtures. The procedure for adjusting the estimated income of a subject property by analysis of income derived from comparable but dissimilar properties will be explained below in connection with the preparation of a rental schedule.

Attention is also called to the fact that income generally declines as building age advances. It stands to reason that, per space unit (all other things remaining equal), more will be offered for a property in its early, or prime of, economic life than for the same property in the middle or late period of its economic life. How to adjust for anticipated decline in the revenue flow is a controversial matter. Many appraisers follow teachings that advocate the selection of a higher rate of amortization under the straight line method of capital recapture to compensate for loss of revenue due to property aging. Based on an investment of $20,000, a remaining economic life of twenty years, a 6 percent interest rate and straight line amortization at 5 percent per year, declining income is demonstrated in the American Institute of Real Estate Appraisers textbook as shown on page 210.[2]

The formula used for computing the annual income decline under the method demonstrated below is:

$$\frac{R \times D}{R + D}$$

---

[2] *The Appraisal of Real Estate* (Chicago, Illinois: American Institute of Real Estate Appraisers, 5th ed., 1967), pp. 286–287.

Investment beginning of first year	$20,000	
Income during first year:		
6% interest on $20,000		$1,200
5% recapture on $20,000	1,000	1,000
Remaining investment	$19,000	
Total income first year		$2,200
Investment beginning of second year	$19,000	
Income during second year:		
6% recapture on $19,000		$1,140
5% recapture on $20,000	1,000	1,000
Remaining investment	$18,000	
Total income second year		$2,140
Investment beginning of third year	$18,000	
Income during third year:		
6% interest on $18,000		$1,080
5% recapture on $20,000	1,000	1,000
Remaining investment	$17,000	
Total income third year		$2,080

In this equation, R = the interest rate and D = the rate of recapture. Substituting the rates used above, the percentage annual income decline measures:

$$\frac{.06 \times .05}{.06 + .05} = \frac{.0030}{.11} = .0273, \text{ or } 2.73\%$$

The logic employed to justify the use of a method of depreciation to offset an anticipated loss in the flow of income appears highly questionable. The selection of the appropriate rate of future depreciation must be based on the characteristics of the property, its quality of construction, and market practices for depreciation in typical use. The rate of amortization logically has no relationship to the quantity, quality, or pattern of the income stream. Since the value formula is designated as $V = I/R$, where "I" represents capitalizable income and "R" the rate of capitalization, it is mathematically incorrect and logically indefensible to adjust the denominator in an equation (the rate of capitalization in this instance) to reflect anticipated changes (decline of income) in the numerator. Furthermore, an income decline based on an equal percentage curve suggests a precision in income forecasting that is insupportable in the light of real estate market operations. In this connection it appears justified to repeat the adage, "Two wrongs don't make a right." If the income flow—on the basis of study of similar properties—is expected to decline, then it is the appraiser's clear-cut responsibility to forecast the pattern of this

decline and to capitalize the diminishing returns accurately and professionally. Often, too, attempts are made to stabilize future returns by
arithmetic averaging. Such a procedure is unscientific, since early dollar
returns under discounting procedure have greater weight in relation to
present value than equal dollar returns in late property life.

It is possible, however, to stabilize accurately a declining income stream
implicit in the straight line method of capitalization, to derive a present
value equivalent to that of an ordinary annuity by use of the following
formula:

$$I\left(\frac{1/a_n}{i+D}\right)$$

In which:

$$I = \text{first year income}$$
$$1/a_n = \text{annuity rate of capitalization (reciprocal of Inwood Factor)}$$
$$i = \text{interest rate}$$
$$D = \text{annual straight line rate of recapture}$$

Example: An income of $1,000 per year declining under straight line
assumption over a period of forty years at 7 percent interest equals a
value of

$$\$1,000 \div .095 \ (.07 + .025) = \$10,526$$

To stabilize this income stream, we derive a ratio by the formula noted
above as follows: $1,000 $\times$ (.075 $\div$ .095) = $789.47.[3] Thus whether
we capitalize a declining income beginning with $1,000 under the straight
line method, or capitalize a stabilized income of $789.47 under the annuity
or Inwood method of capitalization the answers are identical. To proof:

1. Straight line capitalization $1,000 $\div$ .095 = $10,526
2. Inwood method of capitalization $789.4 x 13.337 = $10,526

An early and noteworthy attempt to measure income decline by classes
and kinds of real property was made by Frederick M. Babcock in *The
Valuation of Real Estate*.[4] The reader is referred to Chapter 27 of this
book for an excellent discussion of the development of income decline
premises. In practice, the mathematical theory underlying Babcock's prem-

---

[3] This amount was derived with the aid of the above formula as follows:

$$\frac{I}{13.33171} \div (.07 + .025) = .075009 \div .095 = .78947$$

$1,000 $\times$ .78947 = $789.47

[4] Frederick M. Babcock, *The Valuation of Real Estate* (New York: McGraw-Hill
Book Co., Inc., 1932).

ises proved difficult to explain and more difficult for practitioners and laymen alike to understand. Consequently, little is currently known—and still less is applied—of Babcock's declining income premise findings. A more direct and mathematically less cumbersome method of accounting for income flow variations is explained below.

Study of income behavior of various types of properties over past years should enable an appraiser to forecast income expectancy as affected by building age and the space competition of new construction. The diagram shown in Figure 14.1 illustrates an anticipated income pattern of a 16-unit apartment building in a moderate size commercial community.

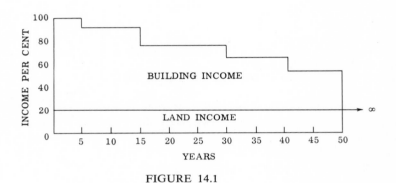

FIGURE 14.1

Typical Income Flow for an Apartment Property
Over an Economic Life Period of Fifty Years

This diagram, supported by income experience data of comparable buildings, indicates that earnings on completion of improvements and full occupancy will remain stable for an operating period of about five years. Building age and obsolescence as well as anticipated building competition are expected to cause a decline in building income at that life stage of approximately 10 percent. Income at this lower level is expected to prevail for a period of another ten years, at which time continued obsolescence and space supply competition will cause a further drop in income of about 15 percent, or to a level of 75 percent of the income earned during initial years of property life. This level of income expectancy, as shown, is to prevail for a period of fifteen years, or until at building age thirty (mid-life). At this time, and again at building age forty, a decline of 10 percent, respectively, is anticipated in rental receipts. The income level during the last, or late building life, period is at a rate of 55 percent of the amount earned during the early years after building completion.

To capitalize this changing income flow does not require special mathematical skill or the use of special capitalization tables. Each level of future income is merely converted into a sum of present worth and discounted to the date of the appraisal. The recommended procedure for capitalizing this declining income will be demonstrated and explained in Chapter 18.

The accurate construction of a schedule of anticipated income, on which the value of a property is to be based, is a responsibility which the appraiser cannot evade by hiding in the process of income forecasting behind a straight line method of capital recapture. For long-lived properties the application of straight line accounting to appraisal theory becomes increasingly more difficult to justify, especially in the light of ever more sophisticated market investment practices.

QUALITY AND DURATION OF INCOME

The value of property varies not only with the quantity or amount of dollars, but also with income quality and its duration. The quality of income generally is dependent on the kind and character of tenants, the type of long- or short-term leases, the degree and extent of space competition (both current and anticipated) over the economic life of the subject property, and the stability of economic conditions in the subject market area. As a matter of practice, differences in the quality of income among properties should not be reflected in upward or downward adjustments of the amount of anticipated income. Quality differentials should rather be a matter for separate and analytical considerations in the selection of the applicable interest rate at which the net income flow is to be capitalized. The analysis and correlation of market rates of interest for purposes of selecting or constructing rates of capitalization will be demonstrated and discussed in Chapter 16.

The duration of income is directly proportional to the remaining useful or economic life of the land improvements.[5] The income attributable to land under fee simple ownership is always deemed to extend into perpetuity. Improvements, however, are subject to physical wear, tear, and the forces of obsolescence, and income to be derived from employment of depreciable assets will cease when their value reaches zero. In predicting the economic lifespan of property improvements, the appraiser must consider.

1. The physical and functional characteristics of the building improvements, and

---

[5] The remaining economic life employed here should be the same as that used for estimating accured depreciation in the cost approach.

2. The economic forces which operate on the demand side for the kind of utility or amenity offered by the subject improvement.

The physical characteristics set the outer limit of duration of useful life. Therefore, the type of architecture, the quality of materials used, the workmanship employed, and the physical conditions of maintenance and repair must be considered in establishing the maximum number of years of utility life. More important as a mortality factor, however, are the environing economic forces which bring about building obsolescence. Otherwise identical improvements will have different economic lives depending on their location within or among communities. In rapidly growing cities, building obsolescence is accelerated as a result of important changes in land use and consequent significant increases in land value. A study in Jacksonville, Florida, disclosed a shift of the 100 percent business location over a distance of several blocks as a result of new and redevelopment construction activity during the past decade. The impact of the automobile, community decentralization, development of suburban shopping centers, and location of new industries in suburban areas are largely responsible for shifting land values and increased economic mortality of building improvements in central business locations.

Where buildings are relatively new, errors in the prediction of remaining building life have a generally minor effect on the overall estimate of total property value. This is true for two reasons: First, because of the relatively minor weight given to the value of distant future income in the discounting or capitalization process; and, second, because increased building obsolescence has historically been accompanied by rising land values which often more than compensate for the economic sacrifice of remaining building life. Where buildings are in middle or late life, however, an error in the anticipated duration of income may importantly affect the value estimate. To predict accurately remaining economic building life requires judgment based on intimate knowledge of community and neighborhood forces affecting property value, as detailed in Chapters 6 and 7. It is for this reason, among others, that property appraising as an applied art is largely limited to local practitioners who keep their fingers on the economic pulse of their community.

RENTAL SCHEDULE CONSTRUCTION AND ANALYSIS

In forecasting income for existing or proposed properties, the appraiser must look to the market for income experience data of properties comparable to the one under appraisal. Through cooperating broker-appraisers or property management firms it is possible to secure rental amounts paid on a per room or per apartment basis for residential properties, and a square foot or front foot basis for commercial or business properties. With the aid of this information, the appraiser can construct a rental schedule which—after adjustments for differences in building age, construction, and attributes of neighborhood, location, and site facilities—can serve as a basis for rental estimates of the subject property.

Rental schedules for the various units of space to be offered are most realistically established on a market comparative basis. This is effectively done by rating the subject property in relation to like properties in similar neighborhoods for which accurate rental data is available. The comparison approach, though simple in application, relies on sound judgment for effective use. Comparison is generally made with a number of typical space units, and price adjustments for the subject property are based on quantitative and qualitative differences. For example, in the pricing of an apartment unit consideration should be given to the following: area of floor space, number of bathrooms, quality of construction, amount of decorative features, efficiency of floor location, type and quality of elevator service, nature and quality of janitorial services, reputation of the building, and characteristics of tenants. In addition, the location of the building in relation to public conveniences, and the quality rating of neighborhood and trends must both be considered. Assuming that a standard unit in an ideal neighborhood rents for $250 per month and the comparative rating for the subject property is 90 percent, then the estimated fair rental is judged to be $225 per month. If a detailed comparison is made for each space unit with four or more selected and comparable units, a fairly accurate and reliable rental schedule for appraisal purposes can be established.

Most helpful in the estimation of anticipated rental income is a rental formula developed by Leo J. Sheridan and William Karkow, two well-known Chicago building managers. (Copies of the Sheridan-Karkow formula are available through the National Association of Building Owners and Managers, Chicago, Illinois.) This table, coupled with rental experience data collected on a local level, should provide the appraiser with excellent guides in revenue forecasting.

OWNER'S INCOME STATEMENTS AND ADJUSTMENTS

In the appraisal of existing properties from which income experience data is obtainable, it is customary to request that the owner furnish an operating statement for at least three years previous. This statement can then be analyzed and reconstructed in conformity with income expectancy under typical managerial operating care and sound appraisal practices.

The income data supplied by the owner is generally labeled *as reported.* The average shown for the three-or-more-year income period is then modified to reflect typical operations, and the amounts used for appraisal purposes are labeled *as adjusted.*[6] Where adjustments reflect more than the rounding of dollar amounts, it is essential that an explanation be fully described in the body of the valuation report or added as a footnote. Typical adjustments may show rental income for the owner- or janitor-occupied apartment, or they may reflect increases or decreases in existing rentals where such rentals are out of line with market rental comparisons.

Owners' statements also generally reflect rentals on an as-is basis and thus include built-in vacancies and rent collection losses, if any. To indicate operation under typical management, it is preferable to estimate gross revenue collectable under 100 percent occupancy and then to subtract for normal vacancy and collection losses that prevail for this type of property in the community market area. Generally, vacancy and collection deductions are calculated as a percentage of gross revenue, varying from a minimum of 2 percent to as high as 50 percent in summer resort areas. In college towns, where school facilities are inoperative during the summer months, vacancy ratios in apartments that cater to students and faculty personnel must be calculated to indicate *realizable* rather than *potential* income.

In appraisal terminology, the amount left after deductions for vacancy and collection losses are made is referred to as *effective gross revenue.* Even in rare instances where owners report no vacancies or collection loses over past years, the appraiser must provide for such contingencies in accordance with typical loss ratios reported for similar properties in the community. The exception, of course, would be where an entire property is under firm lease to a responsible tenant over a period of years.

In forecasting income for capitalization in the determination of value of proposed construction, or in the determination of land value under a hypothetical highest and best use, care must be taken to account for land income and capital investment losses (income foregone) during the period of construction. The present worth of such losses, discounted at the rate of interest applicable to the type of property, must be subtracted from the present worth of estimated future income to derive a net value as of the date of the appraisal. Consideration, too, must be given to high vacancy ratios during initial months or years of the property's operation. Typical sound management calls for careful tenant selection, and larger office and business properties may require periods of two or more years

---

[6] See the following chapter for suggested method to adjust reported operating incomes and expenses.

to reach full occupancy. Such revenue losses also must be accounted for in the valuation process via the income approach.

INCOME ADJUSTMENT FOR CHANGES IN THE PURCHASING POWER OF THE DOLLAR

Fortunately for the real estate appraiser, the anticipated income stream forecast over the economic life of a property need not be adjusted for possible changes in the purchasing power of the dollar. As previously indicated, future income, through the process of capitalization, is converted into a sum of present dollars for which the property is to be exchanged in the open market. Assuming freedom from mortgage debts and other financial encumbrances as well as freedom from restrictions on income such as rent control, a property is deemed competitively free to adjust itself to future changes in the purchasing power of the dollar. However, in a study of income performance over many past years, or in accepting the historical income flow of similar properties as a guide to the forecasting of an anticipated income flow for a given property, it is necessary to adjust past income to reflect changes in the purchasing power of the dollar. This can readily be done with the aid of price level indices published by the U. S. Bureau of Labor Statistics. Thus a rising income stream over thirty or more elapsed years may actually, after dollar purchasing power adjustment, disclose a declining trend in real operating income. Care must be taken, however, to restrict the use of dollar purchasing power adjustment factors to past income only. Where future income is sluggish in adjusting itself to market dollar forces of inflation or deflation —as in the case of long-term lease arrangements—it is best to reflect this rigidity in income flow as a factor of negative income quality, and to adjust the rate of capitalization by an appropriate increase in the risk factor component of the rate of capitalization. A study of the income-to-price relationship of similarly afflicted properties will disclose directly the rate of capitalization applied by investors to like properties in the open market. For a full discussion of the derivation of the capitalization rate, the reader is referred to Chapter 16.

READING AND STUDY REFERENCES

1. *The Appraisal of Real Estate* (Chicago: American Institute of Real Estate Appraisers, 1967), chap. 15.
2. Babcock, Frederick M., *The Valuation of Real Estate* (New York: McGraw-Hill Book Company, Inc., 1932), chaps. 19–21.

3. Bowes, Eugene G., "How to Estimate Gross Income and Operating Costs," *Real Estate Appraisal Practice* (Chicago: American Institute of Real Estate Appraisers, 1958), pp. 173–181.
4. Gibbons, James E., "Income Forecasts," *The Appraisal Journal* (October 1960), pp. 505–09.
5. Horton, E. B., Jr., "How to Use Income and Expense Estimates," *The Appraisal Journal* (July 1959), pp. 341–348.
6. Kahn, Sanders A., Frederick E. Case, and Alfred Schimmel, *Real Estate Appraisal and Investment* (New York: The Ronald Press Company, 1963), chap. 9.
7. McMichael, Stanley L., *McMichael's Appraising Manual*, 4th ed. (Englewood Cliffs, N.J.: Prentice-Hall, Inc., 1951), chap. 9.
8. Ring, Alfred A., "Income Forecasting and Income Conversion," *The Appraisal Journal* (October 1950), pp. 481–86.

The development and use of the gross income multiplier (see Chapter 10, page 145) seems to by-pass completely the need for operating expense forecasting and analysis. Professional appraisers nevertheless should not neglect this important phase of the income approach to value. Further study of the reasons first noted in Chapter 10 will disclose that failure to analyze expense schedules and operating property performance may

15

Operating Expense
Forecasting and Analysis

be the cause of substantial errors in the final estimate of value.

The apparent neglect of operating expense data and their analysis is accounted for by acceptance of the belief that properties of given classifications— residential, apartment house, office buildings, and so on—are characterized by identity in operating performance and similarity of expense-to-income ratios. To assume this is to ignore differences in types of buildings, quality of construction, building volume, age of improvements, architectural design, building features, vacancy ratios, location characteristics, and types of tenants. Since net (operating) income is the basis of value, under the income approach, failure to forecast anticipated operating expenses accurately is bound to be reflected in grossly unreliable appraisal reporting.

INCOME DEDUCTIONS VERSUS
OPERATING EXPENSES

An understanding of accounting procedure proves helpful in identifying and classifying expenditures which are personal in character, or which are of the nature of income deductions as opposed to expenditures that are essential to the operation of a property. Confusion often arises because of differences in treatment of certain expenses under conventional profit and loss accounting as compared with income and expense classification of expenditures for appraisal purposes. To illustrate: Two of the most important outlays incurred in connection with ownership of real property are: (1) mortgage interest and mortgage amortization payments, and (2) allowances or expense charges for investment losses due to depreciation (amortization) of the property. There is no question concerning the fact that under conventional accounting both of these expenditures—i.e., mortgage interest as well as depreciation charges—are costs of ownership. But in the appraisal of real property, mortgage interest charges are considered operating costs only when evaluating the *equity* (i.e., the owner's interest in the property exclusive of the mortgage lien). When borrowing funds, an investor, as a rule, engages in *trading on the equity*. Under such circumstances he finds it profitable to borrow funds at interest rates lower than the property is expected to earn as an operating entity. In deriving gains from interest differentials between the rate of property earnings and the cost of borrowing money, the owner is assuming investment risks for which—if his efforts are successful—he is being duly compensated. But such financial dealings are personal in character (a business venture within itself) and must be classified as income deductions and not as expenditures essential to the operation of a property. A commodity, as has been pointed out in foregoing chapters, can logically have only one value based on F.O.B. delivery at a given time and place. The price of a given commodity may and generally does vary with the terms and conditions of sale; but commodity value must necessarily and consistently be measured in relation to net income derived under typical management, free and clear of all encumbrances, including mortgage liens.

Once the value of a property has been established, free and clear of all encumbrances, due price allowance must be made for favorable or unfavorable terms of sale which attach to the subject property. Because of the importance of "tax shelter" opportunities that enable an owner to convert operating net income into a category of capital gain which is taxed at one-half or less of the rate applicable to earned income, a separate chapter will deal exclusively with equity financing and the methods by which equity yields realized can be computed under varying assumptions and conditions. More and more the tax bracket into which individual investors fall influences their price decisions personally and the market value of income-producing properties which attract given classes of buyers, generally. For more on this subject, the reader is referred to Chapter 21 on Equity Financing.

Appropriate treatment of depreciation allowances, too, pose a problem to the uninformed. Depreciation is definitely an expense of operation, and provision for loss of value (consumed as a result of operation) must be provided for somewhere in the valuation process.

It is often stated that depreciation should not be included as an expense item in the operating schedule because the amount of annual depreciation cannot be known until value, which is the crux of the appraisal problem, has been established. Statements such as these, however, are the result of circular reasoning. It is true that value is not known; but income is known, and so is the rate of depreciation—which is traditionally added to the rate of interest for capitalization purposes. By applying the rate of depreciation (as a percentage of the total rate of capitalization) to the net operating income, the depreciation charge in dollars per annum *can* be determined as an operating expense even though value is not known. To illustrate: Suppose a property produces a net operating income—before interest and depreciation charges—in the amount of $8,000; assuming a rate of interest of 6 percent and a rate of depreciation under straight line accounting of 2 percent, the capitalized value of $8,000 at 8 percent is $100,000.

In the above assumption it is known that the rate of depreciation is 2 percent out of a total rate of capitalization of 8 percent, and that, therefore, 25 percent (2 percent ÷ 8 percent) of net income, represents provision for depreciation. Since 25 percent of $8,000 is $2,000, this leaves $6,000 as net income after depreciation but before interest. Capitalizing $6,000 at 6 percent interest yields a value of $100,000, identical to that obtained by capitalizing $8,000 at an 8 percent rate of capitalization.

To use another illustration employing sinking fund provisions for future depreciation, let us assume a property produces a net operating income of $10,000 before interest and depreciation. If the rate of interest is 6 percent, and a 2½ percent sinking fund over forty years of economic life requires a rate of depreciation of 1.5 percent,[1] then the total rate of capitalization is 7.5 percent. Capitalizing $10,000 at 7.5 percent produces a present value of $133,333.33. Since it is known that a rate of 1.5 percent is reserved for depreciation, the amount of depreciation can be determined by applying the percentage ratio of 1.5 percent to 7.5 percent, or 20 percent, to the income stream; 20 percent of $10,000 is $2,000, leaving a net in-

---

[1] Sinking fund factor for forty years at 2½ percent interest is .014836.

come to interest—after depreciation—of $8,000. Capitalizing $8,000 at 6 percent interest yields a value of $133,333.33, or the same as that obtained by capitalizing $10,000 at 7.5 percent. The above illustrations make clear that if the rate of depreciation is known, then this rate as a percentage of the total rate of capitalization can be applied to net income for a determination of the amount that represents annual recapture of depreciation of capital *before* value is known.

Appraisal practice, however, sanctions the combining of a rate of interest with a rate of depreciation to form a rate of capitalization for income conversion of depreciable property into value. For this reason depreciation as a rule is not included as an operating expense. To do so would include this charge twice: once as an expense of operations, and again in the process of capitalization by combining a rate of the investment (amortization rate) with a rate on the investment to form a rate of capitalization. The method and procedure for developing rates of capitalization will be the subject of discussion in Chapter 16.

Other owner's income deductions which must be excluded as operating expenses include outlays such as charitable contributions, traffic or other fines, entertainment expenses, cost of lawsuits, damage awards, and similar extraneous and personal expenditures.

INCOME TAX AND PROPERTY TAX
CONSIDERATIONS

Personal and corporate income taxes, too, must be excluded as costs of operation. Income tax payments vary with the income brackets into which the taxable earnings of individuals and corporations fall. Such payments are important to a purchaser of property, and may influence his decision as to whether to buy a given property; but the value of the commodity (property) must be found free and clear of such variable and personal considerations. Otherwise, the art of real estate appraising would lose its general applicability as a guide to market value.

Real estate (property) taxes are correctly classified as an operating expense. The omission of property taxes would overstate the net operating income used for capitalization purposes and, as a consequence, the answer sought in the valuation problem. On important occasions, however, the value to be used for tax purposes is at issue, as in the case in a *tax certiorari* proceeding.[2] To include as an operating expense a tax payment made on what is believed to be an excessive assessment would lower both net

---

[2] If an owner believes that the assessed value of his property is too high, and is unable to secure a reduction upon protest to the tax officials, he can appeal to the courts. Such a court case is known as a *certiorai* proceeding.

income and value, as compared with the fair market value that would prevail under equalized tax assessment practices. Where value for tax purposes is at issue—and this is an exception rather than a rule—property taxes as an amount can also be excluded from the operating expense schedule, and taxes as a rate (percent per hundred dollars of assessed value) can be added to the rate of capitalization. In such instances the appraiser must not put into the problem an operating expense amount which depends on the value sought. Thus, if the rate of capitalization is 8 percent and the rate of taxation based on market value is 20 mills, or 2 percent, value for tax purposes can be derived by capitalizing net income before interest, amortization, and property taxes by a combined rate of 10 percent. The application and solution of a *certiorari* tax valuation problem will be demonstrated in connection with other case study problems in Appendix 2, page 495.

OPERATING EXPENSE OUTLAYS AND CLASSIFICATIONS

In nearly all appraisal problems it becomes necessary to reconstruct operating expense schedules and to adjust—over the remaining economic life of the property—expenditures in accordance with those estimated to be incurred under typical management and operation. This requires knowledge of property care and maintenance, as well as the analysis of operating performance of comparable properties in similar locations.

Operating expense schedules generally are arranged to provide for recording of costs under the following headings:

1. Fixed charges.
2. Operating and maintenance costs.
3. Repairs and reserves for replacements.

Fixed charges are those which as a rule vary little, if at all, with occupancy from year to year. In this category would fall property taxes and insurance for fire, theft, and comprehensive hazards.

Operating and maintenance costs would include expenditures for periodic maintenance, management, janitorial care, heating, utilities, and miscellaneous building supplies.

Repairs and reserves for replacement would cover outlays on a pro rata basis of the estimated service life of furnishings and fixtures. For instance, if an apartment building contains twenty refrigerators each having an estimated service life of ten years, the reserve for replacement in this case would call for expense provision equal to costs of two refrigerators annually. Similarly if each of the twenty apartments is decorated once every fourth year, annual provision would include the cost of twenty divided by four—or five apartments typically during any one year. Where exterior fronts, roofing, and plumbing are replaced at service life intervals like provision would be made, generally on a straight line accounting basis.

It is recommended that operating expense schedules be reconstructed in accordance with the accounting procedure followed by the National Association of Building Owners and Managers. This permits comparison of expense estimates with those typically incurred for similar properties and, as reported annually by the Association in its *Building Experience and Exchange Reports,* available through the Chicago office of the Association. Cost comparisons for apartment or office buildings can readily be made from these reports on a per square foot basis of rentable space for the following items:

Operations.   Cleaning; electrical system; heating and ventilating; plumbing system; elevator; general expenses for offices; and general expenses for the entire building.

Construction.   Alterations; repairs and maintenance; and decorating costs.

Fixed charges. Fire and other hazard insurance; taxes; and depreciation. Allowance for depreciation, although not used as an expense in the capitalization process, gives a clue to the length of economic lives of buildings, as well as to the methods and market rates of depreciation employed under typical management.

Typical income and operating expenditures for high-rise modern office buildings, based on studies published by the American Institute of Real Estate Appraisers and the National Associations of Building Owners and Managers, have been classified on a per square foot basis as follows:

For operating expense data and comparative performance statistics of hotels and motor courts, informative reports are published by Horwath and Horwath, accountants and consultants,[3] and Harris, Kerr, Forster and Company, accountants and auditors.[4] The former report presents illustrated trends of business and operating ratios of 100 hotels located in 53 cities. Information in this report provides comparative statistics over a thirty-year period as to total sales, room sales, restaurant sales,

---

[3] *Hotel Operations in 1967,* by Horwath and Horwath, Hotel Accountants and Consultants, New York, N. Y.

[4] *Trends in the Hotel Business 1967,* by Harris, Kerr, Forster and Company, New York, N. Y.

See also: *Economic Factors and Case Studies in Hotel and Motel Valuation,* second edition, published by 1967 Education Committee of the American Institute of Real Estate Appraisers.

	Amount	Percent of Revenue
Gross Revenue	$5.25	100.00
Occupancy—Ratio		96.00
Effective Revenue	5.04	100.00
Operating Expenses		
Cleaning	.65	12.90
Electricity	.22	4.37
Heat—fuel	.18	3.57
Air conditioning	.24	4.76
Plumbing	.04	.79
Elevator	.16	3.17
Administration	.23	4.56
General	.16	3.17
Management	.25	4.96
Total operating costs	$2.13	42.26
Alterations and repairs:		
Tenant alterations	.07	1.39
General repair	.09	1.79
Tenant decorating	.05	.99
Total Alterations and repairs	.21	4.17
Fixed charges:		
Taxes and Insurance	.82	16.27
Depreciation (reserve)	.30	5.95
Total fixed charges:	1.12	22.22
Total operating costs	3.46	68.65
Net operating income after allowance for accrued depreciation	1.58	31.35

room rates, and room occupancies. Detail data for major cities is given for average hotel expenditures as follows:

Administrative and general expenses.
Payroll taxes and employee benefits.
Advertising and promotion.
Heat, light and power expenditures.
Repairs and maintenance.
Replacements, improvements, and additions.

The latter report provides statistics for 400 hotels and 100 motor courts. This publication emphasizes trends of hotel and motel income and expenses, earnings on capitalization, occupancy ratios, room rates, and disposition of the hotel dollar. For purposes of hotel and motor court appraising, these two publications offer important statistical data which are most useful in a study of comparative income and expense performance.

OPERATING EXPENSE SCHEDULE
RECONSTRUCTION

An owner's typical expense statement for a twenty-unit apartment house may contain information as follows:

OWNER'S OPERATING EXPENSE STATEMENT
For the Year 19--

Revenue			$26,000
Operating expenses:			
Taxes		$2,500	
Insurance			
Fire	$300		
Theft	50		
Liability	40		
		390	
Maintenance			
Janitor—exclusive of apartment		1,000	
Heat—oil		1,200	
Water		150	
Electricity		225	
Repairs—miscellaneous		200	
Elevator—contract		400	
Replacements			
1 refrigerator		250	
1 stove		400	
Decorating—6 apartments		900	
Mortgage—Interest		600	
Amortization		500	
Paving assessment		1,000	
Depreciation		2,225	
Total operating expenses			$11,940
Net operating income			$14,060

A reconstructed owner's operating expense statement for appraisal report analysis and valuation of the subject property is presented as follows:

RECONSTRUCTED OPERATING EXPENSE STATEMENT
For the Year 19--

	As Reported	As Adjusted	Reference
Revenue	$26,000	$27,200	1
Vacancy & collection losses 5%		1,360	2
Effective revenue		$25,840	
Operating expenses:			
Fixed expenses:			
Taxes	2,500	2,500	
Insurance	390	475	3
Maintenance costs:			
Management 10%		2,600	4
Janitor	1,000	2,200	5
Heat	1,200	1,200	
Water	150	150	
Electricity	225	225	
Miscellaneous—supplies		80	6
Elevator—contract service	400	400	
Miscellaneous—repairs	200	260	7
Repairs and replacements:			
Refrigerators	250	500	8
Stoves	400	250	9
Decorating	900	750	10
Roof replacement		600	11
Plumbing and electrical		1,200	12
Furniture—lobby and halls		200	13
Other expenses:	4,325		14
Total operating expenses	$11,940	$13,590	
Net operating income—before depreciation	$14,060	$12,250	

Operating expense ratio $13,590 ÷ $25,840 = 53%

The reference numbers noted in the reconstructed operating statement are a guide to explanatory footnotes as follows:

1. Revenue was adjusted upward in the amount of $1,200 to include rental value of $100 per month for an apartment occupied by the resident janitor.
2. Vacancy and collection losses, based on community rental study and records of local boards of realtors, typically amount to 5 percent of gross income at 100 percent occupancy. This rental loss was provided to cover vacancy contingencies over the remaining income life of the property.

3. Insurance coverage was increased to 80 percent of co-insurance requirements.

4. Management costs for comparable properties equal 10 percent of effective gross revenue. Subject building is owner-managed.

5. Janitorial expenses were adjusted to include cost (income foregone) of apartment furnished for his use.

6. Miscellaneous supplies for cleaning were estimated at a cost of $4 per apartment.

7. Miscellaneous repairs increased to equal typical expenditures estimated at 1 percent of construction cost-new.

8. Refrigerator expenses adjusted to provide for two per year. Service life is ten years, or $20 \div 10 = 2$.

9. Stove replacement adjusted to provide for purchase of two per year.

10. Decorating expenses were adjusted to provide for refinishing of each apartment once every four years at a cost of $150 each.

11. Roof replacement required once every twenty years at a cost of $12,-000 (5 percent of $12,000 = $600).

12. Plumbing and electrical replacements based on the service life of fixtures of twenty years, or 5 percent of $24,000 = $1,200.

13. Lobby and hall furnishings at cost of $2,000 are replaceable every ten years, or at cost of $200 per year.

14. Other expenses shown in the owner's statement were omitted as follows:

    a. Mortgage interest and amortization payments are income deductions, not property expenses. Financing arrangements benefit the owner and not the subject property.

    b. Paving assessments are capital improvement outlays which increase the value of land.

    c. Depreciation is included as a rate of return to the property owner in the building rate of capitalization. To include it here would provide a dual return.

For greater accuracy in appraisal reporting and to provide assurance that income and expense forecasting reflects feasible performance capacity of the subject property, it is recommended that the appraiser analyze, whenever possible, income and expense accounting statements for a period of at least three full years. Income or expenditures in any one year may prove to be nonrecurable or not indicative of normal, i.e., typical, operations. Analysis of a number of years of property operating performance will enable the appraiser to "normalize" operating trends, and to forecast with greater accuracy the anticipated income stream for the remaining economic life of the improvements which are under value study.

THE SIGNIFICANCE OF OPERATING EXPENSE RATIOS

Although revenue and operating expenses are independently estimated, a definite relationship exists between them. The amount of rental income for given types of properties varies directly with the amount and quality of services, furnishings, and facilities offered the tenants. Increased revenue from superior conveniences and amenities provided occupants is in turn based on higher operating outlays to supply these services. Characteristically, however, while gross revenue rises and falls in proportion to percent of occupancy, operating expenses are relatively inflexible. Property taxes and insurance payments do not diminish, even where the property at times is 100 percent vacant. Heating, cooling, and janitorial services, too, remain relatively constant. Except for managerial service cost—which is considered a percentage of the effective gross revenue—other expense charges are relatively inflexible.

The inelasticity of operating expenses impairs the quality of net income which is derived from properties with high operating expense ratios. To illustrate: Suppose two properties, *A* and *B*, each yield a net income of $20,000 as follows:

	A	*B*
Effective revenue	$100,000	$40,000
Operating expense	80,000	20,000
Net operating income	$ 20,000	$20,000

Property *A*, as shown, has an operating ratio (operating expenses divided by effective gross revenue) of 80 percent. The operating ratio for property *B* is 50 percent. A decline in gross revenue of only 10 percent will, for property *A*, cause a decrease of 50 percent in the available net income. A decrease of 20 percent in revenue will wipe out property *A*'s net income entirely. Property *B*, however, will experience a much less drastic decline in its net income. A decrease of 10 and 20 percent in revenue causes only a drop of 20 and 40 percent respectively in the net income of property *B*. High operating ratios thus impair the quality of anticipated income. Increased risk of operation as measured by high operating ratios necessitates, as will be explained more fully in the following chapter, a selection of a higher rate of capitalization—which in turn results in a lower value estimate of the property. Everything else remaining equal, the income stream of $20,000 from property *B* is worth more than the identical income anticipated from property *A*, the difference in value being a direct reflection of the investor's unwillingness to gamble with economically sensitive income returns.

Knowledge of typical operating expense ratios is helpful in judging efficiency of operating performance. If typical residential properties indicate prevailing operating ratios between 35 and 45 percent of effective revenue, an operating ratio of 55 percent for a subject property should be cause for inquiry to ascertain the reason for such poor performance.

Many factors such as poor construction, mismanagement, and neighborhood decline may underlie the increased economic hazards reflected by the excessive operating ratio.

Typical operating expense ratios for various types of properties may fall into the following percentage ranges:

Residential, single-family structures	35—40%
Apartment buildings—walk up	40—50%
Apartment buildings—automatic elevator	55—65%
Apartment buildings—manual elevator	60—70%
Office buildings	40—50%
Store and loft buildings	50—60%

These expense ratios [5] vary from area to area with local rental customs and community building use regulations. Like other rules of thumb, operating ratios should not be used as a prime measure of value, but rather should serve as an indicator to judge the reasonableness of the results obtained through reconstruction of owner's income and expense operating statements. An excessively high—or unusually low—operating ratio may be a warning sign that re-analysis of income-expense data is warranted to safeguard against errors through acts of omission or commission.

CAPITAL EXPENDITURES

Care should also be taken in the analysis of operating expenses to exclude outlays or investments for capital improvements. Additions of porches, bathrooms, carports, or utility rooms, for instance, increase property value. As a rule improvements of this kind also increase the service utility of the property, and produce greater amounts of rentals or amenities to the occupying owner. The test of whether an expenditure is a true operating expense or not rests on the nature of the expenditure and the necessity of the outlay in relation to the operating care and maintenance of the property. Intimate knowledge of operating performance of the various property types for which appraisal opinions are to be rendered is a prerequisite to sound and professional appraisal practice.

READING AND STUDY REFERENCES

1. *The Appraisal of Real Estate* (Chicago: American Institute of Real Estate Appraisers, 1967), chap. 16.

---

[5] Exclusive of provisions, or reserves, for amortization (recapture) of capital investment.

2. Babcock, Frederick M., *The Valuation of Real Estate* (New York: McGraw-Hill Book Company, Inc., 1932), chap. 22.

3. Bowes, Eugene G., "How to Estimate Gross Income and Operating Costs," *Real Estate Appraisal Practices* (American Institute of Real Estate Appraisers, 1958), pp. 173–81.

4. Hanav, Yoshio, "Operating Statement—Income and Expenses," *The Real Estate Appraiser* (July 1966), pp. 2–14.

5. Horton, E. B., Jr., "How to Use Income and Expense Estimates," *The Appraisal Journal* (July 1959), pp. 341–48.

6. Kahn, Sanders A., Frederick E. Case, and Alfred Schimmel, *Real Estate Appraisal and Investment* (New York: The Ronald Press Company, 1963), chap. 9.

7. McMichael, Stanley L., *McMichael's Appraising Manual,* 4th ed. (Englewood Cliffs, N.J.: Prentice-Hall, Inc., 1951), chap. 9.

The most important, perhaps the most controversial, and yet the least known phase of property valuation revolves about the procedure for the determination of a market rate of capitalization through which estimated future net income can be converted into a sum of present value. The rate of capitalization acts as a lever which pushes income into a height of value, as shown in Figure 16.1.

The lower the rate of capitalization, the higher the value per dollar of in-

16 Determining the Rate

of Capitalization

come. The conversion power—as in all interest functions—is geometric in character, as is demonstrated in Fig. 16.1 by the capitalization of an income of $1.00 at selected rates of interest.

As indicated in Fig. 16.1, an increase in the rate of interest from 2 percent to 4 percent lowers capitalized value by 50 percent. If 4 percent is the correct rate and 2 percent is used, the increase in capitalized value is 100 percent. Again, the difference between a 5 percent and a 6 percent rate of capitalization is only 1 percentage point; but the value impact of this difference is one-fifth (20 percent) or one-sixth (16.67 percent) depending on which rate forms the correct base for the conversion of income into value.

The basic relationship of income to value through the use of a rate or reciprocal conversion factor is expressed by the formulae $V = I/R$ or $V = I \times F$.

FIGURE 16.1

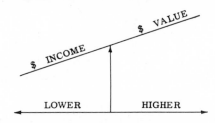

LOWER   HIGHER

RATE OF CAPITALIZATION

GEOMETRIC IMPACT OF RATES OF CAPITALIZATION
ON CONVERSION OF INCOME INTO VALUE

Income	Rate %	Reciprocal Factor	Value
$1.00	.01	100.00	$100.00
1.00	.02	50.00	50.00
1.00	.04	25.00	25.00
1.00	.08	12.50	12.50
1.00	.16	6.25	6.25

In these formulae the symbols used represent the following:

V = present worth of future rights to income.

I = net (operating) income before payments of interest on the investment and provisions for amortization (depreciation) of the investment.

R = Rate of capitalization or rate of interest on investment applicable to the conversion of income (over limited property life or in perpetuity) into value.

F = Reciprocal of rate of capitalization. A convenience factor employed to convert income into value by process of multiplication rather than division.

Whenever two of the factors represented by the symbols in the above formulae are known, the third or unknown factor can be calculated mathematically. Thus if value and income amounts are known, the rate of capitalization or the reciprocal rate factor can be calculated by application of the formulae $R = I/V$ or $F = V/I$. Likewise, applicable income is ascertained by use of the formulae $I = V \times R$ or $I = V/F$. The following diagrams provide handy memory tools for ready appraisal reference:

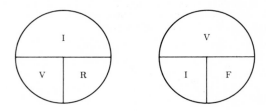

Appraisers often spend hours if not days in the analysis of income and operating expense statements in order to derive with accuracy the potential net income essential to a measure of market (investment) value. By comparison, relatively little time is employed in the selection of the applicable and essential rate of capitalization. This despite the fact that an error of only 1 percentage point (use of 8 percent in place of a 7 percent rate of interest) causes an error of 12.5 percent in the final estimate of value. It seems advisable, therefore, to spend less time on auditing of minor accounts and more time on the study of market indexes which offer an insight into investors risk rate motivations.

Why is it so difficult to derive a correct rate of capitalization? This is a question often raised. The answer evolves about the problems encountered in ferreting out accurate information for objective analysis of the varied and numerous subjective reasons motivating buyers to purchase properties at given prices and times. But even if buyer motives were known, it is still essential to extract reliable and accurate information concerning the net (operating) income of a subject property.

Generally, real property is purchased for one of the following reasons:

1. *Investment.* In this classification fall all buyers who intend to hold property for its income or, if vacant land, to develop it into an income producing investment.
2. Purchase for owners use or pleasure. Under this category fall home owners, store owners and other individuals who acquire property for purposes other than investment or speculation. In such cases property utility in terms of income producing capacity must be estimated (imputed).
3. *Speculation.* This classification includes those whose principal motive in buying is to profit from the resale of the property at some future time. Properties purchased for speculation, such as vacant land, may produce no income at all; in fact the income may be negative, in the form of outlays for taxes and other related costs of ownership.
4. Combination of investment and speculation or purchase in order to better the income tax position of the buyer.

Where speculation or motives other than investment buying are prime reasons for a purchase, the sale price of the property in relation to its income, if any, is of little aid to the appraiser in his search for applicable market rates of capitalization. In fact such sales, if used, may prove highly misleading as indicators of prevailing yields on real estate investments. This can be illustrated by a hypothetical sale as follows:

Suppose that a parking lot which nets an operating income of $2,000 sold at a price of $35,000. Suppose further that community growth and development support a conclusion that this net income will increase in four years' time by at least 50 percent, or to $3,000, and will stabilize at that amount. Using the formula $R = I/V$, and based on current earnings and property sales price, a market rate of capitalization of 5.71 percent is obtained ($2,000 ÷ $35,000). This rate, however, is not a true reflection of the capitalization rate, which by necessity must be based on *future*—not past or present—income prospects and operations of the property over its *entire* economic life. The true capitalization rate in this instance, if not otherwise known, may be derived with the following formula:

$$P = I_1 \frac{1 - \dfrac{I}{(+i)^n}}{i} + \frac{I_2}{i\,(1+i)^n}$$

Where P = price paid for the land or interest.
I_1 = present net income.
n = number of years over which present income is expected.
I_2 = prospective (future) income after n periods, into perpetuity.
i = capitalization rate.

In the above formula, where all factors with the exception of i (the rate of capitalization) are known, by solving for i a capitalization rate of 7.84 percent is obtained. That is, if an annuity of $2,000 per annum for a period of four years is discounted to present worth at 7.84 percent, and added to the present worth of a perpetuity of $3,000 at 7.84 percent beginning four years hence, a sum of $35,000 would result—which equals, of course, the sum paid for this hypothetical interest in realty.

As demonstrated above, extreme care must be taken in the use of market rates, particularly in abnormal or controlled markets. In the illustration offered, the capitalization rate exceeded the market earnings-price ratio by 2.13 percent. The use of earnings-price ratios in place of the effective capitalization rate for properties having like present but dissimilar future incomes would cause sizable errors in the appraiser's final value estimate.

To illustrate further: Suppose 40 acres of rur-urban property is purchased at a price of $1,000 per acre in anticipation that it will increase to

$4,000 per acre in ten years time. Suppose, further, that the land is rented for cattle-grazing purposes and produces a rent just equal to taxes and miscellaneous outlays leaving a zero operating income. Under traditional analysis where the appraiser relates current income to current market prices, the resultant rate of capitalization would be zero since no net income is realized by the purchaser. Should this property, however, sell for $4,000 per acre as anticipated ten years later, the resultant increment in value represents a yield of nearly 15 percent per annum. Reference to a compound annuity table will confirm that $1.00 invested at 15 percent compound interest will grow to $4.05 in ten years' time. The necessity to consider both appreciation and depreciation of the investment during the period of ownership is most essential and will be given further and more detailed consideration in Chapter 21 on Equity Financing.

Most appraisers would find themselves at a loss if the application of the income approach and the selection of a rate of capitalization had to be substantiated solely by analysis of investment sales in their community. Real estate transactions are traditionally private and confidential in nature and factual income data is often difficult to obtain. More difficult still is selecting those sales which could be usefully employed for statistical income analysis.

Although real estate as a commodity is local in character, the financing and purchase of real estate—both for investment and speculative purposes—have characteristics of a national market. The mobility of credit and the flexibility of investment buying with income reserves and surpluses accumulated by insurance companies, investment firms, and labor union pension funds has—as is the case with "arbitrage" in the stock and commodity markets—channeled funds into community areas where the investment returns in relation to capital risks are highest. The existence of a national real estate investment market makes available for real properties national income and rate-of-return statistics which are compiled by investment firms and real estate analysts. These national indices of investment yields, when adjusted for community and regional risks for given classes of real properties, can be used as effective guides in judging the reasonableness of rates of capitalization secured from market analysis of comparable sales.

KINDS OF INTEREST RATES AND
CAPITALIZATION

It may prove helpful to enumerate and briefly explain the kinds of and purposes served by various types of rates in common use today. Appraisers should recognize and differentiate among the following:

1. Interest rate.
2. Rate of capitalization.
3. Over-all rate of capitalization.
4. Building rate of capitalization.
5. Land rate of capitalization.
6. Rate of investment recapture, or amortization.
7. Split rate:
   (a) Mortgage rate.
   (b) Equity rate.
8. Composite rate.

The *interest rate* is in effect a measure of the cost of money, and represents "wages" paid for the use of capital. It is a return on the investment and must be high enough to attract capital to a particular kind of investment. The interest rate as here defined is based on the continued and unimpaired existence of the property as an investment entity. The rate does not include any provision for depreciation or depletion. The interest rate is a market phenomenon and varies in amount with the supply and demand of money, and with the quality characteristics of the investment proper. The interest rate as a composite annual return per dollar of investment is influenced by the following market forces:

1. Rate of interest on government bonds on guaranteed bank deposits.
2. Burden of management or cost of maintaining the investment, including bookkeeping, collecting, inspection, and fund supervision expenses.
3. Relative liquidity of the investment for conversion into cash.
4. Risk of loss of income and investment due to competition or operation of economic forces as reflected by the position of the business cycle.

As a rule, the interest rate on government bonds establishes the lower limit of the interest rate. Where money is used for the purchase of mortgages, equities, or in outright ownership of property, management of the investment creates burdens for which the investor seeks compensation in addition to the rate of interest paid on bonds or bank deposits. This burden is currently quoted at ½ of 1 percent for mortgage and ¾ percent to 1 percent on real estate equity or outright property ownership. Liquidity, too, is important to many investors who seek flexibility of transfer of investment interests. It is estimated that nonliquidity of real estate as an investment adds from 1 to 2 percent to the basic bond or bank rate of interest. Risk of loss of income may be as low as 1 percent for conventional mortgages and may reach a high of 10 percent or even more for specialized farm or industrial property. Although it is theoretically possible to build up a rate of interest by independent consideration of the economic forces which make up the rate as a composite whole, in practice reliance must be placed on analysis of market operations for a determination of the rate that accurately measures the investment cost of money. The rate of interest is basic to a derivation of a rate of capitalization, and the market methods available for obtaining and adjusting rates of interest will be discussed below.

The *rate of capitalization* expresses in percentage form the relationship between the net income of a property (net before interest payments and depreciation charges) and the value or price at which the property sold. The rate of capitalization is always a composite of (1) the rate of interest, and (2) the rate of amortization or depreciation of the investment. In instances where the investment or any part of it will maintain its level of value into perpetuity, the rate of amortization for that part or for the investment as a whole, as the case may be, is zero.

The rate of interest and rate of capitalization are often used interchangeably as if their meaning were one and the same. It is this kind of loose thinking which confuses the uninformed and leads to erroneous value conclusions. It is true that in all instances where amortization of the investment need not be provided for, the rate of interest and the rate of capitalization are identical. But even in such cases it is best to be consistent and to speak of a rate of capitalization rather than a rate of interest when converting income into value. The latter term should be used only when reference is made to a return on the investment representing "wages" paid for the use of capital. It would also contribute to clarity of thinking if the term *rate of capitalization,* whenever used in appraisal practice, be modified to indicate whether use is made of this rate as an overall, a building, or a land rate of capitalization.

The *overall* rate of capitalization is a ratio indicating the relationship of net (operating) income of the entire property (land and building) in relation to value or price of the entire property. The overall rate of capitalization is, as a rule, always greater than the land rate of capitalization, and less than the building rate of capitalization. To illustrate: If a building valued at $16,000 produces a net income of $1,440, the building rate of capitalization is $1,440 ÷ $16,000, or 9 percent. If the land on which this building stands is valued at $4,000 and yields an income of $240, then the land rate of capitalization is $240 ÷ $4,000, or 6 percent. The overall rate of capitalization would be obtained by dividing the combined land and building (property) income by the combined land and building (property) value. In this illustration the overall rate equals $1,680 ÷ $20,000, or 8.4 percent. This overall rate can then be checked by weighting the building and the land (split) rates of capitalization on the basis of a building-to-land ratio of 80 percent and 20 percent respectively of total property value as follows:

Building rate of capitalization, .09 × .80 =   .072
Land rate of capitalization, .06 × .20 =   .012
                                                               ———
Total property, or overall, rate of capitalization = .084, or 8.4 percent

When property income (for both land and building) is converted directly into value by use of an overall rate of capitalization, the method of valuation is called *direct capitalization*. The direct method of capitalization is not recommended for use when other and more precise methods of capitalization, as will be demonstrated in the following chapters, are available. The use of an overall rate assumes that the subject property is identical in building characteristics, building age, and land-to-building value ratio to the comparable properties from which the overall rate was derived. This in practice is rarely the case.

The *building rate of capitalization* is a ratio of building net income (before interest and amortization) to the value of the building. Since building income must cover both a return on the investment and amortization of the building investment over the remaining economic life of the building, the rate of capitalization applicable to the building must also be a composite of a rate on and a rate of the investment. The rate of amortization generally is based on one of the theoretical methods of depreciation explained in Chapter 12. To illustrate: If the rate of interest for a building investment is 7 percent and the rate of amortization is 2 percent (straight line depreciation based on fifty-year remaining life) then the building rate of capitalization is 7 percent plus 2 percent, or 9 percent. As the remaining building life shortens, the building rate of capitalization will increase—assuming no change in the rate of interest. To illustrate: Where the remaining economic life is estimated at twenty years, the straight line rate of amortization is 5 percent. This rate, when added to the 7 percent rate of interest, equals 12 percent building rate of capitalization. The *land rate of capitalization* is a ratio of net income derived from land to the value or price paid for the land. Where property rights are held in fee simple ownership, income from land is assumed to extend into perpetuity, and no provision need be made for depreciation of the land investment. However, where land is subject to depletion of its mineral or other resources, or where ownership is for a period of years as in a leasehold estate, a rate of depreciation or amortization must be calculated and added to the rate of interest to provide for a return of the land investment over the terminal years of ownership. In appraisal problems in which the capitalization of land income involves perpetuity, the land rate of capitalization and the land rate of interest are one and the same.

The *rate of amortization* provides for a return or recapture of the investment over the economic life of the property. This rate of depreciation is based, as a rule, on one of the theoretical, or age-life, methods explained in Chapter 12. The selection of the appropriate rate at which an investment is to be amortized is most important because of the impact that differences in rates have on capitalized value. This is illustrated by the amortization provisions necessary to return an investment over a forty-year life period under depreciation methods as indicated below:

Method	*Rate of Amortization*
Straight line	.025
[1] Sinking fund (3%)	.0133
[1] Annuity (6%)	.0065

The straight line method of providing for future depreciation as compared with the annuity method, as shown above, requires nearly four times the dollar provisions necessary under the latter method. Considering the important differences in leverage that small differences in rates of capitalization cause in the results obtained under the income approach to value, it is evident that the selection of the method and rate of amortization must be undertaken with great care.

In practice, the sinking fund method of capital recapture is rarely used. Where the straight line method of recapture is applied to reflect a declining income stream over the life of the investment, it is recommended to "stabilize" the declining income and to capitalize under the annuity, or Inwood method, for correctly applied and identical appraisal results.[2] Except for short-lived properties or for provision of reserves for the replacement of furniture and fixtures, the use of the straight line method of capitalization is not recommended.

Split rates of interest are better described as *fractional rates* because they apply to fractions of a property. The term *split rate* was coined because fee interests in real estate were split among classes of investors. The split rates best known are those that represent interest yields on mortgages and equity. As a rule, mortgage rates for given types of properties are readily obtainable from individual or institutional lenders. Equity rates, too, are quoted by investment firms, although such rates vary considerably with classes of real property, quality, amount of investment, and the economic rating of the community. Where the mortgage and equity rates can be secured with reasonable accuracy the property investment rate of interest can be computed by weighting the fractional rates, as will be demonstrated below under the *band of investment* method for selecting rates of interest.

The *composite rate of capitalization* is of relative recent origin. This

---

[1] See Sinking Fund Table in Appendix 3, page 569-575.

[2] See Chapter 14 for mathematical procedure to stabilize declining income streams.

rate is applied in the capitalization of a stabilized or level payment over a relative short period of ownership of about ten to fifteen years at a preselected yield to the equity owner rather than a rate applicable to the property as an investment entity. The composite rate, as will be more fully demonstrated in the chapter on Equity Financing, is precalculated to provide the desired equity yield—as influenced by mortgage interest rates and amortization terms, and anticipated percent depreciation or appreciation of the property as a whole over the ownership period. In effect the equity yield as reflected in the composite rate is that yield or rate of interest at which the present worth of the stabilized income stream plus the present worth of the equity reversion at time of sale equals the equity (cash) value of the property, exclusive of the mortgage debt, on date of purchase. Composite rates of capitalization for selected yield and mortgage interest rates over typical mortgage terms and ownership life periods have been precomputed and published as "Ellwood Tables." [3]

AVAILABLE METHODS FOR SELECTION OF THE RATE OF CAPITALIZATION

The basic problem in the construction of a rate of capitalization centers about the selection of a basic rate of interest to which the rate of amortization applicable to the subject property can be added. To find the basic rate of interest the appraiser must analyze market transaction data under one or more of the following rate-selection methods:

1. The market investment quality comparison method.
2. The band of investment method.
3. The banker's rate selection method.
4. The built-up method.

THE MARKET INVESTMENT QUALITY COMPARISON METHOD

As illustrated in Table 16.1, this method is based on the analysis of four or more recent and comparable sale transactions involving properties similar in class and kind to that of the subject property. For each sale property the appraiser must obtain (1) the stabilized operating income; (2) the percentage of operating income requisite for depreciation or amortization of the property; (3) the price paid for the property; and (4) the quality rating of the subject property as compared with the sale property. The method for obtaining this quality rating is illustrated in Table 16.2.

---

[3] L. W. Ellwood, *Elwood Tables for Real Estate Appraising and Financing* (Chicago, Illinois: American Institute of Real Estate Appraisers, 1967).

The percentage of estimated building depreciation as a ratio to operating income before depreciation can be calculated by either the straight line or annuity method of capital amortization. The latter method is recommended for use, but should be consistent with the capitalization method applied to income of the subject property. Where possible, as is the case in the analysis demonstrated in Table 16.1, the sale properties should be comparable to the subject property and to one another as to remaining economic life. Where this is true, a uniform rate of capital recapture can be applied. The derivation of a market investment rate of interest is illustrated as follows:

TABLE 16.1

THE MARKET INVESTMENT QUALITY COMPARISON METHOD FOR
SELECTING A MARKET RATE OF INTEREST

Item	Sale No.	1	2	3	4
1	Operating income	$8,250	11,250	8,000	7,700
2	Estimated building depreciation at 15%	$1,238	1,688	1,200	1,150
3	Net operating income	$7,012	9,562	6,800	6,550
4	Sale price of property	$90,000	110,000	80,000	75,000
5	Rate of interest earned (Item 3 divided by item 4)	7.8%	8.7%	8.5%	8.7%
6	Comparative quality rating (See Table 16.2)	.95	1.10	1.05	1.10
7	Adjusted rate of interest (Item 5 divided by item 6)	8.2%	7.9%	8.1%	7.9%
8	Correlated rate of interest applicable to subject property and based on reliability of sales information		8%		

The quality investment attributes as applied in Item 6 of Table 16.1 were obtained by analysis as follows:

TABLE 16.2

COMPARATIVE INVESTMENT QUALITY RATINGS

			Sale No.			
Quality Factor	*Ideal*	*1*	*2*	*3*	*4*	*Subject*
Certainty of gross	15	15	12	12	12	15
Extent of competition	25	25	20	22	20	20
Expense operating ratio	20	20	15	17	15	20
Salability of property	10	10	10	10	10	10
Stability of value	30	25	25	25	25	25
Total	100%	95%	82%	86%	82%	90%
Ratio of subject to sale property		.95	1.10	1.05	1.10	1.00

The percent ratings assigned to quality of income factors in Table 16.2 for the ideal property are merely suggestive. These ratings can be changed to fit local market investment characteristics. The ratings assigned to the sale properties as well as to the subject property could also be on a better or poorer or same quality basis for each investment, and only a total percentage rating could be assigned to indicate the appraiser's judgment as to the overall quality of an investment.

The market investment quality comparison method, when diligently and accurately applied, should yield reliable indices of market interest rates which the appraiser can use with professional confidence in the income-capitalization approach to value.

THE BAND OF INVESTMENT METHOD

The widespread use of mortgage debt financing in real estate purchase transactions—it is estimated that 85 percent of all real estate purchases involve some form of mortgage debt—makes it possible to calculate a rate of interest by weighting the fractional rates of mortgages and equity where they are known or readily quoted in the investment market. To illustrate: Suppose quality apartment properties could be financed as follows:

> 1st   mortgage—50% of value—at 6% interest
> 2nd mortgage—20% of value—at 8% interest
> Equity   —30% of value—at 12% interest

Based on this information a rate of interest for capitalization purposes can be constructed as follows:

>   6% 1st mortgage interest times .50(% value) = 3.0%
>   8% 2nd mortgage interest times .20(% value) = 1.6%
> 12% equity rate of interest times .30(% value) = 3.6%
>
> Total weighted rate of interest = 8.2%

The accuracy of this rate of interest can be proved as follows: A $100,000 apartment property at 8.2 percent interest must produce a return on the investment in the amount of $8,200. This income would be distributed as follows:

> 1st   mortgage—$50,000 @ 6% = $3,000
> 2nd mortgage—$20,000 @ 8% = $1,600
> 12% equity —$30,000 @ 12% = $3,600
>
> Total interest return $8,200

The band of investment method has been further refined to give weight to length and terms of mortgage amortization provisions. Tables under this method for various mortgage-equity ratios have been developed by Mr. L. W. Ellwood,[4] and the derivation and application of pre-computed composite rates will be further illustrated in Chapter 21 on Equity Financing.

THE BANKER'S RATE SELECTION METHOD

An opportune and useful procedure for the selection of interest rates applicable to various classes of property is provided by a back-door approach to investment risk analysis. Investment bankers and lending institutions generally base approval of mortgage loan applications—among other credit requirements—upon favorable and relatively risk-free earning capacity of the property offered as collateral. Depending on the kind and character of the income-producing property—residential, apartment, commercial, industrial, or farm—lenders stipulate the rate of mortgage interest to be charged and set the maximum value of the mortgage loan in relation to guiding safety margins that anticipated earnings must provide as cover for the interest (debt) charges that are due periodically. To assure sufficient income for payment of mortgage interest during the ups and downs of business cycle periods, interest coverage, at certain loan-to-value ratios, may be set conservatively as follows for different classes of property:

Class of Property	Interest to be Earned	Loan Ratio
Residential	2 times	75%
Apartment	2½ times	70%
Stores—100% location	2 times	60%
Industrial	3 times	55%
Special-purpose	4 times	50%

With the aid and knowledge of investment loan practices, the appraiser can derive a rate of interest applicable to a property as a whole as follows: Suppose loan requirements for an apartment property stipulate that:

1. Mortgage interest to be earned 2½ times.
2. Ratio of loan to value to equal 60 percent.
3. Rate of mortgage interest 6 percent.

Suppose further that an analysis of past earnings over a period of three to five years supports net income expectations in the amount of $9,000

---

4 *Ellwood Tables for Real Estate Appraising and Financing* (Chicago, Illinois: American Institute of Real Estate Appraisers, 1967).

annually. The property interest rate is then derived mathematically by solving for imputed loan data as shown below:

1. Amount of maximum interest payment:
   Income of \$9,000 $\div$ 2.5 (interest coverage) = \$3,600
2. Amount or value of mortgage loan:
   $$V = \frac{I}{R} = \$3,600 \div .06 \text{ (mortgage interest)} = \$60,000$$
3. Value of entire property:
   Mortgage of \$60,000 $\div$ .60 (loan-to-value ratio) = \$100,000
4. Earnings rate for entire property:
   $$R = \frac{I}{V} = \$9,000 \div \$100,000 = .09, \text{ or } 9\%$$
5. Rate of equity earnings:
   $$R = \frac{I}{V} = 5,400 \div 40,000 \text{ (equity interest)} = .135, \text{ or } 13.5\%$$

The accuracy of the findings can now be proven by weighting the fractional rates as shown:

Mortgage rate of 6% times .60 (mortgage ratio) = 3.6%
Equity rate of 13.5 times .40 (equity ratio) =   5.4%
_____
Property earnings or interest rate =   9.0%

THE BUILT-UP METHOD

To select a rate of interest for capitalization purposes under this method requires independent determination of the factors that enter into the construction of a composite market rate of interest. To reiterate, these factors are comprised of the following:

1. Pure interest (interest on government bonds).
2. Burden of monetary (not physical) management.
3. Nonliquidity of the investment.
4. Risk of ownership (loss of capital).

Conceivably, a 9 percent rate of return on an apartment property could be said to include fractional rates as follows:

Pure interest	3.25%
Burden management	1.00
Nonliquidity of investment	1.25
Risk	3.50
	_____
Total rate of interest	9.0 %

Logically, a breakdown of a composite interest rate as shown above would be difficult to support. It may be possible to obtain with reasonable accuracy the first three fractional rate quotations from financial institutions or investment services. The risk element, however, which may constitute the largest single force influencing the magnitude of the interest rate, cannot rationally be determined without analysis of rates of capitalization at which like properties exchange in the market. This leads the appraiser back to the application of the market investment quality comparison method, with the aid of which a rate of interest is directly determined. The build-up method cannot be classified as a primary procedure under which an interest rate can be independently determined. This method, however, has useful applications—not as a means for mathematical appraisal exercise, but as a breakdown or analytical device to measure comparative market risks of different classes of property or to measure risks ascribable to the location of like properties.

Once the market rate of interest has been established with professional care by one of the methods outlined above, this rate may then be applied as a rate of capitalization for incomes extending into perpetuity. For building improvements or for limited land income, a rate of amortization typical for the class of property and based on the remaining estimated economic life of the investment must be added to convert the rate of interest into a rate of capitalization.

READING AND STUDY REFERENCES

1. *The Appraisal of Real Estate* (Chicago: American Institute of Real Estate Appraisers, 1967), chap. 17.

2. Babcock, Frederick M., *The Valuation of Real Estate* (New York: McGraw-Hill Book Company, Inc., 1932), chaps. 28 & 29.

3. Gibbons, James E., "Capitalization Rates and their Selection," *The Residential Appraiser* (November 1961), pp. 3–8.

4. Kahn, Sanders A., Frederick E. Case, and Alfred Schimmel, *Real Estate Appraisal and Investment* (New York: The Ronald Press Company, 1963), chap. 10.

5. McMichael, Stanley L., *McMichael's Appraising Manual*, 4th ed. (Englewood Cliffs, N.J.: Prentice-Hall, Inc., 1951), chap. 5.

6. Mercer, George L., "Proper Selection of Capitalization Rates," *The Real Estate Appraiser* (September 1964), pp. 13–19.

7. Nelson, Roland D., "Overall Rate—Band of Investment Style," *The Appraisal Journal* (January 1969), pp. 25–30.

8. Sadisky, William V., "Relationship of the Cost of Borrowed Money to Capitalization Rates," *The Appraisal Journal* (January 1968), pp. 9–14.

9. Smith, Lawrence E., Sr., "Choosing the 'Cap Rate'," *The Residential Appraiser* (March 1961), pp. 7–10.

An understanding of mathematics as applied to compound interest functions is considered the most important basic tool of property appraising. The entire concept of value is based on a determination of the present worth of future (dollar) rights to income. To convert future income, or, for that matter, future commitments (liabilities) into a sum of present worth or present liability requires not only the application of mathematics but

17 *Mathematics of*

Property Valuation

also a knowledge of the functions and purposes served by established mathematics tables.

There are many types of special-purpose mathematics tables in current use. Each table is designed as an aid in solving often-repeated problems and to save the user the laborious work and time which basic calculations would otherwise require. In succeeding chapters, reference will be made to special-purpose tables of which a professional appraiser should have knowledge as an expert in his field —even though he may never apply such tables or may even disagree with the underlying theory that caused the author to develop the table in question. Among the special tables often used for professional appraisers are the following:

1. Inwood (coefficient) table.
2. Hoskold (sinking fund) premise table.
3. Ring capitalization (straight line) table.
4. Babcock (declining income) premise tables.
5. Ellwood (investment) tables.

A brief description of the derivation and function of each of the above-named special purpose tables will be given following a detailed explanation and demonstration of standard tables which are in general use and which serve as basic tools in appraisal practice. These standard tables are as follows:

1. Compound amount of 1 (interest) table.
2. Present worth of 1 (discount) table.
3. Future worth of an annuity of 1 table.
4. Present worth of an annuity of 1 table.
5. Sinking fund (amortization) table.
6. Amount whose present value is 1 table.

COMPOUND AMOUNT OF 1 (INTEREST) TABLE

This compound interest table rightfully may be called the mother table, from which all basic tables used in appraisal practice are derived. An understanding of the function and derivation of this table is most important, for it will permit the ready computation of rates and factors contained in all the standard tables named above. The ability to construct a compound interest or discount factor, too, may fill a vital need—especially at times when prepared tables at required interest rates are not available. At the outset, the reader is cautioned to keep in mind that interest tables do not make valuations; they are merely tools in the appraisal process, furnishing, as needed, ready-made calculations.

The compound amount of 1 interest table is based on the premise that $1 deposited at the beginning of a period—usually a year—earns interest that accrues during the period and which becomes part of the principal at the end of that period or the beginning of the second year (or interest) period. The interest earned during the second year is again added to become part of the principal on which interest is earned during the third year (or interest) period. This continues for the number of required periods of interest compounding called for in the appraisal problem. The interest earned and added to the principal during each period increases in geometric progression, as is evident from the equation $s = p(1 + i)^n$. The symbols in this equation represent the following:

s = the original investment plus the compound interest accumulations.
p = the original investment.
i = the rate of interest used per period.
n = the periods of compounding.

In the compound amount of 1 table, p stands for $1.00. To solve a problem involving X dollars, X is substituted for p. A compound amount of 1 table at selected rates of interest is presented in Appendix 3, pages 566 to 589. The derivation of this table can be illustrated as follows:

DERIVATION OF COMPOUND AMOUNT OF 1 AT FIVE PERCENT INTEREST

n Periods	Amount at Beginning	Interest at 5 Percent	Amount at End	Progression Formula
1	1.000 000	.050 000	1.050 000	$(1 + i)$
2	1.050 000	.052 500	1.102 500	$(1 + i)^2$
3	1.102 500	.055 125	1.157 625	$(1 + i)^3$
4	1.157 625	.057 881	1.215 506	$(1 + i)^4$
5	1.215 506	.060 753	1.276 281	$(1 + i)^5$
49	10.401 270	.520 063	10.921 333	$(1 + i)^{49}$
50	10.921 333	.546 067	11.467 400	$(1 + i)^{50}$

If the appraiser is interested in knowing the amount to which $1.00 will grow at 5 percent compound interest over a five-year period he merely refers to the compound interest rate table at that rate and for that period and finds the amount as 1.276 281. If the original amount is $200, then the compounded principal and interest equals $200 × 1.276 281, or $255.26.

Typical Use of Compound Interest Table. An investor purchased a property five years ago for $10,000. If this property is to be sold today, how much must the owner realize in order to have his original investment returned plus 5 percent compound interest? Assuming for purposes of this illustration no other capital or expense outlays, and no change in the purchasing power of the dollar, the answer is $10,000 × 1.276 281, or $12,762.81. An investor may wish to know the number of years required for an investment to double itself at 8 percent compound interest. Reference to the Compound Amount of $1.00 table at 8 percent on page 580 will indicate that $1.00 will accumulate at that rate to $1.999 in nine years' time, thus providing a ready answer to this and similar growth of investment problems.

PRESENT WORTH OF 1 (DISCOUNT) TABLE

In appraisal practice, it is often known that a certain amount will become due or will be realized a given number of years from now. The question confronting the appraiser then may be: What is the present worth of this amount today? The present worth of 1 table shown in Appendix 3, page 590 provides the answer at selected interest rates for the amount of $1.00. If X dollars are involved, the amount shown for $1.00 is merely multiplied by X. The present worth of a sum due in the future may be defined as that amount today which, if invested at compound interest over the period involved, will grow to that sum at the interest rate specified.

The present worth of 1 table in effect bears a reciprocal relationship to the compound amount of 1 table. To illustrate: If $1.00 at 5 percent will grow to $1.05 at the end of one year, then $1.00 due one year from a given date has a present worth at 5 percent interest (discount) of $1.00 $\times$ $\dfrac{1}{1.05} = \$1.00 \times .952381$, or $.95. If $1.00 is due two years from today at 5 percent, the answer is secured by multiplying $1.00 $\times \dfrac{1}{1.1025}$ or $1.00 $\times .907023 = \$.91$. The equation for the present value of an amount then becomes $p = \dfrac{s}{(1 + i)^n}$ In this equation, $p =$ the present worth in dollars and $s =$ the sum due at a future time. The construction of the present worth table can be illustrated as follows:

DERIVATION OF PRESENT WORTH OF 1 AT FIVE PERCENT
COMPOUND (DISCOUNT) INTEREST

n Periods	Compound Amount of 1	Present Worth of 1 [1]	Factor Formula
1	1.050 000	.952 381	$\dfrac{1}{(1 + i)}$
2	1.102 500	.907 030	$\dfrac{1}{(1 + i)^2}$
3	1.157 625	.863 838	$\dfrac{1}{(1 + i)^3}$
4	1.215 506	.822 703	$\dfrac{1}{(1 + i)^4}$
5	1.276 281	.783 526	$\dfrac{1}{(1 + i)^5}$
49	10.921 333	.091 564	$\dfrac{1}{(1 + i)^{49}}$
50	11.467 400	.087 204	$\dfrac{1}{(1 + i)^{50}}$

[1] Reciprocal of compound amount of 1.

Typical Use of Present Worth of 1 Table. Suppose at the time of purchase of a property it is known that the porch floor must be replaced five years hence. The cost of this replacement is estimated at $500. The question is: How much should be subtracted from the purchase price to provide for this future expenditure? If the interest rate is 5 percent, the answer is $500 × .783526, or $391.76. Proof: If $391.76 is invested today at 5 percent compound interest, this amount at the end of the five-year period will grow to $391.76 × 1.276281 (compound amount of 1 at 5 percent), or $500. To illustrate further: Supposing a property is under a fifty-year lease and will at the expiration of the lease period have an estimated worth of $50,000, what is the present value of this reversionary right at a rate of 5 percent interest? The answer is $50,000 × .087204, or $4,-360.20. To prove this answer: If $4,360.20 is multiplied by the compound amount of 1 at 5 percent interest for fifty years (11.4674), the total will equal a sum of $50,000.

FUTURE WORTH OF AN ANNUITY OF 1 TABLE

The tables explained above apply to a single sum either invested at the beginning, or anticipated at the end, of a given time. The remaining tables to be explained and demonstrated apply to periodic payments called *annuities*. An *annuity* is defined as a *series of periodic payments usually, but not necessarily, equal in amount*. Annuity payments or earnings can occur either at the beginning of each period (advance rental payments) or at the end of each period, such as amortization payments or business earnings accounted for at the end of the fiscal period. An annuity payment made at the beginning of each period is called an *annuity due*. An annuity payment made at the end of each year is called an *ordinary annuity*. Since advance income payments are the exception rather than the rule, emphasis is given here to the development and explanation of the future worth of an *ordinary annuity* table. Such a table is in effect an addition of the compound interest amounts of *each payment* over the periods (years) that each payment remains invested. To illustrate: Suppose periodic payments of $1.00 are made annually at the end of each period for five years. If the interest rate at which these annuity payments are to be compounded is 5 percent, the total sum of these payments, plus interest earned, can be derived with the aid of the compound amount of 1 table, as shown in Figure 17.1.

The last payment under an ordinary annuity is made at the end of the last period and thus accumulates no interest, as is shown in Figure 17.1. The next to the last payment is invested for a one-year period, the one before that for a two-year period, and so forth. As an equation, the sum total of the compound amount of an ordinary annuity may be expressed as follows:

$$s_5 = 1 + (1+i) + (1+i)^2 + (1+i)^3 + (1+i)^4$$

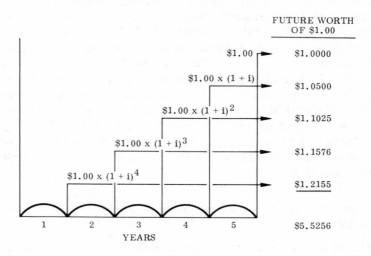

FIGURE 17.1

CONSTRUCTION OF FUTURE WORTH OF AN ORDINARY ANNUITY OF $1
OVER A FIVE-YEAR PERIOD—AT 5 PERCENT COMPOUND INTEREST

A reduced formula which may be applied in the computation of any number of periodic payments at any rate of interest is:

$$S_n = \frac{(1 + i)^n - 1}{i}.$$

The construction of a future worth of an ordinary annuity table in relation to the compound amount of 1 table can be shown as follows:

DERIVATION OF A FUTURE WORTH OF 1 TABLE AT FIVE PERCENT INTEREST
UNDER ORDINARY ANNUITY PAYMENTS

n Periods (End of Period)	Compound Amount of 1	Cumulative Amounts Future Worth of 1
1	1.000 000	1.000 000
2	1.050 000	2.050 000
3	1.102 500	3.152 500
4	1.157 625	4.310 125
5	1.215 506	5.525 631
49	10.401 270	198.426 663
50	10.921 333	209.347 996

Typical Use of Future Worth of 1 Per Period Table. Suppose operating costs on a vacant property covering taxes, insurance, and related maintenance amounted to $500 per annum over a five-year period. How much must the property owner add to the compounded amount of his original investment in order to recover these expenditures plus interest. By reference to the future worth of 1 table the answer is derived by simply multiplying the periodic outlays of $500 by the fifth-year factor of 5.525 631. This equals a sum of $2,762.82.

To illustrate further: Suppose a sum of $100 is set aside annually to amortize an investment. How much will be accumulated in the sinking fund at the end of fifty years, assuming an interest rate of 5 percent. Again by reference to a future worth of 1 table the answer is secured by multiplying $100 by the fifty-year factor of 209.347 996. This equals a sum of $20,934.80. For a future worth of 1 table at selected rates of interest, see Appendix 3, page 573. When annuity payments are made at the beginning of each period (annuity due), the appropriate factor can be secured from the future worth of 1 table by subtracting the amount of 1.00000 from the ordinary annuity factor shown in the $n + 1$ column. To illustrate: The future worth of 1 of an annuity due over four years at 5 percent = 5.525 631 (five-year ordinary annuity factor) minus 1.000 000, or 4.525 631.

PRESENT WORTH OF AN ANNUITY OF 1 TABLE

This table is used more than any other in appraisal practice. It provides factors indicating the present worth of an ordinary annuity of 1. Most income payments or earnings obtained from the use of real property have the characteristics of an annuity. To find the present worth of an income stream under the earnings approach to value it is merely necessary to convert (capitalize) the estimated annual earnings into a sum of present value by use of this table. The procedure for converting estimated operating (net) income into value and the techniques of capitalization will be explained in succeeding chapters. In this chapter, effort will be made to explain the derivation of the present worth of an annuity table and to demonstrate its use.

It will be recalled that the present worth of 1 table provided (discount) factors for the measurement of present value of a single payment or sum of money due at some future time. In effect an annuity is merely a series of future income payments, and the sum total of the present worth of all payments can be derived as demonstrated in Figure 17.2. Assuming an annual income of $1.00 at the end of each year for a period of five years

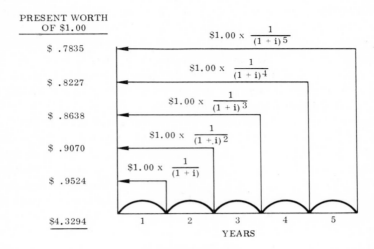

FIGURE 17.2

CONSTRUCTION OF PRESENT WORTH OF AN ORDINARY ANNUITY OF $1.00
OVER A FIVE-YEAR PERIOD—AT 5 PERCENT COMPOUND INTEREST

and an interest rate of 5 percent, the present worth of this annuity can be computed as shown in Figure 17.2.

The equation for deriving the present value of an annuity may be constructed as follows:

$$a_n = (1+i)^{-1} + (1+i)^{-2} + (1+i)^{-3} + (1+i)^{-4} + (1+i)^{-5} \ldots$$

This equation is mathematically reduced to:

$$a_n = \frac{1 - (1+i)^{-n}}{i}$$

The present worth table of 1 per annum at compound interest can be constructed in relation to the present worth of 1 table as on page 255.

Inspection of the table below will disclose that the increase in the present worth of an annuity is at a diminishing rate as future and equal periodic payments are added. The expectancy of $1.00 due fifty years from the present date increases the present value of a forty-nine-year annuity (at 5 percent rate of interest) by only $.087. Even if an annuity should be expected to be forthcoming for thousands of years, the present value

DERIVATION OF PRESENT WORTH OF 1 PER ANNUM AT FIVE PERCENT
INTEREST PAYMENTS AT END OF PERIOD

n Periods	Present Worth of 1	Cumulative Present Worth of 1 Per Annum
1	.952 381	.952 381
2	.907 030	1.859 410
3	.863 838	2.723 248
4	.822 703	3.545 951
5	.783 526	4.329 477
49	.091 564	18.168 722
50	.087 204	18.255 926

of such an annuity will never quite equal the sum obtained by capitalizing such an annuity into perpetuity through use of the formula
$V = \dfrac{I}{R}$. At a rate of 5 percent interest, the present worth of an annuity
of $1.00 extending into perpetuity equals $\dfrac{1}{.05}$, or $20. Proof: If a sum of
$20 is invested, or deposited with a bank that pays 5 percent interest,
the annual income as long as the deposit is kept intact (into perpetuity) is
$20. $\times$ .05, or $1.00. The perpetuity factor for a sum of $1.00 at any
rate of interest is merely the sum of $1.00 divided by the rate of interest
as follows:

Income		Rate of Interest		Perpetuity Factor
$1.00	÷	.04	=	25.00
1.00	÷	.05	=	20.00
1.00	÷	.06	=	16.67
1.00	÷	.07	=	14.29
1.00	÷	.08	=	12.50

Thus where income (as is the case with nondepreciable land) is anticipated to extend unendingly into the future, i.e., perpetuity, the value
of such income is obtained by dividing it by the applicable market-
determined rate of interest or, conversely, multiplying same by the perpetuity (rate reciprocal) factor as demonstrated above.

Typical Use of Present Worth of 1 Per Annum Table. Suppose a five-
year lease calls for net rental payments at the end of each year in the
amount of $1,000. If this lease is offered for sale and the rate of interest
is 5 percent, what is the present value of this series of income payments?
The answer is $1,000 $\times$ 4.329477 (Present Worth of an Annuity of 1. See
Appendix 3, page 596), which equals a sum of $4,329.48. Or, suppose a

property in new condition is estimated to yield $10,000 net annually over a remaining building life of fifty years: What is the present value of this annuity? Answer: $10,000 × 18.255 926, or $182,559.26. Occasionally, valuation problems deal with annuity payments that are received at the beginning of each payment period. The appropriate factor for *beginning-of-period* payments can be secured by adding the amount of 1.000 000 to the present worth factor of an ordinary annuity shown in the *n*—1 column. To illustrate: The present worth of $100 to be received at the beginning of each year for five years is $100 × 4.545 951 (fourth-year present worth factor of 3.545 951 + 1.000 000), or $454.60.

SINKING FUND (AMORTIZATION) TABLE

In all valuation problems in which buildings or other types of property have limited economic lives, provisions must be made for the amortization of that portion of the investment which is consumed annually by use or lessened in value by other causes of depreciation. In instances where the annual provisions for amortization can be set aside in a sinking fund to accumulate at moderate (safe) rates of interest over the economic life of the property, or where the periodic amortization provisions can be reinvested in like or similar investment properties at risk rates of interest, it is necessary to calculate the amount of annual provisions for amortization—or to know the rate per dollar of investment that must be set aside to provide for a return of capital. A useful and ready-made table, known as a sinking fund or amortization table, gives annuity amounts at various rates of compound interest whose future value is 1. To illustrate: If an amount of $1.00 is to be accumulated at 5 percent compound interest over a period of four years, how much must be set aside annually? The amount whose future value is $1 at 5 percent can be found by reference to the Sinking Fund Table in Appendix 3, page 574. The amount as indicated opposite the fourth year period is .232 012 or $.232 012 per dollar of investment value. The accuracy of this rate or amount can be proven by use of the Future Worth of An Annuity of 1 Table in Appendix 3. An annuity of $1 over four years at 5 percent compound interest equals $4.310 125 (see table, page 574). By multiplying this accumulation factor by the sinking fund rate of .232 012, a sum of $1.000 is obtained. If the property is worth $10,000, then the amount to be set aside annually over a four-year period at 5 percent interest to equal this sum is $10,000 × .232 012, or $2,320.12.

The sinking fund or amortization rate table has a reciprocal relationship to the future worth of an annuity of 1 table. Thus any factor at a given rate shown in the future worth of an annuity table, when divided into 1, will yield a sinking fund factor of 1 at the same rate of interest.

This reciprocal relationship and derivation of the Sinking Fund Table at 5 percent interest is demonstrated below.

DERIVATION OF A SINKING FUND TABLE AT FIVE PERCENT COMPOUND INTEREST

n Periods (End of Period)	*Future Worth of* Annuity of 1	Reciprocal of Future Worth or Sinking Fund Rate
1	1.000 000	1.000 000
2	2.050 000	.487 805
3	3.152 500	.317 209
4	4.310 125	.232 012
5	5.525 631	.180 975
49	198.426 663	.005 040
50	209.347 996	.004 777

Typical Use of Sinking Fund Table. A building worth $20,000 is to be amortized over a period of forty years at 6 percent interest. For appraisal purposes, the following answers may be required:

1. The rate of annual provision.
2. The amount of the annual provision.
3. Proof that the amount computed is correct.
4. The amount of amortization that will be accumulated at the end of 30 years of building life.
5. The percent accrued depreciation at the end of 30 years.

Solutions:

1. The rate of annual provision is found in the sinking fund table (see page 401) and the rate indicated under 6 percent opposite 40 years is .006 462.
2. The amount of the annual provision is $20,000 × .006 462, or $129.24.
3. Proof: $129.24 × 154.761 966 (future worth of an ordinary annuity over 40 years at 6 percent interest) equals $20,000.
4. The amount of amortization at the end of 30 years will be $129.24 × 79.058 186 30 (future worth of an annuity of 1 over 30 years at 6 percent interest), which equals $10,217.48.
5. The percent accrued depreciation can be derived by (a) dividing $10,217.48 by the total value of $20,000, or (b) multiplying the sinking fund rate of .006 462 (40-year factor) by the future worth of an annuity of 1 rate of 79.058 186 (30-year factor). Either method of calculation will yield identical answers of 51.09 percent.

AMOUNT WHOSE PRESENT VALUE IS 1

Frequently an appraiser is asked how much net income a property of a given value must produce in order to provide a fair return on the investment and amortization of the investment over the economic life of the property at market rates of interest. Whenever a mortgage loan is applied for, it must be calculated in advance how much the periodic payments amount to in order to yield interest on the mortgage and a return of the loan principal over the life period of the mortgage. Where the value of a property or the amount of a loan is known, the annuity income—or loan payment per dollar of present value—can be obtained from a special table in which the amounts, whose present value is 1, are calculated at selected rates of interest. A table of this kind is shown in Appendix 3, page 596.

The annuity payment table for an amount whose present value is 1 has a reciprocal relationship to the present worth of an annuity of 1 table and may be constructed as shown below:

DERIVATION OF AN ANNUITY PAYMENT TABLE FOR AN AMOUNT WHOSE PRESENT
VALUE IS 1 AT FIVE PERCENT INTEREST

n Periods (End of Period)	*Present Worth of* An Annuity of 1	*Reciprocal of Present Worth* Annuity (Payment of 1 Table)
1	.952 381	1.050 000
2	1.859 410	.537 805
3	2.723 248	.367 209
4	3.545 951	.282 012
5	4.329 477	.230 975
49	18.168 722	.055 040
50	18.255 925	.054 777

Typical Use of Amount Whose Present Value is 1 Table. Suppose a property is worth $30,000 and has an economic life of fifty years. How much must this property return as net income anually to provide interest and amortization at 6 percent interest? The annuity necessary to warrant an amount whose present value is 1 at 6 percent interest is .063 444 (see Appendix 3, page 599). Multiplying this amount by $30,000 gives the answer of $1,903.32. The rate of .063444 used in this illustration is in fact a composite of the interest rate on the investment, or .06 plus the sinking fund rate for fifty years at 6 percent, or .003 444. To derive the amount whose present value is 1 for a four-year period at 5 percent interest, all that is necessary (if this special table is not available) is to make reference to a sinking fund table and to add the rate of interest to the rate shown as follows: Sinking fund rate for four years at 5 percent = .23012 + .05 interest equals .282012, which is the annual amount necessary to provide a return *on* and *of* an investment of $1.00 for a four-year period at 5 percent interest.

A table showing the amount whose present value is 1 is especially useful in connection with mortgage-loan financing. This table provides the exact amounts which must be repaid over the loan period at given rates of interest for every dollar borrowed. Attention is called to the fact that interest and amortization payments on mortgage loans are generally computed over monthly rather than annual periods of time. Where this is the case the interest rate must be divided in the same proportion that the year is divided into smaller parts. To illustrate: If a $10,000 mortgage is made at 6 percent over twenty years and is to be amortized monthly, the twenty-year loan period is divided by 12 (months of the year) to obtain 240 monthly payment periods. Likewise, the annual interest of .06 must be divided by 12 to obtain the rate per payment period, which in this case is .005, or ½ of 1 percent. By reference to a table showing the amount whose present value is 1, the payment per $1.00 is obtained opposite 240 (*n*) periods under the ½ percent interest column. This amount is .007 165. Multiplying this rate of payment per $1.00 of loan by $10,000 indicates monthly payments of $71.65 will be necessary to pay interest at the annual rate of 6 percent (½ percent each month) and to amortize the $10,000 over a period of 240 months. An amortization schedule for the first 3 months of this loan would show entries as follows:

AMORTIZATION SCHEDULE OF A MORTGAGE LOAN OF $10,000 PROVIDING MONTHLY AMORTIZATION OVER A TWENTY-YEAR PERIOD AT FIVE PERCENT INTEREST

Year and Month	Monthly Payment	Interest at .005 Per Period	Amortization of Loan	Remaining Loan Balance
				$10,000.00
0–1	$ 71.65	$ 50.00	$21.65	
0–2	71.65	49.89	21.76	9,978.34
0–3	71.65	49.78	21.87	9,934.72
. . .	. . . .	. . . .	. . . .	. . . .
Totals	$17,196.00	$7,196.00	$10,000	

The various interest and annuity tables discussed in this chapter must be thoroughly understood by all professional appraisers. A complete book of mathematical tables [2] and a good electric (preferably printing) calculator should be part of every appraisal office. Further illustrations and applications of the various interest and annuity tables will be encountered in the chapters dealing with capitalization methods and techniques.

THE IMPORTANCE OF LOGARITHMIC TABLES AND FUNCTIONS

At the outset of this chapter it was stated that the basic compound interest table derived by the formula $S = (1 + i)^n$ is the mother table from which all other interest tables explained above can be readily de-

---

[2] *Financial Compound Interest and Annuity Tables* (Boston, Mass.: Financial Publishing Co., 4th ed., 1966) is recommended.

rived. It is important, therefore, that professional appraisers learn how to compute the compound amount of 1. Occasions arise when prepared tables at required percentages are not available, or where unusually long property lifespans go far beyond the number of compound periods covered in available table publications. The capitalization of income from a power dam, or the computation of its reversionary value when its economic life is judged to be three hundred or more years, may be such an instance.

To find the compound amount of 1 requires raising the amount of 1 plus the rate of interest (at which 1 is to be compounded) to a power equal to that of the number of interest periods involved. To find the compound amount of 1 at 5 percent interest over a period of five years— $(1 + i)^5$—it is necessary to raise 1.05 to the fifth power, as follows:

1.00	$\times$ 1.05 = 1.050 000	1.157 625 $\times$ 1.05 = 1.215 506
1.05	$\times$ 1.05 = 1.102 500	1.215 506 $\times$ 1.05 = 1.276 282
1.1025	$\times$ 1.05 = 1.157 625	

To raise 1.05 to a power of 50, or 500, or higher by simple arithmetic would be a most laborious if not an impossible task. A number, however, can be raised to any conceivable power with relative ease through the use of logarithmic tables.

It is not intended in this chapter to teach the use of logarithmic tables, nor to explain the principle underlying the theory of logarithms or its geometric functions. All that is intended is to state briefly the purposes which logarithmic tables serve and to recommend that interested students or professional appraisers unacquainted with these tables acquire a set, together with instructions for their use, through any bookstore or library.

A logarithm expresses a number in decimals of the power of 10. Adding the log of 1.05 to the log of 1.05 has the same effect as raising 1.05 to the second power; 20 times the log of 1.05 in effect raises 1.05 to its 20th power. To find the compound amount of $(1.05)^{50}$ merely requires looking up the log of 1.05, multiplying it by 50, and looking up the antilog to obtain the answer sought. To illustrate:

Log of 1.05   = 0.0211893
Log 0.0211893 $\times$ 50 = 1.059 465
Antilog 1.059 465   = 11.4674

The amount of 11.4674 thus obtained equals the amount shown under the compound amount of 1 table at 5 percent interest opposite the *n*, or time period of 50. (See Appendix 3, page 573.)

Those familiar with the operation of a slide rule may know that multi-

plication and division by this device are possible because of the logarithmic scale to which the numerals from 1 to 10 are patterned. Possession
of a slide rule, working knowledge of its application, and familiarity with
logarithmic tables, are highly recommended, if not essential, to all practicing appraisers.

SPECIAL PURPOSE TABLES

To permit ready and more rapid conversion of operating income into
value, a number of special purpose tables have been developed and published for use by property appraisers. Although all value problems can
be solved without reference to precomputed tables and it is often advisable
not to employ or rely on special purpose tables especially when testifying
in court as an expert witness,[3] nevertheless, every professional appraiser
must be acquainted with such tables, their derivation, and with circumstances under which such tables may be correctly applied.

THE INWOOD (COEFFICIENT) TABLE

This is the oldest, best known and most frequently applied capitalization
table. This table in essence is a summation of the present worth of $1.00
for each of the future years in which a level income (same amount each
year) is expected over the remaining economic life of the property. The
Inwood factor for a sum of $1.00 to be received over a period of forty
years at 8 percent is 11.9246. This factor is precomputed as shown in
Appendix 3 page 605 and is obtained by addition of the present worth of
$1 at 8 percent $\frac{1}{1.08} + \frac{1}{(1.08)^2} + \frac{1}{(1.08)^3} \cdots \frac{1}{(1.08)^{40}}$ or by the short-
cut method under which the rate of interest is added to the sinking fund
factor at the same rate for the number of years over which the income is
to be capitalized. This rate combination is then divided into the sum of
1.00. The reciprocal thus obtained is the Inwood factor. To illustrate:
Interest rate of .08 plus sinking fund factor at 8 percent for forty years
.00386 equals a capitalization rate of .08386. The reciprocal of this
rate is $\frac{1}{.08386}$ which equals the Inwood factor of 11.9246. To capitalize
an estimated level income of $1,000 per year for a period of forty years
under the Inwood method at 8 percent interest requires only the multiplication of $1,000 by the Inwood factor of 11.9246 to obtain the present value
of the property in the amount of $11,924.60.

---

[3] Experience has shown that laymen and jurors have difficulty in understanding
the use and purpose of complex mathematical tables and as a result become wary of
the findings and judge the integrity of the man rather than the accuracy of the
mechanisms of valuation.

THE HOSKOLD FACTOR TABLE

The Hoskold annuity factor is constructed in a similar fashion as the Inwood annuity factor. The only difference between these two methods of capitalization is that the sinking fund rate of depreciation or recapture is always at a lower, lesser, or "safer" rate than the rate of interest employed as a return on the invested capital. To illustrate: If the rate of interest is found to be 8 percent and the "safe" rate of capital recapture is 3 percent, then the rate of capitalization for an income stream over a period of forty years is .08 percent plus .01326 (3% S.F.) or .09326. The Hoskold factor is merely the reciprocal of the rate of capitalization or 1 ÷ .09326 which equals 10.723. Thus an income of $1,000 due each year over a period of forty years is worth, under the Hoskold method of valuation at the rates stated above, the sum of $1,000 × 10.723 or $10,-723. A Hoskold factor table for a sinking fund rate of 3 percent and interest rates of 5 to 10 percent inclusive is precomputed for ready use as shown on page 616 of Appendix 3.

THE RING FACTOR TABLE

The third most popular method of capitalization calls for straight line depreciation of invested capital. The rate of recapture is obtained by dividing 100 percent by the number of years of remaining building or property life. For an investment life of forty years the rate of recapture per year is 100 percent divided by 40 or 2.5 percent. This rate, when added to the interest rate, forms the rate of capitalization. Thus if the interest rate is 8 percent, and the straight line recapture rate is 2.5 percent, the rate of capitalization is 10.5 percent. To permit use of the value formula: $V = I \times F$ and to provide a table that is similar in construction and use as the Inwood and Hoskold tables of capitalization, the author has precomputed reciprocals of straight line rates of capitalization for years of one to fifty and at interest rates from 6 to 10 percent. These reciprocal rates comprise the Ring factor Table as shown in Appendix 3 page 614.

THE BABCOCK PREMISE FACTOR TABLE

This precomputed capitalization table was developed by Frederick M. Babcock and first published in book form in 1932.[4] In essence, Babcock established curves for declining income streams based on patterns as follows:

---

[4] Frederick M. Babcock, *The Valuation of Real Estate* (New York, N.Y.,: McGraw-Hill Publishing Company, Inc., 1932).

Premise No. 1. Assumed the income before depreciation to occur in *equal* installments over a given economic life without decline. Discounting this income represented by a sum of $1.00 at compound interest rates resulted in factors (under Premise No. 1) identical to and equal in all respect to the Inwood factors at the identical rates of interest.

Premise No. 2 assumed a gradual decline of an income stream equal to a curve as shown in Figure 17.3 below. Discounting this declining income stream beginning with 1.00 at the end of year one and reaching zero in year "n" plus 1, to a present worth at selected rates of interest yielded a Babcock Premise No. 2 factor for ready use. To illustrate: Based on an interest rate of 8 percent and an economic life of forty years, the Inwood or Premise No. 1 factor is 11.9246. For a declining income in accordance with Premise No. 2, the Babcock factor is 10.9702 or 92 percent of value under Premise No. 1 where the interest rate is 8 percent and the income life is forty years.

Premises No. 3 and 4 are similarly computed by discounting to present worth at various rates of interest, income streams that decline as shown in Figure 17.3 below for properties with a remaining economic life of 40 years. For an income stream declining over forty years at 8 percent compound interest, the Babcock factors are 9.8134 and 8.7736 under Premises No. 3 and 4 respectively.

Although Babcock factors are rarely used in practice today, the principle of income decline was firmly established by Babcock and newer and, perhaps, simpler methods for obtaining identical value results are illustrated in the chapter following.

ELLWOOD TABLES

These precomputed rates or coefficients were derived under the "band of investment" rate method to reflect mathematically varying combinations of mortgage and equity ratios over investment or ownership life periods of one to thirty years at preselected mortgage interest and equity yield rates. Ellwood tables are not intended to be applied in the conventional valuation of real property where the sale represents a cash or cash equivalent transaction. Rather the Ellwood tables are intended for use in the valuation of *equity* investments where a major part of the total property is encumbered with a level payment mortgage which is scheduled to be amortized monthly over a number of years at a stipulated rate of interest. With aid of the Ellwood tables an appraiser can readily compute the cash outlay that is warranted for the purchase of the equity interest in a property. This cash outlay must equal at stipulated (market determined) equity yield rates the present worth of future rights to income and capital payments as follows:

1. The present worth of the stabilized cash flow—left after mortgage payments covering interest and amortization of principal are met—during the ownership period of the property, and

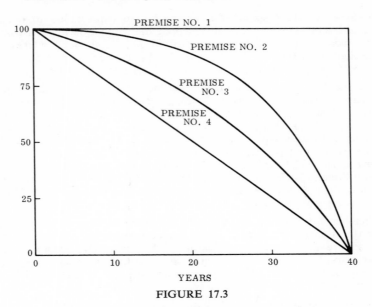

FIGURE 17.3

<small>Babcock Declining Income Premises</small>

2. The present worth of the cash reversion to which the owner is entitled. This is the selling price less the amount of the remaining mortgage principal that is due at the time of sale.

The derivation and application of the precomputed Ellwood tables will be more fully explained and illustrated in Chapter 21 on Equity Financing.

READING AND STUDY REFERENCES

1. *The Appraisal of Real Estate* (Chicago: American Institute of Real Estate Appraisers, 1967), chaps. 17–19.
2. Babcock, Frederick M., *The Valuation of Real Estate* (New York: McGraw-Hill Book Company, Inc. 1932), chaps. 14, 28–29.
3. Ellwood, L. W., "Appraisal Mathematics," *The Appraisal Journal* (April 1963), pp. 165–68.
4. Gushee, Charles H., ed., *Financial Compound Interest and Annuity Tables*, 4th ed. (Boston: Financial Publishing Company, 1968).
5. Holbrook, Jeffery, "The Thinking Man's Capitalization Rate," *The Real Estate Appraiser* (October 1963), pp. 2–8.
6. Hubin, Vincent J., "Some Further Remarks on the Nature, Meaning,

and Use of the 'Cap. Tables'," *The Appraisal Journal* (October 1965), pp. 517–30.

7. Kahn, Sanders A., Frederick E. Case, and Alfred Schimmel, *Real Estate Appraisal and Investment* (New York: The Ronald Press Company, 1963), chap. 11.

8. McMichael, Stanley L., *McMichael's Appraising Manual,* 4th ed. (Englewood Cliffs, N.J.: Prentice-Hall, Inc., 1951), chap. 6.

Appraising, under the income approach to value, calls for aptitude and skill in applying the capitalization process. To capitalize income means to convert or to process earnings anticipated from typical operation of a property into a sum of present worth (capital value). Mathematically, the basic relationship of income to value is expressed by the formula:

$$V = I/R, \text{ or } V = I \times F$$

The symbols used in these alternate

18 *The Income*

Approach to Value

capitalization formulas have meaning as follows:

V = present worth of future rights to income.

I = net operating income *before* providing for interest on the investment and amortization payments of the investment.

R = rate of capitalization—a summation of the rate of interest plus the rate of amortization $(i + r)$.

F = valuation or capitalization factor—a reciprocal of R.

Whether to use formula $V = I/R$ or $V = I \times F$ is optional, so far as the appraiser is concerned, since both equations will yield identical value conclusions. However, it is recommended that, in the selection of a capitalization formula, consideration be given to the technical level of understanding of the valuation report reader, and to present income and capitalization data in logical sequence and simple mathematical style.

The basic value formula $V = I/R$ is applicable to all appraisal problems involving capitalization of future rights to income. Care, however, must be taken to match income and rates of capitalization in relation to the value problem at issue. Thus, if the value of an entire property in fee simple ownership is sought, then I in the capitalization formula must represent total property income and R the total (or overall) property rate at which a fair return *on* and *of* the investment is anticipated. Similarly, if the value of a fractional interest is at issue, then both income and the rate of capitalization must be consistently related to that portion of the entire property, as will be demonstrated below.

CAPITALIZATION ON INCOME EXTENDING INTO PERPETUITY

The indestructible physical characteristics of land permit consideration of income derived from use of land as extending on and on into perpetuity, without termination. Improvements placed on land have finite economic lives; but new improvements can replace old ones, and the cycle of replacement for all practical purposes can be conceived as extending on into infinity.

To illustrate the application of the capitalization process to income extending into perpetuity, it is assumed that a constant, or level, flow of income in the amount of $500 annually is to be converted into value at an interest rate of 5 percent. Applying the formula $V = I/R$, the value obtained equals $500 ÷ .05 = $10,000. The correctness of this answer can be proven by transposing the basic value formula to find income, or I. In this instance, $I = V \times R = $10,000 \times .05 = 500, or the amount necessary annually (into perpetuity) to support a value of $10,000 at an interest rate of 5 percent. The value of $10,000 could also be obtained by use of the formula $V = I \times F$. Since F is the reciprocal of R, the valuation factor is obtained by dividing 1.00 by the rate at which the income is to be capitalized. In this instance $1.00 ÷ .05$ equals a perpetuity factor of 20. Thus $500 \times 20 = $10,000$, a sum equal to that obtained under the alternate capitalization formula used above.

Perpetuity factors at any rate of interest or fraction thereof are derived by simply dividing 1.00 by the rate used for capitalization purposes. With the aid of these valuation factors land value is readily obtained by a simple process of multiplication, as demonstrated above. Perpetuity factors at selected rates of interest are indicated on the next page.

PERPETUITY FACTORS FOR CAPITALIZATION OF NET OPERATING INCOME
AT SELECTED RATES OF INTEREST

Rate	Perpetuity Factor
.04	25.00
.05	20.00
.06	16.67
.07	14.29
.08	12.50
.09	11.11
.10	10.00

CAPTALIZATION OF NONPERPETUITY INCOME

In the valuation of building improvements or property interests with terminal lives, provision must be made to write off, or amortize, the investment over the economic life period of the property. The methods of capitalization used in appraisal practice are named in accordance with the method under which future depreciation, or amortization, is to be provided. When depreciation is calculated under the formula $V = I/R$, the capitalization methods most frequently applied are known as:

1. Straight line capitalization.
2. Sinking fund capitalization.
3. Annuity capitalization.

When use of the reciprocal formula $V = I \times F$ is deemed more practical or convenient, specially prepared factor tables can be applied. In such instances, the capitalization factor method used takes its name from the person who compiled or who popularized the use of the ready-made factor table in question. Using the same order as the capitalization methods listed above, the reciprocal or income conversion methods available for valuation of nonperpetuity income are as follows:

1. Ring factor table of capitalization.[1]
2. Hoskold factor table of capitalization.
3. Inwood factor table of capitalization.

Since the various methods of capitalization, as will be demonstrated below, yield value conclusions that differ importantly from one another,

---

[1] This factor table, for selected rates of interest, was developed by the author and first published in the April, 1960, issue of the *Appraisal Journal,* American Institute of Real Estate Appraisers.

great care must be taken to select the appropriate method that reflects market actions of typical investors. Under no circumstances must the selection of a method of capitalization be contingent upon the value to be found or on preferences voiced either by the appraiser or his client. Identical incomes produce different values under the methods of capitalization named above because of differences in the amount of income set aside under each method to recapture (amortize) the investment value. Everything else remaining equal, the greater the amount that is set aside out of a fixed sum of annual income for amortization purposes the less of the total income remains for the interest earnings on which property value in the final analysis depends.

To illustrate the traditional use of capitalization methods, a simple valuation problem will be assumed, based on the following property and income data:

1. A net income of $1,000 per year.
2. A remaining economic life of 40 years.
3. A 7 percent rate of interest.
4. A sinking fund earning of 3 percent.
5. An annuity rate of 7 percent.
6. A straight line rate of depreciation of 2½ percent over a period of 40 years.

THE STRAIGHT LINE METHOD OF CAPITALIZATION

Based on this method, and using the formula $V = I/R$, the value of a $1,000 net income (net before interest on capital and amortization of capital) estimated to be derived over an investment life period of forty years and capitalized at an interest rate of 7 percent is derived by first substituting income and rate data for the symbols in the value formula. The capitalization equation is then $V = $1,000 divided by .095 (.07 interest plus .025 rate of amortization), giving a present worth of $10,526.32. The accuracy of this value is proven by application of the interest and amortization rates as shown below:

7% return on $10,526.32 =	$ 736.84
2.5% amortization allowance on $10,526.32 =	263.16
Total required annual income	$1,000.00

The depreciation allowance of $263.16 per year without interest over a period of forty years will equal the value of the original investment of $10,-526.32. Using the Ring factor table of capitalization, and the formula

$V = I \times F$, the appraiser can obtain identical value results. Reference to this table (see Appendix 3, page 615) discloses under the 7 percent rate of capitalization and, opposite forty years, a present worth factor per dollar of income of 10.52632. Multiplying the income expectancy of $1,000 by the Ring factor of 10.52632 produces a value of $10,526.32, which is identical to the value found under the $V = I/R$ rate formula above.

A preferred method of capitalization under which identical results can be obtained—but where depreciation under the straight line theory of capital recapture is provided as an *expense* of operations rather than as a *rate* applied to the net income—is demonstrated as follows:

Net income before interest and depreciation	$1,000.00
Depreciation allowance—straight line (40 years)	
$\dfrac{.025}{.095} = .26316$, and $.26316 \times \$1,000 =$	263.16
Net income after depreciation	$ 736.84
Value of property, $736.84 ÷ .07 =	$10,526.32

As the above illustrations demonstrate, the appraiser has an option to either capitalize income *before* depreciation at the selected rate of capitalization, or to capitalize income *after* depreciation at the rate of interest only. Based on the income data given above, the appraiser can either divide $1,000 by .095 or net income after depreciation of $736.84 by the interest rate of .07. Both capitalization options will yield identical value results of $10,526.32.

It is well to emphasize that the appraiser selects by way of market analysis the applicable rate of interest as well as the method and rate of recapture. Since value is always a proportional relationship of income to the rate of capitalization, the net income before depreciation can be divided into interest income and recapture income by the percentage relationship that the interest rate and the recapture rate bear to the combined rate or rate of capitalization. In the above illustration, the rate of capitalization is 9.5 percent of which 7 percent divided by 9.5 percent, or 73.684 percent of total income represents interest return on invested capital and 2.5 percent divided by 9.5 percent represents recapture or depreciation return equal to 26.316 percent.

Since it is readily feasible to separate that portion of net income which must be set aside for recapture (depreciation) it is recommended to do so and to include this amount as an operating expense. This, as explained in Chapter 12, is in full accord with accounting practices followed by C.P.A.'s, investors, tax consultants, and agents of the Bureau of Internal Revenue. No matter which method of capitalization is selected by the appraiser, the ratio that the rate of recapture bears to the combined rate of capitalization always represents the percentage of net income that should be labeled "provision for depreciation" in the operating expense schedule.

Under the straight line method of capitalization, amortization of the investment is provided in equal annual amounts—but as increasing percentages of the remaining value. This can be observed in the table of amortization and the entries derived over the first three years of income life for the investment of $10,526.32 as shown below:

TABLE OF AMORTIZATION FOR AN INVESTMENT OF $10,526.32 OVER A 40-YEAR PERIOD AT 7 PERCENT INTEREST UNDER THE STRAIGHT LINE METHOD

End of Year	Annual Income	7 Percent Interest	2.5 Percent Amortization	Remaining Value
				$10,526.32
1	$ 1,000	$ 736.84	$ 263.16	10,263.16
2	1,000	736.84	263.16	10,000.00
3	1,000	736.84	263.16	9,736.84
..	....	....	....	......
40	1,000	736.84	263.16	0.00
Total	$40,000	$29,473.60	$10,526.40	

In appraisal practice, the use of the straight line method of depreciation is often justified by the assumption that income from the investment will decline as the property ages in direct proportion to the reduced interest earnings derived from the remaining value of the investment at the end of each year. Thus if the remaining value decreases by 263.16 annually, as shown in the above schedule, then income is expected to decrease annually by 7 percent of $263.16, or in the amount of $18.42 over the forty-year economic-income-life period. Based on declining income under this assumption and under the straight line method of capitalization, a schedule of amortization would show entries as follows:

Year	Annual Income	7 Percent Interest On Value Balance	2.5 Percent Amortization	Remaining Value
				$10,526.32
1	$1,000.00	$736.84	$263.16	10,263.16
2	981.58	718.42	263.16	10,000.00
3	963.16	700.00	263.16	9,736.84

The assumption that net income will decline in precise amounts, as indicated in the schedule above, appears difficult to substantiate. Furthermore, it is not orthodox mathematical practice to reflect an anticipated decline in the numerator of the value equation ($V = I/R$) by an upward adjustment of the denominator of the value equation. If income is expected to decline over the life of the investment, why not stabilize the future income stream to reflect this decline rather than tamper with the interest or annuity rate by means of which *all* income should be capitalized? To illustrate: If an income of $1,000 per year over a life period of forty years is expected to decline annually over its remaining economic life, most appraisers at present capitalize this income flow by dividing $1,000 by the rate of interest plus the straight line rate of recapture, or given a rate of 7 percent and a rate of recapture of 2.5 percent the indicated value is obtained as follows: $1,000 ÷ .095 = $10,526.

The same value, however, can be obtained by stabilizing this declining income stream to an amount of $789.50. Capitalizing this *stabilized* income of $789.50 by use of the 7 percent Inwood Factor for forty years of 13.332, or the annuity rate of .075009, an identical value of $10,526 is obtained. To stabilize a declining income stream (under the straight line premise) all the appraiser needs to do is to divide the annuity rate of capitalization at the selected interest rate by the straight line rate of capitalization. In the illustration shown above the 7 percent annuity rate for forty years is .075009, and the straight line rate of capitalization is .095. Dividing the former rate by the latter yields a quotient of 78.950 percent. This is the stabilized income flow per dollar of income which, when capitalized by the Inwood Factor or the annuity rate (reciprocal of Inwood Factor), will give identical value results as those obtained under straight line capitalization. An even more accurate procedure for forecasting a declining income stream and for capitalizing same will be demonstrated under the annuity method of capitalization as demonstrated below.

Further and thoughful consideration will lead the appraiser to realize that most properties are purchased and financed up to 80 or more percent of value by means of a mortgage which is always amortized under the compound interest or annuity Inwood method of financing. If the Inwood or annuity method is applicable to 80 or more percent of property value, one must seriously question the accuracy of straight line recapture and straight line capitalization when applied to the property as a whole.

The use of the straight line method of capitalization, however, may be justified for income to be realized over comparatively short periods of an investment life, or where typical investment practices clearly warrant the use of straight line amortization. For income-producing properties with economic life periods extending over more than ten years, and where declining incomes can be estimated or stabilized with a fair degree of accuracy by market comparison study, the use of the straight line method of capitalization is not recommended nor is it professionally defensible.

THE SINKING FUND METHOD OF CAPITALIZATION

This method of capitalization is based on the premise that the investor has no access or control over the amounts set aside for amortization of the investment and that provisions for capital replacement can be accumulated in a fund, earning compound interest at a safe, or bank, rate of interest. Employing the same valuation data as that used under straight line capitalization, the value of a $1,000 income for a period of forty years at 7 percent interest is derived under the sinking fund (3 percent) rate method as follows: $V = I/R = $1,000 divided by .0832624 (.07 interest plus .0132624 [2] amortization at 3 percent interest), which equals a present worth of $12,010.22. The accuracy of this value is proven by the application of interest and amortization rates as follows:

7% return on $12,010.22 equals	$ 840.72
1.32624% annual sinking fund requirements on $12,010.22 equals	159.28
Total required annual earnings	$1,000.00

The annual depreciation allowance of $159.28, if invested at compound interest at a 3 percent rate over a forty-year period, will equal an amount of $12,010.22.

The application of the sinking fund method, too, can be simplified by the use of a specially prepared table. Applying the formula $V = I \times F$, and with reference to a Hoskold factor table (see Appendix 3, page 616), a factor of 12.01022 is obtained under the 7 percent rate of interest column at 3 percent sinking fund earnings opposite forty years of investment life. Multiplying the factor of 12.01022 by the income of $1,000, a value of $12,010.22 is obtained. This value is identical to that obtained under the $V = I/R$ rate formula equation as used above.

A table of amortization showing the income distribution and value decline of an investment of $12,010.22 over the first three years of income life appears as shown at the top of page 274.

Under the sinking fund theory of capital recapture identical results, too, can be obtained by application of the expense rather than the rate method of capitalization as shown on page 274.

The sinking fund method of capitalization appears designed to serve accounting rather than appraisal purposes. As a rule investment buyers

---

[2] This rate was obtained from the sinking fund table at 3 percent interest. (See Appendix 3, page 569.)

TABLE OF AMORTIZATION FOR AN INVESTMENT OF $12,010.22 OVER A 40-YEAR PERIOD AT 7 PERCENT INTEREST UNDER THE 3 PERCENT SINKING FUND METHOD

Year	Annual Income	7 Percent Interest	3 Percent Sinking Fund Annual	3 Percent Sinking Fund Interest	Total	Remaining Value
						$12,010.22
1	$ 1,000	$ 840.72	$ 159.28	$ —	$159.28	11,850.94
2	1,000	840.72	159.28	4.78	323.34	11,686.88
3	1,000	840.72	159.28	9.70	492.32	11,517.90
..	....	....	....	....	....	......
40	....	....	....	....	....	......
Total	$40,000	$33,628.80	$6,371.20	$5,638.02		

Net income (before interest and amortization)	$ 1,000.00
Depreciation allowance 3% sinking fund (40 years)	
$\dfrac{.0132624}{.0832624}$ = .15928, and .15928 × $1,000 =	159.28
Net income (after depreciation)	$ 840.72
Value of property, $840.72 ÷ .07 =	$12,010.22

of real property have access to all the net income derived from operation of such property, and typically do not set up a fund for amortization of equity interests. The sinking fund method, also, does not provide for declining income as a property ages. It is possible, of course, to consider that the amounts accumulated in the sinking fund are available for reinvestment and that the annual income will decline in proportion to interest earnings on the remaining value, as was the case under straight line amortization. But to assume this method of accounting treatment violates the concept of a "fund" on which the sinking fund or Hoskold method of capitalization is founded.

THE ANNUITY METHOD OF CAPITALIZATION

This method of capitalization is similar in all respects to the sinking fund method except that no fund is established in which the annual amortization provisions are to accumulate. Instead, the periodic payments for amortization of investment capital are made available to the property user or owner for immediate reinvestment in similar or other types of property. The rates of earning for both the property as a whole, and for portions of the investment returned each year through amortization provisions—and which are available for re-investment—are considered as one and the same.

To illustrate again by use of the formula $V = I/R$, the value of a $1,000 income for a life period of forty years at 7 percent interest is: $1,000 divided by .075009 (.07 percent interest plus .005009, the amortization rate at 7 percent), which equals a present worth of $13,331.71. The accuracy of this value conclusion can be proved as follows:

7% return on $13,331.71 =	$ 933.22
.005009 amortization allowance on $13,331.71 =	66.78
Total required annual earnings	$1,000.00

The annual depreciation allowance of $66.78, if reinvested at compound interest of 7 percent over a forty-year period, will equal the original investment of $13,331.71.

The application of the annuity method, too, can be simplified by use of the formula $V = I \times F$ and the Inwood table method of capitalization. By reference to the Inwood table (See Appendix 3, page 601), a factor of 13.33171 is obtained under the 7 percent interest column opposite forty years of income life. Multiplying this factor by the income of $1,000 gives a present value of $13,331.71, which is identical with that obtained under the annuity method of capitalization. The Inwood premise table and the present worth of an annuity of 1 table are one and the same. Amortization of the investment value of $13,331.71 derived under the annuity, or Inwood, method of capitalization is provided as indicated by entries over the first three years of investment life as follows:

TABLE OF AMORTIZATION FOR AN INVESTMENT OF $13,331.71 OVER A 40-YEAR PERIOD AT 7 PERCENT INTEREST UNDER THE ANNUITY METHOD

Year	Annual Income	7 Percent Interest	Amortization	Remaining Value
				$13,331.71
1	$ 1,000	$ 933.22	$ 66.78	13,264.93
2	1,000	928.55	71.45	13,193.48
3	1,000	923.54	76.46	13,117.02
..	....	......	......	......
40	....	......	......	......
Total	$40,000	$26,668.29	$13,331.71	

Study of the amortization schedule shown above will reveal that although the income before depreciation remains stable, the interest or net income on which value in the final analysis is based is declining annually. To say, therefore, that the Inwood method of capitalization should be used when the income flow is constant or stable is a misnomer; for if net income really were stable, then value would not decline as shown in the amortization schedule above. As demonstrated with the straight line and sinking fund methods of capitalization, it would, therefore, be more accurate to extract the amount of recapture (depreciation) and to capitalize the remaining (true) net income by the investment or interest rate as follows:

Net income (before interest and amortization)	$1,000.00
Depreciation allowance @ 7% annuity over 40 years	
$\dfrac{.005009}{.075009} = .06678$, and $.06678 \times \$1,000 =$	66.78
Net income (after depreciation)	$ 933.22
Value of property $933.22 ÷ .07 =	$13,331.71

It is often and erroneously held that the annuity method of capitalization should be applied only to a constant or "level" income flow, or to annuities which are equal in amount throughout the economic life of the investment property. As will be demonstrated, the annuity, or Inwood, method of capitalization can effectively and accurately be applied whether the income flow is increasing, decreasing, or a combination of both. Even deficit income occasionally incurred—as during initial stages of investment operation—can be capitalized by the annuity method and amortized out of future earnings.

To illustrate the application of the annuity method to capitalization of a declining income expectancy from a typical apartment property, it is assumed that field studies of comparable properties support a conclusion that a most probable pattern of income over the economic life expectancy of fifty years will be as follows:

First 5 years	$10,000
Next 15 years	9,000
Next 10 years	7,500
Next 10 years	6,500
Last 10 years	5,500

The present worth of this declining income stream at 7 percent interest is capitalized with the aid of conventional interest and discount tables as at the top of page 277.

The same value conclusion can also be obtained by application of the Inwood factors exclusively as on page 277.

Income Period	Income Expectancy		Present Worth of Annuity of 1		Deferment Factor (P.W. of 1)		Present Value
1–5	$10,000	×	4.1002	×	1.0000	=	$ 41,002
6–20	9,000	×	9.1079	×	.7130	=	58,445
21–30	7,500	×	7.0236	×	.2584	=	13,613
31–40	6,500	×	7.0236	×	.1314	=	5,999
41–50	5,500	×	7.0236	×	.0668	=	2,580
	Total present value						$121,639

Income Period	Income Expectancy	Inwood Factor	Fractional Factors		Present Value
1–5	$10,000	—	4.1002	=	$ 41,005
6–20	9,000	(10.5940–4.1002)	6.4938	=	59,442
21–30	7,500	(12.4090–10.5940)	1.8150	=	13,613
31–40	6,500	(13.3317–12.4090)	.9227	=	5,999
41–50	5,500	(13.8007–13.3317)	.4690	=	2,580
	Total—Inwood Factor		13.3317		
	Total Present Value				$121,639

Where appraisers prefer to stabilize income rather than report detailed valuation results in stages of declining or increasing amounts as shown above, this stabilization can readily be accomplished by transposing the formula $V = I/R$ to $I = V \times R$. By multiplying the present value derived from the declining income flow in the amount of $121,639 by the 7 percent capitalization annuity rate of .07245985 (.07 interest plus .00245985 amortization at 7 percent) a level income flow of $8,813.65 is obtained. A schedule of amortization can now be established using the declining income estimates—or the stablized income amount—as computed above. In both instances the income flow over the fifty-year economic life period will yield an income of 7 percent on the remaining value balances, and amortize the investment value of $121,639 under the annuity method of capitalization.

To demonstrate application of the annuity capitalization procedure where increasing income is anticipated, an income flow over a four-year period is assumed as follows:

$2,000 for the first two years, and
$4,000 for the last two years.

The present worth of this income stream at 6 percent interest is capitalized as shown at the top of page 278.

Income Period	Annual Income	Present Worth of Annuity of 1	Deferment Factor		Present Value
1–2	$2,000	1.83339	1.000	=	$ 3,666.78
3–4	4,000	1.83339	.890	=	6,526.87
	Total present value				$10,193.65

With use of the Inwood factor table, the identical value is derived as follows:

Income Period	Annual Income	Inwood Factor	Fractional Factor		Present Value
1–2	$2,000	—	1.83339	=	$ 3,666.78
3–4	4,000	(3.46511–1.83339)	1.63172	=	6,526.87
	Total Inwood Factor		3.46511		
	Total Present Value				$10,193.65

A schedule of amortization, based on the investment value of $10,-193.65 can now be established to show income distribution to interest and amortization over the four-year economic life period as provided below:

SCHEDULE OF AMORTIZATION FOR AN INVESTMENT OF $10,193.65 OVER A 4-YEAR PERIOD AT 6 PERCENT INTEREST UNDER THE ANNUITY METHOD

Year	Annual Income	6 Percent Interest	Amortization	Remaining Value
				$10,193.65
1	$ 2,000	$ 611.62	$ 1,388.38	8,805.27
2	2,000	528.32	1,471.68	7,333.59
3	4,000	440.01	3,559.99	3,773.60
4	4,000	226.41	3,773.60	0.00
Total	$12,000	$1,806.36	$10,193.65	

To stabilize the increasing income flow shown above, the appraiser applies the income formula $I = V \times R$. Multiplying the present value of the above income stream of $10,193.65 by the capitalization rate of .2885915 (.06 interest plus .2285914 amortization at 6 percent) a level income flow of $2,941.79 is obtained. A schedule of amortization using the stabilized income over a four-year period will amortize the investment of $10,193.65 with identical results as those obtained by use of the increasing flow of income and as shown above.

The annuity, or Inwood, method of capitalization is most always used in connection with capitalization of land income where the period of land ownership does not extend into perpetuity, as is the case under leasehold operation. When the reversionary interest of the fee owner (to whom the land reverts at the end of the lease period) is discounted at the same rate at which the income received by the tenant is capitalized, the value of the parts (into which land ownership is divided) will always equal the value of the land as a whole. Assuming a land value of $100,000 and an interest rate of 6 percent, the value of the split interests at ten-year intervals over a hundred-year period is derived as follows:

I. PRESENT WORTH OF INCOME FLOW TO LAND USER

Years	Income	Inwood Factor	Present Worth of Income	Percent of Total Value
10	$6,000	7.360 087	$44,161	44.2
20	6,000	11.469 921	68,820	68.8
30	6,000	13.764 831	82,589	82.6
40	6,000	15.046 297	90,278	90.3
50	6,000	15.761 861	94,571	94.6
60	6,000	16.161 428	96,969	97.0
70	6,000	16.384 544	98,307	98.3
80	6,000	16.509 131	99,055	99.1
90	6,000	16.578 699	99,472	99.5
100	6,000	16.617 546	99,705	99.7

II. PRESENT WORTH OF FEE OWNER'S (REVERSIONARY) INTEREST

Years	Value of Land	Present Worth Factor	Present Value of Reversion Land	Percent of Total Value
10	$100,000	.558 395	$55,840	55.8
20	100,000	.311 805	31,181	31.2
30	100,000	.174 110	17,411	17.4
40	100,000	.097 222	9,722	9.7
50	100,000	.054 288	5,429	5.4
60	100,000	.030 314	3,031	3.0
70	100,000	.016 927	1,693	1.7
80	100,000	.009 452	945	.9
90	100,000	.005 278	528	.5
100	100,000	.002 947	295	.3

The importance of early years of income life as compared with ownership and income privileges that lie in the distant future can be judged effectively by inspection of the above tables. At 6 percent interest, and under the annuity method of capitalization, the present worth of the income flow over the first twenty years equals 68.8 percent of total property value as compared with 100 percent for income rights that extend into perpetuity. The first forty years represent 90.3 percent of total property value and rights extending beyond eighty years and into perpetuity have a present worth of less than 1 percent of total value.

MORTGAGE DEBT VALUATION

The annuity, or Inwood table, method of capitalization is used almost exclusively in the evaluation of mortgage debts and in the determination of periodic payments necessary to pay off a mortgage loan of a stated amount and over a given period of amortization. The same formula used in the appraisal of an entire property applies to the evaluation of a part or fractional interest of a property. The only difference, so far as mortgage debt valuation is concerned, is in the mechanical application—due to the custom of amortizing loans over monthly rather than annual interest or discount periods.

To illustrate the application of the annuity, or Inwood, capitalization method to mortgage debt valuation, it is assumed that a loan of $5,000 is to be obtained over an eight-year period at 6 percent interest and that interest and amortization payments are due each month during the life of the loan.

The first step in any mortgage loan problem is to determine the number of periodic payments during the life of the loan and the pro rata interest rate that is applicable to each period as a fraction of the annual rate of interest. In the problem stated above, the loan is to be amortized monthly over eight years, hence 8 (years) $\times$ 12 (months) $= 96$ payment periods. The annual rate is 6 percent, hence the rate of interest per period is 6 percent $\div$ 12, or .5, or $\frac{1}{2}$ percent per loan period. Since the problem calls for the determination of periodic loan payments to amortize a mortgage debt of $5,000, the formula used is $I = V \times R$. Substituting value and rate factor data the solution is found by multiplying $5,000 $\times$ .01314143 (.005 interest plus .00814143, rate of amortization). This equals payments of $65.71 per month. The total dollar payments necessary to amortize this loan equal 96 $\times$ $65.71, or $6,308.16. Of this amount, $5,000 is principal and $1,308.16 is interest at $\frac{1}{2}$ percent per month on the remaining balances of the mortgage loan.

Frequently, the value problem calls for a determination of the mortgage loan for stipulated payments and at specified rates of interest. Suppose a borrower wishes to pay $100 per month for a period of five years at 6 percent interest. How much is the loan principal? Applying the value formula $V = I \times F$, $100 is multiplied by the Inwood factor for 60 (monthly) periods at $\frac{1}{2}$ percent per period, or 51.7256. This equals a mortgage loan principal amount of $5,172.56.

SUMMARY

The income approach to value calls for application of the capitalization process and use of the basic formula $V = I/R$, or $V = I \times F$. The first formula gives the appraiser a choice of three methods of capitalization, commonly known as:

1. The straight line rate method.
2. The sinking fund rate method.
3. The annuity rate method.

Where the latter formula is applied, specially prepared factor (premise) tables are available. These factor tables are reciprocals of the rates found under the straight line, sinking fund, and annuity rate methods of capitalization and are in the order given above:

1. The Ring factor table.
2. The Hoskold factor table.
3. The Inwood factor table.

To illustrate the application of the rate and factor methods of capitalization, the following data was assumed: A net income of $1,000 per annum over an economic life period of forty years, a rate of interest of 7 percent, and a 3 percent sinking fund earnings rate. Based on these income rate and property life data, value results were obtained as follows:

Straight Line
    A. Straight line rate capitalization

$$V = I/R = \$1,000 \div .095 = \$10,526.32$$

    B. Ring factor capitalization

$$V = I \times F = \$1,000 \times 10.52632 = 10,526.32$$

Sinking Fund at 3 Percent
    A. Sinking fund rate capitalization

$$V = I/R = \$1,000 \div .0832624 = \$12,010.22$$

    B. Hoskold factor capitalization

$$V = I \times F = \$1,000 \times 12.01022 = 12,010.22$$

Annuity Method
    A. Annuity method rate capitalization

$$V = I/R = \$1,000 \div .07500913 = \$13,331.71$$

    B. Inwood capitalization

$$V = I \times F = \$1,000 \times 13.33171 = 13,331.71$$

The values obtained under the respective methods of capitalization vary from a low of $10,526.32 under the straight line method to a high of $13,331.71 under the annuity method for identical income streams of $1,000 capitalized at 7 percent rates of interest. The difference in value is entirely due to differences in the amounts of income (expressed as a rate per dollar) set aside under each capitalization method for amortization purposes. The greater the portion of net income that is reserved for depreciation anticipated over the economic life span of the property, the lesser the amount that represents interest earnings—and, as a consequence, the smaller the capital value.

In appraisal practice, only one method of capitalization can logically be applied. The selection of the appropriate method of capitalization should not be made haphazardly, nor should the choice be influenced by attempts to obtain high, low, or conservative value estimates. Rather it is the appraiser's duty to study earnings-to-price relationships at which comparable properties have exchanged in the open market, and to use rates as well as methods of capitalization which reflect typical market practices and operations.

READING AND STUDY REFERENCES

1. *Acquisition for Right-of-Way* (Washington, D.C.: American Association of State Highway Officials, 1962), chap. 28.

2. *The Appraisal of Real Estate* (Chicago: American Institute of Real Estate Appraisers, 1967), chaps. 18–19.

3. Babcock, Frederick M., *The Valuation of Real Estate* (New York: McGraw-Hill Book Company, Inc., 1932), chap. 12.

4. Bonner, John T., "The Income Approach—Capitalization," *The Real Estate Appraiser* (January 1963), pp. 2–8.

5. Kahn, Sanders A., Frederick E. Case, and Alfred Schimmel, *Real Estate Appraisal and Investment* (New York: The Ronald Press Company, 1963), chaps. 9 and 10.

6. Kinnard, William N., Jr., *Industrial Real Estate* (Washington, D.C.: Society of Industrial Realtors, 1967), chap. 12, part III F.

7. McMichael, Stanley L., *McMichael's Appraising Manual*, 4th ed. (Englewood Cliffs, N.J.: Prentice-Hall, Inc., 1951), chap. 4.

8. Ring, Alfred A., "The Direct-Ring Method of Capitalization," *The Appraisal Journal* (April 1960), pp. 183–89.

9. Ring, Alfred A., "Streamlining the Income Approach to Value," *The Appraisal Journal* (January-February 1969), pp. 43–47.

10. Ring, Alfred A., "Updating the Earnings Approach to Value," *The Appraisal Journal* (April 1963), pp. 2–9.

11. Wendt, Paul F., "Depreciation and the Capitalization of Income Method," *The Appraisal Journal* (April 1963), pp. 185–93.

In the foregoing chapter, discussion of the income approach to value was limited to application of methods of capitalization. Separate treatment was given to valuation procedure for perpetuity income derived from land and nonperpetuity income derived from either land or building improvements. To promote better understanding of the different methods of capitalization it was assumed that income from land and income from

19 *Residual Techniques* *of Capitalization*

buildings and their respective values can readily be obtained as separate entities, and that summation of the values of the parts will yield an estimate of the value of the whole—i.e., for the entire property.

In everyday practice, when improvements are placed on land to make land productive in conformity with the principle of highest and best use, an economic merger takes place that weds the investment parts into an economic unit, or property, as a whole. Physically we can describe the nature and character of land, and, separately, the amount, kind and quality of the improvements—but income derived from operation is a product of the joint property and not an aggregate of those of its parts. Yet, in valuation procedure it does become necessary to isolate the income attributable to the parts in order to ascertain whether land, in fact, is developed to its highest and best use; and if not, the extent to which value losses are ascribable to the man-made improvements as a measure of functional or economic obsolescence.

THE RESIDUAL CHARACTER OF LAND

As explained in Chapter 9, the value of land is dependent on its utilization in combination with labor and capital investment; and the highest value of land is reached at a point when expenditures for land improvements are in accordance with the principle of highest and best land use. Although value can be assigned to land by studying similar sites which are effectively utilized or which have sold recently in the open market, economic comparability via the market approach is based on judgment and is difficult to achieve—especially where land is found to be best suited for agricultural, industrial, or special-purpose commercial uses. But even where market transactions are considered as reliable indices of value, a check on the accuracy of market forces necessitates the application of the income approach to value.

Economically, land is residual in character. This means that the factors of labor and capital, when combined with land, must be compensated first or they will cease to function and the balance of income which remains is thus residual (left) to land. It is this residual income which, under highest and best utilization, forms the logical basis for land value.

In appraisal practice, land is found either vacant and available for immediate or prospective use or in different stages of utilization. Because of this, various capitalization techniques had to be developed to strengthen the order of income priority of the production factors, as warranted under given and ever-changing socio-economic circumstances. The techniques of capitalization which are generally applied in appraisal practice, and which will be fully explained and demonstrated below, are:

1. The land residual technique.
2. The building residual technique.
3. The property residual technique.

LAND RESIDUAL TECHNIQUE

Where buildings are new and their values are known or can be estimated with reasonable accuracy, the land residual technique is used for estimating land value and for obtaining the value of the property as a whole. Generally this technique of separating property net income into sums attributable to land and buildings is used either when the land is vacant—or assumed to be vacant—and available for development under its highest and best use, or is actually improved with a new building that constitutes the highest and best utilization of property.

Where the property is vacant, or assumed to be vacant, it is the appraiser's responsibility to visualize, specify, and support the kind of land improvements which will yield to land a residual income stream that, on appropriate capitalization, results in the highest present value of the land. This generally involves hypothetical appraising, since the specified improvements in fact may not be built at the time of valuation—or even in the immediate future. Nevertheless, if this capitalization technique is to be accurately applied, the appraiser must carry out the following steps:

1. Describe and justify the type (architecture), kind (materials used), and quality of improvements that are recommended for construction under a program of highest and best land use.
2. Accurately estimate, or ascertain, dependable bids for construction costs of building and related land improvements complete in all respects and ready for operation as of a given date.
3. Estimate the effective gross revenue that can reasonably be obtained under typical management and operation.
4. Estimate the operating expenses to be incurred under typical management, and by subtracting these from the effective gross revenue derive the net operating income before interest and amortization payments.
5. Derive by market study and analysis the rate of interest at which land and building income is to be capitalized.
6. Select the method of capitalization and determine the period of economic life expectancy of the building investment based on the market actions of typical investors who have purchased like or similar properties.
7. Estimate the amount that must be subtracted from the capitalized value of land to account for loss of interest earnings and costs incurred during the period of land development.

Where the land is already improved under a program of highest and best use, and where the buildings are in new condition and in operating order, Steps 1, 2 and 7 above may be eliminated. To illustrate the application of the land residual technique under straight line, sinking fund, and annuity methods of capitalization, the following assumptions are made:

1. Value of building improvements $100,000
2. Estimated remaining economic life   50 years
3. Rate of interest   8%
4. Net operating income $12,500

I. *Land Residual Technique—Straight Line Capitalization*

Net operating income		$12,500
Building rate of capitalization:		
Interest rate	.08	
Amortization rate (100 ÷ 50)	.02	
Total rate	.10	

Income attributable to building:
$$I = V \times R = \$100,000 \times .10 =$$ $10,000

Income attributable to land: $ 2,500
  Land rate of capitalization .08
  Land value, $V = I/R = \$2,500 \div .08 =$ $31,250
Property value:

Land	$31,250	
Building	100,000	
Total	$131,250	

II. *Land Residual Technique—3 Percent Sinking Fund Capitalization*

Net operating income		$12,500
Building rate of capitalization:		
Interest rate	.08	
Amortization rate (S. F. Table)	.008865	
Total rate	.088865	

Income attributable to building:
$$I = V \times R = \$100,000 \times .088865 =$$ 8,887

Income attributable to land: $ 3,613
  Land rate of capitalization .08
  Land value, $V = I/R = \$3,613 \div .08 =$ $45,163
Property value:

Land	$ 45,163	
Building	$100,000	
Total	$145,163	

III. *Land Residual Technique—Annuity Method Capitalization*

Net operating income		$12,500
Building rate of capitalization:		
Interest rate	.08	
Amortization rate (S. F. Table 8%)	.00174	
Total rate	.08174	

Income attributable to building:
$$I = V \times R = \$100,000 \times .08174 =$$ 8,174

Income attributable to land: $ 4,326
  Land rate of capitalization .08
  Land value, $V = I/R = \$4,326 \div .08 =$ $54,075
Property value:

Land	$ 54,075	
Building	100,000	
Total	$154,075	

The same results as demonstrated above can also be obtained by the expense method of capitalization as follows:

I. *Land Residual Technique—Straight Line Expense Method of Capitalization*

Net operating income—before depreciation	$ 12,500
Building depreciation 2% of $100,000 =	2,000
Net income after depreciation	$ 10,500
Value of property: $10,500 ÷ .08 =	$131,250
Value of building	100,000
Value residual to land	$ 31,250

II. *Land Residual Technique—3 Percent Sinking Fund Expense Method of Capitalization*

Net operating income—before depreciation	$ 12,500
Building depreciation .008875 of $100,000 =	887
Net income after depreciation	$ 11,613
Value of property: $11,613 ÷ .08 =	$145,163
Value of building	100,000
Value residual to land	$ 45,163

III. *Land Residual Technique—Annuity Expense Method of Capitalization*

Net operating income—before depreciation	$ 12,500
Building depreciation .00174 of $100,000 =	174
Net income after depreciation	$ 12,326
Value of property: $12,326 ÷ .08 =	$154,075
Value of building	100,000
Value residual to land	$ 54,075

The land residual technique as illustrated above produces significantly different values of land varying from a low of $31,250 under the straight line method of capitalization to a high of $54,075 under the annuity method of capitalization. The cause for this variation, as was explained in Chapter 18, is found in the radically different assumptions that underlie the provision for amortization under each method of capitalization. In the above illustration, amortization for each year of economic life was computed as follows: straight line method, 2 percent; sinking fund (3 percent) method, 0.89 percent; and annuity method, 0.17 percent. This wide variation again points up the professional necessity of selecting with great care the method under which an income flow is to be capitalized. It isn't consistent with operating experience to assume that income will remain constant over the entire period of economic life, nor is it appropriate to provide for income decline through a rate of amortization. Where the income flow pattern can be estimated with reasonable certainty, as illustrated in Chapter 18, page 277, the annuity method of capitalization can be counted on the produce consistent, logical, and professionally defendable value estimates.

THE BUILDING RESIDUAL TECHNIQUE

Where land value is known—or can be established with reasonable certainty under the market approach to value or under the land residual technique of capitalization—the appraiser can determine the portion of total net income that is attributable to the *known,* the land, and make the balance residual to the *unknown,* which in this instance is the building. Generally, the building residual technique of capitalization is applicable when the building improvements are substantially depreciated or do not conform to standards which represent the highest and best use of the land.

To apply the building residual technique the appraiser must obtain or estimate the following:

1. The land value by market, income, or preferably both approaches to value.
2. Estimate the effective gross revenue obtainable under typical management.
3. Estimate the operating property expenditures and derive the net operating income—net, as always, before interest and amortization charges.
4. Derive the rate of interest at which land and building income is to be capitalized.
5. Select the method of capitalization, and determine the remaining economic life expectancy of the building improvements.

To illustrate the application of the building residual technique under straight line, sinking fund, and annuity methods of capitalization the following assumptions are made:

1. Value of land	$40,000
2. Estimated remaining economic life	30 years
3. Rate of land and building interest	8%
4. Net operating income	$12,500

The same results as demonstrated on the following page can also be obtained by the expense method of capitalization as shown on page 290.

As illustrated, under the building residual technique the land value of $40,000 is held constant and the building value varies depending on the method of capitalization employed. The straight line method, again, results in the lowest value—in this case, $82,059—for the building, and the annuity method in the highest value, $104,698. Logically, an identical income stream should not produce so many different values. Again, the

I. *Building Residual Technique—Straight Line Capitalization*

Net operating income		$12,500
Income attributable to land:		
$I = V \times R = \$40,000 \times .08 =$		3,200
Income attributable to building $=$		$ 9,300
Building rate of capitalization:		
Interest rate	.08	
Amortization rate $(100 \div 30)$	.03333	
Total rate	.11335	
Building value:		
$V = I/R = 9,300 \div .11333 =$		$82,059
or $V = I \times F = 9,300 \times 8.82353$ (Ring Factor) $=$		82,059
Property value:		
Land value	$ 40,000	
Building value	82,059	
Total	$122,059	

II. *Building Residual Technique—3 Percent Sinking Fund Capitalization*

Net operating income		$12,500
Income attributable to land:		
$I = V \times R = \$40,000 \times .08 =$		3,200
Income attributable to building $=$		$ 9,300
Building rate of capitalization:		
Interest rate	.08	
Amortization rate (S. F. 3%)	.02102	
Total rate	.10102	
Building value:		
$V = I/R = \$9,300 \div .10102 =$		$92,061
or $V = I \times F = 9,300 \times 9.8991$ (Hoskold) $=$		92,061
Property value:		
Land value	$ 40,000	
Building value	92,062	
Total	$132,062	

III. *Building Residual Technique—Annuity Method of Capitalization*

Net operating income		$12,500
Income attributable to land:		
$I = V \times R = \$40,000 \times .08 =$		3,200
Income attributable to building $=$		$ 9,300
Building rate of capitalization:		
Interest rate	.08	
Amortization rate (S. F. 8%)	.008827	
Total rate	.088827	

Building value:
  V = I/R = \$9,300 ÷ .088827 =   \$104,698
  or V = I × F = \$9,300 × 11.2578 (Inwood) =   104,698
Property value:
  Land value   \$ 40,000
  Building   104,698

        Total   \$144,698

reasons for the differences are found in the methods used for providing
for future building depreciation, or amortization. The higher amounts set
aside under straight line amortization leave less net income available as
interest earnings, hence the lower value. For long-lived properties, there
can be only one correct method of amortization. The choice of three
methods has long proved confusing to laymen and real estate practitioners
alike. Where a reasonably accurate estimate of future earnings can be

I. *Building Residual Technique—Straight Line Expense Method of Capitalization*

Net operating income	\$ 12,500.00
Income to land \$40,000 × .08 =	3,200.00
Income to building—before depreciation	\$ 9,300.00
Depreciation on building: $\frac{.03333}{.11333} = .29411$	
and \$9,300 × .29411 =	2,735.28
Building income—after depreciation	\$ 6,564.72
Residual value of building \$6,564.72 ÷ .08 =	\$ 82,059
Add value of land	40,000
Total property value	\$122,059

II. *Building Residual Technique—3 Percent Sinking Fund Expense Method of Capitalization*

Net operating income	\$ 12,500.00
Income to land \$40,000 × .08 =	3,200.00
Income to building—before depreciation	\$ 9,300.00
Depreciation on building: $\frac{.02102}{.10102} = .20807$	
and \$9,300 × .20807 =	1,935.04
Building income—after depreciation	\$ 7,364.96
Residual value of building \$7,364.96 ÷ .08 =	\$ 92,062
Add value of land	40,000
Total property value	\$132,062

III. *Building Residual Technique—Annuity Expense Method of Capitalization*

Net operating income	$ 12,500.00
Income to land $40,000 × .08 =	3,200.00
Income to building—before depreciation	$ 9,300.00
Depreciation on building: $\dfrac{.008827}{.088827} = .099372$	
and $9,300 × .099372 =	924.16
Building income—after depreciation	$ 8,375.84
Residual value of building $8,375.84 ÷ .08 =	$104,698
Add value of land	40,000
Total property value	$144,698

made either on a declining or a stabilized income basis, the annuity method of capitalization gives results which are consistent with monetary compound interest theory and practice (see Chapter 18).

THE PROPERTY RESIDUAL TECHNIQUE

Occasionally, valuation problems arise in which total property income is difficult to allocate to either land or building. This may be the case where building improvements are old, and where there is doubt as to whether or not they constitute the highest and best land use. Then, too, market sales of comparable sites may not be available, and hypothetical analysis of land income and land value may be of doubtful validity because of the location or specialized character of the land. Under such circumstances the appraiser may find the application of the property residual technique a useful tool of valuation.

To employ the property residual technique the appraiser must secure or make the following:

1. An estimate of the effective gross revenue that is obtainable under typical management.
2. An estimate of the net operating income—net before interest and amortization charges.
3. The rate of interest at which the property income is to be capitalized.
4. The method of capitalization to be applied over the remaining economic life of the property.
5. A rough estimate as to the probable land value at the termination of building life.

With the aid of this data, the property residual technique can be applied. For illustration purposes the following will be assumed:

1. An interest rate of 8 percent.
2. A building economic life of 30 years.
3. Net operating income of $12,500.
4. An estimated reversionary land value of $40,000.

Based on these assumptions, the property residual technique will be applied under straight line, sinking fund, and annuity methods of capitalization.

The same results as demonstrated previously can also be obtained by the expense method of capitalization as on pages 293–294.

The property residual technique, too, produces value results which differ importantly, depending on the method of capitalization used to provide for amortization of the nonperpetuity property investment. Again, the low value under the straight line provision results because this method sub-

I. *Property Residual Technique—Straight Line Capitalization*

Net operating income		$12,500
Property rate of capitalization:		
Interest rate	.08	
Amortization rate	.03333	
Total rate	.11333	
Property value of property income:		
$V = I/R = \$12,500 \div .113334 =$		$110,294
or $V = I \times F = \$12,500 \times 8.82353$ (Ring Factor)		110,294
Reversionary value of land:		
$\$40,000 \times .099377 =$		3,975
Property value:		
Value of property income	$110,294	
Present reversionary value of land	3,975	
Total		$114,269

II. *Property Residual Technique—3 Percent Sinking Fund Capitalization*

Net operating income		$12,500
Property rate of capitalization:		
Interest rate	.08	
Amortization rate (F. S. 3%)	.02102	
Total rate	.10102	
Value of property income:		
$V = I/R = \$12,500 \div .10102 =$		$123,739
or $V = I \times F = \$12,500 \times 9.8991$ (Hoskold) $=$		123,739
Present worth of land:		
$\$40,000 \times .099377 =$		3,975
Property value:		
Value of property income	$123,739	
Present reversionary value of land	3,975	
Total		$127,714

III. *Property Residual Technique—Annuity Method Capitalization*

Net operating income		$12,500
Property rate of capitalization:		
Interest rate	.08	
Amortization rate (S. F. 8%)	.008827	
Total rate	.088827	
Value of property income:		
V = I/R = $12,500 ÷ .088827 =		$140,723
or V = I × F = $12,500 × 11.2578 (Inwood) =		140,723
Present worth of land:		
$40,000 × .099377 =		3,975
Property value:		
Value of property income	$140,723	
Present reversionary value of land	3,975	
Total	$144,698	

tracts the highest annual amounts from the income stream for estimated losses due to future depreciation.

Appraisers are cautioned against careless or inopportune use of the property residual technique of valuation where straight line or sinking fund rates of amortization are combined with the interest rate to form a rate of capitalization. The application of straight line and sinking fund amortization rates to total property income in effect applies a rate of depreciation to the land in excess of that sanctioned by sound appraisal practice for a period extending over the life of the building. Thus the longer the economic life of the property, the greater the error in the estimate of value under straight line and sinking fund methods of capitalization. The built-in errors can readily be detected by reference to the value results obtained above under the building residual and property residual techniques. It will be noted that for both techniques the basic

I. *Property Residual Technique—Straight Line Expense Method of Capitalization*

Net operating income—before depreciation		$ 12,500.00
Property depreciation $= \dfrac{.03333}{.11333} = .29411$		
and $12,500 × .29411 =		3,676.37
Property income—after depreciation		$ 8,823.63
Property value: $8,823.63 ÷ .08 =		$110,294
Add reversionary value of land:		
$40,000 × .099377 =		3,975
Total property value		$114,269

II. *Property Residual Technique—3 Percent Sinking Fund Expense Method of Capitalization*

Net operating income—before depreciation	$ 12,500.00
Property depreciation $= \dfrac{.02102}{.10102} = .20807$	
and $12,500 $\times$ .20807 $=$	2,600.88
Property income—after depreciation	$ 9,899.12
Property value $=$ $9,899.12 $\div$ .08 $=$	$123,739
Add reversionary value of land: $40,000 $\times$ .099377 $=$	3,975
Total property value	$127,714

III. *Property Residual Technique—Annuity Expense Method of Capitalization*

Net operating income—before depreciation	$ 12,500.00
Property depreciation $= \dfrac{.008827}{.088827} = .099372$	
and $12,500 $\times$ .099372 $=$	1,242.16
Property value—after depreciation	$ 11,257.84
Property value $11,257.84 $\div$ .08 $=$	$140,723
Add reversionary value of land: $40,000 $\times$ .099377 $=$	3,975
Total property value	$144,698

income, building, and land value data are identical as follows: net operating income, $12,500; building or property life, thirty years; land value, $40,000; and 8 percent interest rate. The value results obtained on the basis of these identical assumptions compare as follows:

Method of Capitalization	Building Residual	Property Residual
Straight Line	$122,055	$114,269
3% Sinking Fund	132,062	127,714
Annuity	144,698	144,698

Only under the annuity method of capitalization are identical value results consistently obtained using both residual techniques, where the underlying income and property data remain equal. The substantial error under the straight line method points up, once more, the fallacy of mixing an interest-bearing rate of capitalization with a noninterest-bearing rate of amortization.

Nevertheless, the property residual technique under the annuity, or In-wood, method of capitalization serves a useful appraising function. There are occasions when neither land nor building value can be obtained with reasonable accuracy. Under such circumstances the application of either the land or building residual techniques is inappropriate. If these tech-niques are used, they will magnify the basic error where value of land or building is assumed. The property residual technique, it may be pointed out, also assumes a land value in the distant future. Does not such an unreliable forecast invalidate the use of this method also? It does not, because in the property residual technique only the reversionary (present worth)—not the full—value of the land is included in the appraisal esti-mate. The effect of a possible error in computing the future value of the land is thus minimized, if not neutralized. To illustrate: Assume that in the problem used above the land value as applied proved to be $50,000 instead of $40,000. What is the impact of this $10,000 error on the present value estimate? The answer is as follows:

I. Assumed land value of $40,000.
    1. Value of property income (see preceding page = $140,723
    2. Reversionary land value ($40,000 × .099377) =   3,975

        Total property value $144,698

II. Assumed land value of $50,000.
    1. Value of property income as above = $140,723
    2. Reversionary land value ($50,000 × .099377) =   4,969

        Total property value $145,692

The difference in the two appraisals is $994, or approximately ⅔ of 1 percent of the present value estimate. Since appraisals of such magni-tude as those derived above are generally rounded off to the nearest thou-sand dollars, the present value effect of the error of $10,000 in the assumed land value, thirty years removed from date of the appraisal, is of little present-worth consequence.

DIRECT CAPITALIZATION

The value of income-producing property can also be obtained by the rather simple and direct method of relating the income earned by the subject property as a whole (land and improvements) to an overall or combined rate of capitalization derived from market analysis of com-parable income producing properties. Thus if like properties produce a net income—for both land and building—which when divided by the selling prices of these properties yield a rate of 9.5 percent, then it would appear appropriate to find the value of the subject property by relating its income to land and building to this market-determined overall rate simply by use of the formula V = I/R, where "I" represents the net income for the entire property and "R" the overall rate of capitalization as derived above.

The use of direct capitalization, however, is not recommended except for "rough" estimating, or where other and more refined residual methods of capitalization cannot be applied in order to achieve greater accuracy and thus a more reliable value estimate. Overall rate or direct methods of capitalization are subject to all the pitfalls found in similar "nutshell" appraisal practices wherein the monthly or gross annual income multipliers are used, for instance, as direct measures of market value.

It is an accepted fact that real properties are nonhomogeneous in character, and that no two parcels are location or income-producingwise ever alike. Also there are important differences among index sales as to mixture of the investment quantities of land and improvements, age of the structures, and their operating ratios. Then, too, some properties produce less income than others (indicating falsely a low overall rate of return) but which, because of the likelihood of a significant windfall of appreciation, sell at high market prices. Because of these pitfalls, and the danger of committing errors which attend all "short-cut" operations no matter what the field of specialization, the professional appraiser is advised to analyze with care the components which make up the overall rate and to apply these rate components as directed under the appropriate methods and residual techniques of capitalization. It is well to remember the adage: "The longest way around is often the shortest way home."

SUMMARY

In all appraising problems where land and building improvements form an integral whole from which revenue and capitalizable net operating income is derived, the appraiser must apply under the income approach to value (1) the land residual, (2) the building residual, or (3) the property residual techniques of valuation. Which appraisal technique to apply is not a matter of arbitrary selection but rather one dependent on the nature of the valuation data. Where land is developed under a program of highest and best use, and where the improvements are in condition new, it is logical to determine the amount of net income necessary to yield a prevailing (market) rate of interest on the value of the building—plus the amounts which are necessary to amortize periodically the depreciable part of the building investment. The amount of income left is then residual to the land and forms the basis for an estimation of land value via the capitalization, or income, approach. Where land is vacant and available for use, the land residual technique permits study of alternative (hypothetical) land uses in order to determine which use over a period of years produces the highest residual land income and hence the highest present value of the land.

When land is developed with improvements considered to be in middle or late economic life, or which do not represent the highest and best use of the site, it is logical to ascertain first wherever possible the value of the land by either the market comparison method or by a hypothetical analysis of land uses and capitalization of land income under a highest and best program of land utilization. Once the value of land is known the income attributable to land at going rates of interest can be determined, and the balance of the net operating income becomes residual to the building improvements. By capitalization of the residual income under the appropriate method of income conversion, the value of the building is obtained. The building residual technique of capitalization also serves a highly useful purpose in cases where community growth or shifting land uses cause rapid increases in land value and, conversely, accelerates building obsolescence. Where, under this technique of valuation, the net operating income barely covers the income necessary to yield a fair return on the rising value of the land, the appraiser can report the approaching end of a building's economic life and the necessity to plan for reconstruction or rehabilitation to maintain a future flow of income and to preserve the financial integrity of the property as a going investment.

In some instances where buildings are old and land is of specialized nature, or in a location where neither market transactions nor income analysis makes possible a reasonably accurate estimate of land value, it is necessary to treat the property as an integral whole and to apply the property residual technique of valuation. In such instances care must be taken not to use the straight line or sinking fund methods of capitalization, since both of these methods for the duration of the property life apply to land a rate of amortization which is inconsistent with basic theory and practice underlying the valuation of land. If the property residual technique is deemed applicable, the appraiser should estimate with care the pattern of income flow anticipated over the economic lifespan of the property and convert this income stream into a sum of present value under the annuity method of capitalization. To the capitalized value of the property income must then be added the present, or reversionary, worth of the land based on land value when such land is free for sale or use at the end of the economic life of the subject property. Since only the present or reversionary worth of estimated future land value is added to the capitalized value of property income, errors in the estimated land value are minimized under this technique of capitalization, as demonstrated on page 295.

READING AND STUDY REFERENCES

1. *The Appraisal of Real Estate* (Chicago: American Institute of Real Estate Appraisers, 1967), chaps. 18–19.
2. Bowes, Eugene G., "How to Use Residual Techniques," *The Appraisal Journal* (January 1957), pp. 27–34.
3. Campbell, S.J., "The Land Residual Technique," *Appraisal Institute Magazine* (January 1957), pp. 11–12.
4. Kahn, Sanders A., Frederick E. Case, and Alfred Schimmel, *Real Estate Appraisal and Investments* (New York: The Ronald Press Company, 1963), chap. 12.
5. Lum, Y.T., "Value, Leaseholds, and the Appraising of Leaseholds by Residuals," *The Appraisal Journal* (February 1963), pp. 4–11.
6. McMichael, Stanley L., *McMichael's Appraising Manual*, 4th ed. (Englewood Cliffs, N.J.: Prentice-Hall, Inc., 1951), chap. 5.
7. Ring, Alfred A., *Real Estate Principles and Practices,* 6th ed. (Englewood Cliffs, N.J.: Prentice Hall, Inc., 1967), chap. 23.
8. Wall, Norbert F., "A Case Study—Land Residual Technique," *The Real Estate Appraiser* (February 1967), pp. 22–26.

Owners of income-producing real estate often find it profitable to permit others to hire the property at a stipulated fee, or *rental*. Where this is the case, the parties to the transaction enter into an agreement, called a *lease,* which establishes the landlord and tenant relationship. When properly drawn and executed the lease becomes a legal contract binding the parties in accordance with specified terms as to length of possession, use

20 Leasehold Estates and

Leased Fee Appraising [1]

of property, and payments due at periodic intervals.

Broadly speaking, leases are classified as either *short-term* or *long-term* in duration. This division, based on length of time and terms of use, is rather arbitrary. Generally, however, leases extending over ten or more years may appropriately be referred to as having long-term lease characteristics. Such leases, as a rule, are lengthy documents containing many special provisions and landlord-tenant covenants.

Lease agreements are further subclassified as to type, depending on the methods used to determine the amount of

---

[1] The term 'leased fee' as used in this chapter refers to the owner's interest and rights in the property subject to conditions and terms of a written or oral lease agreement. The term 'leasehold estate' refers to the tenant's right—over periods of months or years—to benefit from the use of the property in accordance with a written or oral agreement and the payment of a stipulated periodic rental.

periodic rent payments. The most frequently used types of leases are the following:

1. Flat, straight, or fixed rental leases.
2. Step-up, or graduated rental, leases.
3. Reappraisal leases.
4. Percentage-of-gross-sales leases.
5. Sale and lease-back contract.

The *flat,* or *straight,* lease is one in which the rental is a fixed sum paid periodically throughout the entire lease term. This type of lease, which at one time enjoyed wide use and popularity, has come—at least for long-term leasing—into gradual disuse. The reason, no doubt, is the steadily declining purchasing power of the dollar. Whereas in selling a property the owner can reinvest his equity in another type of property, in a lease his payments are due over a series of future years, and—where rentals are fixed in amount—a declining dollar value deprives the property (or fee) owner of a fair return in proportion to the value of his property as measured in terms of constant dollars.

The *step-up,* or *graduated rental,* lease is intended to give the land user an opportunity to lighten his operating expense burdens during the early formative years of his business enterprise and to give the landlord an opportunity to participate in future business growth through successively higher rental payments. Such lease agreements must be cautiously evaluated, since excessive rental payments historically have proved a prime cause of business failure and resultant bankruptcy.

The *reappraisal* lease, which establishes rentals as a percentage of property value at fixed intervals of three to five years, is rarely used today. This type of lease has proved expensive to maintain, and has been the cause of lengthy litigation where value agreements were difficult to arbitrate because of divergent professional estimates and opinions.

The *percentage-of-gross-sales* lease has gained steadily in popularity and, for short-term commercial leasing, is used most frequently at present. Under this lease, the tenant agrees to pay a stipulated percentage of his gross sales from goods and services sold on the premises. Generally, leases of this kind provide for a minimum rental ranging from 40 to 80 percent of amounts considered fair in relation to property value. Percentage rentals may range from as low as 2 percent of gross sales for department stores or supermarkets to as high as 75 percent for parking-lot operation. Tables for typical percentage rental payments are available through the Institute of Property Management, Chicago, Illinois, and through Prentice-Hall, Inc.[2]

The "sale and lease-back" contract agreement has gained wide popu-

---

[2] McMichael & O'Keefe, *Leases: Short and Long Term* (Englewood Cliffs, N. J.: Prentice-Hall, Inc., 5th ed., 6th printing, 1964).

larity with owners of large industrial and commercial properties. Under this form of agreement the owner, in return for full value, conveys title to his property by deed to a real estate investor or an institutional lender—generally an insurance company—and leases back the property for a long term.

Under provisions of the lease the former owner becomes the lessee and agrees to pay a net rent as well as all operating expenses including taxes, insurance, maintenance, and essential replacements.

The sale and lease-back transaction has many advantages as a mode of real estate ownership and tenant operations:

1. The seller (user of realty) obtains the full cash value of the property which, as a rule, is twice the amount that could be obtained under mortgage financing and this without the burdensome provisions of mortgage debt clauses and the possible threat of foreclosure in case of nonpayment of interest or principal.
2. The seller is able to reinvest the cash in his business enterprise in which as a "specialist" he has greater skill to increase net operating earnings. The sale, too, increases flexibility of capital investment and mobility of the enterprise in case expansion or relocation becomes necessary.
3. The seller, often, secures substantial tax advantages. If the sale yields a price less than book value of the property, the loss can be reflected in income tax reporting. Also, the entire amount paid for rent becomes a business expense, whereas under mortgage borrowing only the interest portion of the debt and accrued depreciation are tax-deductible items.

The purchaser also gains advantages which make the sale and lease-back transaction financially profitable to him:

1. Since the lessee assumes all operating expenses and burden of management, the net income (rent) provides a rate of return generally more favorable than that obtainable under a mortgage debt in investment.
2. Equity ownership provides an excellent hedge against inflation. If the property enhances in value during its investment life, it's the investor who will benefit in the long run.

The advantages to buyer and seller under a sale and lease-back transaction as outlined above are not all-inclusive, but are sufficiently substantial to make consideration of this type of real estate financing worthy of serious and profitable consideration.

IMPORTANCE OF LEASE PROVISIONS

To appraise a leasehold interest or a leased fee estate requires careful study of lease provisions in order to establish the respective rights of parties and their obligations concerning costs of property maintenance and operation. The landlord, for instance, may own both land and building improvements and agree to pay property taxes, hazard insurance, and expenditures for maintenance of building improvements. Interior costs of decorating, repair, and costs of utilities, on the other hand, may be borne by the tenant.

Many long-term leases are for the rental of unimproved land and are called *ground leases*. Agreements of this type usually provide for construction of a building by the tenant. Under ground-lease terms, the tenant as a rule pays all taxes and other maintenance charges, leaving the landlord's rent as *net*. Ground leases generally provide for disposition of the building at the end of the term. The building, although erected at the expense of the tenant, legally becomes real property and is—unless otherwise provided for—the property of the landlord, subject to the tenant's right of possession for the term of the lease. At the end of the lease term the building improvements revert to the landlord or the landlord generally, as agreed on, either pays the tenant for the building a stipulated or appraised value, or renews the lease at his option. Before a tenant proceeds under a long-term ground lease, he must make certain that his income from use of the property covers the following items:

1. The ground rent payable to the owner.
2. Taxes of all kinds and assessments for local improvements.
3. Premiums on policies of insurance against fire, liability suits, workmen's compensation claims, and plate-glass damage.
4. Charges for water, heat, light, and power.
5. Labor and repairs—including all charges for upkeep, maintenance, and service to tenants.
6. Interest on capital invested—that is, on the amount expended in erection of the building.
7. An amount sufficient to amortize the cost of the building during the term of the lease or by the end of the last renewal of the lease.
8. A sufficient amount over and above all the foregoing charges to compensate the operator for his services and the risk involved in the enterprise.[3]

SPLIT INTEREST VALUATION

A lease in effect splits the *bundle of property rights* and transfers the rights to use for a designated period of time from the owner to the tenant. Often the tenant in turn subleases a part or all of his lease interests and thus becomes sandwiched between the owner—to whom he is obligated under the terms of the basic, or original, lease—and the user, or subten-

[3] Alfred A. Ring and Nelson L. North, *Real Estate Principles and Practices* (Englewood Cliffs, New Jersey: Prentic-Hall, Inc., 6th ed., 1967), pp. 315–16.

ant, of the property, from whom he obtains rental payments for the term of the sublease. In fact the secondary, or subsidiary, leases between tenant and subtenant are actually called *sandwich leases* and are evaluated under the income approach in the same manner as other nonperpetuity rights to income.

Valuation of leased fee and leasehold interests are in appraisal practice restricted to the annuity, or Inwood, method of capitalization. It is held that contract rent as specified by lease terms provides a definite and thus predictable income flow, to which neither the straight line nor the sinking fund method of capitalization can be applied with accuracy. Although the same cannot be said for the income flow derived from operation of the property and out of which the tenant discharges his contract rent obligations, the leasehold interest by common agreement in appraisal practice is also capitalized under the Inwood, or annuity, method. This the author believes is a step in the right direction, for the logic which sanctions use of the annuity method for appraisal of leasehold interests will some day cause also the abandonment of straight line and sinking fund methods of capitalization for fee appraising.

In the appraisal of split interests, it is found that as a general rule the value of the sum of the parts of a property equals the value of the property as a whole. There are exceptions to this rule, and the appraiser must be alert to recognize conditions under which the value of the sum of the parts may be more or less than the value of the entire property—under free and clear ownership. The summation value of split interests is greater where the contract rent agreed on by a financially strong tenant exceeds the economic rent which the property is estimated to produce at the time of appraisal. Such excessive income nevertheless may have to be separated and capitalized at higher risk rates of interest, for even financially strong tenants seek to correct inequities. Where lease terms are restrictive to the point that the tenant is unable to make effective use of the property, the reduced income flow would cause the value of the parts to be less than the value of the property as a whole.

In all lease appraisal assignments it is advisable to derive the value of the entire property first, as if unencumbered and free for operation under unrestricted fee simple ownership. This total value can then serve as a bench mark, against which the reasonableness of the value of the parts can be judged. Failure to follow this procedure would deprive the appraiser of necessary checks and balances.

It is also of interest to point out that when the contract rent and economic rent are one and the same—assuming for purposes of illustration that the landlord furnishes both land and building improvements—the tenant's interest in the property is of zero value. One might ask why would anyone want to lease a property if the rental paid leaves no monetary interest or value to the leasehold. The answer is obvious: The land or improved property is leased merely as a vehicle for other business operations (selling merchandise, for instance) from which the tenant makes his profit. In all equity, the landowner should get the full return equal to the economic rent attributable to his property investment. Many large business concerns in fact prefer to lease rather than own in order not to tie up thousands of dollars in real estate investments. Such money generally can be more profitably invested in operations in which management has the know-how and skill to make higher interest returns on capital investment.

LEASED FEE VALUATION

The rights of a landlord under the terms of a lease are basically two-fold:

> *First,* he is entitled to receive the contract rent agreed on under terms of the lease for the duration of the lease period, and
>
> *Second,* he is entitled to repossession of the land and all permanent improvements thereon in accordance with lease terms. The right to repossess, better known as the reversionary right, reunites the split interests into fee simple ownership on termination or breach of the lease.

In all leased fee valuations, both of these interests or rights of the fee owner must be considered even though the reversionary rights under traditional long-term (ninety-nine years) leasing may prove of little value consequence.

To demonstrate appraisal practices in leased fee and leasehold valuations, three types of long-term leases will be presented for analysis as follows:

1. A *fixed-rental* lease with a nationally known company. Under terms of this lease, contract rents specified exceed warranted economic rent attributable to the property if free and clear.
2. A *step-up ground* lease, under which contract rentals prove inadequate to yield a fair return on the market value of the property.
3. An *advance-payment* lease, providing for reversion of land and building improvements at termination of the lease.

> *Illustration 1.* A building site in the downtown area of an industrial community was leased twenty years ago to a national concern for a period of forty years at a fixed rental of $10,500 per year. The current market value of the land is estimated at $150,000, and the rate of capitalization for similar land investments is established at 6½ percent. The building, which was erected by the tenant, is considered of no value at the end of the lease term. Based on these facts the value of the leased fee is derived as follows:

Value of the land by market comparison		$150,000
Land rate of capitalization, 6.5%		
Economic rent, $I = V \times R = \$150,000 \times .065 =$	$ 9,750	
Contact rent	$ 10,500	
Economic rent	9,750	
Excess rent	$ 750	
Present worth of economic rent for the remaining		
20 years at 6.5%		
$V = I \times F$ (Inwood) $= \$9,750 \times 11.0185 =$		107,430
Present worth of excess rent for 20 years at 8.0% [4]		
$V = I \times F = \$750 \times 9.8181 =$		7,364
Reversionary land value	$150,000	
Present worth factor—20 years at 6.5% $= .2838$		
Present worth of reversion $(150,000 \times .2838)$		42,570
Total value of leased fee		$157,364

In this illustration the value of the leased fee exceeds the market value of the land precisely by the capitalized amount of the excess rentals. Based on the present value of the economic rent and the present value of the reversion, the sum total of the parts equals the value of the property as a whole. Attention is also called to the fact that the excess rental, though committed for payment by a reliable national concern, was capitalized at an 8 percent rate of interest to indicate the greater risk attached to this excess income. National concerns of good repute—yes, even banks—have closed down in times of stress. Bankruptcy, for instance, would terminate the lease, and in such a contingency only the economic rent could be counted on to support property value. The selection of the risk rate is a matter of judgment based on general economic conditions, the reputation and history of the leasing firm, and the extent and nature of product and space competition.

Increases in the reversionary land value which are due to inflation must be ignored since the appraiser finds value in *present* dollars. Increases in value which are due to supply-demand influenced market conditions, should be considered only where such increases or decreases can be substantiated with a high degree of certainty.

Illustration 2. A city block measuring 200 feet by 200 feet was leased thirty years ago for a period of ninety-nine years. The step-up lease calls for rental payments as follow:

First 25 years	$ 8,000
Next 25 years	9,000
Next 20 years	10,000
Last 29 years	11,000

[4] The likelihood that excess rent may not continue for the period of lease term (e.g., lessee may become bankrupt) warrants application of a higher risk rate to this portion of the total income.

The value of the site on the date of appraisal has a market value of $150,000. It is estimated that this value will remain stable and that this amount may be anticipated at time of land reversion. The rate of interest for similar investments is determined at 6.5 percent. Based on these facts, and using the Inwood factor method of capitalization, the value of the leased fee is obtained as shown:

Value of land by market comparison	$150,000
Land rate of capitalization, 6.5%	
Present worth of rental income: (69 remaining years)	
$9,000 for first 20 years at 6.5 percent interest equals:	
$9,000 × 11.0185 =	99,167
$10,000 for next 20 years at 6.5 percent interest	
deferred for 20 years equals:	
$10,000 × 11.0185 = $110,185 × .2383797 =	31,270
$11,000 for balance of 29 years at 6.5 percent interest	
deferred for 40 years equals:	
$11,000 × 12.90749 = 141,982 × .08054 =	11,436
Present worth of contract rent	$141,873
Add: Reversionary rights to land value of $150,000,	
69 years removed at 6.5 percent, equals:	
$150,000 × .012968 =	1,945
Total value of leased fee	$143,818

The above value can also be obtained by use of the 6.5 percent Inwood factors exclusively without reference to the deferment factors:

Present worth of $9,000 per year for 20 years at 6.5% =		
$9,000 × 11.0185 =		$ 99,167
Present worth of $10,000 per year from		
21st year to 40th year:		
40-year factor	14.1455	
Less 20-year factor	11.0185	
Factor for next 20 years	3.127	
$10,000 × 3.127 =		31,270
Present worth of $11,000 per year from		
41st year to 69th year:		
69-year factor	15.1851	
Less 40-year factor	14.1455	
Factor for last 29 years	1.0396	
$11,000 × 1.0396 =		11,436
Present worth of contract rent		$141,873
(Add land reversion as above)		1,945
Total value of leased fee		$143,818

In this second illustration the lease as originally drawn covered a period of ninety-nine years. On the date of appraisal, thirty years of the total lease period had elapsed and no consideration was given either to past rights or past obligations. The value of the leased fee interest as derived above reflects only the present worth of future rights to income. Attention, too, is called to the fact that the value of the lessor's interest of $143,700 is less than the value of $150,000 which this property would warrant if free from lease obligations. The loss in value in this instance is entirely due to lease term provisions under which the contract rent paid is less than the economic rent which the property can produce under a program of highest and best land use. The lessor's loss is, of course, the lessee's gain whenever the value of the sum of the parts equals the value of the property as a whole.

> *Illustration 3.* A single-story building containing three stores in an 80 percent business district is leased for a period of thirty years. The net rent payable annually in advance is $7,375. The tenant is to pay all taxes, insurance, and related costs of maintenance and repair, and to return the property in operating condition subject only to ordinary wear and tear from building age and use. The value of the land free and clear is $40,000 and the replacement cost new of the building is $60,000. At the termination of the lease period, accrued building depreciation is estimated at 60 percent. Based on these facts, and an interest rate of 7 percent, the value of the leased fee is derived as follows:

Contract rent (for 30 years)		$ 7,375
Present worth of 1 per annum (advance payment)		
at 7% interest		13.278
Present worth of contract rent		$ 97,925
Add revisionary value:		
Land	$40,000	
Building (40%)	24,000	
Total	$64,000	
Present worth of 1 at 7%	.131367	
Present worth of reversion		8,407
Total value of leased fee		$106,332

In this illustration, although the contract rent and the economic rent are approximately identical, the value of the leased fee exceeds the value of the land and building by $6,332. This excess value is entirely caused by contract provisions, which call for annual rental payments in advance.

VALUATION OF LEASEHOLDS

Theoretically, in a free and competitive market the lessee's interest in the property should be of zero value. His profits, as previously explained, should be derived from operation of the business in which he specializes. In practice, however, lease terms are relatively inflexible and, as a consequence, contract rent is greater or lesser than the economic rent the property yields under highest and best use and unencumbered fee simple ownership. To the extent that contract rent exceeds economic rent, the lessee is transferring value from property he owns in buildings or business to the landlord or fee owner. Conversely, where contract rent is less than economic rent the landlord transfers part of his property-value interest to the tenant.

In appraisal practice the value of a leasehold is often obtained by subtracting the value of the leased fee from the value of the property as if free and clear from contract obligations. This short cut procedure for leasehold valuation is not recommended, because an error in calculation of the leased fee interest automatically transfers this error to the leasehold estate whenever value of the parts is considered equal to the value of the whole. For this reason efforts should always be made to establish leasehold values independently by separate discounting of the future rights to leasehold income (positive or negative) into a sum of present value.

The tenant or user of the property has the right to employ the property in accordance with lease terms and to receive the economic rent which the property produces under its highest and best use. Out of this economic rental or income, the tenant pays the contract rent; that which remains, if anything, over the lease period forms the basis for the value of the leasehold estate. To demonstrate the application of leasehold valuation, reference is made to the three illustrations cited above as follows:

Illustration 1.

Economic rent of property	$ 9,750
Contract rent per lease	10,500
Deficit rent from property	($ 750)
Capitalized value of deficit leasehold income:	
$V = I \times F = \$750 \times 9.8181 =$	($ 7,364)

The deficit income was capitalized at an interest rate of 8 percent. (The rate used must be supported by market analysis of interest yields for comparable properties.)

To prove the accuracy of the leasehold valuation a check can now be made as follows:

Valuation of leased fee (see page 305)	$157,364
Add value of leasehold estate (*deficit*)	(7,364)
Value of entire property	$150,000

Illustration 2.

Remaining term of leasehold	69 years	
Economic (stablized) rental	$10,000	
First 20 years:		
Economic rent	$10,000	
Contract rent	9,000	
	―――――	
Excess rent	$ 1,000	
Capitalized at risk rate of 14% [5]		
$V = I \times F = \$1,000 \times 6.623 =$		$ 6,623
Next 20 years:		
Economic rent	$10,000	
Contract rent	10,000	
	―――――	
Excess rent	None	
Capitalized value		None
Last 29 years:		
Economic rent	$10,000	
Contract rent	11,000	
	―――――	
Deficit rent	($ 1,000)	
Capitalized at rate of 14% interest		
69-year (Inwood) factor	7.142	
40-year (Inwood) factor	7.105	
	―――――	
29-year factor—used	.037	
$Value = I \times F = \$1,000 \times .037 =$		($ 37)
		―――――
Value of leasehold estate		$ 6,586
Value check:		
Appraised leased fee value (see page 306)		$143,818
Appraised value of leasehold estate		6,586
		―――――
Value of entire fee		$150,404

The combined value derived above is slightly higher than the value of the property under fee simple ownership. This discrepancy is caused by selection of interest rates—rounded to the nearest quarter of 1 percent —used in the capitalization of split property interests. In appraisal practice the values reported are generally rounded to comply with market practices under which offers to buy and sell are quoted in units of $100 or $500, depending on the value of the investment. In the above case, appraisal findings would undoubtedly be reported as follows:

――――――――

[5] The rate of interest applied to the tenant's (lessee) interest in this illustration was selected for demonstration purposes. In practice a study of leasehold sales or market interest rates at which tenants are attracted to comparable investment properties is necessary to support the applicable rate of interest.

Leased fee	$143,500
Leasehold estate	6,500
Total value of property	$150,000

Illustration 3. In this illustration, lease provisions held the contract rent and economic rent in balance. Under ordinary circumstances in such instances the value of the leasehold estate would be zero. However, business custom and accounting practices typically provide for rental payments at the end of the payment period. This shift in the payment period results in a present worth gain for the leased fee, and a consequent loss to the leasehold estate as illustrated below:

1. Contract rent for 30 years paid annually in advance	$ 7,375
Present worth—advance—of annuity of 1 at 7%	13.278
Present value of contract rent	$97,925
2. Contract rent for 30 years paid annually at end of year	$7,375
Present worth—end of year factor (7%)	12.409
Present value of contract rent	$91,516
Deficit (negative) value of leasehold estate	($ 6,409)

SANDWICH LEASE VALUATION

In instances where a leasehold interest is subleased to a third party the original lessee becomes a sublandlord in his own right, and legally as well as economically is sandwiched between the fee owner—to whom the property reverts at the termination of the original lease—and the user, or subtenant, to whom the leasehold was transferred under separate and specific contract provisions. Investors may find it profitable to acquire long-term ground leases, develop the land, erect building improvements, and sublease the property to one or more tenants for part of or the entire period of the original lease term.

The contract rights and obligations of the sandwich leasehold estate normally are clearly spelled out, and the rights to income are capitalized under the annuity, or Inwood, method in the same manner as demonstrated in the three illustrations shown above. Care must be taken to derive the net rental to which the sandwich owner is entitled and to capitalize this net income (the difference between the contract rent received from the subtenant and the contract rent paid to the fee owner) at the appropriate risk rate of interest. Splitting a fee into one or more leasehold interests also splits property value in accordance with terms of income distribution and relative risk of the split ownership. The general rule that the sum of the parts equals the whole prevails. Differences in rates of interest applied to different levels of ownership merely reflect a redistribution of the risk of rights to income under terms of the lease agreements. The fee owner, like a first mortgagee, occupies a preferred risk position. The sandwich leaseholder has a contractual position similar to that of a second mortgagee, and the rate of interest assigned to this second priority of income is appropriately higher. The user of the property must rely on income from operations of the property, and he assumes all the risks that accompany equity ownership.

To illustrate the application of the income approach to value to a property under sandwich lease agreement, the following data will be used as a basis for appraisal purposes:

A lease from Stem to Bloom was made thirty years ago, for a term of eighty years. Rental payments were agreed upon as follows:

First 20 years	$2,000
Next 20 years	2,500
Last 40 years	3,000

Ten years after the date of original lease Bloom completed a building at a cost of $80,000 and subleased the property to Petal for a period of seventy years. Rental payments on a step-up basis were agreed upon as follows:

First 25 years	$ 9,000
Next 25 years	10,000
Last 20 years	11,000

The property on a free-and-clear basis is estimated to have a market value on the date of appraisal of $70,000 for improvements and $80,000 for land, a total of $150,000. The economic rent is estimated at $12,000. Market analysis indicates risk rates of interest of 7 percent for the leased fee, 8 percent for the sandwich leasehold, and 10 percent for the top leasehold. The lease and improvements have a fifty-year remaining life. Based on this data the value of the respective interests is derived as shown below:

1. *Leased fee* at 7 percent rate of interest:

Contract rent for 10 years, $2,500 × 7.0236 (P.W. factor for 10 years) =	$17,559
Contract rent for 40 years, $3,000 (50-year factor minus 10-year factor or 13.8007 − 7.0236) 6.7771 =	20,331
Present worth of reversion $80,000 × .03395 =	2,716
Total value of leased fee	$40,606

2. *Sandwich lease* at 8 percent rate of interest:

Net contract rent for 5 years, $6,500 ($9,000 — $2,500)
Net contract rent for next 5 years, $7,500 ($10,000 — $2,500)
Net contract rent for next 20 years, $7,000 ($10,000 — $3,000)
Net contract rent for last 20 years, $8,000 ($11,000 — $3,000)

Value:

$6,500 × 3.9927 (P.W. factor—first 5 years) =	$25,953
$7,500 × 2.7174 next 5 years (6.7101 — 3.9927) =	20,381
$7,000 × 4.5477 next 20 years (11.2578 — 6.7101) =	31,834
$8,000 × .9757 last 20 years (12.2336 — 11.2578) =	7,806
Total value of sandwich leasehold	$85,974

3. *Top leasehold* at 10 percent rate of interest

Net income for 5 years, $3,000 ($12,000 — $ 9,000)
Net income for 25 years, $2,000 ($12,000 — $10,000)
Net income for 20 years, $1,000 ($12,000 — $11,000)

Value:

$3,000 × 3.7908 (P.W. factor—5 years) =	$11,372
$2,000 × 5.6361 next 25 years (9.4269 — 3.7908) =	11,272
$1,000 × .4879 last 20 years (9.9148 — 9.4269) =	488
Total value of top leasehold	$23,132

Combined value of lease interests:

Leased fee	$ 40,605
Sandwich leasehold	85,974
Top leasehold	23,132
Total	$149,711

In appraisal practice the above value results would be rounded and reported as follows:

Leased fee	$ 40,750
Sandwich leasehold	86,000
Top leasehold	23,250
Total	$150,000

SUMMARY

A lease agreement is a formal, legally binding contract between two or more parties providing for a definite split of the bundle of rights between the owner of the fee, or landlord, and the leasehold user, or tenant. Under lease terms, definite or determinable rental payments are agreed on and paid at designated time intervals monthly, quarterly, semiannually, or annually, in advance or at the end of the time period.

The landlord, or fee owner, generally is entitled to the contract rent for the duration of the lease and to the reversion of the land and improvements—the latter as specified under lease contract terms. The tenant, or leasehold estate owner, is entitled to the economic rent, out of which he pays the contract rent. The difference between the economic and contract rent constitutes the net income upon which the value of the leasehold is based. Under a sandwich lease agreement a further split of the leasehold interest is agreed upon and a third, or sandwich leasehold, interest is established. The value of this interest is based on the difference between the contract rent obtained from the top leaseholder and the contract rent paid to the owner of the leased fee.

It is the appraiser's responsibility to examine the lease agreements carefully, to evaluate the property under free-and-clear ownership, to establish the risk rates of interest applicable to the split property interests, and to determine, by capitalization of income under the annuity, or Inwood, method, the value of the various interests or rights to the property. Under typical circumstances, the combined value of the various interests should equal the value of the property as a whole—unencumbered. Where the sum of the parts does not equal the whole (property) an explanation must be offered to substantiate the validity and accuracy of the value findings. As in all valuation problems, accuracy of factual data and soundness of appraisal judgment—rather than mathematical skill—are basic to accurate and reliable value conclusions.

READING AND STUDY REFERENCES

1. *Acquisition for Right-of-Way* (Washington, D.C.: American Association of State Highway Officials, 1962), chaps. 31–32.
2. *The Appraisal of Real Estate* (Chicago: American Institute of Real Estate Appraisers, 1967), chap. 25.
3. Babcock, Frederick M., *The Valuation of Real Estate* (New York: McGraw-Hill Book Company, Inc., 1932), chaps. 24–25.
4. *Condemnation Appraisal Practice* (Chicago: American Institute of Real Estate Appraisers, 1961), pp. 397–406, 418–21.
5. Dalgety, George S., "The Appraisal of Long-Term Leaseholds," *The Appraisal Journal* (April 1948), pp. 165–73.
6. Free, Robert L. "The Appraisal of Sandwich Leases," *The Appraisal Journal* (July 1958), pp. 354–59.
7. Kahn, Sanders A., Frederick E. Case, and Alfred Schimmel, *Real*

Estate Appraisal and Investment (New York: The Ronald Press Company, 1963), chap. 22.

8. McMichael, Stanley L., *McMichael's Appraising Manual,* 4th ed. (Englewood Cliffs, N.J.: Prentice-Hall, Inc., 1951), chaps. 33–34.

9. Shenkel, William M., "Valuation of Leased Fees and Leasehold Interests," *The Appraisal Journal* (October 1965), pp. 487–98.

10. Warwick, Samuel C., "Leasehold Interest Paradox," *The Real Estate Appraiser* (March 1966), pp. 30–33.

Ever since the introduction of *Ellwood Tables for Real Estate Appraising and Financing,*[1] a keen interest has developed among professional appraisers in the application of a more sophisticated method of capitalization that will give effect to profitable equity yields which accrue to investors under mortgage debt financing of real property. Although Ellwood's pre-computed tables for mortgage-equity financing are of relatively recent origin, the

21 Equity Appraising

and Financing

concept of "leverage" or trading on the equity for purposes of increasing owners' interest earnings on cash investment is as old as civilization. In fact, mortgage lending and equity investment practices date back to Biblical days. (See Nekemiah, Chapter 5, Versus 1 to 7.) Extensive use of credit, however, as a major source of real estate financing did not become popularized until the beginning of the twentieth century.

TRADING ON THE EQUITY

Apart from the necessity to borrow funds, probably the greatest justification for incurring indebtedness is to be found in the principle of trading on the equity. In conformity with this principle, it is economically advisable to borrow funds

[1] L. W. Ellwood, *Ellwood Tables for Real Estate Appraising and Financing* (Chicago: American Institute of Real Estate Appraisers, 1967).

when the use of such funds brings a higher rate of return than the rate, or cost, of borrowing. To illustrate: Assume that a property costing $100,000 brings in a gross rental of $17,500 per annum, and that this property was purchased for all cash and thus is free and clear of monetary encumbrances. If the taxes, repairs, and other operating expenses including provision for depreciation (recapture) amount to $7,500 annually then the net income is $10,000 or 10 percent on the owner's investment. Now suppose the owner mortgages the property for $50,000 at 7 percent interest per annum. The interest on $50,000 amounting to $3,500 would reduce the net income to $6,500; but since the owner's equity investment is now only $50,000, his equity rate of return (yield) has increased from 10 percent to 13.5 percent per annum. Suppose, further, that a mortgage in the amount of $75,000 was obtainable at 7 percent. The interest on this indebtedness would increase to $5,250 and, conversely, would decrease the net income to equity to $4,750. This income, however, in relation to the equity investment of $25,000, represents an interest yield—as a result of trading on the equity —at a rate of 19 percent per annum.

To recapitulate:	*Case No. 1*	*Case No. 2*
Investment value	$100,000	$100,000
Net income to property	10,000	10,000
Overall rate of earning	10%	10%
Mortgage loan	50,000	75,000
Loan interest at 7%	3,500	5,250
Equity value	50,000	25,000
Equity net income	6,500	4,750
Equity yield—percent	13.5	19.0

The above illustration was offered in order to emphasize at the outset of this chapter the distinction that need and must be made between the earnings capacity of a property under free and clear ownership and equity yields obtainable under favorable mortgage debt financing or "trading on the equity." Thus, although a given property earns a maximum rate of 10 percent per annum, the equity yield through increased leverage can almost be doubled as noted above. From an economic point of view, trading on the equity does not increase the earnings of the property but rather compensates the borrower for the additional risks assumed in securing the safety of borrowed funds and in guaranteeing the priority of interest and amortization payments to which the lender—under the financial mortgage agreement—has a legal claim.

When property is unimproved, or inadequately improved, borrowing to erect a suitable improvement is invariably an advantage. An annual loss or a very small annual return may be turned into an annual income commensurate with the value of the property. The land may be valuable, but it will yield its economic rent only when improved with a building; and it is often a financial advantage to obtain a mortgage loan to pay all or part of the cost of such building. Suppose that a parcel of unimproved land is worth $100,000. The taxes amount to $2,000 and the loss of interest on the money invested in land is 7.0 percent or $7,000, a total annual loss of $9,000 to the owner. To save this loss the owner puts up a building costing $300,000, and he borrows this whole amount on a mortgage at 7.0 percent. The land and building together produce a rent income of $60,000, and the taxes, depreciation, and other charges are $27,000, leaving a net rental of $33,000. Out of this net rental, $21,000 is paid as interest on the money borrowed, leaving $12,000 for the equity owner—this being 12 percent on his cash investment which is still $100,000. He has, therefore, stopped his loss, and now has an income of $12,000.

It is probable that in cases of this kind the amount of depreciation of the building would be represented by a corresponding annual payment to reduce the amount of the mortgage over the years of indebtedness. More likely, the amount of depreciation permitted as a write-off under the Internal Revenue Code will provide a tax shelter (tax-free income) to the extent that allowable deductions exceed mortgage amortization. This excess write-off, or at least to the extent to which mortgage amortization as dollar amounts exceed accrued depreciation as a loss in value, increases the equity portion of the total investment and thus converts the excess amount that reverts to the owner at the time of property sale into a "capital gain." The total amount of equity realized or recaptured at the time of property sale, if greater than the original equity investment, further increases the equity yield as will be demonstrated below.

PROPERTY APPRAISING VERSUS EQUITY
APPRAISING AND FINANCING

Prior to illustrating the application of the mortgage-equity method of capitalization it is essential that the appraiser fully realizes the distinction that must be made between valuation of real property as an economic whole or entity, and valuation of the "equity investment" under market regulated mortgage-equity methods of financing.

Market value is best defined as the "present worth of future rights to income." To be accurate, market value must be based on income produced under:

1. Fee simple ownership, irrespective of financial encumbrances.
2. Typical property management, and
3. Utilization of property under a program of highest and best use.

Once market value has been established, so to speak on F.O.B. typical financial terms, then the "price" which the investor is warranted in paying for the property can be ascertained by adding or subtracting from market value benefits or detriments attributable to personal or financial attributes such as reputation of, or extraordinary management (good will), title encumbrances (good or bad leases, easements, and so on) and good or bad financial terms of sale. To do otherwise would inject price-influencing personal causes into the capitalization process and cloud, if not prevent, objective analysis and price adjustment of comparable sales in order to derive an accurate measure of present worth of the subject property.

Those who apply and defend the mortgage-equity method of capitalization as a means for estimating property value reject the idea that property should be appraised as though free and clear of financial encumbrances. Instead it is claimed that the investor will secure as much of the purchase price as the "traffic will bear" through mortgage debt financing at rates and terms prevailing in the market. Further, it is refuted that value must be based on income derived over the economic life of the property; rather it is deemed an accepted and observable fact that the customary period of ownership is short lived—ten to fifteen years—and that income projections, therefore, should be of equal short-term duration. At the termination of the investment life the property is sold, the remaining equity investment (sale price less remaining mortgage debt) reverts back to the owner, and the cycle of ownership from cash to cash position is completed.

Failure to differentiate between the mortgage-equity *"price"* methods of capitalization and the more conventional income *"value"* methods of capitalization, as explained above, is responsible for the confusion of minds found not only among earnest students of appraising but also among most professional appraisers who find themselves lost in mathematical equations. Semantics, too, aggravate the issue at hand. Whereas value should represent the "present" worth of future rights to income and be free from influences of dollar inflation or deflation (income and value when unencumbered will rise and fall like a ship at sea with the level of prices) the mortgage-equity approach to value yields a "price" that includes the benefits of terms of financing, the impact of leverage, and the inflationary or deflationary effects on equity investment which result in capital gain. Further complicating matters is the fact that under the conventional method of income capitalization the appraiser is given the option to use, as he deems best applicable, the straight line or annuity residual techniques of determining land and building value as demonstrated in Chapter 19. Under the mortgage-equity method of capitalization, the appraiser is restricted to the use of an overall rate of capitalization and to the conversion of a "stabilized" or level income derived for the property as a whole rather than for land and improvements as separate and distinct value parts.

To illustrate the application of the mortgage-equity method of capitalization, the following appraisal problem is presented:

> A department store property has been leased to a national chain for a term of ten years at a rental of $22,000 per annum. Owner's, taxes, insurance, and exterior maintenance costs total $6,000 per year leaving a net rental before recapture or depreciation in the amount of $16,000. Mortgage money of $135,000 can be obtained to finance the purchase of this property at 7.5 percent interest with full amortization over twenty years payable monthly in the amount of $1,088, or a total of $13,056, per year covering mortgage interest and amortization. The property is anticipated to decrease in value over the ten-year ownership period and bring at time of sale $160,000. The owner seeks an appraisal of this income property specifying an equity yield of 10 percent.

Solution:

1. Net income		$ 16,000	
2. Mortgage interest and principal—annual		13,056	
3. Equity income—cash flow		$ 2,944	
4. Present value of equity income of $1.00 at 10% compound interest—Inwood factor, 10-year period		6.1446	
Present worth of equity income for 10-year period = $2,944 × 6.1446 =			$18,090
5. Sale price of property		$160,000	
6. Remaining value of mortgage:			
a) Monthly mortgage payments	$1,088		
b) Remaining payment period—10 years —Inwood factor for 120 months at rate of 7.5% per annum	84.245		
c) Mortgage balance on date of sale $1,088 × 84.245		$91,659	
7. Value of equity on date of sale		$68,341	
8. Reversionary value:			
a) Present worth of $1.00 at 10% for income due 10 years from date of appraisal =		.3855	
9. Present worth of reversion $68,341 × .3855 =			$ 26,345
10. Total present value of equity at 10% interest =			44,435
11. Add mortgage loan value on date of appraisal			135,000
12. Total value of property			$179,435

13. Overall rate of capitalization
R = I/V = $16,000 ÷ 179,435 = 8.92%
Proof:

Value of property		$179,435
Mortgage loan		135,000
Equity cash value		$ 44,435
Net income flow	$16,000	
Annual-level mortgage payments	13,056	
Equity cash flow	$ 2,944	
Present worth of cash flow at 10% $2,944 × 6.1446 (Inwood factor for 10 years)		$18,090
Present worth of equity reversion ($44,436 − $18,090) =		$ 26,345
Future worth of $26,345 at 10% $26,345 × 2.594 (F.W. of $1.00) =		$ 68,431
Add remaining value of mortgage loan at time of sale		91,659
Value of property on date of sale		$160,000

The distribution of net income—before recapture—to equity and level mortgage payments, and the changing relationship of the mortgage amortization and mortgage interest components over the ten-year ownership period is graphically shown in Figure 21.1 below. The pattern of changes

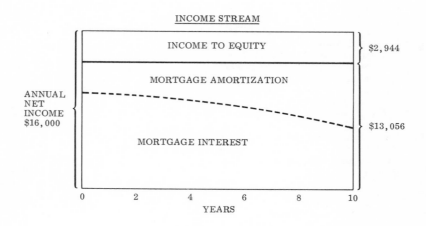

FIGURE 21.1

in capital formation caused by property depreciation, declining mortgage debt balances, and increasing equity over the ownership period are presented in Figure 21.2.

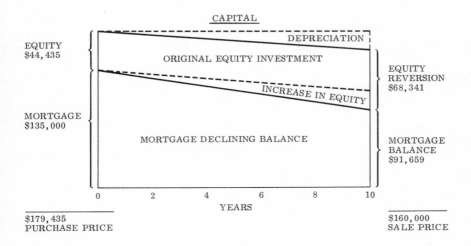

FIGURE 21.2

In the above illustration the equity yield was obtained from the investor. The yield rate can also be obtained from market study of comparable properties. Where a sale price is firm and the mortgage terms and rate are known, the equity interest yield rate can be obtained by analysis as follows:

Suppose a property was bought eight years ago for $300,000. Of this purchase price, $200,000 was financed by a twenty-five-year mortgage at 6 percent interest. The level mortgage payments totaled $15,468 per year. The average annual net income produced by this property during the term of ownership was $24,500. The property brought on date of sale—eight years from date of purchase a price of $255,000. What is the yield on the equity's investment?

Solution:

1. Original purchase price	$300,000
2. Mortgage loan	200,000

3. Original cash investment		$100,000
4. Sales price—8 years later		$255,000
5. Mortgage balance—8 years later:		
a) Monthly level payments	$1,289	
b) Inwood factor ½% for 204 periods =	127.6975	
Mortgage balance $1,289 × 127.6975 =		$164,602
6. Reversion to equity on date of sale		$ 90,398
7. Income from property		24,500
8. Mortgage loan payments		15,468
9. Income to equity (cash flow) annually		$ 9,032
"Trial" interest yield rate of 8%		
10. Present worth of income stream at 8% $9,032 × 5.747		
(Inwood factor for 8 years) =		$ 51,907
11. Present worth of reversion at 8% $90,398 × .5403		
(P. W. of $1.00 — 8 years) =		$ 48,842
12. Total value of equity indicated by yield rate of 8% =		$100,749
13. Present worth of income stream at 9% $9,032 × 5.535		
(Inwood factor for 8 years) =		$ 49,992
14. Present worth of reversion at 9% $90,398 × .5019		
(P. W. of $1.00 — 8 years) =		$ 45,371
Total value of equity indicated by yield rate of 9%		$ 95,363

To determine the precise yield rate that falls between 8 and 9 percent, it is necessary to interpolate as follows:

Value of equity at 8% interest =	$100,749
Value of equity at 9% interest =	95,363
Difference caused by 1% rate of interest =	$ 5,386
Value of equity at 8% interest	$100,749
Value of equity at "X"% interest	100,000
Difference of 8% over "X"%	$ 749

Thus the actual rate is 749 ÷ 5,386 of 1 percent above the yield rate of 8 percent or .00139. This fractional rate when added to the trial rate of .08 determines the accurate yield rate of .08139 or 8.14 percent.

Suppose the appraiser is called on to ascertain the amount that the property for which a yield rate of 8.14 percent was computed above should have sold for in order to yield a 10 percent rate of interest to the owner. The answer would be derived as follows:

1. Value of income stream at 10% $9,032 × 5.335	
(8 year Inwood factor at 10%) =	$ 48,186
2. Present value of property reversion = $100,000	
less $48,186 =	51,814

3. Future worth of property 8 years hence is $51,814 ×
   2.144 (F. W. of $1.00 at 10%) =   111,089
4. Add mortgage loan balance on date of sale (see
   above illustration)   164,602

5. Sale price of property to yield 10 percent interest
   to owner $275,691

Conversely, it could be asked how much should the owner have paid for the property on date of purchase to yield an interest rate of 10 percent where the anticipated sale price of $255,000, the equity reversion of $90,392, and all other factors given in the problem above remain constant.

Solution:

1. Present value of income stream at 10% as above
   ($9,032 × 5.335) = $ 48,186
2. Present worth of reversion at 10% $90,398 × .4665 =
   (P. W. of $1.00) =   42,171

3. Value of equity cash investment to yield an interest
   rate of 10% = $ 90,357
4. Add amount of original mortgage loan of   200,000

5. Purchase price of property to yield 10% of equity
   investment. $290,357

The above illustrations support the fact that the equity yield which comparable sales support or which an investor demands is that rate at which the stabilized cash flow to equity when capitalized to present worth over the years of ownership plus the present worth of the equity reversionary interests (sale price less mortgage balance) at time of sale equal the cash value [2] of the equity on date of purchase. It should be held clearly in mind that since a property's income-producing capacity is unaffected by terms of financing, the interest yield to an owner will vary with his ability to obtain the best bargain possible by "trading on the equity," i.e., by obtaining the largest possible mortgage in relation to total property value at the lowest possible rate of interest over the longest possible years which are short of the economic life of the property as a whole.

As demonstrated above, given a level income and a stated purchase price at appraised value, the equity yield rate will increase or decrease with appreciation or depreciation of the property over the ownership period. The impact on equity yield rates resulting from property price increases or

---

[2] Cash value of equity is the cash amount paid for the property over and above the existing mortgage debt on date of purchase of the subject property.

decreases can best be visualized by graphic presentation as shown in Figure 21.3 below.

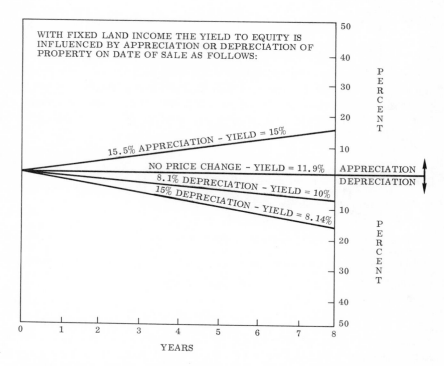

WITH FIXED LAND INCOME THE YIELD TO EQUITY IS INFLUENCED BY APPRECIATION OR DEPRECIATION OF PROPERTY ON DATE OF SALE AS FOLLOWS:

15.5% APPRECIATION - YIELD = 15%

NO PRICE CHANGE - YIELD = 11.9%

8.1% DEPRECIATION - YIELD = 10%

15% DEPRECIATION - YIELD = 8.14%

APPRECIATION

DEPRECIATION

YEARS

PROSPECTS FOR YIELD ON EQUITY INVESTMENT BASED ON ⅔ MORTGAGE AT 6% INTEREST OVER A TWENTY-FIVE AMORTIZATION PERIOD

ELLWOOD'S TABLES FOR CAPITALIZATION

It is now brought to the attention of our readers that the solutions to the equity yield problems as demonstrated above in the mortgage-equity method of capitalization were obtained without aid of any formulas or specially derived coefficients or factors other than those found in standard compound interest tables such as presented and illustrated in the chapter on Mathematics of Property Valuation. Special purpose tables such as named Babcock, Inwood, Hoskold, Ring and Ellwood do, however, play an important role in the valuation process for they are intended to save considerable work-time in the appraisal process by offering precomputed rates, factors, or income derivations applicable to an amount or percentage of $1.00. Once we establish the impact of a method of capitalization on the value of an income stream of $1.00, the appraiser can readily compute the value of "X" dollars by multiplication or division, as the case might be, by simple reference to the appropriate factor table.

Mr. L. W. Ellwood, who for many years served as supervisor in the Mortgage Loan Division of the New York Life Insurance Company developed, by following essentially the same mathematical steps as illustrated in the equity value problems above, precomputed "overall rates of capitalization" which permit ready and instant capitalization of a stabilized income stream over specified years of ownership periods at market-determined mortgage loan terms and prevailing equity yield rates applicable to the subject property.

The basic formula applied by Ellwood [3] in the development of precomputed (mortgage-equity leveraged) rates of capitalization is as follows:

$$R = Y - MC + (dep.\ 1/S_n)\ or\ (-\ app.\ 1/S_n)$$

These symbols have meaning as follows:

R = Over-all rate of capitalization.
Y = Equity yield rate demanded by prudent investors.
M = Ratio of mortgage to total investment, i.e. 60%, 70%, etc.
C = Mortgage coefficient. This coefficient is derived by the formula: $C = Y + (P \times 1/S_n) - f$. Here, Y represents the equity yield; p, the proportion or percentage of the loan paid off; $1/S_n$, the sinking fund rate at the equity yield rate for given or "n" years of ownership; and, f, the annual level mortgage loan payment per dollar of debt.
$1/S_n$ = Represents the sinking fund factor at equity yield rate which is multiplied by the percentage of appreciation or depreciation estimated to occur over the years of ownership. This derived portion of the sinking fund factor is added in case of depreciation, and subtracted in case of property appreciation.

To demonstrate the development of a "band of investment" mortgage-equity weighted rate of capitalization the following market-derived data is applied:

1. Mortgage loan funds available over twenty-five-year loan period for 70 percent of value at 7 percent interest compounded monthly.
2. Equity yield is 12 percent on cash investment.
3. Ownership period from date of purchase to date of sale is ten years.
4. Net income before recapture or debt service is $47,675.
5. Depreciation is estimated at 1.5 percent per year or a total of 15 percent over the ten-year period.

---

[3] L. W. Ellwood, *Ellwood Tables for Real Estate Appraising and Financing* (Chicago: American Institute of Real Estate Appraisers, 1967).

Solution:

$$R = Y - MC + dep.\ 1/S_n$$
$$R = .12 - (.70 \times .04736\,^*) + (.15 \times .0570)$$
$$R = .12 - .0332 + .00855$$
$$R = .09535$$

$$^*C = .12 + (.21364^1 \times .057^2) - .08482^3$$
$$C = .12 + .0121775 - .08482$$
$$C = .04736$$

Value of property = $47,675 \div .09535$ =	$500,000
Mortgage loan of 70% =	350,000
Equity cash investment =	$150,000

Proof:

Total Income	$47,675
Debt service payments $350,000 \times .0848$ (mortgage constant)	29,680
Cash to equity	$17,995

Present worth of cash flow at 12% = $17,995 \times 5.6503$ (Inwood Factor) =	$101,677
Present worth of reversion, 12%, 10 years = $425,000 ($500,000 less 15%) less mortgage balance of $(.786 \times \$350,000)$ $275,100 = $149,900 \times .322$ (P. W. of $1.00 at 12%) =	48,268
Total present value of equity	$149,945

Rounded to $150,000

The value of $500,000 as obtained above, based on an income stream of $47,675 per annum to be derived from a property to be owned over a period of ten years where 70 percent mortgage funds can be obtained at 7 percent interest over twenty-five-year loan periods and where equity yields must bring 12 percent to the owner-investor, could have been capitalized directly by reference to an Ellwood table for real estate appraising and financing or could be computed by the long method or formula method as demonstrated above. The important thing is that the appraiser "knows" the means and ways for computing value under the mortgage-

---

[1] 1.00 — (Monthly mortgage payments of .007068 per $1.00 of loan, times Inwood factor for 180 months at 7% of 111.256) = .78636 remaining mortgage principal, or .21364 per dollar of loan paid off in ten years time.

[2] Sinking fund factor for 10 years at 12% = .057.

[3] Mortgage constant payment per month of .007068 times 12 = annual constant of .08482.

equity method of capitalization, and understands the difference between "property appraising" free and clear of debt encumbrances and mortgage-equity valuation to reflect leveraged income derived from "trading on the equity."

SUMMARY

It is most important that a clear destinction be made between property appraising on the one hand, and mortgage-equity appraising on the other. In the former case, the appraiser is charged with the responsibility to estimate "objectively" the present worth of a property which is or can be employed under a program of highest and best utilization and which is managed in accordance with practices deemed typical in the market area. A property thus utilized can conceivably have only one market value but may, because of available alternate means of mortgage-equity terms of financing and wide differences in buyers, abilities to trade on the equity have a substantial range of subjective values to individual or corporate owners.

Much of the confusion in appraisal practice is due to the failure to distinguish between objective value as measured in present worth and number of "current" purchasing power dollars and subjective value (price) which gives weight to terms of the sale, entrepreneurial skill of trading on the equity, tax position of the buyer, and price increments or decrements caused by inflation or deflation. For the sake of clarity as well as for professional purity in appraisal theory and practice, it is strongly recommended that value be estimated objectively first on a free and clear basis, i.e., free of all encumbrances; and second, that price adjustments be made and identified to reflect available terms of financing, tax shelter opportunities, and other tax or ownership benefits which accrue to a specific owner or a group of owners. Such value report presentation will then enable the client or report reader to accept, reject, or modify the appraisal expert's conclusions.

The impact of trading on the equity caused by increasing mortgage loan leverage is apparent from the alternate methods of financing as summarized below:

Example No.	*1*	*2*	*3*	*4*
Market value	$100,000	$100,000	$100,000	$100,000
Net income	10,000	10,000	10,000	10,000
Overall rate—percent	10	10	10	10
Mortgage loan of	60,000	70,000	80,000	90,000
Interest cost at 7%	4,200	4,900	5,600	6,300
Income to equity	5,800	5,100	4,400	3,700
Cash value of equity	40,000	30,000	20,000	10,000
Equity yield—percent	14.5	17.0	22.0	37.0

Thus, though the property income and property value remain constant, equity yields can be increased from a low of 14.5 percent to a high of 37.0 percent depending on mortgage-equity ratios or leverage. If the interest rate applicable to the mortgage loan can be lowered because of an owner's increased security status, the equity yield will grow inversely higher.

Perhaps the greatest pitfall in appraisal practice is to include in the measure of current equity yields the impact of price inflation that is estimated to incur ten or more years from date of appraisal. As a recent study statistically demonstrates,[4] it required a "nominal" yield of 10.8 percent on 1968 capital investment to earn an effective yield of 6.0 percent in terms of purchasing power dollars. The constant erosion of the purchasing power of the dollar is also dramatically evident from the diagram presented below. Also applying future depreciation or appreciation estimates to the total property (both land and building) is counter to conventional accounting and appraisal practices.

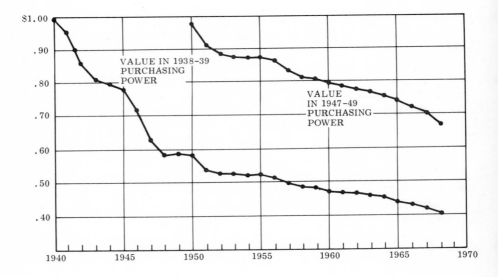

On the plus side, the Ellwood precomputed tables for mortgage-equity appraising are most useful in measuring quickly by reference to a precomputed table the effects of "leverage" or trading on the equity and in ascertaining the income tax impact as well as the financial investment cash

---

[4] *The Appraiser* (Chicago, Illinois: American Institute of Real Estate Appraisers, Vol. 25, No. 1, 1969).

requirements of the equity owner. Care, however, must be taken not to confuse equity appraising with property appraising where "present worth" of land and building improvements are to be the measure of market value.

READING AND STUDY REFERENCES

1. Arnold, Robert S., "Ellwood Revisited—and Perhaps Simplified," *The Appraisal Journal* (October 1966), pp. 502–510.
2. Dasso, Jerome, "Understanding the Mortgage—Equity Capitalization Technique," *The Real Estate Appraiser* (September-October 1968), pp. 27–31.
3. Ellwood, Leon W., "Capitalization of Income is Not Enough," *Appraisal Digest* (January-March 1960), pp. 19–21.
4. Ellwood, L. W., *Ellwood Tables for Real Estate Appraising and Financing*, 2nd ed. (Chicago: American Institute of Real Estate Appraisers, 1967), chaps. 1, 3–5.
5. Ellwood, L. W., "Influence of the Available Mortgage on Value," *The Appraisal Journal* (October 1949), pp. 446–53.
6. Gibbons, James E., "Mortgage Equity Capitalization: Ellwood Method," *The Appraisal Journal* (April 1966), pp. 196–202.
7. Kinnard, William N., Jr., *Industrial Real Estate* (Washington, D.C.: Society of Industrial Realtors, 1967), chap. 2, part III F, 10a.
8. McMichael, Stanley L., *McMichael's Appraising Manual*, 4th ed. (Englewood Cliffs, N.J.: Prentice-Hall, Inc., 1951), chap. 8.
9. Ratcliff, Richard U., *Real Estate Analysis* (New York: McGraw-Hill Book Company, Inc., 1961), chap. 6.
10. Torry, William W., "The Ellwood Tables: A Critique," *The Appraisal Journal* (July 1966), pp. 339–52.

Ownership of real property is widely distributed, and is cherished by millions of American homeowners and real estate investors. This right to use and control property is legally recognized and is given express protection by the United States Constitution. As explained more fully in Chapter 3, property ownership is conceived of as a *bundle of rights* in which the individual sticks that make up this bundle confer on an owner the following privileges:

22

Condemnation Appraising
Practices and Procedures

1. To enter upon the premises or decline to enter.
2. To use the realty or decline to use it.
3. To sell the property rights wholly or separately or refuse to dispose of them.
4. To lease or decline to lease.
5. To donate, dispose by will, or give away the property interest—partially or totally.
6. To peaceful possession and quiet enjoyment.

These rights to the control and enjoyment of property under allodial ownership are inviolate and exclusive, except for superior and sovereign rights of government exercised for the mutual welfare of the community, state, or nation. These sovereign powers are exercised to safeguard the health, welfare, and morality of the public at large and are enforced as needed by taxation, police-power regulations, and the acquisition of property under the sovereign right of eminent domain.

POWER OF EMINENT DOMAIN

In the final analysis, the strength of private ownership is derived from the strength and power of a sovereign government formed to enforce and protect such rights as are vested in the individual under constitutional guardianship. It is fundamental, therefore, that rights essential to the maintenance and welfare of society must be paramount to those claimed by individuals in the pursuit of their separate interests. The right to expropriate private property for public use is legally known as the power of *eminent domain*. This power is well defined in 10 Cal. Juris. Sec. 2 as follows:

> Eminent domain is the right of the people or government to take private property for public use, whenever the exigencies of the public cannot be adequately met and provided for in any other way. . . . Eminent domain is justifiable only because the power makes for the common benefit.

To prevent arbitrary and confiscatory taking of private property by legislative or executive decree, the drafters of the U.S. Constitution have provided safeguards which U.S. courts throughout history have zealously enforced. These safeguards read as follows:

1. *Fifth Amendment,* ". . . nor shall private property be taken for public use, without just compensation."
2. *Fourteenth Amendment,* Section 1. ". . . nor shall any state deprive any person of life, liberty, or property without due process of law . . ."

Individual states, generally, have patterned their respective constitutions to safeguard against the taking of private property except where (1) public necessity has been shown, (2) due process of law is followed, and (3) just compensation is paid to the owner.

DUE PROCESS OF LAW

The acquisition of private property in a condemnation action must conform to legal processes established under law. Procedures vary among states and within federal jurisdictions, but generally petition or prayer for taking of private property must provide more or less for the following:

1. Authority and necessity of taking.
2. Indication of public use for which land is condemned.
3. Survey of land and description.

4. Complaint and summons of owners.
5. Interest to be acquired.
6. Necessary parties defendant.
7. Legal testimony before proper tribunal.
8. Prayer that property be condemned.

Unless the prescribed legal steps are carefully followed, due process may be declared lacking, and the condemnation action invalidated on account of error or omission of proceeding. Constitutional or statutory provisions by the various states further detail due process to include the following:

1. Process, service, and publication of public action.
2. Trial procedures.
3. Form of verdict by court in jury trials.
4. Appeal and review by court appeal.
5. Allocation of cost of proceedings.
6. Payment into court prior to taking.

JUST COMPENSATION

The payment of just compensation for the taking of property under eminent domain proceedings is assured by constitutional guaranty. The right to such payments is not questioned. The crux of the problem is a determination of the amount of payments due and the valuation procedure on which such payments are based.

Compensation generally is restricted to the value of the property physically taken, and to offset a loss in value, if any, to the remaining parcel on account of severance of a part from the unity of a whole property. In evaluating just compensation, care must be taken to exclude losses incurred by the exercise of the police power of government, which in most states and legal jurisdictions are not compensable. Thus losses incurred through changes in zoning, change in level or grade of roads, construction, or elimination of public improvements and business losses in general are not compensated unless specifically provided for under statutory law or permissible under court instruction. Only losses attributable to the property as a result of physical taking, and as measured by a diminution of value subsequent to the taking, are generally permitted as evidence for a court determination of just compensation.

MEANING OF VALUE

Value has many meanings to many persons. (See Chapter 1.) Because of the failure of the appraisal prefession to establish a clear-cut definition of value based on the laws of economics (specifically, the law of supply and demand) higher courts had to fill the void and interpret value for purposes of litigation. Most courts have held value to mean *market value* or its equivalent—a warranted market price obtainable as a result of open and free bartering between willing, ready, and informed buyers and sellers.

The definition of market value most frequently quoted in court proceedings and accepted for publication as recommended appraisal terminology by the American Institute of Real Estate Appraisers is based on a California court decision and reads: [1]

> Market value is the highest price estimated in terms of money which a property will bring if exposed for sale in the open market, allowing a reasonable time to find a purchaser who buys with knowledge of all the uses to which it is adapted and for which it is capable of being used.

The emphasis placed on market price as evidence of market value is further shown by another court decision which reads as follows: [2]

> The market value of land taken for a public use is the price for which it could have been sold by a person desirous of selling to a person willing to buy, neither acting under compulsion and both exercising intelligent judgment.

The "willing buyer, willing seller" concept so frequently stressed in conventional appraisal practice has little practical application in condemnation proceedings. This is so because the seller as a rule is *not* willing and, in fact, is praying for relief in court. This is supported by the following quotation: [3]

> The willing buyer and seller theory is a mere academic enunciation. The theory is correct in principle. The fact does not obtain in practice. It is a mere deduction of what ought to happen.

Court decisions appear to sustain the principle of equity in condemnation under which the property owner is to be left whole in terms of dollars. It is the court's intention to leave his cash position, as measured by the value of his property before and after the taking, intact.

MEASURES OF VALUE

Where, as a result of condemnation for public use, an owner is deprived of *all* his real property holdings at a given location, the loss in value must

---

[1] *Appraisal Terminology and Handbook,* American Institute of Real Estate Appraisers (Chicago, Illinois: The Institute, 5th ed., 1967), p. 131; based on People *v.* Ricciardi, 23 Cal. 2d 390, 144 p. 2d 799 (1943).

[2] Baltimore and Ohio Railroad Company *v.* Bonafield's Heirs, 90 SE 868, 79 W. Va. 287.

[3] *Real Estate Appraising* (Chicago, Illinois: The Appraisal Division of the National Association of Real Estate Boards, 1927), p. 121.

equal the value of the entire property. Little difficulty, as a rule, is encountered by professional appraisers in estimating the market value of an entire property in accordance with prevailing appraising principles and practices and as outlined in preceding chapters. Generally the things to be considered in a determination of market value, and as gleaned from a condensation of court decisions, include among others the following: [4]

1. A view of the premises and its surroundings.
2. A description of the physical characteristics of the property and its situation in relation to the points of importance in the neighborhood.
3. The price at which the land was bought, if sufficiently recent to throw light on present value.
4. The price at which similar neighboring land has sold, at or about the time of taking.
5. The opinion of expert witnesses.
6. A consideration of the uses for which the land is adapted and for which it is available.
7. The cost of the improvements less depreciation, if they are such as to increase the market value of the land.
8. The net income from the land, if the land is devoted to one of the uses to which it could be most advantageously and profitably applied.

It is in *partial* taking that substantial differences arise among opposing expert witnesses as to value losses resulting from expropriation plus losses inflicted on the remainder of the property because of property *severance*.

The steps essential to a measurement of value losses in case of partial taking of real property are threefold:

1. Estimate the value of the property under consideration as a whole, free from encumbrances and restrictions except those imposed by public authorities. This market value is to be based on a cash or cash equivalent market transaction.
2. Apportion this value—for the entire property—between the value of the property actually taken and the remainder property left to the owner.
3. Estimate the damages, if any, caused to the remainder property as a result of severance of the part taken under the power of eminent domain.

The value of the part taken, plus damages resulting from severance, comprises the amount due the owner as fair compensation. This amount, however, cannot logically exceed the value of the entire property prior to taking as calculated under the first step above. In the valuation of the part taken, courts have ruled that the part under appraisal must be evaluated as a part of the whole and not as a free-standing and separate parcel. A strip

---

[4] Phillip Nichols, *Nichols on Eminent Domain,* IV (Albany, New York: Matthew Bender & Company, Inc., 1957), p. 52.

of land five feet deep and a hundred feet long may have little value if offered for sale and use; but the same strip of land may make an important contribution to value if added to a parcel ninety-five feet deep in an area where a minimum depth of a hundred feet is necessary under zoning regulations for a given highest and best land use. In considering what constitutes the whole property where several parcels are under one ownership at a given location, the appraiser should be guided by court-proved rules which establish economic unity in accordance with:

1. Contiguity of location.
2. Unity of ownership.
3. Unity of use as evidenced by economic unity (utility) rather than physical unity.

In the estimation of value for the property as a whole, land and improvements must also be considered as an integral whole and not as independent and unrelated parts. Only after value for the entire property has been ascertained can allocation logically be made to fractional portions of the land or to land and buildings as respective parts. To illustrate: Where one-half of a tract of land is taken, and where the value of the entire tract is estimated to be $20,000, the value of the part taken—as a part of the whole—is deemed to be $10,000. However, if the two halves of the tract of land under value consideration were offered for sale as separate parcels, each may bring only $6,000 because of size and the resultant change in the economically feasible highest and best land use. Courts have consistently ruled that an owner's property must be left economically whole in terms of value, and in the illustration cited above would rule on —or instruct the jury to consider—the value of the land taken as a part of the whole and not as a separate parcel unrelated to the owner's entire property from which it is taken. The methods used most frequently in the valuation of property where there is partial taking are:

1. The equal-unit-value (plus severance damages, if any) method.
2. The before-and-after valuation method.

The *equal-unit-value* method, often referred to as the *square-foot* method of land valuation, is a compromise designed to distribute the value of the whole over the physical units contained in the entire parcel affected by the taking. Otherwise, in the condemnation of a strip of land for street-widening purposes, it may be argued that the front part of a lot is more valuable than the rear portion which is remote from access and thus considered less serviceable. Opponents, on the other hand, may argue— and rightfully so—that the economic effect of condemnation of a strip of land for road-widening purposes is simply to reduce the lot in depth, leaving street rights and frontage intact. The economic effect of taking thus is deemed to be from the rear of the property rather than from the front area where the physical severance is to take place. Under the equal-unit-value method the value of the part taken to the value of the whole is intended to be in the same ratio that the physical units of land taken bear to the total land units of the property as a whole.

The *before-and-after* method of land valuation appears to be more equitable in measuring value losses sustained by the condemnee. This method, however, may unavoidably include benefits accruing to a property as a result of the proposed public improvements. For this reason, this method of valuation is used more often as a check on the accuracy of valuation obtained by the equal-unit-value (plus severance damages, if any) method rather than as an independent measure of just compensation. In some state jurisdictions, such as in Florida, consideration of benefits resulting from proposed public improvements is specifically ruled out by constitutional or statutory provisions. To quote from the Florida Constitution, Article 16, Section 29:

> No private property, nor right of way shall be appropriated to the use of any corporation or individual until full compensation therefore shall be first made to the owner, or first secured to him by deposit of money, which compensation, irrespective of any *benefits* [5] from any improvement proposed by such corporation or individual, shall be ascertained by a jury of twelve men in a court of competent jurisdiction as shall be prescribed by law.

The taking of a part of an owner's property often causes value losses to the remainder property as a result of *severance*. To minimize such severance losses, legislation in many states permits condemning authorities to offset damages caused by severance against benefits (value increments) brought about by the public improvements (for which the property was partially taken). Under no circumstances, however, should value benefits be given consideration in estimating the value of the part (or whole) of a property taken under eminent domain proceeding.

SEVERANCE DAMAGE

In brief, *severance damage* constitutes a loss in value of the part of a property remaining after taking as compared with the value of the remainder when considered as a part of the whole. Severance damage in essence is a measure of depreciation attributable to a remainder property as a result of one or more of the following:

---

[5] Italics supplied for emphasis.

1. Change in highest and best use of the property subsequent to the taking.
2. Expenditures necessary to restore or protect the property from hazards caused by the taking of property.
3. Increased cost of operation or, conversely, a lowering of net income on which value is based.

Where a strip of land is taken for construction of a limited access highway across an industrial property and the remainder land is cut off from railroad sidings and road access, a change in the highest and best use to a lower and possibly agrcultural land use is likely. The difference in value under the prevailing use prior to land-taking, as compared with the highest and best use subsequent to the land-taking, constitutes the amount of severance to which the owner is entitled as just compensation in addition to the value of the land taken.

Where, as a result of the taking, expenditures are incurred to make repairs on remaining improvements—or where, for instance, fencing is necessary to guard cattle against the hazards of a proposed railroad right-of-way—such expenditures are recognized as severance damage for which compensation is due. It is important to recognize that severance damages claimed against the building improvements because of road hazards or the destruction of amenities caused by increased proximity to a new road right-of-way can logically be incurred only for the useful (economic) life of the building, and cannot extend into perpetuity as is the case with damage to land.

TREATMENT OF BENEFITS

Public improvements generally are intended to create benefits for the community as a whole, and specifically for the area in which the improvements are directly located. These benefits, although rarely mutually exclusive, must for purposes of court presentation be identified as follows:

1. Benefits which accrue to the community as a whole, and which in a few states such as Alabama, New Mexico, New York, North Carolina, South Carolina, Virginia, and Wisconsin, are permitted as "offset" against damages claimed as a result of the taking of private property. In other state jurisdictions, however, general benefits must be excluded from consideration in the determination of both the value of the part taken and in the loss of value suffered as a result of the taking by the remainder property.
2. Special benefits which accrue to the adjoining properties, and particularly to the property for which severance damages are claimed. In some states special benefits may be set off against both the value of the part taken and the damages claimed to the remainder property. In other states only the damages to the remainder or severed land may be

reduced by the value of such special benefits as are directly related to the public improvements for which the taking of property was authorized. For a listing of states and special condemnation laws applicable to each, see *Condemnation Appraisal Handbook,* by George L. Schmutz, revised by Edwin M. Rams, and published by Prentice-Hall, Inc., Englewood Cliffs, New Jersey, 1963, pp. 133, 134.

CONSEQUENTIAL DAMAGE

Broadly speaking, *consequential damage* to property includes all damage suffered by a property owner, including the loss attributable to severance. In practice, however, the term has come to denote damage suffered by owners as a result of proposed public improvements where no real property is physically taken. A change in road grade, the construction of a bridge, the bypassing of a town, the relocation of a road, the construction of a sewage treatment plant—all are instances where neighboring or abutting property owners may suffer losses due to a diminution in the value of their property. Such losses, if ascribable to the exercise of the police power of government, are not compensable. It seems inequitable that some owners, where there is some taking of physical land, are being compensated for consequential damages where such contribute to a lowering of value of the remainder property, while other owners suffering like damage—but where there is no taking of property—are left without recourse for compensation. Often suit is brought by owners so affected, and their action at court is termed *inverse condemnation.* That is, suit is instituted by them for relief under the laws of equity rather than by the condemnor as is the case in usual eminent domain court action. It is seldom that compensation is judicially ordered in such instances unless property losses can directly be linked to the physical taking of an owner's property.

EXCESS CONDEMNATION

Public improvements in general, and road improvements in particular, create benefits that often reflect substantial increment in the value of abutting and neighboring lands. When such value increments are substantial an attempt is made, where permissible under law, to channel the benefits for disposition by public authority for the good of all within the state or community. Construction of parks, parkways, recreation centers, and planned public buildings are instances of this. In New York State, excess condemnation is permissible under state law. Thus, if it is estimated that the value benefits of a proposed garden parkway may extend up to 500 feet on either side of a 100-foot limited access roadbed, condemning authorities may acquire by eminent domain action a strip of land 1,100 feet in width. After completion of the parkway, the adjacent land may be leased for concessionary use by restaurant and gas station chain operators; or the land may be resold to private owners at prices which may recoup the increment in land value. Such gains may go far to offset the costs of construction, betterments, and capital improvements. The entire theory of excess condemnation is still in the development stage. Wisely used, this practice could prevent windfall gains by land speculators and place much-needed public improvement programs on a self-liquidating, pay-as-you-go financial basis.

THE EXPERT WITNESS

Increasingly, professional appraisers are called on to testify as expert witnesses in condemnation trials. Many facetious definitions of an "expert" are given. He has been called "a person fifty or more miles away from home," or, "someone who has learned to carry a briefcase with dignity." Such definitions are offered to belittle professional skill that usually can be acquired only through years of hard work and study, field experience, careful preparation, and training. The dean of appraisers, the late George Schmutz, defined an expert witness as [6]

> . . . one who is possessed of peculiar knowledge and experience that are not common to persons generally, and who has an opinion based upon such knowledge and experience that is peculiarly fitted for assisting the court, or jury, in determining an issue, such as the amount of damage measured in terms of dollars.

This definition implies that the appraiser, as an expert, merely testifies as to his *opinion* of value. It is the court or jury that *determines* value. This the appraiser must firmly keep in mind, or he will jeopardize his case by being accused of usurping the functions of both court and jury. Whereas an expert can express opinions and conclusions based on facts, laymen as a rule are restricted to confining their testimony to recitation of statements concerning facts.

Before accepting an assignment to serve as an expert witness, the appraiser must make certain that he will be allowed to testify as an *independent* agent, free from bias and pressure to produce a "favorable" opinion. Unfortunately, many clients through their advocate attorneys shop around for "experts" whose judgment can be swayed. Professional appraisers are subject to censure on ethical and moral grounds if they serve as advocates rather than as free and independent agents. Appraisal fees, too, should be

---

[6] George L. Schmutz, *Condemnation Appraisal Handbook* (Englewood Cliffs, N. J.: Prentice-Hall, Inc., 1963), p. 360.

based on time, expense, and degree of professional responsibility assumed, and should *not* be made contingent on the value reported, the amount of the verdict, or the winning of the case.

PRETRIAL PREPARATION

Testimony to be offered by an expert witness should be backed by a detailed appraisal report in which the value conclusions reached are fully documented. The report need not be and generally is not submitted as a court exhibit, and it cannot be demanded for inspection by the opposing counsel unless the report is referred to and used as a basis for testifying under direct examination. Comprehensive appraisal preparation permits the client's lawyer to familiarize himself with factual details and the technical terminology peculiar to the case. Visual aids, where possible, should be employed. Subdivision maps, photographs, plot plans, market, cost, and income summary sheets should be submitted for court exhibit and to facilitate data presentation at the time of the trial.

It is well, too, for the appraiser and trial attorney to agree on the order of data presentation, and to outline the questions and answers to be asked and given during direct examination. The sequence of questions asked generally falls into categories pertaining to:

1. Qualifications of witness.
2. Examination of subject property.
3. Method used in arriving at an estimate of value.
4. Opinion of value.

Care should be taken to present in simple but impressive manner the qualifications of the expert witness. Even when opposing counsel stipulates that, in the interest of time, he accepts the witness as qualified to testify as an expert, the client's lawyer should nevertheless—if only for the court's benefit—qualify the witness as an expert in his field. It is the jury or court that sets the value, and the witness's testimony bears greater weight if extensive experience and knowledge in the field of property appraising back up the expert's findings. Qualifying questions should inform the court as to the expert's background and experience on such points as:

1. Occupation.
2. Place and geographic extent of business or profession.
3. Education and degrees earned.
4. Membership in professional associations.
5. Years of experience as an appraiser.
6. Types of clients served.
7. Types of properties appraised.
8. Appraisal courses completed or taught.

9. Publication of appraisal articles.
10. Experience in related fields of real estate brokerage and property management.

The questions asked pertaining to the examination of the subject property should establish a thorough familiarity with details of land and site improvements. Here the direct testimony should bring forth answers to such questions as:

1. Please describe and clearly identify the subject property.
2. When did you last inspect the property?
3. Have you examined the building plans and specifications for estimating cost of reproduction of the improvements?
4. What is the age of the structure and what methods were used to determine accrued depreciation?
5. Have you compared the subject property with other similar properties that have sold in recent times?
6. Did you verify the income experience of this property? Have expenditures been verified?
7. What is the present and foreseeable future highest and best use of the subject property?

The next group of questions under direct examination explores the method used in arriving at an estimate of value. Since any testimony offered at this stage of the court proceedings is subject to rebuttal during cross-examination, the appraiser should be careful not to present details of estimating that later may be questioned to pinpoint errors of judgment or of facts. Care must also be taken so as not to testify that value was derived by the summation method; that is, an estimation of the value of the lot separately, to which was then added the value of the improvements less accrued depreciation. Land and buildings thereon are merged as an operating unit and any division of the whole into arbitrary parts in some state jurisdictions may be charged as constituting *hypothetical* appraising, which is contrary to accepted valuation theory and practice.

It is best to generalize and to explain in simple, nontechnical words the methods used in estimating value. The appraiser, for instance, may state: "I have examined the property; considered its location within the neighborhood; inspected the site; checked public records for legal description and zoning, deed restrictions, and assessment data; studied comparable sales, and analyzed other general and specific factual data deemed essential to the formation of a prefessional opinion of value."

It is advisable, too, at this point for counsel to request that the witness describe and explain the comparable sales which he considered in formulating an estimate of market value. The witness should request permission to refer to a large subdivision map, which should be marked for identification as a court exhibit that jurors may study and to which they may refer during their deliberation. On this map the subject property should be prominently marked in crayon, and the sale properties numbered and marked with crayons of different colors. As each sale property is identified, the transaction price should be stated, the seller and buyer named, the date of sale specified, and the terms of sale at which the transaction closed given. The appraiser should make certain that each sale was verified with the purchaser, seller, or real estate broker as to date of sale, transaction price, and terms of sale. Under no circumstances is it wise to rely on documentary stamps as evidence of market prices at which the comparable sales exchanged. Even if stamp data is considered accurate, the jury or court could be adversely influenced by lack of sale confirmation and by admission from the witness that revenue stamps can readily and legally be overstated to deliberately mislead those who rely on such evidence as a guide to market value.

The final category of questions concerns the *opinion* of value. Counsel as a rule asks: "As a result of your investigation, and by reason of your experience, have you formed an opinion of value for the subject [identify by name] property as of a specified date [date of taking]?" The witness, of course, answers in the affirmative. Counsel then may ask witness to state his professional opinion concerning:

1. Value of the entire property as a whole.
2. Value of the part taken when considered as a part of the whole or as a separate parcel when such testimony is deemed advantageous to the interests of the condemnee.
3. Value of the remainder considered as part of the property as a whole.
4. Value of the remainder as a separate parcel subsequent to the taking of a part of the property as constituted prior to the taking.
5. Severance damage attributable to the remainder property (the difference between Items 3 and 4 above).

Where permissible, expert opinion may relate directly to the value of the entire property before the taking and the value of the remainder after the taking. This simplifies proceedings and yields directly the amount of compensation (the difference between before-and-after value as a result of condemnation) to which the owner is entitled to cover both the taking of a part of his property and the severance damages caused to the remainder. As explained above in the discussion of severance damages, care must be taken to exclude benefits which may accrue as a result of the road or public improvements at issue. The appraiser must, of course, be prepared to testify as to the extent and possible effects of potential benefits caused by the public improvements, provided such questions are raised with the permission of the court (and undoubtedly over the objection of counsel for the condemnee).

Following the statement of value opinion, the expert witness generally is called on to give his reason for the conclusions reached either as to the value of the property as a whole or the allocation of this value to the parts and the severance damages effected as a consequence. The answer merely calls for a summary of the important conclusions reached as a result of the appraisal investigation and a re-emphasis of market cost or income data which supports the expert opinion.

CROSS-EXAMINATION

It is under cross-examination that the competence of the appraiser and his quality as an expert witness come to light. Many appraisers—although thorough, diligent, and accurate in their value findings—lack personality, experience on the witness stand, diction, and the ease that flows from a broad educational background. Such men, through indecision, lack of confidence, and inability to think quickly while on their feet may undo in a few minutes the work of many days or weeks of preparation. Other witnesses have an oversized ego which causes them to falter or to explode when—directly or by implication—their integrity or competence is questioned. Fear of seeing their findings exposed to ruthless analysis and their community reputation jolted by clever lawyers who go all out to destroy the effectiveness of their testimony keeps many otherwise qualified professional appraisers from accepting assignments that require as a condition subsequent defense of these findings in court.

Yet those who enter the appraisal profession should be trained to take the stand as expert witnesses. As a first step, personal fear must be overcome and confidence acquired that due care was taken in the process of estimating value as a means of aiding the court in reaching a just decision. The court and jurors usually frown on personal abuse and on tricky behavior unbecoming to a man of law. The witness should remind himself that his counsel is his silent partner, that unfair or misleading questions will be objected to when raised, and that the court and jurors are intelligent observers seeking truth rather than entertainment by a pyrotechnical display of legal skill.

The witness should listen to questions earnestly and carefully. Where the intent of the question is not clear, a clarification should be asked for. Answers should be short, simple, polite, and directed to the jury or court. When yes or no answers are requested the witness should comply, but ask permission to explain his answer when clarification is deemed essential. To illustrate, a series of yes or questions may be as follows:

1. Are you representing the condemnee?
2. Have you served him professionally previously?
3. Are you paid by him for your services?
4. You would not be testifying without promise of pay, would you?
5. Your opinion of value is bought, is it not?

Certainly Questions 4 and 5 should be explained, since bias is implied that may influence the court's decision. To Question 4 the witness should add that as a member of the appraisal profession he is not accustomed to volunteer his services, and that as an independent fee appraiser he gladly serves all who call on him for professional aid. To Question 5 the witness, after a firm "No," should state that although his services are paid for, his opinion of value is based on facts gathered and studied during the course of the investigation; and that the findings and opinions stated would be the same no matter who engaged his services or agreed to defray professional costs and fees.

The cross-examiner must be expected to do all in his power to attempt to weaken or even discredit the value testimony of the opposing expert witness. Questions asked are generally designed to cast doubt where possible on such matters as:

1. Adequacy of experience or education.
2. Familiarity with the subject property or subject area and neighborhood.
3. Adequate preparation or omission of relevant data.
4. Freedom from bias or incompetence.
5. Correctness of computations or validity of valuation premises.

In preparing his valuation report and in planning the sequence of his testimony the appraiser, with the aid of his lawyer, should anticipate probable questions that may be raised during cross-examination and be ready to offer clear and convincing answers. In an article published in the October 1959 issue of *Right of Way,* official publication of the American Right of Way Association, Mr. John P. Horgan, lawyer and specialist in condemnation trials for the California Division of Highways, offered the following ten courtroom commandments as a guide to real estate appraisers:

1. Thou shalt not lie nor be evasive.
2. Thou shalt not exaggerate the "highest and best use."
3. Thou shalt not testify to a dictated appraisal.
4. Thou shalt carefully examine and evaluate all comparable sales.
5. Thou shalt be wary of capitalizing hypothetical income on vacant land.
6. Thou shalt be judicious in the exercise of thy right to explain thy answer.
7. Thou shalt not clothe thyself in the garments of infallibility.
8. Thou shalt remember that thou art an impartial witness, not an advocate.
9. Thou shalt so live with thyself that thy testimony would be the same if appearing for the opposing party.
10. Thou shalt always remember to control thy temper on cross-examination and retain a sense of humor.

READING AND STUDY REFERENCES

1. Kahn, Sanders A., Frederick E. Case, and Alfred Schimmel, *Real Estate Appraisal and Investment* (New York: The Ronald Press Company, 1963), chaps. 3–8, 10, 33, 41.
2. Bowes, Watson A., "The Function of the Appraiser in Condemnation," *The Appraisal Journal* (July 1958), pp. 407–14.
3. *Condemnation Appraisal Practice* (Chicago: American Institute of Real Estate Appraisers, 1961).
4. Deutsch, Joseph S., "Fundamentals of Appraising for Condemnation," *Appraisal Digest* (September 1963), pp. 12–16.
5. Enfield, Clifton W. and William A. Mansfield, "Special Benefits and Right-of-Way Acquisition," *The Appraisal Journal* (October 1957), pp. 551–65.
6. MacBride, Dexter D., *Power and Process, A Commentary On Eminent Domain and Condemnation,* ASA Monograph No. 1 (Washington, D.C.: American Society of Appraisers, January 1969).
7. McMichael, Stanley L., *McMichael's Appraising Manual,* 4th ed. (Englewood Cliffs, N.J.: Prentice-Hall, Inc., 1951), chap. 32.
8. *Condemnation Appraisal Practice* (Chicago: American Institute of Real Estate Appraisers, 1961), parts II, III, IV.
9. Theiss, William R., "Distinction Between General and Special Benefits," *The Appraisal Journal* (April 1963), pp. 267–70.

During the past three decades, real estate appraising has developed into a well-defined art practiced professionally by thousands of qualified appraisers. Owners and investors in real property—including banking institutions, insurance companies, government agencies, brokerage firms, and commercial and industrial institutions—have come to rely on this profession as a reliable guide to property value. Annually, thousands of business

23 *Appraisal Planning*

and Reporting

men and women attend appraisal demonstration and extension courses conducted under the auspices of the American Institute of Real Estate Appraisers and the Society of Real Estate Appraisers. An ever-increasing number of colleges, universities, and commercial schools, too, offer courses in the art of valuation for degree credit and on an extension and short-course basis.

As an art, real estate appraising is patterned in accordance with well defined ground rules, which as a whole are contained in an orderly plan of action known as the *appraisal process*. It is with the aid of this process that the professional appraiser seeks to reach a sound conclusion or estimate of value. The orderly steps and considerations of the appraisal process include the following:

1. Determine the appraisal problem.
2. Determine the purpose which the appraisal is to serve.
3. Secure a full and accurate description of the property to be appraised.

4. Make a preliminary estimate of the time, labor, and expense involved in the completion of the appraisal assignment, and secure a written request for the appraisal services in which should be stated the fee agreed on for services to be rendered.
5. Plan the appraisal, assign the work details, and assemble the essential appraisal data.
6. Make a study of the general economic, social, and political influences which bear on the value of the property to be appraised.
7. Analyze the appraisal data, and reach a value conclusion under each of the following approaches to value: cost, market, and income.
8. Correlate the value findings.
9. Submit an appraisal report.[1]

The first and most important step in the process is to determine the appraisal problem. Some owners, buyers, or investors are not only interested in ascertaining an accurate estimate of value but also expect information regarding ownership or title interests, rights of tenants, property encroachments, claims of mortgagees and other lienors, conditions shown by accurate survey, tax liens, violations, and so forth. The appraiser should not accept the valuation assignment unless the client clearly understands the limits of the appraiser's professional responsibility and the area of study to which his specialized knowledge is confined. The appraiser, in essence, practices in the field of economics—for value is in fact the heart of economics. The appraiser should not consider himself a lawyer, architect, builder, engineer, surveyor, or title abstractor. If his client requests information in these specialized fields, authority should be secured to engage such qualified experts as the problem necessitates, arranging for independent compensation of the outside firms or individuals called on for the specified service. Unless otherwise stated, the appraiser must assume (1) that the title is held in fee simple and that no legal claims, easements, restrictions, or other rights affect the title or use of the property except those stated to the appraiser by the applicant: (2) that the title and his valuation are subject to corrections which an accurate survey of the property may reveal; (3) that the sale of the property will be on a cash or cash equivalent basis, since good or cumbersome financial arrangements do affect the price at which the property may sell in the market; and (4) that no responsibility can be taken by the appraiser for matters legal in character.

Some valuation problems, too, require special owner or tenant cooperation or aid from neighboring property owners or users. Where such is the case, the assignment must be accepted contingent on the cooperation of the parties involved. Only when the problem is clearly defined, and its

---

[1] Alfred A. Ring and Nelson L. North, *Real Estate Principles and Practices* (Englewood Cliffs, N. J.: Prentice-Hall, Inc., 6th ed., 1967), Chapter 23.

limits are known and understood, should the appraiser proceed further with the steps of the appraisal process.

Next, it is essential that the appraiser be provided with a clear statement as to the purpose which the appraisal is to serve. Even though only one value can exist for market purposes at a given time and place, different valuation purposes may warrant greater stress being laid on one or the other of the three value approaches—or the inclusion of special appraisal details in the final report of value. It can readily be seen that different interests are served if the valuation is for one or the other of the following purposes:

1. Purchase, sale, or exchange of property.
2. Fire insurance or hazard underwriting.
3. Valuation for utility rate determination.
4. Investment or mortgage loan security.
5. Inheritance, property tax, or assessments.
6. Inventory or accrued depreciation.
7. Equity appraising or financing.

In each instance a different interest is served, and different valuation details warrant emphasis and inclusion in the appraisal report. For instance, a report for fire insurance purposes would principally stress replacement costs as evidence of value, and the report would detail with great accuracy the construction features and material elements that make up the property improvements. For mortgage loan purposes, on the other hand, property income, its remaining economic life, and its ready marketability would receive major stress—with replacement cost, less depreciation, merely serving as a ceiling of value beyond which lenders, as a rule, are restricted or unwilling to go.

To avoid possible misunderstanding or claims that the purpose of the appraisal influenced the value found, the professional appraiser should not only include a clear statement of the purpose which the appraisal is to serve but also a clear-cut definition of the term *value* as used in his report. Failure to do so may cause serious misunderstanding and, where warranted, even disciplinary action under the code of ethics to which all professional appraisers, as members of their respective appraisal societies, subscribe. The date of the appraisal, too, should be fixed and prominently stated. Values are subject to constant shifts because the laws of supply and demand operate in a dynamic society which experiences sudden and often unexpected changes. Then, too, value for specific purposes may have to be stated as of a given day in the past.

A full and accurate description of the property is next in order. Not only must the exact limits of the area under appraisal be known, but the full legal property description must be cited in order to leave no doubt as to the precise location and identity of the realty covered in the valuation report. Although various kinds of property descriptions may be used, it is best to rely on one shown in the last deed of record. Should property analysis disclose encumbrances which limit in any way an owner's rights under fee simple title or impede in any way the utilization of the property under a program of highest and best use, then such financial encumbrances on ownership or use limitations must be clearly identified and the impact on value of such limitations made clear to the reader of the appraisal report.

Before proceeding with the valuation assignment, it is essential that the appraiser make a preliminary but careful estimate of the time, labor, and expense involved in completing the appraisal request. This preliminary estimate should serve as a guide in setting a fair appraisal fee commensurate with the responsibility and service requirements assumed. Many real estate boards recommend to broker members a percentage fee of their value findings. Where the recommended fee, for instance, is one-half of one percent of property value, the warranted appraisal fee on a $20,000 property would be $100. This method of service fee determination, however, appears illogical and is subject to censure on ethical grounds. The temptations would indeed be great to boost value findings as a means of increasing service fees. The ethics code of the American Institute of Real Estate Appraisers specifically condemns this practice and stipulates that it is unethical for an appraiser to accept an engagement to appraise a property if his employment or fee is contingent on his reporting a predetermined or specified amount of value, or is otherwise contingent upon any finding to be reported.

Once the fair fee has been ascertained, the client should be so informed. If the fee, as generally is the case, proves acceptable, the appraiser should request written confirmation of his professional assignment and the fee should be stipulated in the letter of request or should be noted by the appraiser in his letter of acceptance. The fee seldom covers any appearance or testimony by the appraiser before any court, commission, or other body; to avoid later dispute, this should be clearly understood at the time of engagement and stated in the appraisal report itself.

Once the appraisal assignment and service fee are mutually agreed on, steps are taken to plan the work details and to assemble the essential appraisal data. Much of the necessary general data pertaining to social, political, and economic influences on value are directly obtainable from office (appraisal plant) files or may be taken from previous appraisal reports in which the general value comments are deemed sufficiently recent and applicable to be of interest to the case at hand. General data bearing on value of the subject property and not available from the appraisal plant should be secured whenever possible from primary sources. Data applicable to the site, improvements, and immediate environment must be obtained through personal inspection and through a detailed inventory of neighborhood, site, and improvement data that bear directly or indirectly on property values. Many forms have been devised by private firms and governmental agencies to aid the appraiser in the laborious task of gathering field data to insure that no important matter pertaining to the property is inadvertently omitted.

VALUE CORRELATION

Once the general and specific data applicable to the subject property are assembled, the appraiser proceeds with an analysis of the data under each of the value approaches—market, income, and cost. Although the importance of each of the three approaches to value may vary, depending on the kind and nature of the property and the purpose which the appraisal is to serve, nevertheless it is important to consider each approach to value as a separate entity under the appraisal process and to reach independent value conclusions in relation to replacement costs less accrued depreciation, market sales of comparable properties, and capitalization of net income derived from property operation under typical ownership and management. These independent but related estimates of value must then be correlated into a sum representing the appraiser's considered judgment of final value conclusion.

Correlation of the value estimates should under no circumstances be considered as a mathematical process involving mere averaging of the estimates derived under the independent value approaches. Rather, care must be taken in weighing the results on the basis of accuracy and completeness of data and in the light of market conditions that prevail on the date of the appraisal. Whenever significant differences exist in the estimates derived under the three value approaches, the appraiser, as a first step, should review the data assembled under each approach and check the mathematical procedures which underlie the answer. Under the cost approach, for instance, a recheck should be made of the size of the structure and the volume of square or cubic feet reported. The cost factor, too, may be in error or inapplicable to the type and kind of structure under appraisal. More likely than not, the error may rest in the derivation of the amount of accrued depreciation. The economic age may have been misstated or an omission may have been made in the listing and weighing of the causes which account for total accrued depreciation. Under the market approach, judgment errors are easily committed. The transaction prices of the comparable properties may not reflect true property values, or the properties selected may not represent real comparability. Too, the judgment weights assigned may warrant a careful recheck. The income approach is also fraught with appraising pitfalls. The revenue flow may be over- or understated, allowances for vacancy and collection losses may have been omitted, operating expenses may not reflect operation under competent and efficient management, the remaining life of the property may be in error—and so may be the rate of capitalization—which especially warrants close inspection as to its appropriateness. The application of a rate of 8 percent instead of 9 percent may not appear serious to the uninformed, but the value results would differ by one-sixth or one-seventh, or approximately 11 to 12.5 percent depending on which rate is the appropriate one.

If, after careful recheck of the various steps in each approach, significant differences still exist in the value estimates under each approach, the appraiser must consider the results in the light of the problem and the purposes which the appraisal is to serve. Thus, for mortgage loan purposes, the income-producing capacity of the property is all-important. For inheritance tax, condemnation, or sale purposes, the market data (provided the market is sufficiently active to prove guiding) should be given greatest stress. For fire insurance or protection against other hazards, the replacement cost may prove all-important. It is in the correlation of the value estimates that the experience, skill, and judgment of the appraiser can find no substitute. It is the human factor in the equation which causes real estate appraising to be a personal art rather than an objective science.

THE APPRAISAL REPORT

The final step in the appraising process is the preparation of a comprehensive appraisal report. At one time an oral opinion or a letter of valuation sufficed. Such practices, however, are frowned on today and professional appraisers are advised to furnish their clients with a narrative appraisal report in which their value findings, along with the contingent conditions on which the appraisal is based, are clearly set forth. No particular style of report is copyrighted, nor is any one form recommended. A good report, nevertheless, is one in which the data presented are so convincingly analyzed that the reader inevitably is led to the same value conclusions as those reached by the appraiser. As a rule, the data should be sufficiently self-supporting to permit judgment adjustment by the reader or client if he so chooses.

The following are deemed essential to a well-written and comprehensive appraisal report:

1. A letter of transmittal in which the value findings and the effective date of the appraisal are recorded. This letter, too, should state the number of pages contained in the report in order to forestall possible deletion of important pages or data by unauthorized persons.
2. A table of contents which permits quick reference to particular report material.
3. Two clear and preferably large (8″ x 10″) photographs showing front and side views of the property appraised.
4. A complete and accurate legal description.

5. A statement as to the purpose of the appraisal and definition of the term *value* as used by the appraiser.

6. A statement of highest and best use of the property, and whether the present improvements meet the test.

7. A summary statement of important conclusions, particularly those in which the report reader has a prime interest, to wit: taxes, assessments, operating income, operating expenses, and so forth.

8. An analysis of the general social, political, and economic influences on value, particularly in reference to the nation, the region, the city, and the neighborhood or environing area.

9. A factual presentation of site, building, and property data. An inventory should be presented of the important site utilities and building construction features.

10. An explanation of the appraisal process and the methods by which the value conclusions were derived.

11. An analysis of the cost approach to value, followed by schedules showing unit cost deviations and depreciation calculations.

12. An analysis of the market approach to value. Separate comparative tables should be included showing sales considered in arriving at the market value of (1) the land and (2) the property as a unified whole.

13. An analysis of the income approach to value, showing sources of revenue, allowances due to anticipated vacancies and collection losses, operating expenses, rates of capitalization, and process employed in the discounting of the anticipated income into a present sum of value.

14. A correlation of the value estimates derived under the cost, market, and income approaches to value. The weights, if any, assigned to each approach or the methods of selection of one estimate in preference to another should be clearly set forth and explained.

15. A statement of limiting conditions in which the appraiser sets forth the areas—as in fields of surveying, engineering, or law—in which he disclaims liability.

16. A certification of value in which the appraiser professionally warrants his findings and disclaims any personal interest in the property that could possibly influence his value findings.

17. A statement of qualifications of the appraiser, setting forth briefly his educational, professional background, and experience qualifications allowing him to render value opinions.

18. Addenda material containing some or all of the following: location sketch of the property, a plot plan, floor plan, and a subdivision map and city map on which markings indicate the subject property in relation to important business and civic centers; also, where deemed of interest, additional photographs of neighboring properties and street views, showing improvements north, south, east, and west of the subject property.

THE ANALYTICAL, OR DEMONSTRATION, APPRAISAL REPORT

Students of real estate appraising at many colleges and candidates who seek professional affiliation with the American Institute of Real Estate

Appraisers or the Society of Real Estate Appraisers are required to submit in partial fulfillment of prerequisites for the respective professional membership designations,[2] fully documented narrative appraisal reports of various types of real property to demonstrate their competence and soundness of judgment in the compilation and interpretation of valuation data and the logical presentation of such data in report form. As a student's guide, and for illustration purposes, a comprehensive demonstration report of an apartment property is presented in Appendix 1.

The difference between a demonstration and a professional narrative appraisal report lies mainly in the requirement that all data sources, sequence, and analysis of pertinent facts and value conclusions must be documented and justified in a demonstration appraisal report. Whereas the professional appraiser may, on the basis of experience and reputation, reach certain conclusions or make certain assumptions, the student appraiser must follow step-by-step orderly reporting and miss no link in welding the chain of value conclusion. A professional appraiser may categorically stipulate that a rate of capitalization of 8 percent is deemed applicable to the subject property, or that the cost of reproduction of building improvement is estimated at $1.35 per cubic foot, and offer no documentary evidence to support his statements. A student appraiser cannot rely on personal skill, maturity of judgment, or years of appraisal experience to justify assumptions or conclusions. The reader of the demonstration report must literally be led along the path of the appraisal process and given an opportunity to judge the technical skill of the writer on the basis of sufficiency of report data, soundness of data interpretation, and extent to which the value conclusions reached are warranted.

SHORT-FORM APPRAISAL REPORTING

Government agencies and lending institutions prefer standarized form reports in connection with routine appraising of properties offered as loan collateral. Although such forms leave little room for justification of appraisal judgment, uniformity of data reporting facilitates loan processing and supervision on the basis of comparability of report features in relation to minimum standards which properties must meet to prove acceptable. An appraisal form widely used for reporting on residential properties by the Mortgage Guaranty Insurance Corporation of Milwaukee, Wisconsin, is reproduced below:

---

[2] Prevailing professional designations offered are as follows:
A.S.A., Member American Society of Appraisers.
R.M., Residential Member—American Institute of Real Estate Appraisers.
M.A.I., Member American Institute of Real Estate Appraisers.
S.R.A., Senior Residential Appraiser, Society of Real Estate Appraisers.
S.R.E.A., Senior Real Estate Appraiser, Society of Real Estate Appraisers.

APPRAISER'S REPORT

FOR SINGLE FAMILY RESIDENTIAL PROPERTY

Applicant: ....

Property Address: ....

State: ....

City: ....

File No. ....

Diagram of Buildings (Show dimensions on foundations, additions, porches; give story heights and specify whether full foundations and cellar are under house)

STAPLE PHOTO HERE

LAND, GROUNDS & UTILITIES

Size of Lot .... X .... Zoning and restrictions .... feet. Land is: low ☐ swampy ☐ filled ☐

At ☐ above ☐ below ☐ grade ☐ Condition: Good ☐ Fair ☐ Poor ☐ Drainage: Good ☐ Fair ☐ Poor ☐

Graded ☐ Sodded ☐ Shrubbery ☐ Condition: Good ☐ Fair ☐ Poor ☐ Sidewalk: ....

Street: Graded ☐ Kind of pavement ....

Accepted by city? .... Curb ☐ Gutter ☐. Well water: Depth ....

City Water ☐ Gas ☐ Electricity ☐ Connected to house? ...... Septic tank ☐ City sewer ☐ Connected to house? ....

NEIGHBORHOOD FACILITIES:

Transit facilities: Type .... Distance ....

Churches .... miles. Grammar school .... miles. High school .... miles. Stores .... miles.

New section ☐ Old section ☐ Ave. age of buildings .... Ave. type buildings: ....

Classification of area: Best ☐ Good ☐ Ave. ☐ Poor ☐

(1-2 fam., rooming, etc.)

354

Characteristics: Occupants of area:- Wage earner ☐ Small salaried man ☐ First class business and professional man ☐ Most fashionable ☐

Density of dwellings within 500-ft. radius: 100% built up ☐ 75% ☐ 50% ☐ 25% ☐ 10% ☐ Less than 10% ☐

Distance from built-up district .... Neighborhood nuisances ....

Kind of commercial buildings within radius of 500 ft. ....

Transition—To Business ☐ To Apartment ☐ To Industry ☐ None ☐ Roomers in this property ☐ In this section ☐

% vacancies in this section............ Reasons ....

SUBJECT PROPERTY:

Does subj. conform?............ Row House ☐ Semi-Detached ☐ Detached ☐ Corner ☐

Size and value of this building compared with surrounding buildings: Larger ☐ Same ☐ Smaller ☐

Size and value of this lot compared with surrounding lots: Larger ☐ Same ☐ Smaller ☐

Classification of buildings in the area: Best ☐ Ave. ☐ Substandard ☐

GARAGE

Capacity......cars. Size....X..... Attached ☐ In basement ☐ Detached ☐ Material of construction............

Roof: Flat ☐ Pitched ☐ Material .... Type of floor material ....

Type and No. of Doors:............ Garage Condition: Good ☐ Fair ☐ Poor ☐

Driveway: Private ☐ Mutual ☐ Kind............ Driveway Condition: Good ☐ Fair ☐ Poor ☐

MAIN BUILDING: No. of family units .... Rooms per unit:............ No. of stories ....

Exterior: Type of siding material:............

Condition of siding: Good ☐ Fair ☐ Poor ☐ Condition Paint on Body: Good ☐ Fair ☐ Poor ☐

Paint on Exterior Trim: Good ☐ Fair ☐ Poor ☐

Roof: Type .... Material............ Condition: Good ☐ Fair ☐ Poor ☐

Leaders and Gutters: Type: .... Condition: Good ☐ Fair ☐ Poor ☐

Flashing: Type: .... Condition: Good ☐ Fair ☐ Poor ☐

(Over)

355

Interior:

Foundation: Thickness.................... Material.................... Water proofed....................

Basement under entire building ☐. If not, under what part.................... Kind of floor....................

Type & size of beam.................... Columns.................... Joists....X...., o.c.......... Span....................

Equipment:

Heating Plant: Type.................... Fuel.................... Age; No. of Units....................

Is radiation adequate: .... Condition: ....

Air conditioned? .... Insulated? .... How? ....

Hot Water: Type.................... Adequate? .... Condition: ....

Plumbing: Type Piping; Brass ☐ Galvanized ☐ Copper ☐ Lead ☐ Condition ....

Type and No. of Plumbing Fixtures: .... Grade of Fixtures: ....

Flooring: Single ☐ Double ☐ Kind of wood .... Condition ....

Interior Wall: Plaster ☐ Dry Wall ☐ Other ☐ Condition ....

Paper ☐ Paint ☐ Both ☐ . Condition: Good ☐ Fair ☐ Poor ☐

Ceilings: Kind.................... Condition: Good ☐ Fair ☐ Poor ☐

Interior Trim: Material....................

Condition: Good ☐ Fair ☐ Poor ☐ Hardware: Good ☐ Fair ☐ Cheap ☐

Doors: Material.................... Finish.................... Condition ....

Is House Weather Stripped?.................... Storms ☐ Screens ☐ Type & Condition ....

Electric Fixtures: Good ☐ Fair ☐ Cheap ☐ Outlets: Is number adequate for each room? ....

Extras: Built in oven & range; Dishwasher, Intercom, Fireplaces, etc.....................

....

| | Basement | 1st Floor | 2nd Floor |

Room Layout: (LR, DR, etc.):

No. Closets:

Attic, Porches, etc:

General: Taxes:.................... This Property Could Be Rented For $.................... Marketability is:....................

Age of Building: Actual.................... Effective.................... Est. Remaining Econ. Life....................

356

VALUATION

By Cost Approach:

Land: .... ft. @ $.............. = ... $..............

Land improvements .... v .... $..............

Main Bldg: .... ft. @ $.............. = $..............

Additions: .... ft. @ $.............. = $..............

Depreciation: .... % = $..............

Value of Main Building: .... $..............

Garage: .... $..............

Other Buildings: .... $..............

Value of Property by Cost Approach: .... $..............

	Address	Date, Sale Price	Sq. Ft.	Adjusted Value*
No. 1	....	....	....	....
No. 2	....	....	....	....
No. 3	....	....	....	....

* Adjustment for difference in size, equipment, buildings, land.

Value of Property by Market Approach: .... $..............

Fair Market Value .... $..............

Remarks as to factors affecting the marketability of this property:

....

....

....

....

I have personally inspected the above property.

Date.............. .... Appraiser

357

READING AND STUDY REFERENCES

1. *Acquisition for Right-of-Way,* "Correlation and Final Value Estimate" (American Association of State Highway Officials, 1962), pp. 367–70.

2. *The Appraisal of Real Estate* (Chicago: American Institute of Real Estate Appraisers, 1967), chaps. 23–24.

3. Hollebaugh, Clifford W., "Correlation—The 'Heart' of the Appraisal Process," *The Appraisal Journal* (April 1962), pp. 17–20.

4. Kahn, Sanders A., Frederick E. Case, and Alfred Schimmel, *Real Estate Appraisal and Investment* (New York: The Ronald Press Company, 1963), chap. 15.

5. Kinnard, William N., Jr., *An Introduction to Appraising Real Property* (Chicago: Society of Real Estate Appraisers, 1968), chap. 17.

6. Ring, Alfred A., "Correlation is the Secret of Appraisal Success," *Technical Valuation* (February 1954), pp. 31–33.

7. Vaughan, John L., "The Purpose of the Appraisal," *Appraisal and Valuation Manual,* Vol. 2 (1956–1957).

Appraising has come a long way since value judgments were chiefly rendered by real estate brokers to facilitate the meeting of minds in connection with buyer-seller transactions. Today there exists an ever-increasing demand for accurate valuation and general appraisal services on the part of industry, business, civic and public organizations, and related professions. This growth and development of technical appraising is in

24

Professional Standards

and Responsibilities

no small measure due to the individual efforts of leading appraisers who have won great respect for their profession by insistence that value findings be expressed in detailed, logical, and comprehensive narrative reports. Nevertheless, no matter how great the technical skill ascribable to a given field of specialization, the ingredients that cause an individual, or the profession which he serves, to become favorably recognized are to be found in the human element of service to an ideal.

The older professional callings in the fields of medicine, law, and the chemical and biological sciences have conclusively demonstrated that worthwhile achievements—and public acceptance of the status of members as experts or scientists—are founded on unselfish devotion to a cause. Basically, the essentials that underlie worthwhile professional conduct include the following:

359

1. Integrity.
2. Intellect.
3. Education.
4. Judgment.

The Bible asserts that man cannot live by bread alone. This implies that economic activities in any field of human endeavor need to be supplemented and guided by social and moral considerations. *Integrity* is an inner force that flows from a wholesome personal and professional philosophy of life which inspires trust and confidence in others. Integrity is akin to honor and service, and both are basic to a genuine display of sincerity of purpose in the discharge of professional responsibility. It is integrity that propels man to render his best service, independent of the financial reward offered him to solve a given problem or to report on his findings or investigations.

The service motive, to be fruitful, must be reinforced with *intellect*. This is the power of reasoning as distinguished from the faculty of absorbing knowledge. Without intellect, the power of knowing gained from study and experience remains limited. Some men are by nature blessed, it seems, with more intellect than are others. But unless such talents are put to use, atrophy—a form of mental rigor mortis—may rob the possessor of his native advantage.

Important as these sources of professional strength are, integrity and intellect cannot stand alone. Both of these qualities must be supplemented by education. One must consciously make efforts to discipline his mind through study and instruction. The art of learning is essential in order for professional men to keep abreast with modern developments in theory and in practice. Education, it should be emphasized, need not be formal in character. Although study in college or trade school is economical and time-saving in the long run, informal education can be gained through experience, intensive reading, attendance at seminars, workshops, and through related organizational and professional activities. It is in this area of self-study that professional groups render their most valuable service to fellow members.

Judgment, the final ingredient that characterizes a professional man, is the ability to consider and weigh relevant data in order to reach a sound and reasonable conclusion. Of the qualities that go to make up a professional man, judgment is the most difficult to cultivate. Judgment cannot readily be transferred from one person to another. Experience, it is agreed, has proved to be the best teacher of judgment.

IMPORTANCE OF PROFESSIONAL CONDUCT

The more specialized a given activity and the greater the required personal skill, the less the public appears to know about the quality and technical phases of the service rendered. To safeguard the general public against the malpractices of the few, and to promote the general interest of its members, professional societies are formed. Through them, intensive efforts are made to develop and maintain high standards of conduct.

As an organized profession, appraising dates back only to the year 1932, when the American Institute of Real Estate Appraisers was founded. In 1935, another group of specialists organized the Society of Real Estate Appraisers. Both organizations are international in scope, with cooperating chapters in Europe and Canada. Since 1935, other organizations which embrace valuation on a broader scale have been founded. For example, the members of the American Society of Appraisers are interested in the technical appraising of industrial plant equipment, securities, intangibles, and chattel fixtures.

Although real estate appraising has developed during the past thirty years into the most specialized branch of the real estate business, relatively few practitioners have achieved true professional standing. This is because relatively few real estate firms or individuals devote their working time exclusively to real estate appraising. Most members of the two leading appraising organizations depend on other income from collateral interests in brokerage, investment, management, or mortgage-financing fields of the real estate business. The collateral activities are by no means deemed a handicap, for the best known and most respected appraisers are those who have had a broad background in related real estate activities and whose judgments are tempered by wide and personal experience in all the varied phases of the real estate business. Having achieved, however, the experience and perception essential to the makeup of a qualified appraiser, professional status can be claimed only by those who devote their full time and specialized energies to activities which sharpen their value judgments, strengthen their value know-how, and enhance the integrity and quality of their services to clients and to the general public.

PROFESSIONAL QUALIFICATIONS

Although ever greater stress is laid on adequate selection and analysis of appraisal data, the value conclusions reached by real estate practitioners constitute at best an informed estimate, the soundness of which largely depends on the quality of judgment possessed by the appraiser. To perfect the practice of real estate appraising and to safeguard against incompetence, appraisal societies are setting ever higher standards as requisites for membership. For instance, to be eligible for membership in the American Institute of Real Estate Appraisers, and thus be privileged to use the coveted M.A.I. designation after his name, a candidate must be at least thirty years of age, have a minimum of five years of appraisal experience, possess the equivalent of a high school education, submit three acceptable narrative appraisal reports covering different classes of real estate property, and must pass two written examinations—each eight hours in duration—in order to demonstrate his ability to cope with valuation theory questions and case study problems. Even when meeting the above requirements, a candidate may still be short of the 120 points required for membership unless he has a college education, more than five years' appraising practice, and collateral business experience, and unless he submits additional appraisal reports or requests additional examinations to satisfy the credit points set as a minimum by the admissions committee of the Appraising Institute. These stringent admission requirements account for the fact that the Institute has less than 5,000 M.A.I.'s as members. Many times more than the number of professional appraisers now practicing are needed, however, if the demand for competent real property valuation services is to be met adequately. To this end, a comprehensive nationwide educational program is being sponsored by the American Institute of Real Estate Appraisers and the Society of Real Estate Appraisers in cooperation with leading universities and colleges throughout the nation.

STANDARDS OF PROFESSIONAL CONDUCT

All professional societies have established rules of conduct or codes of ethics. Generally, rules of conduct are intended not only to safeguard the interests of individual members from one another but also to assure the public of professional services that will instill confidence and bring honor to the organization at large. To assure this, membership is restricted to those of proved technical competence who are known for adherence to high moral standards and a display of unquestionable personal integrity. Rules of conduct, by and large, are promulgated to promote and protect the common good as follows:

1. The interest of the public.
2. The interest of the client.
3. The interest of fellow members and the profession at large.

The *interest of the public* is deemed adversely affected whenever the appraiser fails to act as an independent agent. It is true that the appraiser must be hired by someone, and that he owes his loyalty to his principal; but the value findings must not be slanted or biased because of it. Value found must be objective and independent of the client's cause or the compensation paid for services rendered. Based on premises clearly set forth in the body of the appraisal report, the value conclusions reached must be independently supportable no matter whose cause is being served.

In the interest of the public, the appraiser must be careful to base value on factual and reliable data and not on hypothetical assumptions or on questionable and uncertain future benefits. To ignore legal property-use restrictions, or to base value on hoped-for changes in area zoning, is a violation of public trust. The appraisal report must be written for the benefit of the uninformed reader, who will act on the findings in good faith. Care, too, must be taken not to appraise fractional parts of a property, especially where the sum of the parts appraised as if independent property units does not equal the value of the entire property when appraised as an integral whole. Fractional appraising is deemed unethical whenever the report—intentionally or otherwise—misleads the reader.

The appraiser would also be guilty of professional misconduct if he should accept an assignment for valuation of a property in which he has an undisclosed financial interest. No man can serve two masters and serve them well, especially where a conflict of interests beclouds the independence of action on which objective value must rest to be publicly acceptable.

The *interests of the client* impose further obligations on the professional appraiser. The most important of these is not to reveal the value findings to anyone unless specifically authorized to do so by the client or compelled to do so by court order. Communications between appraiser and client are not privileged under common law as are those of physicians, clergymen, and lawyers. Nevertheless, every precaution must be taken to keep a client's trust confidential and to protect his interests at all times.

Clients, too, have a right to expect that an appraiser will not accept an assignment for which he has no previous experience or for which he is not qualified professionally. It would be considered a violation of professional trust for an appraiser to accept an assignment to evaluate a citrus grove or an industrial park if his previous appraisal experience was limited to urban and primarily residential properties. The appraiser can, of course, affiliate himself with another member of his profession who is qualified to render the specialized service, provided the client is duly informed and the appraisal report discloses the cooperative efforts of the parties involved.

Appraisers must take care to keep their client's relationship above-board. The fees charged should bear a reasonable relationship to quantity and character of service, and to professional responsibility assumed in the discharge of the assignment. As a rule, fees should be calculated on a per diem basis for personnel employed (professional responsibility assumed), plus direct and indirect expenses chargeable to the assignment. It is considered unethical to accept a commission in lieu of a stipulated fee or to accept gifts and services or undisclosed payments. To do so destroys the standing of the appraiser as an independent member of his profession, at least in the eyes of the public. Such conduct, of course, casts a shadow on all who strive diligently to uphold and enhance the dignity of this specialized calling.

The American Institute of Real Estate Appraisers, in its Regulation

No. 10, recommends that its members certify a statement in each appraisal report, substantially as follows:

> I the undersigned do hereby certify that to the best of my knowledge and belief the statements contained in this appraisal and upon which the opinions expressed herein are based, are correct, subject to the limiting conditions herein set forth; also that this appraisal has been made in conformity with the Professional Standards of the American Institute of Real Estate Appraisers of the National Association of Real Estate Boards.

The interests of the members and the profession at large, too, are guided by written and implied rules of conduct. Most professional organizations deem it unethical for a member to conduct himself in such a manner as to prejudice the professional status or reputation of other members or that of the association under whose auspices he practices. Appraisers thus should not solicit assignments nor advertise professional attainments or services except as authorized and in a dignified manner. Generally, announcements are limited to business cards, directory listings, and newspaper notices containing only the member's name, his professional designation, his telephone number, and his business address.

Most recent regulations caution members of the appraisal profession not to enter into competitive bidding for appraisal assignments. It is considered undignified to offer services, when it is known that the assignment will go to the lowest bidder. Service is two-dimensional: qualitative as well as quantitative. Bidding suggests uniformity of product service which in practice does not exist. Experience, judgment, skill, integrity, and education are intangible ingredients which are difficult to subject to measurement under standard specifications in accordance with which service is to be performed. Some government agencies are still guilty of requesting bids and assigning appraisal service on the basis of cost, without due consideration of the experience, skill, and reputation which affect the quality of the service sought.

APPRAISER'S RULES OF CONDUCT

Whether or not a real estate appraiser belongs to one or more of the leading appraisal institutes or societies, he should be aware of and adhere to the guiding rules of conduct on which the growth and development of appraisal service as a professional calling depend. Under these rules, the appraiser must:

> 1. *Willingly share knowledge and professional experiences.* No man can live unto himself alone. Exchange of experiences and knowledge enriches performance, creates mutual trust, and inspires public confidence. Cooperation, especially through affiliation with professional

organizations, has increased the demand significantly for specialized appraisal service during the past ten years. Members are urged to publish research findings and to participate in educational seminars and workshops in which new theories and practices can be explored and tested. It is in the field of education that professional organizations have made their greatest contributions.

2. *Encourage higher standards and service performance.* The transition from oral and letter reporting to preparation of lengthy and detailed narrative reports in which value conclusions are logically derived and supported is largely due to friendly competition encouraged among professional appraisers to promote higher performance standards. Professional service, if worthy of its name, should be documented and rendered with pride. It is facetiously said that doctors bury their mistakes, but appraisers exhibit theirs for all to see. Increased stress on higher standards and service performance will weed out the incompetent and create interest among the college-trained to share in the challenging opportunities that appraisal service promises to offer in the years to come.

3. *Never speak ill or disparagingly about a fellow appraiser.* Greatness cannot be achieved by pulling others down. One does not become taller by making others smaller. Disparaging talk—even when warranted—leaves a bitter taste, often traced to envy. How much more cheerful and impressive it is to subscribe to the theory that all persons, including fellow competitors, are striving to do well in accordance with their talents and abilities. In the long run, reputation based on quality performance standards will bring the best men to the top in a free and competitive society.

4. *Seek no unfair advantage.* It is disappointing that many otherwise informed men still subscribe to the erroneous philosophy that the goods of the world or of a nation, or the income derived from a service, are all as limited in quantity as is the size of a given pie. To secure a larger slice, those who hold to this philosophy must necessarily connive to shrink the shares of others, or freeze them out entirely. Progress in all phases of life, as well as our high standard of living, is proof that bigger pies—and not more slices of an existing pie—increase the wealth of a nation. This is apparent in most professions, too, where despite increasing membership growth work loads and work opportunities have not diminished.

5. *Avoid controversy.* Do not wash soiled linen in public. There is a saying that you may win an argument, but you may lose a friend. The professional man should avoid arguments; but, when unavoidable, his disputes should not be aired in public. More often than not, differences of opinion arise because of misunderstandings, statements of half-truth, or quotations taken out of context. Where differences of opinions do arise they can generally be talked out in gentlemanly fashion and under circumstances wherein men of honor can agree to disagree.

6. *Abide by rules and regulations, and encourage opportunities for professional education.* Most men are understandably rebellious at heart and inclined to disregard rules and regulations when such seem to work against them. Man naturally seeks to be free from fetters. He wants to enjoy rights, but he objects to obligations. Yet rights cannot

exist without obligations. The right to live imposes the obligation not to kill. The right to free speech imposes the obligation to allow others to do likewise. Rights without obligations lead to anarchy and chaos. Rules and regulations are intended to maximize the common good either of a people or of a given clan or profession. Every individual gain is obtained at a sacrifice of social costs. Control of some sort is needed to keep a balance between incentive (profit) motives and those aimed at the exploitation of the weak, uninformed, or the public at large. Violations of rules and regulations and unprofessional conduct are often traceable to ignorance or lack of understanding. Enlightenment through education has proved the bulwark of professionalism. Every support should be given to efforts intended to spread the gospel of professional truth and know-how.

7. *Keep confidential matters entrusted in good faith.* Every code of ethics, from the oldest to the youngest professions, stresses the importance of "privileged communication." It seems to bolster one's ego to possess information that others long to know, and it is the devilish urge to be magnanimous by sharing such important matters with others that inclines the weak to discuss private matters with the wrong people. The Golden Rule should have special meaning to men of professional status. Once a trust is violated, it is difficult to regain public confidence. Worse still, a breach of conduct undermines strength of character and may lead to misfeasance in client relations that may have serious repercussions to the practitioner as an individual and to the profession of which he is a part.

8. *Not undermine a fellow practitioner's professional relations with others, nor attempt to create closed-shop appraisal practices in his community.* Experience in all parts of the country supports the conclusion that the demand for qualified appraisers outruns the available supply. Commercial banks, insurance firms, business establishments, investors, and industry rely increasingly on independent appraisers for guidance in their loan and investment policies. Healthy competition is good for trade as well as for professional growth and development. In a progressive society, standing still means going backwards. An attempt to keep qualified practitioners from serving the community is a sign of weakness and stagnation. A "let-the-best-man-win" philosophy is essential to keeping good men at the top.

9. *Not solicit employment of a fellow practitioner's office or field personnel without his full knowledge and permission.* It is considered poor practice to encourage transfer of working personnel from one office to another. Employees are not subject to the same stringent regulations or codes of ethics that bind their professional employers, and inevitable comparison of office policies and practices may cast doubts on uniformity and quality of service that may adversely affect the integrity of the profession as a whole. Where a spirit of friendly cooperation rather than competition prevails, employees, too, will find their working environment more congenial. Instill a feeling of belonging and a sense of loyalty among those who serve you. Where such feelings prevail, employment problems cease to exist.

10. *Conduct his work so as to achieve a high regard in his community and make fellow members of the appraisal profession thankful for his wholesome influence.* There are many things in life which money

cannot buy, and reputation is among them. Unfortunately, too many people consider short-run monetary gains without thoughtful deliberation as to the long-term effects of their actions. Where love of work, interest, and service are prime considerations in the discharge of professional duty, success is bound to follow. The sense of a job well done in an atmosphere of confidence and public recognition provides the lasting compensation that is reflected in a firm's shield of honor. It is the hope of all to carry this shield on without blemish from one generation to another.

For reference and guidance of men engaged as real estate appraisers the code of ethics of the American Institute of Real Estate Appraisers is quoted below: [1]

Land is the basic source of all wealth. Real estate wisely used and widely allocated in private ownership is essential to our national well being. Upon its intelligent and proper evaluation depend the investments and lifetime savings of our people and their confidence in the economy which sustains our free institutions.

The functions of the real estate appraiser are strictly professional in character; he is charged with solemn business, civic, and social responsibilities.

Recognizing these obligations, we mutually pledge to each other our knowledge, our experience, and our sacred honor. Each member of the American Institute of Real Estate Appraisers agrees that he will:

1. Conduct his professional activities in a manner that will reflect credit upon himself, other real estate appraisers, and the American Institute of Real Estate Appraisers.
2. Protect the professional reputation and prospects of other real estate appraisers who subscribe to and abide by this Code of Ethics.
3. Acknowledge the contribution of others who participate professionally with him in an appraisal.
4. Secure appraisal assignments by referral and through recognition of his professional competence without unprofessional solicitation or advertisement, without payment or acceptance of commission, without unprofessional fee bidding, and without contingencies dependent on findings, conclusions, or value reported.
5. Accept only those appraisal assignments relating to which he has no current or prospective unrevealed personal interest or bias and which he is qualified to undertake and complete without his professional standing or integrity being placed in jeopardy.
6. Preserve a professional confidential relationship with his client, revealing or reporting only to his client his conclusions and valuation.
7. Render properly and adequately developed valuations without advocacy for accommodation of any particular interests, being factual, objective, unbiased, and honest in presenting his oral or written analyses, conclusions, and opinions.

---

[1] *The Appraisal of Real Estate* (Chicago, Illinois: American Institute of Real Estate Appraisers, 5th ed., 1967), pp. 430–37.

8. Cooperate with the Institute and its officers in all matters, including investigation, censure, discipline, or dismissal of members who, by their conduct, prejudice their professional status or the reputation of the Institute.

9. Conform in all respects to this Code of Ethics and to the Standards of Professional Conduct adopted by the American Institute of Real Estate Appraisers as the same may be amended from time to time.

For further reference and guidance of those engaged as real estate appraisers, the code of ethics and the standards of professional practice of the Society of Real Estate Appraisers are quoted below as follows: [2]

STANDARDS OF PROFESSIONAL PRACTICE AND CONDUCT

ADOPTED BY BOARD OF GOVERNORS FEBRUARY 9, 1968

PREAMBLE

The Society of Real Estate Appraisers was founded to elevate the standards of the appraisal profession, to aid in the solution of the many problems of the profession in appraising real estate, and to designate certain members as having attained certain skills and knowledge. The members are pledged to maintain a high level of trust and integrity in their practice.

CODE OF ETHICS

This Code of Ethics is a set of dynamic principles guiding the appraiser's conduct and way of life. It is the appraiser's duty to practice his profession according to this Code of Ethics.

Each member agrees that he shall:

I. Conduct his activities in a manner that will reflect credit upon himself, other real estate appraisers, and the Society of Real Estate Appraisers.

II. Cooperate with the Society of Real Estate Appraisers and its officers in all matters, including, but not limited to the investigation, censure, discipline, or dismissal of members, who by their conduct prejudice their professional status or the reputation of the Society of Real Estate Appraisers.

III. Obtain appraisal assignments, prepare appraisals, and accept compensation in a professional manner in accordance with the provisions of the Standards of Professional Practice and Conduct of the Society of Real Estate Appraisers.

---

[2] *The Real Estate Appraiser* (Chicago, Illinois: Society of Real Estate Appraisers, Vol. 34, No. 3, 1968), pp. 14–16.

IV. Accept only those appraisal assignments for which he has adequate time, facilities, and technical ability to complete in a competent professional manner, and in which he has no current or unrevealed interest.

V. Render properly developed, unbiased, and objective value opinions.

VI. Prepare an adequate written appraisal for each real estate appraisal assignment accepted.

VII. Reveal his value conclusions and opinions to no one other than his client, except with the permission of the client or by due process of law, and except when required to do so to comply with the rules of the Society of Real Estate Appraisers.

VIII. Conform in all respects to this Code of Ethics, the Standards of Professional Practice and Conduct, and the Bylaws of the Society of Real Estate Appraisers as the same may be amended from time to time.

STANDARDS OF PROFESSIONAL PRACTICE

I. *Valuation Practices*

A. Prudent and logical appraisal practice suggests these recommended steps in reaching a supportable conclusion of value:

1. The description or identification of the subject property:

a. The appraiser should include a legal description, street address, or other means of specifically and adequately locating the property being appraised.

b. The appraiser should consider matters relating to title that may affect the final value conclusions, such as:

1) The nature of the ownership, i.e., fee simple, or an explanation of other division of ownership interest.

2) Easements, restrictions, encumbrances, leases, reservations, covenants, contracts, declarations, special assessments, ordinances, or other items of a similar nature.

c. Each appraisal should be predicated on a valuation of the land for its highest and best use as though unimproved and capable of development to its most profitable legal use. The highest and best use of the property as presently improved may or may not result in a value conclusion exceeding the value of the land alone. The appraiser should support his estimates of highest and best use.

d. The appraiser should include an accurate and adequate description of the political, social, and economic factors affecting the property including the effect on both the land and the physical improvement on and to the land.

e. The appraiser should consider all physical, functional, and economic factors as they may affect the value conclusion.

2. Purpose of the appraisal and definition of the value estimated:

a. The appraiser should state the purpose of the appraisal, and clearly define the value estimated.

3. Effective date of the appraisal:

a. The date of the value estimate ordinarily should be the date of the last property inspection except when the appraisal requires a prior date.

4. Data collection, analysis and interpretation:
   a. The appraiser should recognize that each of the approaches to value are functions of market phenomena.
   b. The appraiser should consider appropriate units of comparison and also whenever possible, practical and appropriate adjustments should be made for all factors of dissimilarity.
   c. The comparable sales approach (when applicable):
      1) The appraiser should collect, inspect, verify, analyze, and correlate such comparable sales as are available to indicate a value conclusion. No pertinent information shall be withheld. The pertinent comparable sales should be identified by address, and incorporated into the appraisal report itself.
   d. The income approach (when applicable):
      1) When applicable to income-producing properties, the appraiser should collect, inspect, verify, analyze, and correlate such comparable rentals as are available to indicate an appropriate estimate of the economic rental value of the property being appraised. No pertinent information shall be withheld.
      2) When applicable to income-producing properties, the appraiser should collect, verify, analyze, and correlate such data on comparable operating expenses as are available to support an appropriate estimate of all operating expenses of the property being appraised. No pertinent information shall be withheld.
      3) When applicable to income-producing properties, the appraiser should collect, verify, analyze, and correlate such comparable data relating to an appropriate capitalization rate or rates to be applied to the estimated net income to indicate a proper value conclusion. No pertinent information shall be withheld.
      4) When applicable to income-producing properties, the method process and technique of capitalization used should be appropriate to the type and characteristics of the property being appraised.
      5) In the case of single-family dwellings, the appraiser should collect, inspect, verify, analyze, and correlate such data on comparable sales and rentals as are available to indicate a value conclusion by use of the gross rent multiplier technique. No pertinent information shall be withheld.
   e. The cost approach (when applicable):
      1) The appraiser should collect, verify, analyze, and correlate such comparable cost data as are available for use in estimating the cost new of the subject property.
      2) The appraiser should collect, verify, analyze, and correlate such comparable data as are available to support and explain the difference between cost new and present worth of the improvements (accrued depreciation) reflecting items of deterioration and obsolescence. No pertinent information shall be withheld. The appraiser

should qualify the data sources and cost methodology used in his cost estimate.

5. Correlation and final value estimate:

   a. In the final value estimate, the appraiser should consider the purpose which the appraisal serves, the type of property being appraised, and the relative weights which typical users or investors would accord to the quality and quantity of data available and analyzed within the approaches used.

6. Special and limiting conditions:

   a. It should be the duty of the appraiser to support the validity and feasibility of any special and limiting conditions or assumptions under which his appraisal is made. Unquestioning acceptance of an opinion motivated by advocacy such as an attorney's does not relieve the appraiser of his responsibility to provide valid support for such conditions and assumptions.

7. Appraiser's certification:

   a. The appraiser should certify that he has personally inspected the subject property; that to the best of his knowledge and belief the statements and opinions contained in the resulting report are correct; that no pertinent information has knowingly been withheld; that he has no present or contemplated future interest in the property appraised; and that the amount of his fee is not contingent on reporting a predetermined value or on the amount of the value estimate. Any exceptions should be clearly stated.

   b. While the appraiser is ultimately responsible for any report to which he has affixed his signature, he should acknowledge those phases of the appraisal process performed by others under his supervision and, when appropriate, they should become signatories to the report.

B. It is unethical for an appraiser to estimate fractional parts of a property so that the reported value exceeds the value that would be derived if the property were considered separately as a whole.

C. It is unethical for an appraiser to base his value conclusion on the assumed completion of public or private improvements unless he clearly defines the conditions, extent, and effects of such assumption. Any such assumption must be predicated on sound valuation principles.

II. *Reporting Practices*

A. An adequate written appraisal containing a supported value shall be prepared for each appraisal assignment accepted, and shall include the following as minimum requirements:

1. An adequate and definite description of the property being appraised.

2. The purpose of the appraisal and a definition of the value estimated.

3. The effective date of the appraisal.

4. The date and reasoning supporting the value conclusion which may include the comparable sales approach, the income approach, and the cost approach. The exclusions of any of the usual three approaches must be explained and supported.

5. The final estimate of value.

6. Special and limiting condition, if any.
7. The appraiser's certification and signature.

B. A true copy of each appraisal shall be prepared and retained by the appraiser, and shall be sent on request to a duly constituted Professional Practice Committee of the Local Chapter or of the International Society of Real Estate Appraisers.

C. It is unethical to issue a separate appraisal report on only a part of a whole property without stating that it is a fractional appraisal and, as such, subject to use in a manner consistent with such limitation.

D. It is unethical to issue a separate appraisal report when another appraiser assigned to appraise the same property has had a part in the formation of the opinion of value.

E. It is unethical for an appraiser to reveal in any way the substance of any appraisal without permission of the client except under due process of law, or when required to do so in compliance with the rules and regulations of the Society of Real Estate Appraisers.

STANDARDS OF PROFESSIONAL CONDUCT

I. It is unethical for an appraiser to become an advocate of any opinion other than his unbiased and objective value conclusion.

II. It is unethical for an appraiser to conduct himself in any manner that will prejudice his professional status or the reputation of any appraisal organization or any other appraiser.

III. It is unethical to accept an assignment to appraise a property of a type with which he has had no previous experience unless in making the appraisal he associates with an appraiser who has had experience with the type of property under appraisement, or makes full disclosure of the degree of his experience, background, and training to the client.

IV. It is unethical for an appraiser to:
a. Contract for or accept compensation for appraisal services in the form of a commission, rebate, division of brokerage commissions, or any similar forms;
b. Receive or pay finder's or referral fees;
c. Compete for any appraisal engagement on the basis of bids when the amount of the fee is the basis for awarding the assignment, but this is not to be construed as precluding the submission of a proposal for services.
d. Accept an assignment to appraise a property for which his employment or fee is contingent on his reporting a predetermined conclusion;
e. Make his compensation on any basis other than a fair professional fee for the responsibility entailed and the work and expense involved.

V. It is unethical for an appraiser to attempt to supplant another appraiser after definite steps have been taken toward the employment of such other appraiser.

VI. It is unethical for an appraiser to advertise or solicit appraisal business in any manner not consonant with accepted professional practice.

VII. It is unethical for an appraiser to claim professional qualifications which may be subject to erroneous interpretation, or to state professional qualifications which he does not possess. Specifically, Associates of the Society of Real Estate Appraisers do not have the Society's professional endorsement and cannot refer to their affiliation.

VIII. It is unethical to fail to report to the Society the actions of any member who, in the opinion of the reporting member, has violated this Standards of Professional Practice and Conduct.

READING AND STUDY REFERENCES

1. Burlake, J. M., "Conflict of Interest in Appraising," *Technical Valuation* (October 1961), pp. 35–38.

2. Davis, W. D., "Professional Standards and the Appraiser's Future," *The Real Estate Appraiser* (May 1963), pp. 2–7.

3. Dolman, John P., "Responsibilities of the Appraiser," *The Appraisal Journal* (January 1962), pp. 49–52.

4. Gillespie, John, "An Appraisal of the Profession of Appraising," *The Residential Appraiser* (June 1962), pp. 19–20.

5. Kahn, Sanders A., Frederick E. Case, and Alfred Schimmel, *Real Estate Appraisal and Investment* (New York: The Ronald Press Company, 1963), chap. 1.

6. Kinnard, William N., Jr., *An Introduction to Appraising Real Property* (Chicago: Society of Real Estate Appraisers, 1968), chap. 18.

7. Ring, Alfred A., "Appraising—What it Takes to be an Expert," *The Real Estate Appraiser* (May 1965), pp. 23–28.

8. Ring, Alfred A., "A Professional Philosophy," *The Review* (March 1953), pp. 12–14.

9. Smith, Walstein, Jr., *Is the Appraisal Witness Qualified?* (Chicago: Society of Real Estate Appraisers, 1968).

Appendix I

Sample Appraisal Form

The reader's attention is called to the fact that there is considerable leeway in methods and procedures governing appraisal report presentation of valuation data. The demonstration and narrative reports presented herein represent one possible way of handling the appraisal problems among several acceptable alternatives.

DEMONSTRATION APPRAISAL REPORT

FOR AN APARTMENT HOUSE PROPERTY

ALFRED A. RING, S.R.A., M.A.I.

Appraiser

PART I

GENERAL INFORMATION

ALFRED A. RING, S.R.A., M.A.I.
Appraiser

Valuation Report

for

Apartment House Property

Prepared for

Mr. Thomas B. Wright, President
Bankers Trust Company
204 N. W. Main Street
Gainesville, Florida

ALFRED A. RING, S.R.A., M.A.I.
Appraiser

202 Matherly Hall
West University Avenue
Gainesville, Florida 32601
January 15, 19--

Mr. Thomas B. Wright, President
Bankers Trust Company
204 N. W. Main Street
Gainesville, Florida 32601

Dear Mr. Wright:

In compliance with your request, the undersigned has completed
an appraisal of the twelve unit apartment house property located at
312 - 320 S. W. 10th Street in Gainesville, Florida. This property is
located as shown in the attached location sketch and is more fully and
legally described in the body of this report.

Please be informed that a careful and personal inspection was
made of this apartment house site and its building improvements. Due
consideration was given to all factors and forces that influence property
value at the subject location.

The attached report contains an analysis of general and specific
data which was deemed essential to support the estimate of value as
reported herein under the cost, income and market approaches to value.

As a result of my investigation and detailed findings, it is
my considered and professional opinion that the apartment house property
described herein warrants a market value as of January 10, 19-- in the
amount of:

One Hundred Seventeen Thousand Dollars

($117,000)

ALFRED A. RING, S.R.A., M.A.I.
Appraiser

Mr. Thomas B. Wright
January 15, 19--
Page 2

  Please feel free to let me know if you desire additional
information concerning this report or if we may be of further
assistance in this matter.

       Respectfully submitted,

       Alfred A. Ring, S.R.A., M.A.I.

       Consultant - Appraiser

ALFRED A. RING, S.R.A., M.A.I.
Appraiser

Table of Contents

Part I

General Information

Part II

Analysis and Value Conclusions

ALFRED A. RING, S.R.A., M.A.I.
Appraiser

ALFRED A. RING, S.R.A., M.A.I.
Appraiser

ALFRED A. RING, M. A. I.
Appraiser

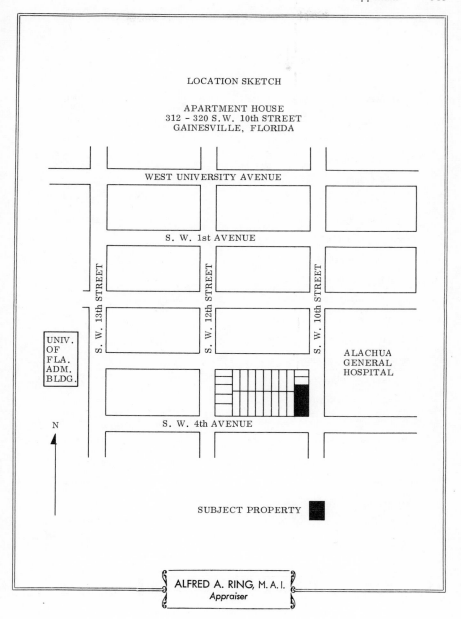

LOCATION SKETCH

APARTMENT HOUSE
312 – 320 S.W. 10th STREET
GAINESVILLE, FLORIDA

WEST UNIVERSITY AVENUE

S. W. 1st AVENUE

S. W. 13th STREET

S. W. 12th STREET

S. W. 10th STREET

UNIV. OF FLA. ADM. BLDG.

ALACHUA GENERAL HOSPITAL

N

S. W. 4th AVENUE

SUBJECT PROPERTY

ALFRED A. RING, M.A.I.
Appraiser

Summary of Important Conclusions

Final estimate of value	$117,000
Value of land	13,500
Value of building improvements	103,500
Value estimate under:	
Cost approach	120,700
Market approach	119,300
Income approach	117,100
Effective revenue	$ 18,938
Operating expenses	8,159
Operating income	10,779
Rate of Capitalization:	
Return "on" the investment	8.5%
Amortization rate per annum	.338%
Assessment and tax data:	
County $93,690 taxes	$ 1,907
City $93,690 taxes	937
Building area	11,340 sq. ft.
Building replacement cost--new	$130,110
Remaining economic building life	40 years
Effective age	10 years
Chronological building age	12 years
Accrued depreciation	$ 22,892
Per cent building depreciation	16.8%

ALFRED A. RING, S.R.A., M.A.I.
Appraiser

Purpose of the Appraisal

The purpose of this appraisal is to establish an estimate of
market value of the apartment house property described herein as of
January 10, 19--. This report is prepared to furnish a guide as to the
sales price that the subject property should command if exposed for sale
in the open market on date of this appraisal.

Definition of Market Value

Market value, for purposes of this report, is defined as follows:

The estimated price in terms of money which a
property will bring if exposed for sale in the open
market, allowing a reasonable time to find a
purchaser who buys with knowledge of all the
uses to which the property is adopted and for
which it is capable of being used.

In this definition it is assumed that the transaction is based
on cash or cash equivalent considerations. Favorable or unfavorable
terms of sale are bound to affect the transaction price which this
property can command in the open market.

ALFRED A. RING, S.R.A., M.A.I.
Appraiser

It is further assumed that title to the property is good and
marketable and that fee simple ownership is to be transferred free from
all encumbrances except for those specified in the deed of public records.

Legal Description

The subject property is legally described as follows:

"Lots 22, 23 and 24, Block 5, as known and
numbered on the Plat of University Heights,
recorded in Mortgage Book 104, page 10 and
in Plat Book "A", page 99, Official Records
Book 60, page 605 of the public records of
Alachua County, Florida."

Statement of Highest and Best Use

It is the appraiser's opinion that the subject property as
found on the date of inspection, January 10, 19--, was improved in
accordance with the principle of highest and best use.

By highest and best use is meant that program of land use or
employment which will preserve the utility of the land and yield a net
income flow that forms, when appropriately capitalized, the highest
present value of the land. The subject property is zoned R-3 permitting
high-density, multi-family dwellings.

ALFRED A. RING, S.R.A., M.A.I.
Appraiser

PART II

ANALYSIS AND VALUE CONCLUSIONS

ALFRED A. RING, S.R.A., M.A.I.
Appraiser

<u>General, Social, Economic, and</u>

<u>Political Data Influencing Value</u>

<u>National Data</u>:

Approximately two-thirds of the nations's wealth consists of real estate, and any governmental acts designed to infringe upon private control of real estate are bound to be reflected in the future trend of property values.

Two forces are currently at work that indirectly influence property values. One is continued efforts towards socialization of our resources. This socialization, in the form of increased taxes to support "government in business," reduces the available private income that forms the basis of economic values. Unless the march of the "welfare state" is halted, real estate as an investment will decline in popularity and value.

The counteracting force is the government's active interest in underwriting the cause of home ownership. The Federal Housing Administration, the Veterans' Administration (with its loan program), and many other related Federal agencies make possible "pay-as-you-live" purchase plans, with the aid of which homes can be bought using future income rather than capital savings as in the past. This governmental effort and direct subsidy has increased tremendously the demand for home sites and homes. The trend is still strong, and both political parties have committed themselves to continuing the liberalization of underwriting home purchase plans.

ALFRED A. RING, S.R.A., M.A.I.
Appraiser

The latter force, at present and for some years to come, out-weighs the threat of the first sufficiently to make home ownership still one of the soundest investments in America today.

This valuation report is also predicated on the assumption that no "hot" war will erupt in the foreseeable future. The out-break of a shooting war would cause an exodus of students and faculty from this university city and diminish the demand for housing. This in turn would adversely affect the value of residential and apartment house properties at the subject location.

Experts predict a rise in U. S. population reaching 225 million persons by 1980, and a 50-million increase in the decade following, reaching a total of 260 million persons by the end of 1990. This population expansion will cause an estimated demand for new housing at a level of 1.3 to 1.5 million dwellings per annum.

Individual standards of living, too, continue to rise with the over-all economic growth of the country. A minimum increase in U. S. economic potential is forecast at a rate of 5 per cent per annum over the next ten years, as compared with a 3.5 per cent annual growth factor (in constant dollars) over the past decade.

Based on these forecasts the investment and ownership outlook for residential real estate from a national point of view is considered favorable.

ALFRED A. RING, S.R.A., M.A.I.
Appraiser

State and Regional Data:

The economic outlook for Florida is bright. This state constitutes one of the few remaining frontiers in U. S. land development,
and significant population shifts because of immigration and decentralization exert a favorable influence on this state's economy.

Florida's increase in population at a rate of 200,000 persons
per annum has caused the state to advance in population rank from
20th in 1950 to 9th in 1970. Since land and realty values are sensitive
to population changes, this favorable growth in Florida should
act as a substantial cushion for any general economic recession which
may materialize in the years to come.

Florida, too, is excelling in its three major economic
activities: tourism, industry, and agriculture. The steady and wholesome increase in family income, savings, and capital outlays at average
rates exceeding those for the nation as a whole make Florida one of the
best regions in America for capital investment in land and land improvements.

The favorable climate which attracts between 12 and 15 million
visitors to Florida each year is recognized as the state's principal
economic asset. However, the political climate is also favorable.
Florida has no state income or inheritance taxes and corporate tax
burdens are competitive with those of other southern states. Home owners
enjoy a $5,000 homestead tax exemption which shifts the incidence of
local taxes upon out-of-state tourists by means of a 4 per cent sales
tax.

ALFRED A. RING, S.R.A., M.A.I.
Appraiser

Experts generally agree that Florida's economy is on a sound footing and that the outlook for land and real estate investment throughout the state is excellent.

City Data:

Gainesville is the political and administrative center of Alachua County and is located approximately seventy-two miles southwest of Jacksonville, Florida. It is the largest city in the county, housing a population of 60,000 persons within the geographic limits of twenty-six square miles.

A direct relationship exists between the growth of the University of Florida and the growth of Gainesville as a community. This is evident from the fact that almost one-third of the total working population of the greater Gainesville area is employed by the University.

As with Florida as a whole, Gainesville has a cosmopolitan population, with various racial and cultural groups being represented both at the University and in the city. The colored population of the greater Gainesville area is less than 20 per cent, and no racial problems are apparent.

Gainesville is increasingly developing into a distribution and manufacturing center for North Central Florida. Among the light industries in the Gainesville area are electronic microwave production, the manufacturing of crates and boxes, poultry processing, printing and binding, metal foundries, lumber treating, the making of pine products, the manufacturing of concrete blocks, the production of masonry paints,

ALFRED A. RING, S.R.A., M.A.I.
Appraiser

cane syrup manufacture, bottling plants, and others. Over 3,700 persons are currently employed in the city's industrial plants and its environs, forming a total annual payroll of over $13,500,000.

In addition to the persons employed in industry and the retailing and wholesaling trades, the University of Florida employs over 6,500 persons in both academic and non academic capacities, with an annual payroll of over $52,000,000.

Gainesville has a modified city manager form of government. Five city commissioners are elected at large on a nonpartisan ballot. The city manager is professionally trained and has direct control over all governmental activities except finance, public utilities, law enforcement and the courts. The city owns and operates its own municipal power-generating and water-treatment plants. Utility rates are competitive with rates charged by the Rural Electrification Administration (REA), which supplies electricity in environing county areas.

Gainesville is served by both the Atlantic Coast Line Railway and the Seaboard Air Line Railway. Two passenger-bus lines, Greyhound and Trailways, operate through the local terminal, with forty buses entering and leaving daily. In addition, there is a local bus service with convenient schedules throughout the city. The Gainesville Airport is located five miles north of the city and is served by Eastern Air Lines. U. S. Highway 441, a major north-south arterial highway and Interstate 75 pass through the city. At the present time four-lane construction is authorized for an eventual four-lane highway from

ALFRED A. RING, S.R.A., M.A.I.
Appraiser

Gainesville to Orlando. State Roads 24, 20, 26, 331, and 329 afford connecting links to other cities in the state.

A police force of seventy-five men has an organized detective and traffic division to serve the city. The fire department has fifty-four men and nine pieces of motor equipment. The fire insurance rates are in the lowest bracket of any city of comparable size in the state.

Property taxes are levied at a rate of 10 mills and 20 mills respectively by city and county governments. This tax millage, however, is applied to assessed valuations that average 80 per cent of market value for city and county tax purposes.

Detailed facts and figures about Gainesville are provided in a booklet published by the local chamber of commerce. Generally, the outlook for real estate investment in Gainesville, the state's tenth largest city, is excellent.

ALFRED A. RING, S.R.A., M.A.I.
Appraiser

Neighborhood Data

The subject property is situated in a nearly 100 per cent developed area containing some of the oldest development in Gainesville. There is virtually no vacant land available in the neighborhood at the present time.

The neighborhood is located immediately to the East of the University of Florida campus. The area is bounded on the West by SW 13th Street; the North by University Avenue; the East by SW 10th Street to 5th Avenue thence South from 5th Avenue to SW 9th Street; and the South by SW 8th Avenue.

The area is predominantly zoned R-3, which permits occupancy by high-density, multi-family dwellings. The highest uses permitted by this zoning is apartments, townhouses, multiple dwellings, fraternities, dormitories and customary accessory buildings.

All public and quasi-public utilities such as gas, water, telephones, sewerage, electricity and cable TV are available in the area. The neighborhood has adequate fire and police protection.

Existing single-family residences average from 30 to 60 years in age; while apartment houses in the area tend to vary from new to 20 years in age. The neighborhood trend is toward construction of multi-unit apartment buildings. The trend is expected to continue with some redevelopment of existing residential properties for apartments and student oriented housing.

ALFRED A. RING, S.R.A., M.A.I.
Appraiser

The area is predominantly inhabited with students since the
University is within 5 minutes walking time from any location within
the neighborhood. Occupants of nearly all single-family residential
houses tend to be elderly couples or students.

The neighborhood is conveniently located - not only abutting
the University - but also near the central business district and Santa
Fe Junior College. Most public conveniences and facilities such as
bus routes, neighborhood shopping, churches, etc., are available in or
near the area. Neighborhood vacancies are relatively high in the Summer
months due to the proximity and reliance on the University. This likewise
contributes to relatively high tenant turnover in the area.

In view of the favorable location near the University of
Florida and the buffer zones created on the South by the sorority houses,
on the East by Alachua General Hospital and on the North by University
Avenue, the area is expected to maintain its appeal for University
oriented housing in the foreseeable future. Consequently, property
values should remain relatively stable, or even increase as the area
redevelops with apartment houses and University related structures.

ALFRED A. RING, S.R.A., M.A.I.
Appraiser

Site Data

The subject site is a corner lot situated on the Northwest corner of the intersection of SW 10th Street and SW 4th Avenue. The lot is rectangular in shape, fronting 150' on SW 10th Street to a depth of 120' along SW 4th Avenue. (See Addenda for plot plan.) No corner lot or depth factor adjustments are applied to the subject site since neither of these are expected to affect the utility of the lot for apartment houses purposes.

The abutting streets are dual-lane and are fitted with concrete curbs and gutters. The lot is of even contour and of sandy soil which permits ready absorption of normal rainfall. The site is shaded by several very large oak trees that enhance the location.

The plot is serviced by city water, electricity, natural gas, sewerage service, telephone service and cable TV. A fire hydrant is located at the corner of the lot. Mail is delivered daily. The subject site and surrounding area are moderately landscaped and appear well maintained.

The area to the East of the site is occupied by the Alachua General Hospital, while the lots to the South, West and North are improved with residential homes and apartment houses. The site, as well as most of the neighborhood, is zoned R-3, which permits apartments and University oriented multiple-family high-density site utilization.

ALFRED A. RING, S.R.A., M.A.I.
Appraiser

Property Data

The site is improved with three two-story concrete block structures. Each building contains four apartments, each containing two bedrooms, living-room, kitchen-dining room combination and one full bath. The floor plans for all 12 units are identical. An asphalt surfaced parking area for apartment residents is located on the rear 20 feet of the site.

The buildings are attractively designed and meet accepted architectural standards. The improvements are constructed of 8" x 8" x 16" concrete blocks. The sub-flooring is of concrete slab. The finished ground flooring is of terrazzo, the second floor is of hardwood construction. Windows are of aluminum frame and jalousie type, with tile window stools throughout. The structures appear to be in good consision. No cracks or settling was observed.

The flat roof is of tar and gravel, and was found to be in good condition. Interior walls are stucco. The bathrooms have tile wainscotting.

Each structure measures 70' x 27' x 22' (height), and contains 3,780 square feet of floor space (both floors), or a total of 83,186 cubic feet. Each building has a basement containing 3,000 additional cubic feet. The laundry facilities (coin-operated washer and dryer) are located in the basements of the two outside buildings.

Each apartment contains about 837 square feet, is well designed, and provides privacy with reference to location of bedrooms and bath. Room sizes are above average. (See Floor Plan in Addenda).

ALFRED A. RING, S.R.A., M.A.I.
Appraiser

The kitchen is conveniently arranged and well placed. The units are well ventilated, and have good lighting. Storage space is adequate.

Each building contains two furnished apartments upstairs and two unfurnished units downstairs. The furnished apartments are carpeted throughout, except for the kitchen area which is covered with asphalt tile. These units contain adequate furnishings for this price class.

All units contain:

1. A split-system central heating and air conditioning unit. The heating furnace has a 75,000 BTU output, while the condenser output of the air conditioner is two tons (24,000 BTU);

2. an electric range;

3. a refrigerator; and

4. a 30 gallon gas hot water heater.

The basements in the two outside buildings each contain:

1. a coin-operated washer;

2. a coin-operated dryer; and

3. a 30 gallon gas hot water heater.

A 3' x 30' stoop covers the front and rear entrances of each building. The site contains about 1,224 square feet of concrete sidewalks and 550 square yards of asphalt surfaced parking area.

The chronological age of the buildings is 12 years, while the effective age is estimated to be 10 years. The remaining economic life of the structures is estimated to be 40 years. See the depreciation schedule for the estimated economic lives of equipment, fixtures and building parts.

ALFRED A. RING, S.R.A., M.A.I.
Appraiser

See the Addenda for detailed information on the plot plan
and floor plan. Photographs of the kitchen, living room, and various
views of the site and improvements are also presented in the Addenda.

Room Layout and Orientation

Each unit in the three structures contains identical room
layout and orientation as described below.

Living Room. This room is 15.6' x 14.0', and contains a 4' x 8' picture
window. The area contains 4 electrical outlets and two air conditioning
outlets. The room has doors and openings to the stairwell, kitchen-
dining room area, and small hallway leading to the bath and bedrooms.
The ceiling is 8.5' in height.

Kitchen - Dining Room Combination. This area is located opposite the
living-room and is 11.4' x 14.3'. Entrance to the rear stairwell and
living-room may be made from this room. The kitchen has floor and wall
cabinets containing 11.4 linear feet. The floor cabinets have a formica
top and contain a double sink. The room contains two ceiling lights and
a 4' x 6' window. A refrigerator, electric range, a 10" exhaust fan
and range hood, and 3 electric outlets are located in the kitchen-dining
room area.

ALFRED A. RING, S.R.A., M.A.I.
Appraiser

Hall area. A small hall area, measuring about 3' x 4' connect the two bedrooms and bathroom areas with the living room. A 6.7' x 2.0' closet is located off the hall and contains the Lennox heating furnace (the air conditioning unit is located on a concrete slab on the ground outside the building). A second closet - located between the two bedroom entrances serves as a linen closet, and measures 1.7' x 6.7'. A third closet, which is situated by the bathroom entrance, serves as a storage closet, and also contains a 30 gallon gas hot water heater. This closet is 2.0' x 6.7'.

Master Bedroom. This room, measuring 12.8' x 15.0', contains a 4.0' x 6.0' picture window on one side of the room and a 3.2' x 4.3' window on the adjoining corner wall. A 12.8 linear foot closet and vanity is located along one of the walls. An overhead light and two electrical outlets are available in this room.

Second Bedroom. The second bedroom has two windows, each measuring 3.0' x 4.2'. A light fixture, two electrical outlets, and 11.4 linear foot closet (which contains a vanity) are located in this 11.4' x 12.2' corner room.

Bathroom. The bathroom floor is tiled with ceramic, while the walls are half tiled - with full tile around the tub-shower combination. The bathroom contains a tub, lavatory, toilet, mirror, and light. The room is ventilated with a 2.0' x 3.0' window over the tub.

ALFRED A. RING, S.R.A., M.A.I.
Appraiser

Stair-well. The stair-well, which is 8.0' wide, provides a front and rear entrance to each unit in the building. The front stair-well, providing entrance to each living-room, is carpeted throughout, while the rear stair-well, providing entrances to the kitchen-dining room area, has a hardwood finished floor over a plywood subflooring.

Utility Room. Entrance to this 8' x 16' basement is gained from the rear of the building. The area contains a coin-operated washer and dryer, and a gas-fired 30 gallon hot water heater. The fuse boxes are located in this room.

ALFRED A. RING, S.R.A., M.A.I.
Appraiser

The Appraisal Process

The valuation of property is generally undertaken by one of three approaches:

1. Summation, or Cost, Approach

2. Comparison, or Market, Approach

3. Economic, or Income, Approach

In this instance all three approaches to value were used to provide means for checking and counterchecking the results obtained. A correlation of the three approaches was made, and the final value was based on the appraiser's judgment of the comparative reliability of the method used. Brief descriptions of the basic procedure for each valuation approach follows:

Summation, or Cost Approach

Under this method, value is derived by estimating the replacement cost new of the building and other improvements, based on today's labor and material prices and present construction techniques. From this total a subtraction is made for accrued depreciation and the land value found by market comparison is then added to derive a summation estimate of value. In deriving the cost of the building, the total square feet contained within the outer walls of the structure were multiplied by the cost per square foot applicable to this type of structure. The square foot method rather than the cubic foot method of estimating was used because the former is quoted more readily by builders in this area.

ALFRED A. RING, S.R.A., M.A.I.
Appraiser

Comparison, or Market, Approach

Under this approach an estimate of value is derived by comparing the property under appraisal with other "bench mark" properties of similar size, quality and location that sold in recent times.

Economic, or Income, Approach

This approach is of primary importance in ascertaining the value of income-producing properties, such as apartments, commercial and industrial properties since value may be defined as "the present worth of future rights to income, or utility." Thus in the present report, the income approach is expected to provide the most reliable index of value.

The value estimate under this approach is derived by ascertaining the economic rent of the property (i.e., that income which is ascribable to the land under its highest and best use), deducting all reasonable operating expenses (as would be expected to be experienced under typical management), and then capitalizing the resultant net operating income by an appropriated rate of capitalization to obtain the present value of the forecasted income stream. This method provides an objective estimate of what a prudent investor would pay for the subject property - being sufficiently informed and having adequate time under normal conditions.

ALFRED A. RING, S.R.A., M.A.I.
Appraiser

Determination of Land Value by Market Comparison

A survey was made of land sales which have occurred in R-3 zoned areas (multi-family) or higher density areas in Gainesville within the past three years. Although about fifteen transactions were investigated, only reliable sales, which were considered to be comparable to the subject, were chosen to provide a basis for deriving land value in the subject location.

The four comparable land sales were confirmed as to price, terms and special circumstances of the transactions with the grantor or grantee. The prices of the sale lots were adjusted for differences (versus the subject site) in neighborhood, location, site facilities, plottage size and shape, and other adjustments in order to make the sale properties as nearly as possible comparable with the subject plot. Each of the sales were assigned a comparability rating - based on the adjustments - which was then applied to the price per square foot (adjusted for time) to derive a comparable value per square foot applicable to the subject location.

Market analysis indicates that land values in Gainesville have increased at an average rate of 10% over the past several years. This rapid rise can primarily be attributed to an increasing level of inflation, and to above state average population increases in Gainesville and Alachua County.

Sale No. 1 is situated near the border of the subject neighborhood and is considered to be only slightly inferior to the subject as to location and neighborhood. The site is similar to the subject with

ALFRED A. RING, S.R.A., M.A.I.
Appraiser

regards to site facilities and physical characteristics (terrain, etc.).

A time adjustment of 30% was made since the sale occurred three years ago. The subject site is judged – on the basis of the comparison factors – to about 15% better than land sale no. 1.

Sale No. 2 is a large tract (about 2.42 acres) located on the Archer Road across from the VA Hospital. The property was zoned R-3 at the time of the sale, but has since been rezoned B-P (Business Professional). Mr. Hanes, one of the parties to the transaction, indicated that the purchase price reflects the expected rezoning. It is judged that the higher zoning increased the value of the plot by about 50%. Thus, the sale price would need to be adjusted to about 67% of the actual consideration paid in order to reflect what the estimated transaction price would have been if no change in R-3 zoning had been expected.

The site is comparable to the subject with regards to location, neighborhood, and site facilities. A time adjustment of 10% was made to reflect the date of sale, and an over-all subject rating of 67% was assigned on the basis of the required adjustments and comparability with Sale No. 2.

Sale No. 3 is located just off North 13th Street at the 1500 block. The adjoining street does not have curbs and gutters, but the site is serviced by all utilities. The location and neighborhood are judged to be inferior to the subject site.

ALFRED A. RING, S.R.A., M.A.I.
Appraiser

The lot is zoned R-P (Residential Professional) - which is a slightly higher zoning than the subject (R-3). However, the grantee indicated that the site would probably be used for apartments; thus zoning is not expected to significantly effect the value of the sale versus subject site.

A time adjustment of 5% was made to reflect the date of the sale. Over-all, the subject is rated to be about 20% better than the vacant sale lot.

Sale No. 4, located just off South 13th Street at the 1900 block, is zoned R-3, and is serviced by all utilities. The adjoining street is, however, not curbed and guttered. The location and neighborhood are generally considered to be inferior to the subject property.

The date of sale and transaction price is adjusted to reflect the fact that the property was purchased on an option. In other words, it is assumed that the "meeting of the minds" occurred when the option was purchased. A time adjustment of 20% was required. The subject site was rated 20% better due to superior location, neighborhood, and site facilities.

The adjusted value per square foot of each land sale provides an indication of the value of the subject site since each was adjusted to provide for comparability. It is then necessary to correlate the land sales to yield a single indication of value per square foot of the subject land. Sale No. 3 was the most comparable since the adjustments were most reliable; while sale no. 2 was the least comparable (bought based on B-P zoning).

ALFRED A. RING, S.R.A., M.A.I.
Appraiser

Correlation weights of 25%, 15%, 35%, and 25% were assigned to sales 1-4 respectively based on their relative comparability with the subject site. Based on the correlation, a square foot value of $.75 was derived for the subject location - yielding a land value based on market comparison of $13,500 (18,000 sq. ft. @ $.75).

Detailed adjustments and calculations for the index sales are shown in the following recapitulation sheet.

ALFRED A. RING, S.R.A., M.A.I.
Appraiser

Land Value by Market Comparison: Recapitulation

Sale Reference No.	1	2	3	4
Report page				
Transaction Price	$5,000	$115,000	$45,000	$33,300
Date of Sale (time elapsed)	3 years	1 year	6 months	2 years
Time Adjustment Factor	1.30	1.10	1.05	1.20
Price Adjusted for Time	$6,500	$126,500	$47,250	$39,960
Size of Plot (sq.ft.)	8,750	105,464	88,205	61,768
Price per square foot	$.743	$1.199	$0.536	$0.647

Adjustment Factors: Subject by Comparison is (has):

Neighborhood	Better	Better	Better	Better
Location	Better	Same	Better	Better
Site facilities	Same	Same	Better	Better
Plot size & shape	Better	Poorer	Same	Same
Other Adjustments	None	Lower Zoning	Lower Zoning	None
Subject property rating	1.15	0.67	1.20	1.20
Comparable Value per square foot	$0,854	$0.804	$0.643	$0.776
Correlated Value per square foot		$0.75		

Value of Subject Land

Size of plot: 150' x 120' = 18,000 Sq. Ft.

Value per square foot   = $0.75

Land Value based on
Market Comparison   = 18,000 S.F. @ $0.75 = $13,500

ALFRED A. RING, S.R.A., M.A.I.
Appraiser

Property Value - Market Sale Analysis

  The market data approach is based on a comparison of prices
paid for similar properties in recent months. Adjustments are made for
differences in time, lot sizes (land is removed before further adjustments
are made), and other features of the subject property versus comparative
improved property sales. Adjusted sale prices are commonly analyzed on
the basis of apartment units, rooms, square feet, and gross income
multiplier.

  The sale prices are first adjusted for time differences
(versus the present) in order to obtain an estimation of what the
properties would bring if sold today. For the improved property sales,
it is estimated - based on market analysis - that about a 6% per annum
upward trend in prices has prevailed. This annual increase in sale
prices is due primarily to the current high levels of inflation and to
upward trending land values in the Gainesville area.

  Although a 10% annual time differential seems to be warranted
for unimproved land sales, only a 6% factor appears justified for
improved property sales in the Gainesville area due largely to leverage
of accrued building depreciation. Older apartment properties also are
unable to adjust their rental incomes upward at a sufficient rate to
keep pace with inflation and changing land values.

  In addition to the time adjustment, the transaction price is
adjusted to reflect differences in size of units (square feet),
effective age (years), type and quality of construction, general

ALFRED A. RING, S.R.A., M.A.I.
Appraiser

condition of the improvements, and extent of amenities of the sale
property versus the subject. A rating is assigned to each sale in
order to facilitate over-all comparability, yielding an adjusted
estimate which can be used to indicate the building value of the subject
property on a per unit, per room, and per square foot basis.

     The four recent sale properties used to derive market value
via this approach were chosen on the basis of comparability with the
subject. All properties were verified as to date and transaction price
with the grantor(s) or grantee(s). Data on the improvements were
obtained where possible from the current owner. Each sale site and its
improvement was carefully inspected to ascertain and evaluate comparability with the subject property.

     Sale No. 1 is abutting the subject property on the northern
boundary, and hence is highly comparable as to location, neighborhood,
site facilities, terrain, etc.

     The improvement is constructed of brick, and contains four
apartments - each unit having two bedrooms, living-room, dining-room,
kitchen and bath. The building has an estimated effective age of 20
years and contains about 4,177 square feet. The structure, which is
not air conditioned, appears to be in very good condition.

     A time adjustment of +3% was made to reflect the date of the
sale (six months ago). The subject property, due primarily to a 10 year
lower effective age, is judged to be 15% better than the sale property.
The indicated building value - after the adjustments - is computed on a
per unit, per room, and per square foot basis to yield translatable

ALFRED A. RING, S.R.A., M.A.I.
Appraiser

indicies of value for the subject property. A gross income multiplier
for the sale property was derived by dividing the unadjusted transaction
price by the gross annual revenue. See the recapitulation sheet for a
detailed presentation and analysis of the key market data.

Sale No. 2 is situated in the same neighborhood as the subject
property, and is comparably located. The plot has all site facilities
and has similar physical features (e.g., terrain) as the subject lot.

The site is improved with a two-story concrete block
structure containing 8 apartments - each unit having two bedrooms, living-
room, kitchen and bath. The effective age is estimated to be 15 years.
The building contains about 6,950 square feet, and is in poorer general
condition than the subject. The units are not air conditioned.

A time adjustment of 12% was required. The sale property was
generally comparable as to size of units, effective age, type of
construction, etc. Over-all the subject property is judged 10% better
than the sale property which is considered to be the most comparable of
the four properties with the subject. A gross multiplier of 6.25 was
obtained for sale no. 2.

Sale No. 3 is located on NW 5th Avenue in the 1500 block. The
site is roughly comparable with the subject as to neighborhood and
location. All site facilities are available.

The site is improved with two four-unit single-story concrete
block structures containing a total of about 4,200 square feet. Each
unit contains one bedroom, living-room, kitchen and bath. The buildings
have an estimated effective age of 8 years, and are air conditioned. The
property has been poorly maintained.

ALFRED A. RING, S.R.A., M.A.I.
Appraiser

The property sold 14 months ago, requiring a 7% time adjustment. In view of the small size of the rooms, and poor general
condition, the subject property is rated 15% better than sale no. 3.

Sale No. 4, located on N.W. 4th Avenue in the 1600 block, is
more poorly situated with respect to location and neighborhood than the
subject site. All site facilities are available.

The improvements are of concrete block single-story construction.
12 units are contained in three four-unit structures, each unit having
one bedroom, living-room, kitchen and bath. The three buildings contain
a total of about 5,616 square feet, and have an estimated effective age
of 6 years. The structures, which are air conditioned, have been poorly
maintained.

An adjustment of 12% was made to reflect the fact that the
sale occurred two years ago. The subject property is rated 20% better
than sale no. 4 in view of the small size of the rooms, the poorer
quality of construction, and the poor condition of the buildings.

After adjusting the four sales for comparability with the
subject, the indicated building value per unit, per room, per square
foot, and based on the gross income multiplier, were computed for each
sale property. The indicated market value of the subject property was
then derived from the correlated indicies of value provided by the sale
properties.

ALFRED A. RING, S.R.A., M.A.I.
Appraiser

The reasons for value weights assigned each sale property has been footnoted on the recapitulation sheet. In general, the weights, of course, reflect the degree of comparability of each sale property with the subject with regards to the various units of measure (per apartment, per room, etc.), and over-all comparability.

Based on the indicated correlated value per apartment, the market value of the subject property is $119,500, including land and improvements; while the value based on a per room basis is $120,200. The indicated value, based on the gross multiplier, is $119,300.

The final indicated value of the subject property, based on the market approach, is $119,300. This value estimate is based primarily on the gross income multiplier indication of value since no adjustments were required – while extensive adjustments were needed to derive the other value estimates. It should be noted that all indicies of value based on the market approach fall within a $900 range.

A detailed presentation and analysis of the key market data is contained in the following recapitulation sheet.

ALFRED A. RING, S.R.A., M.A.I.
Appraiser

Property Value by Market Comparison: Recapitulation

Sale Reference No.	1	2	3	4
Report Page				
Address	1005 SW 3rd Ave.	1236 SW 1st Ave.	1533 NW 5th Ave.	1624-32 NW 4th Ave.
Transaction Price	$41,500	$79,500	$74,200	$78,000
Date of Sale (time elapsed)	6 months	2 years	14 months	2 years
Time Adjustment Factor	1.03	1.12	1.07	1.12
Price Adjusted for Time	$42,745	$89,040	$79,394	$87,360
Size of Plot (sq. ft.)	12,000	12,826	22,400	27,600
Land Value	$9,000	$9,620	$16,800	$20,700
Depreciated Building Value	$33,745	$79,420	$62,594	$66,660
Adjustment Factors: Subject by Comparison is (has):				
Size of Units	-20%	-4%	+60%	+80%
Effective Age (years)	+10	+5	-2	-4
Type of Construction	Poorer	Same	Same	Same
Construction features	Better	Same	Same	Same
Quality of Construction	Same	Same	Better	Better
General condition	Same	Better	Better	Better
Amenities (air conditioning, etc.)	Better	Better	Better	Better
Subject property rating	1.15	1.10	1.15	1.20
Adjusted Building value	$38,807	$87,362	$71,983	$79,992
Number of Units	4	8	8	12
Number of Rooms	16	32	24	36

ALFRED A. RING, S.R.A., M.A.I.
Appraiser

Property Value by Market Comparison: Recapitulation (cont).

Building Area (sq.ft.)   4,177   6,950   4,200   5,616

Indicated Building Value:

Per Unit	$9,702	$10,920	$9,000	$6,666
Per Room	$2,426	$2,730	$3,000	$2,222
Per Square Foot	$9.29	$12.57	$17.14	$14.24
Gross Annual Revenue	$6,000	$12,000	$9,120	$15,120
Gross Multiplier	6.9	6.25	8.1	5.15

Market Value of Subject Property

12 apartments @ $8,834[1] per unit = $106,008

Add Land Value   13,500

    Indicated Value on Unit
    Comparison Basis (rounded) $119,500

48 rooms @ $2,222[2]   = $106,656

Add: Land Value   13,500

    Indicated Value on Room
    Comparison Basis (rounded) $120,200

None of the sale properties were comparable

    on a square foot basis with the subject

    property due to the wide variations in

    volume of building area (subject =

    10,044 sq.ft.) and type of construction.

Gross income ($19,080 x 6.25[3] (multiplier)   = $119,250

    Indicated Value on Basis of Gross

      Income Multiplier (rounded)   = $119,300

    Indicated Value via Market Approach[4]   = $119,300

ALFRED A. RING, S.R.A., M.A.I.
Appraiser

(1)
  Sale properties 2 and 4 were weighted 40% each to reflect their higher degree of comparability with the subject (No. 2 requires the fewest adjustments; while No. 4 has the same number of buildings and units as subject). Sale No. 3 was weighted only 20% (8 units vs. 12 for subject), and Sale No. 1 received no weight since it contains only 4 units.

(2)
  Sale No. 4 was weighted 100% since it was the only property having 12 units (same as subject), and has the most comparable number of total rooms.

(3)
  Since sale no. 2 is most comparable over-all (namely, same location and neighborhood, same type of construction and construction features, and the fewest adjustments for size of units and effective age), the gross multiplier was based principally on this sale. Note also that the multipliers of the other sale properties bracket the multiplier of sale no. 2.

(4)
  The indicated value via the market approach was based on the gross income multiplier since fewer adjustments are required, and since sale no. 2 is most comparable – of the sales – with the subject property. Note that this indicated value is within $1,000 of the value indicated on the basis of units and rooms.

ALFRED A. RING, S.R.A., M.A.I.
Appraiser

The Cost Approach To Value

Unit cost estimates for the subject property could not be obtained from market cost comparison since no similar buildings were constructed nor have sold in recent times. Reliance on base unit costs was placed on cost estimates obtained from three leading builders in the Gainesville area. The consensus of these builders is that buildings comparable to the subject property, exclusive of equipment and furnishings can be constructed on date of the appraisal for $10.25 per square foot. Based on this estimate the depreciated replacement cost of the subject property was obtained as follows:

Base cost per square foot		$10.25
Add: Base cost adjustments:		
Furniture - 6 units @ $1,000 =	$6,000	
Equipment laundry room - 2 @ $600 =	1,200	
Ranges - 12 @ $200 =	2,400	
Refrigerators - 12 @ $200 =	2,400	
Total	$12,000	
Cost of adjustments per square foot: $12,000 ÷ 11,340 =		1.05
Adjusted cost per square foot		11.30

Estimated replacement cost, new:

   Main buildings:

      11,340 sq. ft. @ $11.30 = $128,142

ALFRED A. RING, S.R.A., M.A.I.
Appraiser

Add: Parking area - asphalt

        550 sq. yds. @ $1.75   =   963

     Sidewalks -

        1,224 sq. ft. @ $.50   =   612

     Landscaping   =   300

Total estimated replacement cost,

   new - all improvements $130,110

Less: Accrued Depreciation

   (see schedule)   22,892

Depreciated replacement cost $107,218

Add: Value of Land - by comparison

   18,000 sq. ft. @ $0.75   =   13,500

Indicated Value via Cost Approach $120,718

             Rounded to $120,700

ALFRED A. RING, S.R.A., M.A.I.
Appraiser

Depreciation Schedule

Physical Deterioration

Curable:

    Deferred Maintenance:

        Resurface parking area

            550 sq. yds. @ \$1.00 =   \$ 550

        Refinish terrazzo floors

            6 @ \$50 =   300

    Total deferred maintenance   \$ 850

    Reserve for Replacement*:

        Refrigerators: $12/15 \times \$2,400$ =   \$1,920

        Ranges: $12/15 \times \$2,400$ =   1,920

        Water Heaters: $12/15 \times \$980$ =   784

        Dryers: $5/10 \times \$400$ =   200

        Washers: $5/10 \times \$400$ =   200

        Roof: $12/20 \times \$1,360$ =   816

        Plumbing & Electrical:

            $12/25 \times \$4,500$ =   2,160

        Furniture: $12/15 \times \$6,000$ =   4,800

        Carpets: $4/12 \times \$3,000$ =   1,000

        Heating & Air Conditioning:

            $12/15 \times \$6,600$ =   5,280

---

*Reserves for replacement are based on straight line depreciation.

ALFRED A. RING, S.R.A., M.A.I.
Appraiser

Painting & Decorating:

    exterior - 4/5 x $1,200 = $ 960

    interior - 2/5 x $1,200 =   480

    Total Reserves for Replacement $20,520

Incurable:

    Liability to replace, based on diminished

        utility and caused by effective age of

        10 years, at 8.5% rate of interest

    Present worth factor 50 years   =   11.5656

    Present worth factor 40 years   =   11.3145

    Liability factor   =   0.2511

    Incurable loss:

        0.2511 ÷ 11.5656 = .0217 or

        2.17% of $116,235   =   2,522

Total Physical Deterioration $22,892

Functional Obsolescence:

    Curable: None

    Incurable: None

    Total Functional Obsolescence   None

Economic Obsolescence:

    Incurable: None

Total Estimate of Accrued Depreciation $22,892

Per Cent Accrued Depreciation:

    $22,892 ÷ $130,110   =   16.8%

ALFRED A. RING, S.R.A., M.A.I.
Appraiser

Income Approach To Value

The income approach for apartment house properties is the most reliable indication of value. The purchaser in effect relates the purchase price to the anticipated net income which will provide a return on and of his total investment over the remaining economic life of the income producing property.

The first step under the income approach is to determine the economic rent which the property can produce under typical management. This economic rent was derived by market comparison with similar apartment properties as shown on the "Economic Rent Schedule" below.

Economic Rent Schedule

Rental Reference No.	1	2	3	4
Name of Apts.	May Apts.	Parklane Apts.	Thomas Apts.	Tyson Apts.
Address	1210 SW 3rd Ave.	1306 SW 13th St.	1716 NW 3rd Ave.	1508 NW 4th Ave.
Number of units	12	12	12	8
Number of rooms	48	48	48	32
Gross sq. ft. - bldg.	8,750	8,208	10,200	6,000
Gross sq. ft. - apt.	729	684	850	750
Gross annual rent - bldg.	$16,920	$16,320	$18,000	$9,120
Gross annual rent - apt. furnished	$1,500	$1,440	$1,500	---
unfurnished	$1,320	$1,200	---	$1,140
Gross annual rent - per sq. ft.:				

ALFRED A. RING, S.R.A., M.A.I.
Appraiser

furnished	$2.06	$2.11	$1.76	---
unfurnished	$1.81	$1.90	---	$1.52

Gross annual rent - per room:

furnished	$375	$360	$375	---
unfurnished	$330	$300	---	$285

Adjustment Factors: Subject by comparison is (has):

Size of apt (sq.ft.)	+108	+153	Same	+87
Quality & finish	Better	Better	Same	Better
Location	Same	Better	Better	Better
Amenities	Better	Same	Better	Better
Tenantry	Better	Better	Better	Better
Subject property rating:	1.15	1.20	1.10	1.25

Indicated rental:

per apartment:

furnished	$1,725	$1,728	$1,650	---
unfurnished	$1,515	$1,440	---	$1,425

per square foot:

furnished	$2.36	$2.53	$1.94	---
unfurnished	$2.08	$2.28	---	$1.90

per room:

furnished	$431	$432	$413	---
unfurnished	$380	$360	---	$356

ALFRED A. RING, S.R.A., M.A.I.
Appraiser

Indicated economic rent for subject property:

	Correlated* Rental	Rounded to Nearest $5 per month
per apartment:		
furnished	$1,684	$1,680
unfurnished	1,474	1,500
per square foot:		
furnished	$2.27	$2.27
unfurnished	2.09	2.09
per room:		
furnished	$426	$420
unfurnished	369	375

Indicated economic rent for subject property:

6 furnished   units @ $1,680   = $10,080

6 unfurnished units @ $1,500   =   9,000

          Total economic rent $19,080

_____

*The rentals were assigned weights based on their relative comparability with the subject property as follows:

Property No. 1:   50% / 50% for furn. & unfurn. apartments respectively

Property No. 2:   20% / 25% for furn. & unfurn. apartments respectively

Property No. 3:   30% / -- for furn. & unfurn. apartments respectively

Property No. 4:   --- / 25% for furn. & unfurn. apartments respectively

Totals   100% 100% for furn. & unfurn. apartments respectively

ALFRED A. RING, S.R.A., M.A.I.
Appraiser

Based on rental analysis as shown above the subject property can command an income as follows:

    Furnished apartment $140 per month or $1,680 per annum

    Unfurnished apartment $125 per month or $1,500 per annum

These rental estimates were confirmed and judged accurate by leading Realtors in the community.

A detailed application of the income approach to value is as follows:

Gross Revenue - stabilized - per year		$18,800*
Less 2% vacancy & collection losses		376
Effective revenue		$18,424

Less Operating Expenses:

Fixed expenses

Real Estate taxes	$2,844	
Insurance	170	
Pest Control	65	

Maintenance

Management	1,500	
Utilities	850	
Heating & Air Conditioning	200	
Repairs	200	

*To reflect declining income over the economic building life the gross revenue of $19,320 was stabilized at $18,800 to reflect a rental decline of $10 per month per apartment at 10 year intervals.

ALFRED A. RING, S.R.A., M.A.I.
Appraiser

Reserve for replacement

Refrigerators	160	
Ranges	160	
Water Heaters	65	
Dryers	40	
Washers	40	
Heating & Cooling Equipment	440	
Furniture	400	
Carpets	250	
Decorating	480	
Plumbing & Electrical	180	
Roof	80	

Total Operating Expenses	8,124
Net stabilized income	$10,300
Less income attributable to land	
$13,500 x .085 =	1,148
Income attributable to building	$ 9,152

Capitalized value of building income over

   remaining economic life of 40 years at

   8.5% interest under the annuity method =

$9,152 x 11.31452 (Inwood Factor) =	$103,550
Add Land Value – by Comparison	13,500
Value Via income approach	$117,050

Rounded to $117,000

ALFRED A. RING, S.R.A., M.A.I.
Appraiser

Rate of Capitalization

The rate of capitalization was derived from analysis of market transaction of comparable income producing properties.[1] This rate was then further tested for accuracy via the band of investment method as follows:

Property Sale No.	1	2	3	4
1. Reported operating income	$4,500	$7,800	$7,300	$7,500
2. Sale Price of Property	$41,500	$79,500	$74,200	$78,000
3. Indicated Land Value	$9,000	$9,620	$16,800	$20,700
4. Residual building value	$32,500	$69,880	$57,400	$57,300
5. Over-all rate of capitalization	10.85	9.81	9.84	9.62
6. Remaining life of property	30	35	42	44
7. Rate of annual depreciation[2]	2.5	2.0	1.5	1.5
8. Ratio of building value	78.3	87.9	77.4	73.5

---

[1] These are the same sale properties previously analyzed under the market comparison approach to value.

[2] Market indicated depreciation rates of 1.5% for first 10 years of effective age, 2% for next ten years and 2.5% for properties aged 20 years and more.

ALFRED A. RING, S.R.A., M.A.I.
Appraiser

Rate of Capitalization (cont.)

9. Adjusted rate of recapture	2.0	1.76	1.16	1.10
10. Rate of return (Item 5 less item 9)	8.85	8.05	8.68	8.52
11. Subject property rating	.95	1.05	.975	1.00
12. Adjusted interest rate	8.41	8.45	8.46	8.52
13. Rounded to	8.5%			

Band of Investment Approach

Loan and Equity Per Cent of Value		Current Yield Rates	Weighted Rates
First Mortgage	.70 x	7.75	5.425
Second Mortgage	.15 x	9.00	1.350
Equity	.15 x	12.50	1.875
		Composite Rate	8.650

Rounded to 8.5%

ALFRED A. RING, S.R.A., M.A.I.
Appraiser

Correlation of Value Estimates

Value via cost approach $120,700

Value via market approach   119,300

Value via income approach   117,000

Final estimate of value $117,000

Explanation of correlation judgement:

The cost approach is a reliable guide to value where the
buildings are new and the site has been put to its highest and best
use. However, when depreciation must be estimated to reflect physical
deterioration, and functional and economic obsolescence, it becomes
increasingly difficult to accurately estimate value by this approach.
In the present appraisal, the cost approach is used as an index of
value to check the final indication of value derived by the other
approaches, and thus has not been assigned any weight in the final
value conclusion.

The market approach yields a reliable indication of value
where sales are recent and reasonably similar to the subject property.
However, where sales are one to three years old and extensive adjustments
are required to make the sale and subject properties comparable, the
value estimate by this approach can serve only as a guide to value –
providing a useful check on the accuracy of the income approach. Since
only one of the sales occurred within the last year and considerable

ALFRED A. RING, S.R.A., M.A.I.
Appraiser

adjustments were necessary, no weight has been assigned to this approach in the final estimate of value.

The income approach is of primary importance in ascertaining the value of income-producing property since value may be defined as "the present worth of future rights to income, or utility." In the present appraisal, sufficiently comprehensive income and expense data was available to process a reliable indication of value for the subject apartment house.

Complete reliance was placed on the income approach in this report since the property is income-producing and in view of the relative reliability of the three approaches. The value estimates by the cost and market approaches are within 3% (or $3600) of the value conclusion obtained by the income approach, providing a useful check on the accuracy of the final estimate of value of $117,000 for the subject apartment house.

ALFRED A. RING, S.R.A., M.A.I.
Appraiser

Trial interest yield rate of 9%

    Present worth of $8,928 for 5 years

        $8,928 x 3.890 = $34,730

    Present worth of reversion of

        $126,637 x .65 =   82,314

    Total present value of equity at 9% $117,044

Interpolation for accurate yield rate:

    1. Equity value at 8%   = $121,890

        Equity value at 9%   =   117,044

        Difference caused by 1% = $ 4,846

    2. Equity value at 8%   = $121,890

        Equity value at x%   =   120,000

        Difference $ 1,890

    Derivation of yield rate:

    $1,890 ÷ $4,846 = .39

    'x' = 8% + .39% = 8.39%

ALFRED A. RING, M. A. I.
Appraiser

Statement of Limiting Conditions

The market value set forth in this appraisal report is subject to the following limiting conditions:

1. This property has been appraised as though free of liens and encumbrances other than those contained in the deed of record.

2. No responsibility is to be assumed for matters legal in nature, nor is any opinion of title rendered by this report. Good title is assumed.

3. Both legal description and dimensions are taken from sources thought to be authoritative; however, no responsibility is assumed for either unless a survey, by a competent surveyor or engineer, is furnished to the appraiser.

4. The sale of the subject property is assumed to be on an all cash basis. Financial arrangements would affect the price at which the property may sell for if placed on the market.

5. The appraiser, by reason of this report, is not required to give testimony in court, with reference to the appraised property, unless arrangements for such a contingency have been previously agreed upon.

ALFRED A. RING, S.R.A., M.A.I.
Appraiser

6. The physical condition of the improvements was based on visual inspection. No liability is assumed for the soundness of the structure since no engineering tests were made of the buildings.

7. Possession of any copy of this report does not carry with it the right of publication, nor may it be used for any purpose by anyone, except the addressee (Mr. Thomas B. Wright) and the property owner, without the previous written consent of the appraiser, and, in any event, only may be revealed in its entirety.

ALFRED A. RING, S.R.A., M.A.I.
Appraiser

Certification

This is to certify that the undersigned has made a careful personal inspection of the property legally described herein and that all findings, statements and opinions submitted in this report are correct to the best of his knowledge.

This appraisal was prepared for demonstration purposes and the valuation estimate certified below is not contingent on any monetary fees or interests whatsoever.

The appraiser has no present or prospective interest in the subject property and the fee agreed upon is in no way related or contingent upon the value reported.

It is further certified that this appraisal has been made in conformity with the professional standards of the American Institute of Real Estate Appraisers and the Society of Real Estate Appraisers of which the undersigned is a member.

The market value of the property as described herein is certified as of January 10, 19--, to be:

One Hundred Seventeen Thousand Dollars

($117,000)

Certified by,

Alfred A. Ring, M.A.I., S.R.A.

Consultant - Appraiser

ALFRED A. RING, S.R.A., M.A.I.
Appraiser

Qualifications of Appraiser

Education

Bachelor of Science - Magna Cum Laude - 1942
Master of Business Administration - 1945
Doctor of Philosophy - 1947
New York University

Professional Membership

Gainesville Board of Realtors
Florida State Association of Realtors (Life Member)
National Association of Real Estate Boards
Director, Jacksonville Chapter, Society of Real Estate
    Appraisers
American Institute of Real Estate Appraisers
Society of Real Estate Appraisers
American Economic Association
Southern Economic Association

Experience

Professor of Real Estate and Chairman of Department
    University of Florida

University Appraiser since 1951

Dean of American Institute Urban and Farm Appraising
    Courses at University of Florida

Member Faculty of New York University, Department of
    Real Estate, 1941 - 1947

Senior Estimator, Westchester Lighting Company, Mount
    Vernon, New York, 1935 - 1941

Certified Verterans' Administration Appraiser and Compliance
    Inspector

Expert witness in Florida Circuit Court

ALFRED A. RING, S.R.A., M.A.I.
Appraiser

Publication

        Co-author: "Real Estate Principles and Practices,"
        6th Edition, Prentice-Hall, Inc., 1967.

        Author: "Question and Problems in Real Estate Principles
        and Practices," Revised Edition, Prentice-Hall, Inc.,
        1967.

        Author: "The Valuation of Real Estate," 2nd ed.,
        Prentice-Hall, Inc., 1970.

        Author of articles on Appraisal subject published in:
        Appraisal Journal, Society of Residential Appraisers
        Review, Technical Valuation, Journal of Living,
        Encyclopedia Americana, Economic Leaflets, University
        of Florida.

Appraisal Clients

        University of Florida
        Florida State Road Department
        Alachua County Commissioners
        Alachua County School Board
        Marion County Commissioners
        U. S. Army Corps of Engineers
        First National Bank of Gainesville
        Veterans' Administration
        Catholic Student Center of Gainesville
        Attorneys in Jacksonville and Gainesville
        Numerous private clients throughout Florida

Remarks

        For additional and personal data, please refer to listing in:

        1. Who's Who in American Education

        2. Who's Who in the South and Southeast

        3. American Men of Science III

ALFRED A. RING, S.R.A., M.A.I.
Appraiser

Part III

ADDENDA

ALFRED A. RING, S.R.A., M.A.I.
Appraiser

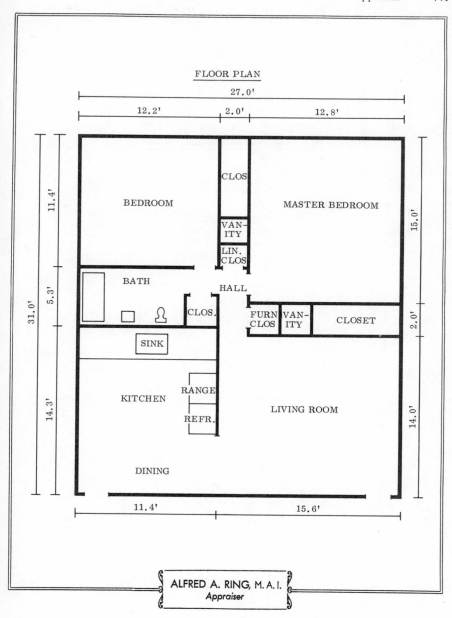

FLOOR PLAN

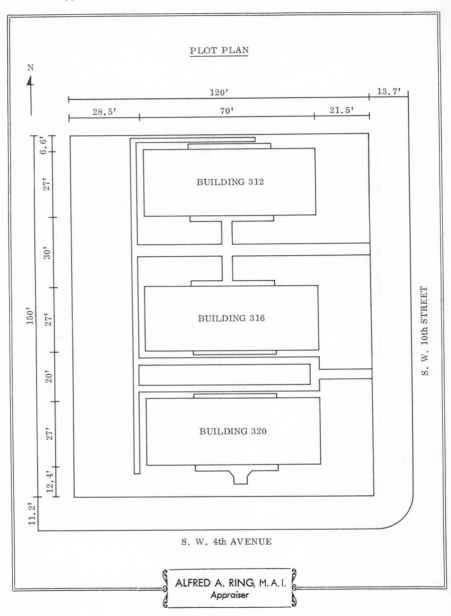

PLOT PLAN

N

120'   13.7'

28.5'   70'   21.5'

6.6'

27'

BUILDING 312

30'

150'   27'

BUILDING 316

20'

27'

BUILDING 320

12.4'

11.2'

S. W. 10th STREET

S. W. 4th AVENUE

ALFRED A. RING, M. A. I.
Appraiser

Additional Photographs

of

Subject Property

View of Interior Court

View of Kitchen Equipment

ALFRED A. RING, S.R.A., M.A.I.
Appraiser

Land Sale No. 1

Location: Intersection SW 8th Avenue and SW 9th Street

Legal Description: Porters Addition, Plat Book A-54, West ½ of Lots 111
and 112 as per Official Records Book 382, Page 223
of the Public Records of Alachua County, Florida.

Lot Size: 140' x 62.5' (8,750 S.F.)

Date of Sale: April 8, 19--

Grantors: Wilbur and Francis W. Bishop, et. al.

Grantee: Donald I. Grauer

Indicated Price: $5,000

Revenue Stamps: Florida Documentary $15.00

Deed Book: OR 382, Page 223

Transaction confirmed by Mr. Bishop.

Remarks: Situated in slightly poorer neighborhood and location
than subject. Same site facilities as subject. The
vacant lot is zoned R-3 (multiple family - high
density) and is sufficiently large to permit 4 one-
bedroom apartment units.

ALFRED A. RING, S.R.A., M.A.I.
Appraiser

Land Sale No. 2

Location: Intersection SW 16th Street and Archer Road

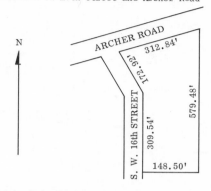

Legal Description: McDonald Acres, Plat Book D-22, Lot 2, as per Official
Records Book 488, Page 173 of the Public Records of
Alachua County, Florida.

Lot Size: Irregular lot containing circa 105,646 square feet
(about 2.42 acres).

Date of Sale: January 18, 19--

Grantors: Ida M. and R. W. Munson

Grantees: E. Finley Cannon, Jr., and wife, May S. Cannon, et. al.

Indicated Price: $115,000

Revenue Stamps: Florida Documentary $345.00

Deed Book: OR 486, Page 173

Transaction confirmed by Mr. Myrl J. Hanes.

Remarks: The site is situated in a desirable location across the
street from the VA and University Hospitals. Same site
facilities as the subject. The property was zoned R-3
at the time of sale but has since been rezoned B-P
(Business Professional). Mr. Hanes indicated that the
purchase price reflects the expected rezoning.

ALFRED A. RING, S.R.A., M.A.I.
Appraiser

Land Sale No. 3

Location: Intersection NW 12th Street and NW 15th Avenue

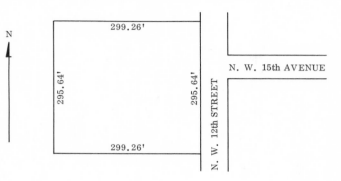

Legal Description: J. B. Bailey Estate, Deed Book K-203, S. 295.64 ft. of
N. 473.64 ft. of E. 299.26 ft. of E ½ of Lot 3 as per
Official Records Book 527, Page 231 of the Public
Records of Alachua County, Florida.

Lot Size: 295.64' x 299.26' (88,205 S.F.)

Date of Sale: September 4, 19--

Grantors: Emmette E. and Bertha Lee Holloway

Grantee: Stephen Shey

Indicated Price: $45,000

Revenue Stamps: Florida Documentary $135.00

Deed Book: OR 527, Page 231

Transaction confirmed by Mr. Shey.

Remarks: The site is in a slightly poorer neighborhood and
location than the subject, and does not have curbs and
gutters abutting the plot. The vacant lot is zoned R-P
(Residential Professional), but the grantee indicated
the site was purchased for the purpose of erecting
apartments (which is permitted in R-P zoning).

ALFRED A. RING, S.R.A., M.A.I.
Appraiser

Land Sale No. 4

Location: Intersection S. W. 19th Avenue and S. W. 14th Street

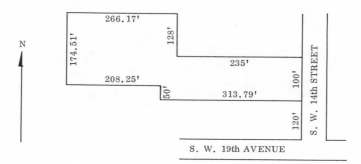

Legal Description: Commence at a point 3480.9 ft. S/LY + 355.5 ft. W/LY
from NE Corner of Section POB S. 100 ft., W/LY 313.79 ft.,
N/LY 50 ft., W/LY 208.25 ft., N/LY 174.51 ft., E/LY
266.17 ft., S. 128 ft., E/LY 235 ft. POB, as per Offical
Records Book 477, Page 44 of the Public Records of
Alachua County, Florida.

Lot Size: Irregular lot containing circa 1.418 acres, more or
less (ca. 61,768 S.F.)

Date of Sale: Early 19-- (option) - November 7, 19-- (deed)

Grantors: Rodger Q. and Blanche F. Bault

Indicated Price: $33,300 (includes option price)

Revenue Stamps: Florida Documentary $84.90

Deed Book: OR 477, Page 44

Transaction confirmed by Mr. Stephen Shey.

Remarks: Situated in poorer neighborhood and location than
subject. Site not serviced by curbs and gutters.
Same R-3 zoning as subject.

ALFRED A. RING, S.R.A., M.A.I.
Appraiser

Property Sale No. 1

Location: 1005 SW 3rd Avenue

Legal Description: University Heights, Lots 20 and 21 of Block 5, as per
                   Mortgage Book 104, Page 10 of the Public Records of
                   Alachua County, Florida.

Property Data: Brick construction containing 4 apartments - each unit
                       having two bedrooms, living room, dining room, kitchen
                       and bath. The building has an estimated effective age
                       of 20 years and contains about 4,177 square feet. The
                       structure appears to be in very good condition. The
                       units are not air conditioned.

Lot Data: The site abuts the subject lot, and is adequately
                       drained and nicely landscaped. The lot has all site
                       facilities and is in same neighborhood and location as
                       the subject.

Lot Size: 100' x 120' (12,000 sq. ft.)

Indicated Price: $41,500

Date of Sale: October 5, 19 --

Grantors: Mary L. and E. W. Moeller

Grantees: Darell E. and Mary I. McCloud

ALFRED A. RING, S.R.A., M.A.I.
Appraiser

Property Sale No. 1 (cont.)

Deed Book: 534, Page 272

Revenue Stamps: Florida Documentary $124.50

Sale confirmed by Mrs. Mary Moeller.

ALFRED A. RING, S.R.A., M.A.I.
Appraiser

Property Sale No. 2

Location: 1236 SW 1st Avenue

Legal Description: University Place, Lots 17 and 18 of Block 3, as per
                           Plat Book A-77 and Official Records Book 433, Page 111
                           of the Public Records of Alachua County, Florida.

Property Data: Concrete block construction containing 8 apartments –
                           each unit having two bedrooms, living room, kitchen
                           and bath. Effective age is estimated to be 15 years.
                           Structure is in poorer condition than subject and
                           contains about 6,950 square feet. The units are not
                           air conditioned.

Lot Data: The site is situated in the same neighborhood as the
                           subject, and has a comparable location. All site
                           facilities are available. The site is very comparable
                           with the subject plot.

Lot Size: 106' x 121' (12,826 sq. ft.)

Indicated Price: $79,500

Date of Sale: March 23, 19 --

Grantors: Cyrus W. and Gloria I. Durbin

Grantee: Jack C. May

ALFRED A. RING, S.R.A., M.A.I.
Appraiser

Property Sale No. 2 (cont).

Deed Book: 433, Page 111

Revenue Stamps: Florida Documentary $225.00

Sale confirmed by Mr. Jack C. May.

ALFRED A. RING, S.R.A., M.A.I.
Appraiser

Property Sale No. 3

Location: 1533 N. W. 5th Avenue

Legal Description: Leonard Subdivision Lot 55 as per Plat Book A-44.
                   Commence NW Corner of Lot 3 E. 418.13 feet POB, E.
                   160.17 feet, S. 138.30 feet, W. 161.38 feet, N. 139.93
                   feet to POB as recorded in Official Records Book 477,
                   Page 407 of the Public Records of Alachua County,
                   Florida.

Property Data: Concrete block single-story construction. Two four-
                   unit buildings containing a total of about 4,200 square
                   feet, and having an estimated effective age of 8 years.
                   The structures have been poorly maintained. The
                   apartments have air conditioning.

Lot Data: The plot is furnished with all site facilities.
                   Location and neighborhood are comparable with the
                   subject site.

Lot Size: ca. 161' x 139' (22,400 sq.ft.)

Indicated Price: $74,200

Date of Sale: December 1, 19--

Grantors: James L. and Ruby D. Sanders

Grantee: Jack L. and Sally C. Giles

ALFRED A. RING, S.R.A., M.A.I.
Appraiser

Property Sale No. 3 (cont.)

Deed Book: 477, Page 407

Revenue Stamps: Florida Documentary $222.60

Sale confirmed by Dr. Jack Giles.

ALFRED A. RING, S.R.A., M.A.I.
Appraiser

Property Sale No. 4

Location: 1624 - 32 N. W. 4th Avenue

Legal Description: Leonard Subdivision Lot 55 as per Plat Book A-44.
                         W. 208.2 feet of Lot 4 as recorded in Offical Records
                         Book 429, Page 330 of the Public Records of Alachua
                         County, Florida.

Property Data: Concrete block single-story construction. Three four-
                         unit buildings containing a total of about 5,616
                         square feet, and having an estimated effective age of
                         6 years. The structures are in poorer general
                         condition than the subject property. The apartments
                         have air conditioning.

Lot Data: The site is situated in a poorer neighborhood than
                         subject, but has only a slightly less desirable
                         location. The plot has all site facilities.

Lot Size: 132.5' x 208.3' (27,600 sq. ft.)

Indicated Price: $78,000

Date of Sale: March 2, 19--

Grantor: Florida Tile Roof, Inc.

Grantees: A. W. and Mary Elizabeth Row

ALFRED A. RING, S.R.A., M.A.I.
Appraiser

Property Sale No. 4 (cont.)

Deed Book: 429, Page 330

Revenue Stamps: Florida Documentary $234.00

Sale confirmed by Mr. Row.

ALFRED A. RING, S.R.A., M.A.I.
Appraiser

Area Map

of

Subject and Sale Properties

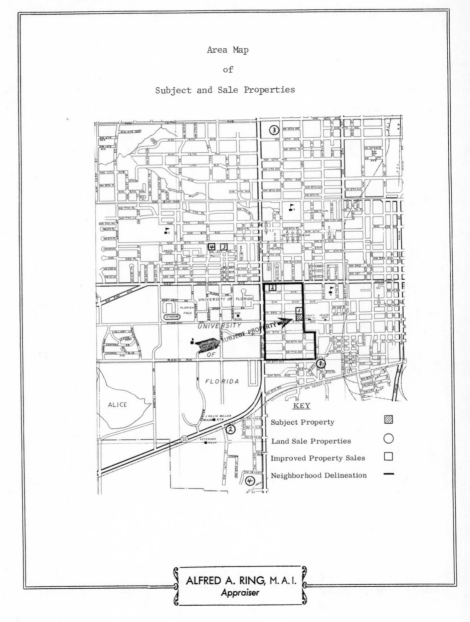

KEY

Subject Property	▨
Land Sale Properties	○
Improved Property Sales	□
Neighborhood Delineation	—

ALFRED A. RING, M.A.I.
Appraiser

NARRATIVE APPRAISAL REPORT

FOR

SINGLE FAMILY RESIDENCE

ALFRED A. RING, S.R.A., M.A.I.
Appraiser

Valuation Report

for

Single Family Residence

Prepared for

Mr. John B. Hopeful

16 N. W. 20th Terrace

Gainesville, Florida

ALFRED A. RING, S.R.A., M.A.I.
Appraiser

Route 3, Box 186 A-1
Gainesville, Florida
January 15, 19--

Mr. John B. Hopeful
16 N. W. 20th Terrace
Gainesville, Florida

Dear Mr. Hopeful:

In compliance with your request the undersigned has
completed an appraisal of residential property owned and occupied
by you at 16 N. W. 20th Terrace in Gainesville, Florida. This
property is legally described as follows:

> Lot 3 and the North five feet of lots 1 and 2 and the
> South fifteen feet of lot 4, Block 2 College Court
> Subdivision as recorded in public records of Alachua
> County, Florida.

Please be informed that a careful and personal inspection
was made of this residential site and its building improvements and
that due consideration was given to all factors and forces that influence property value at the subject location.

The attached report contains an analysis of general and
specific data which was deemed essential to support the estimate
of value as reported herein under the cost, market and income
approaches to value.

As a result of my investigation and findings it is my
considered and professional opinion that your residential property,
as described above, warrants a market value as of the date of this
appraisal in the amount of _____

ALFRED A. RING, S.R.A., M.A.I.
Appraiser

Mr. John B. Hopeful
Page 2
January 15, 19--

Sixteen Thousand Five Hundred Dollars

($16,500)

Should questions arise in connection with this report or
if I can be of further assistance in this or other matters, please
feel free to call upon me.

Respectfully submitted,

Alfred A. Ring, S.R.A., M.A.I.
Consultant - Appraiser

ALFRED A. RING, S.R.A., M.A.I.
Appraiser

ALFRED A. RING, M. A. I.
Appraiser

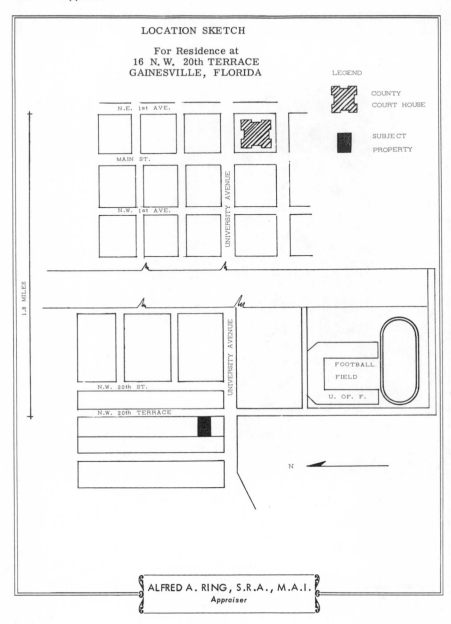

LOCATION SKETCH

For Residence at
16 N. W. 20th TERRACE
GAINESVILLE, FLORIDA

LEGEND

COUNTY
COURT HOUSE

SUBJECT
PROPERTY

N.E. 1st AVE.

MAIN ST.

N.W. 1st AVE.

UNIVERSITY AVENUE

1.8 MILES

UNIVERSITY AVENUE

N.W. 20th ST.

N.W. 20th TERRACE

FOOTBALL
FIELD

U. OF. F.

N

ALFRED A. RING, S.R.A., M.A.I.
Appraiser

Purpose of the Appraisal

The purpose of this appraisal is to establish an estimate of market value of the residential property described herein as of January 15, 1970. This report is prepared to furnish a guide as to the sales price that the subject property should command if exposed for sale in the open market on the date of this appraisal.

Definition of Market Value

Market value, for purposes of this report, is defined as follows:

The estimated price in terms of money which a property will bring if exposed for sale in the open market, allowing a reasonable time to find a purchaser who buys with knowledge of all the use to which the property is adopted and for which it is capable of being used.

In this definition it is assumed that the transaction is based on cash or cash equivalent considerations. Favorable or unfavorable terms of sale are bound to affect the transaction price which this property can command in the open market.

ALFRED A. RING, S.R.A., M.A.I.
Appraiser

It is further assumed that title to the property is good and marketable and that fee simple ownership is to be transferred free from all encumbrances except for those specified in the deed of public records.

Legal Description

Lot 3, and North 5 feet of lots 1 and 2 and South 15 feet of lot 4, Block 2, College Court Subdivision, as recorded in the public records of Alachua County, Florida.

Statement of Highest and Best Use

It is the appraiser's opinion that the subject property as found on the date of inspection, January 15, 19--, was improved in accordance with the principle of highest and best land use.

By highest and best use is meant that program of land use or employment which will preserve the utility of the land and yield a net income flow that forms, when appropriately capitalized, the highest present value of the land.

ALFRED A. RING, S.R.A., M.A.I.
Appraiser

Assessment and Tax Data

The subject property is assessed for ad valorem tax purposes by the city and county governments for the current year as follows:

Agency	Tax Number	Assessment	Tax Amount
County	6460 - 94	$14,000	$285.00
City	6460 - 94	14,000	140.00
	Total		$425.00

ALFRED A. RING, S.R.A., M.A.I.

Appraiser

Neighborhood Data:

The subject property is located in a fully developed neighborhood that enjoys an air of quality and social refinement. The homes
are 15 to 20 years of age, of varied but pleasing architecture, well
set back from the street line, and in excellent physical condition.
A wide double-lane boulevard, divided by an attractively landscaped
parkway separates the community homes on opposing sides. The lots
are of generous size, varying from 75' to 100' in width and 120' to 140'
in depth. The homes are well placed, assuring a maximum of privacy and
quiet enjoyment.

The neighborhood encompasses an area of six square blocks
and is well protected geographically, as well as by zoning and deed
restriction, from detrimental influences. The physical boundaries of the
neighborhood are University Avenue on the south, N. W. 5th Avenue on the
north, N. W. 22nd Street on the west, and N. W. 17th Street on the east.

All public utilities -- gas, water, telephones, sewerage
(both drain and sanitary), and electricity -- are available. The area
is frequently patrolled, assuring adequate fire and police protection.
City bus lines servicing this neighborhood at 30-minute intervals come
within one block of the subject property.

There is an excellent grade school within four blocks of the
property, and ample opportunities for recreational activities are found
on the campus of the University of Florida, which adjoins the neighborhood and extends south and eastward over an area comprising more than

ALFRED A. RING, S.R.A., M.A.I.
Appraiser

300 acres. The main shopping center is reached by bus or car in a few minutes' drive. The distance is about one and one-half miles; however, small shops catering to neighborhood customers are located within a half mile distance. Two excellent high schools are located within one and a quarter miles from the subject property and land has been acquired within four blocks by school authorities, who contemplate the erection of a modern high school to serve this neighborhood.

The city has twenty-two churches, mostly of Protestant denomination, all of which are centrally located within a radius of two miles, and readily accessible by public or private transportation.

The neighborhood population is wholly professional, and College Court is occupied almost entirely by University personnel. The street often is referred to as "Professors' Row." The income averages about $12,500 per annum. The stability of this income is well reflected in pride of home ownership as shown by housing and lawn care. Owner occupancy is rated at 95 per cent. Property turnover is at a minimum.

Continued growth of the University of Florida and of Gainesville proper assures this neighborhood of an active demand for residential housing far beyond the remaining economic life of the subject property described below.

ALFRED A. RING, S.R.A., M.A.I.
Appraiser

Site Data:

Subject site is geographically situated on the west side of
Northwest 20th Terrace, approximately 125' north of University Avenue.
It is rectangular in shape, having a frontage of 70' on a paved street
and a depth of 130'.

Northwest 20th Terrace is a dual-lane thoroughfare, divided
by an attractively landscaped parkway. Concrete curbing and gutters
facilitate surface drainage. The building site is fairly even in
contour, slightly above street level, with a natural slope toward the
rear. The sandy soil permits ready absorption of normal rainfall.

The plot is serviced by both sanitary and storm sewers. City
water, electricity, and gas are available and connected to the site.
Mail is delivered daily and bus transportation is within a few hundred
feet. Exceptionally well-maintained landscaping and desirable shade
trees provide very pleasant surroundings.

Although the adjoining lot on the south is unimproved, it is
zoned for lower residential purposes, which permits the erection of
four-unit-type multiple dwellings. There is a fraternity house directly
across the street from the subject site. In the appraiser's opinion
the nearness of student housing facilities does not create a detrimental
influence. Investigation disclosed that the neighborhood occupants
are mostly University professors who do not find fraternity and student
housing objectionable. It is further reasonable to assume that the
subject property, if offered for sale on the open market, would

ALFRED A. RING, S.R.A., M.A.I.
Appraiser

attract University personnel who no doubt share the opinion of the
other residents.

Property Data:

The Building

The lot is improved with a one-story bungalow-type house of
1427 square feet area containing three bedrooms, a dining room, a
living room, a study, a hall, a kitchen, one and one-half baths, and a
screened-in porch. The residence is a detached wooden structure,
shingled with cypress, conforming in design and size with the surrounding
residences and with accepted architectural standards. It is so placed
that ample privacy is obtained; the front door opens south of the porch
so that entrance from the street is indirect. The garage, completely
detached from the house, is located at the rear of the lot.

The house is squarely placed on a continuous brick foundation
extending to a mean height of eighteen inches above grade. Adequate
ventilation is provided through screened openings, and metal shields
are provided to prevent termites from reaching the joists. The house
is in good condition; the structural members are sound; no evidence of
rot, sagging, or uneven settling is present.

The gable-type roof is of asphalt shingle in excellent repair.
All gutters, conductors, and flashings are of copper. All windows are
frame-sash-type and double hung. Outside steps are made of brick.

ALFRED A. RING, S.R.A., M.A.I.
Appraiser

Interior walls and ceilings are of sand-finish plaster and in very good condition. The floors are of a good quality hardwood oak throughout over pine subflooring. All closets provide for air circulation through built-in screened ventilators in the ceiling. The attic, which is accessible through two large trap doors (hall and study closet), is sufficiently high to serve for storage of light furniture and goods.

The effective age of this structure is 20 years. The remaining economic life is estimated to be 25 years. Equipment includes a 36-inch attic fan, an 85,000-B.T.U. thermostat-controlled gas space heater, and two gas space heaters each of 20,000-B.T.U. rating. Hot water is supplied by a G.E. 40-gallon electric heater. The kitchen is wired for an electric stove. Hot and cold water connections are piped for an automatic washing machine.

ALFRED A. RING, S.R.A., M.A.I.
Appraiser

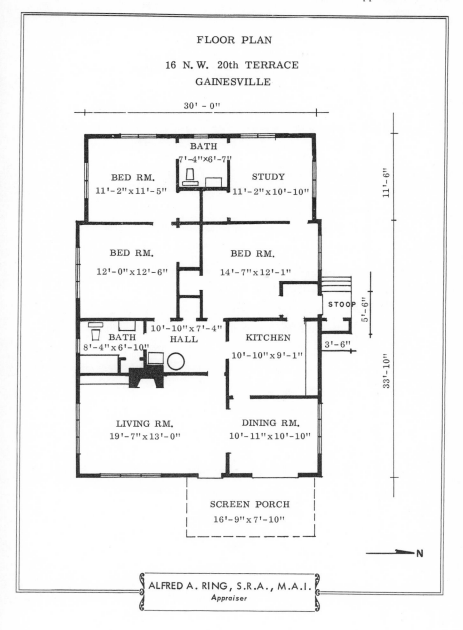

FLOOR PLAN

16 N. W. 20th TERRACE
GAINESVILLE

BATH
7'-4"×6'-7"

BED RM.
11'-2" x 11'-5"

STUDY
11'-2" x 10'-10"

BED RM.
12'-0" x 12'-6"

BED RM.
14'-7" x 12'-1"

STOOP

BATH
8'-4" x 6'-10"

HALL
10'-10" x 7'-4"

KITCHEN
10'-10" x 9'-1"

3'-6"

LIVING RM.
19'-7" x 13'-0"

DINING RM.
10'-11" x 10'-10"

SCREEN PORCH
16'-9" x 7'-10"

30' - 0"

11'-6"

5'-6"

33'-10"

N

ALFRED A. RING, S.R.A., M.A.I.
Appraiser

Market Approach to Value

In the determination of value via the market approach, four sales were analyzed as follows:

Sale No. 1 is located in the same block as the subject property and is identified by the street address of 208 N. W. 20 Terrace. This property sold a year ago for $16,000 and was purchased by B. F. Meter and wife. The lot size is identical to the subject property. Time adjustment due to inflation is judged to be plus 10%. The over-all rating for the subject property is 95% because of differences in effective age. All other building features appear comparable. The adjusted sales value is $16,720.

Sale No. 2 is also located within the subject block at 123 N. W. 20th Terrace. This property has an 80 feet frontage as compared with 70 feet for the subject property. This property was purchased by K. L. Mitch and wife six months ago for $18,500. The subject property is smaller in building size by 285 square feet. The subject property rating is 85% and the lot value adjustment is minus $500. The adjusted sales price is $16,086.

Sale No. 3 is better located at 1717 N. W. 7th Place on a larger lot which is priced $1,500 more than the lot value estimated for the subject property. The property sold three months ago to E. G. Folk and wife for $16,800. Time adjustment was rated at plus 2% and the over-all comparability for the subject property because of better construction features is 1.10%. The adjusted price is $17,200.

ALFRED A. RING, S.R.A., M.A.I.
Appraiser

Sale No. 4 is also better located at 1730 N. W. 11th Road causing an estimated land value differential of $2,750. The subject property is larger by 127 square feet and is better in construction features and condition. The sale property was bought four weeks ago by C. F. Cain and wife for $16,500. There is no time adjustment, however, the rating for the subject property is 15% superior. The adjusted price is $15,813.

The four sales were correlated giving a value weight of 50% to sale no. 1, 30% to sale no. 2 and 10% each to sales 3 and 4. The correlated market value on the basis of these sales is $16,500.

ALFRED A. RING, S.R.A., M.A.I.
Appraiser

The Cost Approach to Value

Determination of Base Unit Cost Factor:

Based on the unit-in-place cost method of building construction, the subject property -- free of special features -- would require
an expenditure of $8.00 per sq. ft. This basic cost factor is verified
by special cost studies recently concluded by local builders.

Cost factor derivation:

Basic unit cost per sq. ft. $8.00

Add special features:

Brick fireplace	$ 550	
Tile work in kitchen and bath	425	
Additional millwork allowance	275	
Additional half bath	325	
Additional closets	180	
Waterlines for automatic washer	100	
Total extras	$1,855	

Extra costs per sq. ft.

    $1,855 ÷ 1,427 sq. ft. =   1.30

Adjusted cost per sq. ft. $9.30

ALFRED A. RING, S.R.A., M.A.I.
Appraiser

The Cost Approach to Value:

Estimated replacement cost, new:

    Main dwelling

1,427 sq. ft. @ 9.30 =	$13,271	
131 sq. ft. screened porch @ $4.00 =	524	
19 sq. ft. side stoop @ 5.00 =	95	
500 sq. ft. garage @ 5.00 =	2,500	
Total replacement cost -- new		$16,390

Value of landscaping, walk, drive and equipment

36" Coolair attic fan -- installed	$ 225	
35,000--B.T.U. Cor Air thermostatically controlled gas space heaters	250	
Two 20,000--B.T.U. gas room heaters	50	
Venetian blinds	110	
Aluminum "Flow Breeze" awning	100	
Landscaping	150	
Walks and drives	175	
Total		1,060
Total replacement cost -- all improvements		$17,450
Less accrued depreciation (see schedule)		4,376
Depreciated replacement cost		$13,074
Add value of land -- by comparison		3,500
Value via cost approach		$16,574

Rounded to $16,550

ALFRED A. RING, S.R.A., M.A.I.
Appraiser

Depreciation Schedule

Physical Deterioration

Curable:

Refinish floors	$ 325	
Repair window screens	65	
Reserve for heating equipment		
based on 4 year use	105	

Incurable:

Liability to replace

based on effective age

of 20 years is (12%)[1]   1,967

Total physical deterioration $2,462

Functional Obsolescence

Curable:

Relocate hot water heater

from hallway to attic $ 175

Replace two outmoded light

fixtures   100

$ 275

[1] Per cent liability based on 8% rate of interest (see schedule for 45 year economic life --- Appendix III).

ALFRED A. RING, S.R.A., M.A.I.
Appraiser

Incurable:

    Value loss due to sales resistance

        because of poor floor plan and

        inferior room arrangement. This

        estimate is based on a market

        sale resistance rate of 10% of

        replacement cost new $1,639

Total functional obsolescence $1,914

Economic Obsolescence   none

Total accrued depreciation $4,376

ALFRED A. RING, S.R.A., M.A.I.
Appraiser

Income Approach to Value

        The income approach to value is of minor significance in the valuation of single-family residential properties. This is the case because most properties of this type are under homeowner occupancy and amenities (or "psychic income") derived from ownership do not lend themselves readily to economic measurement.

        An attempt, however, was made to determine what comparable properties rent for in similar locations. Rentals ranged from $175 per month for homes in relatively new condition to $120 per month for homes in late life. A stabilized income of $145 per month reflects the income-producing capacity of this property over the remaining estimated economic life of 30 years. This rental estimate was confirmed and judged accurate by leading Realtors in the Gainesville community.

        The rent multiplier for Gainesville based on sale of comparable properties is 110.

        Value based on rent multiplier

           110 x $145 = $15,950 rounded to $16,000

ALFRED A. RING, S.R.A., M.A.I.
Appraiser

Correlation of Value Estimates

The current market conditions in Gainesville reflect an active demand for residential homes. An informed seller, however, would consider the depreciated reproduction cost of similar property as a ceiling of value. The income approach for residential property was given little weight.

In consideration of all the forces which influence value, the appraiser has applied the following judgment weights in the derivation of the final estimate of value:

	Value Estimate	Value Weight	Value Influence
Market	$16,500	.35	$ 5,775
Cost	16,550	.60	9,930
Income	16,000	.05	800
Total			$16,505
Final estimate of value			$16,500

Explanation of Value Weights:

The value weights as applied above are justified as follows: The market is active for new homes which sell at replacement cost new. Hence the cost approach is of greatest present influence as a market price determinant. The weight assigned for this measure of value is 60 per cent.

ALFRED A. RING, S.R.A., M.A.I.
Appraiser

The demand for older homes is slow and appears subject to less accurate price adjustments in the market. The assigned weight is 35 per cent. The income approach is of negligible importance in the value of residences -- hence the low correlation weight of 5 per cent.

ALFRED A. RING, S.R.A., M.A.I.
Appraiser

Statement of Limiting Conditions

This appraisal is subject to the following limiting conditions:

1. The property is free and clear of all liens and encumbrances other than those listed in the deed of record.

2. The appraiser did not search validity of title nor does he assume responsibility for corrections which a survey of the property may reveal.

3. The sale of this property will be on an all-cash basis -- since financial arrangements, good or cumbersome, are bound to affect the price at which this property may sell in the market.

4. The information contained herein is not guaranteed, but it was gathered from reliable sources which are believed to be accurate.

5. No responsibility is assumed for matters legal in character.

6. Sketches are accurate only for purposes of approximation.

7. This report is not to be reproduced in part or as a whole without written consent of the appraiser.

ALFRED A. RING, S.R.A., M.A.I.
Appraiser

Certification

This is to certify that the undersigned has made a careful personal inspection of the property legally described herein and that all findings, statements and opinions submitted in this report are correct to the best of his knowledge.

This appraisal was prepared for demonstration purposes and the valuation estimate certified below is not contingent on any monetary fees or interests whatsoever.

The appraiser has no present or prospective interest in the subject property and the fee agreed upon is in no way related to or contingent upon the value reported.

It is further certified that this appraisal has been made in conformity with the professional standards of the American Institute of Real Estate Appraisers and the Society of Real Estate Appraisers, of which the undersigned is a member.

The market value of the property as described herein is certified as of January 15, 19-- to be:

Sixteen Thousand Five Hundred Dollars

($16,500)

Certified by

Alfred A. Ring

Alfred A. Ring, M.A.I., S.R.A.

Consultant - Appraiser

ALFRED A. RING, S.R.A., M.A.I.

Appraiser

Appendix II

Problems in Property Appraising

Problems:

1. Distinguish wealth from property and state why the valuator is concerned with the appraisal of property rather than with the appraisal of wealth.

For answer see page 523.

2. (a) Define: (1) price, (2) value, (3) cost, and (4) warranted value. (b) How does value differ from utility, scarcity, and subjective value?

For answer see page 523.

3. Brown bought a building from which he anticipates, at the time of purchase, $2,000 in operating income (per annum). Ten years later, having maintained the building in full repair, his operating income remained at $2,000 per annum. He anticipates the same level of income throughout the future service life of this building. Has the passage of time, assuming all other things remain equal, affected the value of this building? Explain.

For answer see page 523.

4. Mr. Baker is asked by his employer to appraise a combination garage and loft building which the owner has offered as security for a $20,000 loan. Mr. Baker proceeds to the site and after careful, detailed inspection estimates that the replacement cost of this structure and land is $30,000. He reports his valuation and recommends that, based on this security, the loan be granted. Do you agree with Mr. Baker? State your reasons.

For answer see page 523.

5. Can zoning regulations prevent value decline in residential districts? Discuss.

For answer see page 524.

6. It is stated that "where the building codes or local conditions make construction more costly in one city than another, the general land values are lower." Is this statement true? Give your reason.

For answer see page 524.

7. Assume that the net income from the ownership of land is $200 and that the current rate of interest (capitalization rate) is 5 per cent. Assume further that a tax of $20 is levied on this land which reduces the net income to $180. Compute the following:

(a) The land value prior to imposition of the tax.

    (b) The land value after the tax levy.

    (c) The amount of capital levy imposed by this tax if the capitalization rate falls to 4 per cent.

For answer see page 524.

8. Why must the appraiser under the income approach to value consider past managerial practices? Explain.

For answer see page 524.

9. In the valuation process what significance should the appraiser attach to (a) present income, (b) past income, and (c) anticipated income?

For answer see page 524.

10. If one dollar is invested in a fund at 5 per cent compound interest for a period of 12 years, how much will be in the fund at the beginning of the 13th year?

For answer see page 524.

11. If five dollars is invested at 6 per cent compound interest for a period of 10 years, how much _interest_ will this investment earn?

For answer see page 524.

12. Johnson purchased a vacant lot for $2,000. Ten years later he offers this lot for sale. How much must this lot sell for to return to Johnson his original purchase price plus interest at 5 per cent? (Do not assume any outlays other than the initial purchase price.)

For answer see page 525.

13. What is meant by "present value of an amount due at some given future time"?

For answer see page 525.

14. It is expected that a property will have a value of $20,000 upon the expiration of a lease which has ten years to run. What is the present value of this reversion at 6 per cent?

For answer see page 525.

15. In appraising a building the appraiser intends to make a lump-sum deduction for the poor condition of the roof. He expects the present roof to last about five years. He is informed by a contractor that a new roof will cost $2,000. At 5 per cent what amount should the appraiser deduct from today's valuation?

For answer see page 525.

16. (a) What is an annuity? (b) What is the compound amount of an annuity?

For answer see page 525.

17. B has paid $100 in taxes each year on a vacant lot which he purchased ten years ago for $3,000. Assuming interest rates at 6 per cent, how much is his total investment to date?

For answer see page 525.

18. X leased a vacant lot which he is using as a commercial parking lot. The lease calls for an annual payment of $600 per annum. X has been paying on this leasehold for a period of five years. If the interest rate is 7 per cent, what is the cost of this leasehold to date?

For answer see page 525.

19. (a) Explain what is meant by "present value of an annuity."
(b) What is the present value of $1.00 due each year for a period of three years? Interest rates are 6 per cent.

For answer see page 525.

20. (a) The net income of a downtown apartment house is estimated at $4,000 per annum. If the economic life of this structure is 50 years and the capitalization rate is 8 per cent, what is the present value of this income flow? Use annuity method of capitalization. (b) Assuming that the land on which this apartment house stands has a value of $15,000, how much must be added to the present value of the estimated income flow of $4,000 for 50 years to determine the present value of the entire property? Assume 6 per cent interest on the land value.

For answer see page 525.

21. Define: (a) capitalization, (b) perpetuity, (c) rate of capitalization, and (d) rate of interest.

For answer see page 525.

22. Capitalize the following at 8 per cent:
   (a) an income flow (annuity) of $500 per annum for 15 years.
   (b) an income flow (annuity) of $500 per annum for 100 years.
   (c) an income flow of $500 per annum in perpetuity.

For answer see page 526.

23. The economic rent for a certain city lot is anticipated to be as follows:

At end of first year	$200
At end of second year	225
At end of third year	225
At end of fourth year	250
At end of fifth year	275
At end of sixth year and to perpetuity	300

Estimate the present value of this property. Assume interest at 6 per cent

   (a) Estimate the present value of this property. Assume interest at 6 percent.

(b) **Stabilize** (find the weighted average annual income) this income stream. Use 6 percent interest.

For answer see page 526.

24. Determine the present value of a leased fee at 6 per cent which calls for yearly returns as follows:

1st to 5th year inclusive	$800 per annum
6th to 10th year inclusive	$1,000 per annum
11th to 30th year inclusive	$1,200 per annum
Land value (if free and clear):	$20,000. Land rate is 6 per cent.

For answer see page 526.

25. Estimate the present value of a building which has an anticipated remaining economic life of 30 years. The predicted residual building returns are as follows:

First and second year	$4,000 per annum
Third and fourth year	$5,000 per annum
Thereafter for 26 years	$4,500 per annum

The rate of capitalization is 7 per cent.

For answer see page 527.

26. The construction cost of a 10-story apartment house is $250,000. The building represents the highest and best use and has an estimated total economic life of 40 years, over which period the net income will be sufficient to amortize the above investment at 8 per cent interest. The 100' × 100' plot on which this apartment house stands has an estimated value of $50,000. Assuming 6 per cent interest on this amount, what is the combined income necessary to warrant this investment under (a) straight line method and (b) Inwood or annuity method of capitalization.

For answer see page 527.

27. Define: (a) effective gross revenue; (b) occupancy ratio; (c) collection losses; (d) net operating income (earning expectancy); (e) operating ratio (expense ratio); (f) fixed charges; (g) equity income; (h) trading on the equity; (i) yield on equity investment.

For answer see page 528.

28. Two properties have the following income schedules:

	Property A	Property B
Revenue	$100,000	$40,000
Operating expense	80,000	20,000
Operating income	$ 20,000	$20,000

Which property has greater value? Why? Explain your reasoning.

For answer see page 528.

29. If $1,000 is to be accumulated under the sinking fund method over a period of 20 years, how much must be placed annually into the fund if compound interest rates are 3 per cent?

For answer see page 528.

30. What is interest?

For answer see page 528.

31. What component parts make up the total rate of interest?

For answer see page 528.

32. Explain what is meant by (a) over-all capitalization rates and (b) fractional rates.

For answer see page 529.

33. An owner of a $10,000 residential home wishes to secure a first mortgage loan and is offered by a finance company.the following terms:
    1. A $5,000 (50 per cent) loan at 5 per cent interest.
    2. A $6,000 (60 per cent) loan at 6 per cent interest.
    3. A $7,000 (70 per cent) loan at 8 per cent interest.
Since the first $5,000 can be obtained at 5 per cent interest, but the entire amount must bear 6 per cent if the loan is $6,000 and 8 per cent if the loan is $7,000, determine the interest rates that apply to each additional $1,000 above the initial $5,000 under (a) $6,000 and (b) $7,000 mortgage loan terms.

For answer see page 529.

34. Compute the over-all capitalization rates from the data given below:

Property A	Land value	$ 2,500	Capitalization rate	"	6%
	Building value	7,500	"	"	8%
	Total value	$10,000	"	"	?
Property B	Land value	$ 5,000	Capitalization rate	"	6%
	Building value	5,000	"	"	9%
	Total value	$10,000	"	"	?
Property C	Land value	$ 7,500	Capitalization rate	"	7%
	Building value	2,500	"	"	9%
	Total value	$10,000	"	"	?

For answer see page 529.

35. You are called upon to appraise the value of a store property. After thorough and careful analysis you determine the following facts:
    1. Revenue—$18,000.
    2. Operating expenses (exclusive of depreciation)—$6,000
    3. Economic life of improvement—30 years.
    4. A 2/3 mortgage can be obtained at 6 per cent interest.
    5. The 1/3 equity interest rate is 12 per cent.
    6. The value of the land 30 years hence is $40,000—land interest
    7. Market warrants use of annuity method of capitalization.
From this data, derive:
    (a) The value of the entire property.

(b) The over-all capitalization rate.

For answer see page 529.

36. Assume the following:
    1. Income of $5,000 per annum.
    2. A 60 per cent mortgage on the value of the property.
    3. Mortgage interest at 5 per cent.
    4. Mortgage interest is earned (required) 2.5 times.
Based upon these facts, determine the over-all rate of capitalization.

For answer see page 530.

37. Two identical structures (residences) are erected on opposite
sides of the same street. The same builder and identical building
designs are employed. The contract specified that the builder should
be compensated at a cost-plus-10-per cent basis with a maximum expenditure of $10,000 per structure. The final costs were as follows;
Building A—$9,000; Building B—$9,500. The higher cost of building B
was caused by the existence of rock which had to be blasted out of place.
The land for each structure (50' × 100') was purchased for $1,000 per
lot. Based on the above data discuss the following:
    (a) Have the buildings different values? Explain.
    (b) Are the lots identical in value?
    (c) What is the nature of the expenditure for blasting the rock?
        Does it add to or detract from, the value of (1) the building
        and (2) the land?

For answer see page 530.

38. In appraising a vacant business lot on Main Street, no comparable
sales could be found. The lot size is 50'× 100'. The most profitable
use is estimated to be a one-story building containing 100,000 cu. ft.
estimated to cost 35¢ per cu. ft. The net income of the land and building is estimated at $4,500 per year before depreciation. Assuming an
interest rate of 6 per cent and an economic building life of 40 years,
what land value is indicated by the capitalization approach? Use
straight line method of capitalization.

For answer see page 530.

39. A building 40 years old is located in a strong central business
district and has shown profitable operating returns throughout its
entire history. It is now proposed to modernize the structure at a
cost of $150,000. The land has a value of $200,000. Taxes are estimated at $14,500 per annum after modernization. An appraisal of the
structure made from plans indicates that after modernization, the
building will be worth $250,000. Depreciation has been charged in the
past at $2\frac{1}{2}$ per cent and will be charged in the future at $2\frac{1}{2}$ per cent.
The present owner, who has owned the property since the building was
originally constructed, expects to hold the property and seeks a return of 7 per cent net on his investment.
    (a) On the basis of a land investment of $200,000, what is the
        owner's net investment after remodeling?

(b) What is the net rental required to pay 7 per cent and to liqui-
date the owner's depreciable investment in 40 years?
Assuming the property is placed on the market and is sold at its
value, not its cost:
(c) What net rental would a prudent buyer require assuming a
7 per cent return and liquidation of his depreciable investment in 25 years?
(d) Explain how a prudent buyer would establish the equitable net
rent.

For answer see page 529.

40. There are three residual methods of processing the net income
from a property. Assume you are appraising an old 4-story brick and
frame, furnished apartment property, on a $10,000 lot, and that you
have found that the property for some time to come should produce a
net income before interest and depreciation of $6,000. Further as-
sume that the furnishings in use in the building have a ten-year remaining useful life, that 10 per cent is to be earned on their present
value of $5,500, that 8 per cent is an acceptable rate of interest re-
turn, and that the building has a remaining economic life of 25 years.
(a) Which one of the residual methods do you use in arriving at
an estimate of the value to assign to the structure?
(b) What is the indicated value of the structure? Show your computations. Use the straight line method of capitalization.

For answer see page 530.

41. Mr. A is the fee owner of a vacant lot. He enters into a ground
lease with Mr. B for a term of 50 years. The net ground rental re-
served in the lease by Mr. A is:
$ 9,000 per year during the first five years
10,000 per year during the next ten years
12,000 per year during the remainder of the term
Mr. B, the lessee, erected a building on the leased land at a highest
and best use cost of $200,000. Assume that you have appraised the
market value of the freehold (that is, the market value of the entire
property—land and building as a unit) lease free ten years later, and
found the total market value of the property to be $400,000. You are
to appraise the market value of the leased fee (the interest of the
lessor, Mr. A) and also appraise the value of the leasehold (the lessee's interest, Mr. B), as of today, ten years after date of lease.
After having made an analysis of the site, you have concluded that the
land, if vacant, as of the date of the appraisal has a market value of
$240,000, and that ground leases for 25 years or more in this vicinity
are customarily based upon a net interest return of 6 per cent. What
is the indicated market value of:
(a) The lessor's interest.
(b) The lessee's interest.

Assume that the building has a total economic life of 40 years from
the date of its completion, and that it is to be depreciated at $2\frac{1}{2}$ per
cent of its cost for each year of its life.

For answer see page 530.

42. Assume that you have a lot 50' × 150' to a 20' paved alley in the center of the 80 per cent business block in a good, stable community, and that the lot has a current market value, if vacant, of $2,000 per front foot. A new one-story modern brick store building 50' × 100' with 16' ceiling height and single-span truss roof has just been completed at a cost of $6.00 per sq. ft. and leased for 10 years at $22.00 per front foot per month. The new building is assumed to have a 50-year economic life from the date of its completion. Expenses are as follows:

Management	5 per cent of effective rental schedule.
Repair and maintenance	1 per cent of building cost new.
Reserve for alteration and replacement	$120 per front foot each 10 years.
Insurance	$1.00 per hundred on 80 per cent co-insurance per year.
Taxes	2 per cent of cost of land and building.
Vacancies and credit losses	3 per cent of gross rental schedule.

Find value, assuming:
(a) Straightline method of depreciation and 6 per cent rate of interest.
(b) Inwood method of capitalization at 6 per cent.
(c) Hoskold method of capitalization at 6 per cent risk rate and 3 per cent safe rate of interest.

For answer see page 530.

43. Mr. A, the owner of the fee in a parcel of vacant land, leased the property to Mr. B for a term of 50 years at a net rent of $3,000 per year. Mr. B immediately erected a commercial building on the lot and, 5 years later, subleased to Mr. C at a rent equivalent to $ 8,000 per year net, for 45 years. The vacant lot has a fair market value of $75,000. The economic rental value of the property is $12,000 per year net. As of today (15 years after date of original lease from A to B) on an 8 per cent basis for Mr. A's interest, and assuming the building to be valueless at the end of the lease:
(a) What is the value of the interest of Mr. A?
(b) What is the value of the interest of Mr. B?
(c) What is the value of the interest of Mr. C?
Show your computations.

For answer see page 531 .

44. A real estate investor sold two parcels of property; one was an office building for which he received $75,000 and on which he made a capital gain of 25 per cent; the other was an apartment building for which he also received $75,000 and on which he suffered a loss of 25 per cent. How much did the seller gain or lose? Show all computations.

For answer see page <u>531</u>.

45. An improved property sold for $150,000. Of this, $25,000 was imputed to land. The stabilized net income was $14,000 per annum. The building has a remaining life of 20 years. 6 per cent is required to attract capital to land investment of this type.
Problem: find rates applicable to the building as follows:
 (a) Building rate of capitalization.
 (b) Interest rate under straight line depreciation—for building only.
 (c) Interest rate under Inwood premise valuation—for building only.

For answer see page <u>531</u>.

46. Find value of the following corner lot: Assume 100 feet depth as standard.

For answer see page <u>532</u>.

47. A 6 percent first mortgage in the amount of $10,000 is to be amortized monthly over 4 years. How much is due periodically?

For answer see page <u>532</u>.

48. A prospective homeowner can afford to pay $60 monthly for interest and principal. Assuming he can secure an 8-year 4 per cent amortizing mortgage, how much can he borrow?

For answer see page <u>532</u>.

49. Set up a schedule of amortization for the $10,000 mortgage (as computed in Question 47) and show <u>all</u> captions, headings and entries for a two-month period.

For answer see page <u>532</u>.

50. Compute an Inwood factor and a 3 per cent Hoskold factor assuming a rate of interest of 6 per cent and an income life of 30 years.

For answer see page <u>532</u>.

51. Based on the facts detailed below, determine via the income approach the value of the apartment property:
 (a) Building contains 40 apartments renting at $45.50 (average rental) each per month. Remaining building life is estimated at 40 years.

(b) The land—via market approach—is valued at $20,000.
(c) Interest rates in the area of 7. 5 percent.
(d) The following expenses are listed for the calendar year:

Taxes on land and building	$2,400
Power and light	200
Depreciation provision	1,600
Repairs	800
Renovating and painting	1,200
Janitor expense	2,000
Extermination	60
Replacements:	
40 ranges (8-year life)	3,000
40 refrigerators (12-year life)	6,000
New roof	1,100
Legal fees	120
Corporation tax	300
Income taxes	350
Mortgage interest	1,200
Mortgage amortization	1,000
Management fees	1,200
Water	450
Fire insurance (3-year policy)	600
Paving assessment	400
Promotion and advertising	250

For answer see page <u>533</u>.

52. An apartment house was leased by A to B, and subleased by
B to C. Based on the terms given below, determine the value of the
sandwich lease hold. Use a rate of 6.5 per cent.
    (a) Lease from A to B, provides for rentals as follows:
                5 years at $1,000 per year
                15 years at $1,200 per year
    (b) Lease from B to C calls for rentals as follows:
                10 years at $1,500
                10 years at $1,800

For answer see page <u>534</u> .

53. Outline a procedure or plan for estimating the anticipated revenue
flow for a new 10-story office building located in a large commercial
city.

For answer see page <u>535</u> .

54. The anticipated net income flow from an office building is estimated to be as follows:

Years	Net Income
First 5 years incl.	$1,600 per annum
Next 5 years incl.	2,000 per annum
Next 20 years	2,400 per annum

The interest rate is 7.5 per cent

(a) What is the present value of this interest? Use the annuity method of capitalization.

(b) Suppose the land has an estimated market value of $10,000. Determine the total value of the property.

For answer see page 535.

55. You, the owner of a city lot 100' × 100', have the choice of erecting either one of the following improvements:

(a) A 10-story apartment house at a cost of $100,000
(b) A 20-story office building at a cost of $250,000

The largest net return over a period of ten years is estimated to be derived from the 10-story apartment house. However, beginning ten years from now, it is estimated that the 20-story structure would bring the higher net return. Which structure would you erect? Give your reasons.

For answer see page 536.

56. In estimating capitalizable "net" income for office or apartment properties, should depreciation expense be subtracted from effective gross revenue? Explain your reasons fully.

For answer see page 536.

57. Will the appraiser, in his work, have to give consideration to the fact that money can change in value because of inflation or deflation? Explain.

For answer see page 536.

58. An apartment house which represents the highest and best use has been completed at a cost of $150,000. The anticipated net income from this improvement, which has an estimated economic life of 40 years, is as follows:

First year	$ 9,500
Second year	$12,000
Third year and thereafter	
for 37 years	$14,000

Based on an interest rate of 8 per cent, determine the appraised value of this property. Use the Inwood method of capitalization.

For answer see page 537.

59. A skyscraper office building on Madison Avenue in New York City was assessed for $7,500,000 and the property tax at 30 mills per dollar based on this value was set at $225,000. The owners claimed overassessment and instituted certiorari proceedings to reduce taxes in conformity with fair market value. Assuming a land value of $2,000,000, a net income before interest and amortization but after taxes (as billed) of $570,000, a rate of interest of 7.5 per cent, and a rate of depreciation of 2.5 per cent, determine the following:

(a) The capitalized value of the property.
(b) Property taxes based on this value.
(c) Net income after (fair) taxes.

For answer see page 538.

60. A commercial property producing a stabilized annual income of $50,000
is offered for sale to the Goodrich Investment Corporation. The purchase
is subject to an existing 25 year amortizing mortgage of $300,000 financed at
7 percent interest. The monthly level mortgage payments amount to $2,120.
The Goodrich Investment Corporation seeks an equity return of 12 percent
over an ownership period of 10 years. The property is estimated to depreciate a
rate of 2 percent per year and realize $400,000 on date of sale. The unpaid
mortgage balance 10 years from now eill be $235,902.
Problem: Find the purchase price that will yield a 12 percent return.

For an answer, see page 539.

61. A property is offered to the Upland Corporation for $400,00. There
is an existing 20 year $280,000 mortgage at 7.5 per cent interest. Level
debt service payment amounts to $2,256 per month. The property is scheduled
to be held for a period of 5 years. The annual stabilized propeety income is $36,
Depreciation is estimated at 1.5 per cent per year.

For answer see page 539.

Case Study No. 1

Land Development Approach to Value

A 100 acre tract of land within city limits is to be subdivided into 210 building sites.

There is active demand for homes in the $25,000 to $30,000
price bracket. The average price per home is estimated at $28,500.
The ratio of land to property value in like subdivisions is one to six
($1.00 land to $5.00 building investment).

The proposed subdivision is to be improved with all required
city utilities including 60 feet wide paved roads fitted with concrete
curbs and gutters, water, drainage and sanitary disposal. Telephone
and electric service facilities including street lights are to be
supplied through underground cables laid in steel conduit.

Analysis of development plans indicate improvement measurements as follows:

15,000 lineal feet of streets @ $9 per lineal foot;

15,500 lineal feet of water mains @ $4 per lineal foot;

15,500 lineal feet of sanitary and drainage sewer mains @
$4.50 per lineal foot;

210 water and sewage distribution connections @ $180 per lot.

The developer is to receive a refund of $90 under city
regulations at time each lot is tapped on to the main and becomes
active by customer use.

Electric underground facilities cost $450 per building site. No extra cost for telephone lines or site connections are chargeable to the developer.

Site clearing, grading and landscaping are subcontracted at a cost of $80 per building lot.

Planning, engineering and supervision costs are estimated at $12,000.

Legal expenses, taxes, advertising and field overhead costs are estimated at 4.5% of gross sales.

Selling expenses (brokers and sales expense commissions) are fixed by custom at 10% of selling prices.

Developers profits average 12% of selling prices. The cost of capital -- interest charges -- currently are 8.5%.

The investment period is scheduled to extend over a three year period. Lot sales of 70 per year are considered a reasonable certainty.

Based on market analysis and the information, as stated above, supplied by informed sources, derive the land value of the undeveloped tract of land under alternative options as follows:

1. The development for the entire 210 lot subdivision is to be completed and all utilities to be installed without delay.

2. The development and installation of utilities is to be phased equally over the three year development period with 1/3 of the costs to be incurred each year. Under this extended (delayed) construction program street

improvement and utility installation costs will be
increased by 10%.

Which program of development (1 or 2) is preferable. Explain
your answer by stating the underlying reasons.

Case Study No. 2

Apartment House Property

Based on field and property data noted below, estimate the following:

1. Value under cost approach
2. Value under market approach
3. Value under income approach
4. Final estimate of value based on correlation of value findings. Give narrative statement supporting judgement weights applied in the derivation of the final estimate of value.

Neighborhood - Location

The subject property is located in a desirable residential area zoned R-3 for high rise apartments. The neighborhood area is 95 per cent developed with a variety of apartment structures ranging in height from three to eight stories. Structures vary in age from two to twenty years. All are in good physical conditions.

The area is well located within walking distance of a good grade school, within two blocks of neighborhood shopping and six blocks from the University campus. A bus stop is one-half block to the north at the intersection of N. W. Beach Boulevard and N. W. 14th Street. The distance to the central city is 3 miles and bus transportation is available at 30 minute intervals from 6 a.m. to 7 p.m. and every hour from 7 p.m. to 2 a.m.

The occupants of the area are mostly college students who in groups of 2 to 4 share occupancy. The vacancy ratio reported averages 6 to 8 per cent.

The trend is for continued land use as apartment development. The rental range for unfurnished apartments is $90 to $100 for two room, kitchen and bath, and $110 to $125 for 3 room, kitchen and bath apartments. The property is located in the middle of the block on N. W. 14th Street between N. W. Beach Boulevard to the West and N. W. 5th Avenue to the East. The site measures 100 feet on N. W. 14th Street to a depth of 150 feet.

Improvement Data

The subject apartment is a 5-story masonry structure. The exterior walls are brick veneer over concrete blocks. A partial basement contains the manager's apartment, the heater, air conditioning, and elevator equipment and adequate storage facilities for tenants. There are 40 - 2 room and bath apartments and 20 - 3 room and bath apartments. Each apartment is equipped with an electric range, dishwasher and refrigerator.

The building measures 80 feet on N. W. 14th Street to a depth of 90 feet. The over-all building height is 56 feet.

The building roof is "built up" and topped with marble chits as protection against heavy rains. Windows are of aluminum sash and of awning type manufacture.

The floors are carpeted throughout over left on concrete subfloors. The basement apartment has vinyl tile over concrete slab. The basement utility area is reinforced concrete.

Interior walls are furred out, insulated, and finished with dry wall masonry boards. Good quality paint is used throughout except for feature walls which are attractively finished with wall paper. Interior trim is white spruce.

2-room apartments contain 500 square feet and 3-room apartments contain 700 square feet. All bathrooms are fully tiled and fitted with pastel colored fixtures. Each apartment has extra clothes closets off the entrance foyer and a walk-in closet in the master bedroom. Kitchen floors are covered with grease-proof vinyl tile.

The entire structure is centrally heated and air conditioned with a "climatrol" Carrier furnace and condenser. Two standard, automatic elevators serve the building. Off street parking is adequate. The remaining economic life is 50 years. Accrued depreciation is negligible. There is no deferred maintenance. Lobby furniture is valued at $1,500. Land value is well established at $3.50 per square foot.

Assessment and Insurance Data

The subject property is assessed for ad valorem tax purposes at $275,000. Taxes are levied at 13.65 mills by the county and at 8.35 mills by the city.

Comprehensive and fire insurance is based on 80% of building replacement cost new. The insurance rate is 35¢ per $100 per year. Public liability insurance costs $125 per year.

Comparative Sales

Sale No.	1	2	3	4
Date of Sale	Current	6 mo. ago	Current	2 years ago
Sale Price	$470,000	$240,000	$490,000	$576,000
Land Value	$45,000	$22,000	$48,000	$60,000
No. of Apts.	69	40	65	87
No. of Rooms	158	94	151	206
Effective Revenue	$68,115	$34,300	$70,500	$83,450
Operating Ratio	42%	40%	42%	39%
Remaining Economic Life	45 years	40 years	50 years	48 years
Effective age	5 years	10 years	none	2 years

Time adjustment: 6 month - none. 1 year + 5%. 2 years + 10%. Apply the straight line method of depreciation in analyzing the market data approach to value. Except for age, apartment structures are comparable in all respects including location.

Revenue and Expense Data

Rental Income -- 30 - 2 Room Apts @ $ 90

              10 - 2 Room Apts @ $100

              15 - 3 Room Apts @ $110

               5 - 3 Room Apts @ $125

               1 - Basement   @ $ 75*

Vacancy and Collection loss allowance 7.5%

_____

*No revenue is collected from superintendent who occupies unfurnished basement apartment. The rental amount is considered part of superintendent's wages.

Operating Expenditures:

Management 5% of effective gross income	
Payroll -- Superintendent and labor	$ 3,000
Electricity	1,200
Water & sewage charge	1,400
Heating fuel	1,300
Legal and administrative	500

Painting and decorating -- every 3 years
    $120 for 2 Room Apts and $160 for 3 Room Apts
    Exterior maintenance every 5 years -- $4,000	

Supplies and services	450
Corporate income tax	9,000
Elevator contract	1,000
Amortization	15,000
Repairs and general maintenance	700
Interest on mortgages	22,000

Reserve for replacements:

Ranges -- 15 year life	Cost each	$	120
Refrigerators -- 15 year life	Cost each		160
Dishwashers -- 12 year life	Cost each		140
Lobby furniture -- 10 year life			
Equipment -- furnace & pumps -- 15 year life			15,000

Apply the annuity method of capitalization in deriving value via the income approach to value.

The market indicates availability of mortgage funds up to 60% of property value at 7.5 per cent interest. Equity funds are obtainable at 10% interest.

Cost Data

Analysis of comparable buildings constructed in recent months as well as information obtained from informed investor - builders supports a replacement cost new of $.95 per cubic foot exclusive of furniture and kitchen equipment (ranges, refrigerators and dishwashers). Depreciation is considered negligible. The estimated economic life of the subject property is 50 years.

Case Study No. 3

Retail Store Property

Based on field data presented below, analyze the pertinent
information and set up schedules essential to the derivation of
estimates as follows:

1. Value of land

2. Cost Approach to value

3. Market comparison approach to value

4. Rate of interest applicable to subject property

5. Income approach to value

6. Correlation and final estimate of value.

In all schedules justify -- by explanatory statements -- the
conclusions reached.

Purpose of Appraisal

To estimate the market value of the subject property for
possible sale or long term lease purposes.

Street Address

925 Broadway, Capital City

Legal Description

The East one half (E½) of the East one half (E½) of Lot 6,
Block 42 Old Survey of Capital City, as per public records, Lincoln
County, Any State.

Highest and Best Use

The subject property conforms to existing zoning regulations
and constitutes the highest and best use of the site.

By highest and best use is meant that legal program of land
utilization which will preserve the utility of the property and yield
an income which when appropriately capitalized aggregates the highest
present value to the land.

National Data

The continued high level of economic activity accounts
largely for the firm and steady upward trend in land and realty values
throughout the nation. Inflationary tendencies too during the past
few years have caused real estate values to move upward significantly.
The over all increase in property values appears attributable to the
following favorable causes:

1. Continued unexpected population increases.
2. Extraordinary family formation - caused by "undoubling"
   within family units and higher economic standards of
   living.

3. Increase in marriage rates.

4. Pension and annuity plans.

Politically, too, the U. S. Government is taking a positive interest in facilitating the acquisition of realty for home and investment purposes. Activities of the H. H. F. A., the F. H. A. and the V. A. are geared to make ownership of realty possible to any and all who meet the necessary minimum income criteria. All signs point to continued government action to encourage a ready flow of mortgage funds at favorable rates of interest.

In the present and "planned" political and financial climate, investment in real property - when appropriately considered and executed - should prove economically rewarding.

City Data

The community is best known as a trading center for Lincoln County with a population of 80,000 people. The city is bisected by four important U. S. Highways and is well located midway between two large commercial cities 110 miles to the North - East and 90 miles to the South - West.

In proportion to its size the community is one of the leading cities in the state. Its diverse economic activities assure continuous population growth and relative freedom from adverse effects of extreme swings of the business cycle.

Neighborhood Data

The subject property is located in the "hub" of the City and within the old Court House Square. This central business neighborhood encompasses approximately eight blocks bounded by Washington Street on the North, Birch Street on the East, Fort Bliss Avenue on the South and Coal Street on the West.

The construction of neighborhood shopping centers on Main Street and on Gulf Boulevard during the past eight years have diverted business activity from the subject location. The removal of the old County Court House and its relocation two blocks Northwesterly of the business center has also affected adversely the purchasing power of the number of store locations that are vacant and for rent and from the reduction of land value on the West and South side of the Square from an estimated $1,500 per front foot in 1956, to $1,000 per front foot in 1966.

There is every indication that property values on the Square are about to stabilize. The city has purchased the old Hotel property and has announced plans to convert the entire East block of the Square into a park and parking lot facility. This form of urban renewal should benefit materially the remaining business properties by eliminating available store competition and further by attracting shoppers from outlying areas to the central city. The store facilities to the South and East of the city Square are expected to benefit substantially from the construction of expanded parking lot facilities.

Generally, it is deemed that the neighborhood properties in the "hub" of the City can anticipate a stable and gradually improving financial and value position in the years ahead.

Site Data

The subject property is located on the South side of the City Square and in the center of the block bounded by Broadway on the North, Magnolia Street on the West, Main Street on the East, and Ft. King Avenue on the South.

The lot location is above street grade and measures 32 feet East and West and 119 feet North and South. The stair area is jointly owned and used, 1.5 feet of space belongs to each of the adjoining properties. Entire stair well is 3 feet wide. All streets in the area are paved and fitted with sidewalks, curb and gutters. All public utilities including storm and sanitary sewage, gas, telephone, electricity, and city water are available and connected to the site. Fire and police protection are deemed adequate and efficient.

Improvement Data

The improvements consist of a two story structure built of solid brick, painted white with a stuccoed store front facade. Girders are of wood as are the studs of the interior plastered walls. The roof is "built up" with layers of tar mopped roofing felt. Upstairs windows are of aluminum sash and of awning type manufacture. Store windows are of standard sheet glass.

The store area is served with two water closets and two lavatories, all in working condition. There are no water closet facilities in the upstairs storeroom areas. Electric wiring has been replaced in the downstairs store area and in the front one-half of the upstairs area. The rear upstairs storage area has old fashioned open wiring that should be replaced to eliminate a possible fire hazard.

The store finished flooring is of carpeting in the customer display area and of asphalt tile over concrete slab subflooring in the storage and work areas. The upstairs floors are of hard strip pine over rough pine subflooring.

The building is approximately eighty years old and appears structurally in sound condition. The effective economic age is forty-five years. The store front will have to be modernized in three to five years. Complete renovation including rewiring in the downstairs and upstairs area will be required at the termination of the present lease at an estimated cost of $3,500.

The store area is served with a modern gas fired "heat pump" of Arkla Servel Sun Valley manufacture, that provides all year heat and air conditioning.

The remaining economic life under normal maintenance is estimated to be fifteen years. Accrued depreciation not including deferred maintenance is estimated at $1\frac{1}{2}$ per cent over the effective building age.

Building Cost

Replacement cost - new is based on comparative building costs
and estimated @ $7.50 per square foot for the downstairs area, @ $6.50
per square foot for the upstairs area and @ $5.25 per square foot for
the "lean to" structure.

The heating and air conditioning system is only three years
old and has a present value of $3,500.

Present Occupancy

The subject property is presently leased for $457 per month
payable in advance for the downstairs and upstairs areas. The "lean
to" is rented on a month to month basis for $35. Properties in this
commercial area are rented for periods of 5 to 10 years with options
to renew for a like period. Present lease expires at end of current
month.

All interior repairs and decorating are the responsibility of
the lessee. Lessee too pays increases in taxes over those paid at time
of lease date. The lessor pays for taxes which currently amount to
$750 per year, plus special sewer and water tax of $55 per year.
Insurance cost is $275, Management fees 10% and exterior maintenance
and repairs average $400. This remaining economic life is 15 years.
Recapture of capital is calculated under the straight line method.
The heating and air conditioning system has an estimated life of 15 years.

Market Data

Sale No. 1 -- Unimproved site

Date of Sale	Six months ago
Sale price	$45,000
Lot size	40' x 115'
Location	corner
Subject rating	.95

Sale No. 2 -- Unimproved site

Date of Sale	Current
Sale price	$50,000
Lot size	44' x 110'
Location	corner
Subject rating	.90

Sale No. 3 -- Unimproved site

Date of Sale	Two years ago
Sale price	$30,000
Lot size	40' x 110'
Location	Interior lot
Subject rating	1.25

Sale No. 4 -- Unimproved site

Sale price	$60,000
Date of Sale	Current
Lot size	60' x 100'
Location	Interior
Subject rating	1.00

Sale No. 5 -- Store Property

Sale Price	$49,000
Date of sale	One year ago
Reported gross	$7,200
Estimated operating ratio	35 per cent
Building effective age	30 years
Remaining Economic life	20 years
Inprovement -- Property ratio	30 per cent
Building area	7,800 sq. ft.

Sale No. 6 -- Store and Loft Property

Sale price	$45,000
Date of Sale	6 months ago
Reported gross	$6,500
Estimated operating ratio	32 per cent
Building effective age	28 years
Remaining economic life	20 years
Improvement -- Property ratio	35 per cent
Building area	7,750 sq. ft.

Sale No. 7

Sale Price	$56,000
Date of Sale	1 year ago
Reported gross	$8,300
Estimated operating ratio	38 per cent
Building effective age	35 years
Remaining economic life	20 years

Sale No. 7 (cont.)

Improvement -- Property ratio	25 per cent
Building area	7,700 sq. ft.

Sale No. 8

Sale price	$45,000
Date of Sale	Current
Reported gross	$6,450
Estimated operating ratio	35 per cent
Building effective age	25 years
Remaining Economic life	20 years
Improvement -- Property ratio	26 per cent
Building area	5,320 sq. ft.

Market price adjustments are as follows:

Sales 6 months ago	5 per cent up
Sales 1 year ago	10 per cent up
Sales 2 years ago	15 per cent up

Straight line recapture of building investment is customarily applied to store buildings in the subject area.

Case Study No. 4

Store and Office Building

Analyze the field data and information obtained from reliable
sources as set forth below, and prepare schedules to support the
following:

1. Cost Approach to Value

2. Income Approach to Value

3. Market data approach to Value

4. Correlation of Value estimates and final Value
    conclusion.

Site Data

The subject store and office building is favorably located
south of the county court house at the intersection of Pine and Broad
Street. The site fronts on Pine Street for a distance of 110 feet to
a depth of 120 feet.

The site is level, above street grade and is furnished with
all city utilities as well as with natural gas, telephone and T.V. cable
services. Parking is provided across the street on a site 100' x 125'
which is leased for a period of 10 years with option to renew for an
additional 5 year lease term at a monthly rental of $800.

Improvement Data

      The subject property is a 4-story steel reinforced structure faced with natural rock stones. It was built five years ago and is in excellent physical condition. No deferred maintenance was observed.

      The structure contains stores and offices on the ground floor, offices on the second, third and fourth floors and a fully equipped restaurant on the fourth floor. A single automatic elevator serves the building.

      The interior walls are furred out, plastered and covered with washable wallpaper in the hallways. The interiors of all offices are mahogany paneled. Doors are of solid oak, mahogany stained and fitted with high grade solid brass door locks and hinges. Floors are of reinforced concrete and covered with wall-to-wall nylon carpet layed over cotton felt. Ceilings are soundproofed with accoustical tile. Picture window construction admits adequate daylight. Artificial lighting is recessed and flurescent to simulate daylight effect. The structure is fully and thermostatically heated. Air conditioned cooling capacity is 105 tons output.

      Each office has outside exposure providing good lighting throughout. The remaining economic life is estimated at 45 years.

Building Cost Data

      The structure contains 34,340 square feet. Replacement cost new is confirmed by local builders and architects at $20.50 per square foot exclusive of carpets, drapes and restaurant furnishings and equipment.

The replacement cost of furnishings and fixtures is as follows:

Carpets and Drapes $37,500

Restaurant furnishings   38,000

Income and Expense Data

The subject property has a total net rentable area of 26,000 square feet. The ground floor contains 5,500 square feet and rents at $5.25 per square foot. Upstairs offices occupy 19,500 square feet and rent for $4.75 per square foot. The restaurant is leased for a period of five (5) years at $1,450 per month. All offices and stores are under lease for periods of five to ten years.

Operating expenses experienced by the subject property appear in line with average office building operating costs as reported by the Research Division of the National Association of Building Owners and Managers. Applicable operating expenditures based on net rentable square foot area is as follows:

Cleaning	49.5¢
Electric	18.5
Heat	5.2
Air conditioning	15.8
Plumbing	2.4
Elevator	13.3
General Expense	13.5
General Repairs	8.2
Alterations	3.4
Decorating	4.7

Depreciation (recapture)   22.6

Management   12.5

Mortgage Amortization   32.4

Taxes and Insurance   82.3

Estimated life of restaurant
      furnishings   10 years

Estimated life of carpets and
      drapes   20 years

Market Indicies

Comparative sales indicate a unit value for the land at $10 per square foot. Similar buildings have been acquired at 6 times the annual gross income.

Investment capital is available as follows:

1st Mortgage 2/3 of Value @ 6%

2nd Mortgage 1/5 of Value @ 8%

Equity   @ 15%

The remaining economic life is 45 years. The annuity method of capitalization is indicated.

SUGGESTED ANSWERS

TO

CASES AND PROBLEMS

Suggested Answers:

1. All physical and tangible items which have attributes of, or claims to objects of, value are classified as <u>wealth</u>. <u>Property</u> is a right to control, use, and own wealth. Property as here defined is intangible. The appraiser is concerned with the evaluation of (property) rights in and to wealth. The larger the rights, as a general rule, the greater the future benefits and hence the greater the present value.

2. (a) <u>Value</u> is the present worth of future rights to income—or in terms of barter, the power of a good or service to command other goods or services in exchange. <u>Price</u> is the monetary measure of dollar value given in exchange for a good or service. Price may be more or less than value. It is only when the price paid is <u>warranted</u> that price and value are in equilibrium. <u>Cost</u> is a monetary measure of past sacrifices of the factors of production or expenditure for a good or service. Costs may further be identified as historical, original, replacement, or reproduction depending on meaning of the term. <u>Warranted</u> <u>Value</u> (or <u>market</u> <u>value</u>) is the highest price which a good or service can command in the open market if exposed for sale, assuming willing, ready, and fully informed buyers and sellers who transfer respective rights within a reasonable time on a cash or cash equivalent basis. (b) To possess value a product must have the following characteristics: utility, scarcity, and demand. It must also be transferable as to control from one to another. Each characteristic is important, but power to fill a need (utility) or scarcity standing alone does not create value in the absence of the other and necessary characteristics. Subjective value is a measure of worth to an individual. Value, unless limited in meaning by the use of adjective, is recognized as objective in character.

3. Yes—assuming all other things remain equal—the passage of time has affected the value of this property. The building is ten years older and thus nearer the end of its economic life. Value is based on the present worth of future rights to income and these inevitably are reduced as the structure ages, even though annual income does not diminish.

4. By use of the cost approach only, Mr. Baker could commit a serious error in value. A hotel in the desert costs as much if not more to construct than a hotel in a large city when built in conformity with the concept of highest and best land use. The value of the desert hotel no doubt is zero. To establish value for loan purposes, Mr. Baker should check the findings derived under the cost approach with value results obtained under the market and income approaches to value.

5. No, zoning regulations cannot prevent value decline. Zoning regulations are intended to retard value declines in residential areas. Zoning regulations, however, apply to land uses and not to people. The infiltration of a lower social or economic group of residents will affect value adversely no matter how well designed or enforced zoning regulations are in a given neighborhood or community.

6. This statement is true. Where legal requirements cause an increase in construction costs without offsetting benefits resulting from a better housing product, land values will tend to be lower. Land is "residual" in character under a highest and best use. Legal impediments that lower income inevitably lower the value of land that is subject to adverse controls. This is especially true where communities are competing with each other for population growth and economic development.

7. All other things remaining equal, a decline in income because of the imposition of added taxes lowers the value of the affected property.
    (a) The value of the land prior to the imposition of the tax was:
           $V = I/R$ or $\$200 \div .05 =$ $\$4,000$
    (b) The value of the land after the tax levy is:
           $V = I/R$ or $\$180 \div .05 =$ $\underline{3,600}$
           Capital levy = $\overline{\$\ \ \ 400}$
    (c) Levy at 4% = $V = I/R = \$20 \div .04 =$ $\$\ \ \ 500$

8. To the extent that past managerial practices influence future income favorably or unfavorably, value is affected. Past managerial practices are of interest to an appraiser because exceptional management over past years may reduce future operating costs and produce a flow of income in excess of that which ordinarily can be anticipated under "typical" operations. Conversely, poor management over past years may cause excessive operational outlays in future years in order to bring the property up to the income performance expected under "typical" management and operation.

9. Past and present income serve as bench marks for forecasting the anticipated future flow of income. Value should always be based on future rights to income and not on established past or present income.

10. One dollar invested at 5 per cent compound interest will grow over a period of 12 years to 1.7959 dollars, or $1.80. See future worth (compound amount) of 1 table in Appendix 3.

11.
    Compound amount of $1.00 at 6 per cent for 10 years = $1.7908
    Compound amount of $5.00 at 6 per cent for 10 years =
            5 × 1.7908 = $8.95
            Original investment $\underline{5.00}$
            Interest earned $3.95

12.

> $1.00 invested at compound interest of 5 per cent over a period of
> 10 years = $1.6289
>
> $2,000 invested at 5 per cent compound interest over
> 10 years = $2,000 × 1.6289 = $3,257.80

This is the amount the property must realize to return the original investment plus compound interest at 5 per cent.

13. The present value of an amount due at some given future time is the "discounted" present value of that future amount or a sum which invested today at compound interest will grow to the amount due at the given future time.

14. The present worth of $1.00 due ten years hence at 6 per cent = $.5584. The present worth of $20,000 = 20,000 × .5584 = $11,168. To state it differently, $11,168, if invested at compound interest of 6 per cent over a period of 10 years, will grow to $20,000.

15. The present worth of $1.00 due five years hence at 5 per cent interest is $.7835.[1] The present worth of $2,000 = $2,000 × .7835 = $1,567.

16. (a) An annuity is a periodic amount paid or received regularly over a specified time. The periodic payments generally are, but need not necessarily be, equal in amount. (b) The compound amount of an annuity is the future accumulated sum obtained from uninterrupted investment of the periodic amounts (annuity) at compound interest over a specified time.

17. Original investment of $3,000 at 6 per cent compound interest
over 10 years should grow to $3,000 × 1.79[1] or $5,370

Annuity of $100 at 6 per cent compound interest over
10 years should grow to $100 × 13.18[1] or 1,318

Total investment at end of tenth year $6,688

18. An annuity of $600 invested at compound interest of 7 per cent over 5 years will grow to $600 × 5.75[2] or $3,450. This amount represents the cost of the leasehold to date.

19. (a) The present value of an annuity is the total discounted present worth of each annuity payment. (b) Present value of an annuity of $1.00 at 6 per cent interest over a period of three years is $2.67. (See present worth of annuity table in Appendix 3.)

20. (a) One dollar per year at 8 per cent over 50 years is worth today $12.2335. $4,000 per year is worth today $4,000 × 12.2335[2], or $48,934. (b) Present worth of $1.00 due 50 years hence at 6 per cent is $.05429.[2] The present worth of $15,000 = $15,000 × .05429 = $814.35. The total value of the entire property is:

---

[1] Factors taken from compound interest table in Appendix 3.
[2] Factors taken from compound interest table in Appendix 3.

Present worth of 50-year income stream $48,934
Reversionary (present) value of land   814
Total present value of property $49,748

21. (a) Capitalization is the process used in the conversion of a future stream of income into a present sum or value. (b) Perpetuity is unending expectancy of income or events into infinity. (c) Rate of capitalization is the "rate" used in the conversion of a future stream of income into a sum of present worth. For depreciable property, this rate is a composite of the rate of interest plus the rate of amortization or depreciation. (d) Rate of interest is a measure of the wages of capital or the cost of money. It is a return on the investment and is exclusive of a rate of amortization or depreciation. Where such rates (for losses in value) are added the rate of interest becomes a rate of capitalization.

22.
(a) $500 × 8.559 (P.W. of annuity at 8 per cent) = $4,280
(b) $500 × 12.494 (P.W. of annuity at 8 per cent) = $6,247
(c) $500 × 12.5 or $500 ÷ .08   = $6,250

23. (a)

Year	Income		P.W. Factor		Present Worth
1	$ 200	×	.9434	=	$ 188.68
2	225	×	.8900	=	200.25
3	225	×	.8396	=	188.91
4	250	×	.7921	=	198.03
5	275	×	.7473	=	205.51
6	300	×	16.6667 =		
	$5,000	×	.7473	=	3,736.50

Total present value $4,717.88

(b) If V   I/R, then I   V x R
     I $4,717.88 x .06 (perpuity rate)
     $283.0728

Proff   V   I/R $283.0728   .06 $4,717.88

24.

Year	Income		6 Per Cent P.W. Factor		6 Per Cent Discount Factor		Present Worth
1- 5	$ 800	×	4.2124		—	=	$ 3,370
6-10	1,000	×	4.2124	×	.7473	=	3,148
11-30	1,200	×	11.4699	×	.5584	=	7,686
	Land value		$20,000	×	.1741	=	3,482

Total present value of property $17,686

25.

Year	Income	7 Per Cent P.W. Factor		7 Per Cent Discount Factor		Present Worth
1- 2	$4,000	1.808		—	=	$ 7,232
3- 4	5,000	1.808	×	.8734	=	7,896
5-30	4,500	11.826	×	.7629	=	40,599
		Total value				$55,727

Alternate Solution

Year	Income		Inwood Factors	Deferment Factor		Present Worth
1 - 5	$800	x	(4. 2124-0. 0000)	4. 2124	=	$3,370
6 - 10	1,000	x	(7. 3601-4. 2124)	3.1477		3,148
11 - 30	1, 2000	x	(13. 7648-7. 3601)	6.4047		7,686
Land value 20,000			x	.1741	=	3,482
	Total present value					$17,686

26. (a) Straight line method of capitalization:
Income to building:
$$l = V \times R = \$250,000 \times .105(.08 + .025) \qquad = \$26,250$$
Income to land:
$$\$50,000 \times .06 \qquad = \underline{\quad 3,000}$$
Total Income $29,250

(b) Inwood, or annuity, method of capitalization:
Income to building:
$$\$250,000 \times .08386 (.08 + .00386 \qquad = \$20,965$$
Income to land:
$$\$50,000 \times .06 \qquad = \underline{\quad 3,000}$$
Total Income $23,965

(b) Alternate method of capitalization
Income to building:
$$250,000 \div 11.9246 \text{ (Inwood factor at 8\%)} \qquad = \$20,965$$
Income to land:
$$\$50,000 \times .06 \qquad = \underline{\quad 3,000}$$
Total Income $23,965

27. (a) <u>Effective gross revenue</u> is the amount of realizable revenue anticipated after deduction of vacancy and collection losses. (b) <u>Occupancy ratio</u> is a ratio or per cent of rentable space occupied to total available rentable space in a building. (c) <u>Collection losses</u> are uncollectable rent. (d) <u>Net operating income</u> is income after deduction of operating costs from effective gross revenue. It is capitalizable income before interest charges on the investment and amortization charges to recapture the investment over the estimated economic life of the property. (e) <u>Operating ratio</u> is a per cent relationship of operating expenses to effective gross revenue. (f) <u>Fixed charges</u> are expenditures such as taxes, fuel costs, and insurance which do not vary significantly with occupancy or operation of the property. (g) <u>Equity income</u> is income left after deduction for costs (interest and amortization) of borrowed mortgage-funds. (h) <u>Trading on the</u>

equity is the practice of borrowing funds at a rate less than that earned by the property as a whole. Trading on the equity increases the rate of earnings on the equity capital. (i) Yield on equity investment is a percentage ratio of equity income to equity capital.

28. Property B has the greater value because of its favorable operating ratio as compared with Property A. The income from B is less risky than income from Property A; hence income from B will be capitalized at a lower rate of interest. A 20 per cent drop in revenue wipes out the net income for A but lowers the net income for B only by $8,000, or 40 per cent.

29. The 3 per cent sinking fund table (see Appendix 3) shows a rate per dollar of .0372. Multiplying this by $1,000 gives the answer of $37.20. If $37.20 is placed in a sinking fund annually at 3 per cent compound interest over a period of 20 years, the fund will accumulate to $1,000 over this period of time.

30. Interest is a wage paid for the use of capital. It is the cost of money.

31. The component parts of interest are:
    1. A safe (U.S. Bond) rate.
    2. A rate for nonliquidity of investment.
    3. A rate of management (management of the security and not of the property).
    4. A rate to reflect risk of the investment.

32. (a) Over-all rates of capitalization ratio are derived by dividing net income before interest and amortization by total value (land and improvements) of the property. (b) Fractional rates are ratios derived by dividing income attributable to a fraction of the property by the value of the part. Thus mortgage rates, equity rates, land rates, and building rates are fractional rates.

33.

(a)
$6,000 loan @ 6 per cent	=	$360 interest
$5,000 loan @ 5 per cent	=	250 interest
$1,000 additional loan	=	$110 interest or 11 per cent

(b)
$7,000 loan @ 8 per cent	=	$560 interest
$6,000 loan @ 6 per cent	=	360 interest
$1,000 additional loan	=	$200 interest or 20 per cent

34.

Property A	.25 × 6% =	1.5%
	.75 × 8% =	6.0%
	Total =	7.5%
Property B	.50 × 6% =	3.0%
	.50 × 9% =	4.5%
	Total =	7.5%
Property C	.75 × 7% =	5.25%
	.25 × 9% =	2.25%
	Total =	7.5%

35.
    Effective gross revenue $18,000
    Operating expenses   6,000
    Operating income $12,000
    Rate of interest: 2/3 of 6% = 4%
                1/3 of 12% = 4%
    Interest rate   8%
    Inwood Factor 30 years @ 8% = 11.258
    Value of income stream $12,000 x 11.258 = $135,096
    Add land reversion: $40,000 x .0994 = 3,976
            Total Value $139,072
    Over-all rate of capitalization
    $12,000 ÷ 139.072 = 8.63%

36. Income of $5,000 ÷ 2.5 = $2,000 maximum interest
    $2,000 interest ÷ .05 (mortgage rate) = $40,000 mortgage
    $40,000 mortgage ÷ .60 (mortgage to value ratio) = $66,667 or
        value of entire property
    $5,000 income ÷ $66,667 (value) = 7.5% rate of capitalization
    (over-all rate)

37. (a) No, the buildings have identical values. The extra cost of
blasting rock is a charge ascribable to land. (b) After blasting, yes—
before blasting, no. The value of lot B before blasting was only $500.
(c) The nature of blasting expenditures is a land development cost
chargeable to land to bring it up to its highest and best use.

38. Building value 100,000 cu. ft. × .35 = $35,000
    Total income before interest and depreciation is $4,500
    Income to building:
        $35,000 × .085 =   2,975
    Income to land $1,525
    Value of land $1,525 ÷ .06 = $25,417

39.
    (a) $350,000 ($200,000 land plus $150,000 cost of remodeling)

    (b) $200,000 @ 7% = $14,000
        150,000 @ 9.5% =   14,250
        Taxes   14,500
          Total net rental $42,750

    (c) $200,000 @ 7% = $14,000
        250,000 @ 11% (7% + 4%) = 27,500
        Taxes   14,500
          Total net rental $56,000

    (d) As shown in (c), above, the prudent buyer wants a return on
        the investment at the going rate, plus amortization require-
        ments to depreciate the investment over the estimated re-
        maining life of the improvements, plus property taxes due.

40.

   (a) Whenever land value is known with accuracy, the appraiser should use the building residual method of capitalization.

   (b)

Net income	$6,000
Income to land $10,000 × .08 =	800
Income to furnishings $5,500 × .20 =	1,100
Net income residual to building	$4,100

Building value = $4,100 ÷ .12 = $34,167

41.

   (a) The lessor's interest

$10,000 (for 5 years) × 4.2124 =	$ 42,124
12,000 (for next 35 years) × 10.8339	
(15.0463 - 4.2124) =	130,007
Land reversion = $240,000 × .0972 =	23,328
Total lessor's interest	$195,459

   (b) The lessee's interest

1. Land income $240,000 × .06 =	$ 14,400
Less contract rent for 5 years	10,000
Net to lessee	$ 4,400
2. Land income next 35 years	$ 14,400
Less contract rent	12,000
Net to lessee	$ 2,400

Value: 4,400 × 4.2124 =	$ 18,535
2,400 x 10.8339 (15.0463 - 4.2124)	26,001
Total value in land	$ 44,536
Value of building as appraised	160,000
Total value, lessee	$204,536

Summary:

Lessor's interest	$195,459
Lessee's interest	204,536
Total	$399,995
Say	$400,000

42.

Gross revenue $22 × 12 × 50 =		$13,200
Less vacancy and collection losses @ 3% =		396
Effective gross revenue		$12,804
Less operating expenses:		
Management cost 5%	$ 640	
Repairs & maintenance	300	
Reserve for replacement	600	
Insurance	240	
Taxes	2,600	
Total expenses		$ 4,380
Operating income		$ 8,424
Income to land: $100,000 @ 6%		6,000
Income to building		$ 2,424

(a) Building value—straight line capitalization

$2,424 ÷ .08 = $ 30,300
Add land value   100,000
        Total value $130,300

(b) Building value—Inwood method

$2,424 × 15.76 = $ 38,202
Add value of land   100,000
        Total value $138,202

(c) Building value—Hoskold method

$2,424 × 14.521 = $ 35,199
Add value of land   100,000
        Total value $135,199

43.

(a) Mr. A's interest:

Income of $3,000 x 11,655 (Inwood) $34,965
Land reversion $75,000 x .06763   5,072
        Total $40,037

(b) Mr. B's interest at 8%:

Income of $8,000 - $3,000 = $5,000 x 11.665 = $58,275

(c) Mr. C's interest at 8%:

Income of $12,000 - $8,000 = $4,000 x 11.655 = $46,620

In practice the interests of B and C are capitalized at a higher rate -- perhaps 10 and 12 percent respectively.

44.

Office building:
        Sale price $75,000 at 125% of cost
        Cost = $75,000 ÷ 1.25 = $60,000
        Gain = $75,000 - $60,000 = $15,000
Apartment building:
        Sale price: $75,000 at 75% of cost
        Cost = $75,000 ÷ 75 = $100,000
        Loss = $100,000 - $75,000 = $25,000
        Net loss = $25,000 - $15,000 $10,000

45.

Total value $150,000
Building value   125,000
Land value   25,000

Total income $14,000
Land income $25,000 x .06   1,500
Building income $12,500

(a) Building -- over-all rate $12 500 ÷ $125,000 =.10 or 10%
(b) Building rate   .10
    Depreciation rate (straight line)   .05
    Interest rate   .05 or 5%
(c) Building rate -- Inwood factor   10.0000
        (Factor = Value ÷ Income)
    7.5% Inwood factor   10.194
    8.0% Inwood factor   9.818
    .5% differential factor   .376

7. 5% Inwood factor 　　　　　　　　10.194
　X% Inwood factor 　　　　　　　　10.000
　　X　differential 　　　　　　　　　.194

$$\frac{X}{.5} = \frac{.194}{.376} \quad \text{hence, } X = .258$$

Interest rate $= 7.5\% + .258\% = 7.758\%$

46.

Lot A = 100' × \$300 = 　　　　　　　　　　\$30,000
　　　　Corner value = 100' × \$200 × .72 = 　　14,400
　　　　Total　　　　　　　　　　　　　\$44,400

Lot B = 25 × \$300 × 1.09 = 　　　　　　　　8,175

Lot C = 25 × \$200 = 　　　　　　　　　　5,000
　　　　　　　Total value　　　　　　　\$57,575

47.　4 years　48 months
　　6% interest　1/2% interest per month
　　1　V x R　\$10,000 x .023485　\$234. 85

48.　V = I x F or 1/R
　　V = 　\$60　x 42.580318　= \$2,554. 82
　　V = \$60 = .023485 　=　\$2554. 82

49.　Table of Amortization for a \$10,000 Mortgage over 8 years
　　@ 6 percent Interest per annum.

Year	Month	Periodic Payment	1/2 Percent Interest	Amortization	Remaining Value
0	1	\$131.41	50.00	81.41	\$10,000.00
0	2	\$131.41	49.59	81.82	9,918.59
					9,836.77

50.

Inwood factor:　Rate "on"　=　　　　　.06
　　　　　　　Rate "of"　=　　　　　.012649
　　Total annuity rate　　=　　　　　.072649
　Factor=1 -.072649=13.7648

Hoskold factor:　Rate "on"　=　　　　.06
　　　　　　　Rate　"of"　=　　　　.021019
　　Total sinking fund (3%) rate　　　.081019
　Factor=1 -.081019　12.3428

51.

		As Reported	As Adjusted
Gross revenue ($45.50 × 12 × 40)		$21,840	
Collection and vacancy losses 5%[3]		1,092	
Effective gross revenue		$20,748	

Operating Expenses	As Reported	As Adjusted
Taxes on land and building	$2,400	$2,400
Power and light	200	200
Depreciation provision[4]	1,600	
Repairs	800	800
Renovating and painting	1,200	1,200
Janitor expense	2,000	2,000
Extermination	60	60
Replacements: 40 ranges[5] (8-year life)	3,000	375
Replacements: 40 refrigerators[6] (12-year life)	6,000	500
New roof[7]	1,100	55
Legal fees	120	120
Corporation tax[8]	300	
Income tax[9]	350	
Mortgage interest[10]	1,200	
Mortgage amortization[11]	1,000	

[3]It is good business practice to provide for collection and vacancy losses. By experience such losses and vacancies average currently 5 per cent of gross revenues.

[4]In appraising, depreciation provision should not be treated as an operating expense. The capitalization process already provides for a return of the building's capital value. If depreciation is to be treated as an expense item then the remaining net income must be capitalized as a perpetuity. It is customary to capitalize over the life of the building, however. Depreciation, thus, is automatically cared for through amortization in the capitalization process.

[5 & 6]Since the equipment has 8- and 12-year service lives, the expenses per annum should only include the proportionate share of such expenses, in this case as follows:
Ranges $3,000 ÷ 8 = 375 per annum
Refrigerators $6,000 ÷ 12 = 500 per annum

[7]Expenditure for a new roof based on 20-year life.

[8 & 9]Corporation taxes and income taxes are not operating expenses but rather income expenses. Personal or corporate taxes are not considered in the appraising of real property.

[10 & 11]Mortgage payments or amortization are not considered unless the problem calls for valuation of the equity. Property is always appraised on a cash sale basis; adjustments may then be made for the nature of the sale terms.

Management fees[12]	1,200	1,037
Water	450	450
Fire insurance		
(3-year policy)	600	200
Paving assessment[13]	400	
Promotion and advertising[14]	250	250
Liability and comprehensive		
insurance[15]		100

Adjusted operating expenses	$ 9,747
Net income (before depreciation, amortization, and interest)	$ 11,001
Income attributable to land:	
7.5% of $20,000 =	1,500
Income attributable to building	$ 9,501
Building value (present worth, of an annuity of $9,501 for 40 years at 7.5%)	
9,501 × 12.5944 =	$119,659
Add land value (via market approach)	20,000
Total value of apartment property	$139,659

52. Value of 20-Year Sandwich Leasehold:

	First 5 Years	Next 5 Years	Next 10 Years
Payments by C to B	$1,500	$1,500	$1,800
Payments by B to A	1,000	1,200	1,200
Surplus income to B	$ 500	$ 300	$ 600

The value of the sandwich leasehold is derived by capitalizing (finding the present worth of) an annuity as follows:

First 5 years $500 per year or $500 × 4.1557 =	$2,077.85
Next 5 years 300 per year or 300 × 3.0331 (7.1888 - 4.1557) =	909.93
Next 10 years 600 per year or 600 × 3.8297 (11.0185 - 7.1888) =	2,297.82
Total value of sandwich leasehold	$5,285.60

---

[12]Management fees are generally standardized at 5 per cent of effective gross revenue.

[13]Paving assessment is not considered as operating expenses. Such expenditures are considered capital additions. This assessment will be reflected in the increased land value.

[14]Such expenses need be carefully checked to ascertain whether or not they are a part of management costs and are to be excluded.

[15]Not reported in original schedule. This insurance expense is a necessary operating item.

53. The anticipated revenue from a new office building can be estimated by comparison with rentals derived from comparable office buildings in the area under study. Adjustments are made for neighborhood, site location and facilities, building newness, services, and conveniences. On the basis of this comparison a rental schedule for the subject property can be established with reasonable accuracy.

54. This problem involves the capitalization of discounting to present worth of a varying annuity at 7.5% interest as follows:

First five-year income	$1,600 per year or		
	1,600 × 4.0459	=	$ 6,473.44
Next five-year income	$2,000 per year or		
	2,000 × 2.8182		
	(6.8641 - 4.0459)	=	5,636.40
Next twenty-year income	$2,400 per year or		
	2,400 × 4.9463		
	(11.8104 - 6.8641)	=	11,871.12

Total Present Worth of Income for Next 30 Years $23,980.96

Add present value of land (land will be free in 30 years)
$10,000 × .1142   =   1,142.00

Total value of property $25,122.96

Rounded to $25,125

This problem may also be solved as follows:

	Annuity Factor	Present Worth or Discount Factor	
Present worth of first five-year annuity of	$1,600 = 1,600 × 4.0459 × 1.000000		= $ 6,473.44
Present worth of next five-year annuity of	$2,000 = 2,000 × 4.0459 × .696559		= 5,636.42
Present worth of next twenty-year annuity of	$2,400 = 2,400 × 10.1945 × .485194		= 11,871.14

Total Present Worth for 30-Year Income $23,981.00

Add present value of land (discounted over 30 years)
$10,000 × .1142   =   1,142.00

Total value of property $25,123.00

Rounded to $25,125

55. This problem involves the theory or concept of land utilization. Land at any one time can only have one "highest and best" use. The "highest and best" use of land is that use which will yield to land the highest present value (derived by discounting residual net land income under the most profitable future use). In this problem consideration must be given to the fact that apartment or office buildings have an estimated life of 50 or more years. Thus, the higher net income derived from the office building from the 11th to the 50th year will undoubtedly more than offset the anticipated loss of income over the first ten years. To illustrate:

Suppose the net income to land from the 10-story apartment house is estimated over the life of the building at $2,000 per annum. The income to land under the 20-story office building is estimated to be $1,500 for the first ten years and $3,000 thereafter for 40 years. The present value of the land under use:

(a) (over 50 years only) at 5% is $2,000 × 18.2559 or $36,511.80
Under use:

(b) land value is $1,500 × 7.7217 (first 10 years)   = $11,582.55
　　　　　　　$3,000 × 10.5342 (next 40 years)
　　　　　　　　　　　　(18.2559 – 7.7217)   =   31,602.60
Total value under use (b) $43,185.15
Differential to land: use (b) over (a)   = $ 6,673.35

56. If the loss in dollars due to depreciation could be estimated with reasonable accuracy, the depreciation amount could be treated as an operating cost and the net income <u>after depreciation</u> capitalized by the rate of interest in the same manner that income to land is capitalized. In practice, however, depreciation is estimated as a "rate" per annum and this rate of amortization or rate of future depreciation is added to the prevailing interest rate to form a rate of capitalization. In this case depreciation as an amount must not be deducted as an operating expense. To do so would penalize the property twice and lower the value accordingly—and erroneously.

57. In estimating the <u>present</u> value of property, the appraiser must give consideration to estimates or predictions of revenues and expenses also in <u>present</u> dollars. Thus, logically and consistently the appraiser should <u>not</u> give consideration to future trends or changes in the value of money. Under a system of free enterprise a change in the value of money reflects itself in an adjusted price-level. Thus if money value goes down—normally—both revenues and expenses will rise and the price of the property will move upward proportionately. Of course if the appraiser should have <u>valid</u> (supportable) reason to anticipate restrictions in the rise of revenues (through rent control) but no restriction in the rise of expenses, he will have to give consideration to such value hazards. Normally, however, such hazards are given weight in the selection of a higher rate of capitalization to reflect this added risk.

58.

	1st Year	2nd Year	3rd to 40th Year
Net income	$ 9,500.00	$12,000.00	$14,000.00

Building life—40 years
Building cost—$150,000
Building rate—8%
Building returns

	1st Year	2nd Year	3rd to 40th Year
150,000 + 11.9246 =	12,579.04[16]	12,579.04	12,579.04
Residual land income	(3,079.04)	(579.04)	1,420.96

Land value at end of
    3rd year

	1st Year	2nd Year	3rd to 40th Year
$1,420.96 + .08 =			17,762.00[18]
Present value factor 8%	0.9259	0.8573	0.8573

Present value of land

	1st Year	2nd Year	3rd to 40th Year
returns	(2,850.88)[17]	(496.41)[17]	15,227.36[19]

Land value = $15,227.36 - $496.41 - $2,850.88 = $11,880.07

Summary

Land value	$ 11,880.07
Building value	150,000.00
Total	$161,880.07

---

[16]Under the highest and best use, building cost equals value. Therefore the problem calls for determination of the income necessary to provide a return on the investment (in this case 8 per cent) and a return of the investment (amortization) over the life of the property.

Since Value = Income × Annuity Present Worth Factor, Income must equal Value ÷ Annuity Present Worth Factor, or 150,000 ÷ 11.9246 = $12,579.04.

[17]Land income and land value under the highest and best use is always residual. In this instance the net income for the first and second year is insufficient to meet required building returns, thus leaving to land a discounted deficit of $2,850.88 and $496.41 in these two years respectively. Such deficits result in negative value items which must be subtracted from the positive value item.

[18]Income to land is generally capitalized into perpetuity. In this instance the stabilized income at the end of the third year is so capitalized.

[19]The same present value factor is used in the third year as in the second. The reason for this is that the capitalization process already includes the discounting of income anticipated to begin with a year hence.

59.

(a) Net income after taxes $570,000
    Taxes as billed   225,000
    Net income before taxes,
      interest, and amortization $795,000
    Land rate of capitalization:
      Interest rate   .075
      Tax rate   .030
      Total rate   .105
    Land income: $I = V \times R$
      $\$2,000,000 \times .105 =$ 210,000
    Income residual to building $585,000
    Building value:
      Interest rate   .075
      Depreciation rate   .025
      Tax rate   .030
      Total rate   .13
    Value: $V = I/R$
      $\$585,000 \div .13 =$ $4,500,000
    Property value:
      Building $4,500,000
      Land   2,000,000
      Total $6,500,000

(b) Property taxes:
    $\$6,500,000 \times .03 =$ $195,000

(c) Net income after taxes:
    $\$795,000 - 195,000 =$ $ 600,000

60. Property income $50,000
    Mortgage – debt service payments   25,440
    Equity – cash flow $24,560

  (a) Present worth of cash flow – 10 years
      at 12% $\equiv 24,560 \times 5.65 =$ $138,764

      Present worth of cash-reversion on
      date of sale:
            Selling price $400,000
            Market

(b) Present worth of reversionary equity =
$164,098 x .322 (12%) =   52,840
(c) Total present worth of equity $19 1,604
(d) Add present value of mortgage   300,000
(e) Purchase price to yield 12% rate of equity return $ 491,604
        Rounded to $ 491,600

61. Solution:
    Purchase price $ 400,000
    Mortgage loan   280,000
    Cash-equity investment   120, 000

    Selling price $400,000 x .925 =
    Mortgage balance - 15 years remaining - $ 370,000
      $2,256 monthly payment x 107.8734 (180
      month factor at 7.5%) =   243,363
    (a) Reversion to equity $126,637
       Revenue $36,000
       Debt service   27,072
    (b) Cash flow $ *

    Trial interest yield rate of 8%
      Present worth of $8,928 for 5 years =
        $8,928   3.993 = $ 35,650
      Present worth of reversion of
        $126,637 x .681 =   86,240
        Total present value of equity at 8% $1 21,890

    Trial interest yield rate of 9%
      Present worth of $8,928 for 5 years
        $8,928 x 3.890 = $ 34,730
      Present worth of reverison of
        $126,637 x .645   81,680
        Total present value of equity at 9% $ 116,410

    Interpolation for accurate yield rate:
     1. Equity value at 8%   = $121,890
        Equity value at 9%   =   116, 410
        Difference $ 1,890
     2. Equity value at 8%   121,890
        Equity value at x%   120,000
        Difference $ 1,890

    Rate to be added to .08 =
     $1,890 -- $5,380   .0035   .03   .0835
     or 8.35%

Case Study No. 1

Suggested Solution

Development of the entire subdivision without delay.

Gross Sales 210 sites @ $4,750 =		$ 997,500
Add refund @ $90 per lot times 210 =		18,900
Total Sales and Refund		$1,016,400
Less Sales Expense 10% of $997,500 =	$ 99,750	
Legal and other expenses		
4.5% of $997,500 =	44,888	
Total Sales and Legal Costs		144,638
Gross sales before costs of development		
profit and interest		$ 871,762
Cost of Development		
Streets 15,000 L.F. @ $9 =	135,000	
Water 15,500 L.F. @ $4 =	62,000	
Sewer 15,500 L.F. @ $4.50 =	69,750	
Site preparation 210 x $80 =	16,800	
Electric facilities 210 x $450 =	94,500	
Water & Sewage connections		
210 x $180	37,800	
Planning & Engineering cost	12,000	
Total Development Costs	$427,850	

Interest on development costs:

$427,850 ÷ 2.554* = $167,522

$167,522 x 3 = $502,566 - $427,850 =   74,716

Development Costs plus Interest	502,566
Proceeds from sale before profit and interest	$ 369,196
Less Developer's Profit 12% of $997,500 =	119,700
Proceeds from sale -- before interest	$ 249,496

Proceeds per year = 249,496 ÷ 3 - $83,165

Present worth of 83,165 over 3 years @ 8.5% = $83,165 x 2.554* =

$212,403 or rounded to $2,125 per acre for 100 acres equals

$212,500

---

*Present worth of an annuity of $1 over 3 years at 8.5% interest.

Case Study No. 1

Alternate Solution

Gross Sales 210 sites @ $4,750 = $ 997,500

    Refunds 210 sites @ $90 =   18,900

Total Proceeds $1,016,400

Less Selling and legal expenses   144,638

Gross Sales -- before development costs,

    profit and interest $ 871,762

Less profit 12%   119,700

Gross after profit $ 752,062

Present worth of Income -- 3 years delayed

    $752,062 ÷ 3 = $250,687 x 2.554* = $640,254

    Less Development Costs   =   427,850

Value of Undeveloped Land   = $212,404

Rounded to $212,500

_____

*Present worth of an annuity of $1 over 3 years at 8.5% interest.

<u>Solution No. 2</u>

<u>Development in stages over 3 year period</u>

Gross Sales 70 lots @ $4,750 =		$332,500
Add Refunds -- 70 times $90 =		6,300
Total Gross per year		$338,800

Development Costs per year

    $427,850 + $42,785* = $470,635

$470,635 ÷ 3 =	$153,545	
Interest on Development Costs		
1 year 8.5% of $153,545 =	13,051	
Selling expense 10% of $332,500 =	33,250	
Legal Expense etc. 4.5% of $332,500 =	14,962	
Profit 12% on $332,500 =	39,900	
Total Development Charges		254,708
Net Proceeds per year		$ 84,092
Present Worth of $84,092 x 2.554** =		214,771

Rounded to <u>$214,800</u>

---

    *Added Cost for piecemeal development over three equal stages.

    **Present worth of an annuity of $1 over 3 years at 8.5% interest.

Note: Since sales of 70 lots per year are deemed reasonably certain,
it is recommended that development of the entire subdivision be
undertaken and completed as a single project. This will incur
a saving of approximately $3,000, as compared with development
phased out and delayed over the three year period.

Case Study No. 2

Suggested Solution

1. Cost Approach to Value

Replacement Cost New: Building Cubic

    Contents = 80' x 90' x 56' = 403,200 cu. ft.

        403,200 cu. ft. x $.95 = $383,040

    Add cost of furniture equipment:

        60 ranges @ $120 =   7,200

        Furniture   1,500

        60 Refrigerators @ $160 =   9,600

        60 Dishwashers @ $140 =   8,400

Total Costs New $409,740

Less Accrued Depreciation   none

Depreciated Replacement Cost -- New $409,740

Add Land Value by Comparison

    15,000 sq. ft. x $3.50 =   52,500

        Total Value -- **under** Cost Approach $462,240

Rounded to $462,000

2. Market Approach To Value

Sale No.	1	2	3	4
Sale Price	$470,000	240,000	490,000	576,000
Time Adjustment	none	none	none	1.10
Adjusted Price	$470,000	240,000	490,000	633,600
Land Value	$ 45,000	22,000	48,000	60,000
Dep. Building Value	$425,000	218,000	442,000	573,600
Per cent condition	.90	.80	1.00	.96
Adjusted Cost New	$472,200	272,500	442,000	597,500
No. Apartments	69	40	65	87
No. Rooms	158	94	151	206
Cost New per Apt.	$ 6,843	6,813	6,800	6,868
Cost New per Room	$ 2,989	2,899	2,927	2,900
Gross Income	$ 68,115	34,300	70,500	83,450
Gross Multiplier	6.9	7.0	6.95	6.9

Market Value of Subject Property

1. 60 apartments @ $6,800* per apartment = $408,000

   Add Land Value   52,500

                      Indicated Value $460,500

2. 140 Rooms @ $2,925* per room = $409,500

   Add Land Value   52,500

                      Indicated Value $462,000

3. Gross Income $66,322 x 6.95* (multiplier) = $460,938

*Market indexes based principally on sale No. 3, because no adjustment for condition of age of building was necessary.

Indicated Value Via Market Approach

$461,000

3. Income Approach To Value

Gross Revenue

30 Apts. @ 90 x 12 =		$32,400
10 Apts. @ 100 x 12 =		12,000
15 Apts. @ 110 x 12 =		19,800
5 Apts. @ 125 x 12 =		7,500
Total Revenue		$71,700
Less 7.5% Vacancy & Collection Losses		5,378
Effective Revenue		$66,322

Less Operating Expenses

Management 5% =	$3,316	
Real Estate Taxes		
City $275,000 @ 13.65 =	3,754	
County 275,000 @ 8.35 =	2,296	
Insurance .0035 x $327,800 =	1,150	
Liability	125	
Payroll	3,000	
Electricity	1,200	
Water & sewage service	1,400	

Heating fuel	$1,300	
Legal, etc.	500	
Painting and decorating	2,667	
Exterior repairs	800	
Supplies	450	
Elevator Contract	1,000	
Repairs general	700	

Reserve for Replacements

Ranges $7,200 ÷ 15 =	480	
Refrigerators $9,600 ÷ 15 =	640	
Dishwashers $8,400 ÷ 12 =	700	
Lobby Furnishings $1,500 ÷ 10 =	150	
Equipment $15,000 ÷ 15 =	1,000	

Total Operating Expense & Reserves	26,628
Operating Income -- before depreciation	$39,694

Interest rate 8.5%

Income to Land

8.5% x $52,500 =	4,462
Income residual to building	$35,323

Building Value

35,232 x 11.566 =	$407,493
Add Land Value of	52,500
Total Value -- Earnings Approach	$459,993

Rounded to $460,000

Alternate Income Valuation

Net building income before depreciation $35,232

Depreciation Reserve =

    Depreciation Rate   .0014634 = 1.6925%

    Annuity Rate   .08646334

Annual Depreciation

    1.6925 x 35,232 =   596

Net property income - after depreciation

    ($39,694 - 596) = $ 39,098

Value of property $39,098 ÷ .085 =   459,976

Rounded to $460,000

4. Correlation

    Analysis of Valuation data discloses the following conclusions:

        1. Cost Approach $462,000

        2. Market Approach   461,000

        3. Income Approach   460,000

    Since only four sales were available for comparison purposes and considerable adjustments were necessary to compensate for time of sale, rate of depreciation and differences in land value, the market approach in this instance is not wholly reliable as an index of value.

The cost approach tends to set the ceiling of value and proves reliable only if truly comparable replacement costs could be obtained. A change on only 1 cent in the cubic cost of re-construction would cause a value difference in excess of $4,000 for the subject property. For this reason the cost approach was used only as a check on the reliability of the final estimate of value.

The income approach provides for the subject property a strong indication of value. This for two reasons: 1. Value is defined as the present worth of future rights to income and 2. the value is based on established and competitive income on which investors rely for value comparison with alternate and similar investment properties and/or opportunities.

Based on the considerations detailed above, it is the appraisers professional and considered opinion that the apartment property warrants a value as of the date of this appraisal in the amount of:

Four Hundred Sixty Thousand Dollars

($460,000)

Certified by

John Doe, M.A.I.

Appraiser

Case Study No. 3

Suggested Solution

Land Value

Sale No.	1	2	3	4
Price	$45,000	50,000	30,000	60,000
Time adjustment	1.05	1.00	1.15	1.00
Price-Adjusted	$47,250	50,000	34,500	60,000
Front feet	40	44	40	60
Area	4,600	4,840	4,400	6,000
Price per ft. ft.	$1,181	1,136	863	1,000
Price per sq. ft.	$10.27	10.33	7.84	10.00
Adjustment ratio	.95	.90	1.25	1.00
Adjusted price - ft. ft.	$1,122	1,022	1,079	1,000
Adjusted price - sq. ft.	$10.20	9.30	9.80	10.00

Sale No. 4 required no adjustment and is judged most comparable. Sale No. 4 also falls well within the limits of comparable value set by sales 1 to 3.

The indicated value of the subject property -- based on market comparison -- is:

32 front feet @ $1,000 = $32,000

Cost Approach To Value

Main Building Area:		Square Feet
Downstairs		2,876
Upstairs		1,900
Lean-to		263

Replacement Cost New:

Downstairs	2,876 sq. ft. @ $7.50 =	$21,470
Upstairs	1,900 sq. ft. @ $6.50 =	12,350
Lean-to	263 sq. ft. @ $5.25 =	1,380
Total Replacement Cost New		$35,300

Deferred Maintenance:

Ceiling repairs and redecoration throughout	$ 3,500	
Wear, tear and obsolescence based on effective age of 45 years at 1.5% per year = 67.5% of $35,300 =	23,828	
Total Accrued Depreciation		27,328
Depreciated Building Value		$ 7,972
Add Land Value -- By Comparison		32,000
Total Value Via Cost Approach		$39,972

Rounded to $40,000

Interest Rate From Market Data

Sale No.	5	6	7	8
A. Price	$49,000	45,000	56,000	45,000
B. Building Value %	.30	.35	.25	.26
C. Building Value --				
Amount	$14,700	15,750	14,000	11,700
D. Effective Gross	$7,200	6,500	8,300	6,450
E. Operating ratio %	35	32	38	35
F. Net Income	$4,680	4,438	5,146	4,192
G. Depreciation - ratio	5%	5%	5%	5%
H. Depreciation - Amount	$735	788	700	585
I. Net interest income	$3,945	3,650	4,446	3,607
J. Interest rate				
(I ÷ A)	8.05	8.1	7.94	8.0

Based on market analysis of comparable properties on interest ratio of 8% is indicated.

Market Approach To Value

Sale No.	5	6	7	8
Sale Price	$49,000	45,000	56,000	45,000
Date of Sale	1 year ago	6 mo. ago	1 year ago	current
Time Adjustment	1.10	1.05	1.10	1.00
Adjusted Price	$53,900	47,250	61,600	45,000

Sale No.	5	6	7	8
Land Value	$37,730	30,713	46,200	33,300
Dep. Building Value	$16,170	16,537	15,400	11,700
Effective age -				
Adjustment	.75	.75	.75	.75
Adjusted Building value	$12,128	12,403	11,550	8,775
Building Area -- sq. ft.	7,800	7,750	7,700	5,320
Building Value per sq. ft.	1.55	1.60	1.50	1.65
Gross Multiplier	6.8	6.9	6.75	6.98

A depreciated building value of $1.60 is indicated per square foot. The gross multiplier is 6.9. Based on these indexes of value the market approach yields the following value results:

Building value	5,039 sq. ft. @ $1.60 =	$ 8,062
Add Land Value of		32,000
Total Value		$40,062
Gross Income	$5,900 x 6.9 =	40,700

Rounded to $40,500

Income Approach to Value

Gross Income		$ 5,900
Vacancy & Collection loss 2%		118
Effective Gross Income		$ 5,782

Operating Expenses

R.E. Taxes	$750	
Special Tax	55	
Insurance	275	
Exterior Expense	400	
Management	578	
Total Operating Expense		2,058
Net income -- before depreciation		$ 3,722

Less income to land

$32,000 @ 8% =		2,560
Income to building		$ 1,162
Building Value		
$1,162 ÷ 14.67 =		7,921
Add Land Value		32,000
Total Value		$39,921

Rounded to $39,900

Correlation

Value under Cost Approach	$40,000
Value under Market Approach	40,500
Value under Income Approach	39,900

The analysis of market cost and income data support an estimate of $40,000 for the subject property.

Case Study No. 4

Suggested Solution

1. Cost Approach To Value

Replacement Cost New:

Building: 34,400 sq. ft. @ $20.50 =	$703,970	
Carpets and drapes	37,500	
Restaurant furnishings	38,000	
Total replacement cost – new		$779,470

Less accrued depreciation:

Building – 26,000 sq. ft. @ $1.13			
(22.6¢ x 5 years)[1]	=	$ 29,380	
Carpets and drapes –			
$37,500 @ 2.5% (5% x 5 yrs.)[1]	=	9,375	
Restaurant furnishings –			
$38,000 @ 50% (10% x 5 yrs.)[1]	=	19,000	$ 57,755
Depreciated replacement cost			$721,715
Add: Land value – 13,200 sq. ft. @ $10. =			132,000
Value via cost approach			$853,715

Rounded to $853,700

---

[1]Based on straight line depreciation.

2. Income Approach To Value

Gross Revenue

Ground floor - 5,500 sq. ft. @ $5.25   = $ 28,875

Upstairs offices -

19,500 sq. ft. @ $4.75   =   92,625

Restaurant -

$1,450/mo. x 12 mos.   =   17,400

Total annual revenue $138,900

Less: vacancy & collection losses (negligible)[2]   -0-

Effective revenue $138,900

Less: operating expenses

Cleaning	$0.495	per sq. ft.
Electric	.185	"
Heat	.052	"
Air conditioning	.158	"
Plumbing	.024	"
Elevator	.133	"
General Expense	.135	"
General Repairs	.082	"
Alterations	.034	"
Decorating	.047	"

---

[2]Vacancy and collection losses are assumed to be negligible since the building space is under leases for periods of five to ten years, and in view of the favorable location of the property.

Management   .125 per sq. ft.

Taxes and insurance   .823   "

                                      $2.293 per sq. ft.

Total fixed expenses & maintenance costs   =

   26,000 sq. ft. @ $2.293   = $59,618

   Replacement of carpets and drapes   =   1,875[1]

   Replacement of restaurant furniture =   3,800[2]

   Parking lot $800/mo. x 12   =   9,600

      Total operating expenses $ 74,893

Net operating income - before interest and amortization $ 64,007

   Less: income attributable to land

      $132,000 @ 7.5%[3] =   9,900

   Income attributable to building $ 54,107

---

[1] Based on 20 year life - straight line depreciation.

[2] Based on 10 year life - straight line depreciation.

[3] The interest rate is calculated by the "band of investment" method as follows:

      6.0% x .667   =   .040

      8.0% x .200   =   .016

   15.0% x .133   =   .020

          .076 = 7.6%

Rounded to 7.5%

Capitalized value of building income over

    remaining economic life of 45 years at 7.5%

    interest under the annuity income method =

    $54,107 x 12.8186 = $693,576

Add: land value   132,000

    Total value $825,576

Rounded to <u>$825,600</u>

3. <u>Market Approach To Value</u>

    Gross Income $138,900 x 6.0 (multiplier) =   <u>$833,400</u>

4. <u>Correlation</u>

    The following value estimates were derived from an analysis of the

    available valuation data:

        Cost Approach $853,700

        Market Approach   833,400

        Income Approach   825,600

    The cost approach is useful as a guide to value since it

generally serves as a ceiling of value. Secondary reliance, however,

must be attributed to this approach where the improvement is not

new, and where more reliable estimates are provided by the other

approaches to value. Thus the cost approach, yielding an estimate

within about 2½% of the final estimate, was used only as a check on

the reliability of the final estimate of value.

    Market value may be defined as the estimated price which a

property will bring in the open market - given sufficient time

and assuming knowledgeable buyer and seller. This definition encompasses both the "barter" and "productivity" aspects of the concept of value since, in effect, the former is based (at least implicitly) on the latter.

The final estimate of value, in the present case, is based entirely on the market comparison approach since no adjustments were required. The income approach - which yields an estimate that is within about 1% of the final estimate - is used to check the reliability of the market approach.

The subject property in the opinion of the appraiser warrants a value as of the date of this appraisal in the amount of:

Eight Hundred and Thirty-Three Thousand Dollars

($833,000)

Appendix III

General Tables

Appendix III

Future Worth of A Deposit of $1.00 Compounded
At   1/2   Per Cent Interest
Per Period As Follows:

Number Of Periods	Growth Of $1.00[1]	Growth Of $1.00 Per Period[2]	Deposit Needed To Accumulate $1.00[3]
1	1.005 000	1.000 000	1.000 000
2	1.010 025	2.005 000	.498 753
3	1.015 075	3.015 025	.331 672
4	1.020 151	4.030 100	.248 133
5	1.025 251	5.050 251	.198 010
6	1.030 378	6.075 502	.164 595
7	1.035 529	7.105 879	.140 729
8	1.040 707	8.141 409	.122 829
9	1.045 911	9.182 116	.108 907
10	1.051 140	10.228 026	.097 771
11	1.056 396	11.279 167	.088 659
12	1.061 678	12.335 562	.081 066
13	1.066 986	13.397 240	.074 642
14	1.072 321	14.464 226	.069 136
15	1.077 683	15.536 548	.064 364
16	1.083 071	16.614 230	.060 189
17	1.088 487	17.697 301	.056 506
18	1.093 929	18.785 788	.053 232
19	1.099 399	19.879 717	.050 303
20	1.104 896	20.979 115	.047 666
21	1.110 420	22.084 011	.045 282
22	1.115 972	23.194 431	.043 114
23	1.121 552	24.310 403	.041 135
24	1.127 160	25.431 955	.039 321
25	1.132 796	26.559 115	.037 652

---

[1]How $1 left at compound interest will grow (deposit made at beginning of period). Formula: $s = P (1 + i)^n$

[2]How $1 deposited periodically will grow (deposit made at end of period). For deposits made at the beginning of the period, subtract 1. from the amount shown in the following period.
Formula: $S_n = \dfrac{(1 + i)^n - 1}{i}$

[3]Periodic deposit that will grow to $1 at a future date (deposits made at end of period). Formula: $\dfrac{1}{S_n} = \dfrac{i}{(1 + i)^n - 1}$

Future Worth of A Deposit of $1.00 Compounded
At   1/2   Per Cent Interest
Per Period As Follows:

Number Of Periods	Growth Of $1.00[1]	Growth Of $1.00 Per Period[2]	Deposit Needed To Accumulate $1.00[3]
26	1.128 460	27.691 911	.036 112
27	1.144 152	28.830 370	.034 686
28	1.149 873	29.974 522	.033 362
29	1.155 622	31.124 395	.032 129
30	1.161 400	32.280 017	.030 979
31	1.167 207	33.441 417	.029 903
32	1.173 043	34.608 624	.028 895
33	1.178 908	35.781 667	.027 947
34	1.184 803	36.960 575	.027 056
35	1.190 727	38.145 378	.026 215
36	1.196 681	39.336 105	.025 422
37	1.202 664	40.532 785	.024 671
38	1.208 677	41.735 449	.023 960
39	1.214 721	42.944 127	.023 286
40	1.220 794	44.158 847	.022 646
41	1.226 898	45.379 642	.022 036
42	1.233 033	46.606 540	.021 456
43	1.239 198	47.839 572	.020 903
44	1.245 394	49.078 770	.020 375
45	1.251 621	50.324 164	.019 871
46	1.257 879	51.575 785	.019 389
47	1.264 168	52.833 664	.018 927
48	1.270 489	54.097 832	.018 485
49	1.276 842	55.368 321	.018 061
50	1.283 226	56.645 163	.017 654

---

[1]How $1 left at compound interest will grow (deposit made at beginning of period). Formula: $s = P (1 + i)^n$

[2]How $1 deposited periodically will grow (deposit made at end of period). For deposits made at the beginning of the period, subtract 1. from the amount shown in the following period.
Formula: $S_n = \dfrac{(1 + i)^n - 1}{i}$

[3]Periodic deposit that will grow to $1 at a future date (deposits made at end of period). Formula: $\dfrac{1}{S_n} = \dfrac{i}{(1 + i)^n - 1}$

Future Worth of A Deposit of $1.00 Compounded
At   3   Per Cent Interest
Per Period As Follows:

Number Of Periods	Growth Of $1.00[1]	Growth Of $1.00 Per Period[2]	Deposit Needed To Accumulate $1.00[3]
1	1.030 000	1.000 000	1.000 000
2	1.060 900	2.030 000	.492 611
3	1.092 727	3.090 900	.323 530
4	1.125 509	4.183 627	.239 027
5	1.159 274	5.309 136	.188 355
6	1.194 052	6.468 410	.154 598
7	1.229 874	7.662 462	.130 506
8	1.266 770	8.892 336	.112 456
9	1.304 773	10.159 106	.098 434
10	1.343 916	11.463 879	.087 231
11	1.384 234	12.807 796	.078 077
12	1.425 761	14.192 030	.070 462
13	1.468 534	15.617 790	.064 030
14	1.512 590	17.086 324	.058 526
15	1.557 967	18.598 914	.053 767
16	1.604 706	20.156 881	.049 611
17	1.652 848	21.761 588	.045 953
18	1.702 433	23.414 435	.042 709
19	1.753 506	25.116 868	.039 814
20	1.806 111	26.870 374	.037 216
21	1.860 295	28.676 486	.034 872
22	1.916 103	30.536 780	.032 747
23	1.973 587	32.452 884	.030 814
24	2.032 794	34.426 470	.029 047
25	2.093 778	36.459 264	.027 428

[1]How $1 left at compound interest will grow (deposit made at beginning of period). Formula: $s = P (1 + i)^n$

[2]How $1 deposited periodically will grow (deposit made at end of period). For deposits made at the beginning of the period, subtract 1. from the amount shown in the following period. Formula: $S_n = \dfrac{(1 + i)^n - 1}{i}$

[3]Periodic deposit that will grow to $1 at a future date (deposits made at end of period). Formula: $\dfrac{1}{S_n} = \dfrac{i}{(1 + i)^n - 1}$

Future Worth of A Deposit of $1.00 Compounded
At   3   Per Cent Interest
Per Period As Follows:

Number Of Periods	Growth Of $1.00[1]	Growth Of $1.00 Per Period[2]	Deposit Needed To Accumulate $1.00[3]
26	2.156 591	38.553 042	.025 938
27	2.221 289	40.709 634	.024 564
28	2.287 928	42.930 923	.023 293
29	2.356 566	45.218 850	.022 115
30	2.427 262	47.575 416	.021 019
31	2.500 080	50.002 678	.019 999
32	2.575 083	52.502 759	.019 047
33	2.652 335	55.077 841	.018 156
34	2.731 905	57.730 177	.017 322
35	2.813 862	60.462 082	.016 539
36	2.898 278	63.275 944	.015 804
37	2.985 227	66.174 223	.015 112
38	3.074 783	69.159 449	.014 459
39	3.167 027	72.234 233	.013 844
40	3.262 038	75.401 260	.013 262
41	3.359 899	78.663 298	.012 713
42	3.460 696	82.023 196	.012 192
43	3.564 517	85.483 892	.011 698
44	3.671 452	89.048 409	.011 230
45	3.781 596	92.719 861	.010 785
46	3.895 044	96.502 457	.010 363
47	4.011 895	100.396 501	.009 961
48	4.132 252	104.408 396	.009 578
49	4.256 219	108.540 648	.009 213
50	4.383 906	112.796 867	.008 865

[1]How $1 left at compound interest will grow (deposit made at beginning of period). Formula: $s = P(1 + i)^n$

[2]How $1 deposited periodically will grow (deposit made at end of period). For deposits made at the beginning of the period, subtract 1. from the amount shown in the following period. Formula: $S_n = \dfrac{(1 + i)^n - 1}{i}$

[3]Periodic deposit that will grow to $1 at a future date (deposits made at end of period). Formula: $\dfrac{1}{S_n} = \dfrac{i}{(1 + i)^n - 1}$

Future Worth of A Deposit of $1.00 Compounded
At   4   Per Cent Interest
Per Period As Follows:

Number Of Periods	Growth Of $1.00[1]	Growth Of $1.00 Per Period[2]	Deposit Needed To Accumulate $1.00[3]
1	1.040 000	1.000 000	1.000 000
2	1.081 600	2.040 000	.490 196
3	1.124 864	3.121 600	.320 349
4	1.169 859	4.246 464	.235 490
5	1.216 653	5.416 323	.184 627
6	1.265 319	6.632 975	.150 762
7	1.315 932	7.898 294	.126 610
8	1.368 569	9.214 226	.108 528
9	1.423 312	10.582 795	.094 493
10	1.480 244	12.006 107	.083 291
11	1.539 454	13.486 351	.074 149
12	1.601 032	15.025 805	.066 552
13	1.665 974	16.626 838	.060 144
14	1.731 676	18.291 911	.054 669
15	1.800 944	20.023 588	.049 941
16	1.872 981	21.824 531	.045 820
17	1.947 900	23.697 512	.042 199
18	2.025 817	25.645 413	.038 993
19	2.106 849	27.671 229	.036 129
20	2.191 123	29.778 079	.033 582
21	2.278 768	31.969 202	.031 280
22	2.369 919	34.247 970	.029 199
23	2.464 716	36.617 889	.017 309
24	2.563 304	39.082 604	.025 587
25	2.665 836	41.645 908	.024 012

---

[1]How $1 left at compound interest will grow (deposit made at beginning of period). Formula: $s = P(1 + i)^n$

[2]How $1 deposited periodically will grow (deposit made at end of period). For deposits made at the beginning of the period, subtract 1. from the amount shown in the following period.
Formula: $S_n = \dfrac{(1 + i)^n - 1}{i}$

[3]Periodic deposit that will grow to $1 at a future date (deposits made at end of period). Formula: $\dfrac{1}{S_n} = \dfrac{i}{(1 + i)^n - 1}$

Future Worth of A Deposit of $1.00 Compounded
At   4   Per Cent Interest
Per Period As Follows:

Number Of Periods	Growth Of $1.00[1]	Growth Of $1.00 Per Period[2]	Deposit Needed To Accumulate $1.00[3]
26	2.772 470	44.311 745	.022 567
27	2.883 369	47.084 214	.021 239
28	2.998 703	49.967 583	.020 013
29	3.118 651	52.966 286	.018 880
30	3.243 398	56.084 938	.017 830
31	3.373 133	59.328 335	.016 855
32	3.508 059	62.701 469	.015 949
33	3.648 381	66.209 527	.015 104
34	3.794 316	69.857 909	.014 315
35	3.946 089	73.652 225	.013 577
36	4.103 933	77.598 314	.012 887
37	4.268 090	81.702 246	.012 240
38	4.438 813	85.970 336	.011 632
39	4.616 366	90.409 150	.011 061
40	4.801 021	95.025 516	.010 523
41	4.993 061	99.826 536	.010 017
42	5.192 784	104.819 598	.009 540
43	5.400 495	110.012 382	.009 090
44	5.616 515	115.412 877	.008 665
45	5.841 176	121.029 392	.008 262
46	6.074 823	126.870 568	.007 882
47	6.317 816	132.945 390	.007 522
48	6.570 528	139.263 206	.007 181
49	6.833 349	145.833 734	.006 857
50	7.106 683	152.667 084	.006 550

---

[1]How $1 left at compound interest will grow (deposit made at beginning of period). Formula: $s = P(1 + i)^n$

[2]How $1 deposited periodically will grow (deposit made at end of period). For deposits made at the beginning of the period, subtract 1. from the amount shown in the following period. Formula: $S_n = \dfrac{(1 + i)^n - 1}{i}$

[3]Periodic deposit that will grow to $1 at a future date (deposits made at end of period). Formula: $\dfrac{1}{S_n} = \dfrac{i}{(1 + i)^n - 1}$

Future Worth of A Deposit of $1.00 Compounded
At   5   Per Cent Interest
Per Period As Follows:

Number Of Periods	Growth Of $1.00[1]	Growth Of $1.00 Per Period[2]	Deposit Needed To Accumulate $1.00[3]
1	1.050 000	1.000 000	1.000 000
2	1.102 500	2.050 000	.487 805
3	1.157 625	3.152 500	.317 209
4	1.215 506	4.310 125	.232 012
5	1.276 282	5.525 631	.180 975
6	1.340 096	6.801 913	.147 017
7	1.407 100	8.142 008	.133 820
8	1.477 455	9.549 109	.104 722
9	1.551 328	11.026 564	.090 690
10	1.628 895	12.577 893	.079 505
11	1.710 339	14.206 787	.070 389
12	1.795 856	15.917 127	.062 825
13	1.885 649	17.712 983	.056 456
14	1.979 932	19.598 632	.051 024
15	2.078 928	21.578 564	.046 342
16	2.182 875	23.657 492	.042 270
17	2.292 018	15.840 366	.038 699
18	2.406 619	28.132 385	.035 546
19	2.526 950	30.539 004	.032 745
20	2.653 298	33.065 954	.030 243
21	2.785 963	35.719 252	.027 996
22	2.925 261	38.505 214	.025 971
23	3.071 524	41.430 475	.024 137
24	3.225 100	44.501 999	.022 471
25	3.386 355	47.727 099	.020 952

---

[1]How $1 left at compound interest will grow (deposit made at beginning of period). Formula: $s = P(1 + i)^n$

[2]How $1 deposited periodically will grow (deposit made at end of period). For deposits made at the beginning of the period, subtract 1. from the amount shown in the following period. Formula: $S_n = \dfrac{(1 + i)^n - 1}{i}$

[3]Periodic deposit that will grow to $1 at a future date (deposits made at end of period). Formula: $\dfrac{1}{S_n} = \dfrac{i}{(1 + i)^n - 1}$

Future Worth of A Deposit of $1.00 Compounded
At   5   Per Cent Interest
Per Period As Follows:

Number Of Periods	Growth Of $1.00[1]	Growth Of $1.00 Per Period[2]	Deposit Needed To Accumulate $1.00[3]
26	3.555 673	51.113 454	.019 564
27	3.733 456	54.669 126	.018 292
28	3.920 129	58.402 583	.017 123
29	4.116 136	62.322 712	.016 046
30	4.321 942	66.438 848	.015 051
31	4.538 029	70.760 790	.014 032
32	4.764 941	75.298 829	.013 280
33	5.003 189	80.063 771	.012 490
34	5.253 348	85.066 959	.011 755
35	5.516 015	90.320 307	.011 072
36	5.791 816	95.836 323	.010 434
37	6.081 407	101.628 139	.009 840
38	6.385 477	107.709 546	.009 284
39	6.704 751	114.095 023	.008 765
40	7.039 989	120.799 774	.008 278
41	7.391 988	127.839 763	.007 822
42	7.761 588	135.231 751	.007 395
43	8.149 667	142.993 339	.006 993
44	8.557 150	151.143 006	.006 616
45	8.985 008	159.700 156	.006 262
46	9.434 258	168.685 164	.005 928
47	9.905 971	178.119 422	.005 614
48	10.401 270	188.025 393	.005 318
49	10.921 333	198.426 663	.005 040
50	11.467 400	209.347 996	.004 777

---

[1]How $1 left at compound interest will grow (deposit made at beginning of period). Formula: $s = P (1 + i)^n$

[2]How $1 deposited periodically will grow (deposit made at end of period). For deposits made at the beginning of the period, subtract 1. from the amount shown in the following period. Formula: $S_n = \dfrac{(1 + i)^n - 1}{i}$

[3]Periodic deposit that will grow to $1 at a future date (deposits made at end of period). Formula: $\dfrac{1}{S_n} = \dfrac{i}{(1 + i)^n - 1}$

Future Worth of A Deposit of $1.00 Compounded
At   6   Per Cent Interest
Per Period As Follows:

Number Of Periods	Growth Of $1.00[1]	Growth Of $1.00 Per Period[2]	Deposit Needed To Accumulate $1.00[3]
1	1.060 000	1.000 000	1.000 000
2	1.123 600	2.060 000	.485 437
3	1.191 016	3.183 600	.314 110
4	1.262 477	4.374 616	.228 591
5	1.338 226	5.637 093	.177 396
6	1.418 519	6.975 319	.143 363
7	1.503 630	8.393 838	.119 135
8	1.593 848	9.897 468	.101 036
9	1.689 479	11.491 316	.087 022
10	1.790 848	13.180 795	.075 868
11	1.898 299	14.971 643	.066 793
12	2.012 196	16.869 941	.059 277
13	2.132 928	18.882 138	.052 960
14	2.260 904	21.015 066	.047 585
15	2.396 558	23.275 970	.042 963
16	2.540 352	25.672 528	.038 952
17	2.692 773	28.212 880	.035 445
18	2.854 339	30.905 653	.032 357
19	3.025 600	33.759 992	.029 621
20	3.207 135	36.785 591	.027 185
21	3.399 564	39.992 727	.025 005
22	3.603 537	43.392 290	.023 046
23	3.819 750	46.995 828	.021 278
24	4.048 935	50.815 577	.019 679
25	4.291 871	54.864 512	.018 227

[1] How $1 left at compound interest will grow (deposit made at beginning of period). Formula: $s = P(1 + i)^n$

[2] How $1 deposited periodically will grow (deposit made at end of period). For deposits made at the beginning of the period, subtract 1. from the amount shown in the following period. Formula: $S_n = \dfrac{(1 + i)^n - 1}{i}$

[3] Periodic deposit that will grow to $1 at a future date (deposits made at end of period). Formula: $\dfrac{1}{S_n} = \dfrac{i}{(1 + i)^n - 1}$

Future Worth of A Deposit of $1.00 Compounded
At   6   Per Cent Interest
Per Period As Follows:

Number Of Periods	Growth Of $1.00[1]	Growth Of $1.00 Per Period[2]	Deposit Needed To Accumulate $1.00[3]
26	4.549 383	59.156 383	.016 904
27	4.822 346	63.705 766	.015 697
28	5.111 687	68.528 112	.014 593
29	5.418 388	73.639 798	.013 580
30	5.743 491	79.058 186	.012 649
31	6.088 101	84.801 677	.011 792
32	6.453 387	90.889 778	.011 002
33	6.840 590	97.343 165	.010 273
34	7.251 025	104.183 755	.009 598
35	7.686 087	111.434 780	.008 974
36	8.147 252	119.120 867	.008 395
37	8.636 087	127.268 119	.007 857
38	9.154 252	135.904 206	.007 358
39	9.703 507	145.058 458	.006 894
40	10.285 718	154.761 966	.006 462
41	10.902 861	165.047 684	.006 059
42	11.557 033	175.950 545	.005 683
43	12.250 455	187.507 577	.005 333
44	12.985 482	199.758 032	.005 006
45	13.764 611	212.743 514	.004 700
46	14.590 487	226.508 125	.004 415
47	15.465 917	241.098 612	.004 148
48	16.393 872	256.564 529	.003 898
49	17.377 504	272.958 401	.003 664
50	18.420.154	290.335 905	.003 444

---

[1]How $1 left at compound interest will grow (deposit made at
beginning of period). Formula: $s = P(1 + i)^n$

[2]How $1 deposited periodically will grow (deposit made at end
of period). For deposits made at the beginning of the period,
subtract 1. from the amount shown in the following period.
Formula: $S_n = \dfrac{(1 + i)^n - 1}{i}$

[3]Periodic deposit that will grow to $1 at a future date (deposits
made at end of period). Formula: $\dfrac{1}{S_n} = \dfrac{i}{(1 + i)^n - 1}$

Future Worth of A Deposit of $1.00 Compounded
At   7   Per Cent Interest
Per Period As Follows:

Number Of Periods	Growth Of $1.00[1]	Growth Of $1.00 Per Period[2]	Deposit Needed To Accumulate $1.00[3]
1	1.070 000	1.000 000	1.000 000
2	1.144 900	2.070 000	.483 092
3	1.225 043	3.214 900	.311 052
4	1.310 796	4.439 943	.225 228
5	1.402 552	5.750 739	.173 891
6	1.500 730	7.153 291	.139 796
7	1.605 781	8.654 021	.115 553
8	1.718 186	10.259 803	.097 468
9	1.838 459	11.977 989	.083 486
10	1.967 151	13.816 448	.072 378
11	2.104 852	15.783 599	.063 357
12	2.252 192	17.888 451	.055 902
13	2.409 845	20.140 643	.049 651
14	2.578 534	22.550 488	.044 345
15	2.759 032	25.129 022	.039 795
16	2.952 164	27.888 054	.035 858
17	3.158 815	30.840 217	.032 425
18	3.379 932	33.999 033	.029 413
19	3.616 528	37.378 965	.026 753
20	3.869 684	40.995 492	.025 393
21	4.140 562	44.865 177	.022 289
22	4.430 402	49.005 739	.020 406
23	4.740 530	53.436 141	.018 714
24	5.072 367	58.176 671	.017 189
25	5.427 433	63.249 038	.015 811

---

[1]How $1 left at compound interest will grow (deposit made at beginning of period). Formula: $s = P (1 + i)^n$

[2]How $1 deposited periodically will grow (deposit made at end of period). For deposits made at the beginning of the period, subtract 1. from the amount shown in the following period.
Formula: $S_n = \dfrac{(1 + i)^n - 1}{i}$

[3]Periodic deposit that will grow to $1 at a future date (deposits made at end of period). Formula: $\dfrac{1}{S_n} = \dfrac{i}{(1 + i)^n - 1}$

Future Worth of A Deposit of $1.00 Compounded
At   7   Per Cent Interest
Per Period As Follows:

Number Of Periods	Growth Of $1.00[1]	Growth Of $1.00 Per Period[2]	Deposit Needed To Accumulate $1.00[3]
26	5.807 353	68.676 470	.014 561
27	6.213 868	74.483 823	.013 426
28	6.648 838	80.697 691	.012 392
29	7.114 257	87.346 529	.011 449
30	7.612 255	94.460 786	.010 586
31	8.145 113	102.073 041	.009 797
32	8.715 271	110.218 154	.009 073
33	9.325 340	118.933 425	.008 408
34	9.978 114	128.258 765	.007 797
35	10.676 581	138.236 878	.007 234
36	11.423 942	148.913 460	.006 715
37	12.223 618	160.337 402	.006 237
38	13.079 271	172.561 020	.005 795
39	13.994 820	185.640 292	.005 387
40	14.974 458	199.635 112	.005 009
41	16.022 670	214.609 570	.004 660
42	17.144 257	230.632 240	.004 336
43	18.344 355	247.776 496	.004 036
44	19.628 460	266.120 851	.003 758
45	21.002 452	285.749 311	.003 500
46	22.472 623	306.751 763	.003 260
47	24.045 707	329.224 386	.003 037
48	25.728 907	353.270 093	.002 831
49	27.529 930	378.999 000	.002 639
50	29.457 025	406.528 929	.002 460

[1]How $1 left at compound interest will grow (deposit made at beginning of period). Formula: $s = P (1 + i)^n$

[2]How $1 deposited periodically will grow (deposit made at end of period). For deposits made at the beginning of the period, subtract 1. from the amount shown in the following period. Formula: $S_n = \dfrac{(1 + i)^n - 1}{i}$

[3]Periodic deposit that will grow to $1 at a future date (deposits made at end of period). Formula: $\dfrac{1}{S_n} = \dfrac{i}{(1 + i)^n - 1}$

Future Worth of A Deposit of $1.00 Compounded
At   7 1/2   Per Cent Interest
Per Period As Follows:

Number Of Periods	Growth Of $1.00[1]	Growth Of $1.00 Per Period[2]	Deposit Needed To Accumulate $1.00[3]
1	1.075 000	1.000 000	1.000 000
2	1.155 625	2.075 000	.481 928
3	1.242 297	3.230 625	.309 538
4	1.335 469	4.472 922	.223 568
5	1.435 629	5.808 391	.172 165
6	1.543 302	7.244 020	.138 045
7	1.659 049	8.787 322	.113 800
8	1.783 478	10.446 371	.095 727
9	1.917 239	12.229 849	.081 767
10	2.061 032	14.147 087	.070 686
11	2.215 609	16.208 119	.061 697
12	2.381 780	18.423 728	.054 278
13	2.560 413	20.805 508	.048 064
14	2.752 444	23.365 921	.042 797
15	2.958 877	26.118 365	.038 287
16	3.180 793	29.077 242	.034 391
17	3.419 353	32.258 035	.031 000
18	3.675 804	35.677 388	.028 029
19	3.951 489	39.353 192	.025 411
20	4.247 851	43.304 681	.023 092
21	4.566 440	47.552 532	.021 029
22	4.908 923	52.118 972	.019 187
23	5.277 092	57.027 895	.017 535
24	5.672 874	62.304 987	.016 050
25	6.098 340	67.977 862	.014 711

[1] How $1 left at compound interest will grow (deposit made at beginning of period). Formula: $s = P(1 + i)^n$

[2] How $1 deposited periodically will grow (deposit made at end of period). For deposits made at the beginning of the period, subtract 1. from the amount shown in the following period. Formula: $S_n = \frac{(1 + i)^n - 1}{i}$

[3] Periodic deposit that will grow to $1 at a future date (deposits made at end of period). Formula: $\frac{1}{S_n} = \frac{i}{(1 + i)^n - 1}$

Future Worth of A Deposit of $1.00 Compounded
At 7 1/2 Per Cent Interest
Per Period As Follows:

Number Of Periods	Growth Of $1.00[1]	Growth Of $1.00 Per Period[2]	Deposit Needed To Accumulate $1.00[3]
26	6.555 715	74.076 201	.013 500
27	7.047 394	80.631 916	.012 402
28	7.575 948	87.679 310	.011 405
29	8.144 144	95.255 258	.010 498
30	8.754 955	103.399 403	.009 671
31	9.411 577	112.154 358	.008 916
32	10.117 445	121.565 935	.008 226
33	10.876 253	131.683 380	.007 594
34	11.691 972	142.559 633	.007 015
35	12.568 870	154.251 606	.006 483
36	13.511 536	166.810 476	.005 994
37	14.524 901	180.332 012	.005 945
38	15.614 268	194.856 913	.005 132
39	16.785 339	210.471 181	.004 751
40	18.044 239	227.256 520	.004 400
41	19.397 557	245.300 759	.004 077
42	20.852 374	264.698 315	.003 778
43	22.416 302	285.550 689	.003 502
44	24.097 524	307.966 991	.003 247
45	25.904 839	332.064 515	.003 011
46	27.847 702	357.969 354	.002 794
47	29.936 279	385.817 055	.002 592
48	32.181 500	415.753 334	.002 405
49	34.595 113	447.934 835	.002 232
50	37.189 746	482.529 947	.002 072

---

[1]How $1 left at compound interest will grow (deposit made at beginning of period). Formula: $s = P (1 + i)^n$

[2]How $1 deposited periodically will grow (deposit made at end of period). For deposits made at the beginning of the period, subtract 1. from the amount shown in the following period. Formula: $S_n = \dfrac{(1 + i)^n - 1}{i}$

[3]Periodic deposit that will grow to $1 at a future date (deposits made at end of period). Formula: $\dfrac{1}{S_n} = \dfrac{i}{(1 + i)^n - 1}$

Future Worth of A Deposit of $1.00 Compounded
At   8   Per Cent Interest
Per Period As Follows:

Number Of Periods	Growth Of $1.00[1]	Growth Of $1.00 Per Period[2]	Deposit Needed To Accumulate $1.00[3]
1	1.080 000	1.000 000	1.000 000
2	1.166 400	2.080 000	.480 769
3	1.259 712	3.246 400	.308 034
4	1.360 489	4.506 112	.221 921
5	1.469 328	5.866 601	.170 456
6	1.586 874	7.335 929	.136 315
7	1.713 824	8.922 803	.112 072
8	1.850 930	10.636 628	.094 015
9	1.999 005	12.487 558	.080 080
10	2.158 925	14.486 562	.069 029
11	2.331 639	16.645 487	.060 076
12	2.518 170	18.977 126	.052 695
13	2.719 624	21.495 297	.046 522
14	2.937 194	24.214 920	.041 297
15	3.172 169	27.152 114	.036 830
16	3.425 943	30.324 283	.032 977
17	3.700 018	33.750 226	.029 629
18	3.996 019	37.450 244	.026 702
19	4.315 701	41.446 263	.024 128
20	4.660 957	45.761 964	.021 852
21	5.033 834	50.422 921	.019 832
22	5.436 540	55.456 755	.018 032
23	5.871 464	60.893 296	.016 422
24	6.341 181	66.764 759	.014 978
25	6.848 475	73.105 940	.013 679

---

[1]How $1 left at compound interest will grow (deposit made at beginning of period). Formula: $s = P (1 + i)^n$

[2]How $1 deposited periodically will grow (deposit made at end of period). For deposits made at the beginning of the period, subtract 1. from the amount shown in the following period. Formula: $S_n = \dfrac{(1 + i)^n - 1}{i}$

[3]Periodic deposit that will grow to $1 at a future date (deposits made at end of period). Formula: $\dfrac{1}{S_n} = \dfrac{i}{(1 + i)^n - 1}$

Future Worth of A Deposit of $1.00 Compounded
At 8 Per Cent Interest
Per Period As Follows:

Number Of Periods	Growth Of $1.00[1]	Growth Of $1.00 Per Period[2]	Deposit Needed To Accumulate $1.00[3]
26	7.396 353	79.954 415	.012 507
27	7.988 061	87.350 768	.011 448
28	8.627 106	95.338 830	.010 489
29	9.317 275	103.965 936	.009 619
30	10.062 657	113.283 211	.008 827
31	10.867 669	123.345 868	.008 107
32	11.737 083	134.213 537	.007 451
33	12.676 050	145.950 620	.006 852
34	13.690 134	158.626 670	.006 304
35	14.785 344	172.316 804	.005 803
36	15.968 172	187.102 148	.005 345
37	17.245 626	203.070 320	.004 924
38	18.625 276	220.315 945	.004 539
39	20.115 298	238.941 221	.004 185
40	21.724 521	259.056 519	.003 860
41	23.462 483	280.781 040	.003 561
42	25.339 482	304.243 523	.003 287
43	27.366 640	329.583 005	.003 034
44	29.555 972	356.949 646	.002 802
45	31.920 449	386.505 617	.002 587
46	34.474 085	418.426 067	.002 390
47	37.232 012	452.900 152	.002 208
48	40.210 573	490.132 164	.002 040
49	43.427 419	530.342 737	.001 886
50	46.901 613	573.770 156	.001 743

---

[1]How $1 left at compound interest will grow (deposit made at beginning of period). Formula: $s = P(1 + i)^n$.

[2]How $1 deposited periodically will grow (deposit made at end of period). For deposits made at the beginning of the period, subtract 1. from the amount shown in the following period. Formula: $S_n = \dfrac{(1 + i)^n - 1}{i}$

[3]Periodic deposit that will grow to $1 at a future date (deposits made at end of period). Formula: $\dfrac{1}{S_n} = \dfrac{i}{(1 + i)^n - 1}$

Future Worth of A Deposit of \$1.00 Compounded
At 8 1/2 Per Cent Interest
Per Period As Follows:

Number Of Periods	Growth Of \$1.00[1]	Growth Of \$1.00 Per Period[2]	Deposit Needed To Accumulate \$1.00[3]
1	1.085 000	1.000 000	1.000 000
2	1.177 225	2.085 000	.479 616
3	1.277 289	3.262 225	.306 539
4	1.385 859	4.539 514	.220 288
5	1.503 657	5.925 373	.168 766
6	1.631 468	7.429 030	.134 607
7	1.770 142	9.060 497	.110 369
8	1.920 604	10.830 639	.092 331
9	2.083 856	12.751 244	.078 424
10	2.260 983	14.835 099	.067 408
11	2.453 167	17.096 083	.058 493
12	2.661 686	19.549 250	.051 153
13	2.887 930	22.210 936	.045 023
14	3.133 404	25.098 866	.039 842
15	3.399 743	28.232 269	.035 420
16	3.688 721	31.632 012	.031 614
17	4.002 262	35.320 733	.028 312
18	4.342 455	39.322 995	.025 430
19	4.711 563	43.665 450	.022 901
20	5.112 046	48.377 013	.020 671
21	5.546 570	53.489 059	.018 695
22	6.018 028	59.035 629	.016 939
23	6.529 561	65.053 658	.015 372
24	7.084 574	71.583 219	.013 970
25	7.686 762	78.667 792	.012 712

[1]How \$1 left at compound interest will grow (deposit made at beginning of period). Formula: $s = P (1 + i)^n$

[2]How \$1 deposited periodically will grow (deposit made at end of period). For deposits made at the beginning of the period, subtract 1. from the amount shown in the following period. Formula: $S_n = \dfrac{(1 + i)^n - 1}{i}$

[3]Periodic deposit that will grow to \$1 at a future date (deposits made at end of period). Formula: $\dfrac{1}{S_n} = \dfrac{i}{(1 + i)^n - 1}$

Future Worth of A Deposit of $1.00 Compounded
At 8 1/2 Per Cent Interest
Per Period As Follows:

Number Of Periods	Growth Of $1.00[1]	Growth Of $1.00 Per Period[2]	Deposit Needed To Accumulate $1.00[3]
26	8.340 137	86.354 555	.011 580
27	9.049 049	94.694 692	.010 560
28	9.818 218	103.743 741	.009 639
29	10.652 766	113.561 959	.008 806
30	11.558 252	124.214 725	.008 051
31	12.540 703	135.772 977	.007 365
32	13.606 663	148.313 680	.006 742
33	14.763 229	161.920 343	.006 176
34	16.018 104	176.683 572	.005 660
35	17.379 642	192.701 675	.005 189
36	18.856 912	210.081 318	.004 760
37	20.459 750	228.938 230	.004 368
38	22.198 828	249.397 979	.004 010
39	24.085 729	271.596 808	.003 682
40	26.133 016	295.682 536	.003 382
41	28.354 322	321.815 552	.003 107
42	30.764 439	350.169 874	.002 856
43	33.379 417	380.934 313	.002 625
44	36.216 667	414.313 730	.002 414
45	39.295 084	450.530 397	.002 220
46	42.635 166	489.825 480	.002 042
47	46.259 155	532.460 646	.001 878
48	50.191 183	578.719 801	.001 728
49	54.457 434	628.910 984	.001 590
50	59.086 316	683.368 418	.001 463

---

[1]How $1 left at compound interest will grow (deposit made at beginning of period). Formula: $s = P(1 + i)^n$

[2]How $1 deposited periodically will grow (deposit made at end of period). For deposits made at the beginning of the period, subtract 1. from the amount shown in the following period.
Formula: $S_n = \dfrac{(1 + i)^n - 1}{i}$

[3]Periodic deposit that will grow to $1 at a future date (deposits made at end of period). Formula: $\dfrac{1}{S_n} = \dfrac{i}{(1 + i)^n - 1}$

Future Worth of A Deposit of $1.00 Compounded
At   9   Per Cent Interest
Per Period As Follows:

Number Of Periods	Growth Of $1.00[1]	Growth Of $1.00 Per Period[2]	Deposit Needed To Accumulate $1.00[3]
1	1.090 000	1.000 000	1.000 000
2	1.188 100	2.090 000	.478 469
3	1.295 029	3.278 100	.305 055
4	1.411 582	4.573 129	.218 669
5	1.538 624	5.984 711	.167 092
6	1.677 100	7.523 335	.132 920
7	1.828 039	9.200 435	.108 691
8	1.992 563	11.028 474	.090 674
9	2.171 893	13.021 036	.076 799
10	2.367 364	15.192 930	.065 820
11	2.580 426	17.560 293	.056 947
12	2.812 665	20.140 720	.049 651
13	3.065 805	22.953 385	.043 567
14	3.341 727	26.019 189	.038 433
15	3.642 482	29.360 916	.034 059
16	3.970 306	33.003 399	.030 300
17	4.327 633	36.973 705	.027 046
18	4.717 120	41.301 338	.024 212
19	5.141 661	46.018 458	.021 730
20	5.604 411	51.160 120	.019 546
21	6.108 808	56.764 530	.017 617
22	6.658 600	62.873 338	.015 905
23	7.257 874	69.531 939	.014 382
24	7.911 083	76.789 813	.013 023
25	8.623 081	84.700 896	.011 806

---

[1]How $1 left at compound interest will grow (deposit made at beginning of period). Formula: $s = P(1 + i)^n$

[2]How $1 deposited periodically will grow (deposit made at end of period). For deposits made at the beginning of the period, subtract 1. from the amount shown in the following period. Formula: $S_n = \dfrac{(1 + i)^n - 1}{i}$

[3]Periodic deposit that will grow to $1 at a future date (deposits made at end of period). Formula: $\dfrac{1}{S_n} = \dfrac{i}{(1 + i)^n - 1}$

Future Worth of A Deposit of $1.00 Compounded
At   9   Per Cent Interest
Per Period As Follows:

Number Of Periods	Growth Of $1.00[1]	Growth Of $1.00 Per Period[2]	Deposit Needed To Accumulate $1.00[3]
26	9.399 158	93.323 977	.010 715
27	10.245 082	102.723 135	.009 735
28	11.167 140	112.968 217	.008 852
29	12.172 182	124.135 356	.008 056
30	13.267 678	136.307 539	.007 336
31	14.461 770	149.575 217	.006 686
32	15.763 329	164.036 987	.006 096
33	17.182 028	179.800 315	.005 562
34	18.728 411	196.982 344	.005 077
35	20.413 968	215.710 755	.004 636
36	22.251 225	236.124 723	.004 235
37	24.253 835	258.375 948	.003 870
38	26.436 680	282.629 783	.003 538
39	28.815 982	309.066 463	.003 236
40	31.409 420	337.882 445	.002 960
41	34.236 268	369.291 865	.002 708
42	37.317 532	403.528 133	.002 478
43	40.676 110	440.845 665	.002 268
44	44.336 960	481.521 775	.002 077
45	48.327 286	525.858 734	.001 902
46	52.676 742	574.186 021	.001 742
47	57.417 649	626.862 762	.001 595
48	62.585 237	684.280 411	.001 461
49	68.217 908	746.865 648	.001 339
50	74.357 520	815.083 556	.001 227

---

[1]How $1 left at compound interest will grow (deposit made at beginning of period). Formula: $s = P (1 + i)^n$

[2]How $1 deposited periodically will grow (deposit made at end of period). For deposits made at the beginning of the period, subtract 1. from the amount shown in the following period.
Formula: $S_n = \dfrac{(1 + i)^n - 1}{i}$

[3]Periodic deposit that will grow to $1 at a future date (deposits made at end of period). Formula: $\dfrac{1}{S_n} = \dfrac{i}{(1 + i)^n - 1}$

Future Worth of A Deposit of $1.00 Compounded
At 9 1/2 Per Cent Interest
Per Period As Follows:

Number Of Periods	Growth Of $1.00[1]	Growth Of $1.00 Per Period[2]	Deposit Needed To Accumulate $1.00[3]
1	1.095 000	1.000 000	1.000 000
2	1.199 025	2.095 000	.477 327
3	1.312 932	3.294 025	.303 580
4	1.437 661	4.606 957	.217 063
5	1.574 239	6.044 618	.165 436
6	1.723 791	7.618 857	.131 253
7	1.887 552	9.342 648	.107 036
8	2.066 869	11.230 200	.089 046
9	2.263 222	13.297 069	.075 205
10	2.478 228	15.560 291	.064 266
11	2.713 659	18.038 518	.055 437
12	2.971 457	20.752 178	.048 188
13	3.253 745	23.723 634	.042 152
14	3.562 851	26.977 380	.037 068
15	3.901 322	30.540 231	.032 744
16	4.271 948	34.441 553	.029 035
17	4.677 783	38.713 500	.025 831
18	5.122 172	43.391 283	.023 046
19	5.608 778	48.513 454	.020 613
20	6.141 612	54.122 233	.018 477
21	6.725 065	60.263 845	.016 594
22	7.363 946	66.988 910	.014 928
23	8.063 521	74.352 856	.013 449
24	8.829 556	82.416 378	.012 134
25	9.668 364	91.245 934	.010 959

[1]How $1 left at compound interest will grow (deposit made at beginning of period). Formula: $s = P(1 + i)^n$

[2]How $1 deposited periodically will grow (deposit made at end of period). For deposits made at the beginning of the period, subtract 1. from the amount shown in the following period.
Formula: $S_n = \dfrac{(1 + i)^n - 1}{i}$

[3]Periodic deposit that will grow to $1 at a future date (deposits made at end of period). Formula: $\dfrac{1}{S_n} = \dfrac{i}{(1 + i)^n - 1}$

Future Worth of A Deposit of $1.00 Compounded
At 9 1/2 Per Cent Interest
Per Period As Follows:

Number Of Periods	Growth Of $1.00[1]	Growth Of $1.00 Per Period[2]	Deposit Needed To Accumulate $1.00[3]
26	10.586 858	100.914 297	.009 909
27	11.592 610	111.501 156	.008 969
28	12.693 908	123.093 766	.008 124
29	13.899 829	135.787 673	.007 364
30	15.220 313	149.687 502	.006 681
31	16.666 242	164.907 815	.006 064
32	18.249 535	181.574 057	.005 507
33	19.983 241	199.823 593	.005 004
34	21.881 649	219.806 834	.004 549
35	23.960 406	241.688 483	.004 138
36	26.236 644	265.648 889	.003 764
37	28.729 126	291.885 534	.003 426
38	31.458 393	320.614 659	.003 119
39	34.446 940	352.073 052	.002 840
40	37.719 399	386.519 992	.002 587
41	41.302 742	424.239 391	.002 357
42	45.226 503	465.542 133	.002 148
43	49.523 020	510.768 636	.001 958
44	54.227 707	560.291 656	.001 785
45	59.379 340	614.519 364	.001 627
46	65.020 377	673.898 703	.001 484
47	71.197 313	738.919 080	.001 353
48	77.961 057	810.116 393	.001 234
49	85.367 358	888.077 450	.001 126
50	93.477 257	973.444 808	.001 027

---

[1]How $1 left at compound interest will grow (deposit made at beginning of period). Formula: $s = P(1 + i)^n$

[2]How $1 deposited periodically will grow (deposit made at end of period). For deposits made at the beginning of the period, subtract 1. from the amount shown in the following period.
Formula: $S_n = \dfrac{(1 + i)^n - 1}{i}$

[3]Periodic deposit that will grow to $1 at a future date (deposits made at end of period). Formula: $\dfrac{1}{S_n} = \dfrac{i}{(1 + i)^n - 1}$

Future Worth of A Deposit of $1.00 Compounded
At   10   Per Cent Interest
Per Period As Follows:

Number Of Periods	Growth Of $1.00[1]	Growth Of $1.00 Per Period[2]	Deposit Needed To Accumulate $1.00[3]
1	1.100 000	1.000 000	1.000 000
2	1.210 000	2.100 000	.476 190
3	1.331 000	3.310 000	.302 115
4	1.464 100	4.641 000	.215 471
5	1.610 510	6.105 100	.163 797
6	1.771 561	7.715 610	.129 607
7	1.948 717	9.487 171	.105 405
8	2.143 589	11.435 888	.087 444
9	2.357 948	13.579 477	.073 641
10	2.593 742	15.937 425	.062 745
11	2.853 117	18.531 167	.053 963
12	3.138 428	21.384 284	.046 763
13	3.452 271	24.522 712	.040 779
14	3.797 498	27.974 983	.035 746
15	4.177 248	31.772 482	.031 474
16	4.594 973	35.949 730	.027 817
17	5.054 470	40.544 703	.024 664
18	5.559 917	45.599 173	.021 930
19	6.115 909	51.159 090	.019 547
20	6.727 500	57.274 999	.017 460
21	7.400 250	64.002 499	.015 624
22	8.140 275	71.402 749	.014 005
23	8.954 302	79.543 024	.012 572
24	9.849 733	88.497 327	.011 300
25	10.834 706	98.347 059	.010 168

---

[1]How $1 left at compound interest will grow (deposit made at beginning of period). Formula: $s = P(1 + i)^n$

[2]How $1 deposited periodically will grow (deposit made at end of period). For deposits made at the beginning of the period, subtract 1. from the amount shown in the following period. Formula: $S_n = \dfrac{(1 + i)^n - 1}{i}$

[3]Periodic deposit that will grow to $1 at a future date (deposits made at end of period). Formula: $\dfrac{1}{S_n} = \dfrac{i}{(1 + i)^n - 1}$

Future Worth of A Deposit of $1.00 Compounded
At   10   Per Cent Interest
Per Period As Follows:

Number Of Periods	Growth Of $1.00[1]	Growth Of $1.00 Per Period[2]	Deposit Needed To Accumulate $1.00[3]
26	11.918 177	109.181 765	.009 159
27	13.109 994	121.099 942	.008 258
28	14.420 994	134.209 936	.007 451
29	15.863 093	148.630 930	.006 728
30	17.449 402	164.494 023	.006 079
31	19.194 342	181.943 425	.005 496
32	21.113 777	201.137 767	.004 972
33	23.225 154	222.251 544	.004 499
34	25.547 670	245.476 699	.004 074
35	28.102 437	271.024 368	.003 690
36	30.912 681	299.126 805	.003 343
37	34.003 949	330.039 486	.003 030
38	37.404 343	364.043 434	.002 747
39	41.144 778	401.447 778	.002 491
40	45.259 256	442.592 556	.002 259
41	49.785 181	487.851 811	.002 050
42	54.763 699	537.636 992	.001 860
43	60.240 069	592.400 692	.001 688
44	66.264 076	652.640 761	.001 532
45	72.890 484	718.904 837	.001 391
46	80.179 532	791.795 321	.001 263
47	88.197 485	871.974 853	.001 147
48	97.017 234	960.172 338	.001 041
49	106.718 957	1057.189 572	.000 946
50	117.390 853	1163.908 529	.000 859

---

[1]How $1 left at compound interest will grow (deposit made at beginning of period). Formula: $s = P(1 + i)^n$

[2]How $1 deposited periodically will grow (deposit made at end of period). For deposits made at the beginning of the period, subtract 1. from the amount shown in the following period. Formula: $S_n = \dfrac{(1 + i)^n - 1}{i}$

[3]Periodic deposit that will grow to $1 at a future date (deposits made at end of period). Formula: $\dfrac{1}{S_n} = \dfrac{i}{(1 + i)^n - 1}$

Present Worth Of A Future Amount of $1.00
Discounted At   1/2   Per Cent Interest
Per Period As Follows:

Number Of Periods	Present Worth Of $1.00[1]	Present Worth Of $1.00 Per Period[2]	Partial Payment Per $1.00 Of Loan[3]
1	.995 025	.995 025	1.005 000
2	.990 075	1.985 099	.503 753
3	.985 149	2.970 248	.336 672
4	.980 248	3.950 496	.253 133
5	.975 371	4.925 866	.203 010
6	.970 518	5.896 384	.169 595
7	.965 690	6.862 074	.145 729
8	.960 885	7.822 959	.127 829
9	.956 105	8.779 064	.113 907
10	.951 348	9.730 412	.102 771
11	.946 615	10.677 017	.093 659
12	.941 905	11.618 932	.086 066
13	.937 219	12.556 151	.079 642
14	.932 556	13.488 708	.074 136
15	.927 917	14.416 625	.069 364
16	.923 300	15.339 925	.065 189
17	.918 707	16.258 632	.061 506
18	.914 136	17.172 768	.058 232
19	.909 588	18.082 356	.055 303
20	.905 063	18.987 419	.052 666
21	.900 560	19.887 979	.050 282
22	.896 080	20.784 059	.048 114
23	.891 622	21.675 681	.046 135
24	.887 186	22.562 866	.044 321
25	.882 772	23.445 638	.042 652

---

[1]What $1 due in the future is worth today. Formula: $p = \dfrac{s}{(1 + i)^n}$

[2]What $1 payable periodically is worth today (payments made at end of period). For payments made at the beginning of the period, add 1. to the amount shown for the previous period.
Formula: $a_n = \dfrac{1 - (1 + i)^{-n}}{i}$

[3]Periodic payment necessary to pay off a loan of $1. Formula: The sinking fund factor plus the rate of interest.

Present Worth Of A Future Amount of $1.00
Discounted At   1/2   Per Cent Interest
Per Period As Follows:

Number Of Periods	Present Worth Of $1.00[1]	Present Worth Of $1.00 Per Period[2]	Partial Payment Per $1.00 Of Loan[3]
26	.878 380	24.324 018	.041 112
27	.874 010	25.198 028	.039 686
28	.869 662	26.067 689	.038 362
29	.865 335	26.933 024	.037 129
30	.861 030	27.794 054	.035 979
31	.856 746	28.650 800	.034 903
32	.852 484	29.503 284	.033 895
33	.848 242	30.351 526	.032 947
34	.844 022	31.195 548	.032 056
35	.839 823	32.035 371	.031 215
36	.835 645	32.871 016	.030 422
37	.831 487	33.702 504	.029 671
38	.827 351	34.529 854	.028 960
39	.823 235	35.353 089	.028 286
40	.819 139	36.172 228	.027 646
41	.815 064	36.987 291	.027 036
42	.811 009	37.798 300	.026 456
43	.806 974	38.605 274	.025 903
44	.802 959	39.408 232	.025 375
45	.798 964	40.207 196	.024 871
46	.794 989	41.002 185	.024 389
47	.791 034	41.793 219	.023 927
48	.787 098	42.580 318	.023 485
49	.783 182	43.363 500	.023 061
50	.779 286	44.142 786	.022 654

[1] What $1 due in the future is worth today. Formula: $p = \dfrac{s}{(1 + i)^n}$

[2] What $1 payable periodically is worth today (payments made at end of period). For payments made at the beginning of the period, add 1. to the amount shown for the previous period.
Formula: $a_n = \dfrac{1 - (1 + i)^{-n}}{i}$

[3] Periodic payment necessary to pay off a loan of $1. Formula: The sinking fund factor plus the rate of interest.

Present Worth Of A Future Amount of $1.00
Discounted At   3   Per Cent Interest
Per Period As Follows:

Number Of Periods	Present Worth Of $1.00[1]	Present Worth Of $1.00 Per Period[2]	Partial Payment Per $1.00 Of Loan[3]
1	.970 874	.970 874	1.030 000
2	.942 596	1.913 470	.522 611
3	.915 142	2.828 611	.353 530
4	.888 487	3.717 098	.269 027
5	.862 609	4.579 707	.218 355
6	.837 484	5.417 191	.184 598
7	.813 092	6.230 283	.160 506
8	.789 409	7.019 692	.142 456
9	.766 417	7.786 109	.128 434
10	.744 094	8.530 203	.117 231
11	.722 421	9.252 624	.108 077
12	.701 380	9.954 004	.100 462
13	.680 951	10.634 955	.094 030
14	.661 118	11.296 073	.088 526
15	.641 862	11.937 935	.083 767
16	.623 167	12.561 102	.079 611
17	.605 016	13.166 118	.075 953
18	.587 395	13.753 513	.072 709
19	.570 286	14.323 799	.069 814
20	.553 676	14.877 475	.067 216
21	.537 549	15.415 024	.064 872
22	.521 893	15.936 917	.062 747
23	.506 692	16.443 608	.060 814
24	.491 934	16.935 542	.059 047
25	.477 606	17.413 148	.057 428

---

[1]What $1 due in the future is worth today. Formula: $p = \dfrac{s}{(1 + i)^n}$

[2]What $1 payable periodically is worth today (payments made at end of period). For payments made at the beginning of the period, add 1. to the amount shown for the previous period.
Formula: $a_n = \dfrac{1 - (1 + i)^{-n}}{i}$

[3]Periodic payment necessary to pay off a loan of $1. Formula: The sinking fund factor plus the rate of interest.

Present Worth of A Future Amount of $1.00
Discounted At   3   Per Cent Interest
Per Period As Follows:

Number Of Periods	Present Worth Of $1.00[1]	Present Worth Of $1.00 Per Period[2]	Partial Payment Per $1.00 Of Loan[3]
26	.463 695	17.876 842	.055 938
27	.450 189	18.327 031	.054 564
28	.437 077	18.764 108	.053 293
29	.424 346	19.188 455	.052 115
30	.411 987	19.600 441	.051 019
31	.399 987	20.000 428	.049 999
32	.388 337	20.388 766	.049 047
33	.377 026	20.765 792	.048 156
34	.366 045	21.131 837	.047 322
35	.355 383	21.487 220	.046 539
36	.345 032	21.832 252	.045 804
37	.334 983	22.167 235	.045 112
38	.325 226	22.492 462	.044 459
39	.315 754	22.808 215	.043 844
40	.306 557	23.114 772	.043 262
41	.297 628	23.412 400	.042 712
42	.288 959	23.701 359	.042 192
43	.280 543	23.981 902	.041 698
44	.272 372	24.254 274	.041 230
45	.264 439	24.518 713	.040 785
46	.256 737	24.775 449	.040 363
47	.249 259	25.024 708	.039 961
48	.241 999	25.266 707	.039 578
49	.234 950	25.501 657	.039 213
50	.228 107	25.729 764	.038 865

---

[1]What $1 due in the future is worth today. Formula: $p = \dfrac{s}{(1 + i)^n}$

[2]What $1 payable periodically is worth today (payments made at end of period). For payments made at the beginning of the period, add 1. to the amount shown for the previous period.
Formula: $a_n = \dfrac{1 - (1 + i)^{-n}}{i}$

[3]Periodic payment necessary to pay off a loan of $1. Formula: The sinking fund factor plus the rate of interest.

Present Worth Of A Future Amount Of $1.00
Discounted At   4   Per Cent Interest
Per Period As Follows:

Number Of Periods	Present Worth Of $1.00[1]	Present Worth Of $1.00 Per Period[2]	Partial Payment Per $1.00 Of Loan[3]
1	.961 538	.961 538	1.040 000
2	.924 556	1.886 095	.530 196
3	.888 996	2.775 091	.360 349
4	.854 804	3.629 895	.275 490
5	.821 927	4.451 822	.224 627
6	.790 315	5.242 137	.190 762
7	.759 918	6.002 055	.166 610
8	.730 690	6.732 745	.148 528
9	.702 587	7.435 332	.134 493
10	.675 564	8.110 896	.123 291
11	.649 581	8.760 477	.114 149
12	.624 597	9.385 074	.106 552
13	.600 574	9.985 648	.100 144
14	.577 475	10.563 123	.094 669
15	.555 265	11.118 387	.089 941
16	.533 908	11.652 296	.085 820
17	.513 373	12.165 669	.082 199
18	.493 628	12.659 297	.078 993
19	.474 642	13.133 939	.076 139
20	.456 387	13.590 326	.073 582
21	.438 834	14.029 160	.071 280
22	.421 955	14.451 115	.069 199
23	.405 726	14.856 842	.067 309
24	.390 121	15.246 963	.065 587
25	.375 117	15.622 080	.064 012

[1]What $1 due in the future is worth today. Formula: $p = \dfrac{s}{(1+i)^n}$

[2]What $1 payable periodically is worth today (payments made at end of period). For payments made at the beginning of the period, add 1. to the amount shown for the previous period.
Formula: $a_n = \dfrac{1 - (1+i)^{-n}}{i}$

[3]Periodic payment necessary to pay off a loan of $1. Formula: The skinking fund factor plus the rate of interest.

Present Worth Of A Future Amount of $1.00
Discounted At   4   Per Cent Interest
Per Period As Follows:

Number Of Periods	Present Worth Of $1.00[1]	Present Worth Of $1.00 Per Period[2]	Partial Payment Per $1.00 Of Loan[3]
26	.360 689	15.982 769	.062 567
27	.346 817	16.329 586	.061 239
28	.333 477	16.663 063	.060 013
29	.320 651	16.983 715	.058 880
30	.308 319	17.292 033	.057 830
31	.296 460	17.588 494	.056 855
32	.285 058	17.873 551	.055 949
33	.274 094	18.147 646	.055 104
34	.263 552	18.411 198	.054 315
35	.253 415	18.664 613	.053 577
36	.243 669	18.908 282	.052 887
37	.234 297	19.142 579	.052 240
38	.225 285	19.367 864	.051 632
39	.216 621	19.584 485	.051 061
40	.208 289	19.792 774	.050 523
41	.200 278	19.993 052	.050 017
42	.192 575	20.185 627	.049 540
43	.185 168	20.370 795	.049 090
44	.178 046	20.548 841	.048 665
45	.171 198	20.720 040	.048 262
46	.164 614	20.884 654	.047 882
47	.158 283	21.042 936	.047 522
48	.152 195	21.195 131	.047 181
49	.146 341	21.341 472	.046 857
50	.140 713	21.482 185	.046 550

[1]What $1 due in the future is worth today. Formula: $p = \dfrac{s}{(1+i)^n}$

[2]What $1 payable periodically is worth today (payments made at end of period). For payments made at the beginning of the period, add 1. to the amount shown for the previous period.
Formula: $a_n = \dfrac{1 - (1+i)^{-n}}{i}$

[3]Periodic payment necessary to pay off a loan of $1. Formula: The sinking fund factor plus the rate of interest.

Present Worth Of A Future Amount Of $1.00
Discounted At   5   Per Cent Interest
Per Period As Follows:

Number Of Periods	Present Worth Of $1.00[1]	Present Worth Of $1.00 Per Period[2]	Partial Payment Per $1.00 Of Loan[3]
1	.952 381	.952 381	1.050 000
2	.907 029	1.859 410	.537 805
3	.863 838	2.723 248	.367 209
4	.822 702	3.545 951	.282 012
5	.783 526	4.329 477	.230 975
6	.746 215	5.075 692	.197 017
7	.710 681	5.786 373	.172 820
8	.676 839	6.463 213	.154 722
9	.644 609	7.107 822	.140 690
10	.613 913	7.721 735	.129 505
11	.584 679	8.306 414	.120 389
12	.556 837	8.863 252	.112 825
13	.530 321	9.393 573	.106 456
14	.505 068	9.898 641	.101 024
15	.481 017	10.379 658	.096 342
16	.458 112	10.837 770	.092 270
17	.436 297	11.274 066	.088 699
18	.415 521	11.689 587	.085 546
19	.395 734	12.085 321	.082 745
20	.376 889	12.462 210	.080 243
21	.358 942	12.821 153	.077 996
22	.341 850	13.163 003	.075 971
23	.325 571	13.488 574	.074 137
24	.310 068	13.798 642	.072 471
25	.295 303	14.093 945	.070 952

[1] What $1 due in the future is worth today. Formula: $p = \dfrac{s}{(1 + i)^n}$

[2] What $1 payable periodically is worth today (payments made at end of period). For payments made at the beginning of the period, add 1. to the amount shown for the previous period.
Formula: $a_n = \dfrac{1 - (1 + i)^{-n}}{i}$

[3] Periodic payment necessary to pay off a loan of $1. Formula: The sinking fund factor plus the rate of interest.

Present Worth Of A Future Amount Of $1.00
Discounted At   5   Per Cent Interest
Per Period As Follows:

Number Of Periods	Present Worth Of $1.00[1]	Present Worth Of $1.00 Per Period[2]	Partial Payment Per $1.00 Of Loan[3]
26	.281 241	14.375 185	.069 564
27	.267 848	14.643 034	.068 292
28	.255 094	14.898 127	.067 123
29	.242 946	15.141 074	.066 046
30	.231 377	15.372 451	.065 051
31	.220 359	15.592 811	.064 132
32	.209 866	15.802 677	.063 280
33	.199 873	16.002 549	.062 490
34	.190 355	16.192 904	.061 755
35	.181 290	16.374 194	.061 072
36	.172 657	16.546 852	.060 434
37	.164 436	16.711 287	.059 840
38	.156 605	16.867 893	.059 284
39	.149 148	17.017 041	.058 765
40	.142 046	17.159 086	.058 278
41	.135 282	17.294 368	.057 822
42	.128 840	17.423 208	.057 395
43	.122 704	17.545 912	.056 993
44	.116 861	17.662 773	.056 616
45	.111 297	17.774 070	.056 262
46	.105 997	17.880 066	.055 928
47	.100 949	17.981 016	.055 614
48	.096 142	18.077 158	.055 318
49	.091 564	18.168 722	.055 040
50	.087 204	18.255 925	.054 777

---

[1]What $1 due in the future is worth today. Formula: $p = \dfrac{s}{(1 + i)^n}$

[2]What $1 payable periodically is worth today (payments made at end of period). For payments made at the beginning of the period, add 1. to the amount shown for the previous period.
Formula: $a_n = \dfrac{1 - (1 + i)^{-n}}{i}$

[3]Periodic payment necessary to pay off a loan of $1. Formula: The sinking fund factor plus the rate of interest.

Present Worth Of A Future Amount of $1.00
Discounted At   6   Per Cent Interest
Per Period As Follows:

Number Of Periods	Present Worth Of $1.00[1]	Present Worth Of $1.00 Per Period[2]	Partial Payment Per $1.00 Of Loan[3]
1	.943 396	.943 396	1.060 000
2	.889 996	1.833 393	.545 437
3	.839 619	2.673 012	.374 110
4	.792 094	3.465 106	.288 591
5	.747 258	4.212 364	.237 396
6	.704 961	4.917 324	.203 363
7	.665 057	5.582 381	.179 135
8	.627 412	6.209 794	.161 036
9	.591 898	6.801 692	.147 022
10	.558 395	7.360 087	.135 868
11	.526 788	7.886 875	.126 793
12	.496 969	8.383 844	.119 277
13	.468 839	8.852 683	.112 960
14	.442 301	9.294 984	.107 585
15	.417 265	9.712 249	.102 963
16	.393 646	10.105 895	.098 952
17	.371 364	10.477 260	.095 445
18	.350 344	10.827 603	.092 357
19	.330 513	11.158 116	.089 621
20	311 805	11.469 921	.087 185
21	.294 155	11.764 077	.085 005
22	.277 505	12.041 582	.083 046
23	.261 797	12.303 379	.081 278
24	.246 979	12.550 358	.079 679
25	.232 999	12.783 356	.078 227

----

[1]What $1 due in the future is worth today. Formula: $p = \dfrac{s}{(1 + i)^n}$

[2]What $1 payable periodically is worth today (payments made at end of period). For payments made at the beginning of the period, add 1. to the amount shown for the previous period.
Formula: $a_n = \dfrac{1 - (1 + i)^{-n}}{i}$

[3]Periodic payment necessary to pay off a loan of $1. Formula: The sinking fund factor plus the rate of interest.

Present Worth Of A Future Amount Of $1.00
Discounted At   6   Per Cent Interest
Per Period As Follows:

Number Of Periods	Present Worth Of $1.00[1]	Present Worth Of $1.00 Per Period[2]	Partial Payment Per $1.00 Of Loan[3]
26	.219 810	13.003 166	.076 904
27	.207 368	13.210 534	.075 697
28	.195 630	13.406 164	.074 593
29	.184 557	13.590 721	.073 580
30	.174 110	13.764 831	.072 649
31	.164 255	13.929 086	.071 792
32	.154 957	14.084 043	.071 002
33	.146 186	14.230 230	.070 273
34	.137 912	14.368 141	.069 598
35	.130 105	14.498 246	.068 974
36	.122 741	14.620 987	.068 395
37	.115 793	14.736 780	.067 857
38	.109 239	14.846 019	.067 358
39	.103 056	14.949 075	.066 894
40	.097 222	15.046 297	.066 462
41	.091 719	15.138 016	.066 059
42	.086 527	15.224 543	.065 683
43	.081 630	15.306 173	.065 333
44	.077 009	15.383 182	.065 006
45	.072 650	15.455 832	.064 700
46	.068 538	15.524 370	.064 415
47	.064 658	15.589 028	.064 148
48	.060 998	15.650 027	.063 898
49	.057 546	15.707 572	.063 664
50	.054 288	15.761 861	.063 444

[1]What $1 due in the future is worth today. Formula: $p = \dfrac{s}{(1 + i)^n}$

[2]What $1 payable periodically is worth today (payments made at end of period). For payments made at the beginning of the period, add 1. to the amount shown for the previous period.
Formula: $a_n = \dfrac{1 - (1 + i)^{-n}}{i}$

[3]Periodic payment necessary to pay off a loan of $1. Formula: The sinking fund factor plus the rate of interest.

Present Worth Of A Future Amount of $1.00
Discounted At   7   Per Cent Interest
Per Period As Follows:

Number Of Periods	Present Worth Of $1.00[1]	Present Worth Of $1.00 Per Period[2]	Partial Payment Per $1.00 Of Loan[3]
1	.934 579	.934 579	1.070 000
2	.873 439	1.808 018	.553 092
3	.816 298	2.624 316	.381 052
4	.762 895	3.387 211	.295 228
5	.712 986	4.100 197	.243 891
6	.666 342	4.766 540	.209 796
7	.622 750	5.389 289	.185 553
8	.582 009	5.971 299	.167 468
9	.543 934	6.515 232	.153 486
10	.508 349	7.023 582	.142 378
11	.475 093	7.498 674	.133 357
12	.444 012	7.942 686	.125 902
13	.414 964	8.357 651	.119 651
14	.387 817	8.745 468	.114 345
15	.362 446	9.107 914	.109 795
16	.338 735	9.446 649	.105 858
17	.316 574	9.763 223	.102 425
18	.295 864	10.059 087	.099 413
19	.276 508	10.335 595	.096 753
20	.258 419	10.594 014	.094 393
21	.241 513	10.835 527	.092 289
22	.225 713	11.061 240	.090 406
23	.210 947	11.272 187	.088 714
24	.197 147	11.469 334	.087 189
25	.184 249	11.653 583	.085 811

[1]What $1 due in the future is worth today. Formula: $p = \dfrac{s}{(1 + i)^n}$

[2]What $1 payable periodically is worth today (payments made at end of period). For payments made at the beginning of the period, add 1. to the amount shown for the previous period.
Formula: $a_n = \dfrac{1 - (1 + i)^{-n}}{i}$

[3]Periodic payment necessary to pay off a loan of $1. Formula: The sinking fund factor plus the rate of interest.

Present Worth Of A Future Amount of $1.00
Discounted At   7   Per Cent Interest
Per Period As Follows:

Number Of Periods	Present Worth Of $1.00[1]	Present Worth Of $1.00 Per Period[2]	Partial Payment Per $1.00 Of Loan[3]
26	.172 195	11.825 779	.084 561
27	.160 930	11.986 709	.083 426
28	.150 402	12.137 111	.082 392
29	.140 563	12.277 674	.081 449
30	.131 367	12.409 041	.080 586
31	.122 773	12.531 814	.079 797
32	.114 741	12.646 555	.079 073
33	.107 235	12.753 790	.078 408
34	.100 219	12.854 009	.077 797
35	.093 663	12.947 672	.077 234
36	.087 535	13.035 208	.076 715
37	.081 809	13.117 017	.076 237
38	.076 457	13.193 473	.075 795
39	.071 455	13.264 928	.075 387
40	.066 780	13.331 709	.075 009
41	.062 412	13.394 120	.074 660
42	.058 329	13.452 449	.074 336
43	.054 513	13.506 962	.074 036
44	.050 946	13.557 908	.073 758
45	.047 613	13.605 522	.073 500
46	.044 499	13.650 020	.073 260
47	.041 587	13.691 608	.073 037
48	.038 867	13.730 474	.072 831
49	.036 324	13.766 799	.072 639
50	.033 948	13.800 746	.072 460

[1]What $1 due in the future is worth today. Formula: $p = \dfrac{s}{(1 + i)^n}$

[2]What $1 payable periodically is worth today (payments made at end of period). For payments made at the beginning of the period, add 1. to the amount shown for the previous period.
Formula: $a_n = \dfrac{1 - (1 + i)^{-n}}{i}$

[3]Periodic payment necessary to pay off a loan of $1. Formula: The sinking fund factor plus the rate of interest.

Present Worth Of A Future Amount of $1.00
Discounted At 7 1/2 Per Cent Interest
Per Period As Follows:

Number Of Periods	Present Worth Of $1.00[1]	Present Worth Of $1.00 Per Period[2]	Partial Payment Per $1.00 Of Loan[3]
1	.930 233	.930 233	1.075 000
2	.865 333	1.795 565	.556 928
3	.804 961	2.600 526	.384 538
4	.748 801	3.349 326	.298 568
5	.696 559	4.045 885	.247 165
6	.647 962	4.693 846	.213 045
7	.602 755	5.296 601	.188 800
8	.560 702	5.857 304	.170 727
9	.521 583	6.378 887	.156 767
10	.485 194	6.864 081	.145 686
11	.451 343	7.315 424	.136 697
12	.419 854	7.735 278	.129 278
13	.390 562	8.125 840	.123 064
14	.363 313	8.489 154	.117 797
15	.337 966	8.827 120	.113 287
16	.314 387	9.141 507	.109 391
17	.292 453	9.433 960	.106 000
18	.272 049	9.706 009	.103 029
19	.253 069	9.959 078	.100 411
20	.235 413	10.194 491	.098 092
21	.218 989	10.413 480	.096 029
22	.203 711	10.617 191	.094 187
23	.189 498	10.806 689	.092 535
24	.176 277	10.982 967	.091 050
25	.163 979	11.146 946	.089 711

---

[1]What $1 due in the future is worth today. Formula: $p = \dfrac{s}{(1 + i)^n}$

[2]What $1 payable periodically is worth today (payments made at end of period). For payments made at the beginning of the period, add 1. to the amount shown for the previous period.
Formula: $a_n = \dfrac{1 - (1 + i)^{-n}}{i}$

[3]Periodic payment necessary to pay off a loan of $1. Formula: The sinking fund factor plus the rate of interest.

Present Worth Of A Future Amount of $1.00
Discounted At   7 1/2   Per Cent Interest
Per Period As Follows:

Number Of Periods	Present Worth Of $1.00[1]	Present Worth Of $1.00 Per Period[2]	Partial Payment Per $1.00 Of Loan[3]
26	.152 539	11.299 485	.088 500
27	.141 896	11.441 381	.087 402
28	.131 997	11.573 378	.086 405
29	.122 788	11.696 165	.085 498
30	.114 221	11.810 386	.084 671
31	.106 252	11.916 638	.083 916
32	.098 839	12.015 478	.083 226
33	.091 943	12.107 421	.082 594
34	.085 529	12.192 950	.082 015
35	.079 562	12.272 511	.081 483
36	.074 011	12.346 522	.080 994
37	.068 847	12.415 370	.080 545
38	.064 044	12.479 414	.080 132
39	.059 576	12.538 989	.079 751
40	.055 419	12.594 409	.079 400
41	.051 553	12.645 962	.079 077
42	.047 956	12.693 918	.078 778
43	.044 610	12.738 528	.078 502
44	.041 498	12.780 026	.078 247
45	.038 603	12.818 629	.078 011
46	.035 910	12.854 539	.077 794
47	.033 404	12.887 943	.077 592
48	.031 074	12.919 017	.077 405
49	.028 906	12.947 922	.077 232
50	.016 889	12.974 812	.077 072

[1]What $1 due in the future is worth today. Formula: $p = \dfrac{s}{(1 + i)^n}$

[2]What $1 payable periodically is worth today (payments made at end of period). For payments made at the beginning of the period, add 1. to the amount shown for the previous period.
Formula: $a_n = \dfrac{1 - (1 + i)^{-n}}{i}$

[3]Periodic payment necessary to pay off a loan of $1. Formula: The sinking fund factor plus the rate of interest.

Present Worth Of A Future Amount of $1.00
Discounted At   8   Per Cent Interest
Per Period As Follows:

Number Of Periods	Present Worth Of $1.00[1]	Present Worth Of $1.00 Per Period[2]	Partial Payment Per $1.00 Of Loan[3]
1	.925 926	.925 926	1.080 000
2	.857 339	1.783 265	.560 769
3	.793 832	2.577 097	.388 034
4	.735 030	3.312 127	.301 921
5	.680 583	3.992 710	.250 456
6	.630 170	4.622 880	.216 315
7	.583 490	5.206 370	.192 072
8	.540 269	5.746 639	.174 015
9	.500 249	6.246 888	.160 080
10	.463 193	6.710 081	.149 029
11	.428 883	7.138 964	.140 076
12	.397 114	7.536 078	.132 695
13	.367 698	7.903 776	.126 522
14	.340 461	8.244 237	.121 297
15	.315 242	8.559 479	.116 830
16	.291 890	8.851 369	.112 977
17	.270 269	9.121 638	.109 629
18	.250 249	9.371 887	.106 702
19	.231 712	9.603 599	.104 128
20	.214 548	9.818 147	.101 852
21	.198 656	10.016 803	.099 832
22	.183 941	10.200 744	.098 032
23	.170 315	10.371 059	.096 422
24	.157 699	10.528 758	.094 978
25	.146 018	10.674 776	.093 679

[1] What $1 due in the future is worth today. Formula: $p = \dfrac{s}{(1 + i)^n}$

[2] What $1 payable periodically is worth today (payments made at end of period). For payments made at the beginning of the period, add 1. to the amount shown for the previous period.
Formula: $a_n = \dfrac{1 - (1 + i)^{-n}}{i}$

[3] Periodic payment necessary to pay off a loan of $1. Formula: The sinking fund factor plus the rate of interest.

Present Worth Of A Future Amount of $1.00
Discounted At   8   Per Cent Interest
Per Period As Follows:

Number Of Periods	Present Worth Of $1.00[1]	Present Worth Of $1.00 Per Period[2]	Partial Payment Per $1.00 Of Loan[3]
26	.135 202	10.809 978	.092 507
27	.125 187	10.935 165	.091 448
28	.115 914	11.051 078	.090 489
29	.107 328	11.158 406	.089 619
30	.099 377	11.257 783	.088 827
31	.092 016	11.349 799	.088 107
32	.085 200	11.434 999	.087 451
33	.078 889	11.513 888	.086 852
34	.073 045	11.586 934	.086 304
35	.067 635	11.654 568	.085 803
36	.062 625	11.717 193	.085 345
37	.057 986	11.775 179	.084 924
38	.053 690	11.828 869	.084 539
39	.049 713	11.878 582	.084 185
40	.046 031	11.924 613	.083 860
41	.042 621	11.967 235	.083 561
42	.039 464	12.006 699	.083 287
43	.036 541	12.043 240	.083 034
44	.033 834	12.077 074	.082 802
45	.031 328	12.108 402	.082 587
46	.029 007	12.137 409	.082 390
47	.026 859	12.164 267	.082 208
48	.024 869	12.189 136	.082 040
49	.023 027	12.212 163	.081 886
50	.021 321	12.233 485	.081 743

---

[1]What $1 due in the future is worth today. Formula: $p = \dfrac{s}{(1 + i)^n}$

[2]What $1 payable periodically is worth today (payments made at end of period). For payments made at the beginning of the period, add 1. to the amount shown for the previous period.
Formula: $a_n = \dfrac{1 - (1' + i)^{-n}}{i}$

[3]Periodic payment necessary to pay off a loan of $1. Formula: The sinking fund factor plus the rate of interest.

Present Worth Of A Future Amount of $1.00
Discounted At 8 1/2 Per Cent Interest
Per Period As Follows:

Number Of Periods	Present Worth Of $1.00[1]	Present Worth Of $1.00 Per Period[2]	Partial Payment Per $1.00 Of Loan[3]
1	.921 659	.921 659	1.085 000
2	.849 455	1.771 114	.564 616
3	.782 908	2.554 022	.391 539
4	.721 574	3.275 597	.305 288
5	.665 045	3.940 642	.253 766
6	.612 945	4.553 587	.219 607
7	.564 926	5.118 514	.195 369
8	.520 669	5.639 183	.177 331
9	.479 880	6.119 063	.163 424
10	.442 285	6.561 348	.152 408
11	.407 636	6.968 984	.143 493
12	.375 702	7.344 686	.136 153
13	.346 269	7.690 955	.130 023
14	.319 142	8.010 097	.124 842
15	.294 140	8.304 237	.120 420
16	.271 097	8.575 333	.116 614
17	.249 859	8.825 192	.113 312
18	.230 285	9.055 476	.110 430
19	.212 244	9.267 720	.107 901
20	.195 616	9.463 337	.105 671
21	.180 292	9.643 628	.103 695
22	.166 167	9.809 796	.101 939
23	.153 150	9.962 945	.100 372
24	.141 152	10.104 097	.098 970
25	.130 094	10.234 191	.097 712

---

[1]What $1 due in the future is worth today. Formula: $p = \dfrac{s}{(1 + i)^n}$

[2]What $1 payable periodically is worth today (payments made at end of period). For payments made at the beginning of the period, add 1. to the amount shown for the previous period.
Formula: $a_n = \dfrac{1 - (1 + i)^{-n}}{i}$

[3]Periodic payment necessary to pay off a loan of $1. Formula: The sinking fund factor plus the rate of interest.

Present Worth Of A Future Amount of $1.00
Discounted At 8 1/2 Per Cent Interest
Per Period As Follows:

Number Of Periods	Present Worth Of $1.00[1]	Present Worth Of $1.00 Per Period[2]	Partial Payment Per $1.00 Of Loan[3]
26	.119 902	10.354 093	.096 580
27	.110 509	10.464 602	.095 560
28	.101 851	10.566 453	.094 639
29	.093 872	10.660 326	.093 806
30	.086 518	10.746 844	.093 051
31	.079 740	10.826 584	.092 365
32	.073 493	10.900 078	.091 742
33	.067 736	10.967 813	.091 176
34	.062 429	11.030 243	.090 660
35	.057 539	11.087 781	.090 189
36	.053 031	11.140 812	.089 760
37	.048 876	11.189 689	.089 368
38	.045 047	11.234 736	.089 010
39	.041 518	11.276 255	.088 682
40	.038 266	11.314 520	.088 382
41	.035 268	11.349 788	.088 107
42	.032 505	11.382 293	.087 856
43	.029 959	11.412 252	.087 625
44	.027 612	11.439 864	.087 414
45	.025 448	11.465 312	.087 220
46	.023 455	11.488 767	.087 042
47	.021 617	11.510 384	.086 878
48	.019 924	11.530 308	.086 728
49	.018 363	11.548 671	.086 590
50	.016 924	11.565 595	.086 463

[1]What $1 due in the future is worth today. Formula: $p = \dfrac{s}{(1 + i)^n}$

[2]What $1 payable periodically is worth today (payments made at end of period). For payments made at the beginning of the period, add 1. to the amount shown for the previous period.
Formula: $a_n = \dfrac{1 - (1 + i)^{-n}}{i}$

[3]Periodic payment necessary to pay off a loan of $1. Formula: The sinking fund factor plus the rate of interest.

Present Worth Of A Future Amount of $1.00
Discounted At   9   Per Cent Interest
Per Period As Follows:

Number Of Periods	Present Worth Of $1.00[1]	Present Worth Of $1.00 Per Period[2]	Partial Payment Per $1.00 Of Loan[3]
1	.917 431	.917 431	1.090 000
2	.841 680	1.759 111	.568 469
3	.772 183	2.531 295	.395 055
4	.708 425	3.239 720	.308 669
5	.649 931	3.889 651	.257 092
6	.596 267	4.485 919	.222 920
7	.547 034	5.032 953	.198 691
8	.501 866	5.534 819	.180 674
9	.460 428	5.995 247	.166 799
10	.422 411	6.417 658	.155 820
11	.387 533	6.805 191	.146 947
12	.355 535	7.160 725	.139 651
13	.326 179	7.486 904	.133 567
14	.299 246	7.786 150	.128 433
15	.274 538	8.060 688	.124 059
16	.251 870	8.312 558	.120 300
17	.231 073	8.543 631	.117 046
18	.211 994	8.755 625	.114 212
19	.194 490	8.950 115	.111 730
20	.178 431	9.128 546	.109 546
21	.163 698	9.292 244	.107 617
22	.150 182	9.442 425	.105 905
23	.137 781	9.580 207	.104 382
24	.126 405	9.706 612	.103 023
25	.115 968	9.822 580	.101 806

[1]What $1 due in the future is worth today. Formula: $p = \dfrac{s}{(1 + i)^n}$

[2]What $1 payable periodically is worth today (payments made at end of period). For payments made at the beginning of the period, add 1. to the amount shown for the previous period.
Formula: $a_n = \dfrac{1 - (1 + i)^{-n}}{i}$

[3]Periodic payment necessary to pay off a loan of $1. Formula: The sinking fund factor plus the rate of interest.

Present Worth Of A Future Amount of $1.00
Discounted At   9   Per Cent Interest
Per Period As Follows:

Number Of Periods	Present Worth Of $1.00[1]	Present Worth Of $1.00 Per Period[2]	Partial Payment Per $1.00 Of Loan[3]
26	.106 393	9.928 972	.100 715
27	.097 608	10.026 580	.099 735
28	.089 548	10.116 128	.098 852
29	.082 155	10.198 283	.098 056
30	.075 371	10.273 654	.097 336
31	.069 148	10.342 802	.096 686
32	.063 438	10.406 240	.096 096
33	.058 200	10.464 441	.095 562
34	.053 395	10.517 835	.095 076
35	.048 986	10.566 821	.094 636
36	.044 941	10.611 763	.094 235
37	.041 231	10.652 993	.093 870
38	.037 826	10.690 820	.093 538
39	.034 703	10.725 523	.093 236
40	.031 838	10.757 360	.092 960
41	.029 209	10.786 569	.092 708
42	.026 797	10.813 366	.092 478
43	.024 584	10.837 950	.092 268
44	.022 555	10.860 505	.092 077
45	.020 692	10.881 197	.091 902
46	.018 984	10.900 181	.091 742
47	.017 416	10.917 597	.091 595
48	.015 978	10.933 575	.091 461
49	.014 659	10.948 234	.091 339
50	.013 449	10.961 683	.091 227

---

[1]What $1 due in the future is worth today. Formula: $p = \dfrac{s}{(1 + i)^n}$

[2]What $1 payable periodically is worth today (payments made at end of period). For payments made at the beginning of the period, add 1. to the amount shown for the previous period.
Formula: $a_n = \dfrac{1 - (1 + i)^{-n}}{i}$

[3]Periodic payment necessary to pay off a loan of $1. Formula: The sinking fund factor plus the rate of interest.

Present Worth Of A Future Amount of $1.00
Discounted At   9 1/2   Per Cent Interest
Per Period As Follows:

Number Of Periods	Present Worth Of $1.00[1]	Present Worth Of $1.00 Per Period[2]	Partial Payment Per $1.00 Of Loan[3]
1	.913 242	.913 242	1.095 000
2	.834 011	1.747 253	.572 327
3	.761 654	2.508 907	.398 580
4	.695 574	3.204 481	.312 063
5	.635 228	3.839 709	.260 436
6	.580 117	4.419 825	.226 253
7	.529 787	4.949 612	.202 036
8	.483 824	5.433 436	.184 046
9	.441 848	5.875 284	.170 205
10	.403 514	6.278 798	.159 266
11	.368 506	6.647 304	.150 437
12	.336 535	6.983 839	.143 188
13	.307 338	7.291 178	.137 152
14	.280 674	7.571 852	.132 068
15	.256 323	7.828 175	.127 744
16	.234 085	8.062 260	.124 035
17	.213 777	8.276 037	.120 831
18	.195 230	8.471 266	.118 046
19	.178 292	8.649 558	.115 613
20	.162 824	8.812 382	.113 477
21	.148 697	8.961 080	.111 594
22	.135 797	9.096 876	.109 928
23	.124 015	9.220 892	.108 449
24	.113 256	9.334 148	.107 134
25	.103 430	9.437 578	.105 959

---

[1]What $1 due in the future is worth today. Formula: $p = \dfrac{s}{(1 + i)^n}$

[2]What $1 payable periodically is worth today (payments made at end of period). For payments made at the beginning of the period, add 1. to the amount shown for the previous period.
Formula: $a_n = \dfrac{1 - (1 + i)^{-n}}{i}$

[3]Periodic payment necessary to pay off a loan of $1. Formula: The sinking fund factor plus the rate of interest.

Present Worth Of A Future Amount of $1.00
Discounted At 9 1/2 Per Cent Interest
Per Period As Follows

Number Of Periods	Present Worth Of $1.00[1]	Present Worth Of $1.00 Per Period[2]	Partial Payment Per $1.00 Of Loan[3]
26	.094 457	9.532 034	.104 909
27	.086 262	9.618 296	.103 969
28	.078 778	9.697 074	.103 124
29	.071 943	9.769 018	.102 364
30	.065 702	9.834 719	.101 681
31	.060 002	9.894 721	.101 064
32	.054 796	9.949 517	.100 507
33	.050 042	9.999 559	.100 004
34	.045 700	10.045 259	.099 549
35	.041 736	10.086 995	.099 138
36	.038 115	10.125 109	.098 764
37	.034 808	10.159 917	.098 426
38	.031 788	10.191 705	.098 119
39	.029 030	10.220 735	.097 840
40	.026 512	10.247 247	.097 587
41	.024 211	10.271 458	.097 357
42	.022 111	10.293 569	.097 148
43	.020 193	10.313 762	.096 958
44	.018 441	10.332 203	.096 785
45	.016 841	10.349 043	.096 627
46	.015 380	10.364 423	.096 484
47	.014 045	10.378 469	.096 353
48	.012 827	10.391 296	.096 234
49	.011 714	10.403 010	.096 126
50	.010 698	10.413 707	.096 027

[1] What $1 due in the future is worth today. Formula: $p = \dfrac{s}{(1 + i)^n}$

[2] What $1 payable periodically is worth today (payments made at end of period). For payments made at the beginning of the period, add 1. to the amount shown for the previous period.
Formula: $a_n = \dfrac{1 - (1 + i)^{-n}}{i}$

[3] Periodic payment necessary to pay off a loan of $1. Formula: The sinking fund factor plus the rate of interest.

Present Worth Of A Future Amount of $1.00
Discounted At   10   Per Cent Interest
Per Period As Follows:

Number Of Periods	Present Worth Of $1.00[1]	Present Worth Of $1.00 Per Period[2]	Partial Payment Per $1.00 Of Loan[3]
1	.909 091	.909 091	1.100 000
2	.826 446	1.735 537	.576 190
3	.751 315	2.486 852	.402 115
4	.683 013	3.169 865	.315 471
5	.620 921	3.790 787	.263 797
6	.564 474	4.355 261	.229 607
7	.513 158	4.868 419	.205 405
8	.466 507	5.334 926	.187 444
9	.424 098	5.759 024	.173 641
10	.385 543	6.144 567	.162 745
11	.350 494	6.495 061	.153 963
12	.318 631	6.813 692	.146 763
13	.289 664	7.103 356	.140 779
14	.263 331	7.366 687	.135 746
15	.239 392	7.606 080	.131 474
16	.217 629	7.823 709	.127 817
17	.197 845	8.021 553	.124 664
18	.179 859	8.201 412	.121 930
19	.163 508	8.364 920	.119 547
20	.148 644	8.513 564	.117 460
21	.135 131	8.648 694	.115 624
22	.122 846	8.771 540	.114 005
23	.111 678	8.883 218	.112 572
24	.101 526	8.984 744	.111 300
25	.092 296	9.077 040	.110 168

---

[1]What $1 due in the future is worth today. Formula: $p = \dfrac{s}{(1 + i)^n}$

[2]What $1 payable periodically is worth today (payments made at end of period). For payments made at the beginning of the period, add 1. to the amount shown for the previous period.
Formula: $a_n = \dfrac{1 - (1 + i)^{-n}}{i}$

[3]Periodic payment necessary to pay off a loan of $1. Formula: The sinking fund factor plus the rate of interest.

Present Worth Of A Future Amount of $1.00
Discounted At   10   Per Cent Interest
Per Period As Follows:

Number Of Periods	Present Worth Of $1.00[1]	Present Worth Of $1.00 Per Period[2]	Partial Payment Per $1.00 Of Loan[3]
26	.083 905	9.160 945	.109 159
27	.076 278	9.237 223	.108 258
28	.069 343	9.306 567	.107 451
29	.063 039	9.369 606	.106 728
30	.057 309	9.426 914	.106 079
31	.052 099	9.479 013	.105 496
32	.047 362	9.526 376	.104 972
33	.043 047	9.569 432	.104 499
34	.039 143	9.608 575	.104 074
35	.035 585	9.644 159	.103 690
36	.032 349	9.676 508	.103 343
37	.029 408	9.705 917	.103 030
38	.026 735	9.732 651	.102 747
39	.024 304	9.756 956	.102 491
40	.022 095	9.779 051	.102 259
41	.020 086	9.799 137	.102 050
42	.018 260	9.817 397	.101 860
43	.016 600	9.833 998	.101 688
44	.015 091	9.849 089	.101 532
45	.013 719	9.862 808	.101 391
46	.012 472	9.875 280	.101 263
47	.011 338	9.886 618	.101 147
48	.010 307	9.896 926	.101 041
49	.009 370	9.906 296	.100 946
50	.008 519	9.914 814	.100 859

[1] What $1 due in the future is worth today. Formula: $p = \dfrac{s}{(1 + i)^n}$

[2] What $1 payable periodically is worth today (payments made at end of period). For payments made at the beginning of the period, add 1. to the amount shown for the previous period.
Formula: $a_n = \dfrac{1 - (1 + i)^{-n}}{i}$

[3] Periodic payment necessary to pay off a loan of $1. Formula: The sinking fund factor plus the rate of interest.

Present Worth of an Annuity of 1 Table
for Selected Interest Rates
Based on Straight Line Theory of Depreciation
Under the Direct-Ring Method of Capitalization*

Period	6%	7%	8%	9%	10%
1	.94340	.93458	.92593	.91743	.90909
2	1.78571	1.75439	1.72414	1.69492	1.66667
3	2.54237	2.47934	2.41935	2.36222	2.30771
4	3.22581	3.12500	3.03030	2.94118	2.85714
5	3.84615	3.70370	3.57143	3.44828	3.33333
6	4.41176	4.22535	4.05405	3.89560	3.74995
7	4.92958	4.69799	4.48718	4.29448	4.11765
8	5.40541	5.12821	4.87805	4.65116	4.44444
9	5.84416	5.52147	5.23256	4.97240	4.73687
10	6.25000	5.88235	5.55555	5.26316	5.00000
11	6.62651	6.21469	5.85106	5.52761	5.23809
12	6.97674	6.52174	6.12245	5.76934	5.45464
13	7.30337	6.80624	6.37255	5.99089	5.65227
14	7.60870	7.07071	6.60377	6.19464	5.83328
15	7.89474	7.31707	6.81818	6.38284	5.99999
16	8.16327	7.54717	7.01754	6.55738	6.15385
17	8.41584	7.76256	7.20339	6.71953	6.29644
18	8.65835	7.96460	7.37705	6.87002	6.42855
19	8.87850	8.15451	7.53968	7.01262	6.55308
20	9.09091	8.33333	7.69231	7.14286	6.66667
21	9.29204	8.50202	7.83582	7.26639	6.77415
22	9.48276	8.66142	7.97101	7.38253	6.87500
23	9.66387	8.81226	8.09859	7.49182	6.96966
24	9.83607	8.95522	8.21918	7.59492	7.05882
25	10.00000	9.09091	8.33333	7.69231	7.14286

---

*What $1 payable periodically for the remaining economic life of an investment and with annual interest paid on the entire investment is worth today.

Formula: Ring Factor = $\dfrac{1}{\text{Str. Line Rate}}$ or $\dfrac{1}{\text{Int. Rate + Depre. Rate}}$

Present Worth of an Annuity of 1 Table
for Selected Interest Rates
Based on Straight Line Theory of Depreciation
Under the Direct-Ring Method of Capitalization*

Period	6%	7%	8%	9%	10%
26	10.15625	9.21986	8.44156	7.78452	7.22230
27	10.30534	9.34256	8.54430	7.87154	7.29714
28	10.44776	9.45946	8.64197	7.95456	7.36844
29	10.58394	9.57096	8.73494	8.03329	7.43594
30	10.71429	9.67742	8.82353	8.10833	7.50019
31	10.83916	9.77918	8.90805	8.17942	7.56098
32	10.95890	9.87654	8.98876	8.24742	7.61905
33	11.07382	9.96979	9.06593	8.33333	7.69231
34	11.18421	10.05917	9.13978	8.37444	7.72732
35	11.29032	10.14492	9.21053	8.43377	7.77780
36	11.39240	10.22727	9.27835	8.49055	7.82607
37	11.49068	10.30640	9.34343	8.54504	7.87234
38	11.58536	10.38251	9.40594	8.59734	7.92823
39	11.67664	10.45576	9.46602	8.64745	7.95919
40	11.76470	10.52632	9.52381	8.69565	8.00000
41	11.84971	10.59431	9.57944	8.74202	8.03923
42	11.93181	10.65989	9.63303	8.78665	8.07696
43	12.01117	10.72319	9.68469	8.82963	8.11326
44	12.08791	10.78431	9.73451	8.87099	8.14817
45	12.16216	10.84337	9.78261	8.91091	8.18197
46	12.23404	10.90047	9.82906	8.94943	8.21429
47	12.30366	10.95571	9.87395	8.98665	8.24565
48	12.37113	11.00917	9.91736	9.02258	8.27588
49	12.43654	11.06094	9.95935	9.05731	8.30510
50	12.50000	11.11111	10.00000	9.09091	8.33333

*What $1 payable periodically for the remaining economic life of an investment and with annual interest paid on the entire investment is worth today.

Formula: Ring Factor = $\dfrac{1}{\text{Str. Line Rate}}$ or $\dfrac{1}{\text{Int. Rate + Depre. Rate}}$

Present Worth of an Annuity of 1 Table

for Sinking Fund Rate or 3 Per Cent and Selected Speculative

Interest Rates*

(Hoskold Sinking Fund Valuation Premise)

Years	5%	6%	7%	8%	9%	10%
1	.9524	.9434	.9346	.9259	.9174	.9091
2	1.8429	1.8096	1.7774	1.7464	1.7164	1.6874
3	2.6772	2.6074	2.5411	2.4781	2.4182	2.3611
4	3.4599	3.3442	3.2360	3.1345	3.0393	2.9496
5	4.1954	4.0265	3.8706	3.7264	3.5925	3.4680
6	4.8876	4.6599	4.4524	4.2626	4.0883	3.9278
7	5.5400	5.2492	4.9874	4.7504	4.5350	4.3383
8	6.1555	5.7986	5.4808	5.1960	4.9393	4.7068
9	6.7370	6.3118	5.9370	5.6043	5.3069	5.0395
10	7.2870	6.7921	6.3601	5.9798	5.6424	5.3410
11	7.8078	7.2123	6.7532	6.3260	5.9496	5.6155
12	8.3014	7.6651	7.1194	6.6462	6.2320	5.8664
13	8.7697	8.0626	7.4610	6.9430	6.4923	6.0965
14	9.2144	8.4369	7.7805	7.2188	6.7328	6.3081
15	9.6370	8.7899	8.0797	7.4757	6.9557	6.5034
16	10.0391	9.1232	8.3604	7.7154	7.1628	6.6840
17	10.4218	9.4382	8.6242	7.9395	7.3555	6.6815
18	10.7865	9.7363	8.8724	8.1494	7.5353	7.0073
19	11.1341	10.0186	9.1063	8.3463	7.7033	7.1524
20	11.4658	10.2864	9.3270	8.5313	7.8607	7.2878
21	11.7825	10.5405	9.5355	8.7054	8.0082	7.4144
22	12.0850	10.7820	9.7326	8.8694	8.1468	7.5331
23	12.3741	11.0115	9.9193	9.0241	8.2772	7.6444
24	12.6506	11.2300	10.0962	9.1703	8.4000	7.7491
25	12.9152	11.4380	10.2640	9.3086	8.5159	7.8476
26	13.1686	11.6363	10.4234	9.4395	8.6253	7.9404
27	13.4113	11.8253	10.5748	9.5635	8.7287	8.0280
28	13.6438	12.0058	10.7189	9.6812	8.8267	8.1107
29	13.8668	12.1781	10.8560	9.7929	8.9194	9.1890
30	14.0807	12.3427	10.9867	9.8991	9.0074	8.2631

---

*What $1 payable periodically and partially retained in accordance with the Hoskold valuation premise is worth today. Formula: Hoskold Factor equals the reciprocal of the sum of the speculative interest rate and the factor for the rate from the Sinking Fund Table.

Present Worth of an Annuity of 1 Table

for Sinking Fund Rate of 3 Per Cent and Selected Speculative

Interest Rates*

(Hoskold Sinking Fund Valuation Premise)

(Continued)

Years	5%	6%	7%	8%	9%	10%
31	14.2859	12.5002	11.1112	10.0001	9.0910	8.3334
32	14.4830	12.6508	11.2301	10.0963	9.1704	8.4001
33	14.6722	12.7949	11.3435	10.1879	9.2459	8.4634
34	14.8540	12.9329	11.4519	10.2752	9.3178	8.5236
35	15.0287	13.0652	11.5554	10.3585	9.3862	8.5808
36	15.1967	13.1920	11.6545	10.4380	9.4515	8.6353
37	15.3582	13.3135	11.7493	10.5140	9.5137	8.6872
38	15.5137	13.4301	11.8400	10.5866	9.5731	8.7367
39	15.6632	13.5421	11.2969	10.6560	9.6298	8.7840
40	15.8072	13.6496	12.0102	10.7224	9.6841	8.8291
41	15.9458	13.7528	12.0901	10.7860	9.7359	8.8721
42	16.0793	13.8520	12.1667	10.8470	9.7855	8.9133
43	16.2080	13.9474	12.2402	10.9053	9.8330	8.9527
44	16.3319	14.0391	12.3107	10.9613	9.8785	8.9904
45	16.4514	14.1273	12.3785	11.0150	9.9221	9.0265
46	16.5666	14.2121	12.4436	11.0665	9.9639	9.0610
47	16.6776	14.2938	12.5062	11.1160	10.0040	9.0942
48	16.7848	14.3724	12.5663	11.1635	10.0424	9.1259
49	16.8881	14.4481	12.6242	11.2091	10.0793	9.1584
50	16.9879	14.5211	12.6798	11.2530	10.1148	9.1856

*What $1 payable periodically and partially retained in accordance with the Hoskold valuation premise is worth today. Formula: Hoskold Factor equals the reciprocal of the sum of the speculative interest rate and the factor for the rate from the Sinking Fund Table.

STABILIZATION FACTORS*
FOR CONVERSION OF DECLINING INCOME
UNDER STRAIGHT LINE CAPITALIZATION
TO A LEVEL – STABILIZED – INCOME
FOR ANNUITY OR INWOOD METHOD CAPITALIZATION

Economic Life Remaining Years	Rate of Interest At				
	8%	9%	10%	11%	12%
1	1.00000	1.00000	1.00000	1.00000	1.00000
2	.96684	.96351	.96032	.95727	.95435
3	.93880	.93327	.92796	.92304	.91842
4	.91491	.90785	.90135	.89535	.88982
5	.89449	.88653	.87932	.87281	.86691
6	.87695	.86852	.86102	.85437	.84846
7	.86189	.85327	.84581	.83929	.83362
8	.84885	.84035	.83308	.82690	.82164
9	.83763	.82939	.82251	.81679	.81207
10	.82794	.82011	.81373	.80858	.80447
11	.81960	.81227	.80647	.80196	.79852
12	.81242	.80567	.80053	.79671	.79396
13	.80622	.80016	.79571	.79258	.79055
14	.80102	.79561	.79186	.78945	.78814
15	.79656	.79187	.78884	.78716	.78656
16	.79282	.78885	.78656	.78560	.78570
17	.78971	.78648	.78492	.78468	.78545
18	.78714	.78466	.78383	.78428	.78572
19	.78509	.78335	.78324	.78437	.78643
20	.78348	.78247	.78306	.78485	.78752
21	.78227	.78199	.78326	.78568	.78893
22	.78141	.78185	.78378	.78681	.79061
23	.78089	.78202	.78459	.78820	.79252
24	.78064	.78245	.78565	.78980	.79462
25	.78066	.78313	.78691	.79160	.79687
26	.78091	.78402	.78838	.79356	.79927
27	.78136	.78509	.78899	.79564	.80175
28	.78200	.78632	.79175	.79784	.80432
29	.78283	.78772	.79363	.80015	.80697
30	.78377	.78922	.79560	.80252	.80963

*For application of stabilization factors see illustration at end of table.

Economic Life Remaining Years	8%	9%	10%	11%	12%
31	.78486	.79083	.79765	.80492	.81235
32	.78607	.79255	.79978	.80739	.81508
33	.78739	.79434	.80197	.80989	.81782
34	.78881	.79622	.80422	.81242	.82057
35	.79030	.79814	.80648	.81494	.82329
36	.79186	.80011	.80877	.81748	.82600
37	.79349	.80213	.81109	.82001	.82869
38	.79517	.80417	.81341	.82254	.83135
39	.79690	.80625	.81574	.82505	.83398
40	.79867	.80834	.81808	.82755	.83658
41	.80047	.81045	.82040	.83002	.83913
42	.80230	.81257	.82271	.83246	.84164
43	.80416	.81469	.82502	.83487	.84412
44	.80603	.81681	.82730	.83725	.84655
45	.80792	.81893	.82956	.83960	.84893
46	.80982	.82103	.83180	.84191	.85132
47	.81171	.82313	.83401	.84418	.85354
48	.81362	.82522	.83621	.84642	.85579
49	.81553	.82729	.83837	.84861	.85798
50	.81743	.82934	.84049	.85076	.86012

How to use the stabalization factors:

Assumptions,
        Remaining economic building life 50 years
        Net income before depreciation $1,000
        Rate of interest 8%
        Rate of recapture 2%
        Inwood factor at 8% - 50 years = 12.2335

Value under straight line capitalization
$V = I/R = \$1,000 \div .10 = \underline{\$10,000}$

Value under Inwood method of capitalization
$V = I \times F = \$1,000 \times .81743$ (stabalization factor) = $\$817.43 \times$
   12.2335 (Inwood factor) = $\underline{\$10,000}$

THE LIABILITY TO REPLACE
A MEASURE OF INCURABLE PHYSICAL DEPRECIATION
BASED ON INCREASING EFFECTIVE AGE —
FOR PROPERTIES WITH ECONOMIC LIFES OF 5 TO 50 YEARS
AT SELECTED RATES OF INTEREST

Per Cent Liability At Interest Rates Of:

End Of Year	7%	8%	9%	10%	11%	12%
		5 - Year Economic Life				
1	17.39	17.05	16.71	16.38	16.06	15.74
2	36.00	35.46	34.92	34.40	33.88	33.37
3	59.90	55.34	54.77	54.22	53.66	53.12
4	77.21	76.81	76.81	76.02	75.62	75.23
5	100.00	100.00	100.00	100.00	100.00	100.00
		10 - Year Economic Life				
1	7.24	6.90	6.58	6.27	5.98	5.70
2	14.98	14.36	13.76	13.18	12.62	12.08
3	23.27	22.41	21.58	20.77	19.99	19.23
4	32.14	31.11	30.10	29.12	28.17	27.23
5	41.62	40.50	39.39	38.31	37.24	36.20
6	51.77	50.64	49.52	48.41	47.32	46.24
7	62.64	61.59	60.56	59.53	58.51	57.49
8	74.26	73.42	72.59	71.75	70.92	70.09
9	86.69	86.20	85.70	85.20	84.70	84.20
10	100.00	100.00	100.00	100.00	100.00	100.00
		15 - Year Economic Life				
1	3.98	3.68	3.41	3.15	2.91	2.68
2	8.24	7.66	7.12	6.61	6.13	5.69
3	12.79	11.96	11.17	10.42	9.71	9.04
4	17.67	16.60	15.58	14.61	13.69	12.82
5	22.89	21.61	20.38	19.22	18.10	17.04
6	28.47	27.02	25.62	24.28	23.00	21.77
7	34.44	32.86	31.34	29.86	28.44	27.06
8	40.83	39.17	37.56	35.99	34.47	32.99
9	47.67	45.99	44.35	42.74	41.17	39.63
10	54.98	53.35	51.75	50.16	48.60	47.07

Per Cent Liability At Interest Rates Of:

End Of Year	7%	8%	9%	10%	11%	12%
	15 – Year Economic Life – (Continued)					
11	62.81	61.30	59.81	58.32	56.86	55.40
12	71.19	69.89	68.60	67.30	66.02	64.74
13	80.15	79.17	78.18	77.18	76.18	75.19
14	89.74	89.18	88.62	88.05	87.47	86.89
15	100.00	100.00	100.00	100.00	100.00	100.00
	20 – Year Economic Life					
1	2.44	2.19	1.96	1.75	1.56	1.39
2	5.05	4.55	4.09	3.67	3.29	2.94
3	7.84	7.09	6.41	5.78	5.21	4.68
4	10.83	9.85	8.94	8.10	7.34	6.63
5	14.03	12.82	11.70	10.66	9.70	8.82
6	17.45	16.03	14.71	13.46	12.33	11.26
7	21.11	19.50	17.98	16.56	15.24	14.00
8	25.03	23.24	21.56	19.97	18.47	17.07
9	29.22	27.29	25.45	23.71	22.06	20.51
10	33.70	31.66	29.70	27.83	26.05	24.36
11	38.50	36.37	34.32	32.35	31.47	28.67
12	43.64	41.47	39.37	37.34	35.38	33.49
13	49.13	46.97	44.87	42.82	40.83	38.90
14	55.01	52.92	50.86	48.84	46.87	44.96
15	61.30	59.33	57.39	55.47	53.59	51.74
16	68.03	66.27	64.51	62.77	61.04	59.34
17	75.23	73.75	72.27	70.79	69.31	67.84
18	82.93	81.84	80.73	79.61	78.49	77.37
19	91.18	90.57	89.95	89.32	88.69	88.05
20	100.00	100.00	100.00	100.00	100.00	100.00
	25 – Year Economic Life					
1	1.58	1.37	1.18	1.02	.87	.75
2	3.27	2.85	2.47	2.14	1.84	1.59
3	5.08	4.44	3.87	3.37	2.92	2.53
4	7.02	6.16	5.40	4.72	4.12	3.58
5	9.09	8.03	7.07	6.21	5.44	4.77

Per Cent Liability At Interest Rates Of:

End Of Year	7%	8%	9%	10%	11%	12%

25 - Year Economic Life - (Continued)

End Of Year	7%	8%	9%	10%	11%	12%
6	11.31	10.04	8.88	7.85	6.92	6.09
7	13.68	12.21	10.86	9.65	8.55	7.57
8	16.22	14.55	13.02	11.63	10.37	9.23
9	18.94	17.07	15.37	13.81	12.38	11.08
10	21.84	19.82	17.94	16.21	14.62	13.16
11	24.96	22.77	20.73	18.84	17.10	15.49
12	28.28	25.96	23.78	21.74	19.85	18.10
13	31.84	29.40	27.10	24.93	22.91	21.02
14	35.65	33.12	30.72	28.35	26.30	24.23
15	39.73	37.14	34.66	32.31	30.07	27.96
16	44.09	41.48	38.96	36.55	34.25	32.07
17	48.76	46.17	43.65	40.23	38.89	36.66
18	53.75	51.26	48.76	46.37	44.05	41.81
19	59.10	56.69	54.33	52.02	49.77	47.58
20	64.82	62.60	60.40	58.24	56.11	54.04
21	70.93	68.97	67.02	65.08	63.16	61.27
22	77.48	75.86	74.23	72.60	70.98	69.38
23	84.49	83.29	82.09	80.88	79.67	78.45
24	91.98	90.63	90.66	89.99	89.30	88.62
25	100.00	100.00	100.00	100.00	100.00	100.00

30 - Year Economic Life

End Of Year	7%	8%	9%	10%	11%	12%
1	1.06	.88	.73	.61	.50	.41
2	2.19	1.84	1.53	1.28	1.06	.88
3	3.40	2.87	2.41	2.01	1.68	1.40
4	4.70	3.98	3.36	2.82	2.37	1.98
5	6.09	5.18	4.39	3.71	3.13	2.63
6	7.57	6.48	5.52	4.69	3.98	3.36
7	9.16	7.88	6.75	5.77	4.92	4.18
8	10.86	9.39	8.09	6.95	5.96	5.10
9	12.68	11.02	9.55	8.26	7.12	6.12
10	14.63	12.79	11.15	9.69	8.40	7.27

Per Cent Liability At Interest Rates Of:

End Of Year	7%	8%	9%	10%	11%	12%
30 - Year Economic Life - (Continued)						
11	16.71	14.69	12.88	11.27	9.83	8.56
12	18.94	16.75	14.78	13.00	11.41	10.00
13	21.32	18.98	16.84	14.91	13.17	11.61
14	23.87	21.38	19.09	17.01	15.12	13.42
15	26.60	24.97	21.54	19.32	17.29	15.45
16	29.52	26.77	24.21	21.85	19.69	17.72
17	32.65	29.79	27.13	24.65	22.36	20.26
18	35.99	33.06	30.30	27.72	25.33	23.10
19	39.57	36.59	33.76	31.10	28.61	26.29
20	43.40	40.40	37.53	34.82	32.26	29.86
21	47.50	44.51	41.64	38.91	36.31	33.85
22	51.88	48.95	46.13	43.41	40.81	38.33
23	56.57	53.75	51.01	48.35	45.80	43.34
24	61.59	58.94	56.34	53.80	51.34	48.96
25	66.96	64.53	62.14	59.79	57.49	55.25
26	72.70	70.58	68.47	66.37	64.31	62.25
27	78.85	77.11	75.36	73.62	71.89	70.18
28	85.43	84.16	82.88	81.59	80.30	79.02
29	92.47	91.77	91.07	90.36	89.64	88.92
30	100.00	100.00	100.00	100.00	100.00	100.00
35 - Year Economic Life						
1	.72	.58	.46	.37	.29	.23
2	1.50	1.21	.97	.77	.62	.49
3	2.33	1.88	1.52	1.22	.98	.78
4	3.21	2.62	2.12	1.71	1.38	1.11
5	4.36	3.40	2.78	2.25	1.82	1.46
6	5.18	4.26	3.49	2.85	2.32	1.88
7	6.26	5.18	4.27	3.50	2.86	2.34
8	7.42	6.17	5.11	4.22	3.47	2.85
9	8.67	7.25	6.04	5.01	4.15	3.41
10	10.00	8.41	7.04	5.88	4.90	4.07

Per Cent Liability At Interest Rates Of:

End Of Year	7%	8%	9%	10%	11%	12%
35 - Year Economic Life - (Continued)					
11	11.42	9.66	8.14	6.84	5.73	4.79
12	12.94	11.01	9.34	7.89	6.65	5.59
13	14.57	12.47	10.64	9.05	7.67	6.49
14	16.31	14.05	12.06	10.32	8.81	7.50
15	18.18	15.76	13.61	11.72	10.07	8.64
16	20.18	17.60	15.30	13.26	11.47	9.90
17	22.31	19.59	17.14	14.96	13.03	11.32
18	24.60	21.73	19.15	16.82	14.75	12.92
19	27.04	24.05	21.33	18.88	16.67	14.70
20	29.66	26.56	23.72	21.13	18.80	16.69
21	32.46	29.26	26.32	23.61	21.16	18.93
22	35.45	32.18	29.15	26.35	23.78	21.43
23	38.66	35.34	32.23	29.35	26.68	24.23
24	42.09	38.75	35.60	32.65	29.91	27.37
25	45.75	42.43	39.27	36.29	33.49	30.89
26	49.68	46.40	43.26	40.28	37.47	34.83
27	53.88	50.69	47.62	44.68	41.89	39.33
28	58.38	55.32	52.36	49.52	46.79	44.18
29	63.19	60.33	57.55	54.84	52.23	49.71
30	68.33	65.74	63.19	60.69	58.26	55.91
31	73.84	71.58	69.34	67.13	64.97	62.85
32	79.73	77.89	76.05	74.21	72.40	70.62
33	86.04	84.70	83.35	82.00	80.66	79.33
34	92.78	92.06	91.32	90.57	89.83	89.08
35	100.00	100.00	100.00	100.00	100.00	100.00
40 - Year Economic Life					
1	.50	.39	.30	.23	.17	.13
2	1.04	.80	.62	.47	.36	.28
3	1.61	1.25	.97	.75	.58	.44
4	2.22	1.74	1.35	1.05	.81	.62
5	2.88	2.26	1.77	1.38	1.07	.83

Per Cent Liability At Interest Rates Of:

End Of Year	7%	8%	9%	10%	11%	12%
6	3.58	2.83	2.23	1.74	1.36	1.06
7	4.34	3.44	2.72	2.14	1.68	1.32
8	5.14	4.11	3.26	2.58	2.04	1.60
9	6.00	4.82	3.85	3.07	2.44	1.93
10	6.92	5.59	4.50	3.60	2.87	2.29
11	7.91	6.43	5.20	4.19	3.36	2.69
12	8.96	7.33	5.96	4.83	3.90	3.15
13	10.09	8.30	6.79	5.54	4.51	3.65
14	11.30	9.35	7.70	6.32	5.17	4.22
15	12.59	10.48	8.69	7.18	5.91	4.86
16	13.97	11.71	9.77	8.12	6.74	5.57
17	15.45	13.03	10.94	9.16	7.65	6.17
18	17.03	14.46	12.22	10.30	8.66	7.27
19	18.72	16.00	13.62	11.56	9.79	8.27
20	20.54	17.67	15.14	12.94	11.04	9.39
21	22.47	19.46	16.80	14.46	12.42	10.65
22	24.55	21.41	18.61	16.13	13.96	12.06
23	26.77	23.51	20.58	17.97	15.67	13.64
24	29.14	25.77	22.73	20.00	17.56	15.40
25	31.68	28.22	25.07	22.22	19.67	17.38
26	34.40	30.86	27.62	24.67	22.00	19.60
27	37.32	33.72	30.40	27.36	24.59	22.08
28	40.42	36.80	33.43	30.32	27.47	24.86
29	43.75	40.13	36.74	33.58	30.66	27.97
30	47.32	43.73	40.34	37.17	34.21	31.46
31	51.13	47.61	44.27	41.11	38.14	35.37
32	55.21	51.81	48.55	45.45	42.51	39.73
33	59.58	56.34	53.21	50.22	47.36	44.64
34	64.25	61.23	58.30	55.46	52.74	50.13
35	69.24	66.52	63.84	61.24	58.71	56.27
36	74.59	72.22	69.88	67.59	65.34	63.16
37	80.32	78.39	76.47	74.57	72.70	70.87
38	86.44	85.05	83.65	82.25	80.87	79.50
39	92.99	92.24	91.47	90.70	89.94	89.17
40	100.00	100.00	100.00	100.00	100.00	100.00

Per Cent Liability At Interest Rates Of:

End Of Year	7%	8%	9%	10%	11%	12%
			45 - Year Economic Life			
1	.35	.26	.19	.14	.10	.07
2	.73	.54	.40	.29	.21	.16
3	1.13	.84	.62	.46	.34	.25
4	1.55	1.17	.87	.65	.48	.35
5	2.01	1.52	1.14	.85	.63	.47
6	2.50	1.90	1.43	1.07	.80	.60
7	3.03	2.31	1.75	1.32	.99	.74
8	3.59	2.75	2.10	1.59	1.20	.81
9	4.19	3.23	2.48	1.89	1.44	1.09
10	4.84	3.75	2.89	2.22	1.70	1.29
11	5.52	4.31	3.34	2.58	1.98	1.52
12	6.26	4.91	3.83	2.97	2.30	1.78
13	7.05	5.56	4.37	3.41	2.66	2.06
14	7.89	6.27	4.95	3.89	3.05	2.39
15	8.79	7.03	5.58	4.42	3.49	2.74
16	9.76	7.85	6.28	5.00	3.97	3.15
17	10.79	8.73	7.03	5.64	4.51	3.60
18	11.90	9.69	7.85	6.34	5.11	4.10
19	13.08	10.72	8.75	7.12	5.77	4.67
20	14.35	11.84	9.73	7.97	6.51	5.31
21	15.70	13.05	10.80	8.90	7.32	6.02
22	17.15	14.35	11.96	9.93	8.23	6.81
23	18.70	15.76	13.22	11.06	8.24	7.70
24	20.36	17.27	14.60	12.31	10.36	8.70
25	22.14	18.91	16.11	13.68	11.60	9.82
26	24.03	20.69	17.75	15.19	12.97	11.07
27	26.07	22.60	19.53	16.85	14.50	12.47
28	28.24	24.67	21.48	18.67	16.20	14.04
29	30.57	26.90	23.61	20.67	18.18	15.80
30	33.06	29.31	25.92	22.88	20.17	17.77
31	35.72	31.91	28.44	25.31	22.49	19.97
32	38.57	34.73	31.19	27.98	25.07	22.44
33	41.62	37.76	34.19	30.92	27.93	25.21
34	44.89	41.04	37.46	34.15	31.10	28.31
35	48.37	44.58	41.02	37.70	34.62	31.78

Per Cent Liability At Interest Rates Of:

End Of Year	7%	8%	9%	10%	11%	12%

45 - Year Economic Life - (Continued)

End Of Year	7%	8%	9%	10%	11%	12%
36	52.11	48.41	44.90	41.61	38.53	35.67
37	56.11	52.54	49.13	45.91	42.87	40.02
38	60.39	56.00	53.75	50.64	47.69	44.90
39	64.97	61.82	58.77	55.84	53.04	50.36
40	69.86	67.03	64.25	61.56	58.97	56.48
41	75.10	72.65	70.23	67.86	65.56	63.33
42	80.71	78.72	76.74	74.79	72.87	71.00
43	86.71	85.27	83.83	82.40	70.99	79.60
44	93.13	92.35	91.57	90.78	90.00	89.22
45	100.00	100.00	100.00	100.00	100.00	100.00

50 - Year Economic Life

End Of Year	7%	8%	9%	10%	11%	12%
1	.25	.18	.12	.09	.06	.04
2	.51	.36	.26	.18	.13	.09
3	.79	.57	.40	.28	.22	.14
4	1.19	.79	.56	.40	.28	.20
5	1.41	1.02	.74	.52	.37	.27
6	1.76	1.28	.92	.66	.47	.34
7	2.13	1.56	1.13	.82	.59	.42
8	2.52	1.85	1.35	.98	.73	.51
9	2.95	2.18	1.60	1.17	.85	.62
10	3.40	2.53	1.86	1.37	1.00	.73
11	3.83	2.90	2.16	1.59	1.17	.86
12	4.40	3.31	2.47	1.84	1.36	1.01
13	4.96	3.75	2.82	2.11	1.57	1.17
14	5.55	4.22	3.19	2.40	1.80	1.35
15	6.18	4.73	3.60	2.73	2.06	1.55
16	6.86	5.29	4.05	3.09	2.35	1.78
17	7.59	5.88	4.54	3.48	2.67	2.04
18	8.36	6.53	5.07	3.92	3.02	2.32
19	9.20	7.22	5.65	4.40	3.41	2.64
20	10.08	7.98	6.27	4.92	3.85	3.00

Per Cent Liability At Interest Rates Of:

End Of Year	7%	8%	9%	10%	11%	12%
50 - Year Economic Life - (Continued)						
21	11.04	8.79	6.97	5.50	4.33	3.40
22	12.06	9.67	7.71	6.13	4.87	3.85
23	13.15	10.62	8.53	6.83	5.46	4.36
24	14.31	11.64	9.42	7.60	6.12	4.92
25	15.56	12.74	10.39	8.45	6.86	5.56
26	16.89	13.94	11.45	9.38	7.67	6.26
27	18.32	15.22	12.60	10.40	8.57	7.06
28	19.85	16.62	13.86	11.53	9.58	7.95
29	21.49	18.12	15.23	12.77	10.69	8.94
30	23.24	19.74	16.72	14.13	11.93	10.06
31	25.11	21.50	18.35	15.63	13.30	11.30
32	27.11	23.39	20.13	17.28	14.82	12.70
33	29.26	25.44	22.05	19.10	16.51	14.27
34	31.55	27.65	24.17	21.09	18.39	16.02
35	34.00	30.03	26.47	23.29	20.47	17.99
36	36.63	32.61	28.97	25.70	23.78	20.19
37	39.44	35.39	31.70	28.36	25.35	22.65
38	42.45	38.10	34.68	31.28	28.20	25.41
39	45.67	41.64	37.92	34.49	31.36	28.50
40	49.11	45.15	41.45	38.03	34.87	31.96
41	52.79	48.94	45.31	41.91	38.76	35.84
42	56.73	53.03	49.51	46.19	43.08	40.18
43	60.95	57.44	54.09	50.90	47.88	45.05
44	65.46	62.21	59.08	56.06	53.21	59.49
45	70.29	67.36	64.52	61.77	59.12	56.59
46	75.46	72.93	70.45	68.03	65.69	63.43
47	80.98	78.93	76.91	74.92	72.97	71.07
48	86.90	85.42	83.95	82.50	81.05	79.65
49	93.23	92.43	91.63	90.83	90.04	89.25
50	100.00	100.00	100.00	100.00	100.00	100.00

Schedule of Amortization of an Investment of $10,000
Providing for Annual Amortization and Interest
At 8 Per Cent Over A Period of 50 Years

Year	Annual Payment	Interest On Investment At 8%	Amortization Annual	Amortization Cumulative	Remaining Investment
1	$817.43	$800.00	$ 17.43	$ 17.43	$9,982.57
2	817.43	798.60	18.83	36.26	9,963.74
3	817.43	797.10	20.33	56.59	9,943.41
4	817.43	795.47	21.96	78.55	9,921.45
5	817.43	793.72	23.71	102.26	9,897.74
6	817.43	791.82	25.61	127.87	9,872.13
7	817.43	789.77	27.66	155.53	9,844.47
8	817.43	787.56	29.87	185.40	9,814.60
9	817.43	785.17	32.26	217.66	9,782.34
10	817.43	782.59	34.84	252.50	9,747.50
11	817.43	779.80	37.63	290.13	9,709.87
12	817.43	776.79	40.64	330.77	9,669.23
13	817.43	773.54	43.89	374.66	9,625.34
14	817.43	770.03	47.40	422.06	9,577.94
15	817.43	766.24	51.19	473.25	9,526.75
16	817.43	762.14	55.29	528.54	9,471.46
17	817.43	757.72	59.71	588.25	9,411.75
18	817.43	752.94	64.49	652.74	9,347.26
19	817.43	747.78	69.65	722.39	9,277.61
20	817.43	742.21	75.22	797.61	9,202.39
21	817.43	736.19	81.24	878.85	9,121.15
22	817.43	729.69	87.74	966.59	9,033.41
23	817.43	722.67	94.76	1,061.35	8,938.65
24	817.43	715.09	102.34	1,163.66	8,836.34
25	817.43	706.91	110.52	1,274.18	8,725.82

Schedule of Amortization of an Investment of $10,000
Providing for Annual Amortization and Interest
At 8 Per Cent Over A Period of 50 Years

Year	Annual Payment	Interest On Investment At 8%	Amortization Annual	Amortization Cumulative	Remaining Investment
26	$817.43	$698.07	$119.36	$ 1,393.54	$8,606.46
27	817.43	688.52	128.91	1,522.45	8,477.55
28	817.43	678.20	139.23	1,661.68	8,338.32
29	817.43	667.07	150.36	1,812.04	8,187.96
30	817.43	655.04	162.39	1,974.43	8,025.57
31	817.43	642.05	175.38	2,149.81	7,850.19
32	817.43	628.02	189.41	2,339.22	7,660.78
33	817.43	612.86	204.57	2,543.79	7,456.21
34	817.43	596.50	220.93	2,764.72	7,235.28
35	817.43	578.82	238.61	3,003.33	6,996.67
36	817.43	559.73	257.70	3,261.03	6,738.97
37	817.43	539.12	278.31	3,539.34	6,460.66
38	817.43	516.85	300.58	3,839.92	6,160.08
39	817.43	492.81	324.62	4,164.54	5,835.46
40	817.43	466.84	350.59	4,515.13	5,484.87
41	817.43	438.79	378.64	4,893.77	5,106.23
42	817.43	408.50	408.93	5,302.70	4,697.30
43	817.43	375.78	441.65	5,744.35	4,255.65
44	817.43	340.45	476.98	6,221.33	3,778.67
45	817.43	302.29	515.14	6,736.47	3,263.53
46	817.43	261.08	556.35	7,292.82	2,707.18
47	817.43	216.57	600.86	7,893.68	2,106.32
48	817.43	168.51	648.92	8,542.60	1,457.40
49	817.43	116.59	700.84	9,243.44	756.46
50	817.43	60.52	756.91	10,000.35	000.00

DISTRIBUTION OF MORTGAGE PAYMENTS
UNDER THE LEVEL OR CONSTANT PAYMENT PLAN

Based on a $10,000 mortgage--amortized over 25 years at 7 per cent interest, constant payments of $70.70 each, over 300 monthly periods.

Time Of Payment		Amount Of Interest	Amount Of Amorti- zation	Balance Of Principal
Month	Year			$10,000.00
1	1	$58.30	$12.40	$ 9,987.60
2	"	58.30	12.40	9,975.20
3	"	58.20	12.50	9,962.70
4	"	58.10	12.60	9,950.10
5	"	58.00	12.70	9,937.40
6	"	58.00	12.70	9,924.70
7	"	57.90	12.80	9,911.90
8	"	57.80	12.90	9,899.00
9	"	57.70	13.00	9,886.00
10	"	57.70	13.00	9,873.00
11	"	57.60	13.10	9,859.90
12	"	57.50	13.20	9,846.70
1	2	57.40	13.30	9,833.40
2	"	57.40	13.30	9,820.10
3	"	57.30	13.40	9,806.70
4	"	57.20	13.50	9,793.20
5	"	57.10	13.60	9,779.60
6	"	57.00	13.70	9,765.90
7	"	57.00	13.70	9,752.20
8	"	56.90	13.80	9,738.40
9	"	56.80	13.90	9,724.50
10	"	56.70	14.00	9,710.50
11	"	56.60	14.10	9,696.40
12	"	56.60	14.10	9,682.30
1	3	56.50	14.20	9,668.10
2	"	56.40	14.30	9,653.80
3	"	56.30	14.40	9,639.40
4	"	56.20	14.50	9,624.90
5	"	56.10	14.60	9,610.30
6	"	56.10	14.60	9,595.70

Time Of Payment		Amount Of Interest	Amount Of Amortization	Balance Of Principal
Month	Year			
7	3	$56.00	$14.70	9,581.00
8	"	55.90	14.80	9,566.20
9	"	55.80	14.90	9,551.30
10	"	55.70	15.00	9,536.30
11	"	55.60	15.10	9,521.20
12	"	55.50	15.20	9,506.00
1	4	55.50	15.20	9,490.80
2	"	55.40	15.30	9,475.50
3	"	55.30	15.40	9,460.10
4	"	55.20	15.50	9,444.60
5	"	55.10	15.60	9,429.00
6	"	55.00	15.70	9,413.30
7	"	54.90	15.80	9,397.50
8	"	54.80	15.90	9,381.60
9	"	54.70	16.00	9,365.60
10	"	54.60	16.10	9,349.50
11	"	54.50	16.20	9,333.30
12	"	54.40	16.30	9,317.00
1	5	54.30	16.40	9,300.60
2	"	54.30	16.40	9,284.20
3	"	54.20	16.50	9,267.70
4	"	54.10	16.60	9,251.10
5	"	54.00	16.70	9,234.40
6	"	53.90	16.80	9,217.60
7	"	53.80	16.90	9,200.70
8	"	53.70	17.00	9,183.70
9	"	53.60	17.10	9,166.60
10	"	53.50	17.20	9,149.40
11	"	53.40	17.30	9,132.10
12	"	53.30	17.40	9,114.70
1	6	53.20	17.50	9,097.20
2	"	53.10	17.60	9,079.60
3	"	53.00	17.70	9,061.90
4	"	52.90	17.80	9,044.10
5	"	52.80	17.90	9,026.20
6	"	52.70	18.00	9,008.20

Time Of Payment		Amount Of Interest	Amount Of Amorti-zation	Balance Of Principal
Month	Year			
7	6	$52.50	$18.20	$ 8,990.00
8	"	52.40	18.30	8,971.70
9	"	52.30	18.40	8,953.30
10	"	52.20	18.50	8,934.80
11	"	52.10	18.60	8,916.20
12	"	52.00	18.70	8,897.50
1	7	51.90	18.80	8,878.70
2	"	51.80	18.90	8,859.80
3	"	51.70	19.00	8,840.80
4	"	51.60	19.10	8,821.70
5	"	51.50	19.20	8,802.50
6	"	51.30	19.40	8,783.10
7	"	51.20	19.50	8,763.60
8	"	51.10	19.60	8,744.00
9	"	51.00	19.70	8,724.30
10	"	50.90	19.80	8,704.50
11	"	50.80	19.90	8,684.60
12	"	50.70	20.00	8,664.60
1	8	50.50	20.20	8,644.40
2	"	50.40	20.30	8,624.10
3	"	50.30	20.40	8,603.70
4	"	50.20	20.50	8,583.20
5	"	50.10	20.60	8,562.60
6	"	49.90	20.80	8,541.80
7	"	49.80	20.90	8,520.90
8	"	49.70	21.00	8,499.90
9	"	49.60	21.10	8,478.80
10	"	49.50	21.20	8,457.60
11	"	49.30	21.40	8,436.20
12	"	49.20	21.50	8,414.70
1	9	49.10	21.60	8,393.10
2	"	49.00	21.70	8,371.40
3	"	48.80	21.90	8,349.50
4	"	48.70	22.00	8,327.50
5	"	48.60	22.10	8,305.40
6	"	48.40	22.30	8,283.10

Time Of Payment		Amount Of Interest	Amount Of Amorti- zation	Balance Of Principal
Month	Year			
7	9	$48.30	$22.40	$ 8,260.70
8	"	48.20	22.50	8,238.20
9	"	48.10	22.60	8,215.60
10	"	47.90	22.80	8,192.80
11	"	47.80	22.90	8,169.90
12	"	47.70	23.00	8,146.90
1	10	47.50	23.20	8,123.70
2	"	47.40	23.30	8,100.40
3	"	47.30	23.40	8,077.00
4	"	47.10	23.60	8,053.40
5	"	47.00	23.70	8,029.70
6	"	46.80	23.90	8,005.80
7	"	46.70	24.00	7,981.80
8	"	46.60	24.10	7,957.70
9	"	46.40	24.30	7,933.40
10	"	46.30	24.40	7,909.00
11	"	46.10	24.60	7,884.40
12	"	46.00	24.70	7,859.70
1	11	45.80	24.90	7,834.80
2	"	45.70	25.00	7,809.80
3	"	45.60	25.10	7,784.70
4	"	45.40	25.30	7,759.40
5	"	45.30	25.40	7,734.00
6	"	45.10	25.60	7,708.40
7	"	45.00	25.70	7,682.70
8	"	44.80	25.90	7,656.80
9	"	44.70	26.00	7,630.80
10	"	44.50	26.20	7,604.60
11	"	44.40	26.30	7,578.30
12	"	44.20	26.50	7,551.80
1	12	44.10	26.60	7,525.20
2	"	43.90	26.80	7,498.40
3	"	43.70	27.00	7,471.40
4	"	43.60	27.10	7,444.30
5	"	43.40	27.30	7,417.00
6	"	43.30	27.40	7,389.60

Time Of Payment		Amount Of Interest	Amount Of Amorti- zation	Balance Of Principal
Month	Year			
7	12	$43.10	$27.60	$ 7,362.00
8	''	42.90	27.80	7,334.20
9	''	42.80	27.90	7,306.30
10	''	42.60	28.10	7,278.20
11	''	42.50	28.20	7,250.00
12	''	42.30	28.40	7,221.60
1	13	42.10	28.60	7,193.00
2	''	42.00	28.70	7,164.30
3	''	41.80	28.90	7,135.40
4	''	41.60	29.10	7,106.30
5	''	41.50	29.20	7,077.10
6	''	41.30	29.40	7,047.70
7	''	41.10	29.60	7,018.10
8	''	40.90	29.80	6,988.30
9	''	40.80	29.90	6,958.40
10	''	40.60	30.10	6,928.30
11	''	40.40	30.30	6,898.00
12	''	40.20	30.50	6,867.50
1	14	40.10	30.60	6,836.90
2	''	39.90	30.80	6,806.10
3	''	39.70	31.00	6,775.10
4	''	39.50	31.20	6,743.90
5	''	39.30	31.40	6,712.50
6	''	39.20	31.50	6,681.10
7	''	39.00	31.70	6,649.30
8	''	38.80	31.90	6,617.40
9	''	38.60	32.10	6,585.30
10	''	38.40	32.30	6,553.00
11	''	38.20	32.50	6,520.50
12	''	38.00	32.70	6,487.80
1	15	37.80	32.90	6,454.90
2	''	37.70	33.00	6,421.90
3	''	37.50	33.20	6,388.70
4	''	37.30	33.50	6,355.30
5	''	37.10	33.60	6,321.70
6	''	36.90	33.80	6,287.90

Time Of Payment		Amount Of Interest	Amount Of Amorti- zation	Balance Of Principal
Month	Year			
7	15	$36.70	$34.00	$ 6,253.90
8	"	36.50	34.20	6,219.70
9	"	36.30	34.40	6,185.30
10	"	36.10	34.60	6,150.70
11	"	35.90	34.80	6,115.90
12	"	35.70	35.00	6,080.90
1	16	35.50	35.20	6,045.70
2	"	35.30	35.40	6,010.30
3	"	35.10	35.60	5,974.70
4	"	34.90	35.80	5,938.90
5	"	34.60	36.10	5,902.80
6	"	34.40	36.30	5,866.50
7	"	34.20	36.50	5,830.00
8	"	34.00	36.70	5,793.30
9	"	33.80	36.90	5,756.40
10	"	33.60	37.10	5,719.30
11	"	33.40	37.36	5,682.00
12	"	33.10	37.60	5,644.40
1	17	32.90	37.80	5,606.60
2	"	32.70	38.00	5,568.60
3	"	32.50	38.20	5,530.40
4	"	32.30	38.40	5,492.00
5	"	32.00	38.70	5,453.30
6	"	31.80	38.90	5,414.40
7	"	31.60	39.10	5,375.30
8	"	31.40	39.30	5,336.00
9	"	31.10	39.60	5,296.40
10	"	30.90	39.80	5,256.60
11	"	30.70	40.00	5,216.60
12	"	30.40	40.30	5,176.30
1	18	30.20	40.50	5,135.80
2	"	30.00	40.70	5,095.10
3	"	29.70	41.00	5,054.10
4	"	29.50	41.20	5,012.90
5	"	29.20	41.50	4,971.40
6	"	29.00	41.70	4,929.70

Time Of Payment		Amount Of	Amount Of Amorti-	Balance Of
Month	Year	Interest	zation	Principal
7	18	$28.80	$41.90	$ 4,887.80
8	"	28.50	42.20	4,845.60
9	"	28.30	42.40	4,803.20
10	"	28.00	42.70	4,760.50
11	"	27.80	42.90	4,717.60
12	"	27.50	43.20	4,674.40
1	19	27.30	43.40	4,631.00
2	"	27.00	43.70	4,587.30
3	"	26.80	43.90	4,543.40
4	"	26.50	44.20	4,499.20
5	"	26.20	44.50	4,454.70
6	"	26.00	44.70	4,410.00
7	"	25.70	45.00	4,365.00
8	"	25.50	45.20	4,319.80
9	"	25.20	45.50	4,274.30
10	"	24.90	45.80	4,228.50
11	"	24.70	46.00	4,182.50
12	"	24.40	46.30	4,136.20
1	20	24.10	46.60	4,089.60
2	"	23.90	46.80	4,042.80
3	"	23.60	47.10	3,995.70
4	"	23.30	47.40	3,948.30
5	"	23.00	47.70	3,900.60
6	"	22.80	47.90	3,852.70
7	"	22.50	48.20	3,804.50
8	"	22.20	48.50	3,756.00
9	"	21.90	48.80	3,707.20
10	"	21.60	49.10	3,658.10
11	"	21.30	49.40	3,608.70
12	"	21.10	49.60	3,559.10
1	21	20.80	49.90	3,509.20
2	"	20.50	50.20	3,459.00
3	"	20.20	50.50	3,408.50
4	"	19.90	50.80	3,357.70
5	"	19.60	51.10	3,306.60
6	"	19.30	51.40	3,255.20

Time Of Payment		Amount Of	Amount Of Amorti-	Balance Of
Month	Year	Interest	zation	Principal
7	21	$19.00	$51.70	$ 3,203.50
8	"	18.70	52.00	3,151.50
9	"	18.40	52.30	3,099.20
10	"	18.10	52.60	3,046.60
11	"	17.80	52.90	2,993.70
12	"	17.50	53.20	2,940.50
1	22	17.20	53.50	2,887.00
2	"	16.80	53.90	2,833.10
3	"	16.50	54.20	2,778.90
4	"	16.20	54.50	2,724.40
5	"	15.90	54.80	2,669.60
6	"	15.60	55.10	2,614.50
7	"	15.30	55.40	2,559.10
8	"	14.90	55.80	2,503.30
9	"	14.60	56.10	2,447.20
10	"	14.30	56.40	2,390.80
11	"	13.90	56.80	2,334.40
12	"	13.60	57.10	2,276.90
1	23	13.30	57.40	2,219.50
2	"	12.90	57.80	2,161.70
3	"	12.60	58.10	2,103.60
4	"	12.30	58.40	2,045.20
5	"	11.90	58.80	1,986.40
6	"	11.60	59.10	1,927.30
7	"	11.20	59.50	1,867.78
8	"	10.90	59.80	1,808.80
9	"	10.50	60.20	1,747.80
10	"	10.20	60.50	1,687.30
11	"	9.80	60.90	1,626.40
12	"	9.50	61.20	1,565.20
1	24	9.10	61.60	1,503.60
2	"	8.80	61.90	1,441.70
3	"	8.40	62.30	1,379.40
4	"	8.00	62.70	1,316.70
5	"	7.70	63.00	1,253.70
6	"	7.30	63.40	1,190.30

Time Of Payment		Amount Of Interest	Amount Of Amorti- zation	Balance Of Principal
Month	Year			
7	24	$6.90	$63.80	$ 1,126.50
8	"	6.60	64.10	1,062.40
9	"	6.20	64.50	997.90
10	"	5.80	64.90	933.00
11	"	5.40	65.30	867.70
12	"	5.10	65.60	802.10
1	25	4.70	66.00	736.10
2	"	4.30	66.40	669.70
3	"	3.90	66.80	602.90
4	"	3.50	67.20	535.70
5	"	3.10	67.60	468.10
6	"	2.70	68.00	400.10
7	"	2.30	68.40	331.70
8	"	1.90	68.40	262.90
9	"	1.50	69.20	193.70
10	"	1.10	69.60	124.10
11	"	.70	70.00	54.10
12	"	.30	54.10	0.00

PERCENTAGE OF MORTGAGE DEBT REMAINING AT
END OF EACH YEAR FOR MORTGAGE LOAN PERIODS
OF 5 TO 30 YEARS AT 6 PER CENT INTEREST
UNDER MONTHLY CONSTANT PAYMENT DEBT AMORTIZATION

Age Of Loan	Mortgage Loan Periods — Years					
	5	10	15	20	25	30
	Per Cent Mortgage Debt Remaining At End of Each Year*					
1	82.31	92.46	95.76	97.32	98.21	98.77
2	63.53	84.46	91.25	94.48	96.31	97.46
3	43.62	75.97	86.46	91.46	94.30	96.07
4	22.42	66.95	81.39	88.26	92.16	94.59
5	0.00	57.37	75.99	84.86	89.88	93.02
6		47.21	70.27	81.25	87.47	91.36
7		36.41	64.19	77.41	84.90	89.60
8		24.95	57.74	73.34	82.18	87.72
9		12.79	50.89	69.02	79.30	85.72
10		0.00	43.62	64.44	76.23	83.61
11			35.90	59.56	72.97	81.37
12			27.70	54.39	69.52	78.99
13			18.99	48.90	65.85	76.46
14			9.76	43.08	61.95	73.77
15			0.00	36.89	57.82	70.92
16				30.32	53.43	67.89
17				23.35	48.77	64.68
18				15.94	43.82	61.27
19				8.08	38.57	57.64
20				0.00	32.99	53.80
21					27.07	49.72
22					20.78	45.38
23					14.11	40.78
24					7.02	35.90
25					0.00	30.71
26						25.20
27						19.36
28						13.15
29						6.56
30						0.00

*To find remaining mortgage debt for remaining life period of a loan,
multiply the monthly constant mortgage loan payment by "Present Worth of
$1.00" factor — use fractional monthly interest rate for number of
remaining monthly payments. Formula: $a_{\overline{7}|} = \dfrac{1 - v^n}{i}$

PERCENTAGE OF MORTGAGE DEBT REMAINING AT
END OF EACH YEAR FOR MORTGAGE LOAN PERIODS
OF 5 TO 30 YEARS AT 6.5 PER CENT INTEREST
UNDER MONTHLY CONSTANT PAYMENT DEBT AMORTIZATION

| Age Of Loan | Mortgage Loan Periods – Years | | | | | |
| | 5 | 10 | 15 | 20 | 25 | 30 |
	Per Cent Mortgage Debt Remaining At End of Each Year*					
1	82.50	92.65	95.92	97.47	98.34	98.87
2	63.83	84.81	91.56	94.78	96.57	97.67
3	43.91	76.44	86.91	91.90	94.68	96.38
4	22.65	67.52	81.95	88.83	92.66	95.01
5	0.00	57.99	76.66	85.56	90.51	93.55
6		47.83	71.01	82.07	88.21	91.99
7		36.99	64.98	78.34	85.76	90.32
8		25.42	58.55	74.36	83.14	88.54
9		13.08	51.69	70.12	80.35	86.65
10		0.00	44.38	65.59	77.38	84.62
11			36.57	60.76	74.20	82.46
12			28.23	55.60	70.81	80.16
13			19.34	50.10	67.20	77.70
14			9.86	44.24	63.34	75.08
15			0.00	37.97	59.22	72.28
16				31.30	54.83	69.30
17				24.17	50.14	66.11
18				16.56	45.14	62.72
19				8.45	39.81	59.09
20				0.00	34.12	55.22
21					28.05	51.09
22					21.57	46.69
23					14.65	41.99
24					7.28	36.98
25					0.00	31.63
26						25.92
27						19.83
28						13.33
29						6.39
30						0.00

*To find remaining mortgage debt for remaining life period of a loan, multiply the monthly constant mortgage loan payment by "Present Worth of $1.00" factor – use fractional monthly interest rate for number of remaining monthly payments. Formula: $a_7 = \dfrac{1 - v^n}{i}$

PERCENTAGE OF MORTGAGE DEBT REMAINING AT
END OF EACH YEAR FOR MORTGAGE LOAN PERIODS
OF 5 TO 30 YEARS AT 7 PER CENT INTEREST
UNDER MONTHLY CONSTANT PAYMENT DEBT AMORTIZATION

| Age Of Loan | Mortgage Loan Periods – Years | | | | | |
| | 5 | 10 | 15 | 20 | 25 | 30 |
	Per Cent Mortgage Debt Remaining At End of Each Year*					
1	82.68	92.83	96.09	97.61	98.47	99.07
2	64.11	85.14	91.89	95.05	96.82	97.99
3	44.19	76.90	87.39	92.31	95.06	96.84
4	22.84	68.06	82.57	89.36	93.17	95.60
5	0.00	58.58	77.40	86.21	91.15	94.27
6		48.41	71.85	82.82	88.98	92.84
7		37.51	65.91	79.19	86.65	91.31
8		25.82	59.53	75.30	84.15	89.67
9		13.29	52.69	71.12	81.47	87.91
10		0.00	45.36	66.65	78.60	86.02
11			37.49	61.85	75.52	84.00
12			29.07	56.71	72.22	81.84
13			20.03	51.19	68.68	79.51
14			10.33	45.27	64.88	77.02
15			0.00	38.93	60.81	74.34
16				32.13	56.44	71.48
17				24.83	51.76	68.40
18				17.01	46.74	65.11
19				8.62	41.36	61.57
20				0.00	35.59	57.78
21					29.40	53.71
22					22.77	49.35
23					15.65	44.68
24					8.02	39.67
25					0.00	34.29
26						28.53
27						22.36
28						15.73
29						8.63
30						0.00

*To find remaining mortgage debt for remaining life period of a loan, multiply the monthly constant mortgage loan payment by "Present Worth of $1.00" factor – use fractional monthly interest rate for number of remaining monthly payments. Formula: $a_7 = \dfrac{1 - v^n}{i}$

PERCENTAGE OF MORTGAGE DEBT REMAINING AT
END OF EACH YEAR FOR MORTGAGE LOAN PERIODS
OF 5 TO 30 YEARS AT 7.5 PER CENT INTEREST
UNDER MONTHLY CONSTANT PAYMENT DEBT AMORTIZATION

Age Of Loan	Mortgage Loan Periods – Years					
	5	10	15	20	25	30
	Per Cent Mortgage Debt Remaining At End of Each Year*					
1	82.87	93.01	96.24	97.75	98.58	99.16
2	64.41	85.47	92.18	95.33	97.06	98.18
3	44.52	77.35	87.81	92.72	95.41	97.12
4	23.09	68.60	83.10	89.91	93.64	95.97
5	0.00	59.17	78.02	86.87	91.73	94.74
6		49.01	72.55	83.61	89.67	93.41
7		38.05	66.65	80.09	87.45	91.98
8		26.25	60.30	76.29	85.06	90.44
9		13.53	53.45	72.21	82.48	88.78
10		0.00	46.07	67.80	79.71	86.99
11			38.12	63.06	76.72	85.06
12			29.56	57.94	73.49	82.99
13			20.32	52.42	70.02	80.75
14			10.38	46.48	66.28	78.33
15			0.00	40.09	62.24	75.73
16				33.18	57.89	72.93
17				25.75	52.21	69.91
18				17.73	48.16	66.65
19				9.10	42.72	63.15
20				0.00	36.86	59.37
21					30.54	55.29
22					23.73	50.90
23					16.39	46.17
24					8.48	41.08
25					0.00	35.58
26						29.66
27						23.28
28						16.40
29						8.99
30						0.00

---

*To find remaining mortgage debt for remaining life period of a loan, multiply the monthly constant mortgage loan payment by "Present Worth of $1.00" factor – use fractional monthly interest rate for number of remaining monthly payments. Formula: $a_{\overline{7}} = \dfrac{1 - V^n}{i}$

PERCENTAGE OF MORTGAGE DEBT REMAINING AT
END OF EACH YEAR FOR MORTGAGE LOAN PERIODS
OF 5 TO 30 YEARS AT 8 PER CENT INTEREST
UNDER MONTHLY CONSTANT PAYMENT DEBT AMORTIZATION

Age Of Loan	Mortgage Loan Periods – Years					
	5	10	15	20	25	30
	Per Cent Mortgage Debt Remaining At End of Each Year*					
1	83.05	93.19	96.40	97.88	98.69	99.23
2	64.70	85.81	92.50	95.58	97.27	98.33
3	44.82	77.81	88.28	93.10	95.73	97.36
4	23.29	69.16	83.70	90.40	94.07	96.30
5	0.00	59.78	78.75	87.49	92.26	95.16
6		49.63	73.38	84.33	90.31	93.92
7		38.64	67.56	80.91	88.19	92.57
8		26.73	61.27	77.20	85.90	91.12
9		13.83	54.45	73.19	83.42	89.54
10		0.00	47.07	68.84	80.73	87.83
11			39.08	64.13	77.82	85.99
12			30.42	59.04	74.66	83.99
13			21.04	53.52	71.25	81.82
14			10.89	47.54	67.55	79.47
15			0.00	41.06	63.55	76.93
16				34.05	59.21	74.17
17				26.47	54.51	71.19
18				18.23	49.43	67.96
19				9.32	43.20	64.46
20				0.00	37.95	60.67
21					31.49	56.58
22					24.49	52.13
23					16.91	47.32
24					8.71	42.11
25					0.00	36.47
26						30.36
27						23.74
28						16.57
29						8.81
30						0.00

*To find remaining mortgage debt for remaining life period of a loan, multiply the monthly constant mortgage loan payment by "Present Worth of $1.00" factor – use fractional monthly interest rate for number of remaining monthly payments. Formula: $a_{\overline{n}|} = \dfrac{1 - v^n}{i}$

PERCENTAGE OF MORTGAGE DEBT REMAINING AT
END OF EACH YEAR FOR MORTGAGE LOAN PERIODS
OF 5 TO 30 YEARS AT 8.5 PER CENT INTEREST
UNDER MONTHLY CONSTANT PAYMENT DEBT AMORTIZATION

| Age Of Loan | \(\text{Mortgage Loan Periods} - \text{Years}\) ||||||
| | 5 | 10 | 15 | 20 | 25 | 30 |
	Per Cent Mortgage Debt Remaining At End of Each Year*					
1	84.68	93.94	96.84	98.18	98.90	99.31
2	66.56	86.77	93.11	96.03	97.60	98.49
3	46.84	78.96	89.05	93.68	96.18	97.60
4	25.38	70.47	84.63	91.13	94.63	96.63
5	0.00	61.23	79.82	88.36	92.95	95.58
6		51.17	74.58	85.34	91.12	94.43
7		40.22	68.88	82.05	89.12	93.18
8		28.30	62.68	78.47	86.96	91.82
9		15.32	55.93	74.57	84.60	90.34
10		0.00	48.58	70.33	82.03	88.73
11			40.58	65.72	79.23	86.97
12			31.88	60.69	76.19	85.06
13			22.40	55.23	72.88	82.98
14			12.09	49.28	69.28	80.72
15			0.00	42.80	65.35	78.26
16				35.75	61.08	75.58
17				28.08	56.44	72.67
18				19.73	51.38	69.50
19				10.65	45.88	66.04
20				0.00	39.89	62.28
21					33.37	58.19
22					26.27	53.74
23					18.55	48.89
24					10.14	43.61
25					0.00	37.87
26						31.63
27						24.82
28						17.42
29						9.36
30						0.00

*To find remaining mortgage debt for remaining life period of a loan, multiply the monthly constant mortgage loan payment by "Present Worth of $1.00" factor - use fractional monthly interest rate for number of remaining monthly payments. Formula: $a_{\overline{7}} = \dfrac{1 - v^n}{i}$

PERCENTAGE OF MORTGAGE DEBT REMAINING AT
END OF EACH YEAR FOR MORTGAGE LOAN PERIODS
OF 5 TO 30 YEARS AT 9 PER CENT INTEREST
UNDER MONTHLY CONSTANT PAYMENT DEBT AMORTIZATION

Age Of Loan	Mortgage Loan Periods - Years					
	5	10	15	20	25	30
	Per Cent Mortgage Debt Remaining At End of Each Year*					
1	84.86	94.09	96.99	98.29	98.98	99.37
2	66.85	87.07	93.40	96.25	97.78	98.63
3	47.16	79.39	89.48	94.02	96.45	97.81
4	25.61	70.99	85.19	91.59	95.01	96.92
5	0.00	61.80	80.50	88.92	93.43	95.94
6		51.75	75.37	86.00	91.70	94.87
7		40.76	69.76	82.81	89.81	93.70
8		28.74	63.62	79.32	87.74	92.42
9		15.59	56.91	75.51	85.48	91.02
10		0.00	49.56	71.33	83.00	89.49
11			41.53	66.77	80.29	87.82
12			32.74	61.78	77.33	85.99
13			23.13	56.32	74.09	83.98
14			12.61	50.34	70.55	81.79
15			0.00	43.81	66.67	79.40
16				36.66	62.43	76.78
17				28.84	57.79	73.91
18				20.29	52.72	70.78
19				10.94	47.17	67.35
20				0.00	41.10	63.60
21					34.46	59.50
22					27.20	55.01
23					19.26	50.11
24					10.57	44.74
25					0.00	38.87
26						32.44
27						25.42
28						17.74
29						9.33
30						0.00

*To find remaining mortgage debt for remaining life period of a loan,
multiply the monthly constant mortgage loan payment by "Present Worth
of $1.00" factor - use fractional monthly interest rate for number of
remaining monthly payments. Formula: $a_7 = \dfrac{1 - y^n}{i}$

PERCENTAGE OF MORTGAGE DEBT REMAINING AT
END OF EACH YEAR FOR MORTGAGE LOAN PERIODS
OF 5 TO 30 YEARS AT 9.5 PER CENT INTEREST
UNDER MONTHLY CONSTANT PAYMENT DEBT AMORTIZATION

Age Of Loan	Mortgage Loan Periods – Years					
	5	10	15	20	25	30
	Per Cent Mortgage Debt Remaining At End of Each Year*					
1	85.02	94.25	97.11	98.39	99.06	99.44
2	67.13	87.38	93.66	96.48	97.93	98.76
3	47.47	79.83	89.87	94.37	96.70	98.02
4	25.85	71.53	85.70	92.05	95.34	97.20
5	0.00	62.41	81.12	89.50	93.84	96.30
6		52.38	76.08	86.70	92.20	95.32
7		41.36	70.55	83.62	90.39	94.24
8		29.24	64.46	80.23	88.41	93.05
9		15.92	57.77	76.51	86.23	91.74
10		0.00	50.42	72.42	83.83	90.30
11			42.33	67.92	81.19	88.72
12			33.45	62.98	78.29	86.98
13			23.68	57.54	75.11	85.07
14			12.94	51.57	71.60	82.97
15			0.00	45.01	67.75	80.66
16				37.79	63.52	78.12
17				29.85	58.87	75.33
18				21.13	53.76	72.26
19				11.55	48.14	68.89
20				0.00	41.59	65.19
21					35.16	61.11
22					27.69	56.64
23					19.49	51.71
24					10.46	46.30
25					0.00	40.36
26						33.82
27						26.63
28						18.73
29						10.04
30						0.00

*To find remaining mortgage debt for remaining life period of a loan,
multiply the monthly constant mortgage loan payment by "Present Worth
of $1.00" factor – use fractional monthly interest rate for number of
remaining monthly payments. Formula: $a_{\overline{7}} = \dfrac{1 - V^n}{i}$

PERCENTAGE OF MORTGAGE DEBT REMAINING AT
END OF EACH YEAR FOR MORTGAGE LOAN PERIODS
OF 5 TO 30 YEARS AT 10 PER CENT INTEREST
UNDER MONTHLY CONSTANT PAYMENT DEBT AMORTIZATION

Age Of Loan	Mortgage Loan Periods – Years					
	5	10	15	20	25	30
	Per Cent Mortgage Debt Remaining At End of Each Year*					
1	85.19	94.39	97.23	98.49	99.13	99.49
2	67.40	87.67	93.90	96.68	98.09	98.87
3	47.76	80.24	90.23	94.68	96.94	98.19
4	26.06	72.03	86.17	92.46	95.67	97.44
5	0.00	62.96	81.68	90.02	94.26	96.61
6		52.94	76.73	87.32	92.71	95.70
7		41.87	71.25	84.34	91.00	94.69
8		29.64	65.21	81.05	89.10	93.57
9		16.14	58.53	77.41	87.01	92.33
10		0.00	51.15	73.39	84.70	90.97
11			43.00	68.95	82.15	89.46
12			33.99	64.04	79.33	87.80
13			24.04	58.62	76.21	85.96
14			13.05	52.64	72.77	83.93
15			0.00	46.02	68.97	81.68
16				38.72	64.77	79.20
17				30.65	60.13	76.47
18				21.73	55.01	73.44
19				11.88	49.34	70.10
20				0.00	43.09	66.41
21					36.17	62.33
22					28.54	57.82
23					20.10	52.84
24					10.79	47.34
25					0.00	41.26
26						34.55
27						27.14
28						18.95
29						9.90
30						0.00

*To find remaining mortgage debt for remaining life period of a loan, multiply the monthly constant mortgage loan payment by "Present Worth of $1.00" factor – use fractional monthly interest rate for number of remaining monthly payments. Formula: $a_7 = \dfrac{1 - v^n}{i}$

Land Measurement Table

Acreage

Acres	Square Feet	1 Acre Equals Rectangle	
		Width	Length
1	43,560	16.5	2,640.0
2	87,120	33.0	1,320.0
3	130,680	50.0	871.2
4	174,240	66.0	660.0
5	217,800		
6	261,360	75.0	580.8
7	304,920	100.0	435.6
8	348,480	132.0	330.0
9	392,040	150.0	290.4
10	435,600	208.71	208.71

Table of Linear Measure

12 inches (in.)	make	1 foot	(ft.)
3 feet	"	1 yard	(yd.)
5 1/2 yards or 16 1/2 feet	"	1 rod	(rd.)
40 rods	"	1 furlong	(fur.)
8 furlongs, 320 rods, or 5,280 feet	"	1 statute mile	(mi.)

Table of Square Measure

144 square inches (sq. in.)	make	1 square foot	(sq. ft.)
9 square feet	"	1 square yard	(sq. yd.)
30 1/4 square yards	"	1 square rod	(sq. rd.)
40 square rods	"	1 rood	(R.)
4 rods or 43,560 square feet	"	1 acre	(A.)
640 acres	"	1 square mile	(sq. mi.)

Table of Surveyor's Linear Measure

7.92 inches (in.)	make	1 link	(l.)
25 links	"	1 rod	(rd.)
4 rods or 66 feet	"	1 chain	(ch.)
80 chains	"	1 mile	(mi.)

Table of Surveyor's Square Measure

625 square links (sq. l.)	make	1 pole	(P.)
16 poles	"	1 square chain	(sq. ch.)
10 square chains	"	1 acre	(A.)
640 acres	"	1 square mile	(sq. mi.)
36 square miles (6 mi. square)	"	1 township	(Tp.)

Note: 1 acre in square form equals 208.71 feet on each side.